FINITE MATHEMATICS
WITH APPLICATIONS
for Business and Social Sciences

FINITE MATHEMATICS WITH APPLICATIONS

for Business and Social Sciences
Fourth Edition

Abe Mizrahi
Indiana University Northwest

Michael Sullivan
Chicago State University

John Wiley & Sons
New York • Chichester • Brisbane • Toronto • Singapore

To Our Parents With Gratitude

Cover: Photograph by Paul Silverman

Library of Congress Cataloging in Publication Data:

Mizrahi, Abe.
   Finite mathematics with applications for business and
social sciences.

   Includes bibliographies and index.
   1. Business mathematics.   2. Social sciences—
Mathematics.   3. Mathematics—1961–   . I. Sullivan,
Michael, 1942–   II. Title.
HF5695.M66 1983   519   82-17590
ISBN 0-471-05398-8

Printed in the United States of America

10 9 8 7 6 5 4 3 2 1

Preface

First and foremost, this book is student-oriented. It does not dwell on formalities, but appeals to intuition. Abstraction and sophisticated mathematical theory are minimized without sacrificing an understanding of the underlying mathematical concepts. As much as possible, problems are introduced through real-life situations; the mathematics needed to handle similar situations is then developed. This motivation is highlighted by references to current applications in the social, business, and life sciences. In addition, questions from Certified Public Accountant (CPA) Examinations, Certificate in Management Accounting (CMA) Examinations, and Society of Actuaries Examinations have been reproduced at the end of appropriate chapters to contribute further to the relevance of the mathematics in this book. Textual explanations are precise, brief, and to the point, and they are always accompanied by illustrative examples.

- The textual material is interspersed with more than 300 illustrative examples. Almost every new idea is followed by one or two examples demonstrating how related problems can be solved. Often an example is furnished to motivate the need for a difficult concept before a precise definition is given. (See, for instance, pages 71 and 261.) When possible, an outline of steps to follow in solving a problem is given. (See pages 85, 161, and 271.)
- There are over 1700 exercises, most of which are keyed to the illustrative examples. The exercises very in nature and range from drill exercises to those that challenge the superior student. Most exercise sets contain real-world applications of the material. (See pages 144 and 312.) At the end of some chapters, true-false and fill-in-blank questions are provided to aid in the review process. (See pages 145 and 227.)
- Completely worked-out solutions, with illustrations, to odd-numbered problems are given in the back of the book. Completely worked-out solutions to even-numbered problems are available in a supplement to the text. Review exercises are given at the end of each chapter. At the end of most chapters, actual questions from recent CPA Exams, CMA Exams, and Society of Actuaries. Exams are reproduced. (See, for example pages 53 and 147.)
- Every chapter contains word problems as applications, including many real-world applications. (Pages 180 and 288.)
- A second color is used in the text and art to highlight important facts. Over 200 figures illustrate many concepts.
- Flowcharts are utilized whenever possible to outline procedures. See, for instance, pages 101 and 166.

A student study guide and a solutions manual to even-numbered problems will be available.

This is truly a collaborative effort, and the order of authorship signifies alphabetical precedence. We assume equal responsibility for the book's strengths and weaknesses, and welcome comments and suggestions for its improvement.

ORGANIZATION

This book deals with the topics in mathematics that have come to be known as "finite mathematics."

Chapter 1 is the "foundation" or review chapter and covers topics such as real numbers, rectangular coordinates, and linear equations and inequalities, including applications of linear equations.

Chapter 2 introduces matrices, including systems of equations and inverses. Applications to economics (Leontief model), cryptography, demography, and accounting are optional.

Chapter 3 discusses linear programming in two dimensions; Chapter 4 continues the study of linear programming using the simplex method.

Chapter 5 discusses sets, counting principles, permutations, and combinations and forms the basis for the study of probability in Chapter 6. Chapter 7, "Decision Theory," discusses expectation and applications to operations research.

Chapter 8 discusses various applications in probability theory that use Markov chain models. Included here are applications in business and genetics. Chapter 9 surveys game theory and some of its applications to business situations.

Chapter 10, "Statistics," may be covered any time after Chapter 6. Chapter 12 covers applications of matrices to directed graphs. Included here are applications to social psychology (dominance, communication, detection of cliques, and identification of liaison officials). This chapter requires a knowledge of Sections 1 to 3 of Chapter 2. Chapters 11 and 13 are independent of all chapters and may be covered at any time. The diagram on page vii illustrates the dependence/independence of the chapters and summarizes the preceding discussion.

Since topics covered in this type of course vary, we suggest possible plans in the following table.

Time	Material To Be Covered
3 Semester hours	Chapters 1, 2, 3, 4, 5, 6
	or
	Chapters 1, 2, 5, 6, 7, 8
	Chapters 1, 2, 5, 6, 7, 9
	Chapters 1, 2, 5, 6, 7, 10
	Chapters 1, 2, 3, 4 11, 12
6 Semester hours	Entire book

Worked-out solutions to approximately 850 odd-numbered problems are given in the back of the book. Worked-out solutions to approximately 850 even-numbered problems are available in a *Solutions Manual*. Problems with asterisks are to be considered more challenging.

At the end of each chapter, a review of important terms, additional problems, and actual questions from recent CPA, CMA, and Society of Actuaries Exams are included. Finally, the text contains all tables required in the exercises.

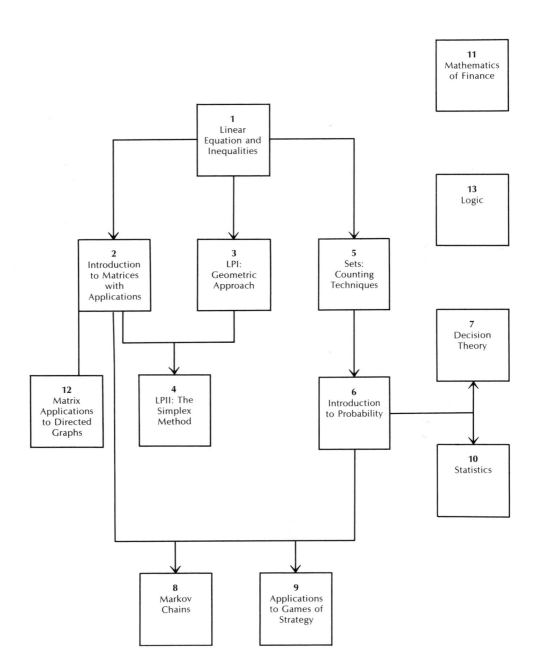

ACKNOWLEDGMENTS

We thank the many students at Indiana University Northwest, and Chicago State University for their comments and criticisms.

We are indebted to Professor William D. Blair, Northern Illinois University; Professor Milton D. Cox, Miami University; Professor Joseph Hansen, Northeastern University; Professor Herbert Hethcote, University of Iowa; Professor Jack Wadhaus, Golden West College; and Professor Robert Wheeler, Northern Illinois University, who used previous editions and provided us with many constructive criticisms and helpful suggestions.

We also thank these reviewers for their suggestions: Professor Charles B. Barker, DeAnza College; Professor William Blair, Northern Illinois University; Professor James C. Frauenthal, SUNY at Stony Brook; Professor Dennis Freeman, Montgomery College; Professor Gerald Hahm, College of St. Thomas; Professor Roy Honda, West Valley College; Professor Arthur Schlissel, Chairman, John Jay College of Criminal Justice; Professor Charles Sheumaker, University of SW Louisiana; and Professor Hubert Walczak, College of St. Thomas.

We especially thank Leroy Peterson and Henry Wyzinski, both at Indiana University Northwest, who checked the accuracy of solutions to all of the exercises.

We also appreciate the patience and skill of Lani Peterson and Katy Sullivan, who typed the revision.

We are grateful to the following organizations who permitted the reproduction of actual questions from previous professional examinations.

American Institute of Certified Public Accountants (CPA Exams)
Educational Testing Service (Actuary Exams)
Institute of Management Accounting of the National Association of Accountants (CMA Exams)

Again we are indebted to the people at Wiley, whose talent played a significant part in the publication of this book. We particularly thank Bob Pirtle, mathematics editor, for his patience and help.

Abe Mizrahi
Michael Sullivan

NEW FEATURES IN THE FOURTH EDITION

The new edition is a much-improved teaching tool because of:

*reorganization of key chapters
1. Material on sets required for the study of probability is placed in the chapter on counting; extraneous set concepts have been removed.
2. Material required for linear programming and matrices is placed in an easy-to-cover Chapter 1.
3. The chapter on matrices (Chapter 2) is placed just after systems of linear equations (Chapter 1); this helps to motivate the power of matrices to solve systems of *n* equations/*n* unknowns—a topic emphasized in this edition.
4. The material on functions now appears in the appendix and can be covered at any time or not at all, at the instructor's discretion.

*exercises and examples
1. Where it seemed helpful, new examples have been added (see Chapter 1, Chapter 2 on matrices, Chapter 4 on the simplex method, Chapter 5 on counting, Chapter 8 on Markov chains, Chapter 10 on statistics, the normal distribution, and Chapter 11 on finance).
2. Where appropriate, additional exercises were added (see Chapter 1, Chapter 2 on matrices, Chapter 5 on counting, Chapter 6 on probability, Chapter 8 on Markov chains, and Chapter 11 on finance).

*new or updated topics
1. A brief discussion on percent and decimals appears in Chapter 1.
2. A short section on prediction and interest appears in Chapter 1 as an application of linear equations.
3. A new section appears in Chapter 2 on solving *n* equations in *n* unknowns.
4. Interest rates in Chapter 11, "Finance," were adjusted to reflect current market conditions; new tables have been compiled to reflect real-life use of interest rates.
5. The CPA, CMA, and Actuary Exams questions were appended to reflect questions occurring during the past four years.
6. Where it seemed appropriate, a set of true/false and fill in the blanks questions appear in the chapter review.
7. Numerous articles have been referenced to allow interested students to seek out relevant applications.

*rewritten material
1. Chapter 1 was redone to emphasize the topics needed for the study of finite mathematics.
2. Chapter 2 now contains a more appropriate example to illustrate the Leontief model.
3. Chapter 4, "Simplex Method," was rewritten to provide more motivation and explanation of the simplex method.

Contents

FINITE MATHEMATICS WITH APPLICATIONS

for Business and Social Sciences

1

Linear Equations and Inequalities

*These sections may be omitted without loss of continuity.

1. Real Numbers

Set

Empty Set

We begin with the idea of a *set*. A *set* is a collection of objects considered as a whole. The objects of a set S are called *elements* of S, or *members* of S. The set that has no elements, called the *empty set* or *null set*, is denoted by the symbol $\emptyset$.

If a is an element of the set S, we write $a \in S$, which is read "a is an element of S" or "a is in S." To indicate that a is not an element of S, we write $a \notin S$, which is read "a is not an element of S" or "a is not in S."

Ordinarily, a set S can be written in either of two ways. These two methods are illustrated by the following example: Consider the set D that has the elements

$$0, 1, 2, 3, 4, 5, 6, 7, 8, 9$$

In this case, we write

$$D = \{0, 1, 2, 3, 4, 5, 6, 7, 8, 9\}$$

This expression is read "D is the set consisting of the elements 0, 1, 2, 3, 4, 5, 6, 7, 8, 9." Here, we list or display the elements of the set D.

Another way of writing this same set D is to write

$$D = \{x \mid x \text{ is a nonnegative integer less than } 10\}$$

This is read "D is the set of all x such that x is a nonnegative integer less than 10." Here, we have described the set D by giving a property that every element of D has and that no element not in D can have.

Counting Numbers

One of the most frequently used set of numbers in finite mathematics is the set of *counting numbers,* namely

$$\{1, 2, 3, 4, \ldots\}$$

These are sometimes referred to as *positive integers*. As the name *counting numbers* implies, they are used to count things. For example, there are 26 letters in our alphabet, and there are 100 cents in a dollar.

Integers

Another important collection of numbers is the set of *integers,*

$$\{0, 1, -1, 2, -2, \ldots\}$$

which consists of the *nonnegative integers,*

$$\{0, 1, 2, 3, \ldots\}$$

and the *negative integers,*

$$\{-1, -2, -3, \ldots\}$$

Integers enable us to handle certain types of situations. For example, if a company shows a loss of \$3 per share, we might decide to denote this loss as a gain of $-\$3$. Then, if this same company shows a profit of \$4 per share next year, the profit over the 2 year period can be obtained by adding -3 to 4, getting a profit of \$1.

However, integers do not enable us to solve *all* problems. For example, can we use an integer to answer the question, "What part of a dollar is 49¢?" Or, can we use an integer to represent the length of a city lot (in feet) if we end up with a length more than 125 feet and less than 126 feet?

Rational Numbers

The answer to both these questions is "No"! We need new or different numbers to handle such situations. These new numbers are called *rational numbers*. To answer the first question, "What part of a dollar is 49¢?" we can say

$$\frac{49}{100}$$

Rational numbers are thus ratios of integers. For a rational number $\frac{a}{b}$, the integer a is called the *numerator,* and the integer b, which cannot be zero, is called the *denominator.*

Examples of rational numbers are $\frac{3}{4}$, $\frac{5}{3}$, $-\frac{2}{7}$, $\frac{100}{3}$, $-\frac{8}{3}$. Since the ratio of any integer to 1 is that integer, the integers are also rational numbers. Thus, $\frac{3}{1} = 3$, $-\frac{2}{1} = -2$, $\frac{0}{1} = 0$.

In this book, we will always write rational numbers in *lowest terms;* that is, the numerator and the denominator will contain no common factors. Thus, $\frac{4}{6}$, which is not in lowest terms, will be written as $\frac{2}{3}$, which is in lowest terms.

In some situations, even a rational number will not accurately describe the situation. For example, if you have an isosceles right triangle in which the two equal sides are 1 foot long, can the length of the third side be expressed as a rational number? See Figure 1.

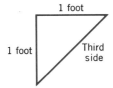

Figure 1

$$\text{Third side} = \sqrt{1 + 1}$$

And how about the value of π (Greek letter "pi")? The Greeks first learned that no matter what two circles are used, the ratio of the circumference to the diameter of the first circle is always the same as the ratio of the circumference to the diameter of the second one. Can this common value, which we call π, be represented by a rational number? See Figure 2.

As it happens, the answer to both these questions is "No." For the first question, we know by the theorem of Pythagoras that the length of the third side is

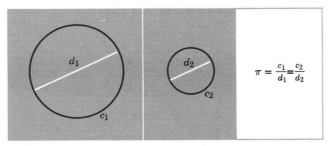

Figure 2

Irrational
Numbers

Real Numbers

$\sqrt{2}$. However, $\sqrt{2}$ is not a rational number—it is not the ratio of two integers. The well-known symbol assigned to the ratio of the circumference to the diameter of a circle is π, which also cannot be expressed as the ratio of two integers. Such numbers as $\sqrt{2}$, π, $\sqrt[3]{5}$, etc., are called *irrational numbers*—numbers that are not rational.

The irrational numbers and the rational numbers together form the *real numbers*.

Decimals and Percents

Decimals

To represent each real number, we use what is commonly referred to as a *decimal representation,* or simply a *decimal.* The table below lists the decimal equivalents of some frequently encountered rational numbers.

Rational Number	Decimal Equivalent
$\frac{1}{2}$	0.5
$\frac{1}{3}$	0.333 . . .
$\frac{2}{3}$	0.666 . . .
$\frac{1}{4}$	0.25
$\frac{3}{4}$	0.75
$\frac{1}{5}$	0.2
$\frac{2}{5}$	0.4
$\frac{3}{5}$	0.6
$\frac{4}{5}$	0.8
$\frac{1}{8}$	0.125
$\frac{3}{8}$	0.375
$\frac{5}{8}$	0.625
$\frac{7}{8}$	0.875

The decimal equivalent of any rational number is obtained by long division: Divide the denominator into the numerator. For example, we find that the decimal equivalent of $\frac{7}{66}$ is 0.10606 . . . as follows:

$$
\begin{array}{r}
0.10606 \\
66\overline{)7.00000} \\
\underline{6\,6} \\
400 \\
\underline{396} \\
400 \\
\underline{396} \\
\text{etc.}
\end{array}
$$

Observe the following fact: The decimal equivalent of a rational number is always one of two types: (*1*) terminating or ending ($\frac{3}{4}, \frac{4}{5}$, etc.) or (*2*) eventually repeating ($\frac{2}{3}$—the 6's repeat; $\frac{7}{66}$—eventually the block 06 repeats).

At first, it may appear that these two types account for all possible decimals.

However, it is relatively easy to construct a decimal that neither terminates nor eventually repeats. For example, the decimal

$$0.123456789101112\ldots$$

where we write down the positive integers one after the other, will neither terminate nor eventually repeat.

In fact, there are an infinite number of such decimals, and they represent the irrational numbers. For example, the real numbers

$$\sqrt{2} = 1.414213\ldots \quad \text{and} \quad \pi = 3.14159\ldots$$

are irrational, since they have decimal representations that neither terminate nor eventually repeat.

Thus, *real numbers* and *all possible decimals* are equivalent concepts. It is this feature of real numbers that provides the "practicality" of real numbers.* In the physical world a changing magnitude, such as the length of a heated rod, the velocity of a particle, and so on, is assumed to pass through every possible magnitude from the initial one to the final one. Since the precise measurement of a magnitude is naturally given by a decimal, the logical equivalent of all possible magnitudes is all possible decimals (real numbers).

In practice, it is usually necessary to represent real numbers by approximations. For example, using the symbol $\approx$, read "approximately equal to," we can write

$$\sqrt{2} \approx 1.4142 \quad \text{and} \quad \pi \approx 3.1416$$

Percents
Many of the problems we shall encounter use *percents* rather than decimals. For example, interest rates and tax rates are almost always expressed as percents. It is easy to convert from a decimal to a percent. Let's look at a few examples.

$$0.15 = 15\% \qquad 0.20 = 20\% \qquad 1.45 = 145\%$$
$$0.08 = 8\% \qquad 0.0525 = 5\tfrac{1}{4}\% \qquad 0.001 = 0.1\%$$

The idea should be clear—to change from a decimal to a percent, move the decimal point two places to the right and add a percent symbol. Reverse this procedure to get from a percent to its decimal equivalent.

Example 1 A resident of Illinois has base income, after adjustments for deductions, of $18,000. The state income tax on this base income is $2\tfrac{1}{2}\%$. What tax is due?

Solution We must find $2\tfrac{1}{2}\%$ of $18,000. We convert $2\tfrac{1}{2}\%$ to its decimal equivalent and then multiply by $18,000.

$$2\tfrac{1}{2}\% \text{ of } \$18{,}000 = (0.025)(\$18{,}000) = \$450$$
$$\uparrow$$
$$\text{Use a}$$
$$\text{calculator}$$

The state income tax is $450.00. ∎

*Other number systems exist that have many applications (such as the complex numbers). In this book, however, we limit our discussion to problems in which only real numbers are used.

Properties of Real Numbers

As an aid to your review of real numbers and their properties, we list several important rules and notations. The letters a, b, c, d represent real numbers; any exceptions will be noted as they occur.

1. *Commutative Laws*
   (a) $a + b = b + a$ (b) $a \cdot b = b \cdot a$

2. *Associative Laws*
   (a) $a + b + c = (a + b) + c = a + (b + c)$
   (b) $a \cdot b \cdot c = (a \cdot b) \cdot c = a \cdot (b \cdot c)$

3. *Distributive Law*
   $a \cdot (b + c) = (a \cdot b) + (a \cdot c)$

4. *Arithmetic of Ratios*

   (a) $\dfrac{a}{b} = a \cdot \dfrac{1}{b}$ $b \neq 0$

   (b) $\dfrac{a}{b} + \dfrac{c}{d} = \dfrac{(a \cdot d) + (b \cdot c)}{b \cdot d}$ $b \neq 0, \quad d \neq 0$

   (c) $\dfrac{a}{b} \cdot \dfrac{c}{d} = \dfrac{a \cdot c}{b \cdot d}$ $b \neq 0, \quad d \neq 0$

   (d) $\dfrac{a}{b} \div \dfrac{c}{d} = \dfrac{a}{b} \cdot \dfrac{d}{c} = \dfrac{a \cdot d}{b \cdot c}$ $b \neq 0, \quad c \neq 0, \quad d \neq 0$

5. *Rules for Division*

   $0 \div a = 0 \quad$ or $\quad \dfrac{0}{a} = 0 \quad$ for any real number a different from 0

   $a \div 0 \quad$ or $\quad \dfrac{a}{0} \quad$ is undefined for any real number a, including 0; *never divide by zero!*

   $a \div a = 1 \quad$ for any real number a different from 0

6. *Cancellation Laws*
   (a) If $a \cdot c = b \cdot c$ and c is not 0, then $a = b$.

   (b) If b and c are not 0, then $\dfrac{a \cdot c}{b \cdot c} = \dfrac{a}{b}$.

7. *Product Law*
   If $a \cdot b = 0$, then either $a = 0$ or $b = 0$.

8. *Rules of Signs*
   (a) $a \cdot (-b) = -(a \cdot b)$ (b) $(-a) \cdot b = -(a \cdot b)$
   (c) $(-a) \cdot (-b) = a \cdot b$ (d) $-(-a) = a$

9. *Agreements: Notations*
   (a) Given $a \cdot b + c$ or $c + a \cdot b$, we agree to multiply $a \cdot b$ first, and then add c.
   (b) A mixed number $3\frac{5}{8}$ means $3 + \frac{5}{8}$; 3 *times* $\frac{5}{8}$ is written as $3(\frac{5}{8})$ or $(3)(\frac{5}{8})$ or $3 \cdot \frac{5}{8}$.

10. *Exponents*
    For any positive integer n and any real number x, we define

    $$x^1 = x, \quad x^2 = x \cdot x, \quad \ldots, \quad x^n = \underbrace{x \cdot x \cdot \ldots \cdot x}_{n \text{ factors}}$$

For any real number $x \neq 0$, we define

$$x^0 = 1, \quad x^{-1} = \frac{1}{x}, \quad x^{-2} = \frac{1}{x^2}, \quad \ldots, \quad x^{-n} = \frac{1}{x^n}$$

11. *Laws of Exponents* (a, x are real numbers; n, m are integers)

(a) $x^n \cdot x^m = x^{n+m}$ (b) $(x^n)^m = x^{nm}$

(c) $(ax)^n = a^n \cdot x^n$ (d) $\left(\dfrac{x}{a}\right)^n = \dfrac{x^n}{a^n}$ $a \neq 0$

(e) $\dfrac{x^n}{x^m} = x^{n-m}$ $x \neq 0$

12. *Roots*

For a positive integer q, the qth root of x, $\sqrt[q]{x}$, is a symbol for the real number which, when raised to the power q, equals x. If q is even and x is positive, then $\sqrt[q]{x}$ is declared to be positive. For example,

$$\sqrt[3]{8} = 2 \quad \text{since } 2^3 = 8 \qquad \sqrt[2]{64} = 8 \quad \text{since} \quad 8^2 = 64$$

Here $\sqrt[3]{x}$ is called the *cube root* of x and $\sqrt[2]{x}$ is called the *square root* of x. Usually, we abbreviate square roots by $\sqrt{}$, dropping the ^{2}. *Be careful! No meaning is assigned to even roots of negative numbers,* since any real number raised to an even power is nonnegative. For example, $\sqrt{4} = 2$, whereas $\sqrt{-4}$ has no meaning in the set of real numbers. On the other hand, $\sqrt[3]{27} = 3$, while $\sqrt[3]{-64} = -4$ since $(-4)^3 = -64$. Thus, meaning is given to odd roots of negative numbers. Finally, following the usual convention, even roots of positive numbers are always positive. Thus, even though $(2)^2 = 4$ and $(-2)^2 = 4$, only the positive root 2 equals $\sqrt{4}$. That is, $\sqrt{4} = 2$.

Example 2

(a) $\dfrac{2}{3} \cdot \dfrac{9}{4} = \dfrac{18}{12} = \dfrac{6 \cdot 3}{6 \cdot 2} = \dfrac{3}{2}$ (b) $\dfrac{1}{2} + \dfrac{3}{4} = \dfrac{2}{4} + \dfrac{3}{4} = \dfrac{5}{4}$

(c) $(-3)^2 = 9$ (d) $-3^2 = -9$

(e) $3 + 4 \cdot 2 = 3 + 8 = 11$ (f) $(3 + 4)^2 = 7^2 = 49$

■

Positive and Negative Numbers

The real numbers can be divided into three nonempty sets that have no elements in common: (*1*) the set of positive real numbers; (*2*) the set with just 0 as a member; and (*3*) the set of negative real numbers. We list some familiar properties:

1. Any real number is either positive or negative or equal to zero.
2. The sum and product of two positive numbers is positive.
3. The product of two negative numbers is positive.
4. The product of a positive number and a negative number is negative.

For real numbers a and b, a is less than b ($a < b$) or b is greater than a ($b > a$) if and only if the difference $b - a$ is a positive real number. For example, $2 < 7$ and $-3 > -6$. It is easy to conclude that

$$a \text{ is positive if and only if} \quad a > 0$$
$$a \text{ is negative if and only if} \quad a < 0$$

If a is less than or equal to b, we write $a \leq b$. If a is greater than or equal to b, we write $a \geq b$. If $a < c$ and $c < b$, we write $a < c < b$. This says that c is between a and b. Similarly, if $a \leq c$ and $c \leq b$, we write $a \leq c \leq b$. The notations $a \leq c < b$ and $a < c \leq b$ are given similar interpretations.

Inequalities obey the following laws:

1. *Addition Law*
   If $a \leq b$, then $a + c \leq b + c$ for any choice of c. That is, the addition of a number to each side of an inequality will not affect the sense or direction of the inequality.

2. *Multiplication Laws*
   (a) If $a \leq b$ and $c > 0$, then $a \cdot c \leq b \cdot c$.
   (b) If $a \leq b$ and $c < 0$, then $a \cdot c \geq b \cdot c$.
   When multiplying each side of an inequality by a number, the sense or direction of the inequality remains the same if we multiply by a positive number; it is reversed if we multiply by a negative number.

3. *Division Laws*
   (a) If $a > 0$, then $\dfrac{1}{a} > 0$.   That is, the reciprocal of a positive number is positive.

   (b) If a, b are positive and if $a < b$, then $\dfrac{1}{a} > \dfrac{1}{b}$.

4. *Trichotomy Law*
   For any two real numbers a, b, one and only one of the following is true: $a < b$, $a = b$, $b < a$.

Example 3   (a) Since $2 < 3$, then $2 + 5 < 3 + 5$, or $7 < 8$.
(b) Since $2 < 3$ and $6 > 0$, then $2 \cdot 6 < 3 \cdot 6$, or $12 < 18$.
(c) Since $2 < 3$ and $-4 < 0$, then $2 \cdot (-4) > 3 \cdot (-4)$, or $-8 > -12$.
(d) Since $3 > 0$, then $\dfrac{1}{3} > 0$.

(e) Since $2 < 3$, then $\dfrac{1}{2} > \dfrac{1}{3}$.

Coordinates

Origin   Real numbers can be represented geometrically on a horizontal line. We begin by selecting an arbitrary point O, called the *origin,* and associate it with the real number 0. We then establish a scale by marking off line segments of equal length (units) on each side of 0. By agreeing that the positive direction is to the right of 0 and the negative direction is to the left of 0, we can successively associate the integers 1, 2, 3, . . . with each mark to the right of 0 and the integers -1, -2, -3, . . . with each mark to the left of 0. See Figure 3.

Figure 3

By subdividing these segments, we can locate rational numbers such as $\frac{1}{2}$ and $-\frac{3}{2}$. The irrational numbers are located by geometric construction (as in the case of $\sqrt{2}$) or by other means. In this way, every point P on the line is associated with a unique real number x, called the *coordinate* of P (see Figure 4). Coordinates establish an ordering for the real numbers; that is, if a and b are coordinates of two points P and Q, respectively, then $a < b$ means that P lies to the left of Q on the line.

Coordinate

Figure 4

Variables

A *variable* is a symbol (usually a letter x, y, etc.) used to represent any real number. An *equation* is a statement involving one or more variables and an "equals" sign ($=$). To *solve* an equation means to find all possible numbers that the variables can assume to make the statement true. The set of all such numbers is called the *solution*. Two equations with the same solution are called *equivalent*.

Equation

Solution

Example 4   Solve the equation: $3x - 8 = x + 4$

Solution   We use the properties of real numbers and proceed as follows:

$$3x - 8 = x + 4$$
$$2x - 8 = 4 \qquad \text{Subtract } x \text{ from both sides}$$
$$2x = 12 \qquad \text{Add 8 to both sides}$$
$$x = 6 \qquad \text{Divide each side by 2}$$

The solution is $x = 6$.

■

Example 5   Solve the equation: $x^2 + x - 12 = 0$

Solution   We factor the left side, obtaining

$$(x - 3)(x + 4) = 0$$

The product law states that either the first factor or the second factor must equal zero. Thus,

$$x - 3 = 0 \qquad \text{or} \qquad x + 4 = 0$$
$$x = 3 \qquad \text{or} \qquad x = -4$$

The solutions to the equation are $x = 3$ or $x = -4$.

■

Inequality

    An *inequality* is a statement involving one or more variables and one of the inequality symbols ($<$, $\leq$, $>$, $\geq$). To *solve* an inequality means to find all possible numbers that the variables can assume to make the statement true. The set of all such numbers is called the *solution*. Two inequalities with the same solution are called *equivalent*.

To find the solution of an inequality, we apply the laws for inequalities.

Example 6   Solve the inequality: $x + 2 \leq 3x - 5$

Solution
$$x + 2 \leq 3x - 5$$
$$-2x \leq -7 \qquad \text{Subtract 2 and then } 3x \text{ from both sides}$$
$$x \geq \frac{7}{2} \qquad \text{Multiply by } -\tfrac{1}{2} \text{ and remember to reverse the inequality because we multiplied by a negative number}$$

The solution is the set of all real numbers to the right of $\frac{7}{2}$, including $\frac{7}{2}$ (see Figure 5).

Figure 5

In graphing the solution to an inequality, our practice will be to use a filled-in circle (●) if the number is included (such as $\frac{7}{2}$ in Figure 5) and an open circle (○) if the number is to be excluded.

Exercise 1

Solutions to Odd-Numbered Problems begin on page 551.

In Problems 1–8 represent each rational number as a decimal.

1. $\frac{1}{2}$ 2. $\frac{3}{4}$ 3. $\frac{13}{8}$ 4. $\frac{15}{8}$
5. $\frac{4}{3}$ 6. $\frac{5}{3}$ 7. $\frac{1}{6}$ 8. $\frac{5}{6}$

In Problems 9–16 write each decimal as a percent.

9. 0.45   10. 0.85   11. 1.12   12. 1.25
13. 0.06   14. 0.07   15. 0.0025   16. 0.0015

In Problems 17–24 write each percent as a decimal.

17. 42%   18. 7.25%   19. 0.2%   20. 300%
21. 0.001%   22. 4.3%   23. 73.4%   24. 92%

In Problems 25–28 write each rational number in lowest terms.

25. $\frac{2}{40}$ 26. $\frac{25}{45}$ 27. $\frac{6}{8}$ 28. $\frac{8}{24}$

In Problems 29–32 calculate the indicated quantity.

29. 15% of 1000   30. 20% of 500   31. 18% of 100   32. 10% of 50

In Problems 33–46 find the solution x of each equation.

33. $2x + 5 = 7$ 34. $x + 6 = 2$
35. $6 - x = 0$ 36. $6 + x = 0$
37. $3(2 - x) = 9$ 38. $5(x + 1) = 10$

39. $\dfrac{4x}{3} + \dfrac{x}{3} = 5$ 40. $\dfrac{2x}{5} + \dfrac{x}{5} = 9$

41. $\dfrac{3x - 5}{x - 3} = 1$ 42. $\dfrac{2x + 1}{x - 1} = 3$

43. $x^2 - x - 12 = 0$ 44. $x^2 + 7x = 0$
45. $x^2 - 5x + 6 = 0$ 46. $x^2 - x - 6 = 0$

In Problems 47–58 find x.

47. $x = 3^2$ 48. $x = 2^3$ 49. $x = 2^{-3}$ 50. $x = 3^{-2}$
51. $x = -3^2$ 52. $x = (-3)^2$ 53. $x^3 = 8$ 54. $x^5 = -32$
55. $2^x = 4$ 56. $3^x = 81$ 57. $4^x = 4^5$ 58. $2^x = 2^{10}$

In Problems 59–62 replace the * by $<$, $>$, or $=$.

59. $\frac{1}{3} * 0.33$ 60. $\frac{1}{4} * 0.25$ 61. $3 * \sqrt{9}$ 62. $\pi * \frac{22}{7}$

In Problems 63–70 find the solution.

63. $3x + 5 \le 2$ 64. $14x - 21x + 16 \le 3x - 2$
65. $3x + 5 \ge 2$ 66. $4 - 5x \ge 3$
67. $-3x + 5 \le 2$ 68. $8 - 2x \le 5x - 6$
69. $6x - 3 \ge 8x + 5$ 70. $-3x \le 2x + 5$

2. Rectangular Coordinates

Consider two lines, one horizontal and the other vertical. Call the horizontal line *x-axis* the *x-axis* and the vertical line the *y-axis*. Assign coordinates to points on these *y-axis* lines, as described previously, by using their point of intersection as the origin O and using a convenient scale on each. We follow the usual convention that points on the *x*-axis to the right of O are associated with positive real numbers, those to the left of O with negative numbers, those on the *y*-axis above O are associated with positive real numbers, and those below O with negative real numbers. This gives the origin a value of zero on both the *x*-axis and the *y*-axis. See Figure 6 on page 12.

Any point P in the plane formed by the *x*-axis and *y*-axis can then be located *Ordered Pair* by using an *ordered pair* of real numbers. Let x denote the signed distance of P from the *y*-axis (signed in the sense that if P is to the right of the *y*-axis, then $x > 0$ and if P is to the left of the *y*-axis, then $x < 0$); and let y denote the signed *Coordinates* distance of P from the *x*-axis. The ordered pair (x, y), the *coordinates of P,* then gives us enough information to locate the point P. We can assign ordered pairs of real numbers to every point P, as shown in Figure 7 on page 12.

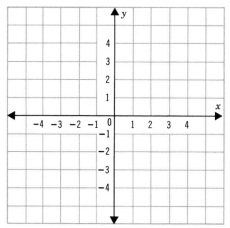

Figure 6

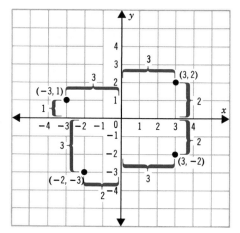

Figure 7

Abscissa
Ordinate

If (x, y) are the coordinates of a point P, then x is called the *abscissa* of P and y is the *ordinate* of P. For example, the coordinates of the origin O are $(0, 0)$. The abscissa of any point on the y-axis is 0; the ordinate of any point on the x-axis is 0.

Rectangular
Coordinate System

The coordinate system described here is a *rectangular* or *cartesian coordinate system* and divides the plane into four sections called *quadrants* (see Figure 8).

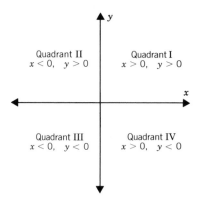

Figure 8

Quadrants

In quadrant I, both the abscissa x and the ordinate y of all points are positive; in quadrant II, $x < 0$ and $y > 0$; in quadrant III, both x and y are negative; and in quadrant IV, $x > 0$ and $y < 0$.

RENÉ DESCARTES (1596–1650), after whom the cartesian coordinate system was named, was born in La Haye, France. After spending several years participating in various wars, he published a treatise introducing analytic geometry. In addition to being a mathematician, he was a respected philosopher and theologian.

Graphs

When a specified relationship between x and y is given, its *graph* consists of the set of points (x, y) in the plane that obey the given relationship. To draw a graph, plot a sufficient number of points to see a pattern.

Example 1   Graph the set of points (x, y) given by the equation

$$y = x$$

Solution   We wish to locate all points (x, y) for which the abscissa x and ordinate y are equal. Some of these points are

$$(0, 0), (0.1, 0.1), (1, 1), (1.5, 1.5), (3, 3), (-3, -3), (-0.2, -0.2), (8, 8)$$

The graph is given in Figure 9. ◼

Example 2   Graph the set of points (x, y) given by the equation

$$y = 2x + 5$$

Solution   We want to find all points (x, y) for which the ordinate y equals twice the abscissa x plus 5. To locate some of these points (and thus to get an idea of the pattern of the graph), let us *assign* some numbers x and find corresponding values for y. Thus:

$$\begin{array}{ll} \text{If} \quad x = 0, & y = 2 \cdot 0 + 5 = 5 \\ \text{If} \quad x = 1, & y = 2 \cdot 1 + 5 = 7 \\ \text{If} \quad x = -5, & y = 2 \cdot (-5) + 5 = -5 \\ \text{If} \quad x = 10 & y = 2 \cdot 10 + 5 = 25 \end{array}$$

We form the points (x, y), namely $(0, 5)$, $(1, 7)$, $(-5, -5)$, and $(10, 25)$. By connecting these points, we obtain the graph. See Figure 10. ◼

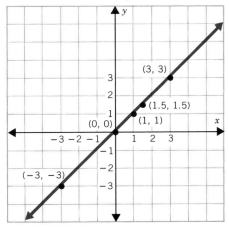

Figure 9

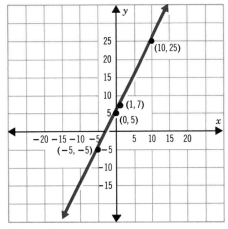

Figure 10

Exercise 2
Solutions to Odd-Numbered Problems begin on page 551.

1. Find the coordinates of each point in Figure 11.
2. Locate the points $(3, -2)$, $(-2, 3)$, $(5, 0)$, $(-3, -4)$, and $(0, 8)$ using Figure 11 as a background.

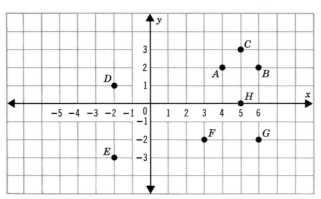

Figure 11

In Problems 3–6 use Figure 11, where $A = (a_1, a_2)$, $B = (b_1, b_2)$, $C = (c_1, c_2)$, and $F = (f_1, f_2)$, to compute each quantity.

3. $\dfrac{f_2 - a_2}{f_1 - a_1}$ 4. $\dfrac{f_2 - c_2}{f_1 - c_1}$ 5. $\dfrac{a_2 - c_2}{a_1 - c_1}$ 6. $\dfrac{a_2 - b_2}{a_1 - b_1}$

In Problems 7–10 copy the tables at the right and fill in the missing values of the given equations. Use these points to graph each equation.

7. $y = x - 3$

x	0		2	-2	4	-4
y		0				

8. $y = -3x + 3$

x	0		2	-2	4	-4
y		0				

9. $2x - y = 6$

x	0		2	-2	4	-4
y		0				

10. $x + 3y = 9$

x	0		2	-2	4	-4
y		0				

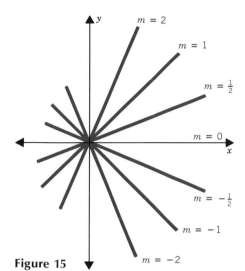

Figure 15

Example 3   The graph of the equation $x = 3$ is a vertical line (see Figure 16).

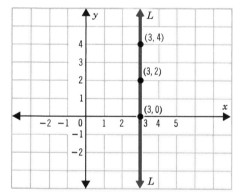

Figure 16

Now let L be a nonvertical line with slope m and containing (x_1, y_1). For (x, y) any other point on L, we have

$$m = \frac{y - y_1}{x - x_1} \qquad \text{or} \qquad y - y_1 = m(x - x_1)$$

Point-Slope Form   **An equation of a nonvertical line of slope m that passes through the point (x_1, y_1) is**

$$y - y_1 = m(x - x_1)$$

Example 4   An equation of the line with slope 4 and passing through the point $(1, 2)$ is

$$y - 2 = 4(x - 1)$$
$$y = 4x - 2$$

See Figure 17.

In Problems 11–20 graph the set of points (x, y) that obey the given equation.

11. $y = 3x$ 12. $y = 4x$
13. $y = 2x - 3$ 14. $y = 2x + 1$
15. $y = 0$ 16. $x = 0$
17. $y = -2x - 3$ 18. $y = -2x - 4$
19. $3x + 2y + 6 = 0$ 20. $2x - 3y + 12 = 0$

21. Graph the equations in Problems 17 and 18 on the same coordinate system. Do you notice anything?

3.   The Straight Line

Linear Equation   In this section, we study a certain type of equation, the *linear equation,* and its graph, the *straight line.* We begin with the result from plane geometry that there is one and only one line L containing two distinct points P and Q. See Figure 12.

Figure 12

If P and Q are each represented by ordered pairs of real numbers, the following definition can be given:

Slope of a Line   **Let P and Q be two distinct points with coordinates (x_1, y_1) and (x_2, y_2), respectively. The *slope* m of the line L containing P and Q is defined by the formula***

$$m = \frac{y_2 - y_1}{x_2 - x_1} \qquad \text{if} \quad x_1 \neq x_2$$

*The following argument, involving similar triangles, shows that the slope of a line L is the same no matter what two distinct points are used: Let L be a nonvertical line joining P and Q and let X and Y be any other two distinct points on L. Construct the triangles depicted in the figure. Since triangle PQA is similar to triangle XYB (why?), it follows that the lengths of the corresponding sides are in proportion. That is, $|AQ|/|BY| = |AP|/|BX|$ or $|AQ|/|AP| = |BY|/|BX|$. But the slope m of L is $|AQ|/|AP|$, and by the foregoing equality, we see that $m = |BY|/|BX|$. In other words, since X and Y are *any* two points, the slope m of a line L is the same no matter what points on L are used to compute m.

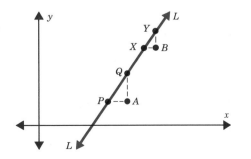

If $x_1 = x_2$, the slope m of L is *undefined* **(since this results in division by zero) and L is a** *vertical line*.

We can also write the slope m of a nonvertical line as

$$m = \frac{\text{change in } y}{\text{change in } x} = \frac{\Delta y}{\Delta x}$$

That is, the slope m of a nonvertical line L is the ratio of the change in the ordinates from P to Q to the change in the abscissas from P to Q. In other words, the slope m of a line L equals the "rise over run" of the line. See Figure 13.

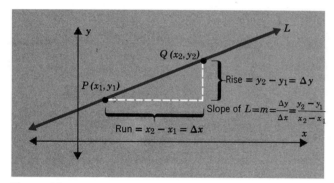

Figure 13

Since

$$\frac{y_2 - y_1}{x_2 - x_1} = \frac{y_1 - y_2}{x_1 - x_2}$$

the result is the same whether the changes are computed from P to Q or from Q to P.

Example 1   The slope m of the line joining the points $(1, 2)$ and $(5, -3)$ may be computed as

$$m = \frac{-3 - 2}{5 - 1} = \frac{-5}{4} \qquad \text{or as} \qquad m = \frac{2 - (-3)}{1 - 5} = \frac{5}{-4} = \frac{-5}{4}$$

To get a better idea of the meaning of the slope of a line L, consider the following example.

Example 2   Compute the slopes of the lines L_1, L_2, L_3, and L_4 containing the following pairs of points. Graph each line.

$$
\begin{array}{lll}
L_1: & P = (2, 3) & Q_1 = (-1, -2) \\
L_2: & P = (2, 3) & Q_2 = (3, -1) \\
L_3: & P = (2, 3) & Q_3 = (5, 3) \\
L_4: & P = (2, 3) & Q_4 = (2, 5)
\end{array}
$$

Solution   Let m_1, m_2, m_3, and m_4 denote the slopes of the lines L_1, L_2, L_3, and L_4, respectively. Then

$$m_1 = \frac{-2 - 3}{-1 - 2} = \frac{-5}{-3} = \frac{5}{3} \qquad \text{A rise of 5 over a run of 3}$$

$$m_2 = \frac{-1 - 3}{3 - 2} = \frac{-4}{1} = -4$$

$$m_3 = \frac{3 - 3}{5 - 2} = \frac{0}{3} = 0$$

$$m_4 = \text{ is undefined}$$

The graphs of these lines are given in Figure 14.

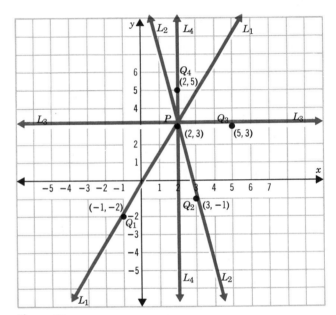

Figure 14

As Figure 14 indicates, when the slope m of a line is positive, the line *slants upward* from left to right (L_1); when the slope m is negative, the line *slants downward* from left to right (L_2); when the slope $m = 0$, the line is horizontal (L_3); and when the slope m is undefined, the line is vertical (L_4). Figure 15 on page 18 illustrates the slopes of several lines. Note the pattern.

Equations of Lines

A vertical line is given by the equation

$$x = a$$

where a is a given real number.

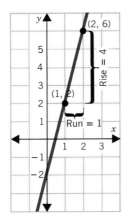

Figure 17

Example 5 Find an equation of the line L passing through the points $(2, 3)$ and $(-4, 5)$. Graph the line L.

Solution Since two points are given, we first compute the slope of the line:

$$m = \frac{5 - 3}{-4 - 2} = \frac{2}{-6} = \frac{-1}{3}$$

Using the point $(2, 3)$ (we could use the other point instead, if we wished), and the fact that the slope $m = \dfrac{-1}{3}$, the point–slope equation of the line is

$$y - 3 = \frac{-1}{3}(x - 2)$$

See Figure 18 for the graph.

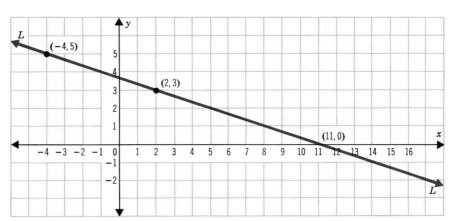

Figure 18

Another form of the equation of the line graphed in Example 5 can be obtained by multiplying both sides by 3 and collecting terms.

$$3(y - 3) = 3(-1/3)(x - 2) \qquad \text{Multiply by 3}$$
$$3y - 9 = -1(x - 2)$$
$$3y - 9 = -x + 2$$
$$x + 3y - 11 = 0$$

This last form is referred to as the *general form,* because every line has an equation that can be written this way.

General Form   **The equation of a line L is in *general form* when it is written as**
$$Ax + By + C = 0$$
where A, B, C are three real numbers with either $A \neq 0$ or $B \neq 0$.

Intercepts   **The points at which the graph of a line L crosses the axes are called** *intercepts.* **The x-*intercept* is the abscissa of the point at which the line crosses the x-axis, and the y-*intercept* is the ordinate of the point at which the line crosses the y-axis.**

For example, the line L in Figure 19 has x-intercept 3 and y-intercept -4. The intercepts are $(3, 0)$ and $(0, -4)$.

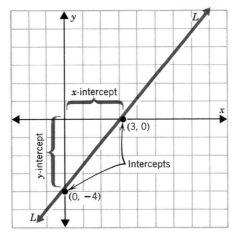

Figure 19

Example 6   Find the intercepts of the line $2x + 3y - 6 = 0$. Graph this line.

Solution   To find the point at which the graph crosses the x-axis—that is, to find the x-intercept—we need to find the number x for which $y = 0$. Thus, we set $y = 0$ to get
$$2x + 3(0) - 6 = 0$$
$$2x - 6 = 0$$
$$x = 3$$

The x-intercept is 3. To find the y-intercept, we set $x = 0$ and solve for y:
$$2(0) + 3y - 6 = 0$$
$$3y - 6 = 0$$
$$y = 2$$
The y-intercept is 2.

We now know two points on the line: $(3, 0)$ and $(0, 2)$. See Figure 20 for the graph.

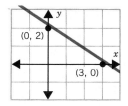

Figure 20

Another useful equation of a line is obtained when the slope m and y-intercept b are known. Since in this event we know both the slope m of the line and a point $(0, b)$ on the line, we may use the point–slope form to obtain the following equation:

$$y - b = m(x - 0) \qquad \text{or} \qquad y = mx + b$$

Slope–Intercept Form   **An equation of a line L with slope m and y-intercept b is**
$$y = mx + b$$

When the equation of a line is written in slope–intercept form, it is easy to find the slope m and y-intercept b of the line. For example, suppose the equation of a line is

$$y = -2x + 3$$

Compare it to $y = mx + b$:

$$y = -2x + 3$$
$$\uparrow \qquad \uparrow$$
$$y = \ \ mx + b$$

The slope of this line is -2 and its y-intercept is 3. Let's look at another example.

Example 7   Find the slope m and y-intercept b of the line L given by $2x + 4y - 8 = 0$. Graph the line.

Solution   To obtain the slope and y-intercept, we transform the equation to its slope-intercept form. Thus, we need to solve for y:

$$2x + 4y - 8 = 0$$
$$4y = -2x + 8$$
$$y = \left(\frac{-1}{2}\right)x + 2$$

The coefficient of x, $-\frac{1}{2}$, is the slope, and the y-intercept is 2. To graph this line, we need two points. Normally, the easiest points to locate are the intercepts. Since the y-intercept is 2, we know one intercept is $(0, 2)$. To obtain the x-intercept, set $y = 0$ and solve for x. When $y = 0$, we have

$$2x - 8 = 0$$
$$x = 4$$

Thus, the intercepts are $(4, 0)$ and $(0, 2)$, as shown in Figure 21.

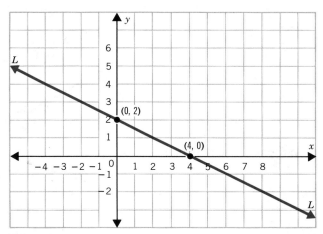

Figure 21

Exercise 3
Solutions to Odd-Numbered Problems begin on page 553.

In Problems 1–6 find the slope m of the line joining the given pair of points.

1. $P = (2, 3)$ $Q = (0, 1)$
2. $P = (1, 1)$ $Q = (5, -6)$
3. $P = (-3, 0)$ $Q = (-5, -4)$
4. $P = (4, -3)$ $Q = (0, 0)$
5. $P = (0.1, 0.3)$ $Q = (1.5, 4.0)$
6. $P = (-3, -2)$ $Q = (6, -2)$

In Problems 7–18 find a general equation for the line having the given properties.

7. Slope = 2;   passing through $(-2, 3)$
8. Slope = 3;   passing through $(4, -3)$
9. Slope = $-\frac{2}{3}$;   passing through $(1, -1)$
10. Slope = $\frac{1}{2}$;   passing through $(3, 1)$
11. Passing through $(1, 3)$ and $(-1, 2)$
12. Passing through $(-3, 4)$ and $(2, 5)$
13. Slope = -3; y-intercept = 3
14. Slope = -2; y-intercept = -2
15. x-intercept = 2; y-intercept = -1
16. x-intercept = -4; y-intercept = 4
17. Slope undefined;   passing through $(1, 4)$
18. Slope undefined;   passing through $(2, 1)$

In Problems 19–24 find the slope and y-intercept of the given line. Graph each line.

19. $3x - 2y = 6$ 20. $4x + y = 2$

21. $x + 2y = 4$
22. $-x - y = 4$
23. $x = 4$
24. $y = 3$

In Problems 25–28 find an equation of the line.

25.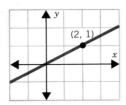

26.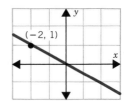

27.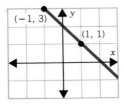

28.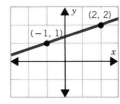

29. *Temperature Conversion.* The relationship between Celsius (°C) and Fahrenheit (°F) for measuring temperature is linear. Find an equation relating °C and °F if 0°C corresponds to 32°F and 100°C corresponds to 212°F. Use the equation to find the Celsius measure of 70°F.

4.   Parallel and Intersecting Lines

Let L and M be two lines. Exactly one of the following three relationships must hold for the two lines L and M:

1. All the points on L are the same as the points on M.
2. L and M have no points in common.
3. L and M have exactly one point in common.

Identical Lines

   If the first relationship holds, the lines L and M are called *identical lines*. In this case, their slopes and their intercepts will be the same.

   When two lines (in a plane) have no points in common, they are said to be

Parallel Lines   *parallel*. Look at Figure 22.

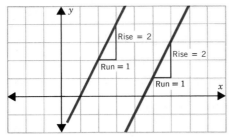

Figure 22

For two lines that are parallel, equal runs result in equal rises. This suggests the following:

Two nonvertical lines are parallel if and only if their slopes are equal.

Example 1

Show that the lines given by the equations below are parallel:

$$L:\quad 2x + 3y - 6 = 0 \qquad M:\quad 4x + 6y = 0$$

Solution

To see if these lines have equal slopes, we put each equation into slope–intercept form:

$$
\begin{array}{ll}
L:\quad 2x + 3y - 6 = 0 & \qquad M:\quad 4x + 6y = 0 \\
\qquad 3y = -2x + 6 & \qquad\qquad 6y = -4x \\
\qquad y = \dfrac{-2}{3}x + 2 & \qquad\qquad y = \dfrac{-2}{3}x \\
\qquad \text{Slope} = -2/3 & \qquad\qquad \text{Slope} = -2/3
\end{array}
$$

Since each has slope $-\frac{2}{3}$, the lines are parallel. See Figure 23. ∎

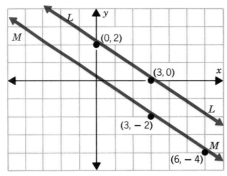

Figure 23

Intersecting Lines

If two lines L and M have exactly one point in common, then L and M are said to *intersect*, and the common point is called the *point of intersection*.

Example 2

Find the point of intersection of the two lines:

$$L:\quad x + y - 5 = 0 \qquad M:\quad 2x + y - 6 = 0$$

Solution

Let the coordinates of the point of intersection of L and M be (x_0, y_0). Since (x_0, y_0) is on both L and M, we must have

$$x_0 + y_0 - 5 = 0 \quad \text{and} \quad 2x_0 + y_0 - 6 = 0$$

Solving for y_0 in each equation, we get

$$y_0 = 5 - x_0 \qquad\qquad y_0 = 6 - 2x_0$$

Setting these equal, we obtain

$$5 - x_0 = 6 - 2x_0$$
$$x_0 = 1$$

Since $x_0 = 1$, then $y_0 = 5 - x_0 = 4$. Thus, the point of intersection of L and M is $(1, 4)$. To check this result, we verify that $(1, 4)$ is on both L and M:

$$x + y - 5 = 0 \qquad 2x + y - 6 = 0$$
$$1 + 4 - 5 = 0 \qquad 2 \cdot 1 + 4 - 6 = 0$$

This verifies that $(1, 4)$ is the point of intersection. The graphs of the lines are given in Figure 24.

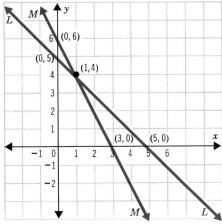

Figure 24

Systems of Equations

A *system of two linear equations in two unknowns* x and y is of the form

$$L: \quad Ax + By + C = 0$$
$$M: \quad A_1x + B_1y + C_1 = 0$$

where A, B, C, A_1, B_1, C_1 are real numbers.

A *solution* (x, y) of such a system is an ordered pair of real numbers that satisfies both equations. Finding the solution (x, y) of a system of two linear equations in two unknowns is the same as finding the point P of intersection of the two lines determined by the equations. Of course, if the equations of a system represent parallel lines, there will be no solution; if the equations represent identical lines, any point P on the line will be a solution of the system of equations (in this case, there is an infinite number of solutions).

Thus, a system of two linear equations in two unknowns will have:

1. Exactly one solution—the lines intersect
2. No solution—the lines are parallel
3. Infinitely many solutions—the lines are identical

Example 3 Determine whether the following systems of equations have one solution, no solution, or infinitely many solutions:

(a) $x + y + 2 = 0$
$4x + 4y + 8 = 0$

(b) $x + y + 2 = 0$
$2x + 2y + 14 = 0$

(c) $x + y + 2 = 0$
$2x - y + 4 = 0$

Solution Put each equation in slope–intercept form:

(a) $x + y + 2 = 0$ $\qquad\qquad 4x + 4y + 8 = 0$
$ y = -x - 2 \qquad\qquad\qquad 4y = -4x - 8$
$ y = -x - 2$

The lines are identical since they have equal slopes and equal y-intercepts. The system has infinitely many solutions.

(b) $x + y + 2 = 0$ $\qquad\qquad 2x + 2y + 14 = 0$
$ y = -x - 2 \qquad\qquad\qquad 2y = -2x - 14$
$ y = -x - 7$

The lines are parallel since they have equal slopes (-1) and different y-intercepts. The system has no solution.

(c) $x + y + 2 = 0$ $\qquad\qquad 2x - y + 4 = 0$
$ y = -x - 2 \qquad\qquad\qquad y = 2x + 4$

The lines intersect since they have unequal slopes. The system has exactly one solution.

We can solve systems of equations with exactly one solution by using two basic methods:*

METHOD 1: Substitution

METHOD 2: Add and subtract.

Substitution The *substitution method* was used in Example 2. The steps to follow are:

STEP 1: Pick one of the equations and solve for one of the unknowns in terms of the other.

STEP 2: Substitute this expression for the same unknown in the other equation.

STEP 3: Solve this equation.

STEP 4: Use the solution found in Step 3 in either of the original equations to get the value of the other unknown.

Let's look at an example.

Example 4 Use the substitution method to find the solution of the system:

$$2x + y + 6 = 0$$
$$4x - 2y + 4 = 0$$

*A third method is given in Chapter 2.

Solution STEP 1: We choose to solve for y in the first equation since this results in the easiest algebra:

$$2x + y + 6 = 0$$
$$y = -2x - 6$$

STEP 2: We replace y in the second equation by this expression:

$$4x - 2(-2x - 6) + 4 = 0$$

STEP 3: Simplify and solve this equation:

$$4x + 4x + 12 + 4 = 0$$
$$8x + 16 = 0$$
$$x = -2$$

STEP 4: Replace x by -2 in the first equation:

$$2(-2) + y + 6 = 0$$
$$-4 + y + 6 = 0$$
$$y + 2 = 0$$
$$y = -2$$

The solution of the system is $x = -2$, $y = -2$. ■

Add and Subtract The steps used in the *add and subtract method* are listed below:

STEP 1: Multiply each equation by an appropriate nonzero constant so that one of the unknowns drops out when the equations are added (or subtracted).

STEP 2: Add (or subtract) the equations and solve the resulting equation.

STEP 3: Use the solution found in Step 2 in either of the original equations to get the value of the other unknown.

Let's redo the system in Example 4, using the add and subtract method.

Example 5 Use the add and subtract method to solve the system:

$$2x + y + 6 = 0$$
$$4x - 2y + 4 = 0$$

Solution STEP 1: The add and subtract method eliminates one of the variables by adding (or subtracting) the two equations. If we choose to eliminate y in this case, we multiply the first equation by 2, obtaining the equivalent system

$$4x + 2y + 12 = 0$$
$$4x - 2y + 4 = 0$$

STEP 2:   Now, when we add these equations, we obtain

$$8x + 16 = 0$$
$$x = -2$$

STEP 3:   To find y, use $x = -2$ in one of the original equations, say the first one:

$$2(-2) + y + 6 = 0$$
$$y = -2$$

Thus, the solution of the system is $x = -2$, $y = -2$. Figure 25 illustrates the two lines.

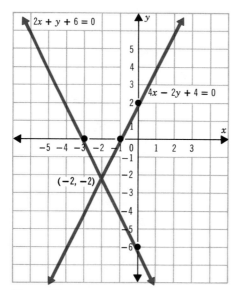

Figure 25

Example 6   Nutt's Nuts, a store that specializes in selling nuts, sells cashews for $1.50 per pound and peanuts for $0.80 per pound. At the end of the month it is found that the peanuts are not selling well. In order to sell 30 pounds of peanuts more quickly, the store manager decides to mix the 30 pounds of peanuts with some cashews and sell the mixture of peanuts and cashews for $1.00 a pound. How many pounds of cashews should be mixed with the peanuts so that the profit remains the same?

Solution   There are two unknowns: the number of pounds of cashews (call this x) and the number of pounds of the mixture (call this y). Since we know that the number of pounds of cashews plus 30 pounds of peanuts equals the number of pounds of the mixture, we can write

$$y = x + 30$$

Also, in order to keep profits the same, we must have

$$\begin{pmatrix} \text{Pounds of} \\ \text{cashews} \end{pmatrix} \cdot \begin{pmatrix} \text{Price per} \\ \text{pound} \end{pmatrix} + \begin{pmatrix} \text{Pounds of} \\ \text{peanuts} \end{pmatrix} \cdot \begin{pmatrix} \text{Price per} \\ \text{pound} \end{pmatrix} = \begin{pmatrix} \text{Pounds of} \\ \text{mixture} \end{pmatrix} \cdot \begin{pmatrix} \text{Price per} \\ \text{pound} \end{pmatrix}$$

That is,

$$(1.50)x + (0.80)(30) = (1.00)y$$
$$\tfrac{3}{2}x + 24 = y$$

Thus, we have a system of two linear equations in two unknowns to solve, namely,

$$y = x + 30$$
$$y = \tfrac{3}{2}x + 24$$

Using the substitution method, we find

$$\tfrac{3}{2}x + 24 = x + 30$$
$$\tfrac{1}{2}x = 6$$
$$x = 12$$

The store manager should mix 12 pounds of cashews with 30 pounds of peanuts. See Figure 26.

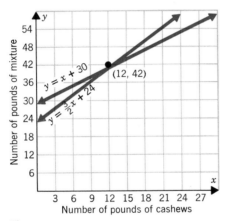

Figure 26

Exercise 4
Solutions to Odd-Numbered Problems begin on page 553.

In Problems 1–4 show that the lines are parallel by finding the slope of each line and showing they are equal.

1. $x + y = 10$
    $3x + 3y = 1$

2. $x - y = 5$
    $-2x + 2y = 7$

3. $2x - 3y + 8 = 0$
    $6x - 9y + 2 = 0$

4. $4x - 2y + 7 = 0$
    $-2x + y + 2 = 0$

In Problems 5–8 find the point of intersection of each pair of lines. Use the substitution method.

5. $x + y - 5 = 0$
    $3x - y - 7 = 0$

6. $2x + y - 7 = 0$
    $x - y + 4 = 0$

7. $3x - 2y + 5 = 0$
   $3x + y - 2 = 0$

8. $4x + y - 6 = 0$
   $4x - 2y = 0$

In Problems 9–14 find the point of intersection of each pair of lines. Use the add and subtract method.

9. $2x - 3y + 4 = 0$
   $3x + 2y - 7 = 0$

10. $3x - 4y - 2 = 0$
    $2x + 5y - 9 = 0$

11. $3x - 4y + 8 = 0$
    $2x + y - 2 = 0$

12. $5x + 2y - 15 = 0$
    $2x - 3y - 6 = 0$

13. $-2x + 3y - 7 = 0$
    $3x + 2y - 9 = 0$

14. $-3x + 4y - 10 = 0$
    $2x - 3y + 7 = 0$

In Problems 15–20 determine whether the system of equations has one solution, no solution, or infinitely many solutions.

15. $L:$ $2x - 3y + 6 = 0$
    $M:$ $4x - 6y + 7 = 0$

16. $L:$ $4x - y + 2 = 0$
    $M:$ $3x + 2y = 0$

17. $L:$ $-2x + 3y + 6 = 0$
    $M:$ $4x - 6y - 12 = 0$

18. $L:$ $2x + 3y - 5 = 0$
    $M:$ $5x - 6y + 1 = 0$

19. $L:$ $3x - 3y + 10 = 0$
    $M:$ $x + y - 2 = 0$

20. $L:$ $2x - 5y - 1 = 0$
    $M:$ $x - 2y - 1 = 0$

21. Find an equation of the line passing through $(1, 2)$ and parallel to $2x - y = 6$.

22. Find an equation of the line passing through $(-1, 3)$ and parallel to $x + y = 4$.

23. *Mixture Problem.* Sweet Delight Candies, Inc. sells boxes of candy consisting of creams and caramels. Each box sells for $4.00 and holds 50 pieces of candy (all pieces are the same size). If the caramels cost $0.05 to produce and the creams cost $0.10 to produce, how many caramels and creams should be in each box for no profit or loss? Would you increase or decrease the number of caramels in order to obtain a profit?

24. *Mixture Problem.* The manager of Nutt's Nuts regularly sells cashews for $1.50 per pound, pecans for $1.80 per pound, and peanuts for $0.80 per pound. How many pounds of cashews and pecans should be mixed with 40 pounds of peanuts to obtain a mixture of 100 pounds that will sell at $1.25 a pound so that the profit or loss is unchanged?

25. *Investment Problem.* Mr. Nicholson has just retired and needs $6000 per year in income to live on. He has $50,000 to invest and can invest in AA bonds at 15% annual interest or in Savings and Loan Certificates at 7% interest per year. How much money should be invested in each so that he realizes exactly $6000 in income per year?

26. Mr. Nicholson finds after 2 years that because of inflation he now needs $7000 per year to live on. How should he transfer his funds to achieve this amount? (Use the data from Problem 25.)

27. Joan has $1.65 in her piggy bank. She knows she only placed nickels and quarters in the bank and she knows that, in all, she put 13 coins

in the bank. Can she find out how many nickels she has without breaking her bank?

28. *Mixture Problem.* A coffee manufacturer wants to market a new blend of coffee that will cost $2.90 per pound by mixing $2.75 per pound coffee and $3 per pound coffee. What amounts of the $2.75 per pound coffee and $3 per pound coffee should be blended to obtain the desired mixture? [*Hint:* Assume the total weight of the desired blend is 100 pounds.]

29. *Mixture Problem.* One solution is 15% acid and another is 5% acid. How many cubic centimeters of each should be mixed to obtain 100 cc of a solution that is 8% acid?

30. *Investment Problem.* A bank loaned $10,000, some at an annual rate of 8% and some at an annual rate of 18%. If the income from these loans was $1000, how much was loaned at 8%? How much at 18%?

31. The Star Theater wants to know whether the majority of its patrons are adults or children. During a week in July, 5200 tickets were sold and the receipts totaled $11,875. The adult admission is $2.75 and the children's admission is $1.50. How many adult patrons were there?

32. After 1 hour of a car ride, 1/3 of the total distance is covered. One hour later, the car is 18 miles past the halfway point. What is the speed of the car (assume it is constant for the entire trip) and what is the total distance to be covered? How long will the trip take? [*Hint:* Distance = Speed • Time.]

5. Applications*

Simple Interest

A knowledge of interest—whether on money borrowed or on money saved—is of ultimate importance today. The old adage "Neither a lender nor a borrower be" is not true in this age of charge accounts and golden passbook savings plans.

Interest

Principal

Rate of Interest

Interest is money paid for the use of money. The total amount of money borrowed (whether by an individual from a bank in the form of a loan or by a bank from an individual in the form of a savings account) is called the *principal*. The *rate of interest* is the amount charged for the use of the principal for a given period of time (usually on a yearly or *per annum* basis). The rate of interest is generally expressed as a *percent*.

Simple Interest *Simple interest* **is interest computed on the principal for the entire period it is borrowed.**

*This section may be omitted without loss of continuity.

Example 1   If $250 is borrowed for 9 months at a simple interest rate of 8% per annum, what will be the interest charged?

Solution   The actual period the money is borrowed for is 9 months, or 3/4 of a year. Thus, the interest charged will be the product of the principal ($250) times the annual rate of interest (0.08) times the period of time held expressed in years (3/4):

$$\text{Interest charged} = \$(250)(0.08)\left(\frac{3}{4}\right) = \$15$$

In general, if a principal of P dollars is borrowed at a simple interest rate r expressed as a decimal, for a period of t years, the interest I charged is

$$I = Prt$$

The amount A owed at the end of a period of time is the sum of the principal and the interest. That is,

$$A = P + I = P + Prt$$

Example 2   If $500 is borrowed at a simple interest rate of 10% per annum, the amount A due after t years is

$$A = \$500 + \$500(.10)t = \$500 + \$50t$$

Thus, the amount due after 2 years is

$$A = \$500 + \$50(2) = \$600$$

The amount due after 6 months (1/2 year) is

$$A = \$500 + \$50(1/2) = \$525$$

The equation

$$A = 500 + 50t$$

is a linear equation in which A and t are the variables. If we graph this equation using A for the vertical axis and t for the horizontal axis, we can see how the amount A changes over time (see Figure 27). The slope of the line (50) equals the constant annual interest due on the loan.

Break-Even Point

In many businesses, the cost C of production and the number x of items produced can be expressed as a linear equation. Similarly, sometimes the revenue R obtained from sales and the number x of items produced can be expressed as a linear equation. When the cost C of production exceeds the revenue R from sales, the business is operating at a loss; when the revenue R exceeds the cost C, there is a profit; and when the revenue R and the cost C are equal, there is no profit or loss—this is usually referred to as the *break-even point*.

Break-Even Point

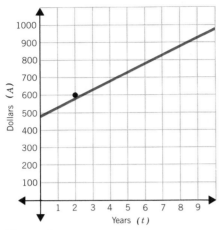

Figure 27   **Figure 28**

Example 3   Sweet Delight Candies, Inc. has daily fixed costs from salaries and building operations of $300. Each pound of candy produced costs $1 and is sold for $2 per
pound. What is the break-even point—that is, how many pounds of candy must
be sold daily to guarantee no loss and no profit?

Solution   The cost C of production is the fixed cost plus the variable cost of producing x
pounds of candy at $1 per pound. Thus,

$$C = \$1 \cdot x + \$300 = x + 300$$

The revenue R realized from the sale of x pounds of candy at $2 per pound is

$$R = \$2 \cdot x = 2x$$

The break-even point is the point where these two lines intersect. Setting $R = C$,
we find

$$2x = x + 300$$
$$x = 300$$

That is, 300 pounds of candy must be sold in order to break even.

■

In Figure 28, we see a graphical interpretation of the break-even point for
Example 3. Note that for $x > 300$, the revenue R always exceeds the cost C so that
a profit results. Similarly, for $x < 300$, the cost exceeds the revenue, resulting in a
loss.

Example 4
Pricing Candy   After negotiations with employees of Sweet Delight Candies and an increase in
the price of chocolate, the daily cost C of production for x pounds of candy is

$$C = \$1.05x + \$330$$

Solution   (a)   If each pound of candy is sold for $2, how many pounds must be sold daily
to break even?

(b)   If the selling price is increased to $2.25 per pound, what is the break-even point?

(c)   If it is known that at least 325 pounds of candy can be sold daily, what price should be charged per pound to guarantee no loss?

Solution   (a)   If each pound is sold for $2, the revenue R from sales is

$$R = \$2x$$

where x represents the number of pounds sold. When we set $R = C$, we find that the break-even point is the solution of

$$2x = 1.05x + 330$$
$$0.95x = 330$$
$$x = \frac{33,000}{95} = 347.37$$

Thus, if 347 pounds of candy are sold, a loss is incurred; if 348 pounds are sold, a profit results.

(b)   If the selling price is increased to $2.25 per pound, the revenue R from sales is

$$R = \$2.25x$$

The break-even point is the solution of

$$2.25x = 1.05x + 330$$
$$1.2x = 330$$
$$x = \frac{3300}{12} = 275$$

With the new selling price, the break-even point is 275 pounds.

(c)   If we know that at least 325 pounds of candy will be sold daily, the price per pound p needed to guarantee no loss (that is, to guarantee at worst a break-even point) is the solution of

$$325p = (1.05)(325) + 330$$
$$325p = 671.25$$
$$p = \$2.07$$

We should charge at least $2.07 per pound to guarantee no loss, provided at least 325 pounds will be sold.   ∎

Example 5   A producer sells items for $0.30 each. If the cost for production is

$$C = \$0.15x + \$105$$

where x is the number of items sold, find the break-even point. If the cost can be changed to

$$C = \$0.12x + \$110$$

would it be advantageous?

Solution   The revenue R received is

$$R = \$0.3x$$

The break-even point is the solution of

$$0.3x = 0.15x + 105$$
$$0.15x = 105$$
$$x = 700$$

Thus, for the first cost, the break-even point is 700 items.

To determine the answer to the second part, we find that the break-even point at the new cost is $x = 611.11$. The old break-even point was $x = 700$. Thus, the new cost will require fewer items to be sold in order to break even. Management should probably change over to the new cost. See Figure 29.

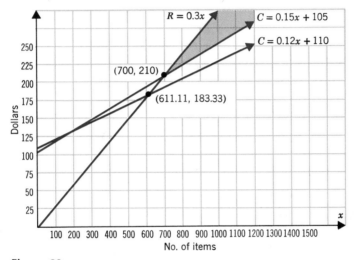

Figure 29

Prediction
Linear equations are sometimes used as predictors of future results. Let's look at an example.

Example 6   In 1981 the cost of an average home was $60,000. One year later the average home sold for $66,000. Assuming this pattern continues, that is, assuming that the increase will remain at $6000 per year, develop a formula for predicting the cost of an average home in 1985. What will it cost in 1990?

Solution   We agree to let x represent the year and y represent the cost. We seek a relationship between x and y. Two points on the graph of the equation relating x and y are

$$(1981, 60{,}000) \quad \text{and} \quad (1982, 66{,}000)$$

The assumption that the rate of increase remains constant tells us that the equation relating x and y is linear. The slope of this line is

$$\frac{66{,}000 - 60{,}000}{1982 - 1981} = 6000$$

Using this fact and the point (1981, 60,000), the point–slope form of the equation of the line is

$$y - 60{,}000 = 6000(x - 1981)$$
$$y = 60{,}000 + 6000(x - 1981)$$

For $x = 1985$, we find the cost of an average home to be

$$y = 60{,}000 + 6000(1985 - 1981)$$
$$= 60{,}000 + 6000(4)$$
$$= \$84{,}000$$

For $x = 1990$, we find

$$y = 60{,}000 + 6000(9) = \$114{,}000$$

Figure 30 illustrates the situation.

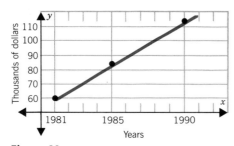

Figure 30

These predictions of future cost are based on the assumption that annual increases remain constant. If this assumption is not accurate, our predictions will be incorrect.

Economics

Supply Equation

Demand Equation

Market Price

The *supply equation* in economics is used to specify the amount of a particular commodity that sellers have available to offer in the market at various prices. The *demand equation* specifies the amount of a particular commodity that buyers are willing to purchase at various prices.

An increase in price p usually causes an increase in the supply S and a decrease in demand D. On the other hand, a decrease in price brings about a decrease in supply and an increase in demand. The *market price* is defined as the price at which supply and demand are equal.

Example 7
Market Price of
Flour

The supply and demand for flour during the period 1920–1935 were estimated as being given by the equations

$$S = 0.8p + 0.5 \qquad D = -0.4p + 1.5$$

where p is measured in dollars and S and D are measured in 50 pound units of flour. Find the market price and graph the supply and demand equations.

Solution

The market price is the point of intersection of the two lines. Thus, the market price p is the solution of

$$0.8p + 0.5 = -0.4p + 1.5$$
$$1.2p = 1$$
$$p = 0.83$$

The graphs are shown in Figure 31.

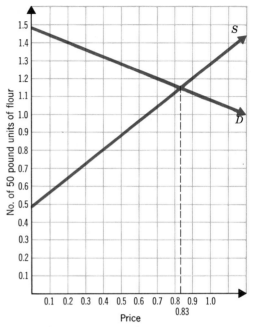

Figure 31

Exercise 5

Solutions to Odd-Numbered Problems begin on page 555.

Simple Interest Problems

1. Suppose you borrow $1000 at a simple interest rate of 18% per annum.
   (a) What is the amount A due after t years?
   (b) How much is due after 6 months?
   (c) How much is due after 1 year?
   (d) How much is due after 2 years?
2. Rework Problem 1 if you borrow $4000 at a simple interest rate of 14%.

Break-Even Problems. In Problems 3–6 find the break-even point for the cost C of production and the revenue R. Graph each result.

3. $C = \$10x + \$600$ $R = \$30x$
4. $C = \$5x + \$200$ $R = \$8x$
5. $C = \$0.2x + \$50$ $R = \$0.3x$
6. $C = \$1800x + \$3000$ $R = \$2500x$

7. A manufacturer produces items at a daily cost of $0.75 per item and sells them for $1 per item. The daily operational overhead is $300. What is the break-even point? Graph your result.
8. If the manufacturer of Problem 7 is able to reduce the cost per item to $0.65, but with a resultant increase to $350 in operational overhead, is it advantageous to do so? Graph your result.

Prediction Problems

9. Suppose the sales of a company are given by

$$S = \$5000x + \$80{,}000$$

where x is measured in years and $x = 0$ corresponds to the year 1980.
   (a) Find S when $x = 0$.
   (b) Find S when $x = 3$.
   (c) Find predicted sales in 1985, assuming this trend continues.
   (d) Find predicted sales in 1988, assuming this trend continues.

10. Rework Problem 9 if the sales of the company are given by

$$S = \$3000x + \$60{,}000$$

Economics Problems. In Problems 11–14 find the market price for each pair of supply and demand equations.

11. $S = p + 1$ $D = 3 - p$
12. $S = 2p + 3$ $D = 6 - p$
13. $S = 20p + 500$ $D = 1000 - 30p$
14. $S = 40p + 300$ $D = 1000 - 30p$

15. *Market Price of Sugar.** The supply and demand equations for sugar from 1890 to 1915 were estimated by H. Schulz to be given by

$$S = 0.7p + 0.4 \qquad D = -0.5p + 1.6$$

Find the market price. What quantity of supply is demanded at this market price? Graph both the supply and demand equations. Interpret the point of intersection of the two lines.

16. The market price for a certain product is $5.00 per unit and occurs when 14,000 units are produced. At a price of $1, no units are manufactured and, at a price of $19.00, no units will be purchased. Find the supply and demand equations, assuming they are linear.

6. Linear Inequalities

We have already discussed linear equations or linear equalities, namely, equations of the form

$$Ax + By + C = 0$$

Linear Inequality

where A, B, C are real numbers. If we replace the equal sign by $>$, $<$, $\geq$, or $\leq$, we obtain a *linear inequality*. The expressions

$$2x + 3y - 6 \geq 0 \qquad \text{and} \qquad 3x - 4y + 7 < 0$$

are examples of linear inequalities.

---

*H. Schulz, *Statistical Laws of Demand and Supply with Special Applications to Sugar,* University of Chicago Press, Chicago, 1928.

The *graph* of a linear inequality is the set of all points (x, y) for which the inequality holds. Let's look at an example.

Example 1   Graph the inequality: $2x + 3y - 6 \geq 0$

Solution   First, we graph the line

$$L: \quad 2x + 3y - 6 = 0$$

Any point on the line L obeys the inequality $2x + 3y - 6 \geq 0$, since we are seeking all points (x, y) for which $2x + 3y - 6$ is greater than *or equal to* zero. See Figure 32.

Now, let's test a few points, such as $(-1, -1)$, $(5, 5)$, $(4, 0)$, $(-4, 0)$, to see if they obey the inequality. We do this by substituting the coordinates of each point into the left member of the inequality and determining whether the result is ≥ 0 or < 0.

	$2x$	$+ 3y$	$- 6$	Conclusion
$(-1, -1)$:	$2(-1)$	$+ 3(-1)$	$- 6 = -2 - 3 - 6 = -11 < 0$	Not part of graph
$(5, 5)$:	$2(5)$	$+ 3(5)$	$- 6 = 25 - 6 = 19 > 0$	Part of graph
$(4, 0)$:	$2(4)$	$+ 3(0)$	$- 6 = 8 - 6 = 2 > 0$	Part of graph
$(-4, 0)$:	$2(-4)$	$+ 3(0)$	$- 6 = -8 - 6 = -14 < 0$	Not part of graph

Notice that the two points $(4, 0)$ and $(5, 5)$ that are part of the graph both lie on one side of L, while the points $(-4, 0)$ and $(-1, -1)$ (not part of the graph) lie on the other side of L. This is not an accident. The graph of the inequality is the shaded region of Figure 33.

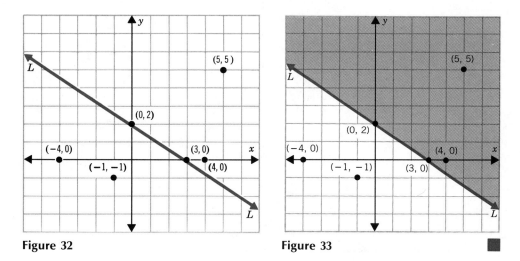

Figure 32   **Figure 33**

Let's outline the procedure for graphing a linear inequality:

1. **Graph the corresponding linear equation, a line L.**
2. **Select a point P not on the line L.**

3. **If the coordinates of this point P satisfy the linear inequality, then all points on the same side of L as the point P satisfy the inequality. If the coordinates of the point P do not obey the linear inequality, then all points on the opposite side of L from P satisfy the inequality.**

Points on the line L itself may or may not obey the inequality. Here is an example of a case when the points on L do not satisfy the inequality.

Example 2 Graph the linear inequality: $2x - y + 4 < 0$

Solution The corresponding linear equation is the line

$$L: \quad 2x - y + 4 = 0$$

For its graph, see Figure 34.

We select a point on either side of L to be tested, for example $(0, 0)$:

$$2(0) - 0 + 4 = 4 > 0$$

Since $(0, 0)$ does not obey the inequality, all points on the opposite side of L from $(0, 0)$ are on the graph.

Since no point on L can be on the graph (why?), the graph is the shaded region of Figure 35 and the line L is dashed to indicate that it is not part of the graph. ■

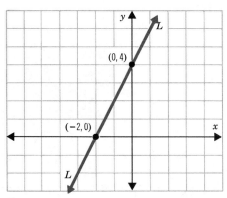

Figure 34

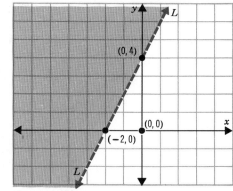

Figure 35

Half-Plane The set of points belonging to the graph of a linear inequality (for example, the shaded region in Figure 35) is sometimes called a *half-plane*.

Systems of Linear Inequalities

In a system of linear inequalities, we want to find all points that simultaneously satisfy each linear inequality of the system. Consider a system of two distinct linear inequalities in two unknowns. There are several types of regions that constitute a solution. For example, suppose L and M are the lines corresponding to two linear inequalities, and suppose L and M intersect. See Figure 36. Then the two lines L and M divide the plane into four regions a, b, c, and d. One of these regions is the solution of the system.

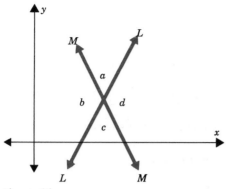

Figure 36

Example 3   Graph the system:

$$2x - y + 4 \leq 0$$
$$x + y + 1 \geq 0$$

Solution   The lines corresponding to these linear inequalities are

$$L: \quad 2x - y + 4 = 0$$
$$M: \quad x + y + 1 = 0$$

The graphs of L and M are shown in Figure 37.

If we graph each linear inequality as a separate problem and then find the region common to the two resulting half-planes, we will have the solution of the system. The cross-hatched region in Figure 38 is the solution. ∎

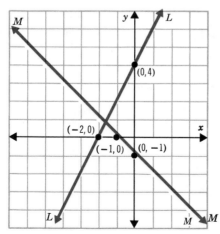

Figure 37

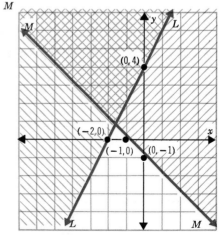

Figure 38

If the lines L and M are parallel, the system of linear inequalities may or may not have a solution. Examples of such situations are given below.

Example 4   Graph the system:

$$2x - y + 4 \leq 0$$
$$2x - y + 2 \leq 0$$

Solution   The lines corresponding to these linear inequalities are

$$L: \quad 2x - y + 4 = 0$$
$$M: \quad 2x - y + 2 = 0$$

These lines are parallel. Their graphs are shown in Figure 39.

    The graphs of the two linear inequalities are shown in Figure 40, and the solution is the cross-hatched region.

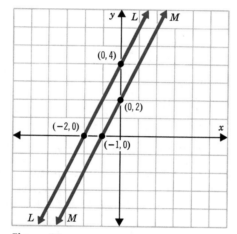

Figure 39

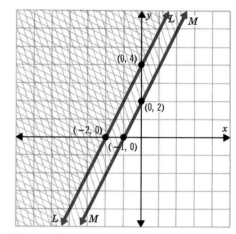

Figure 40

    Notice that the solution of this system is the same as that of the single linear inequality $2x - y + 4 \leq 0$.

Example 5   The solution of the system

$$2x - y + 4 \geq 0$$
$$2x - y + 2 \leq 0$$

is the cross-hatched region in Figure 41.

Example 6   The system

$$2x - y + 4 \leq 0$$
$$2x - y + 2 \geq 0$$

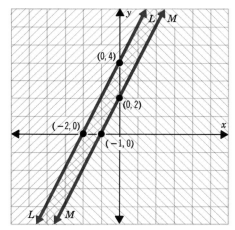

Figure 41

has no solution, as Figure 42 indicates, because the two half-planes have no points in common. ∎

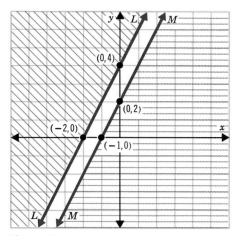

Figure 42

Until now, we have only considered systems of two inequalities in two unknowns. The next example is of a system of four inequalities in two unknowns. As we shall see, the technique for graphing such systems is the same as that used for two inequalities in two unknowns.

Example 7 Graph the system:

$$
\begin{aligned}
x + y - 2 &\geq 0 \\
2x + y - 3 &\geq 0 \\
x &\geq 0 \\
y &\geq 0
\end{aligned}
$$

Solution   Again, we first graph the four lines:

$$L_1: \quad x + y - 2 = 0$$
$$L_2: \quad 2x + y - 3 = 0$$
$$L_3: \qquad\qquad x = 0$$
$$L_4: \qquad\qquad y = 0$$

The graph of the system is the intersection of the four regions determined by each of the four inequalities. See Figure 43. ■

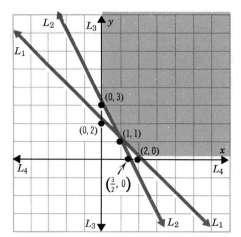

Figure 43   **Figure 44**

Example 8   Graph the system:

$$x + y - 2 \le 0$$
$$2x + y - 3 \le 0$$
$$x \ge 0$$
$$y \ge 0$$

Solution   Since the lines associated with these linear inequalities are the same as those of the previous example, we proceed directly to the graph. See Figure 44. ■

The region determined by the four linear inequalities in Example 8 is a quadrilateral with vertices at the points $(0, 0)$, $(0, 2)$, $(1, 1)$, and $(\frac{3}{2}, 0)$. The vertex $(1, 1)$ is obtained by finding the point of intersection of the lines L_1 and L_2.

Exercise 6
Solutions to Odd-Numbered Problems begin on page 556.

In Problems 1–10 graph each inequality.

1. $x \ge 0$ 2. $y \ge 0$
3. $x \ge 0, \quad y \ge 0$ 4. $x \le 0, \quad y \le 0$

5. $2x - 3y + 6 \leq 0$
6. $3x + 2y - 6 \geq 0$
7. $5x + y + 10 \leq 0$
8. $x - 2y + 4 > 0$
9. $x - 5 \geq 0$
10. $y + 2 \leq 0$

In Problems 11–20 graph each system of linear inequalities.

11.
$$x \geq 0$$
$$y \geq 0$$
$$x + y \leq 2$$

12.
$$x \geq 0$$
$$y \geq 0$$
$$2x + 3y \leq 6$$

13.
$$x \geq 0$$
$$y \geq 0$$
$$x + y \geq 2$$
$$2x + 3y \leq 6$$

14.
$$x \geq 0$$
$$y \geq 0$$
$$x + y \geq 2$$
$$2x + 3y \leq 12$$
$$3x + 2y \leq 12$$

15.
$$x \geq 0$$
$$y \geq 0$$
$$2 \leq x + y$$
$$x + y \leq 8$$
$$2x + y \leq 10$$

16.
$$x \geq 0$$
$$y \geq 0$$
$$2 \leq x + y$$
$$x + y \leq 8$$
$$1 \leq x + 2y$$

17.
$$x \geq 0$$
$$y \geq 0$$
$$x + y \geq 2$$
$$2x + 3y \leq 12$$
$$3x + y \leq 12$$

18.
$$x \geq 0$$
$$y \geq 0$$
$$2 \leq x + y$$
$$x + y \leq 10$$
$$2x + y \leq 3$$

19.
$$x \geq 0$$
$$y \geq 0$$
$$1 \leq x + 2y$$
$$x + 2y \leq 10$$

20.
$$x \geq 0$$
$$y \geq 0$$
$$1 \leq x + 2y$$
$$x + 2y \leq 10$$
$$2 \leq x + y$$
$$x + y \leq 8$$

*7. Mathematical Models

Practical situations usually do not take the form of a mathematical problem since the real world is normally far too complicated and complex to be described precisely. To solve real-world problems, we rely on simplified formulations called *mathematical models*. The purpose of this section is to give you some idea of what mathematical models are, how they are constructed, and how they are interpreted.

Example 1
Free-Falling Body

If a ball is dropped from a height 144 feet above the ground, how far will it have fallen after 2 seconds? How long will it take before the ball strikes the ground?

*This section may be omitted without loss of continuity.

Solution   Assuming air resistance is negligible, it has been determined through experimentation that the distance s a ball falls is given by the equation

$$s = \tfrac{1}{2}gt^2$$

where t is the time measured in seconds, $g \approx 32$ feet per second per second is a constant due to gravity, and s is measured in feet.

After 2 seconds ($t = 2$), we see that the distance s in feet that the ball has fallen is

$$s = \tfrac{1}{2}(32)(2)^2 = 16 \cdot 4 = 64$$

Thus, after 2 seconds, the ball has fallen 64 feet, which means it is 80 feet from the ground.

Now, the ball will strike the ground when it has fallen 144 feet, so the time t needed for this is found by solving

$$144 = 16 \cdot t^2$$
$$t^2 = 9$$

Mathematically, this equation has two solutions:

$$t = \sqrt{9} = 3 \qquad \text{or} \qquad t = -\sqrt{9} = -3$$

Physically, only positive time is meaningful. Thus, the ball is in the air 3 seconds when it strikes the ground.

∎

This example gives us a mathematical interpretation of a physical event. The equation

$$s = \tfrac{1}{2}gt^2$$

is an interpretation of the distance a ball would fall in t seconds.

Next, we look at a business situation and actually construct an equation to represent it.

Example 2
Constructing a
Cost Equation

Suppose a company operates a factory and the fixed cost of operation (the overhead cost for rent, electricity, water, etc.) amounts to $150 per workday. Furthermore, suppose the cost for each item manufactured in the factory is $0.50, that is, the unit cost is $0.50. The operating cost is fixed, but the total cost depends on the number of units produced.

To get a representation for the total cost, we first assign symbols to represent the variable quantities; they are

$$x = \text{Number of units produced per day}$$
$$C = \text{Total daily cost of producing } x \text{ units}$$

From the information given, we can set up the following cost equation:

$$C = \$150 + \$0.50x$$

where $150 is the fixed daily cost and $0.50 is the cost for each unit produced.

∎

The cost equation found in Example 2 represents a simplified version of the actual cost of running the company in question since in computing the cost we have excluded such items as selling expenses, management overhead, and so on. Furthermore, we have assumed that the cost equation is linear, that is, an increase in production of one unit increases the cost by a steady $0.50. Nothing has been said about whether the cost actually is, or should be, related in this way to the number of items produced. However, if the relationship is linear, then certain conclusions can be drawn.

What we have done here is to find a mathematical expression for a business situation in which many assumptions were made; that is, a mathematical model has been designed. The advantage of using a mathematical model is that it allows the full power of mathematics to be utilized in drawing conclusions which may be important for real-world interpretations. The model does *not* have to be an exact duplication of the real world in order to provide results that can be used in a practical way.

Deterministic Model

Probabilistic Model

The model just constructed is an example of a *deterministic model*. It is deterministic in the sense that once the number of items produced is known, the cost is predicted in an *exact* way by the model. This is in contrast to a *probabilistic model*. For example, in a model constructed to predict the weather, once the input is known, the prediction is given in probabilistic terms, such as "There is an 80% chance of rain."

Types of Models **Mathematical models are of two types:** *probabilistic* **and** *deterministic*. **A probabilistic model deals with situations that are random in character. A deterministic model will predict an exact outcome of a situation, based on certain assumptions and laws.**

Chapters 2–4 discuss the mathematics required to handle deterministic models, and Chapters 6–10 consider probabilistic models.

How do you go about constructing a mathematical model? Once a model is constructed, how can you be sure it gives an accurate interpretation? How do you test a model? Many times, the answers to these questions depend on both the degree of accuracy wanted and the degree of difficulty of a particular model. That is, a given physical event can sometimes be interpreted mathematically in more than one way, with one way giving more accurate results, but at the same time requiring more involved computation or deeper mathematical principles. Other times, two different models for the same physical event may not be so easy to distinguish. In these cases, individual or historical biases may decide the "better" model.

Let's follow the historical development of a model from the field of astronomy.

Example 3
A Model in Astronomy*

Early astronomers were concerned with explaining the behavior of the sun, moon, and planets. They watched both the sun and the moon rise in the east

---

*A. Mizrahi and M. Sullivan, "Mathematical Models and Applications," *The Mathematics Teacher,* **66,** 5 (May 1973), pp. 394–402.

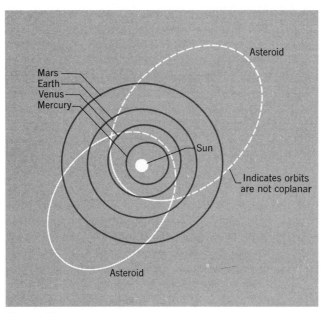

Figure 45

and set in the west and concluded that both the sun and the moon revolved about the earth in circular orbits. This circular orbiting of the sun and moon about the earth is an interpretation of a physical event—a model. Through the use of this model, various conclusions—some of them valid, but most of them false and contradictory—were arrived at.

Because of the many contradictions that arose, the model went through various changes and refinements. Finally, the famous astronomer Kepler proposed a model for planetary motion in which each planet moved about the sun in an elliptical path with the sun fixed at a focus of the ellipse. See Figure 45.

This model led to results that agreed quite closely with the results derived from observation. Thus, a "better" (more accurate) model for explaining planetary motion was discovered.

However, Kepler relied on a theory involving magnetic forces to explain the behavior of planetary motion. Of course, Kepler's magnetic forces were not very

JOHANNES KEPLER (1571–1630) spent several years calculating the mathematical relationships involving the motion of the planets. The forefather of modern astronomy, he was also quite superstitious and was known to have diagramed a horoscope.

ALBERT EINSTEIN (1879–1955) was working for the Swiss Patent Office in 1905 when he published three papers, each of which initiated a new physical theory. One dealt with Brownian motion; another contained the first application of Planck's quantum hypothesis to a subatomic process. (Through this and other papers, Einstein became one of the fathers of quantum theory—yet he never fully accepted this theory.) The third paper contained his *special relativity theory*. This was followed in 1916 by the *general relativity theory* and then by a stubborn search, extending over decades, for a unified theory describing both gravitation and electromagnetism. Einstein came to the United States as a refugee from Hitler's Germany in 1933 and settled in Princeton, New Jersey. In 1939 he signed a letter alerting President Roosevelt to the possibility of an atomic bomb. Throughout his life, Einstein maintained a strong interest in social causes, particularly in world peace, the establishment of a Jewish homeland in Palestine, and civil liberties.

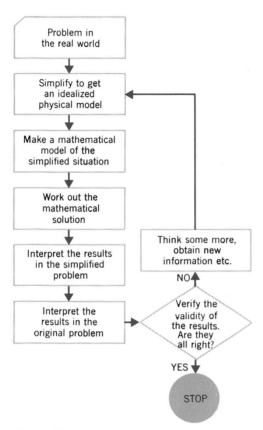

Figure 46

Throughout this course, applications, illustrations, examples, and problems involving real-world situations will be solved or explained through the use of models developed for this purpose. Remember that the solutions given are actually solutions of mathematical models, which are merely interpretations of real-world situations and may only approximate reality.

The following example from the field of biology shows how another model can be constructed.

Example 4*
A Model in
Biology: Mitosis

Biologists are often concerned with the study of the reproduction of cells. They want to know how long it takes for an initial number of cells to grow to a given prescribed number of cells, and they want to know what the rate of growth is for such cells.

To obtain the answers, a model is constructed to accurately describe the situation of cell growth. In the laboratory, a culture that contains cells of the type to be studied is observed. Cells multiply by a process of division called *mitosis:* Each cell grows for a certain period of time and then divides into two separate parts. Each of these parts, in turn, grows and eventually divides into two parts.

---

*A knowledge of function notation is required for this example. Consult the Appendix.

satisfactory, and true understanding of universal gravitation awaited Ne\
who came two generations later. Newton's contribution was to explain
Kepler's model worked. This paved the way for a much more sophisticated
derstanding of a large class of happenings.

Still, slight discrepancies with observed facts were noted in the use o
Kepler model. For example, slight aberrations in the orbit of Mercury were
served, and these could not be explained by Kepler's model. It was Einstein
later refined the model so that the Mercury aberration was taken into accc
Thus, the construction of a model is often an ongoing process, with conti
refinements taking place.

This example illustrates that, in general, mathematics cannot deal directly \
real-world situations. In order to use mathematics to solve problems in the
world, it is necessary to construct a mathematical model in which real-life
jects are represented by mathematical objects.

John Synge* described the modeling process as consisting of three sta

1. A dive from the world of reality into the world of mathematics.
2. A swim in the world of mathematics.
3. A climb from the world of mathematics back into the world of reality, ca
    ing a prediction in our teeth.

The modeling process can be outlined by using a flowchart, such as compu
programmers use. See Figure 46.

To summarize, the flowchart in Figure 46 consists of the following steps:

1. Remove from the original setting only the bare essentials of the real-wo
    problem. This requires thorough examination of the original setting to gε
    direction in determining what is fundamental. The result of such an effort
    a simplified, idealized physical model of the original problem.
2. Make this idealized model the subject of mathematical investigation by ς
    rect translation into mathematical terms. This translation is a mathematic
    model of the idealized physical model of the original problem.
3. Through computation obtain a solution for the mathematical model. In th
    stage there is no reference to the original setting or to the idealized physicε
    model.
4. Interpret the solution in terms of the idealized physical model.
5. Finally, interpret the solution in terms of the original setting.

The validity of a result must be verified and depends upon the extent to which
the model includes all the pertinent facts.

The following example is presented here to illustrate the first two stages of the
modeling process. The third and remaining stages, working out the mathematical solution, requires knowledge of certain mathematical techniques. The purpose of this book is to provide these techniques; you are not expected to be able
to construct mathematical models as a result of completing this chapter.

*John Synge, "Mathematical Education Notes," *American Mathematical Monthly,* **68** (October 1961),
p. 799.

After observing this process for a long time, it can be determined that the time needed for a cell to grow and split into two separate parts is always about the same. Suppose t_0 seconds is the average time required for a single cell to grow and divide into two parts.

For the construction of the model, we *assume* that t_0 seconds is the exact time required for every cell of this type to grow and divide into two parts. Once we have made this assumption, we begin to build our model.

Suppose the function f is the law that relates time t to the number of cells N. That is,

$$N = f(t)$$

If we can find out what the function f is, we have our model.

Now, if we start with a culture containing N_0 cells, we know that at time $t = 0$, there are N_0 cells. That is,

$$N_0 = f(0)$$

After t_0 seconds, each cell has divided into two. Thus, after t_0 seconds there are $2N_0$ cells, or

$$2N_0 = f(t_0)$$

After an additional t_0 seconds, the cells have divided again, giving $4N_0$ cells after $2t_0$ seconds. That is,

$$4N_0 = f(2t_0)$$

Continuing in this way, we obtain

$$8N_0 = f(3t_0) \quad \text{or} \quad 2^3N_0 = f(3t_0)$$
$$16N_0 = f(4t_0) \quad \text{or} \quad 2^4N_0 = f(4t_0)$$
$$\vdots$$
$$2^kN_0 = f(kt_0)$$

This last formula may be used for integral multiples of t_0. To obtain a formula for any time t, we set $t = kt_0$. Then, since $k = t/t_0$, we have

$$f(t) = 2^{t/t_0}N_0$$

Thus, our model for cell division is: For an initial number N_0 of cells, which divide in two every t_0 seconds, there will be

$$2^{t/t_0}N_0$$

cells after t seconds. ■

Mitosis, or division of cells, is a universal process in the growth of living things such as amoebas, plants, and human skin cells. One of the few exceptions are human nerve cells. Of course, the above model is based on an ideal situation in which no cells die and no by-products are produced. In actuality, cells do die and by-products are produced so that after a period of time the growth rate is effectively reduced to almost zero instead of doubling. However, the above model accurately reflects what happens during the growth stage of mitosis.

Exercise 7
Solutions to Odd-Numbered Problems begin on page 558.

1. If a ball is dropped from a height of 16 feet, how long will it take for it to strike the ground? How far did it go in half this time? [*Hint:* $s = 16t^2$, s in feet, t in seconds.]
2. If a ball is dropped from a height of 128 feet, how long will it take for it to strike the ground? How far did it go in half this time?
3. According to one of Kepler's laws of planetary motion, the square of the period T (length of time for one revolution about the sun) of a planet is proportional to the cube of the mean distance x from the sun. Using the fact that the earth is about 93 million miles from the sun, how many earth years does it take for the planet Jupiter, 483 million miles from the sun, to go around the sun?
4. Rework Problem 3 for the planet Mercury, which is 36 million miles from the sun.
5. Construct a model for material decay if half of the original amount remains after a period of 2 years. If you start with 1 ton of such a material, how much remains after 50 years? After 200 years?
6. *Radioactive Decay.* A radioactive substance has a half-life of 8 years. That is, if we start with a given amount of the radioactive substance, then after 8 years only half of the original amount is left.
    (a) How long does it take for $\frac{3}{4}$ of the substance to decay?
    (b) After 28 years, how much is left?
    (c) Assuming that even minute quantities of this substance will have the same half-life, how long does it take for the substance disappear completely?
7. *Cell Growth.* Construct a model for cell growth if each cell in a culture divides into two parts every 5 seconds. If you begin with 1000 such cells, how many are there after 2 minutes? After 1 hour? (Assume the growth stage lasts this long.)

Chapter Review

Important	set
Terms	empty set

set	positive number
empty set	negative number
counting numbers	origin
integers	coordinate
rational numbers	variable
numerator	equation
denominator	solution
irrational numbers	inequality
real numbers	rectangular coordinates
decimals	*x*-axis
percents	*y*-axis

ordered pair	solution of a system of equations
abscissa	substitution
ordinate	add and subtract
quadrants	*simple interest
graphs	*principal
linear equation	*rate of interest
straight line	*amount
slope of a line	*break-even point
vertical line	*prediction
point-slope form	*supply and demand
general form	*market price
intercepts	linear inequality
slope-intercept form	half-plane
identical lines	system of linear inequalities
parallel lines	*deterministic model
intersecting lines	*probabilistic model
system of two linear equations in	*mitosis
two unknowns	

True-False Questions (Answers on page 631)

T F 1. In the slope–intercept equation of a line, $y = mx + b$, m is the slope and b is the x-intercept.

T F 2. The graph of the equation $Ax + By + C = 0$, where A, B, C are real numbers and A, B are not both zero, is a straight line.

T F 3. The y-intercept of the line $2x - 3y + 6 = 0$ is 2.

T F 4. The slope of the line $2x - 4y + 7 = 0$ is $-\frac{1}{2}$.

T F 5. The graph of a single linear inequality is always a half-plane.

Fill in the Blanks (Answers on page 631)

1. If (x, y) are rectangular coordinates of a point, the number x is called the _____ and y is called the _____ .

2. The decimal equivalent of a rational number is either _____ or _____ .

3. The slope of a vertical line is _____ ; the slope of a horizontal line is _____ .

4. If a line slants downward as it moves from left to right, its slope will be a _____ number.

5. If two lines have the same slope but different y-intercepts, they are _____ .

*From optional sections.

Review Exercises
Solutions to Odd-Numbered Problems begin on page 558.

In Problems 1-6 find the solution x of each equation.

1. $3x + 6 = 2x - 1$
2. $-3x - 2 = 2x + 8$
3. $-2(x + 3) = x + 5$
4. $2x - 3 = -2(x + 2)$
5. $\dfrac{4x - 1}{x + 2} = 5$
6. $\dfrac{3x + 2}{2x - 1} = 1$

In Problems 7-10 find the solution of each inequality.

7. $2x - 1 \leq 5$
8. $8x + 1 \geq 9$
9. $3x + 7 \geq -2x + 2$
10. $-3x + 4 \leq 2x - 1$

In Problems 11-14 graph each linear equation.

11. $y = -2x + 3$
12. $y = 6x - 2$
13. $2y = 3x + 6$
14. $3y = 2x + 6$

In Problems 15-18 find a general equation for the line containing each pair of points.

15. $P = (1, 2)$ $\quad Q = (-3, 4)$
16. $P = (-1, 3)$ $\quad Q = (1, 1)$
17. $P = (0, 0)$ $\quad Q = (-2, 3)$
18. $P = (-2, 3)$ $\quad Q = (0, 0)$

In Problems 19-22 find a general equation for the line.

19. Slope is 2;
    x-intercept is -1
20. Slope is -1;
    y-intercept is 1
21. Passing through $(1, 3)$
    with slope 1
22. Passing through $(2, -1)$
    with slope -2

In Problems 23-26 find the slope and y-intercept of each line. Graph each line.

23. $-9x - 2y + 18 = 0$
24. $-4x - 5y + 20 = 0$
25. $4x + 2y - 9 = 0$
26. $3x + 2y - 8 = 0$

In Problems 27-32 determine whether the system of equations has one solution, no solution, or infinitely many solutions.

27. $3x - 4y + 12 = 0$
    $6x - 8y + 9 = 0$
28. $2x + 3y + 5 = 0$
    $4x + 6y + 10 = 0$
29. $x - y + 2 = 0$
    $3x - 4y + 12 = 0$
30. $2x + 3y - 5 = 0$
    $x + y - 2 = 0$
31. $4x + 6y + 12 = 0$
    $2x + 3y + 6 = 0$
32. $3x - y = 0$
    $6x - 2y + 5 = 0$

In Problems 33-36 graph each system of linear inequalities.

33. $2x - 3y + 6 \geq 0$
    $x \geq 0$
    $y \geq 0$
34. $y + 3x \geq 2$
    $x \geq 0$
    $y \geq 0$

35. $y + 2x \geq 4$
    $x + 2y \geq 4$
    $x \geq 0$
    $y \geq 0$

36. $y + 2x \leq 4$
    $x + 2y \leq 4$
    $x \geq 0$
    $y \geq 0$

37. *Investment Problem.* Mr. and Mrs. Byrd have just retired and find that they need $10,000 per year to live on. Fortunately, they have a nest egg of $90,000 which they can invest in somewhat risky B-rated bonds at 16% interest per year or in a well-known bank at 6% per year. How much money should they invest in each so that they realize exactly $10,000 in income each year?

38. *Mixture Problem.* One solution is 20% acid and another is 12% acid. How many cubic centimeters of each solution should be mixed to obtain 100 cc of a solution which is 15% acid?

39. The annual sales of Motors Inc. for the past 5 years are listed in the table.

Year	Units Sold (in thousands)
1977	3400
1978	3200
1979	3100
1980	2800
1981	2200

   (a) Graph this information using the x-axis for years and the y-axis for units sold. (For convenience, use different scales on the axes.)
   (b) Draw a line L that passes through two of the points and comes close to passing through the remaining points.
   (c) Find the equation of this line L.
   (d) Using this equation of the line, what is your estimate for units sold in 1982?

40. *Attendance at a Dance.* A church group is planning a dance in the school auditorium to raise money for its school. The band they will hire charges $500; the advertising costs are estimated at $100; and food is supplied at the rate of $2.00 per person. The church group would like to clear at least $900 after expenses.
   (a) Determine how many people need to attend the dance for the group to break even if tickets are sold at $5 each.
   (b) Determine how many people need to attend in order to achieve the desired profit if tickets are sold for $5 each.
   (c) Answer the above two questions if the tickets are sold for $6 each.

Mathematical Questions
From CPA and CMA Exams
(Answers on page 629)

1. *CPA Exam—November 1976*
   The Oliver Company plans to market a new product. Based on its market studies, Oliver estimates that it can sell 5500 units in 1976. The selling price

will be $2.00 per unit. Variable costs are estimated to be 40% of the selling price. Fixed costs are estimated to be $6000. What is the break-even point?

(a) 3750 units   (b) 5000 units
(c) 5500 units   (d) 7500 units

2. *CPA Exam—November 1976*
The Breiden Company sells rodaks for $6.00 per unit. Variable costs are $2.00 per unit. Fixed costs are $37,500. How many rodaks must be sold to realize a profit before income taxes of 15% of sales?

(a) 9375 units   (b) 9740 units
(c) 11,029 units   (d) 12,097 units

3. *CPA Exam—May 1975*
Given the following notations, what is the break-even sales level in units?

$$SP = \text{Selling price per unit}$$
$$FC = \text{Total fixed cost}$$
$$VC = \text{Variable cost per unit}$$

(a) $\dfrac{SP}{FC \div VC}$ (b) $\dfrac{FC}{VC \div SP}$ (c) $\dfrac{VC}{SP - FC}$ (d) $\dfrac{FC}{SP - VC}$

4. *CPA Exam—November 1976*
At a break-even point of 400 units sold, the variable costs were $400 and the fixed costs were $200. What will the 401st unit sold contribute to profit before income taxes?

(a) $0   (b) $0.50   (c) $1.00   (d) $1.50

Use the following information to answer Problems 5–8:

Akron, Inc. owns 80% of the capital stock of Benson Co. and 70% of the capital stock of Cashin, Inc. Benson Co. owns 15% of the capital stock of Cashin, Inc. Cashin, Inc., in turn, owns 25% of the capital stock of Akron, Inc. These owner-ship interrelationships are illustrated in the following diagram:

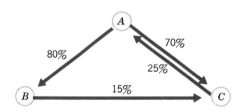

Net income before adjusting for interests in intercompany net income for each corporation follows:

Akron, Inc.	$190,000
Benson Co.	$170,000
Cashin, Inc.	$230,000

The following notations relate to items 5 through 8. Ignore all income tax considerations.

$$A_e = \text{Akron's consolidated net income;}$$
i.e., its net income plus its share of the

consolidated net incomes of Benson
and Cashin
B_e = Benson's consolidated net income;
i.e., its net income plus its share of the
consolidated net income of Cashin
C_e = Cashin's consolidated net income;
i.e., its net income plus its share of the
consolidated income of Akron

5. *CPA Exam—May 1973*
The equation, in a set of simultaneous equations, which computes A_e is:
(a) $A_e = .75(190,000 + .8B_e + .7C_e)$
(b) $A_e = 190,000 + .8B_e + .7C_e$
(c) $A_e = .75(190,000) + .8(170,000) + .7(230,000)$
(d) $A_e = .75(190,000) + .8B_e + .7C_e$

6. *CPA Exam—May 1973*
The equation, in a set of simultaneous equations, which computes B_e is:
(a) $B_e = 170,000 + .15C_e - .75A_e$
(b) $B_e = 170,000 + .15C_e$
(c) $B_e = .2(170,000) + .15(230,000)$
(d) $B_e = .2(170,000) + .15C_e$

7. *CPA Exam—May 1973*
Cashin's minority interest in consolidated net income is:
(a) $.15(230,000)$ (b) $230,000 + .25A_e$
(c) $.15(230,000) + .25A_e$ (d) $.15C_e$

8. *CPA Exam—May 1973*
Benson's minority interest in consolidated net income is:
(a) $34,316   (b) $25,500
(c) $45,755   (d) $30,675

9. *CPA Exam—November 1976*
A graph is set up with "depreciation expense" on the vertical axis and "time" on the horizontal axis. Assuming linear relationships, how would the graphs for straight-line and sum-of-the-years'-digits depreciation, respectively, be drawn?
(a) Vertically and sloping down to the right
(b) Vertically and sloping up to the right
(c) Horizontally and sloping down to the right
(d) Horizontally and sloping up to the right

The following statement applies to items 10 to 12:
In analyzing the relationship of total factory overhead with changes in direct labor hours, the following relationship was found to exist: $Y = \$1000 + \$2X$

10. *CMA Exam—December 1973*
The relationship as shown above is:
(a) Parabolic   (b) Curvilinear
(c) Linear   (d) Probabilistic
(e) None of the above

11. *CMA Exam—December 1973*
    Y in the above equation is an estimate of:
    (a) Total variable costs   (b) Total factory overhead
    (c) Total fixed costs   (d) Total direct labor hours
    (e) None of the above

12. *CMA Exam—December 1973*
    The $2 in the equation is an estimate of:
    (a) Total fixed costs
    (b) Variable costs per direct labor hour
    (c) Total variable costs
    (d) Fixed costs per direct labor hour
    (e) None of the above

2
Introduction to Matrices with Applications

*This section may be omitted without loss of continuity.

1. Preliminary Remarks

In this chapter we survey briefly a branch of mathematics called *linear algebra*. Linear algebra deals with generalizations of numbers, called *vectors* and *matrices*, which are defined in such a way that many of the algebraic properties of the real numbers are retained.

Many situations in both pure and applied mathematics deal with rectangular arrays of numbers. In fact, in many branches of business and the biological and social sciences, it is necessary to express and use a set of numbers in a rectangular array. Let's look at an example.

Example 1   Motors Incorporated produces three models of cars: a sedan, a hard-top, and a station wagon. If the company wishes to compare the units of raw material and the units of labor involved in 1 month's production of each of these models, the rectangular array displayed below may be used to present the data:

	Sedan Model	Hard-Top Model	Station Wagon Model
Units of Material	23	16	10
Units of Labor	7	9	11

The same information may be written concisely as

$$A = \begin{bmatrix} 23 & 16 & 10 \\ 7 & 9 & 11 \end{bmatrix}$$

This array, called a *matrix*, has 2 *rows* (the units) and 3 *columns* (the models). The first row represents units of material and the second row represents units of labor. The first, second, and third columns represent the sedan, hard-top, and station wagon models, respectively.   ■

Example 2   Below are four examples of matrices:

$$A = \begin{bmatrix} 1 & \frac{1}{2} \\ 0 & 2 \end{bmatrix}$$

$$B = \begin{bmatrix} 2 \\ -5 \end{bmatrix}$$

$$C = \begin{bmatrix} 0.01 & 0.02 & 0.07 \\ 0.1 & 0.9 & 0 \end{bmatrix}$$

$$D = \begin{bmatrix} 1.2 & 5 \end{bmatrix}$$

The matrix A has 2 rows and 2 columns; the matrix B has 2 rows and 1 column; C has 2 rows and 3 columns; and D has 1 row and 2 columns.   ■

A formal definition of a matrix as an array of numbers is given below.

Matrix **A** *matrix A* **is a rectangular array of numbers** a_{ij} **of the form**

$$A = \begin{bmatrix} a_{11} & a_{12} & \cdots & a_{1j} & \cdots & a_{1m} \\ a_{21} & a_{22} & \cdots & a_{2j} & \cdots & a_{2m} \\ \vdots & \vdots & & \vdots & & \vdots \\ a_{i1} & a_{i2} & \cdots & a_{ij} & \cdots & a_{im} \\ \vdots & \vdots & & \vdots & & \vdots \\ a_{n1} & a_{n2} & \cdots & a_{nj} & \cdots & a_{nm} \end{bmatrix} \leftarrow i\text{th row}$$

*j*th column

This matrix contains $n \cdot m$ **numbers.**

Row

Column

Each number a_{ij} of the matrix A has two indices: the *row index, i,* and the *column index, j.* The symbols $a_{i1}, a_{i2}, \ldots, a_{im}$ represent the numbers in the *i*th row, and the symbols $a_{1j}, a_{2j}, \ldots, a_{nj}$ represent the numbers in the *j*th column. The numbers a_{ij} of a matrix are sometimes referred to as the *entries* or *components* or *elements* of the matrix. The matrix A above, which has n rows and m columns, can be abbreviated by

$$A = [a_{ij}] \qquad i = 1, 2, \ldots, n; \quad j = 1, 2, \ldots, m$$

Dimension **The** *dimension of a matrix A* **is determined by the number of rows and the number of columns of the matrix. If a matrix** A **has** n **rows and** m **columns, we denote the dimension of** A **by** $n \times m$**, read as "**n *by m***."**

For a 2×3 matrix, remember that the first number 2 denotes the number of rows and the second number 3 is the number of columns. A matrix with 3 rows and 2 columns is of dimension 3×2.

Square Matrix **If a matrix** A **has the same number of rows as it has columns, it is called a** *square matrix.*

Diagonal Entries

In the matrix $A = [a_{ij}]$ above, the entries for which $i = j$, namely $a_{11}, a_{22}, a_{33}, a_{44}$, and so on, form the *diagonal* of A.

Example 3 Examples of square matrices are

$$\begin{bmatrix} 1 & 0 \\ 0 & 1 \end{bmatrix} \qquad \begin{bmatrix} 3 & -3 & 4 \\ 6 & 0 & -3 \\ 1 & 2 & 0 \end{bmatrix} \qquad \begin{bmatrix} 5 & 6 & 0.1 & 0 \\ 0 & 3 & 0.2 & -1 \\ 1 & 2 & 0.3 & -2 \\ 1 & 2 & 0 & -4 \end{bmatrix}$$

$$2 \times 2 \qquad\qquad 3 \times 3 \qquad\qquad\qquad 4 \times 4$$

The diagonal entries of the 2 × 2 matrix are 1, 1; of the 3 × 3 matrix are 3, 0, 0; and of the 4 × 4 matrix are 5, 3, 0.3, −4.

∎

Example 4 In a recent United States census, the following figures were obtained with regard to the city of Glenwood. Each year 7% of city residents move to the suburbs and 1% of the people in the suburbs move to the city. This situation can be represented by the matrix

$$P = \begin{array}{cc} & \begin{array}{cc} \text{City} & \text{Suburbs} \end{array} \\ \begin{array}{c} \text{City} \\ \text{Suburbs} \end{array} & \begin{bmatrix} 0.93 & 0.07 \\ 0.01 & 0.99 \end{bmatrix} \end{array}$$

Here, the entry in row 1, column 2, 0.07, indicates that 7% of city residents move to the suburbs. The matrix P is a square matrix and its dimension is 2 × 2. The diagonal entries are 0.93 and 0.99.

∎

Row and Column Matrix **A** *row matrix* **is a matrix with 1 row of elements. A** *column matrix* **is a matrix with 1 column of elements. Row matrices and column matrices are sometimes referred to as** *row vectors* **and** *column vectors,* **respectively.**

Example 5 The matrices

$$A = \begin{bmatrix} 23 & 16 & 10 \end{bmatrix} \qquad B = \begin{bmatrix} 7 & 9 \end{bmatrix}$$

$$C = \begin{bmatrix} 23 \\ -1 \\ 7 \end{bmatrix} \qquad D = \begin{bmatrix} 16 \\ 9 \end{bmatrix} \qquad E = \begin{bmatrix} 9 \end{bmatrix}$$

have the following dimensions: A, 1 × 3; B, 1 × 2; C, 3 × 1; D, 2 × 1; E, 1 × 1. Here A, B, and E are row vectors and C, D, and E are column vectors.

∎

The matrix $E = [9]$ in Example 5 is a 1 × 1 matrix and, as such, can be treated simply as a real number.

As with most mathematical quantities, we now want to determine various relationships between two matrices. We might ask, "When, if at all, are two matrices equal?"

Let's try to arrive at a sound definition for equality of matrices by requiring equal matrices to have certain desirable properties. First, it would seem necessary that two equal matrices have the same dimension—that is, that they both be $n × m$ matrices. Next, it would seem necessary that their entries be identical numbers. With these two restrictions, we define equality of matrices.

Equality of Matrices **Two matrices A and B are** *equal* **if they are of the same dimension and if corresponding entries are equal. In this case, we write $A = B$, read as "matrix A is equal to matrix B."**

Example 6 In order for the two matrices

$$\begin{bmatrix} p & q \\ 1 & 0 \end{bmatrix} \quad \text{and} \quad \begin{bmatrix} 2 & 4 \\ n & 0 \end{bmatrix}$$

to be equal, we must have $p = 2$, $q = 4$, and $n = 1$. ■

Example 7 Find x and y so that the two matrices given below are equal.

$$A = \begin{bmatrix} x + 2 \\ 3y - 7 \end{bmatrix} \qquad B = \begin{bmatrix} 4 - y \\ x - 3 \end{bmatrix}$$

Solution The matrices A and B are 2×1 matrices—or column vectors. It follows that $A = B$ if

$$x + 2 = 4 - y \quad \text{and} \quad 3y - 7 = x - 3$$

This is a system of two equations in two unknowns, x and y. Solving them, we find that the solutions are

$$x = \frac{1}{2} \qquad y = \frac{3}{2}$$

■

We can check the solution to Example 7 by substituting in A and B:

$$A = \begin{bmatrix} \frac{1}{2} + 2 \\ 3 \cdot \frac{3}{2} - 7 \end{bmatrix} = \begin{bmatrix} \frac{5}{2} \\ -\frac{5}{2} \end{bmatrix} \qquad B = \begin{bmatrix} 4 - \frac{3}{2} \\ \frac{1}{2} - 3 \end{bmatrix} = \begin{bmatrix} \frac{5}{2} \\ -\frac{5}{2} \end{bmatrix}$$

Our answer is verified.

Example 8 Let A and B be two matrices given by

$$A = \begin{bmatrix} x + y & 6 \\ 2x - 3 & 2 - y \end{bmatrix} \qquad B = \begin{bmatrix} 5 & 5x + 2 \\ y & x - y \end{bmatrix}$$

Find x and y so that A and B are equal (if possible).

Solution Both A and B are 2×2 matrices. Thus, $A = B$ if

(a) $x + y = 5$ (b) $6 = 5x + 2$
(c) $2x - 3 = y$ (d) $2 - y = x - y$

Here we have four equations in the two unknowns x and y. From equation (d), we see that $x = 2$. Using this value in equation (a), we obtain $y = 3$. But $x = 2$, $y = 3$ do not satisfy either (b) or (c). Hence, there are *no* values for x and y satisfying all four equations. This means A and B can never be equal. ■

Exercise 1
Solutions to Odd-Numbered Problems begin on page 561.

In Problems 1–8 write the dimension of each matrix.

1. $\begin{bmatrix} 3 & 2 \\ -1 & 3 \end{bmatrix}$ 2. $\begin{bmatrix} -1 & 0 \\ 0 & 5 \end{bmatrix}$ 3. $\begin{bmatrix} 2 & 1 & -3 \\ 1 & 0 & -1 \end{bmatrix}$ 4. $\begin{bmatrix} 1 & 2 \\ 2 & 1 \\ 0 & -3 \end{bmatrix}$

5. $\begin{bmatrix} 4 \\ 1 \end{bmatrix}$ 6. $[2 \quad 1 \quad -3]$ 7. $[2]$ 8. $[0]$

In Problems 9–16 determine whether the given statements are true or false. If false, tell why.

9. $\begin{bmatrix} 0 \\ 1 \end{bmatrix} = [0 \quad 1]$ 10. $\begin{bmatrix} 3 & 2 \\ -1 & 0 \end{bmatrix} = \begin{bmatrix} 3 & 2 \\ -1 & 4 \end{bmatrix}$

11. $\begin{bmatrix} 5 & 0 \\ 0 & 1 \end{bmatrix}$ is square   12. $\begin{bmatrix} 3 & 2 & 1 \\ 4 & -1 & 0 \end{bmatrix}$ is 3×2

13. $\begin{bmatrix} x & 2 \\ 4 & 0 \end{bmatrix} = \begin{bmatrix} 3 & 2 \\ 4 & 0 \end{bmatrix}$ if $x = 3$ 14. $\begin{bmatrix} x & y \\ 0 & 0 \end{bmatrix} = [x \quad y]$

15. $\begin{bmatrix} 5 & 0 \\ 1 & 1 \end{bmatrix} = \begin{bmatrix} 2+3 & 0 \\ 1 & 1 \end{bmatrix}$ 16. $\begin{bmatrix} 1 & 0 \\ 0 & 1 \end{bmatrix} = \begin{bmatrix} 3-2 & 3-3 \\ 3-3 & 3-2 \end{bmatrix}$

17. Find x and z so that

$$\begin{bmatrix} x \\ z \end{bmatrix} = \begin{bmatrix} 4 \\ 3 \end{bmatrix}$$

18. Find x, y, and z so that

$$\begin{bmatrix} x+y & 2 \\ 4 & 0 \end{bmatrix} = \begin{bmatrix} 6 & x-y \\ 4 & z \end{bmatrix}$$

19. Find x and y so that

$$\begin{bmatrix} x-2y & 0 \\ -2 & 6 \end{bmatrix} = \begin{bmatrix} 3 & 0 \\ -2 & x+y \end{bmatrix}$$

20. Find x, y, and z so that

$$\begin{bmatrix} x-2 & 3 & 2z \\ 6y & x & 2y \end{bmatrix} = \begin{bmatrix} y & z & 6 \\ 18z & y+2 & 6z \end{bmatrix}$$

21. XYZ Company produces steel and aluminum nails. One week, 25 gross $\frac{1}{2}$ inch steel nails and 45 gross 1 inch steel nails were produced. Suppose 13 gross $\frac{1}{2}$ inch aluminum nails, 20 gross 1 inch aluminum nails, 35 gross 2 inch steel nails, and 23 gross 2 inch aluminum nails were also made. Write a 2×3 matrix depicting this. Could you also write a 3×2 matrix for this situation?

22. Katy, Mike, and Danny go to the candy store. Katy buys 5 sticks of gum, 2 ice cream cones, and 10 jelly beans. Mike buys 2 sticks of

gum, 15 jelly beans, and 2 candy bars. Danny buys 1 stick of gum, 1 ice cream cone, and 4 candy bars. Write a matrix depicting this situation.

23. Use a matrix to display the information given below, which was obtained in a survey of voters. Label the rows and columns.

351 Democrats earning under $15,000
271 Republicans earning under $15,000
73 Independents earning under $15,000
203 Democrats earning over $15,000
215 Republicans earning over $15,000
55 Independents earning over $15,000

2. Addition of Matrices

Can two matrices be added? And, if so, what is the rule or law for addition of matrices?

Let's return to Example 1 in Section 1. In that example, we recorded 1 month's production of Motors Incorporated by the matrix

$$A = \begin{bmatrix} 23 & 16 & 10 \\ 7 & 9 & 11 \end{bmatrix}$$

Suppose the next month's production is

$$B = \begin{bmatrix} 18 & 12 & 9 \\ 14 & 6 & 8 \end{bmatrix}$$

in which the pattern of recording units and models remains the same.

The total production for the 2 months can be displayed by the matrix

$$C = \begin{bmatrix} 41 & 28 & 19 \\ 21 & 15 & 19 \end{bmatrix}$$

since the number of units of material for sedan models is $41 = 23 + 18$; the number of units of material for hard-top models is $28 = 16 + 12$; and so on.

This leads us to define the sum $A + B$ of two matrices A and B as the matrix consisting of the sum of corresponding entries from A and B.

Addition of Matrices **Let $A = [a_{ij}]$ and $B = [b_{ij}]$ be two $n \times m$ matrices. The** *sum $A + B$* **is defined as the $n \times m$ matrix $[a_{ij} + b_{ij}]$.**

Example 1 (a) $\begin{bmatrix} 23 & 16 & 10 \\ 7 & 9 & 11 \end{bmatrix} + \begin{bmatrix} 18 & 12 & 9 \\ 14 & 6 & 8 \end{bmatrix} = \begin{bmatrix} 23 + 18 & 16 + 12 & 10 + 9 \\ 7 + 14 & 9 + 6 & 11 + 8 \end{bmatrix}$

$$= \begin{bmatrix} 41 & 28 & 19 \\ 21 & 15 & 19 \end{bmatrix}$$

(b) $\begin{bmatrix} 0.6 & 0.4 \\ 0.1 & 0.9 \end{bmatrix} + \begin{bmatrix} 2.3 & 0.6 \\ 1.8 & 5.2 \end{bmatrix} = \begin{bmatrix} 0.6 + 2.3 & 0.4 + 0.6 \\ 0.1 + 1.8 & 0.9 + 5.2 \end{bmatrix}$

$$= \begin{bmatrix} 2.9 & 1.0 \\ 1.9 & 6.1 \end{bmatrix}$$

Notice that it is possible to add two matrices only if their dimensions are the same. Also, the dimension of the sum of two matrices is the same as that of the two original matrices.

The following pairs of matrices cannot be added since they are of different dimensions:

$$A = \begin{bmatrix} 1 & 2 \\ 7 & 2 \end{bmatrix} \qquad \text{and} \qquad B = \begin{bmatrix} 1 \\ -3 \end{bmatrix}$$

$$A = \begin{bmatrix} 2 & 3 \end{bmatrix} \qquad \text{and} \qquad B = \begin{bmatrix} 1 & 1 & 1 \end{bmatrix}$$

$$A = \begin{bmatrix} -1 & 7 & 0 \\ 2 & \frac{1}{2} & 0 \end{bmatrix} \qquad \text{and} \qquad B = \begin{bmatrix} -1 & 2 \\ 3 & 0 \\ 1 & 5 \end{bmatrix}$$

It turns out that the usual rules for the addition of real numbers (such as the commutative laws and associative laws) are also valid for matrix addition.

Example 2   Let

$$A = \begin{bmatrix} 1 & 5 \\ 7 & -3 \end{bmatrix} \qquad \text{and} \qquad B = \begin{bmatrix} 3 & -2 \\ 4 & 1 \end{bmatrix}$$

Then

$$A + B = \begin{bmatrix} 1 & 5 \\ 7 & -3 \end{bmatrix} + \begin{bmatrix} 3 & -2 \\ 4 & 1 \end{bmatrix} = \begin{bmatrix} 1+3 & 5+(-2) \\ 7+4 & -3+1 \end{bmatrix} = \begin{bmatrix} 4 & 3 \\ 11 & -2 \end{bmatrix}$$

$$B + A = \begin{bmatrix} 3 & -2 \\ 4 & 1 \end{bmatrix} + \begin{bmatrix} 1 & 5 \\ 7 & -3 \end{bmatrix} = \begin{bmatrix} 4 & 3 \\ 11 & -2 \end{bmatrix}$$

This leads us to formulate the following property:

If A and B are two matrices of the same dimension, then

$$A + B = B + A$$

That is, matrix addition is *commutative.*

The associative law for addition of matrices is also true. Thus:

If A, B, and C, are three matrices of the same dimension, then

$$A + (B + C) = (A + B) + C$$

For a proof of this result, we let

$$A = [a_{ij}] \qquad B = [b_{ij}] \qquad C = [c_{ij}]$$

Then

$$\begin{aligned}
A + (B + C) &= [a_{ij}] + ([b_{ij}] + [c_{ij}]) = [a_{ij}] + ([b_{ij} + c_{ij}]) \\
&= [a_{ij}] + [b_{ij} + c_{ij}] = [a_{ij} + (b_{ij} + c_{ij})] \\
&= [(a_{ij} + b_{ij}) + c_{ij}] = [a_{ij} + b_{ij}] + [c_{ij}] \\
&= ([a_{ij} + b_{ij}]) + [c_{ij}] = ([a_{ij}] + [b_{ij}]) + [c_{ij}] \\
&= (A + B) + C
\end{aligned}$$

In the proof, we used the fact that addition of real numbers is associative. Where?

The fact that addition of matrices is associative means that the notation $A + B + C$ is *not* ambiguous, since $(A + B) + C = A + (B + C)$.

Zero Matrix   **A matrix in which all entries are zero is called a** *zero matrix*. **We use the symbol 0 to represent a zero matrix of any dimension.**

For real numbers, zero has the property that $0 + x = x$ for any x. An important property of a zero matrix is that $A + \mathbf{0} = A$, provided the dimension of $\mathbf{0}$ is the same as that of A.

Example 3   Let

$$A = \begin{bmatrix} 3 & 4 & -\frac{1}{2} \\ \sqrt{2} & 0 & 3 \end{bmatrix}$$

Then

$$A + \mathbf{0} = \begin{bmatrix} 3 & 4 & -\frac{1}{2} \\ \sqrt{2} & 0 & 3 \end{bmatrix} + \begin{bmatrix} 0 & 0 & 0 \\ 0 & 0 & 0 \end{bmatrix}$$

$$= \begin{bmatrix} 3 + 0 & 4 + 0 & -\frac{1}{2} + 0 \\ \sqrt{2} + 0 & 0 + 0 & 3 + 0 \end{bmatrix} = \begin{bmatrix} 3 & 4 & -\frac{1}{2} \\ \sqrt{2} & 0 & 3 \end{bmatrix} = A$$

If A is any matrix, the *negative of A*, denoted by $-A$, is the matrix obtained by replacing each entry in A by its negative.

Example 4   If

$$A = \begin{bmatrix} -3 & 0 \\ 5 & -2 \\ 1 & 3 \end{bmatrix} \quad \text{then} \quad -A = \begin{bmatrix} 3 & 0 \\ -5 & 2 \\ -1 & -3 \end{bmatrix}$$

For any matrix A, we have the property that

$$A + (-A) = 0$$

Now that we have defined the sum of two matrices and the negative of a matrix, it is natural to ask about the *difference* of two matrices. As you will see, subtracting matrices and subtracting numbers are much the same kind of process.

Difference of Two Matrices **Let $A = [a_{ij}]$ and $B = [b_{ij}]$ be two $n \times m$ matrices. The** *difference* $A - B$ **is defined as the** $n \times m$ **matrix** $[a_{ij} - b_{ij}]$.

Example 5 Let
$$A = \begin{bmatrix} 2 & 3 & 4 \\ 1 & 0 & 2 \end{bmatrix} \quad \text{and} \quad B = \begin{bmatrix} -2 & 1 & -1 \\ 3 & 0 & 3 \end{bmatrix}$$

Then

$$A - B = \begin{bmatrix} 2 & 3 & 4 \\ 1 & 0 & 2 \end{bmatrix} - \begin{bmatrix} -2 & 1 & -1 \\ 3 & 0 & 3 \end{bmatrix}$$

$$= \begin{bmatrix} 2 - (-2) & 3 - 1 & 4 - (-1) \\ 1 - 3 & 0 - 0 & 2 - 3 \end{bmatrix} = \begin{bmatrix} 4 & 2 & 5 \\ -2 & 0 & -1 \end{bmatrix}$$

Notice that the difference $A - B$ is nothing more than the matrix formed by subtracting the entries in B from the corresponding entries in A.

Using the matrices A and B from Example 5, we find that

$$B - A = \begin{bmatrix} -2 & 1 & -1 \\ 3 & 0 & 3 \end{bmatrix} - \begin{bmatrix} 2 & 3 & 4 \\ 1 & 0 & 2 \end{bmatrix}$$

$$= \begin{bmatrix} -2 - 2 & 1 - 3 & -1 - 4 \\ 3 - 1 & 0 - 0 & 3 - 2 \end{bmatrix} = \begin{bmatrix} -4 & -2 & -5 \\ 2 & 0 & 1 \end{bmatrix}$$

Observe that $A - B \neq B - A$, illustrating that matrix subtraction, like subtraction of real numbers, is not commutative.

Exercise 2
Solutions to Odd-Numbered Problems begin on page 561.

In Problems 1–10 use the matrices below to find the indicated expression.

$$A = \begin{bmatrix} 2 & -3 & 4 \\ 0 & 2 & 1 \end{bmatrix} \qquad B = \begin{bmatrix} 1 & -2 & 0 \\ 5 & 1 & 2 \end{bmatrix} \qquad C = \begin{bmatrix} -3 & 0 & 5 \\ 2 & 1 & 3 \end{bmatrix}$$

1. $A + B$
2. $B + C$
3. $A - C$
4. $C - B$
5. $(A + B) - C$
6. $C + (A - B)$
7. $A + (B + C)$
8. $(A + B) + C$
9. $(A - B) - C$
10. $A - (B + C)$

11. Find x, y, and z so that

$$[2 \quad 3 \quad -4] + [x \quad y \quad z] = [6 \quad -8 \quad 2]$$

12. Find x and y so that

$$\begin{bmatrix} 3 & -2 & 2 \\ 1 & 0 & -1 \end{bmatrix} + \begin{bmatrix} x-y & 2 & -2 \\ 4 & x & 6 \end{bmatrix} = \begin{bmatrix} 6 & 0 & 0 \\ 5 & 2x+y & 5 \end{bmatrix}$$

13. The sales figures for two car dealers during June showed that Dealer A sold 100 compacts, 50 intermediates, and 40 full-size cars, while Dealer B sold 120 compacts, 40 intermediates, and 35 full-size cars. During July, Dealer A sold 80 compacts, 30 intermediates, and 10 full-size cars, while Dealer B sold 70 compacts, 40 intermediates, and 20 full-size cars. Total sales over the 3 month period of June–August revealed that Dealer A sold 300 compacts, 120 intermediates, and 65 full-size cars. In the same 3 month period, Dealer B sold 250 compacts, 100 intermediates, and 80 full-size cars.
    (a) Write 2×3 matrices summarizing sales data for June, July, and the 3 month period for each dealer.
    (b) Use matrix addition to find the sales over the 2 month period for June and July for each dealer.
    (c) Use matrix subtraction to find the sales in August for each dealer.

3. Matrix Multiplication

As you shall see, there are two kinds of multiplication involving matrices. We can multiply a real number and a matrix to form a *scalar multiple,* and we can multiply two matrices in *matrix multiplication.*

Scalar Multiple

Before defining *scalar multiple,* let's return to the production of Motors Incorporated during the month specified in Example 1, Section 1 (page 60). The matrix A describing this production is

$$A = \begin{bmatrix} 23 & 16 & 10 \\ 7 & 9 & 11 \end{bmatrix}$$

Let's assume that for 3 consecutive months, the monthly production remained the same. Then the total production for the 3 months is simply the sum of the matrix A taken 3 times. If we represent the total production by the matrix T, then

$$T = \begin{bmatrix} 23 & 16 & 10 \\ 7 & 9 & 11 \end{bmatrix} + \begin{bmatrix} 23 & 16 & 10 \\ 7 & 9 & 11 \end{bmatrix} + \begin{bmatrix} 23 & 16 & 10 \\ 7 & 9 & 11 \end{bmatrix}$$

$$= \begin{bmatrix} 23+23+23 & 16+16+16 & 10+10+10 \\ 7+7+7 & 9+9+9 & 11+11+11 \end{bmatrix}$$

$$= \begin{bmatrix} 3\cdot23 & 3\cdot16 & 3\cdot10 \\ 3\cdot7 & 3\cdot9 & 3\cdot11 \end{bmatrix} = \begin{bmatrix} 69 & 48 & 30 \\ 21 & 27 & 33 \end{bmatrix}$$

In other words, when we add the matrix A 3 times, we multiply each entry of A by 3. This leads to the following definition of scalar multiple.

Scalar Multiple   **Let $A = [a_{ij}]$ be an $n \times m$ matrix and let c be a real number. The** *scalar multiple* cA **of the matrix A and the real number c (called the** *scalar***) is the $n \times m$ matrix $cA = [ca_{ij}]$.**

When multiplying a scalar times a matrix, each entry of the matrix is multiplied by the scalar. Notice that the dimension of A and the dimension of the scalar multiple cA are the same.

Example 1   For
$$A = \begin{bmatrix} 2 \\ 5 \\ -7 \end{bmatrix} \quad \text{and} \quad B = \begin{bmatrix} 20 & 0 \\ 18 & 8 \end{bmatrix}$$

compute: (a) $3A$ (b) $\frac{1}{2}B$

Solution   (a) $3A = 3\begin{bmatrix} 2 \\ 5 \\ -7 \end{bmatrix} = \begin{bmatrix} 3 \cdot 2 \\ 3 \cdot 5 \\ 3 \cdot (-7) \end{bmatrix} = \begin{bmatrix} 6 \\ 15 \\ -21 \end{bmatrix}$

(b) $\frac{1}{2}B = \frac{1}{2}\begin{bmatrix} 20 & 0 \\ 18 & 8 \end{bmatrix} = \begin{bmatrix} \frac{1}{2} \cdot 20 & \frac{1}{2} \cdot 0 \\ \frac{1}{2} \cdot 18 & \frac{1}{2} \cdot 8 \end{bmatrix} = \begin{bmatrix} 10 & 0 \\ 9 & 4 \end{bmatrix}$

Example 2   For
$$A = \begin{bmatrix} 3 & 1 \\ 4 & 0 \\ 2 & -3 \end{bmatrix} \quad \text{and} \quad B = \begin{bmatrix} 2 & -3 \\ -1 & 1 \\ 1 & 0 \end{bmatrix}$$

compute: (a) $A - B$ (b) $A + (-1) \cdot B$

Solution   (a) $A - B = \begin{bmatrix} 1 & 4 \\ 5 & -1 \\ 1 & -3 \end{bmatrix}$

(b) $A + (-1) \cdot B = \begin{bmatrix} 3 & 1 \\ 4 & 0 \\ 2 & -3 \end{bmatrix} + \begin{bmatrix} -2 & 3 \\ 1 & -1 \\ -1 & 0 \end{bmatrix} = \begin{bmatrix} 1 & 4 \\ 5 & -1 \\ 1 & -3 \end{bmatrix}$

The above example illustrates the result that
$$A - B = A + (-1) \cdot B = A + (-B)$$

Matrix Multiplication

We arrive at a definition for multiplying two matrices through the following example.

Example 3   Using the data of 1 month's production of Motors Incorporated from Example 1, Section 1 (page 60), we have

$$A = \begin{matrix} & \text{Sedan} & \text{Hard-top} & \text{Station Wagon} \\ \begin{bmatrix} 23 & 16 & 10 \\ 7 & 9 & 11 \end{bmatrix} \end{matrix} \begin{matrix} \text{Units of material} \\ \text{Units of labor} \end{matrix}$$

Suppose that in this month's production, the cost for each unit of material is $45 and the cost for each unit of labor is $60. What is the total cost to manufacture the sedans, the hard-tops, and the station wagons?

Solution   For sedans, the cost is 23 units of material at $45 each, plus 7 units of labor at $60 each, for a total cost of

$$23 \cdot \$45 + 7 \cdot \$60 = 1035 + 420 = \$1455$$

Similarly, for hard-tops, the total cost is

$$16 \cdot \$45 + 9 \cdot \$60 = 720 + 540 = \$1260$$

Finally, for station wagons, the total cost is

$$10 \cdot \$45 + 11 \cdot \$60 = 450 + 660 = \$1110$$

We can represent the total cost for sedans, hard-tops, and station wagons by the matrix

$$[1455 \quad 1260 \quad 1110]$$

If we represent the cost of units of material and units of labor by the row vector

$$U = [45 \quad 60]$$

the total cost of units for sedans, hard-tops, and station wagons will then be $U \cdot A$. Now $U \cdot A$ is computed as follows:

$$U \cdot A = [45 \quad 60] \begin{bmatrix} 23 & 16 & 10 \\ 7 & 9 & 11 \end{bmatrix}$$

$$= [45 \cdot 23 + 60 \cdot 7 \quad 45 \cdot 16 + 60 \cdot 9 \quad 45 \cdot 10 + 60 \cdot 11]$$

$$= [1455 \quad 1260 \quad 1110]$$

■

In this example, notice that the number of columns of U is the same as the number of rows of A. Also, the number of rows of U is the same as the number of rows of the product $U \cdot A$, and the number of columns of A is the same as the number of columns of the product $U \cdot A$. With this in mind, we define the product of two matrices.

Matrix Multiplication **Let $A = [a_{ij}]$ be a matrix of dimension $n \times m$ and let $B = [b_{jk}]$ be a matrix of dimension $m \times p$. The** *product $A \cdot B$* **is the matrix $C = [c_{ik}]$ of dimension $n \times p$, where the** ik**th entry of C is**

$$c_{ik} = a_{i1}b_{1k} + a_{i2}b_{2k} + a_{i3}b_{3k} + \cdots + a_{im}b_{mk}$$

The element in the ith row and kth column of C, namely, c_{ik}, is obtained by summing the products of the elements of the ith row of A and the corresponding elements of the kth column of B.

The rule for multiplication of matrices is best illustrated by an example.

Example 4   Find the product $A \cdot B$ if

$$A = \begin{bmatrix} 1 & 3 & -2 \\ 4 & -1 & 5 \end{bmatrix} \quad \text{and} \quad B = \begin{bmatrix} 2 & -3 & 4 & 1 \\ -1 & 2 & 2 & 0 \\ 4 & 5 & 1 & 1 \end{bmatrix}$$

Solution   Since A is 2×3 and B is 3×4, the product $A \cdot B$ will be 2×4. To get, for example, the entry in row 2, column 3 of $A \cdot B$, we multiply the entries in row 2 of A by the corresponding entries in column 3 of B and add. That is,

$$\begin{bmatrix} 1 & 3 & -2 \\ 4 & -1 & 5 \end{bmatrix} \qquad \begin{bmatrix} 2 & -3 & 4 & 1 \\ -1 & 2 & 2 & 0 \\ 4 & 5 & 1 & 1 \end{bmatrix}$$

Row 2 of A	Column 3 of B	Product
4	4	16
−1	2	−2
5	1	5
	Sum:	19

This is the entry in row 2, column 3 of $A \cdot B$.

So far, we have

$$A \cdot B = \begin{bmatrix} - & - & - & - \\ - & - & 19 & - \end{bmatrix}$$

To obtain the entry in row 1, column 2, we compute

$$1 \cdot (-3) + 3 \cdot 2 + (-2) \cdot 5 = -3 + 6 - 10 = -7$$

The other entries of $A \cdot B$ are obtained in a similar fashion. The final result—and you should verify this—is

$$A \cdot B = \begin{bmatrix} -9 & -7 & 8 & -1 \\ 29 & 11 & 19 & 9 \end{bmatrix}$$

Let's look at some consequences of the definition of matrix multiplication.

If A is a matrix of dimension $n \times m$ (which has m columns) and B is a matrix of dimension $p \times q$ (which has p rows) and if $m \neq p$, the product $A \cdot B$ is not defined. That is, **multiplication of matrices is possible only if the number of columns of the first equals the number of rows of the second.**

If A is of dimension $n \times m$ and B is of dimension $m \times p$, then the product $A \cdot B$ is of dimension $n \times p$. See Figure 1.

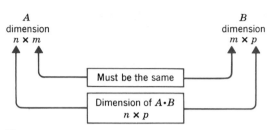

Figure 1

In Example 4, A is of dimension 2×3, B is of dimension 3×4, and we found the product $A \cdot B$ to be of dimension 2×4. Observe that the product $B \cdot A$ is not defined.

Example 5   For

$$A = \begin{bmatrix} 2 & 0 \\ 1 & 5 \end{bmatrix} \quad \text{and} \quad B = \begin{bmatrix} 3 & 2 \\ 1 & 4 \end{bmatrix}$$

compute $A \cdot B$ and $B \cdot A$.

Solution   We observe that the products $A \cdot B$ and $B \cdot A$ are both defined, and so

$$A \cdot B = \begin{bmatrix} 6 & 4 \\ 8 & 22 \end{bmatrix} \qquad B \cdot A = \begin{bmatrix} 8 & 10 \\ 6 & 20 \end{bmatrix}$$

∎

Note from the above example that even if both $A \cdot B$ and $B \cdot A$ are defined, they may not be equal. We conclude that matrix multiplication is not always commutative.

Properties

We continue our study of scalar multiple and matrix multiplication by listing some properties.

Let k and h be two real numbers and let $A = [a_{ij}]$ and $B = [b_{ij}]$, $i = 1, \ldots, n$, $j = 1, \ldots, m$ be matrices of dimension $n \times m$. Then

$$\textbf{(I)} \qquad k(hA) = (kh)A$$
$$\textbf{(II)} \qquad (k + h)A = kA + hA$$
$$\textbf{(III)} \qquad k(A + B) = kA + kB$$

We prove (I) and (II) here; the proof of (III) is left as an exercise (Problem 51, Exercise 3).

(I)   Here

$$k(hA) = k(h[a_{ij}]) = k([ha_{ij}]) = k[ha_{ij}]$$
$$= [kha_{ij}] = (kh)[a_{ij}] = (kh)A$$

(II)   For this property, we have

$$(k + h)A = (k + h)[a_{ij}] = [(k + h)a_{ij}]$$
$$= [ka_{ij} + ha_{ij}] = [ka_{ij}] + [ha_{ij}]$$
$$= k[a_{ij}] + h(a_{ij}) = kA + hA$$

Properties (I)–(III) are illustrated in the following example.

Example 6   For

$$A = \begin{bmatrix} 2 & -3 & -1 \\ 5 & 6 & 4 \end{bmatrix} \quad \text{and} \quad B = \begin{bmatrix} -3 & 0 & 4 \\ 2 & -1 & 5 \end{bmatrix}$$

show that:

Solution   (a) $5[2A] = 10A$ (b) $(4 + 3)A = 4A + 3A$ (c) $3[A + B] = 3A + 3B$

(a) $5[2A] = 5\begin{bmatrix} 4 & -6 & -2 \\ 10 & 12 & 8 \end{bmatrix} = \begin{bmatrix} 20 & -30 & -10 \\ 50 & 60 & 40 \end{bmatrix}$

$10A = \begin{bmatrix} 20 & -30 & -10 \\ 50 & 60 & 40 \end{bmatrix}$

(b) $(4 + 3)A = 7A = \begin{bmatrix} 14 & -21 & -7 \\ 35 & 42 & 28 \end{bmatrix}$

$4A + 3A = \begin{bmatrix} 8 & -12 & -4 \\ 20 & 24 & 16 \end{bmatrix} + \begin{bmatrix} 6 & -9 & -3 \\ 15 & 18 & 12 \end{bmatrix}$

$= \begin{bmatrix} 14 & -21 & -7 \\ 35 & 42 & 28 \end{bmatrix}$

(c) $3[A + B] = 3\begin{bmatrix} -1 & -3 & 3 \\ 7 & 5 & 9 \end{bmatrix} = \begin{bmatrix} -3 & -9 & 9 \\ 21 & 15 & 27 \end{bmatrix}$

$3A + 3B = \begin{bmatrix} 6 & -9 & -3 \\ 15 & 18 & 12 \end{bmatrix} + \begin{bmatrix} -9 & 0 & 12 \\ 6 & -3 & 15 \end{bmatrix}$

$= \begin{bmatrix} -3 & -9 & 9 \\ 21 & 15 & 27 \end{bmatrix}$

In listing some of the properties of matrix multiplication in this book, we agree to follow the usual convention and write $A \cdot B$ as AB, from now on.

Let A be a matrix of dimension $n \times m$, let B be a matrix of dimension $m \times p$, and let C be a matrix of dimension $p \times q$. Then matrix multiplication is *associative.*

That is,

$$A(BC) = (AB)C$$

The resulting matrix ABC is of dimension $n \times q$.

Notice the limitations that are placed on the dimensions of the matrices in order for multiplication to be associative.

Let A be a matrix of dimension $n \times m$. Let B and C be matrices of dimension $m \times p$. Then *matrix multiplication distributes over matrix addition.* **That is,**

$$A(B + C) = AB + AC$$

The resulting matrix $AB + AC$ is of dimension $n \times p$.

Identity Matrix

A special type of square matrix is the *identity matrix,* which is denoted by I_n. It has the property that all its diagonal entries are 1's and all other entries are 0's. Thus,

$$I_n = \begin{bmatrix} 1 & 0 & \cdots & 0 & 0 \\ 0 & 1 & \cdots & 0 & 0 \\ \vdots & \vdots & \ddots & \vdots & \vdots \\ 0 & 0 & \cdots & 1 & 0 \\ 0 & 0 & \cdots & 0 & 1 \end{bmatrix}$$

where the subscript n implies that I_n is of dimension $n \times n$.

Example 7   For

$$A = \begin{bmatrix} 3 & 2 \\ -4 & 5 \end{bmatrix}$$

compute: (a) AI_2 (b) $I_2 A$

Solution

(a) $AI_2 = \begin{bmatrix} 3 & 2 \\ -4 & 5 \end{bmatrix}\begin{bmatrix} 1 & 0 \\ 0 & 1 \end{bmatrix} = \begin{bmatrix} 3 & 2 \\ -4 & 5 \end{bmatrix} = A$

(b) $I_2 A = \begin{bmatrix} 1 & 0 \\ 0 & 1 \end{bmatrix}\begin{bmatrix} 3 & 2 \\ -4 & 5 \end{bmatrix} = \begin{bmatrix} 3 & 2 \\ -4 & 5 \end{bmatrix} = A$

■

This example can be generalized as follows:

If A is a matrix of dimension $n \times m$ and if I_n denotes the identity matrix of dimension $n \times n$, and I_m denotes the identity matrix of dimension $m \times m$, then

$$I_n A = A \qquad \text{and} \qquad AI_m = A$$

The reason for stating two formulas above is that when the matrix A is not square, care must be taken when forming the products AI and IA. For example, if

$$A = \begin{bmatrix} 1 & 2 \\ 3 & 2 \\ 1 & 1 \end{bmatrix}$$

then A is of dimension 3×2 and

$$AI_2 = A \begin{bmatrix} 1 & 0 \\ 0 & 1 \end{bmatrix} = \begin{bmatrix} 1 & 2 \\ 3 & 2 \\ 1 & 1 \end{bmatrix} \begin{bmatrix} 1 & 0 \\ 0 & 1 \end{bmatrix} = \begin{bmatrix} 1 & 2 \\ 3 & 2 \\ 1 & 1 \end{bmatrix} = A$$

Although the product $I_2 A$ is not defined, we can calculate the product $I_3 A$ as follows:

$$I_3 A = \begin{bmatrix} 1 & 0 & 0 \\ 0 & 1 & 0 \\ 0 & 0 & 1 \end{bmatrix} \begin{bmatrix} 1 & 2 \\ 3 & 2 \\ 1 & 1 \end{bmatrix} = \begin{bmatrix} 1 & 2 \\ 3 & 2 \\ 1 & 1 \end{bmatrix} = A$$

Inverse of a Matrix

Inverse   **Let A be a matrix of dimension $n \times n$. A matrix B of dimension $n \times n$ is called an** *inverse* **of A if $AB = BA = I_n$. We denote the inverse of a matrix A, if it exists, by A^{-1}.**

Example 8   Show that $\begin{bmatrix} \frac{1}{2} & -\frac{1}{2} \\ 0 & 1 \end{bmatrix}$ is the inverse of $\begin{bmatrix} 2 & 1 \\ 0 & 1 \end{bmatrix}$.

Solution   Since

$$\begin{bmatrix} 2 & 1 \\ 0 & 1 \end{bmatrix} \begin{bmatrix} \frac{1}{2} & -\frac{1}{2} \\ 0 & 1 \end{bmatrix} = \begin{bmatrix} 1 & 0 \\ 0 & 1 \end{bmatrix}$$

the required condition is met.

Observe that we also could have verified this by showing that

$$\begin{bmatrix} \frac{1}{2} & -\frac{1}{2} \\ 0 & 1 \end{bmatrix} \begin{bmatrix} 2 & 1 \\ 0 & 1 \end{bmatrix} = \begin{bmatrix} 1 & 0 \\ 0 & 1 \end{bmatrix}$$

The next example provides a technique for finding the inverse of a matrix. Although this technique is not the best (see Section 5 for a more efficient method), it is illustrative.

Example 9   Find the inverse of the matrix: $A = \begin{bmatrix} 2 & 1 \\ 0 & 1 \end{bmatrix}$

Solution   We begin by assuming that this matrix has an inverse of the form

$$A^{-1} = \begin{bmatrix} a & b \\ c & d \end{bmatrix}$$

Then the product of A and A^{-1} must be the identity matrix:

$$\begin{bmatrix} 2 & 1 \\ 0 & 1 \end{bmatrix}\begin{bmatrix} a & b \\ c & d \end{bmatrix} = \begin{bmatrix} 1 & 0 \\ 0 & 1 \end{bmatrix}$$

Multiplying the matrices on the left side, we get

$$\begin{bmatrix} 2a + c & 2b + d \\ c & d \end{bmatrix} = \begin{bmatrix} 1 & 0 \\ 0 & 1 \end{bmatrix}$$

The condition for equality requires that

$$2a + c = 1 \qquad 2b + d = 0 \qquad c = 0 \qquad d = 1$$

Thus,

$$a = \tfrac{1}{2} \qquad b = -\tfrac{1}{2} \qquad c = 0 \qquad d = 1$$

Hence, the inverse of

$$A = \begin{bmatrix} 2 & 1 \\ 0 & 1 \end{bmatrix} \quad \text{is} \quad A^{-1} = \begin{bmatrix} \tfrac{1}{2} & -\tfrac{1}{2} \\ 0 & 1 \end{bmatrix}$$

We verify that this is the inverse by computing AA^{-1}:

$$AA^{-1} = \begin{bmatrix} 2 & 1 \\ 0 & 1 \end{bmatrix}\begin{bmatrix} \tfrac{1}{2} & -\tfrac{1}{2} \\ 0 & 1 \end{bmatrix} = \begin{bmatrix} 1 & 0 \\ 0 & 1 \end{bmatrix}$$

■

Sometimes, a square matrix does not have an inverse.

Example 10   Show that the matrix below does not have an inverse.

$$A = \begin{bmatrix} 0 & 1 \\ 0 & 0 \end{bmatrix}$$

Solution   We proceed as in Example 9 by assuming that A does have an inverse. It will be of the form

$$A^{-1} = \begin{bmatrix} a & b \\ c & d \end{bmatrix}$$

The product of A and A^{-1} must be the identity matrix. Thus,

$$\begin{bmatrix} 0 & 1 \\ 0 & 0 \end{bmatrix}\begin{bmatrix} a & b \\ c & d \end{bmatrix} = \begin{bmatrix} 1 & 0 \\ 0 & 1 \end{bmatrix}$$

Performing the multiplication on the left side, we have

$$\begin{bmatrix} c & d \\ 0 & 0 \end{bmatrix} = \begin{bmatrix} 1 & 0 \\ 0 & 1 \end{bmatrix}$$

But these two matrices can never be equal. We conclude that our assumption that A has an inverse is false. That is, A does not have an inverse. ∎

So far, we have shown that a square matrix may or may not have an inverse. The next result tells us that a square matrix will not have more than one inverse.

A square matrix A has at most one inverse. That is, the inverse of a matrix, if it exists, is *unique.*

To verify this, suppose we have two inverses B and C for a matrix A. Then

$$AB = BA = I_n \quad \text{and} \quad AC = CA = I_n$$

Multiplying both sides of $AC = I_n$ on the left by B, we find

$$B(AC) = BI_n = B$$

Similarly, multiplying both sides of $BA = I_n$ on the right by C, we obtain

$$(BA)C = I_n C = C$$

But $B(AC) = (BA)C$. Hence, $B = C$.

What about nonsquare matrices? Can they have inverses? The answer is "No." We have seen that whenever a matrix has an inverse, it will commute with its inverse under multiplication. Therefore, if A is a nonsquare matrix with inverse B, the products AB and BA will not have the same dimension and therefore cannot be equal.

A nonsquare matrix has no inverse.

Exercise 3
Solutions to Odd-Numbered Problems begin on page 562.

In Problems 1–10 let A be of dimension 3×4, let B be of dimension 3×3, let C be of dimension 2×3, and let D be of dimension 3×2. Determine which of the following expressions are defined and, for those that are, give the dimension.

1. BA	2. CD	3. AB	4. DC
5. $(BA)C$	6. $A(CD)$	7. $BA + A$	8. $CD + BA$
9. $DC + B$	10. $CB - A$		

In Problems 11–24 use the matrices below to perform the indicated operations.

$$A = \begin{bmatrix} 1 & 2 \\ 0 & 4 \end{bmatrix} \qquad B = \begin{bmatrix} 1 & 2 & 3 \\ -1 & 4 & -2 \end{bmatrix} \qquad C = \begin{bmatrix} 3 & 1 \\ 4 & -1 \\ 0 & 2 \end{bmatrix}$$

$$D = \begin{bmatrix} 1 & 0 & 4 \\ 0 & 1 & 2 \\ 0 & -1 & 1 \end{bmatrix} \qquad E = \begin{bmatrix} 3 & -1 \\ 4 & 2 \end{bmatrix}$$

11. AB 12. DC 13. BC 14. AA
15. $(D + I_3)C$ 16. $DC + C$ 17. $(DC)B$ 18. $D(CB)$
19. EI_2 20. I_3D 21. $(2E)B$ 22. $E(2B)$
23. $-5E + A$ 24. $3A + 2E$

In Problems 25–30 show that the given matrices are inverses of each other.

25. $\begin{bmatrix} 1 & 2 \\ 2 & 3 \end{bmatrix} \begin{bmatrix} -3 & 2 \\ 2 & -1 \end{bmatrix}$ 26. $\begin{bmatrix} 1 & 5 \\ 2 & 0 \end{bmatrix} \begin{bmatrix} 0 & \frac{1}{2} \\ \frac{1}{5} & -\frac{1}{10} \end{bmatrix}$

27. $\begin{bmatrix} -1 & -2 \\ 3 & 4 \end{bmatrix} \begin{bmatrix} 2 & 1 \\ -\frac{3}{2} & -\frac{1}{2} \end{bmatrix}$ 28. $\begin{bmatrix} 1 & 3 \\ 2 & -1 \end{bmatrix} \begin{bmatrix} \frac{1}{7} & \frac{3}{7} \\ \frac{2}{7} & -\frac{1}{7} \end{bmatrix}$

29. $\begin{bmatrix} 1 & 2 & 3 \\ 2 & 3 & 4 \\ 1 & 2 & 1 \end{bmatrix} \begin{bmatrix} -\frac{5}{2} & 2 & -\frac{1}{2} \\ 1 & -1 & 1 \\ \frac{1}{2} & 0 & -\frac{1}{2} \end{bmatrix}$ 30. $\begin{bmatrix} 1 & 3 & 3 \\ 1 & 4 & 3 \\ 1 & 3 & 4 \end{bmatrix} \begin{bmatrix} 7 & -3 & -3 \\ -1 & 1 & 0 \\ -1 & 0 & 1 \end{bmatrix}$

In Problems 31–36 find the inverse, if it exists, of each matrix.

31. $\begin{bmatrix} 1 & 1 \\ 1 & 2 \end{bmatrix}$ 32. $\begin{bmatrix} 2 & 1 \\ 1 & 1 \end{bmatrix}$ 33. $\begin{bmatrix} 3 & -2 \\ 0 & 2 \end{bmatrix}$

34. $\begin{bmatrix} 4 & -1 \\ -1 & 0 \end{bmatrix}$ 35. $\begin{bmatrix} 3 & 2 \\ 6 & 4 \end{bmatrix}$ 36. $\begin{bmatrix} 4 & 2 \\ 2 & 1 \end{bmatrix}$

37. For

$$A = \begin{bmatrix} 1 & -1 \\ 2 & 0 \end{bmatrix} \qquad \text{and} \qquad B = \begin{bmatrix} 3 & 2 \\ -1 & 4 \end{bmatrix}$$

find AB and BA. Notice that $AB \neq BA$.

38. Show that, for all values a, b, c, and d, the matrices

$$A = \begin{bmatrix} a & b \\ -b & a \end{bmatrix} \qquad \text{and} \qquad B = \begin{bmatrix} c & d \\ -d & c \end{bmatrix}$$

are commutative; that is, $AB = BA$.

39. Let

$$U = \begin{bmatrix} 2 \\ -1 \\ 3 \end{bmatrix} \qquad V = \begin{bmatrix} \frac{1}{2} \\ 0 \\ 1 \end{bmatrix} \qquad W = \begin{bmatrix} -3 \\ -7 \\ 0 \end{bmatrix}$$

Compute the following:
(a) $U + V$ (b) $U - V$ (c) $\frac{1}{2}(U + V)$
(d) $U + V - W$ (e) $2U - 7V$ (f) $\frac{1}{4}U - \frac{1}{4}V - \frac{1}{4}W$

40. Find a_1, a_2, a_3 which satisfy the following:

$$\begin{bmatrix} 2 \\ 1 \\ 0 \end{bmatrix} + \begin{bmatrix} a_1 \\ a_2 \\ a_3 \end{bmatrix} = \begin{bmatrix} 2 \\ -1 \\ 3 \end{bmatrix}$$

41. If possible, find a matrix A such that

$$A\begin{bmatrix} 0 & 1 \\ 2 & -1 \end{bmatrix} = \begin{bmatrix} 2 & 1 \\ -1 & 0 \end{bmatrix} \qquad \textit{Hint:} \text{ Let } A = \begin{bmatrix} a & b \\ c & d \end{bmatrix}.$$

42. For what numbers x will the following be true?

$$[x \quad 4 \quad 1]\begin{bmatrix} 2 & 1 & 0 \\ 1 & 0 & 2 \\ 0 & 2 & 4 \end{bmatrix}\begin{bmatrix} x \\ -7 \\ \frac{5}{4} \end{bmatrix} = \mathbf{0}$$

43. Let

$$A = \begin{bmatrix} 1 & 2 & 5 \\ 2 & 4 & 10 \\ -1 & -2 & -5 \end{bmatrix}$$

Show that $A^2 = \mathbf{0}$. Thus, the rule in the real number system that if $a^2 = 0$, then $a = 0$ does not hold for matrices.

44. What must be true about a, b, c, and d, if we demand that $AB = BA$ for the following matrices?

$$A = \begin{bmatrix} a & b \\ c & d \end{bmatrix} \qquad B = \begin{bmatrix} 1 & 1 \\ -1 & 1 \end{bmatrix}$$

Assume that

$$\begin{bmatrix} a & b \\ c & d \end{bmatrix} \neq \begin{bmatrix} 1 & 0 \\ 0 & 1 \end{bmatrix}$$

45. Let

$$A = \begin{bmatrix} a & b \\ b & a \end{bmatrix}$$

Find a and b such that $A^2 + A = \mathbf{0}$, where $A^2 = AA$.

46. For the matrix

$$A = \begin{bmatrix} a & 1-a \\ 1+a & -a \end{bmatrix}$$

show that $A^2 = AA = I_2$.

47. Find the vector $[x_1 \quad x_2]$ for which

$$[x_1 \quad x_2]\begin{bmatrix} \frac{1}{2} & \frac{1}{2} \\ \frac{1}{4} & \frac{3}{4} \end{bmatrix} = [x_1 \quad x_2]$$

under the condition that $x_1 + x_2 = 1$. Here, the vector $[x_1 \quad x_2]$ is called a *fixed vector* of the matrix

$$\begin{bmatrix} \frac{1}{2} & \frac{1}{2} \\ \frac{1}{4} & \frac{3}{4} \end{bmatrix}$$

48. Mike went to a department store and purchased 6 pairs of pants, 8 shirts, and 2 jackets. Danny purchased 2 pairs of pants, 5 shirts, and 3 jackets. If the pants are $5 each, shirts are $3 each, and jackets are $9 each, use matrix multiplication to find the amounts spent by Mike and Danny.

49. Suppose a factory is asked to produce three types of products, which we will call P_1, P_2, P_3. Suppose the following purchase order was received: $P_1 = 7$, $P_2 = 12$, $P_3 = 5$. Represent this order by a row vector and call it P:

$$P = [7 \quad 12 \quad 5]$$

To produce each of the products, raw material of four kinds is needed. Call the raw material M_1, M_2, M_3, and M_4. The matrix below gives the amount of material needed for each product:

$$Q = \begin{array}{c} \\ P_1 \\ P_2 \\ P_3 \end{array} \begin{array}{cccc} M_1 & M_2 & M_3 & M_4 \\ \begin{bmatrix} 2 & 3 & 1 & 12 \\ 7 & 9 & 5 & 20 \\ 8 & 12 & 6 & 15 \end{bmatrix} \end{array}$$

Suppose the cost for each of the materials M_1, M_2, M_3, and M_4 is $10, $12, $15, and $20, respectively. The cost vector is

$$C = \begin{bmatrix} 10 \\ 12 \\ 15 \\ 20 \end{bmatrix}$$

Compute each of the following and interpret each one:
(a) PQ (b) QC (c) PQC

*50. For a square matrix A, it is always possible to find $A \cdot A = A^2$. It is also clear that we can compute

$$A^n = \underbrace{A \cdot A \cdot \cdots \cdot A}_{n \text{ times}}$$

Find A^2, A^3, and A^4 for each of the following square matrices:

(a) $A = \begin{bmatrix} 1 & 0 \\ 3 & 2 \end{bmatrix}$ (b) $A = \begin{bmatrix} 3 & 1 \\ -2 & -1 \end{bmatrix}$

(c) $A = \begin{bmatrix} 0 & 1 & 1 \\ 0 & -1 & 2 \\ 6 & 3 & -2 \end{bmatrix}$ (d) $A = \begin{bmatrix} 1 & 0 \\ 0 & 1 \end{bmatrix}$

(e) $A = \begin{bmatrix} \frac{1}{2} & \frac{1}{2} \\ \frac{1}{4} & \frac{3}{4} \end{bmatrix}$

Can you guess what A^n looks like for part (d)? For part (e)?

*51. Prove property (III) (page 73.)

4. Row Operations

We begin by considering a system of two equations in two unknowns:

(1)
$$x + 4y = 14$$
$$3x - 2y = 0$$

To find a solution, we multiply the first equation by 3, obtaining $3x + 12y = 42$, and then subtract it from the second:

$$
\begin{array}{rr}
3x - 2y = & 0 \\
3x + 12y = & 42 \\
\hline
-14y = & -42
\end{array}
$$

The original system of equations (1) may now be written as the equivalent system

$$x + 4y = 14$$
$$-14y = -42$$

Dividing the second equation by -14, we get

$$x + 4y = 14$$
$$y = 3$$

To find x, we multiply the second equation by -4 and add it to the first. The result is

(2)
$$x = 2$$
$$y = 3$$

This system of equations has the obvious solution $x = 2$, $y = 3$ and is equivalent to the original system (1), so that the solution of the original system (1) is also $x = 2$, $y = 3$.

We obtained the final system (2) from the original system (1) by a series of operations. Because of its simplicity, the original system could have been solved more quickly by either the substitution method or the add and subtract method (refer to Chapter 1), but we chose the above operations because the *pattern* of the solution shown provides another method for solving a system of equations. The advantages of this third method are:

1. It is algorithmic in character; that is, it consists of repetitive steps so that it can be programmed on a computer.
2. It works on any system of linear equations.

Now, look back at the original system of equations (1):

$$x + 4y = 14$$
$$3x - 2y = 0$$

This can be compactly written as the matrix

$$
\begin{array}{cc}
x & y \\
\end{array}
$$
$$
\left[\begin{array}{cc|c}
1 & 4 & 14 \\
3 & -2 & 0
\end{array}\right]
$$

where it is understood that column 1 is reserved for the coefficients of the variable x, column 2 is for the coefficients of the variable y, and column 3 is for the constants that appear on the right side of the equal sign. We use the vertical bar as a reminder that this is where the equal sign used to be.

Augmented Matrix   **The matrix used to represent a system of equations is called the** *augmented matrix* **of the system.**

Let's repeat the steps we took to solve this system of equations, except now we will manipulate the augmented matrix instead of the equations. For convenience, the equations are listed next to the augmented matrix.

$$\begin{bmatrix} 1 & 4 & | & 14 \\ 3 & -2 & | & 0 \end{bmatrix} \qquad \begin{aligned} x + 4y &= 14 \\ 3x - 2y &= 0 \end{aligned}$$

Multiplying the first *equation* by 3 and subtracting it from the second *equation* corresponds to multiplying the first *row* of the matrix by -3 and adding the result to the second *row*. The result is the matrix

$$\begin{bmatrix} 1 & 4 & | & 14 \\ 0 & -14 & | & -42 \end{bmatrix} \qquad \begin{aligned} x + 4y &= 14 \\ -14y &= -42 \end{aligned}$$

Next, divide the second row of this last matrix by -14 to obtain

$$\begin{bmatrix} 1 & 4 & | & 14 \\ 0 & 1 & | & 3 \end{bmatrix} \qquad \begin{aligned} x + 4y &= 14 \\ y &= 3 \end{aligned}$$

Finally, multiply the second row of this matrix by -4 and add it to the first row to obtain

$$\begin{bmatrix} 1 & 0 & | & 2 \\ 0 & 1 & | & 3 \end{bmatrix} \qquad \begin{aligned} x &= 2 \\ y &= 3 \end{aligned}$$

When manipulations such as the above are performed on a matrix, they are called *elementary row operations*. We now list the three basic types of row operations:

Elementary Row
Operations

1. **The interchange of any 2 rows of a matrix**
2. **The replacement of any row of a matrix by a nonzero scalar multiple of that same row**
3. **The replacement of any row of a matrix by the sum of that row and a scalar multiple of some other row**

An example of each elementary row operation is given below.

Example 1

$$A = \begin{bmatrix} 3 & 4 & -3 \\ 7 & -\frac{1}{2} & 0 \end{bmatrix}$$

1. The matrix obtained by interchanging the first and second rows of A is

$$\begin{bmatrix} 7 & -\frac{1}{2} & 0 \\ 3 & 4 & -3 \end{bmatrix}$$

2. The matrix obtained by multiplying row 2 of A by 5 is

$$\begin{bmatrix} 3 & 4 & -3 \\ 35 & -\frac{5}{2} & 0 \end{bmatrix}$$

We denote this operation by writing $R_2 = 5r_2$, where r_2 denotes the "old" row 2 and R_2 denotes the "new" row 2.

3. The matrix obtained from A by adding 3 times row 1 to row 2 is

$$\begin{bmatrix} 3 & 4 & -3 \\ 7 + 3 \cdot 3 & -\frac{1}{2} + 3 \cdot 4 & 0 + 3 \cdot (-3) \end{bmatrix} = \begin{bmatrix} 3 & 4 & -3 \\ 16 & \frac{23}{2} & -9 \end{bmatrix}$$

We denote this operation by writing $R_2 = r_2 + 3r_1$.

Let's see how row operations are used to solve a system of equations.

Example 2   Solve the system of equations:

$$\begin{aligned} x - \ y &= 2 \\ 2x - 3y &= 2 \end{aligned}$$

Solution   First, we write the augmented matrix:

$$\begin{bmatrix} 1 & -1 & | & 2 \\ 2 & -3 & | & 2 \end{bmatrix} \qquad \begin{aligned} x - \ y &= 2 \\ 2x - 3y &= 2 \end{aligned}$$

Perform the row operation

$$R_2 = -2r_1 + r_2$$

(This has the effect of leaving row 1 fixed and getting a 0 in row 2, column 1.)

$$\begin{bmatrix} 1 & -1 & | & 2 \\ 0 & -1 & | & -2 \end{bmatrix} \qquad \begin{aligned} x - y &= \ \ 2 \\ - y &= -2 \end{aligned}$$

Perform the row operation

$$R_2 = -r_2$$

(This has the effect of getting a 1 in row 2, column 2.)

$$\begin{bmatrix} 1 & -1 & | & 2 \\ 0 & 1 & | & 2 \end{bmatrix} \qquad \begin{aligned} x - y &= 2 \\ y &= 2 \end{aligned}$$

Perform the row operation

$$R_1 = r_2 + r_1$$

(This has the effect of leaving row 2 fixed and getting a 0 in row 1, column 2.)

$$\begin{bmatrix} 1 & 0 & | & 4 \\ 0 & 1 & | & 2 \end{bmatrix} \qquad \begin{aligned} x &= 4 \\ y &= 2 \end{aligned}$$

The solution of the system is $x = 4$, $y = 2$.

Let's summarize the steps to follow in solving a system of n equations in n unknowns using row operations:

1. **Write the augmented matrix corresponding to the system. Remember that the constants must be to the right of the equal sign.**
2. **Perform row operations to get the entry 1 in row 1, column 1.**
3. **Perform row operations that leave the entry 1 obtained in Step 2 undisturbed while getting 0's in the rest of column 1. (We want to get 1's along the diagonal and 0's elsewhere.)**
4. **Perform row operations to get a 1 in row 2, column 2 without disturbing column 1.**
5. **Perform row operations to get 0's in the rest of column 2 without disturbing the entry 1 obtained in Step 4.**
6. **Continue in this way up to and including the last row of the matrix.**

Here is an example of three equations in three unknowns.

Example 3 Solve the system of equations:

$$
\begin{aligned}
x + y + z &= 6 \\
3x + 2y - z &= 4 \\
3x + y + 2z &= 11
\end{aligned}
$$

Solution STEP 1: The augmented matrix corresponding to the system is

$$
\begin{bmatrix}
1 & 1 & 1 & \bigm| & 6 \\
3 & 2 & -1 & \bigm| & 4 \\
3 & 1 & 2 & \bigm| & 11
\end{bmatrix}
$$

STEP 2: Since a 1 appears in row 1, column 1, we can skip to step 3.

STEP 3: Perform the row operations*

$$
\begin{aligned}
R_2 &= -3r_1 + r_2 \\
R_3 &= -3r_1 + r_3
\end{aligned}
$$

Notice that we are leaving row 1 undisturbed:

$$
\begin{bmatrix}
1 & 1 & 1 & \bigm| & 6 \\
0 & -1 & -4 & \bigm| & -14 \\
0 & -2 & -1 & \bigm| & -7
\end{bmatrix}
$$

STEP 4: To get a 1 in row 2, column 2, we use

$$
R_2 = (-1)r_2
$$

Notice that column 1 remains undisturbed:

$$
\begin{bmatrix}
1 & 1 & 1 & \bigm| & 6 \\
0 & 1 & 4 & \bigm| & 14 \\
0 & -2 & -1 & \bigm| & -7
\end{bmatrix}
$$

*You should convince yourself that doing both of these simultaneously is the same as doing the first followed by the second.

STEP 5:   To get 0's in the rest of column 2, we use

$$R_1 = -r_2 + r_1$$
$$R_3 = 2r_2 + r_3$$

Notice that row 2 is left undisturbed:

$$\begin{bmatrix} 1 & 0 & -3 & | & -8 \\ 0 & 1 & 4 & | & 14 \\ 0 & 0 & 7 & | & 21 \end{bmatrix}$$

STEP 6:   Continuing, we seek a 1 in row 3, column 3, so we use

$$R_3 = \tfrac{1}{7}r_3$$

Notice that this is the only choice available to us, since any other choice would disturb the 0's and 1's already obtained:

$$\begin{bmatrix} 1 & 0 & -3 & | & -8 \\ 0 & 1 & 4 & | & 14 \\ 0 & 0 & 1 & | & 3 \end{bmatrix}$$

To get 0's in the rest of column 3, we use

$$R_1 = 3r_3 + r_1$$
$$R_2 = -4r_3 + r_2$$

The result is

$$\begin{bmatrix} 1 & 0 & 0 & | & 1 \\ 0 & 1 & 0 & | & 2 \\ 0 & 0 & 1 & | & 3 \end{bmatrix}$$

The solution of the system is $x = 1$, $y = 2$, $z = 3$.   ■

The method outlined here also reveals systems that have no solution or an infinite number of solutions.

Example 4   Discuss the system

$$3x - 6y = 4$$
$$6x - 12y = 5$$

Solution   The augmented matrix representing this system is

$$\begin{bmatrix} 3 & -6 & | & 4 \\ 6 & -12 & | & 5 \end{bmatrix}$$

Trial and error should convince you that the one way to get a 1 in row 1, column 1 is to use

$$R_1 = \tfrac{1}{3}r_1$$

$$\begin{bmatrix} 1 & -2 & | & \tfrac{4}{3} \\ 6 & -12 & | & 5 \end{bmatrix}$$

To get 0 in row 2, column 1, use

$$R_2 = -6r_1 + r_2$$

$$\begin{bmatrix} 1 & -2 & \Big| & \frac{4}{3} \\ 0 & 0 & \Big| & -3 \end{bmatrix}$$

Let's stop here to look at the actual system of equations:

$$x - 2y = \tfrac{4}{3}$$
$$0x + 0y = -3$$

The second equation can never be true—no matter what the choice of x and y. Hence, there are no numbers x and y that can obey both equations. That is, the system has no solution. ■

Example 5 Discuss the system

$$2x - 3y = 5$$
$$4x - 6y = 10$$

Solution The augmented matrix representing this system is

$$\begin{bmatrix} 2 & -3 & \Big| & 5 \\ 4 & -6 & \Big| & 10 \end{bmatrix}$$

To get a 1 in row 1, column 1, we use

$$R_1 = \tfrac{1}{2}r_1$$

$$\begin{bmatrix} 1 & -\frac{3}{2} & \Big| & \frac{5}{2} \\ 4 & -6 & \Big| & 10 \end{bmatrix}$$

To get a 0 in column 1, row 2, we use

$$R_2 = -4r_1 + r_2$$

$$\begin{bmatrix} 1 & -\frac{3}{2} & \Big| & \frac{5}{2} \\ 0 & 0 & \Big| & 0 \end{bmatrix}$$

The system of equations looks like

$$x - \tfrac{3}{2}y = \tfrac{5}{2}$$
$$0x + 0y = 0$$

The second equation is true for any choice of x and y. Hence, all numbers x and y that obey the first equation are solutions of the system. Since any point on the line $x - \tfrac{3}{2}y = \tfrac{5}{2}$ is a solution, there are an infinite number of solutions. ■

In Section 6 we discuss a method for telling in advance whether a system of equations leads to a unique solution, no solution, or an infinite number of solutions. There, we will also discuss the solution of a system of m equations in n unknowns, where m may be different from n.

We close with a capsule summary of what to expect from any system of two equations with two unknowns.

After completing the steps outlined earlier, one of the following matrices will result for a system of two equations with two unknowns:

$$\begin{bmatrix} 1 & 0 & | & c \\ 0 & 1 & | & d \end{bmatrix}$$ **Unique solution:** $x = c$, $y = d$

$$\begin{bmatrix} a & b & | & c \\ 0 & 0 & | & 0 \end{bmatrix}$$ **Infinite number of solutions:** $ax + by = c$

$$\begin{bmatrix} a & b & | & c \\ 0 & 0 & | & \text{nonzero number} \end{bmatrix}$$ **No solution**

Exercise 4
Solutions to Odd-Numbered Problems begin on page 564.

In Problems 1–4 state the row operation used to transform the matrix on the left to the one on the right.

1. $\begin{bmatrix} 3 & 2 & 1 \\ 2 & 1 & 0 \end{bmatrix}$ $\begin{bmatrix} 2 & 1 & 0 \\ 3 & 2 & 1 \end{bmatrix}$ 2. $\begin{bmatrix} 3 & 2 & 1 \\ 2 & 1 & 0 \end{bmatrix}$ $\begin{bmatrix} 1 & 1 & 1 \\ 2 & 1 & 0 \end{bmatrix}$

3. $\begin{bmatrix} 3 & 2 & 1 \\ 2 & 1 & 0 \end{bmatrix}$ $\begin{bmatrix} 12 & 8 & 4 \\ 2 & 1 & 0 \end{bmatrix}$ 4. $\begin{bmatrix} 3 & 2 & 1 \\ 2 & 1 & 0 \end{bmatrix}$ $\begin{bmatrix} 3 & 2 & 1 \\ 4 & 2 & 0 \end{bmatrix}$

In Problems 5–10 perform the indicated row operation on the matrix

$$\begin{bmatrix} 3 & 6 & 9 \\ 0 & 1 & 4 \\ 1 & 0 & 2 \end{bmatrix}$$

5. $R_1 = r_3$, $R_3 = r_1$ 6. $R_1 = \frac{1}{3}r_1$
7. $R_1 = (-3)r_3 + r_1$ 8. $R_1 = r_2 + r_1$
9. $R_2 = \frac{1}{3}r_1 + r_2$ 10. $R_3 = -\frac{1}{3}r_1 + r_3$

In Problems 11–38 solve each system of equations using the method of row operations.

11. $x + y = 6$
   $2x - y = 0$

12. $x - y = 2$
   $2x + y = 1$

13. $2x + y = 5$
   $x - y = 1$

14. $3x + 2y = 7$
   $x + y = 3$

15. $2x + 3y = 7$
   $3x - y = 5$

16. $2x - 3y = 5$
   $3x + y = 2$

17. $5x - 7y = 31$
   $3x + 2y = 0$

18. $2x + 8y = 17$
   $3x - y = 1$

19. $2x - 3y = 0$
   $4x + 9y = 5$

20. $3x - 4y = 3$
   $6x + 2y = 1$

21. $4x - 3y = 4$
    $2x + 6y = 7$

22. $3x - 5y = 3$
    $6x + 10y = 10$

23. $\frac{1}{2}x + \frac{1}{3}y = 2$
    $x + y = 5$

24. $x - \frac{1}{4}y = 0$
    $\frac{1}{2}x + \frac{1}{2}y = \frac{5}{2}$

25. $x + y = 1$
    $3x - 2y = \frac{4}{3}$

26. $4x - y = \frac{11}{4}$
    $3x + y = \frac{5}{2}$

27. $2x + y + z = 6$
    $x - y - z = -3$
    $3x + y + 2z = 7$

28. $x + y + z = 5$
    $2x - y + z = 2$
    $x + 2y - z = 3$

29. $x + y - z = -2$
    $3x + y + z = 0$
    $2x - y + 2z = 1$

30. $2x - y - z = -5$
    $x + y + z = 2$
    $x + 2y + 2z = 5$

31. $2x + y - z = 2$
    $x + 3y + 2z = 1$
    $x + y + z = 2$

32. $2x + 2y + z = 6$
    $x - y - z = -2$
    $x - 2y - 2z = -5$

33. $x + y - z = 0$
    $2x + 4y - 4z = -1$
    $2x + y + z = 2$

34. $x + y - z = 0$
    $4x + 2y - 4z = 0$
    $x + 2y + z = 0$

35. $3x + y - z = \frac{2}{3}$
    $2x - y + z = 1$
    $4x + 2y = \frac{8}{3}$

36. $x + y = 1$
    $2x - y + z = 1$
    $x + 2y + z = \frac{8}{3}$

37. $x + y + z + w = 4$
    $2x - y + z = 0$
    $3x + 2y + z - w = 6$
    $x - 2y - 2z + 2w = -1$

38. $x + y + z + w = 4$
    $-x + 2y + z = 0$
    $2x + 3y + z - w = 6$
    $-2x + y - 2z + 2w = -1$

In Problems 39–50 discuss each system of equations. Determine whether the system has a unique solution, no solution, or infinitely many solutions. Use matrix techniques.

39. $x - y = 5$
    $2x - 2y = 6$

40. $4x + y = 5$
    $8x + 2y = 10$

41. $2x - 3y = 6$
    $4x - 6y = 12$

42. $2x - 3y = 6$
    $4x - 6y = 8$

43. $5x - 6y = 1$
    $-10x + 12y = 0$

44. $3x + 4y = 7$
    $x - y = 2$

45. $2x + 3y = 5$
    $4x + 4y = 8$

46. $2x - y = 0$
    $4x - 2y = 0$

47. $2x - y - z = 0$
    $x - y - z = 1$
    $3x - y - z = 2$

48. $x + y + z = 3$
    $2x + y + z = 0$
    $3x + y + z = 1$

49. $2x - y + z = 6$
    $3x - y + z = 6$
    $4x - 2y + 2z = 12$

50. $x - y + z = 2$
    $2x - 3y + z = 0$
    $3x - 3y + 3z = 6$

51. *Investment Problem.* An amount of $5000 is put into three investments at rates of 6%, 7%, and 8% per annum, respectively. The total

annual income is $358. The income from the first two investments is $70 more than the income from the third investment. Find the amount of each investment.

52. *Investment Problem.* An amount of $6500 is placed in three investments at rates of 6%, 8%, and 9% per annum, respectively. The total annual income is $480. If the income from the third investment is $60 more than the income from the second investment, find the amount of each investment.

5. Inverse of a Matrix

In this section we discuss another technique for finding the inverse of a matrix. Recall that if A, B, and I_n are square matrices of dimension $n \times n$, then B is an inverse of A if and only if $AB = I_n$, where I_n is the identity matrix. Now, here is an example to illustrate the new technique.

Suppose we want to find the inverse of the matrix

$$A = \begin{bmatrix} 2 & 1 \\ 0 & 1 \end{bmatrix}$$

Assuming A has an inverse, we will denote it by

$$X = \begin{bmatrix} x_1 & x_2 \\ x_3 & x_4 \end{bmatrix}$$

Then the product of A and X is the identity matrix of dimension 2×2. That is,

$$AX = I_2$$

$$\begin{bmatrix} 2 & 1 \\ 0 & 1 \end{bmatrix}\begin{bmatrix} x_1 & x_2 \\ x_3 & x_4 \end{bmatrix} = \begin{bmatrix} 1 & 0 \\ 0 & 1 \end{bmatrix}$$

Performing the multiplication on the left yields

$$\begin{bmatrix} 2x_1 + x_3 & 2x_2 + x_4 \\ x_3 & x_4 \end{bmatrix} = \begin{bmatrix} 1 & 0 \\ 0 & 1 \end{bmatrix}$$

This matrix equation can be written as the following system of four equations in four unknowns:

$$\begin{aligned} 2x_1 + x_3 &= 1 & 2x_2 + x_4 &= 0 \\ x_3 &= 0 & x_4 &= 1 \end{aligned}$$

By inspection, we find the solution to be

$$x_1 = \tfrac{1}{2} \qquad x_2 = -\tfrac{1}{2} \qquad x_3 = 0 \qquad x_4 = 1$$

Thus, the inverse of A is

$$A^{-1} = \begin{bmatrix} \tfrac{1}{2} & -\tfrac{1}{2} \\ 0 & 1 \end{bmatrix}$$

Let's look at what we did more closely. The system of four equations in four unknowns can be written in two blocks as

$$\begin{aligned} \text{(a)} \quad 2x_1 + x_3 &= 1 & \text{(b)} \quad 2x_2 + x_4 &= 0 \\ x_3 &= 0 & x_4 &= 1 \end{aligned}$$

Their augmented matrices are

$$\text{(a)} \quad \begin{bmatrix} 2 & 1 & | & 1 \\ 0 & 1 & | & 0 \end{bmatrix} \quad \text{and} \quad \text{(b)} \quad \begin{bmatrix} 2 & 1 & | & 0 \\ 0 & 1 & | & 1 \end{bmatrix}$$

Since the matrix A appears in both (a) and (b), any row operation we perform on (a) and (b) can be performed more easily on the single augmented matrix that combines the two right-hand columns. We denote this matrix by $A \,|\, I_2$ and write

$$A \,|\, I_2 = \begin{bmatrix} 2 & 1 & | & 1 & 0 \\ 0 & 1 & | & 0 & 1 \end{bmatrix}$$

If we perform row operations on $A \,|\, I_2$, following the steps given in the previous section, we get

$$\begin{bmatrix} 1 & 0 & | & \frac{1}{2} & -\frac{1}{2} \\ 0 & 1 & | & 0 & 1 \end{bmatrix}$$

The 2×2 matrix on the right-hand side of the vertical bar is A^{-1}.

This example illustrates the general procedure:

To find the inverse of a square matrix A of dimension $n \times n$:

1. **Write the augmented matrix $A \,|\, I_n$.**
2. **Using row operations, transform $A \,|\, I_n$ into a matrix of the form $I_n \,|\, B$. This procedure is identical to the one used in the last section. The matrix B is the inverse of matrix A.**

Example 1   Find the inverse of

$$A = \begin{bmatrix} 1 & 1 & 2 \\ 2 & 1 & 0 \\ 1 & 2 & 2 \end{bmatrix}$$

Solution   Since A is of dimension 3×3, we use the identity matrix I_3. The augmented matrix $A \,|\, I_3$ is

$$\begin{bmatrix} 1 & 1 & 2 & | & 1 & 0 & 0 \\ 2 & 1 & 0 & | & 0 & 1 & 0 \\ 1 & 2 & 2 & | & 0 & 0 & 1 \end{bmatrix}$$

We proceed to transform this matrix, using row operations:

Use $\begin{aligned} R_2 &= -2r_1 + r_2 \\ R_3 &= -r_1 + r_3 \end{aligned}$ to get $\begin{bmatrix} 1 & 1 & 2 & | & 1 & 0 & 0 \\ 0 & -1 & -4 & | & -2 & 1 & 0 \\ 0 & 1 & 0 & | & -1 & 0 & 1 \end{bmatrix}$

Use $R_2 = (-1)r_2$ to get $\begin{bmatrix} 1 & 1 & 2 & | & 1 & 0 & 0 \\ 0 & 1 & 4 & | & 2 & -1 & 0 \\ 0 & 1 & 0 & | & -1 & 0 & 1 \end{bmatrix}$

Use $\begin{aligned} R_1 &= -r_2 + r_1 \\ R_3 &= -r_2 + r_3 \end{aligned}$ to get $\begin{bmatrix} 1 & 0 & -2 & | & -1 & 1 & 0 \\ 0 & 1 & 4 & | & 2 & -1 & 0 \\ 0 & 0 & -4 & | & -3 & 1 & 1 \end{bmatrix}$

Use $R_3 = (-\frac{1}{4})r_3$ to get

$$\begin{bmatrix} 1 & 0 & -2 & | & -1 & 1 & 0 \\ 0 & 1 & 4 & | & 2 & -1 & 0 \\ 0 & 0 & 1 & | & \frac{3}{4} & -\frac{1}{4} & -\frac{1}{4} \end{bmatrix}$$

Use $\begin{aligned} R_1 &= 2r_3 + r_1 \\ R_2 &= -4r_3 + r_2 \end{aligned}$ to get

$$\begin{bmatrix} 1 & 0 & 0 & | & \frac{1}{2} & \frac{1}{2} & -\frac{1}{2} \\ 0 & 1 & 0 & | & -1 & 0 & 1 \\ 0 & 0 & 1 & | & \frac{3}{4} & -\frac{1}{4} & -\frac{1}{4} \end{bmatrix}$$

Since the identity matrix I_3 appears on the left side, the matrix appearing on the right is the inverse. That is,

$$A^{-1} = \begin{bmatrix} \frac{1}{2} & \frac{1}{2} & -\frac{1}{2} \\ -1 & 0 & 1 \\ \frac{3}{4} & -\frac{1}{4} & -\frac{1}{4} \end{bmatrix}$$

(You should verify that in fact, $AA^{-1} = I_3$.)

When a matrix A has no inverse, it is not possible to transform $A | I_n$ into the form $I_n | B$.

Example 2 Show that the matrix given below has no inverse.

$$\begin{bmatrix} 3 & 2 \\ 6 & 4 \end{bmatrix}$$

Solution We set up the augmented matrix

$$\begin{bmatrix} 3 & 2 & | & 1 & 0 \\ 6 & 4 & | & 0 & 1 \end{bmatrix}$$

Use $R_1 = \frac{1}{3}r_1$ to get $\begin{bmatrix} 1 & \frac{2}{3} & | & \frac{1}{3} & 0 \\ 6 & 4 & | & 0 & 1 \end{bmatrix}$

Use $R_2 = -6r_1 + r_2$ to get $\begin{bmatrix} 1 & \frac{2}{3} & | & \frac{1}{3} & 0 \\ 0 & 0 & | & -2 & 1 \end{bmatrix}$

The 0's in row 2 tell us we cannot get the identity matrix. This, in turn, tells us the original matrix has no inverse.

The inverse of a matrix can also be used to solve a system of n equations in n unknowns. Let's look at an example.

Example 3 Solve the system of equations

$$\begin{aligned} x + y + 2z &= 1 \\ 2x + y \quad\;\; &= 2 \\ x + 2y + 2z &= 3 \end{aligned}$$

Solution   If we let

$$A = \begin{bmatrix} 1 & 1 & 2 \\ 2 & 1 & 0 \\ 1 & 2 & 2 \end{bmatrix} \qquad X = \begin{bmatrix} x \\ y \\ z \end{bmatrix} \qquad B = \begin{bmatrix} 1 \\ 2 \\ 3 \end{bmatrix}$$

the above system can be written as

$$AX = B$$

From Example 1, we know A has an inverse, A^{-1}. If we multiply both sides of the equation by A^{-1}, we obtain

$$A^{-1}(AX) = A^{-1}B$$
$$(A^{-1}A)X = A^{-1}B$$
$$I_3X = A^{-1}B$$
$$X = A^{-1}B$$

$$X = \begin{bmatrix} \frac{1}{2} & \frac{1}{2} & -\frac{1}{2} \\ -1 & 0 & 1 \\ \frac{3}{4} & -\frac{1}{4} & -\frac{1}{4} \end{bmatrix} \begin{bmatrix} 1 \\ 2 \\ 3 \end{bmatrix} = \begin{bmatrix} 0 \\ 2 \\ -\frac{1}{2} \end{bmatrix}$$

Thus, the solution is

$$x = 0 \qquad y = 2 \qquad z = -\tfrac{1}{2}$$

∎

This method for solving a system of equations is particularly useful for applications in which the constants appearing to the right of the equal sign change while the coefficients of the unknowns on the left side do not. See Problems 35–38 for an illustration. See also Section 7.1 on Leontief models for an application.

Exercise 5
Solutions to Odd-Numbered Problems begin on page 567.

In Problems 1–14 find the inverse of each matrix using the technique of this section.

1. $\begin{bmatrix} 2 & 5 \\ 1 & 3 \end{bmatrix}$
2. $\begin{bmatrix} 4 & 1 \\ 3 & 1 \end{bmatrix}$
3. $\begin{bmatrix} 1 & -1 \\ 3 & -4 \end{bmatrix}$

4. $\begin{bmatrix} 5 & 3 \\ 3 & 2 \end{bmatrix}$
5. $\begin{bmatrix} 2 & 1 \\ 4 & 3 \end{bmatrix}$
6. $\begin{bmatrix} 2 & 3 \\ 2 & -1 \end{bmatrix}$

7. $\begin{bmatrix} 0 & 0 & 1 \\ 0 & 1 & 0 \\ 1 & 0 & 0 \end{bmatrix}$
8. $\begin{bmatrix} -1 & 1 & 0 \\ 1 & 0 & 2 \\ 3 & 1 & 0 \end{bmatrix}$

9. $\begin{bmatrix} 1 & 1 & -1 \\ 3 & -1 & 0 \\ 2 & -3 & 4 \end{bmatrix}$
10. $\begin{bmatrix} 1 & 1 & 1 \\ 2 & 1 & 1 \\ 1 & 1 & 2 \end{bmatrix}$

11. $\begin{bmatrix} 1 & 1 & -1 \\ 2 & 1 & 1 \\ 1 & 0 & 1 \end{bmatrix}$ 12. $\begin{bmatrix} 2 & 3 & -1 \\ 1 & 1 & 1 \\ 0 & 2 & -1 \end{bmatrix}$

13. $\begin{bmatrix} 1 & 1 & 0 & 0 \\ 0 & 1 & -1 & 1 \\ 1 & -1 & 1 & 1 \\ 0 & 1 & 0 & -1 \end{bmatrix}$ 14. $\begin{bmatrix} 1 & 2 & -3 & -2 \\ 0 & 1 & 4 & -2 \\ 3 & -1 & 4 & 0 \\ 2 & 1 & 0 & 3 \end{bmatrix}$

In Problems 15–20 show that each matrix has no inverse.

15. $\begin{bmatrix} 4 & 6 \\ 2 & 3 \end{bmatrix}$ 16. $\begin{bmatrix} -1 & 2 \\ 3 & -6 \end{bmatrix}$ 17. $\begin{bmatrix} -8 & 4 \\ -4 & 2 \end{bmatrix}$

18. $\begin{bmatrix} 2 & 10 \\ 1 & 5 \end{bmatrix}$ 19. $\begin{bmatrix} 1 & 1 & 1 \\ 3 & -4 & 2 \\ 0 & 0 & 0 \end{bmatrix}$ 20. $\begin{bmatrix} -1 & 2 & 3 \\ 5 & 2 & 0 \\ 2 & -4 & -6 \end{bmatrix}$

In Problems 21–34 solve each system of equations by the method of Example 3.

21. $x + y = 6$
    $2x - y = 0$

22. $x - y = 2$
    $2x + y = 1$

23. $2x + 3y = 7$
    $3x - y = 5$

24. $2x - 3y = 5$
    $3x + y = 2$

25. $2x - 3y = 0$
    $4x + 9y = 5$

26. $3x - 4y = 3$
    $6x + 2y = 1$

27. $\frac{1}{2}x + \frac{1}{3}y = 2$
    $x + y = 5$

28. $x - \frac{1}{4}y = 0$
    $\frac{1}{2}x + \frac{1}{2}y = \frac{5}{2}$

29. $2x + y + z = 6$
    $x - y - z = -3$
    $3x + y + 2z = 7$

30. $x + y + z = 5$
    $2x - y + z = 2$
    $x + 2y - z = 3$

31. $2x + y - z = 2$
    $x + 3y + 2z = 1$
    $x + y + z = 2$

32. $2x + 2y + z = 6$
    $x - y - z = -2$
    $x - 2y - 2z = -5$

33. $3x + y - z = \frac{2}{3}$
    $2x - y + z = 1$
    $4x + 2y = \frac{8}{3}$

34. $x + y = 1$
    $2x - y + z = 1$
    $x + 2y + z = \frac{8}{3}$

In Problems 35–38 solve each system by the method of Example 3, that is, by finding A^{-1}.

35. $3x + 7y = 10$
    $2x + 5y = 7$

36. $3x + 7y = -4$
    $2x + 5y = -3$

37. $3x + 7y = 13$
    $2x + 5y = 9$

38. $3x + 7y = 20$
    $2x + 5y = 14$

*39. Show that the inverse of

$$A = \begin{bmatrix} a & b \\ c & d \end{bmatrix}$$

is given by the formula

$$A^{-1} = \begin{bmatrix} \dfrac{d}{\Delta} & \dfrac{-b}{\Delta} \\ \dfrac{-c}{\Delta} & \dfrac{a}{\Delta} \end{bmatrix}$$

where $\Delta = ad - bc \neq 0$. The number Δ is called the *determinant* of A.

6. Systems of *m* Equations in *n* Unknowns

In Section 4 we discussed a method for solving a system of *n* equations in *n* unknowns, which required performing row operations in order to get a matrix having 1's along the diagonal (if possible) and 0's elsewhere. (Refer to page 85 for the steps involved.) The matrix we finally arrive at through this process is said to be in *row-reduced form*.

The precise definition follows:

Row-Reduced Form of a Matrix **Let A be a given matrix of dimension $n \times m$. The *row-reduced form* of A is a matrix obtained from A by a series of row operations and having the following configuration:**

1. **The first *k* rows contain nonzero entries; entries in the remaining rows are all 0's.**
2. **The first nonzero entry in each nonzero row is 1 and it appears to the right of the first nonzero entry of any row above it.**
3. **The first nonzero entry in a nonzero row has 0's above it and below it in its column.**

For any given matrix there is only one matrix that can satisfy all three of these conditions—that is, the row-reduced form of a matrix is unique.

Example 1 The following matrices are in row-reduced form:

$$\begin{bmatrix} 1 & 0 & 0 & 3 \\ 0 & 1 & 0 & 8 \\ 0 & 0 & 1 & -4 \end{bmatrix} \qquad \begin{bmatrix} 0 & 1 & -2 & 0 & 5 \\ 0 & 0 & 0 & 1 & 2 \\ 0 & 0 & 0 & 0 & 0 \end{bmatrix}$$

$$\begin{bmatrix} 0 & 0 \\ 0 & 0 \end{bmatrix} \qquad \begin{bmatrix} 1 & 0 & 0 & 0 \\ 0 & 1 & 0 & 0 \\ 0 & 0 & 0 & 1 \end{bmatrix}$$

You should verify that each of the above matrices satisfies the three conditions.

Example 2   The following matrices are not in row-reduced form:

$$\begin{bmatrix} 1 & 0 & 0 \\ 0 & 0 & 0 \\ 0 & 1 & 0 \end{bmatrix}$$ The second row contains all 0's and the third does not—this violates rule 1.

$$\begin{bmatrix} 1 & 0 & 2 & 4 \\ 0 & 0 & 2 & 3 \\ 0 & 0 & 0 & 1 \end{bmatrix}$$ The first nonzero entry in row 2 is not a 1—this violates rule 2.

$$\begin{bmatrix} 1 & 0 & 5 \\ 0 & 1 & 1 \\ 0 & 1 & 2 \end{bmatrix}$$ The first nonzero entry in the second row does not have zeros above it and below it in its column—this violates rule 3.

Let's review the procedure for getting the row-reduced form of a matrix.

Example 3   Find the row-reduced form of

$$A = \begin{bmatrix} 1 & -1 & 2 \\ 2 & -3 & 2 \\ 3 & -5 & 2 \end{bmatrix}$$

Solution   With $a_{11} = 1$, we want to obtain a matrix in which all the entries in column 1 except a_{11} are 0. We can obtain such a matrix by performing the row operations

$$R_2 = -2r_1 + r_2$$
$$R_3 = -3r_1 + r_3$$

The new matrix is

$$\begin{bmatrix} 1 & -1 & 2 \\ 0 & -1 & -2 \\ 0 & -2 & -4 \end{bmatrix}$$

We want $a_{22} = 1$. By multiplying row 2 by (-1), we obtain

$$\begin{bmatrix} 1 & -1 & 2 \\ 0 & 1 & 2 \\ 0 & -2 & -4 \end{bmatrix}$$

Now column 2 should have 0's except for $a_{22} = 1$. This can be accomplished by applying the row operations

$$R_1 = r_2 + r_1$$
$$R_3 = 2r_2 + r_3$$

The new matrix is

$$\begin{bmatrix} 1 & 0 & 4 \\ 0 & 1 & 2 \\ 0 & 0 & 0 \end{bmatrix}$$

This is the row-reduced form of A.

Example 4   Find the row-reduced form of

$$A = \begin{bmatrix} 1 & -1 & 2 & 2 \\ 2 & -3 & 2 & 1 \\ 3 & -5 & 2 & -3 \\ -4 & 12 & 8 & 10 \end{bmatrix}$$

Solution   To obtain 0's in column 1 under $a_{11} = 1$, we use the row operations

$$R_2 = -2r_1 + r_2 \qquad R_3 = -3r_1 + r_3 \qquad R_4 = 4r_1 + r_4$$

The new matrix is

$$\begin{bmatrix} 1 & -1 & 2 & 2 \\ 0 & -1 & -2 & -3 \\ 0 & -2 & -4 & -9 \\ 0 & 8 & 16 & 18 \end{bmatrix}$$

To get $a_{22} = 1$, we use $R_2 = -r_2$, obtaining

$$\begin{bmatrix} 1 & -1 & 2 & 2 \\ 0 & 1 & 2 & 3 \\ 0 & -2 & -4 & -9 \\ 0 & 8 & 16 & 18 \end{bmatrix}$$

To obtain 0's in column 2 (except for $a_{22} = 1$), we use

$$R_1 = r_2 + r_1 \qquad R_3 = 2r_2 + r_3 \qquad R_4 = -8r_2 + r_4$$

The new matrix is

$$\begin{bmatrix} 1 & 0 & 4 & 5 \\ 0 & 1 & 2 & 3 \\ 0 & 0 & 0 & -3 \\ 0 & 0 & 0 & -6 \end{bmatrix}$$

Next, we use $R_3 = -\frac{1}{3}r_3$; the result is

$$\begin{bmatrix} 1 & 0 & 4 & 5 \\ 0 & 1 & 2 & 3 \\ 0 & 0 & 0 & 1 \\ 0 & 0 & 0 & -6 \end{bmatrix}$$

To obtain 0's in column 4, we use

$$R_1 = -5r_3 + r_1 \qquad R_2 = -3r_3 + r_2 \qquad R_4 = 6r_3 + r_4$$

The result is the matrix

$$\begin{bmatrix} 1 & 0 & 4 & 0 \\ 0 & 1 & 2 & 0 \\ 0 & 0 & 0 & 1 \\ 0 & 0 & 0 & 0 \end{bmatrix}$$

Associated with every matrix A there is a unique row-reduced matrix H, which contains a certain number of rows with nonzero entries. This number is called the *rank* of the matrix A.

Rank

For example, the matrix given in Example 3 is of rank 2 since its row-reduced form has 2 rows with nonzero entries. The rank of the matrix given in Example 4 is 3.

Now that we have introduced the concepts of row operations and rank of matrices, we can discuss the problem of solving a system of m linear equations in n unknowns.

An example of a system of three equations in four unknowns is

$$x_1 + 3x_2 + 5x_3 + x_4 = 2$$
$$2x_1 + 3x_2 + 4x_3 + 2x_4 = 1$$
$$x_1 + 2x_2 + 3x_3 + x_4 = 1$$

System of m Equations in n Unknowns

In general, a system of m linear equations in the n unknowns $x_1, x_2, \ldots, x_n$ is of the form

$$a_{11}x_1 + a_{12}x_2 + \cdots + a_{1n}x_n = b_1$$
$$a_{21}x_1 + a_{22}x_2 + \cdots + a_{2n}x_n = b_2$$
$$a_{31}x_1 + a_{32}x_2 + \cdots + a_{3n}x_n = b_3$$
$$\vdots \qquad \vdots \qquad \qquad \vdots \qquad \vdots$$
$$a_{i1}x_1 + a_{i2}x_2 + \cdots + a_{in}x_n = b_i$$
$$\vdots \qquad \vdots \qquad \qquad \vdots \qquad \vdots$$
$$a_{m1}x_1 + a_{m2}x_2 + \cdots + a_{mn}x_n = b_m$$

where a_{ij} and b_i are real numbers, $i = 1, 2, \ldots, m$, $j = 1, 2, \ldots, n$.

This is a system of *linear* equations because the unknowns $x_1, x_2, \ldots, x_n$ all appear to the first power and there are no products of unknowns. Keep in mind that the subscript on the x is meant only as a distinguishing symbol—it is *not* an exponent. Finally, if we count the number of equations, we conclude that there are m of them, each containing n unknowns $x_1, x_2, \ldots, x_n$.

Solution   **By a *solution* of a system of m equations in n unknowns** $x_1, x_2, \ldots, x_n$ **is meant any ordered set $(x_1, x_2, \ldots, x_n)$ of real numbers for which** each **of the m equations of the system is satisfied.**

To write a system of m equations in n unknowns in matrix form, we define X and B as the column vectors

$$X = \begin{bmatrix} x_1 \\ \vdots \\ x_n \end{bmatrix} \qquad B = \begin{bmatrix} b_1 \\ \vdots \\ b_m \end{bmatrix}$$

Coefficient Matrix Now, we let A denote the *coefficient matrix* of the system, namely

$$A = \begin{bmatrix} a_{11} & a_{12} & \cdots & a_{1n} \\ a_{21} & a_{22} & \cdots & a_{2n} \\ \vdots & \vdots & & \vdots \\ a_{m1} & a_{m2} & \cdots & a_{mn} \end{bmatrix}$$

and the system can be written in matrix form as

$$AX = B$$

Example 5   Consider the following system of three equations in three unknowns:

$$\begin{aligned}
x_1 + x_2 + x_3 &= 6 \\
3x_1 + 2x_2 - x_3 &= 4 \\
3x_1 + x_2 + 2x_3 &= 11
\end{aligned}$$

The matrix form of this system is

$$\begin{bmatrix} 1 & 1 & 1 \\ 3 & 2 & -1 \\ 3 & 1 & 2 \end{bmatrix} \begin{bmatrix} x_1 \\ x_2 \\ x_3 \end{bmatrix} = \begin{bmatrix} 6 \\ 4 \\ 11 \end{bmatrix}$$

The coefficient matrix A is

$$A = \begin{bmatrix} 1 & 1 & 1 \\ 3 & 2 & -1 \\ 3 & 1 & 2 \end{bmatrix}$$

The augmented matrix $A|B$ is

$$A|B = \begin{bmatrix} 1 & 1 & 1 & | & 6 \\ 3 & 2 & -1 & | & 4 \\ 3 & 1 & 2 & | & 11 \end{bmatrix}$$

The row-reduced form of the augmented matrix $A|B$ of a system of equations gives us all the essential information we need to know about the system—provided we remember which unknown is associated with which *column* and we remember the significance of the last *column*. If we perform *row* operations on $A|B$, we obtain a system of equations having the same solutions as that of the original system—since *row* operations will not affect the significance we have placed on the *columns*.

Consistent System

Some systems of equations will not have solutions. Other systems may have more than one solution. If a system of equations has at least one solution, it is called a *consistent system;* otherwise, it is said to be *inconsistent.*

Inconsistent System

The test for whether a system of linear equations has a solution and the test for uniqueness are given below.

Test for Consistency

A system of equations

$$AX = B$$

has at least one solution if and only if

$$\text{Rank } A = \text{Rank } A|B$$

If Rank $A <$ Rank $A|B$ the system has no solution.

Test for Uniqueness

A system of equations

$$AX = B$$

has exactly one solution if and only if

$$\text{Rank } A = \text{Rank } A|B = \text{Number of unknowns}$$

For the system of equations

$$AX = B$$

suppose

$$\textbf{Rank } A = \textbf{Rank } A|B = k$$

$$\textbf{Number of unknowns} = n$$

If $n = k$, the solution is unique.
If $n > k$, there are infinitely many solutions.

Example 6 Solve the system of equations:

$$\begin{array}{rcrcrcr} x_1 &+& x_2 &+& x_3 &=& 6 \\ 3x_1 &+& 2x_2 &-& x_3 &=& 4 \\ 3x_1 &+& x_2 &+& 2x_3 &=& 11 \end{array}$$

Solution The augmented matrix $A|B$ of this system is

$$A|B = \left[\begin{array}{ccc|c} 1 & 1 & 1 & 6 \\ 3 & 2 & -1 & 4 \\ 3 & 1 & 2 & 11 \end{array}\right]$$

As you should verify, the row-reduced form of $A|B$ is

$$\left[\begin{array}{ccc|c} 1 & 0 & 0 & 1 \\ 0 & 1 & 0 & 2 \\ 0 & 0 & 1 & 3 \end{array}\right]$$

We conclude that

$$\text{Rank } A|B = 3$$

The row-reduced form of $A|B$ also provides information about the rank of A, since the row operations used to get the row-reduced form of $A|B$ also give the row-reduced form of A on the left side of the vertical bar. Hence, we conclude that rank $A = 3$. Since rank $A|B = 3$, rank $A = 3$, and the number of unknowns $= 3$, we conclude that the system has a unique solution. Looking at the row-reduced form of $A|B$, we see that the unique solution is

$$x_1 = 1 \qquad x_2 = 2 \qquad x_3 = 3$$

In summary, to solve a system of m equations in n unknowns, we may use the method outlined in Figure 2.

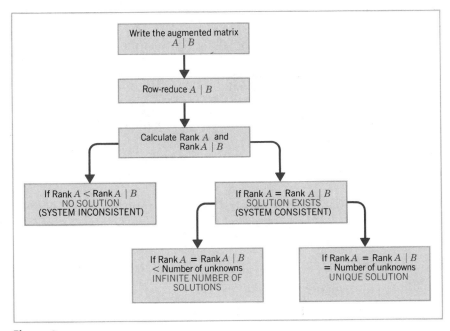

Figure 2

Example 7 Use matrix techniques to find the solution, if it exists, of the system of equations:

$$x_1 + 2x_2 + x_3 = 1$$
$$2x_1 - x_2 + 2x_3 = 2$$
$$3x_1 + x_2 + 3x_3 = 4$$

Solution The augmented matrix $A|B$ is

$$A|B = \begin{bmatrix} 1 & 2 & 1 & | & 1 \\ 2 & -1 & 2 & | & 2 \\ 3 & 1 & 3 & | & 4 \end{bmatrix}$$

The row-reduced form of $A|B$ (as you should verify) is

$$\begin{bmatrix} 1 & 0 & 1 & | & 0 \\ 0 & 1 & 0 & | & 0 \\ 0 & 0 & 0 & | & 1 \end{bmatrix}$$

We conclude that

$$\text{Rank } A = 2 \qquad \text{Rank } A|B = 3$$

By the test for consistency, the system has no solution.

If we write the equations that correspond to the row-reduced matrix of $A \mid B$ in Example 7, we obtain

$$x_1 + x_3 = 0$$
$$x_2 = 0$$
$$0 \cdot x_1 + 0 \cdot x_2 + 0 \cdot x_3 = 1$$

It is clear from the impossibility of the third equation ($0 = 1$), that the system has no solution.

For a system of equations $AX = B$ for which

$$\text{Rank } A = \text{Rank } A \mid B = k < n = \text{Number of unknowns}$$

Parameter
we can solve for some collection of k unknowns in terms of the remaining $n - k$ unknowns. These $n - k$ unknowns are usually referred to as *parameters*. The next example illustrates this situation.

Example 8 Use matrix techniques to find the solution, if it exists, of the system of equations:

$$x_1 + 2x_2 + x_3 = 1$$
$$2x_1 - x_2 + 2x_3 = 2$$
$$3x_1 + x_2 + 3x_3 = 3$$

Solution The augmented matrix is

$$A \mid B = \begin{bmatrix} 1 & 2 & 1 & | & 1 \\ 2 & -1 & 2 & | & 2 \\ 3 & 1 & 3 & | & 3 \end{bmatrix}$$

The row-reduced form of $A \mid B$ (as you should verify) is

$$\begin{bmatrix} 1 & 0 & 1 & | & 1 \\ 0 & 1 & 0 & | & 0 \\ 0 & 0 & 0 & | & 0 \end{bmatrix}$$

We conclude that

$$\text{Rank } A = 2 \qquad \text{Rank } A \mid B = 2$$

The system is consistent. Since the number of unknowns is three, the system has an infinite number of solutions. We proceed to write the equations represented by the row-reduced form of $A \mid B$:

$$x_1 + x_3 = 1$$
$$x_2 = 0$$

Since

$$(\text{Number of unknowns}) - (\text{Rank } A \mid B) = 3 - 2 = 1$$

there is one parameter. If we rewrite the equations as

$$x_1 = 1 - x_3$$
$$x_2 = 0$$

the variable x_3 becomes the parameter.

By assigning arbitrary values to the parameter x_3, we can write down *some* of the infinite number of solutions, as shown in the table below:

Value of x_3 (Arbitrary)	x_1	x_2	Solution (x_1, x_2, x_3)
0	1	0	(1, 0, 0)
−1	2	0	(2, 0, −1)
1	0	0	(0, 0, 1)
5	−4	0	(−4, 0, 5)

Notice that we could just as well have chosen x_1 as the parameter by rewriting the equations as

$$x_3 = 1 - x_1$$
$$x_2 = 0$$

Then, by assigning values of x_1, we would obtain values for x_3.   ∎

Example 9   Use matrix techniques to find the solution, if it exists, of the system of equations:

$$x_1 + 3x_2 + 5x_3 + x_4 = 2$$
$$2x_1 + 3x_2 + 4x_3 + 2x_4 = 1$$
$$x_1 + 2x_2 + 3x_3 + x_4 = 1$$

Solution   The augmented matrix $A|B$ is

$$A|B = \begin{bmatrix} 1 & 3 & 5 & 1 & | & 2 \\ 2 & 3 & 4 & 2 & | & 1 \\ 1 & 2 & 3 & 1 & | & 1 \end{bmatrix}$$

The row-reduced form of $A|B$ (as you should verify) is

$$\begin{bmatrix} 1 & 0 & -1 & 1 & | & -1 \\ 0 & 1 & 2 & 0 & | & 1 \\ 0 & 0 & 0 & 0 & | & 0 \end{bmatrix}$$

We conclude that

$$\text{Rank } A = 2 \qquad \text{Rank } A|B = 2$$

Thus, the system is consistent. Since the system has four unknowns, there are an infinite number of solutions. We proceed to write the equations represented by the row-reduced form of $A|B$:

$$x_1 - x_3 + x_4 = -1$$
$$x_2 + 2x_3 = 1$$

Since

$$(\text{Number of unknowns}) - (\text{Rank } A|B) = 4 - 2 = 2$$

this system has two parameters. If we write this system as

$$x_1 = -1 + x_3 - x_4$$
$$x_2 = 1 - 2x_3$$

then x_3 and x_4 are the parameters. By assigning arbitrary values to x_3 and x_4, we can obtain some of the infinite number of solutions to the system, as shown in the table:

x_3	x_4	x_1	x_2	Solution (x_1, x_2, x_3, x_4)
0	0	−1	1	$(-1, 1, 0, 0)$
1	0	0	−1	$(0, -1, 1, 0)$
0	2	−3	1	$(-3, 1, 0, 2)$

Example 10
Mixing Acids

In a chemistry laboratory one solution is 10% hydrochloric acid (HCl), a second solution contains 20% HCl, and a third contains 40% HCl. How many liters of each should be mixed to obtain 100 liters of 25% HCl?

Solution

Let x_1, x_2, and x_3 represent the number of liters of 10%, 20%, and 40% solutions of HCl, respectively. Since we want 100 liters in all and the amount of HCl obtained from each solution must sum to 25% of 100, or 25 liters, we must have

$$x_1 + x_2 + x_3 = 100$$
$$0.1x_1 + 0.2x_2 + 0.4x_3 = 25$$

Thus, our problem is to solve a system of two equations in three unknowns. By matrix techniques, we obtain the solution

$$x_1 = 2x_3 - 50$$
$$x_2 = -3x_3 + 150$$

where x_3 can represent any real number. Now the practical considerations of this problem lead us to the conditions that $x_1 \geq 0$, $x_2 \geq 0$, $x_3 \geq 0$. In addition, we must have $x_3 \geq 25$ and $x_3 \leq 50$, since otherwise $x_1 < 0$ or $x_2 < 0$. Some possible solutions are listed in the table. The final determination by the chemistry labora-

No. of Liters 10% Solution	No. of Liters 20% Solution	No. of Liters 40% Solution
0	75	25
10	60	30
12	57	31
16	51	33
20	45	35
25	37.5	37.5
26	36	38
30	30	40
36	21	43
38	18	44
46	6	48
50	0	50

tory will more than likely be based on the amount and availability of one acid solution versus others.   ◼

Exercise 6
Solutions to Odd-Numbered Problems begin on page 568.

In Problems 1–6 the rank of the coefficient matrix A, the rank of the augmented matrix $A|B$, and the number of unknowns of a system of equations are given. Tell whether the system is consistent or inconsistent. If it is consistent, tell whether the solution is unique.

1. Rank $A = 2$
    Rank $A|B = 2$
    Number of unknowns = 2

2. Rank $A = 3$
    Rank $A|B = 4$
    Number of unknowns = 4

3. Rank $A = 2$
    Rank $A|B = 3$
    Number of unknowns = 3

4. Rank $A = 3$
    Rank $A|B = 3$
    Number of unknowns = 4

5. Rank $A = 3$
    Rank $A|B = 3$
    Number of unknowns = 5

6. Rank $A = 3$
    Rank $A|B = 3$
    Number of unknowns = 3

In Problems 7–24 use matrix techniques to find the solution, if it exists, of each system of equations.

7. $x + y = 3$
    $2x - y = 3$

8. $x - y = 5$
    $2x + 3y = 15$

9. $3x - 3y = 12$
    $3x + 2y = -3$

10. $6x + y = 8$
    $x - 3y = -5$

11. $3x_1 - 4x_2 = 1$
    $5x_1 + 2x_2 = 19$

12. $2x_1 + 3x_2 = 8$
    $2x_1 - x_2 = 12$

13. $2x_1 + 3x_2 = 5$
    $2x_1 - x_2 = 7$

14. $3x_1 - 4x_2 = 7$
    $5x_1 + 2x_2 = 3$

15. $x_1 - x_2 = 1$
    $x_2 - x_3 = 6$
    $x_1 + x_3 = -1$

16. $2x_1 - x_2 + 3x_3 = 0$
    $x_1 + 2x_2 - x_3 = 5$
    $2x_2 + x_3 = 1$

17. $x_1 + x_2 = 7$
    $x_2 - x_3 + x_4 = 5$
    $x_1 - x_2 + x_3 + x_4 = 6$
    $x_2 - x_4 = 10$

18. $x_1 + x_2 + x_3 + x_4 = 0$
    $2x_1 - x_2 - x_3 + x_4 = 0$
    $x_1 - x_2 - x_3 + x_4 = 0$
    $x_1 + x_2 - x_3 - x_4 = 0$

19. $x_1 + 2x_2 + 3x_3 - x_4 = 0$
    $3x_1 - x_4 = 4$
    $x_2 - x_3 - x_4 = 2$

20. $2x_1 - 3x_2 + 4x_3 = 7$
    $x_1 - 2x_2 + 3x_3 = 2$

21. $x_1 - x_2 + x_3 = 5$
    $2x_1 - 2x_2 + 2x_3 = 8$

22. $x_1 + x_2 + x_3 = 3$
    $x_1 - x_2 + x_3 = 7$
    $x_1 - x_2 - x_3 = 1$

23. $3x_1 - x_2 + 2x_3 = 3$
    $3x_1 + 3x_2 + x_3 = 3$
    $3x_1 - 5x_2 + 3x_3 = 12$

24. $x_1 + x_2 - x_3 = 12$
    $3x_1 - x_2 = 1$
    $2x_1 - 3x_2 + 4x_3 = 3$

*7. Applications

7.1 Leontief Models

The Leontief models in economics are named after Wassily Leontief, who received the Nobel prize in economics in 1973. (See the October 29, 1973 issue of *Newsweek*, p. 94.) These models can be characterized as a description of an economy in which input equals output or, in other words, consumption equals production. That is, the models assume that whatever is produced is always consumed.

Leontief models are of two types: closed, in which the entire production is consumed by those participating in the production; and open, in which some of the production is consumed by those who produce it and the rest of the production is consumed by external bodies.

In the *closed model* we seek the relative income of each participant in the system. In the *open model* we seek the amount of production needed to achieve a forecast demand, when the amount of production needed to achieve current demand is known.

The Closed Model
We begin with an example to illustrate the idea.

Example 1 Three homeowners, Mike, Dan, and Bob, each with certain skills, agreed to pool their talents to make repairs on their houses. As it turned out, Mike spent 20% of his time on his own house, 40% of his time on Dan's house, and 40% on Bob's house. Dan spent 10% of his time on Mike's house, 50% of his time on his own house, and 40% on Bob's house. Of Bob's time, 60% was spent on Mike's house, 10% on Dan's, and 30% on his own. Now that the projects are finished, they need to figure out how much money each should get for his work, including the work performed on his own house, so that each person comes out even. They agreed in advance that the payment to each one should be approximately $300.00.

Solution We place the information given in the problem in a 3×3 matrix, as follows:

	Work done by		
	Mike	Dan	Bob
Proportion of work done on Mike's house	0.2	0.1	0.6
Proportion of work done on Dan's house	0.4	0.5	0.1
Proportion of work done on Bob's house	0.4	0.4	0.3

Next, we define the unknowns:

$$x_1 = \text{Mike's wages}$$
$$x_2 = \text{Dan's wages}$$
$$x_3 = \text{Bob's wages}$$

WASSILY LEONTIEF published his first description of the production interdependence of goods and services for an entire economy in 1936.

*This section may be omitted without loss of continuity.

For each to come out even will require that the total amount paid out by each one equals the total amount received by each one. Let's analyze this requirement, by looking just at the work done on Mike's house. Mike's wages are x_1. Mike's expenditures for work done on his house are $0.2x_1 + 0.1x_2 + 0.6x_3$. These are required to be equal, so

$$x_1 = 0.2x_1 + 0.1x_2 + 0.6x_3$$

Similarly,

$$x_2 = 0.4x_1 + 0.5x_2 + 0.1x_3$$
$$x_3 = 0.4x_1 + 0.4x_2 + 0.3x_3$$

These three equations can be written compactly as

$$\begin{bmatrix} x_1 \\ x_2 \\ x_3 \end{bmatrix} = \begin{bmatrix} 0.2 & 0.1 & 0.6 \\ 0.4 & 0.5 & 0.1 \\ 0.4 & 0.4 & 0.3 \end{bmatrix} \begin{bmatrix} x_1 \\ x_2 \\ x_3 \end{bmatrix}$$

A simple manipulation reduces the system to

$$0.8x_1 - 0.1x_2 - 0.6x_3 = 0$$
$$-0.4x_1 + 0.5x_2 - 0.1x_3 = 0$$
$$-0.4x_1 - 0.4x_2 + 0.7x_3 = 0$$

Solving for x_1, x_2, x_3, we find that

$$x_1 = \tfrac{31}{36}x_3 \qquad x_2 = \tfrac{32}{36}x_3$$

where x_3 is the parameter. To get solutions that fall close to \$300, we set $x_3 = 360$.* The wages to be paid out are therefore

$$x_1 = \$310 \qquad x_2 = \$320 \qquad x_3 = \$360$$

■

The matrix in Example 1, namely,

$$\begin{bmatrix} 0.2 & 0.1 & 0.6 \\ 0.4 & 0.5 & 0.1 \\ 0.4 & 0.4 & 0.3 \end{bmatrix}$$

Input–Output Matrix

is called an *input–output matrix*.

In the general closed model, we have an economy consisting of n components. Each component produces an *output* of some goods or services, which, in turn, is completely used up by the n components. The proportionate use of each component's output by the economy makes up the input–output matrix of the economy. The problem is to find suitable pricing levels for each component so that total income equals total expenditure.

In general, an input–output matrix for a closed Leontief model is of the form

$$A = [a_{ij}] \qquad i, j = 1, 2, \ldots, n$$

*Other choices for x_3 are, of course, possible. The choice of which value to use is up to the homeowners. No matter what choice is made, each homeowner comes out even.

where the a_{ij} represent the fractional amount of goods or services used by i and produced by j. For a closed model, the sum of each column equals 1 (this is the condition that all production is consumed internally) and $0 \leq a_{ij} \leq 1$ for all entries (this is the restriction that each entry is a fraction).

If A is the input–output matrix of a closed system with n components and X is a column vector representing the price of each output of the system, then

$$X = AX$$

We can rewrite the equation above as

$$X - AX = \mathbf{0}$$
$$I_n X - AX = \mathbf{0}$$
$$(I_n - A)X = \mathbf{0}$$

This matrix equation, which represents a system of equations in which the right-hand side is always $\mathbf{0}$, is called a *homogeneous system of equations*. It can be shown that if the entries in the input–output matrix A are positive and if the sum of each column of A equals 1, then this system has a one-parameter solution; that is, we can solve for $n - 1$ of the unknowns in terms of the remaining one, which serves as the parameter. This parameter serves as a "scale factor."

The Open Model

For the open model, in addition to internal consumption of goods produced, there is an outside demand for the goods produced. This outside demand may take the form of exportation of goods or may be the goods needed to support consumer demand. Again, however, we make the assumption that whatever is produced is also consumed.

For example, suppose an economy consists of three industries R, S, and T, and suppose each one produces a single product. We assume that a portion of R's production is used by each of the three industries, while the remainder is used up by consumers. The same is true of the production of S and T. To organize our thoughts, we construct a table that describes the interaction of the use of R, S, and T's production over some fixed period of time. See Table 1.

Table 1

	R	S	T	Consumer	Total
R	50	20	40	70	180
S	20	30	20	90	160
T	30	20	20	50	120

All entries in the table are in appropriate units, say, in dollars. The first row (row R) represents the production in dollars of industry R (input). Out of the total of \$180 worth of goods produced, R, S, and T use \$50, \$20, and \$40, respectively, for the production of their goods, while consumers purchase the remaining \$70 for their consumption (output). Observe that input equals output since everything produced by R is used up by R, S, T, and consumers.

The second and third rows are interpreted in the same way.

An important observation is that the goal of R's production is to produce $70 worth of goods, since this is the demand of consumers. In order to meet this demand, R must produce a total of $180, since the difference $110 is required internally by R, S, and T.

Suppose, however, that consumer demand is expected to change. To effect this change, how much should each industry now produce? For example, in Table 1, current demand for R, S, and T can be represented by a *demand vector:*

Demand Vector

$$D_0 = \begin{bmatrix} 70 \\ 90 \\ 50 \end{bmatrix}$$

But suppose marketing forecasts predict that in 3 years the demand vector will be

$$D_3 = \begin{bmatrix} 60 \\ 110 \\ 60 \end{bmatrix}$$

Here the demand for item R has decreased; the demand for item S has significantly increased, and the demand for item T is higher. Given the current total output of R, S, and T at $180, $160, and $120, respectively, what must it be in 3 years to meet this projected demand?

In using input–output analysis to obtain a solution to such a forecasting problem, we take into account the fact that the output of any one of these industries is affected by changes in the other two, since the total demand for say, R, in 3 years depends not only on consumer demand for R, but also on consumer demand for S and T. That is, the industries are interrelated.

The solution of this type of forecasting problem is derived from the *open Leontief model* in input–output analysis.

To obtain the solution, we need to determine how much of each of the three products R, S, and T is required to produce 1 unit of R. For example, to obtain 180 units of R requires the use of 50 units of R, 20 units of S, and 30 units of T (the entries in column 1). Forming the ratios, we find that to produce 1 unit of R requires $\frac{50}{180} = 0.278$ of R, $\frac{20}{180} = 0.111$ of S, and $\frac{30}{180} = 0.167$ of T. If we want, say, x_1 units of R, we will require $0.278x_1$ units of R, $0.111x_1$ units of S, and $0.167x_1$ units of T.

Continuing in this way, we can construct the matrix

$$A = \begin{matrix} & R & S & T \\ R & \begin{bmatrix} 0.278 & 0.125 & 0.333 \\ S & 0.111 & 0.188 & 0.167 \\ T & 0.167 & 0.125 & 0.167 \end{bmatrix} \end{matrix}$$

Observe that column 1 represents the amounts of R, S, T required for 1 unit of R; column 2 represents the amounts of R, S, and T required for 1 unit of S; and column 3 represents the amounts of R, S, and T required for 1 unit of T. For example, the entry in row 3, column 2 (0.125), represents the amount of T needed to produce 1 unit of S.

As a result of placing the entries this way, if

$$X = \begin{bmatrix} x_1 \\ x_2 \\ x_3 \end{bmatrix}$$

represents the total output required to obtain a given demand, the product AX represents the amounts of R, S, and T required for internal consumption. The condition that production = consumption requires that

Internal consumption + Consumer demand = Total output

In terms of the matrix A, the total output X, and the demand vector D, this requirement is equivalent to the equation

$$AX + D = X$$

In this equation, we seek to find X for a prescribed demand D. The matrix A is calculated as above for some initial production process.*

Example 2 For the data given in Table 1, find the total output X required to achieve a future demand of

$$D_3 = \begin{bmatrix} 60 \\ 110 \\ 60 \end{bmatrix}$$

Solution We need to solve for X in

$$AX + D_3 = X$$

Simplifying, we have

$$[I - A]X = D_3$$

Solving for X, we have

$$X = [I - A]^{-1} \cdot D_3$$

$$= \begin{bmatrix} 0.722 & -0.125 & -0.333 \\ -0.111 & 0.812 & -0.167 \\ -0.167 & -0.125 & 0.833 \end{bmatrix}^{-1} \begin{bmatrix} 60 \\ 110 \\ 60 \end{bmatrix}$$

$$= \begin{bmatrix} 1.6048 & 0.3568 & 0.7131 \\ 0.2946 & 1.3363 & 0.3857 \\ 0.3660 & 0.2721 & 1.4013 \end{bmatrix} \begin{bmatrix} 60 \\ 110 \\ 60 \end{bmatrix}$$

$$= \begin{bmatrix} 178.322 \\ 187.811 \\ 135.969 \end{bmatrix}$$

*The entries in A can be checked by using the requirement that $AX + D = X$, for D = initial demand and X = total output. For our example, it must happen that

Internal consumption + Consumer demand = Total output

$$\begin{matrix} AX & & + & D & = & X \end{matrix}$$

$$\begin{bmatrix} 0.278 & 0.125 & 0.333 \\ 0.111 & 0.188 & 0.167 \\ 0.167 & 0.125 & 0.167 \end{bmatrix} \begin{bmatrix} 180 \\ 160 \\ 120 \end{bmatrix} + \begin{bmatrix} 70 \\ 90 \\ 50 \end{bmatrix} = \begin{bmatrix} 180 \\ 160 \\ 120 \end{bmatrix}$$

Thus, the total output of R, S, and T required for the forecast demand D_3 is

$$x_1 = 178.322 \qquad x_2 = 187.811 \qquad x_3 = 135.969$$

■

The general open model can be described as follows: Suppose there are n industries in the economy. Each industry produces some goods or services, which are partially consumed by the n industries, while the rest are used to meet a prescribed current demand. Given the output required of each industry to meet current demand, what should the output of each industry be to meet some different future demand?

The matrix $A = [a_{ij}]$, $i, j = 1, \ldots, n$, of the open model is defined to consist of entries a_{ij}, where a_{ij} is the amount of output of industry j required for one unit of output of industry i. If X is a column vector representing the production of each industry in the system and D is a column vector representing future demand for goods produced in the system, then

$$X = AX + D$$

From the equation above, we find

$$[I_n - A]X = D$$

It can be shown that the matrix $I_n - A$ has an inverse, provided each entry in A is positive and the sum of each column in A is less than 1. Under these conditions, we may solve for X to get

$$X = [I_n - A]^{-1} \cdot D$$

This form of the solution is particularly useful since it allows us to find X for a variety of demands D by doing one calculation: $[I_n - A]^{-1}$.

We conclude by noting that the use of an input–output matrix to solve forecasting problems assumes that each industry produces a single commodity and that no technological advances take place in the period of time under investigation (in other words, the proportions found in the matrix A are fixed).

Exercise 7.1
Solutions to Odd-Numbered Problems begin on page 570.

In Problems 1–4 find the relative wages of each person for the given closed input–output matrix. In each case, take the wages of C to be the parameter and use $x_3 = C$'s wages $= \$10,000$.

1.
$$
\begin{array}{c c c c}
 & A & B & C \\
A & \frac{1}{2} & \frac{1}{3} & \frac{1}{4} \\
B & \frac{1}{4} & \frac{1}{3} & \frac{1}{4} \\
C & \frac{1}{4} & \frac{1}{3} & \frac{1}{2}
\end{array}
$$

2.
$$
\begin{array}{c c c c}
 & A & B & C \\
A & \frac{1}{4} & \frac{2}{3} & \frac{1}{2} \\
B & \frac{1}{2} & \frac{1}{6} & \frac{1}{4} \\
C & \frac{1}{4} & \frac{1}{6} & \frac{1}{4}
\end{array}
$$

$$
\begin{array}{c}
\begin{array}{ccc} A & B & C \end{array} \\
3. \quad \begin{array}{c} A \\ B \\ C \end{array}
\begin{bmatrix} 0.2 & 0.3 & 0.1 \\ 0.6 & 0.4 & 0.2 \\ 0.2 & 0.3 & 0.7 \end{bmatrix}
\end{array}
\qquad
\begin{array}{c}
\begin{array}{ccc} A & B & C \end{array} \\
4. \quad \begin{array}{c} A \\ B \\ C \end{array}
\begin{bmatrix} 0.4 & 0.3 & 0.2 \\ 0.2 & 0.3 & 0.3 \\ 0.4 & 0.4 & 0.5 \end{bmatrix}
\end{array}
$$

5. For the three industries R, S, and T in the open Leontief model of Example 2 on page 110, compute the total output vector X if the forecast demand vector is

$$
D_2 = \begin{bmatrix} 80 \\ 90 \\ 60 \end{bmatrix}
$$

6. Rework Problem 5 if the forecast demand vector is

$$
D_4 = \begin{bmatrix} 100 \\ 80 \\ 60 \end{bmatrix}
$$

7. A society consists of four individuals: a farmer, a builder, a tailor, and a rancher (who produces meat products). Of the food produced by the farmer, $\frac{3}{10}$ is used by the farmer, $\frac{2}{10}$ by the builder, $\frac{2}{10}$ by the tailor, and $\frac{3}{10}$ by the rancher. The builder's production is utilized 30% by the farmer, 30% by the builder, 10% by the tailor, and 30% by the rancher. The tailor's production is used in the ratios $\frac{3}{10}$, $\frac{3}{10}$, $\frac{1}{10}$, and $\frac{3}{10}$ by the farmer, builder, tailor, and rancher. Finally, meat products are used 20% by each of the farmer, builder, and tailor, and 40% by the rancher. What are the relative wages of each if the rancher's wages are scaled at $10,000?

8. If in Problem 7 the meat production utilization changes so that it is used equally by all four individuals, while everyone else's production utilization remains the same, what are the relative wages?

9. Suppose the interrelationships between the production of two industries R and S in a given year are given in the table:

	R	S	Current Consumer Demand	Total Output
R	30	40	60	130
S	20	10	40	70

If the forecast demand in 2 years is

$$
D_2 = \begin{bmatrix} 80 \\ 40 \end{bmatrix}
$$

what should the total output X be?

7.2 Cryptography

Our second application is to *cryptography*, the art of writing or deciphering secret codes. We begin by giving examples of elementary codes.

Example 1 A message can be encoded by associating each letter of the alphabet with some other letter of the alphabet according to a prescribed pattern. For example, we might have

```
A B C D E F G H I J K L M N O P Q R S T U V W X Y Z
↓ ↓ ↓ ↓ ↓ ↓ ↓ ↓ ↓ ↓ ↓ ↓ ↓ ↓ ↓ ↓ ↓ ↓ ↓ ↓ ↓ ↓ ↓ ↓ ↓ ↓
C D E F G H I J K L M N O P Q R S T U V W X Y Z A B
```

With the above code, the word *BOMB* would become DQOD. ∎

Example 2 Another code may associate numbers with the letters of the alphabet. For example, we might have

```
A  B  C  D  E  F  G  H  I  J  K  L  M  N  O  P  Q  R  S  T  U  V  W  X  Y  Z
↓  ↓  ↓  ↓  ↓  ↓  ↓  ↓  ↓  ↓  ↓  ↓  ↓  ↓  ↓  ↓  ↓  ↓  ↓  ↓  ↓  ↓  ↓  ↓  ↓  ↓
26 25 24 23 22 21 20 19 18 17 16 15 14 13 12 11 10 9  8  7  6  5  4  3  2  1
```

In this code, the word *PEACE* looks like 11 22 26 24 22. ∎

Both the above codes have one important feature in common. The association of letters with the coding symbols is made using a one-to-one correspondence so that no possible ambiguities can arise.

Suppose we want to encode the following message:

BEWARE   THE   IDES   OF   MARCH

If we decide to divide the message into pairs of letters, the message becomes:

BE   WA   RE   TH   EI   DE   SO   FM   AR   CH

(If there is a letter left over, we arbitrarily assign Z to the last position.) Using the correspondence of letters to numbers given in Example 2, and writing each pair of letters as a column vector, we obtain

$$\begin{bmatrix} B \\ E \end{bmatrix} = \begin{bmatrix} 25 \\ 22 \end{bmatrix} \quad \begin{bmatrix} W \\ A \end{bmatrix} = \begin{bmatrix} 4 \\ 26 \end{bmatrix} \quad \begin{bmatrix} R \\ E \end{bmatrix} = \begin{bmatrix} 9 \\ 22 \end{bmatrix} \quad \begin{bmatrix} T \\ H \end{bmatrix} = \begin{bmatrix} 7 \\ 19 \end{bmatrix} \quad \text{etc.}$$

Next, we arbitrarily choose a 2 × 2 matrix A, which we know has an inverse A^{-1} (the reason for this is seen later). Suppose we choose

$$A = \begin{bmatrix} 2 & 3 \\ 1 & 2 \end{bmatrix}$$

Its inverse is

$$A^{-1} = \begin{bmatrix} 2 & -3 \\ -1 & 2 \end{bmatrix}$$

Now, we transform the column vectors representing the message by multiplying each of them on the left by the matrix A:

$$(1) \quad A\begin{bmatrix} B \\ E \end{bmatrix} = A\begin{bmatrix} 25 \\ 22 \end{bmatrix} = \begin{bmatrix} 116 \\ 69 \end{bmatrix}$$

$$(2) \quad A\begin{bmatrix} W \\ A \end{bmatrix} = A\begin{bmatrix} 4 \\ 26 \end{bmatrix} = \begin{bmatrix} 86 \\ 56 \end{bmatrix}$$

$$(3) \quad A\begin{bmatrix} R \\ E \end{bmatrix} = A\begin{bmatrix} 9 \\ 22 \end{bmatrix} = \begin{bmatrix} 84 \\ 53 \end{bmatrix} \quad \text{etc.}$$

The coded message is

$$116 \quad 69 \quad 86 \quad 56 \quad 84 \quad 53 \quad \text{etc.}$$

To decode or unscramble the above message, pair the numbers in 2×1 column vectors. Multiply each of these column vectors by A^{-1} on the left:

$$(1) \quad A^{-1}\begin{bmatrix} 116 \\ 69 \end{bmatrix} = \begin{bmatrix} 25 \\ 22 \end{bmatrix}$$

$$(2) \quad A^{-1}\begin{bmatrix} 86 \\ 56 \end{bmatrix} = \begin{bmatrix} 4 \\ 26 \end{bmatrix}$$

By reassigning letters to these numbers, we obtain the original message.

Example 3 The message to be encoded is

THE   END   IS   NEAR

We agree to associate numbers to letters as follows:

A B C D E F G H I J K L M N O P Q R S T U V W X Y Z
↓ ↓
1 2 3 4 5 6 7 8 9 10 11 12 13 14 15 16 17 18 19 20 21 22 23 24 25 26

The encoded message is to be formed of triplets of numbers.

Solution This time we must divide the message into triplets of letters, obtaining

THE   END   ISN   EAR

in order for the encoded message to have triplets of numbers. (If the message required additional letters to complete the triplet, we would have used Z or YZ.)

Now we choose a 3×3 matrix such as

$$A = \begin{bmatrix} 1 & 0 & 0 \\ 3 & 1 & 5 \\ -2 & 0 & 1 \end{bmatrix}$$

Its inverse is

$$A^{-1} = \begin{bmatrix} 1 & 0 & 0 \\ -13 & 1 & -5 \\ 2 & 0 & 1 \end{bmatrix}$$

The encoded message is obtained by multiplying the matrix A times each column vector of the original message:

$$A\begin{bmatrix} T \\ H \\ E \end{bmatrix} = \begin{bmatrix} 1 & 0 & 0 \\ 3 & 1 & 5 \\ -2 & 0 & 1 \end{bmatrix}\begin{bmatrix} 20 \\ 8 \\ 5 \end{bmatrix} = \begin{bmatrix} 20 \\ 93 \\ -35 \end{bmatrix}$$

$$A\begin{bmatrix} E \\ N \\ D \end{bmatrix} = \begin{bmatrix} 1 & 0 & 0 \\ 3 & 1 & 5 \\ -2 & 0 & 1 \end{bmatrix}\begin{bmatrix} 5 \\ 14 \\ 4 \end{bmatrix} = \begin{bmatrix} 5 \\ 49 \\ -6 \end{bmatrix}$$

$$A\begin{bmatrix} I \\ S \\ N \end{bmatrix} = \begin{bmatrix} 1 & 0 & 0 \\ 3 & 1 & 5 \\ -2 & 0 & 1 \end{bmatrix}\begin{bmatrix} 9 \\ 19 \\ 14 \end{bmatrix} = \begin{bmatrix} 9 \\ 116 \\ -4 \end{bmatrix}$$

$$A\begin{bmatrix} E \\ A \\ R \end{bmatrix} = \begin{bmatrix} 1 & 0 & 0 \\ 3 & 1 & 5 \\ -2 & 0 & 1 \end{bmatrix}\begin{bmatrix} 5 \\ 1 \\ 18 \end{bmatrix} = \begin{bmatrix} 5 \\ 106 \\ 8 \end{bmatrix}$$

The coded message is

$$20 \quad 93 \quad -35 \quad 5 \quad 49 \quad -6 \quad 9 \quad 116 \quad -4 \quad 5 \quad 106 \quad 8 \qquad ■$$

To decode the message in Example 3, form 3×1 column vectors of the numbers in the coded message and multiply on the left by A^{-1}.

Exercise 7.2
Solutions to Odd-Numbered Problems begin on page 570.

1. Using the correspondence

A B C D E F G H I J K L M N O P Q R S T U V W X Y Z
↓ ↓
1 2 3 4 5 6 7 8 9 10 11 12 13 14 15 16 17 18 19 20 21 22 23 24 25 26

and the matrices

$$\text{(I)} \quad A = \begin{bmatrix} 2 & 3 \\ 1 & 2 \end{bmatrix} \qquad \text{(II)} \quad A = \begin{bmatrix} 1 & 0 & 0 \\ 3 & 1 & 5 \\ -2 & 0 & 1 \end{bmatrix}$$

Encode the following messages:

(a) MEET ME AT THE CASBAH
(b) TOMORROW NEVER COMES
(c) THE MISSION IS IMPOSSIBLE

2. Using the correspondence given in Problem 1 and the matrix

$$A = \begin{bmatrix} 2 & 3 \\ 1 & 2 \end{bmatrix}$$

decode the following messages:
(a) 51 30 27 16 75 47 19 10 48 26
(b) 70 45 103 62 58 38 102 61 88 57

3. Using the correspondence given in Problem 1 and the matrix

$$A = \begin{bmatrix} 1 & 0 & 0 \\ 3 & 1 & 5 \\ -2 & 0 & 1 \end{bmatrix}$$

decode the message

$$25 \quad 195 \quad -29 \quad 6 \quad 135 \quad 9 \quad 14 \quad 183 \quad -2$$

7.3 Model: Demography*

A further application of matrices can be made to *demography*, a science of vital statistics, which deals with birth rates, death rates, and population trends.

To project population trends over a time interval of 15 years, three sets of data are needed: (1) the number of living females in different age categories on a given date, (2) the number of surviving females in these age categories 15 years later, (3) the number of daughters born in the time interval of 15 years to mothers in a given age category.

In order to simplify the data involved in such a study, (1) we shall assign daughters born according to the age category of their mother and (2) we shall assume a constant pattern of birth and death for the time interval studied.

Based on the 1940 United States census, we obtain the data matrix for the time interval 1940-1955:

Age	No. of Females Alive (in 1940)	Females Alive 15 Years Later (in 1955)	Daughters Born in 15 Year Interval (1940-1955)
0-14	14,459	16,428	4,651
15-29	15,264	14,258	10,403
30-44	11,346	14,836	1,374

The entries in column 1 of the matrix represent the number of females alive in 1940 for the three age groups specified. The entries in column 2 represent the number of females that are alive in 1955 for each of the three age brackets. For example, the entry 14,258 in row 2, column 2 represents the survivors from the age group 0-14 alive in 1940 (14,459). Similarly, 14,836 represents the number of females alive in 1955 that survived from the 15,264 alive in 1940. The entries in column 3 represent the number of daughters born to females from the three age groups during the 15 year period 1940-1955.

We seek a matrix F, called the *frequency matrix*, which when multiplied by the column vector containing females alive in 1940 will give us a column vector containing females alive in 1955. That is, we seek F so that

$$F \begin{bmatrix} 14,459 \\ 15,264 \\ 11,346 \end{bmatrix} = \begin{bmatrix} 16,428 \\ 14,258 \\ 14,836 \end{bmatrix}$$

*Richard Stone, "Mathematics in the Social Sciences," *Scientific American,* **211,** 3 (September 1964), pp. 168-182.

First, divide the number of daughters born in the 15-year interval (as shown in the third column) by the total number of females (as shown in the first column). The resulting ratios give the frequency for births in a given age group. These ratios are inserted in the first row of the frequency matrix F, as shown below. To obtain the second row, we need to know the survival frequency from the 0–14 age group to the 15–29 age group. The females in the 0–14 age group (14,459) who survived 15 years later number 14,258. Thus, the ratio of survival is $14{,}258 \div 14{,}459$. Since no one in either the 15–29 or the 30–44 age group can be in the 15–29 age group after 15 years have passed, we enter 0's in the rest of row 2. Similarly, row 3 is obtained, and the completed frequency matrix is

$$
\begin{array}{c}
\text{Frequency for births} \\[20pt]
\text{Survival frequency} \\ \text{0–14 to 15–29} \\[10pt]
\text{Survival frequency} \\ \text{15–29 to 30–44}
\end{array}
\quad
\overset{\begin{array}{ccc} 0\text{–}14 & 15\text{–}29 & 30\text{–}44 \end{array}}{
\begin{bmatrix}
\dfrac{4{,}651}{14{,}459} & \dfrac{10{,}403}{15{,}264} & \dfrac{1{,}374}{11{,}346} \\[12pt]
\dfrac{14{,}258}{14{,}459} & 0 & 0 \\[12pt]
0 & \dfrac{14{,}836}{15{,}264} & 0
\end{bmatrix}} = F
$$

The product of this frequency matrix F and the column matrix for females alive in 1940 gives the number of females alive in 1955. That is,

$$
\overset{\text{Frequency matrix } F}{
\begin{bmatrix}
0.32167 & 0.68154 & 0.12110 \\
0.98610 & 0 & 0 \\
0 & 0.97196 & 0
\end{bmatrix}}
\overset{\substack{\text{Females} \\ (1940)}}{
\begin{bmatrix}
14{,}459 \\ 15{,}264 \\ 11{,}346
\end{bmatrix}}
=
\overset{\substack{\text{Females alive 15} \\ \text{years later (1955)}}}{
\begin{bmatrix}
16{,}428 \\ 14{,}258 \\ 14{,}836
\end{bmatrix}}
$$

This is in agreement with our original data, so it indicates that our frequency matrix F has been correctly calculated.

Now, to obtain a projection for 1970, which is 15 years later than 1955, we simply find the product of the square of the frequency matrix F times the column matrix for females in 1940:

$$
F^2
\overset{\substack{\text{Females} \\ (1940)}}{
\begin{bmatrix}
14{,}459 \\ 15{,}264 \\ 11{,}346
\end{bmatrix}}
=
\begin{bmatrix}
0.77554 & 0.33694 & 0.03895 \\
0.31720 & 0.67207 & 0.11942 \\
0.95845 & 0 & 0
\end{bmatrix}
\begin{bmatrix}
14{,}459 \\ 15{,}264 \\ 11{,}346
\end{bmatrix}
=
\begin{bmatrix}
16{,}799 \\ 16{,}200 \\ 13{,}858
\end{bmatrix}
$$

To obtain a projection for 1985 (30 years past 1955), find the product of the cube of the frequency matrix times the column matrix for females in 1940:

$$
F^3
\overset{\substack{\text{Females} \\ (1940)}}{
\begin{bmatrix}
14{,}459 \\ 15{,}264 \\ 11{,}346
\end{bmatrix}}
=
\begin{bmatrix}
0.58172 & 0.56643 & 0.09392 \\
0.76476 & 0.33226 & 0.03841 \\
0.30831 & 0.65323 & 0.11607
\end{bmatrix}
\begin{bmatrix}
14{,}459 \\ 15{,}264 \\ 11{,}346
\end{bmatrix}
=
\begin{bmatrix}
18{,}123 \\ 16{,}565 \\ 15{,}746
\end{bmatrix}
$$

7.4   Model: Reciprocal Holdings

A parent corporation, P, owns, directly or indirectly, a controlling interest in three subsidiaries S_1, S_2, and S_3. The subsidiaries, in turn, own portions of the outstanding stock of the parent company. The percentages of ownership in this particular case are listed in decimal form in Table 2.

Table 2

		Company Whose Stock Is Owned			
		P	S_1	S_2	S_3
Company That Owns Stock	P	0	0.6	0.7	0.84
	S_1	0.05	0	0.1	0.04
	S_2	0.01	0.1	0	0.02
	S_3	0.04	0.1	0.1	0
		0.10	0.8	0.9	0.9

NOTE   Stock which a company owns in itself is not considered "outstanding stock."

As indicated in Table 2, stock that is *internally* held by the four companies consists of 10% of P's stock, 80% of S_1's stock, and 90% of the stock of both S_2 and S_3. Hence, outside stockholders own 90% of P, 20% of S_1, and 10% of S_2 and S_3.

Each of the four legally distinct entities keeps its own accounting records and prepares its own separate balance sheets and income statements. However, since the parent and its subsidiaries generally constitute a *single economic entity* under common management, it is considered necessary in current accounting practice to prepare *consolidated financial statements* for all four companies. The problem in doing this, however, apart from adding together their separate assets, liabilities, revenues, and expenses, is to determine the appropriate interests in these items of each of the respective outside shareholders. This determination is complicated by the reciprocal stock ownership of the companies. Thus, the outside stockholders of any particular company, say S_1, have an interest which is not restricted to the separate assets and income of S_1, but rather includes a share in all four companies by virtue of the interrelated stock ownership.

The solution of the problem may be illustrated by the apportionment of the following net incomes, which are to be interpreted as the separately earned income of each member of the consolidated group:

Company	Net Income
P	$100,000
S_1	40,000
S_2	60,000
S_3	20,000
Total:	$220,000

We define p, s_1, s_2, and s_3 as the total net incomes of P, S_1, S_2, and S_3, respectively, including not only their own separate earnings shown in the table, but also their respective shares of the net income of each other company. Observe that the algebraic sum of p, s_1, s_2, and s_3 will be greater than 220,000, the combined net income of all four companies, since p, s_1, s_2, and s_3 are not mutually exclusive.

The interests of the outside stockholders will be as follows:

Outside Stockholders of	Interest in Income
P	$0.9p$
S_1	$0.2s_1$
S_2	$0.1s_2$
S_3	$0.1s_3$

Moreover, p, s_1, s_2, and s_3 may be formulated by reference to the tables of stock ownership and separate net income as the following system of linear equations:

$$p = \$100,000 + 0.6s_1 + 0.7s_2 + 0.84s_3$$
$$s_1 = \$40,000 + 0.05p + 0.1s_2 + 0.04s_3$$
$$s_2 = \$60,000 + 0.01p + 0.1s_1 + 0.02s_3$$
$$s_3 = \$20,000 + 0.04p + 0.1s_1 + 0.1s_2$$

The solution of this system is best accomplished by matrix methods and will yield an allocation of net income to each of the separate outside stockholder groups such that the sum of the amount allocated will equal the combined net income of the group, that is, $220,000.

7.5 Accounting

Consider a firm that has two types of departments, production and service. The production departments produce goods that can be sold in the market and the service departments provide services to the production departments. A major objective of the cost accounting process is the determination of the full cost of manufactured products on a per unit basis. This requires an allocation of indirect costs, first, from the service department (where they are incurred) to the producing department in which the goods are manufactured and, second, to the specific goods themselves. For example, an accounting department usually provides accounting services for service departments, as well as for the production departments. Thus, the indirect costs of service rendered by a service department must be determined in order to correctly assess the production departments. The total costs of a service department consist of its direct costs (salaries, wages, and materials) and its indirect costs (charges for the services it receives from other service departments). The nature of the problem and its solution are illustrated by the following example.

Example 1 Consider a firm with two production departments, P_1 and P_2, and three service departments, S_1, S_2, and S_3. These five departments are listed in the leftmost column of Table 3 (on page 120). The total monthly costs of these departments are unknown and are denoted by x_1, x_2, x_3, x_4, x_5. The direct monthly costs of the five departments are shown in the third column of the table. The fourth, fifth, and sixth columns show the allocation of charges for the services of $S_1, S_2,$ and S_3 to the various departments. Since the total cost for each department is its direct

Table 3

| Department | Total Costs | Direct Costs, Dollars | Indirect Costs for Services from Departments | | |
			S_1	S_2	S_3
S_1	x_1	600	$0.25x_1$	$0.15x_2$	$0.15x_3$
S_2	x_2	1100	$0.35x_1$	$0.20x_2$	$0.25x_3$
S_3	x_3	600	$0.10x_1$	$0.10x_2$	$0.35x_3$
P_1	x_4	2100	$0.15x_1$	$0.25x_2$	$0.15x_3$
P_2	x_5	1500	$0.15x_1$	$0.30x_2$	$0.10x_3$
Totals			x_1	x_2	x_3

costs plus its indirect costs, the first three rows of the table yield the total costs for the three service departments:

$$x_1 = 600 + 0.25x_1 + 0.15x_2 + 0.15x_3$$
$$x_2 = 1100 + 0.35x_1 + 0.20x_2 + 0.25x_3$$
$$x_3 = 600 + 0.10x_1 + 0.10x_2 + 0.35x_3$$

Let X, C, and D denote the following matrices:

$$X = \begin{bmatrix} x_1 \\ x_2 \\ x_3 \end{bmatrix} \qquad C = \begin{bmatrix} 0.25 & 0.15 & 0.15 \\ 0.35 & 0.20 & 0.25 \\ 0.10 & 0.10 & 0.35 \end{bmatrix} \qquad D = \begin{bmatrix} 600 \\ 1100 \\ 600 \end{bmatrix}$$

Then the system of equations above can be written in matrix notation as

$$X = D + CX$$

which is equivalent to

$$[I_3 - C]X = D$$

The total costs of the three service departments can be obtained by solving this matrix equation for X:

$$X = [I_3 - C]^{-1}D$$

Now,

$$[I_3 - C] = \begin{bmatrix} 0.75 & -0.15 & -0.15 \\ -0.35 & 0.80 & -0.25 \\ -0.10 & -0.10 & 0.65 \end{bmatrix}$$

from which it can be verified that

$$[I_3 - C]^{-1} = \begin{bmatrix} 1.57 & 0.36 & 0.50 \\ 0.79 & 1.49 & 0.76 \\ 0.36 & 0.28 & 1.73 \end{bmatrix}$$

It is significant that the inverse of $[I_3 - C]$ exists, and that all of its entries are nonnegative. Because of this and the fact that the matrix D contains only non-negative entries, the matrix X will also have only nonnegative entries. This means there is a meaningful solution to the accounting problem:

$$X = \begin{bmatrix} 1638.00 \\ 2569.00 \\ 1562.00 \end{bmatrix}$$

Thus, $x_1 = \$1638.00$, $x_2 = \$2569.00$, and $x_3 = \$1562.00$. All direct and indirect costs can now be determined by substituting these values in Table 3, as shown in Table 4.

Table 4

Department	Total Costs, Dollars	Direct Costs, Dollars	Indirect Costs for Services from Departments, Dollars		
			S_1	S_2	S_3
S_1	1629.15	600	409.50	385.35	234.30
S_2	2577.60	1100	573.30	513.80	390.50
S_3	1567.40	600	163.80	256.90	546.70
P_1	3222.25	2100	245.70	642.25	234.30
P_2	2672.60	1500	245.70	770.70	156.20

From Table 4, we learn that department P_1 pays \$1122.25 for the services it receives from S_1, S_2, S_3, and P_2 pays \$1172.60 for the services it receives from these departments. The procedure we have followed charges the direct costs of the service departments to the production departments, and each production department is charged according to the services it utilizes. Furthermore, the total cost for P_1 and P_2 is \$5894.85, and this figure approximates the sum of the direct costs of the three service departments and the two production departments. The results are consistent with conventional accounting procedure. Discrepancies that occur are due to rounding off.

Finally, a comment should be made about the allocation of charges for services as shown in Table 3. How is it determined that 25% of the total cost x_1 of S_1 should be charged to S_1, 35% to S_2, 10% to S_3, 15% to P_1, and 15% to P_2? The services of each department may be measured in some suitable unit, and each department may be charged according to the number of these units of service it receives. If 20% of the accounting items concern a given department, that department is charged 20% of the total cost of the accounting department. When services are not readily measurable, the allocation basis is subjectively determined.

Exercise 7.5
Solutions to Odd-Numbered Problems begin on page 631.

1. Consider the accounting problem described by the data in the table:

Department	Total Costs	Direct Costs, Dollars	Indirect Costs	
			S_1	S_2
S_1	x_1	2000	$\frac{1}{9}x_1$	$\frac{3}{9}x_2$
S_2	x_2	1000	$\frac{3}{9}x_1$	$\frac{1}{9}x_2$
P_1	x_3	2500	$\frac{1}{9}x_1$	$\frac{2}{9}x_2$
P_2	x_4	1500	$\frac{3}{9}x_1$	$\frac{1}{9}x_2$
P_3	x_5	3000	$\frac{1}{9}x_1$	$\frac{2}{9}x_2$
Totals			x_1	x_2

   Determine whether this accounting problem has a solution. If it does, find the total costs. Prepare a table similar to Table 4. Show that the total of the service charges allocated to P_1, P_2, and P_3 is equal to the sum of the direct costs of the service departments S_1 and S_2.

2. Follow the directions of Problem 1 for the accounting problem described by the following data:

Department	Total Costs	Direct Costs Dollars	Indirect Costs for Services from Departments		
			S_1	S_2	S_3
S_1	x_1	500	$0.20x_1$	$0.10x_2$	$0.10x_3$
S_2	x_2	1000	$0.40x_1$	$0.15x_2$	$0.30x_3$
S_3	x_3	500	$0.10x_1$	$0.05x_2$	$0.30x_3$
P_1	x_4	2000	$0.20x_1$	$0.35x_2$	$0.20x_3$
P_2	x_5	1500	$0.10x_1$	$0.35x_2$	$0.10x_3$
Totals		5500	x_1	x_2	x_3

Chapter Review

Important Terms

row	**scalar multiple**
column	**matrix multiplication**
dimension of a matrix	**identity matrix**
diagonal of a matrix	**inverse of a matrix**
square matrix	**augmented matrix**
vector	**row operation**
zero matrix	**row-reduced form of a matrix**

rank
coefficient matrix
consistent system
inconsistent system
test for consistency

test for uniqueness
  parameter
*Leontief model (open and closed)
*input–output matrix

True–False
Questions
(Answers on
page 631)

T   F   1.   Matrices of the same dimension can always be added.
T   F   2.   Matrices of the same dimension can always be multiplied.
T   F   3.   A square matrix will always have an inverse.
T   F   4.   The row-reduced form of a matrix A is unique.
T   F   5.   For the system of equations $AX = B$, if rank A = rank $A|B$ = the number of unknowns, then the system has exactly one solution.

Fill in the Blanks
(Answers on
page 631)

1.   If matrix A is of dimension 3×4 and matrix B is of dimension 4×2, then AB is of dimension _____.

2.   A system of three linear equations in three unknowns has either

_____ solution, or no solutions, or _____

_____ solutions.

3.   A system of equations having no solution is said to be _____.

4.   If A is a matrix of dimension 3×4, the 3 tells the number of

_____ and the 4 tells the number of _____.

5.   If $AB = I$, the identity matrix, then B is called the _____ of A.

Review Exercises
Solutions to Odd-Numbered Problems begin on page 571.

In Problems 1–14 compute the given expression for

$$A = \begin{bmatrix} -2 & 0 & 7 \\ 1 & 8 & 3 \\ 2 & 4 & 21 \end{bmatrix} \qquad B = \begin{bmatrix} 1 & 3 & 9 \\ 2 & 7 & 5 \\ 3 & 6 & 8 \end{bmatrix} \qquad C = \begin{bmatrix} 0 & 1 & 2 \\ 0 & 5 & 1 \\ 8 & 7 & 9 \end{bmatrix}$$

1. $A + B$
2. $B + A$
3. $3(A + B)$
4. $3A + 3B$
5. $3A - 3B$
6. $B - C$
7. $2(5A)$
8. $\frac{3}{2}A$
9. $2A + \frac{1}{2}B - 3C$
10. $A - 2B + 3C$
11. AB
12. BA
13. $(B - A)C$
14. $BC - AC$

15.   Find the inverse of $\begin{bmatrix} 3 & 0 \\ -2 & 1 \end{bmatrix}$

16.   Find the inverse of $\begin{bmatrix} 1 & 2 & 3 \\ 2 & 4 & 5 \\ 3 & 5 & 6 \end{bmatrix}$

*From optimal section.

17. Find the row-reduced form of $\begin{bmatrix} 2 & 0 & 1 \\ 3 & 7 & -1 \\ 1 & 0 & 2 \end{bmatrix}$

18. Find the row-reduced form of $\begin{bmatrix} 2 & -1 & 1 \\ 1 & 1 & -1 \\ 3 & -1 & 1 \end{bmatrix}$

19. Find the solution, if it exists, of the system:

$$2x_1 - x_2 + x_3 = 1$$
$$x_1 + x_2 - x_3 = 2$$
$$3x_1 - x_2 + x_3 = 0$$

20. Find the solution, if it exists, of the system:

$$2x_1 + 3x_2 - x_3 = 5$$
$$x_1 - x_2 + x_3 = 1$$
$$3x_1 - 3x_2 + 3x_3 = 3$$

21. What must be true about x, y, z, w, if the matrices

$$A = \begin{bmatrix} x & y \\ z & w \end{bmatrix} \quad \text{and} \quad B = \begin{bmatrix} 1 & 1 \\ -1 & 1 \end{bmatrix}$$

are to commute? That is, $AB = BA$.

22. Let $t = [t_1 \quad t_2]$, with $t_1 + t_2 = 1$, and let $A = \begin{bmatrix} \frac{1}{4} & \frac{3}{4} \\ \frac{2}{3} & \frac{1}{3} \end{bmatrix}$.
    Find t such that $tA = t$.

*23. Associate numbers to letters as follows:

1 2 3 4 5 6 7 8 9 10 11 12 13 14 15 16 17 18 19 20 21 22 23 24 25 26
↓ ↓
A B C D E F G H I J K L M N O P Q R S T U V W X Y Z

The matrix A used to encode a message has as its inverse the matrix

$$A^{-1} = \begin{bmatrix} 2 & -3 \\ -1 & 2 \end{bmatrix}$$

Decode the message

    11   7   84   51   51   28   66   43   44   29   107   65   64   41

*24. Associate numbers to letters as in Problem 23, and use the matrix

$$A = \begin{bmatrix} 1 & 0 & 0 \\ 3 & 1 & 5 \\ -2 & 0 & 1 \end{bmatrix}$$

to encode the message IT'S OVER

Other Books or Articles

Anton, H. *Elementary Linear Algebra,* 3rd Ed., Wiley, New York, 1981.

Isard, Walter, and Phyllis Kaniss, "The 1973 Nobel Prize for Economic Science," *Science,* (November 9, 1973).

Leontief, Wassily W., *The Structure of American Economy, 1919–1935.* Oxford University Press, New York, 1951.

Ulmer, S. Sidney, "Leadership in the Michigan Supreme Court," in Glendon Schubert, ed., *Judicial Decision-Making,* Free Press, New York, 1963.

3

Linear Programming Part I: Geometric Approach

1. Introduction

The flow of resources in a production process or in the economy involves complex interrelationships among numerous activities. Differences may exist between the processes involved, as well as between the goals to be achieved. Nevertheless, in many cases there are essential similarities in the operation of seemingly very different systems.

In order to analyze such systems, it is necessary first to list the working parts of the system (such as capital, raw materials, and labor force) and then to state the goal or objective to be achieved (such as minimum cost or maximum profit). If the system can be represented mathematically (that is, if a *model* for the system can be found) and if the goal can be similarly quantified, it may be possible to devise a computational scheme for determining the *best* program or schedule of actions among alternatives to achieve the goal. Such schemes are called *mathematical programs*.

Mathematical Program

If the system to be analyzed can be represented by a model consisting of linear inequalities, and if the goal or objective can be expressed as the minimization or maximization of a linear expression, the analysis of the structure is known as a *linear program*. A large class of business, economic, and engineering problems can be represented by linear systems. Other times, a linear program may constitute a good approximation of the conditions of the problem. Of course, for any particular application, it must be determined whether a linear program constitutes a "good enough" approximation. We shall not concern ourselves here with whether a given approximation is "good enough;" we will just concentrate on giving you an introduction to the technique of solving *linear programming problems*.

Linear Program

Historically, linear programs for the solution of problems involving resource allocation were developed during World War II by the United States Air Force. Among those who worked on such problems for the Air Force was George Dantzig, who later gave a general formulation of the linear programming problem and offered a method for solving it. His technique, called the *simplex method*, is discussed in Chapter 4.

Before studying ways to solve a linear programming problem, we give several examples that can be solved using linear programming techniques.

Example 1 A producer of chicken feed is required by the United States Department of Agriculture to furnish a certain amount of nutritional elements (such as vitamins and minerals) per hundred pounds of feed. These elements are found in known proportions in various grains and concentrated supplements whose cost is known. What proportions of these grains and concentrated supplements should be mixed so that the desired amount of nutritional elements is found in the feed and, at the same time, the producer's cost for these elements is least? ∎

Problems like Example 1 are called *diet* or *mixture problems*.

GEORGE DANTZIG is one of the pioneering creators of linear programming, which is one of the most important developments in applied mathematics in the last half-century. He developed the simplex method in 1946.

Example 2   A manufacturer has several production facilities and a number of warehouses. Each production facility can ship goods to any of the warehouses requiring goods. Shipments must be such that each warehouse receives at least as much as its requirements, possibly from more than one source. There is a known cost per unit shipped along each route from production facility to warehouse. The manufacturer wishes to devise a shipping scheme that satisfies the requirements of the warehouses at lowest possible total transportation cost. ∎

Problems like Example 2 are called *transportation problems.*

Example 3   A company manufactures several different products. In making each product, a certain amount of labor, skilled and nonskilled, and a known amount of raw material are used. The company sells each product for a known profit. How much of each product should be manufactured in order to maximize profits? ∎

Each of the above examples has certain similar characteristics. Each requires that a certain quantity, which can be written as a linear equation using the variables involved, be *maximized* or *minimized.* This linear equation is referred to as the *objective function.* Each example further requires that the maximization or minimization occur under certain conditions, or *constraints,* that can be expressed as linear inequalities involving the variables. Problems with these two characteristics can usually be solved by using a linear program.

The next section provides a way of solving certain kinds of linear programming problems by graphical methods. Although the problems we will discuss are too simple to be realistic, they are instructional. In Chapter 4, the simplex method is used to solve more complicated linear programming problems; this method is adaptable to computer systems for relatively fast solutions.

Objective
Function

Constraints

2.   A Geometric Approach to Linear Programming Problems

We will restrict our discussion here to linear programming problems containing only two variables, since it is then possible to represent and solve the problems using graphing techniques.

Every linear programming problem has two components:

1.   A linear objective function to be maximized or minimized
2.   A collection of linear inequalities that must be satisfied simultaneously

Linear Programming Problem   **A** *linear programming problem* **in two variables,** x **and** y, **consists of** *maximizing* **or** *minimizing* **an** *objective function*

$$z = Ax + By$$

where A and B **are given real numbers subject to certain conditions or** *constraints* **expressible as linear inequalities in** x **and** y.

Let's look at this more closely. To maximize (or minimize) the quantity $z = Ax + By$ means to locate the points (x, y) that make the expression for z the largest (or smallest). But not all points (x, y) are eligible. Only the points that obey *all* the constraints are potential solutions. Hence, we refer to such points as *feasible solutions*.

Feasible Solution

In a linear programming problem, we want to find the feasible solution that maximizes (or minimizes) the objective function.

If we graph the constraints of a linear programming problem (a collection of linear inequalities), the resulting set of points is called a *polyhedral set* (its boundary consists of line segments). This polyhedral set of points is *convex;* that is, it has the property that a line segment that joins any pair of points in the set lies entirely in the set. See Figure 1 for some illustrations.

Polyhedral Set

Convex Set

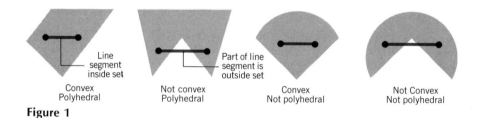

| Line segment inside set | Part of line segment is outside set | | |
| Convex Polyhedral | Not convex Polyhedral | Convex Not polyhedral | Not Convex Not polyhedral |

Figure 1

Solution of a Linear Programming Problem

By a *solution* **to a linear programming problem we mean a point** (x, y) **in the set of feasible solutions together with the value of the objective function at that point, that maximizes (or minimizes) the objective function.**

If none of the feasible solutions maximize (or minimize) the objective function, or if there are no feasible solutions, then the linear programming problem has no solution.

Example 1 Minimize the quantity

$$z = x + 2y$$

subject to the constraints

$$x + y \geq 1 \qquad x \geq 0 \qquad y \geq 0$$

Solution The objective function to be minimized is $z = x + 2y$. The constraints are the linear inequalities

$$x + y \geq 1 \qquad x \geq 0 \qquad y \geq 0$$

The shaded portion of Figure 2 illustrates the set of feasible solutions.

To see if there is a smallest z, we graph $z = x + 2y$ for some choice of z, say

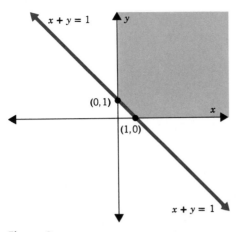

Figure 2

$z = 3$. See Figure 3. By moving the line $x + 2y = 3$ parallel to itself, we can observe what happens for different values of z. Since we want a minimum value for z, we try to move $z = x + 2y$ down as far as possible while keeping some part of the line within the polyhedral convex set of feasible solutions. The "best" solution is obtained when the line just touches one corner, or *vertex*, of the set of feasible solutions. If you refer to Figure 3, you will see that the best solution is $x = 1$, $y = 0$, which yields $z = 1$. There is no other feasible solution for which z is smaller.

Vertex

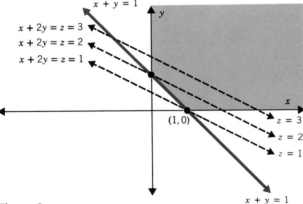

Figure 3

In Example 1, we can see that the feasible solution which minimizes z occurs at a vertex. This is not an unusual situation. If there is a feasible solution minimizing (or maximizing) the objective function, it is *usually* located at a vertex of the set of feasible solutions.

However, it is possible for a feasible solution that is not a vertex to minimize (or maximize) the objective function. This occurs when the slope of the objective function is the same as the slope of one side of the set of feasible solutions. The following example illustrates this possibility.

Example 2   Minimize the quantity

$$z = x + 2y$$

subject to the constraints

$$x + y \geq 1 \qquad 2x + 4y \geq 3 \qquad x \geq 0 \qquad y \geq 0$$

Solution   Again, we first graph the constraints. The shaded portion of Figure 4 illustrates the set of feasible solutions.

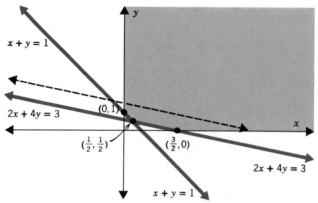

Figure 4

If we graph the objective equation $z = x + 2y$ for some choice of z and move it down, we see that a minimum is reached when $z = \frac{3}{2}$. In fact, any point on the line $2x + 4y = 3$ between $(\frac{1}{2}, \frac{1}{2})$ and $(\frac{3}{2}, 0)$ will minimize the objective function. Of course, the reason any feasible point on $2x + 4y = 3$ minimizes the objective equation $z = x + 2y$ is that these two lines are parallel (both have slope $-\frac{1}{2}$).

■

The next example illustrates a linear programming problem that has no solution.

Example 3   Maximize the quantity

$$z = x + 2y$$

subject to the constraints

$$x + y \geq 1 \qquad x \geq 0 \qquad y \geq 0$$

Solution   First, we graph the constraints. The shaded portion of Figure 5 illustrates the set of feasible solutions.

The graphs of the objective equation $z = x + 2y$ for $z = 2, z = 8$, and $z = 12$ are also shown in Figure 5. Observe that we continue to get larger values for z by moving the graph of the objective function upward. But there is no feasible point that will make z *largest*. No matter how large a value is assigned to z, there is a feasible point that will give a larger value. Since there is no feasible point that

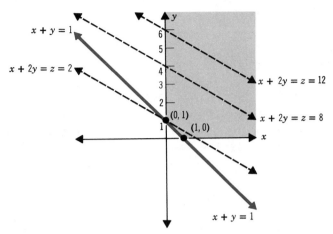

Figure 5

makes z largest, we conclude that this linear programming problem has no solution. ∎

For any linear programming problem that has a solution, the following general result is true:

If a linear programming problem has a solution, it is located at a vertex of the set of feasible solutions; if a linear programming problem has multiple solutions, at least one of them is located at a vertex of the set of feasible solutions. In either case, the corresponding value of the objective function is unique.

Bounded

The result stated above requires knowing in advance whether the linear programming problem has a solution. If the set of feasible solutions is *bounded*—that is, if it can be enclosed within some circle—the linear programming problem will have a solution.

If the set of feasible solutions is not bounded (see Example 3), then the graphs of the objective function for several values of z should be used to determine whether a solution exists or does not exist.

Based on these comments, we can outline a procedure for solving a linear programming problem provided that it has a solution.

1. **Write an expression for the quantity that is to be maximized or minimized (the objective function).**
2. **Determine all the constraints and graph them.**
3. **List the vertices of the set of feasible solutions.**
4. **Determine the value of the objective function at each vertex.**

Let's look at some examples.

Example 4 Maximize and minimize the objective equation

$$z = x + 5y$$

subject to the constraints

① $x + 4y \leq 12$ ② $x \leq 8$ ③ $x + y \geq 2$ ④ $x \geq 0$ ⑤ $y \geq 0$

Solution The objective function and the constraints (numbered for convenience) are given (this will not be the case when we do word problems), so we can proceed to graph the constraints. The shaded portion of Figure 6 illustrates the set of feasible solutions. Since this set is bounded, we know a solution exists.

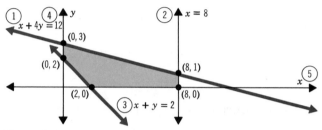

Figure 6

Now we locate the vertices of the set of feasible solutions at the points of intersection of lines ① and ④, ① and ②, ② and ⑤, ③ and ⑤, and ③ and ④. Using methods discussed in Chapter 1 (page 26), we find that the vertices are

$$(0, 3), \quad (8, 1), \quad (8, 0), \quad (2, 0), \quad (0, 2)$$

To find the maximum and minimum value of $z = x + 5y$, we set up a table:

Vertex (x, y)	Value of Objective Equation $z = x + 5y$
(0, 3)	$z = 0 + 5(3) = 15$
(8, 1)	$z = 8 + 5(1) = 13$
(8, 0)	$z = 8 + 5(0) = 8$
(2, 0)	$z = 2 + 5(0) = 2$
(0, 2)	$z = 0 + 5(2) = 10$

The maximum value of z is 15, and it occurs at the point $(0, 3)$.
The minimum value of z is 2, and it occurs at the point $(2, 0)$. ∎

Example 5 Nutt's Nuts has 75 pounds of cashews and 120 pounds of peanuts. These are to be mixed in 1 pound packages as follows: a low-grade mixture that contains 4 ounces of cashews and 12 ounces of peanuts and a high-grade mixture that contains 8 ounces of cashews and 8 ounces of peanuts. A profit of $0.25 per package will be made on the low-grade mixture, and a profit of $0.45 per package will be made on the high-grade mixture. How many packages of each mixture should be prepared to obtain a maximum profit?

Solution   Before applying the method of this chapter to solve this problem, let's discuss a solution that might be suggested by intuition. Namely, since the profit is higher for the high-grade mixture, you might think that Nutt's Nuts should prepare as many packages of the high-grade mixture as possible. If this were done, then there would be a total of 150 packages (8 ounces divides into 75 pounds of cashews exactly 150 times) and the total profit would be

$$150(0.45) = \$67.50$$

As we shall see, this is not the best solution to the problem. This is because there would be several pounds of peanuts left over ($120 - 75 = 45$, to be exact) that would be neither packaged nor sold.

To use more of the peanuts and thus make a higher profit, Nutt's Nuts has to make both high-grade *and* low-grade packages. We are still asking ourselves how many packages of each mixture should be made to obtain the maximum profit, but now we will use linear programming to solve the problem.

We begin by observing that there are two variables, which we name as

$x = $ Number of packages of low-grade mixture
$y = $ Number of packages of high-grade mixture

The quantity to be maximized is the profit, which we denote by P:

$$P = (\$0.25)x + (\$0.45)y$$

This is the objective function. The restrictions on x and y are

$$x \geq 0 \qquad y \geq 0 \qquad \text{Nonnegative constraint}$$

since x and y stand for numbers of packages and negative numbers of packages are meaningless. Also, there is a limit to the number of pounds of cashews and peanuts available. That is, the total number of pounds of cashews cannot exceed 75 pounds (1200 ounces) and the number of pounds of peanuts cannot exceed 120 pounds (1920 ounces). This means that

$$4x + 8y \leq 1200 \qquad \text{Cashew constraint}$$
$$12x + 8y \leq 1920 \qquad \text{Peanut constraint}$$

The constraints of the linear programming problem are

$$x \geq 0 \qquad y \geq 0 \qquad 4x + 8y \leq 1200 \qquad 12x + 8y \leq 1920$$

which may be simplified to

$$\text{①} \; x \geq 0 \quad \text{②} \; y \geq 0 \quad \text{③} \; x + 2y \leq 300 \quad \text{④} \; 3x + 2y \leq 480$$

(Note that we have again numbered the constraints—this will help later.) The graph of the set of feasible solutions is given in Figure 7 on page 136.

Since this set is bounded, we proceed to locate its vertices. The vertices of the set of feasible solutions are the points of intersection of lines ① and ②, ① and ③, ② and ④, and ③ and ④:

$$(0,0), \quad (0,150), \quad (160,0), \quad (90,105)$$

(Notice that the points of intersection of lines ① and ④ and lines ② and ③ are not feasible solutions.) It only remains to evaluate the objective equation at each vertex:

Vertex (x, y)	Value of Objective Equation $P = (\$0.25)x + (\$0.45)y$
$(0, 0)$	$P = (0.25)(0) + (0.45)(0) = 0$
$(0, 150)$	$P = (0.25)(0) + (0.45)(150) = \$67.50$
$(160, 0)$	$P = (0.25)(160) + (0.45)(0) = \$40.00$
$(90, 105)$	$P = (0.25)(90) + (0.45)(105) = \$69.75$

Thus, a maximum profit is obtained if 90 packages of low-grade mixture and 105 packages of high-grade mixture are made. The maximum profit obtainable under the conditions described is $69.75.

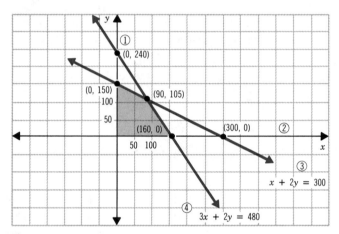

Figure 7

Example 6   Mike's Famous Toy Trucks manufactures two kinds of toy trucks—a standard model and a deluxe model. In the manufacturing process, each standard model requires 2 hours of grinding and 2 hours of finishing, and each deluxe model needs 2 hours of grinding and 4 hours of finishing. The company has 2 grinders and 3 finishers, each of whom work 40 hours per week. Each standard model toy truck brings a profit of $3 and each deluxe model a profit of $4. Assuming every truck made will be sold, how many of each should be made to maximize profits?

Solution   First, we name the variables:

$$x = \text{Number of standard models made}$$
$$y = \text{Number of deluxe models made}$$

The quantity to be maximized is the profit, which we denote by P:

$$P = \$3x + \$4y$$

This is the objective function. To manufacture one standard model requires 2 grinding hours and to make one deluxe model requires 2 grinding hours. Thus, the number of grinding hours for x standard and y deluxe models is

$$2x + 2y$$

But the total amount of grinding time available is 80 hours per week. This means we have the constraint

$$2x + 2y \leq 80 \qquad \text{Grinding time constraint}$$

Similarly, for the finishing time we have the constraint

$$2x + 4y \leq 120 \qquad \text{Finishing time constraint}$$

Simplifying each of these constraints and adding the nonnegativity constraints $x \geq 0$ and $y \geq 0$, we may list all the constraints for this problem.

$$x + y \leq 40 \qquad x + 2y \leq 60 \qquad x \geq 0 \qquad y \geq 0$$

Figure 8 illustrates the set of feasible solutions, which is bounded.
The vertices of the set of feasible solutions are

$$(0, 0), \quad (0, 30), \quad (40, 0), \quad (20, 20)$$

The table lists the corresponding values of the objective equation:

Vertex (x, y)	Value of Objective Equation $P = \$3x + \$4y$
$(0, 0)$	$P = 0$
$(0, 30)$	$P = \$120$
$(40, 0)$	$P = \$120$
$(20, 20)$	$P = 3(20) + 4(20) = \$140$

Thus, a maximum profit is obtained if 20 standard trucks and 20 deluxe trucks are manufactured. The maximum profit is $140.

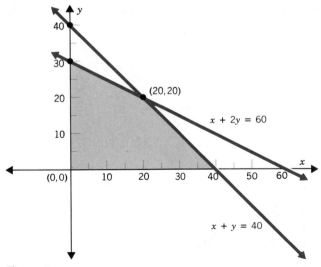

Figure 8

Example 7
Investment
Strategy

A retired couple have up to $30,000 they wish to invest in fixed-income securities. Their broker recommends investing in two bonds: one a AAA bond yielding 12%; the other a B⁺ bond paying 15%. After some consideration, the couple decide to invest at most \$12,000 in the B$^+$-rated bond and at least \$6000 in the AAA bond. They also want the amount invested in the AAA bond to exceed or equal the amount invested in the B$^+$ bond. What should the broker recommend if the couple (quite naturally) want to maximize their return on investment?

Solution First, we name the variables:

$$x = \text{Amount invested in AAA bond}$$
$$y = \text{Amount invested in B}^+ \text{ bond}$$

The quantity to be maximized—return on investment—which we denote by P, is

$$P = 0.12x + 0.15y$$

This is the objective function. The conditions specified by the problem are:

Up to \$30,000 available to invest	$x + y \leq 30,000$
Invest at most \$12,000 in B$^+$ bond	$y \leq 12,000$
Invest at least \$6000 in AAA bond	$x \geq 6,000$
Amount in AAA bond must exceed or equal amount in B$^+$ bond	$x \geq y$

In addition, we must have the conditions $x \geq 0$ and $y \geq 0$. The total list of constraints is

① $x + y \leq 30,000$ ② $y \leq 12,000$ ③ $x \geq 6000$

④ $x \geq y$ ⑤ $x \geq 0$ ⑥ $y \geq 0$

Figure 9 illustrates the set of feasible solutions, which is bounded. The vertices of the set of feasible solutions are

(6000, 0), (6000, 6000), (12,000, 12,000), (18,000, 12,000), (30,000, 0)

The corresponding return on investment at each vertex is:

$$P = 0.12(6000) + 0.15(0) = \$720$$
$$P = 0.12(6000) + 0.15(6000) = 720 + 900 = \$1620$$

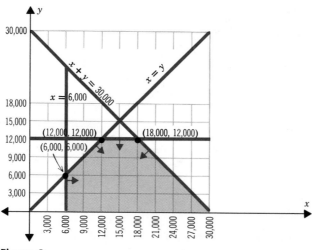

Figure 9

$$P = 0.12(12,000) + 0.15(12,000) = 1440 + 1800 = \$3240$$
$$P = 0.12(18,000) + 0.15(12,000) = 2160 + 1800 = \$3960$$
$$P = 0.12(30,000) + 0.15(0) = \$3600$$

Thus, the maximum return on investment is $3960, obtained by placing $18,000 in the AAA bond and $12,000 in the B$^+$ bond.

∎

Example 8
Urban Economics
Model*

This example concerns reclaimed land and its allocation into two major uses—agricultural and urban (or nonagricultural). The reclamation of land for urban purposes cost $400 per acre and for agricultural uses, $300. The primal problem is that the reclamation agency wishes to minimize the total cost C of reclaiming the land:

$$C = \$400x + \$300y$$

where x = the number of acres of urban land and y = the number of acres of agricultural land. Although this equation can be minimized by setting both x and y at zero, that is, reclaiming nothing, the problem derives from a number of constraints due to three different groups.

The first is an urban group, which insists that at least 4000 acres of land be reclaimed for urban purposes. The second group is concerned with agriculture and says that at least 5000 acres of land must be reclaimed for agricultural uses. Finally, the third group is concerned only with reclamation and is quite uninterested in the use to which the land will be put. The third group, however, says that at least 10,000 acres of land must be reclaimed. The primal problem and the constraints can, therefore, be written in full as follows:
Minimize

$$C = \$400x + \$300y$$

subject to the constraints

$$x \geq 4000$$
$$y \geq 5000$$
$$x + y \geq 10,000$$

Figure 10 on page 140 illustrates the set of feasible solutions, which is not bounded. However, it is apparent that this problem has a solution since lowering the graph of the objective function (dashed black line) will eventually lead to a smallest value for C.

The combination of urban and agricultural land at the vertex (4000, 6000) reveals that if 4000 acres are devoted to urban purposes and 6000 acres to agricultural purposes, the cost is a minimum and is

$$C = (\$400)(4000) + (\$300)(6000) = \$3,400,000$$

∎

*This example is adapted from Maurice Yeates, *An Introduction to Quantitative Analysis in Economic Geography,* McGraw-Hill, New York, 1968.

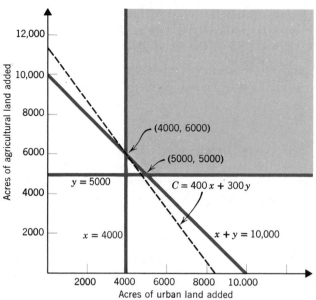

Figure 10

Model: Pollution Control

The following model is taken from a paper by Robert E. Kohn.* In this paper, a linear programming model is proposed that can be useful in determining what air pollution controls should be adopted in an airshed. The methodology is based on the premise that air quality goals should be achieved at the least possible cost. Advantages of the model are its simplicity, its emphasis on economic efficiency, and its appropriateness for the kind of data that are already available.

To illustrate the model, consider a hypothetical airshed with a single industry, cement manufacturing. Annual production is 2,500,000 barrels of cement. Although the kilns are equipped with mechanical collectors for air pollution control, they are still emitting 2 pounds of dust for every barrel of cement produced. The industry can be required to replace the mechanical collectors with four-field electrostatic precipitators, which would reduce emissions to 0.5 pound of dust per barrel of cement or with five-field electrostatic precipitators, which would reduce emissions to 0.2 pound per barrel. If the capital and operating costs of the four-field precipitator are $0.14 per barrel of cement produced and of the five-field precipitator are $0.18 per barrel, what control methods should be required of this industry? Assume that, for this hypothetical airshed, it has been determined that particulate emissions (which now total 5,000,000 pounds per year) should be reduced by 4,200,000 pounds.

If C represents the cost of control, x is the number of barrels of annual cement production subject to the four-field electrostatic precipitator (cost is $0.14 a barrel of cement produced and pollutant reduction is $2 - 0.5 = 1.5$ pounds of particulates per barrel of cement produced), and y is the number of barrels of annual cement production subject to the five-field electrostatic precipitator

*R. E. Kohn, "A Mathematical Programming Model for Air Pollution Control," *School Science and Mathematics* (June 1969), pp. 487–499.

(cost is $0.18 a barrel and pollutant reduction is $2 - 0.2 = 1.8$ pounds per barrel of cement produced), then the problem can be stated as follows:
Minimize

$$C = \$0.14x + \$0.18y$$

subject to

$$x + y \leq 2,500,000$$
$$1.5x + 1.8y \geq 4,200,000$$
$$x \geq 0$$
$$y \geq 0$$

The first equation states that our objective is to minimize air pollution control costs; the second that barrels of cement production subject to the two control methods cannot exceed the annual production; the third that the particulate reduction from the two methods must be greater than or equal to the particulate reduction target; and the last two expressions mean that we cannot have negative quantities of cement. Figure 11 illustrates a graphic solution to the problem.

The least costly solution would be to install the four-field precipitator on kilns producing 1,000,000 ($x = 1,000,000$) and the five-field precipitator on kilns producing 1,500,000 ($y = 1,500,000$) barrels of cement at a cost of $C = \$410,000$.
A further analysis of this type of problem is found in Chapter 4.

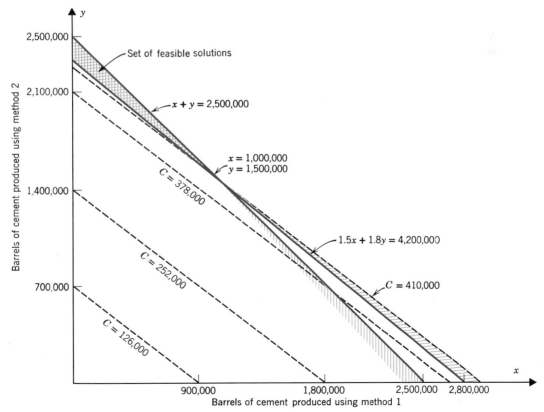

Figure 11

Exercise 2
Solutions to Odd-Numbered Problems begin on page 572.

In Problems 1–6 the figure below illustrates the graph of the set of feasible solutions of a linear programming problem. Find the maximum and minimum values of each objective function.

1. $z = 2x + 3y$ 2. $z = 3x + 27y$ 3. $z = x + 8y$
4. $z = 3x + y$ 5. $z = x + 6y$ 6. $z = x + 5y$

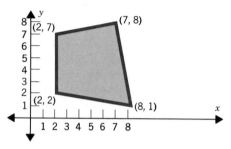

In Problems 7–14 maximize (if possible) the quantity $z = 5x + 7y$ subject to the given constraints.

7. $x \geq 0$ 8. $x \geq 0$
         $y \geq 0$ $y \geq 0$
    $x + y \leq 2$ $2x + 3y \leq 6$

9. $x \geq 0$ 10. $x \geq 0$
         $y \geq 0$ $y \geq 0$
    $x + y \geq 2$ $x + y \geq 2$
  $2x + 3y \leq 6$ $2x + 3y \leq 12$
                              $3x + 2y \leq 12$

11. $x \geq 0$ 12. $x \geq 0$
         $y \geq 0$ $y \geq 0$
    $2 \leq x + y$ $2 \leq x + y$
  $x + y \leq 8$ $x + y \leq 8$
  $2x + y \leq 10$ $1 \leq x + 2y$
                           $x + 2y \leq 10$

13. $x \geq 0$ 14. $x \geq 0$
         $y \geq 0$ $y \geq 0$
  $x + 3y \geq 6$ $2x + 3y \geq 12$

In Problems 15–20 minimize (if possible) the quantity $z = 2x + 3y$ subject to the given constraints.

15. $x \geq 0$ 16. $x \geq 0$
         $y \geq 0$ $y \geq 0$
  $x + y \geq 2$ $2x + y \geq 2$

17. $x \geq 0$ 18. $x \geq 0$
         $y \geq 0$ $y \geq 0$
  $x + y \geq 2$ $2 \leq x + y$
  $2x + 3y \leq 12$ $x + y \leq 10$
  $3x + y \leq 12$ $2x + 3y \leq 6$

19. $x \geq 0$
    $y \geq 0$
    $1 \leq x + 2y$
    $x + 2y \leq 10$

20. $x \geq 0$
    $y \geq 0$
    $1 \leq x + 2y$
    $x + 2y \leq 10$
    $2 \leq x + y$
    $x + y \leq 8$

In Problems 21–26 find the maximum and minimum values (if possible) of the given objective function subject to the constraints

$$x \geq 0 \qquad y \geq 0 \qquad x + y \leq 10 \qquad 2x + y \geq 10 \qquad x + 2y \geq 10$$

21. $z = x + y$
22. $z = 2x + 3y$
23. $z = 5x + 2y$
24. $z = x + 2y$
25. $z = 3x + 4y$
26. $z = 3x + 6y$

27. In Example 5 (page 134), if the profit on the low-grade mixture is $0.30 per package and the profit on the high-grade mixture is $0.40 per package, how many packages of each mixture should be made for a maximum profit?

28. Using the information supplied in Example 6 (page 136), suppose the profit on each standard model is $4 and the profit on each deluxe model is $4. How many of each should be manufactured in order to maximize profit?

29. Using the information supplied in Example 6 (page 136), suppose the profit on each standard model is $4 and the profit on each deluxe model is $3. How many of each should be manufactured in order to maximize profit?

30. *Investment Strategy.* An investment broker wants to invest up to $20,000. She can purchase a type A bond yielding a 10% return on the amount invested and she can purchase a type B bond yielding a 15% return on the amount invested. She also wants to invest at least as much in the type A bond as in the type B bond. She will also invest at least $5000 in the type A bond and no more than $8000 in the type B bond. How much should she invest in each type of bond to maximize her return?

31. A factory manufactures two products, each requiring the use of three machines. The first machine can be used at most 70 hours; the second machine at most 40 hours; and the third machine at most 90 hours. The first product requires 2 hours on Machine 1, 1 hour on Machine 2, and 1 hour on Machine 3; the second product requires 1 hour each on Machines 1 and 2 and 3 hours on Machine 3. If the profit is $40 per unit for the first product and $60 per unit for the second product, how many units of each product should be manufactured to maximize profit?

32. *Diet Problem.* A diet is to contain at least 400 units of vitamins, 500 units of minerals, and 1400 calories. Two foods are available: F_1, which costs $0.05 per unit, and F_2, which costs $0.03 per unit. A unit of food F_1 contains 2 units of vitamins, 1 unit of minerals, and 4 calories; a unit of food F_2 contains 1 unit of vitamins, 2 units of minerals, and 4 calories. Find the minimum cost for a diet that consists of a mixture of these two foods and also meets the minimal nutrition requirements.

33. *Diet Problem.* Danny's Chicken Farm is a producer of frying chickens. In order to produce the best fryers possible, the regular chicken feed is supplemented by four vitamins. The minimum amount of each vitamin required per 100 ounces of feed is: Vitamin 1, 50 units; Vitamin 2, 100 units; Vitamin 3, 60 units; Vitamin 4, 180 units. Two supplements are available: Supplement I costs $0.03 per ounce and contains 5 units of Vitamin 1 per ounce, 25 units of Vitamin 2 per ounce, 10 units of Vitamin 3 per ounce, and 35 units of Vitamin 4 per ounce. Supplement II costs $0.04 per ounce and contains 25 units of Vitamin 1 per ounce, 10 units of Vitamin 2 per ounce, 10 units of Vitamin 3 per ounce, and 20 units of Vitamin 4 per ounce. How much of each supplement should Danny buy to add to each 100 ounces of feed in order to minimize his cost, but still have the desired vitamin amounts present?

34. *Optimal Use of Land.* A farmer has 70 acres of land available on which to grow some soybeans and some corn. The cost of cultivation per acre, the workdays needed per acre, and the profit per acre are indicated in the table:

	Soybeans	Corn	Total Available
Cultivation Cost per Acre	$60	$30	$1800
Days of Work per Acre	3 days	4 days	120 days
Profit per Acre	$300	$150	

As indicated in the last column, the acreage to be cultivated is limited by the amount of money available for cultivation costs and by the number of working days that can be put into this part of the business. Find the number of acres of each crop that should be planted in order to maximize the profit.

35. The manager of a supermarket meat department finds that there are 160 pounds of round steak, 600 pounds of chuck steak, and 300 pounds of pork in stock on Saturday morning. From experience, the manager knows that half these quantities can be sold as straight cuts. The remaining meat will have to be ground into hamburger patties and picnic patties for which there is a large weekend demand. Each pound of hamburger patties contains 20% ground round and 60% ground chuck. Each pound of picnic patties contains 30% ground pork and 50% ground chuck. The remainder of each product consists of an inexpensive nonmeat filler which the store has in unlimited quantities. How many pounds of each product should be made if the objective is to maximize the amount of meat used to make the patties?

36. J. B. Rug Manufacturers has available 1200 square yards of wool and 1000 square yards of nylon for the manufacture of two grades of carpeting: high-grade, which sells for $500 per roll, and low-grade, which sells for $300 per roll. Twenty square yards of wool and 40 square yards of nylon are used in a roll of high-grade carpet, and 40

square yards of nylon are used in a roll of low-grade carpet. Forty work-hours are required to manufacture each roll of the high-grade carpet, and 20 work-hours are required for each roll of the low-grade carpet, at an average cost of $6.00 per work-hour. A maximum of 800 work-hours are available. The cost of wool is $5.00 per square yard and the cost of nylon is $2.00 per square yard. How many rolls of each type of carpet should be manufactured to maximize income? [*Hint:* Income = Revenue from sale − (Production cost for material + labor)]

*37. The rug manufacturer in Problem 36 finds that maximum income occurs when no high-grade carpet is produced. If the price of the low-grade carpet is kept at $300 per roll, in what price range should the high-grade carpet be sold so that income is maximized by selling some rolls of each type carpet? Assume all other data remain the same.

*38. Maximize

$$P = 2x + y + 3z$$

subject to

$$x + 2y + z \le 25$$
$$3x + 2y + 3z \le 30$$
$$x \ge 0 \qquad y \ge 0 \qquad z \ge 0$$

[*Hint:* Solve the constraints three at a time, find the points that are in the set of feasible solutions, and test each of them in the objective function. Assume a solution exists.]

Chapter Review

Important Terms	mathematical program	polyhedral set
	linear program	convex set
	objective function	solution of a linear programming
	constraints	problem
	linear programming problem	vertex
	feasible solution	bounded

True–False Questions (Answers on page 631)

T F 1. The graph of the set of constraints of a linear programming problem, under certain conditions, could have a circle for a boundary.

T F 2. The objective function of a linear programming problem is always a linear expression involving the variables.

T F 3. In a linear programming problem, there may be more than one point that maximizes or minimizes the objective function.

T F 4. Some linear programming problems will have no solution.

T F 5. If a linear programming problem has a solution, it is located at the center of the set of feasible solutions.

Fill in the Blanks
(Answers on
page 631)

1. In a linear programming problem, the quantity to be maximized or minimized is referred to as the _____ function.
2. The points that obey the collection of constraints of a linear programming problem are called _____ solutions.
3. The graph of the constraints of a linear programming problem is a set of points that is both _____ and _____.
4. A linear programming problem will always have a solution if the set of feasible solutions is_____.
5. If a linear programming problem has a solution, it is located at a _____ of the set of feasible solutions.

Review Exercises
Solutions to Odd-Numbered Problems begin on page 577.

1. Maximize and minimize (if possible) the quantity

$$z = 15x + 20y$$

subject to the constraints:

(a) $3x + 4y \leq 12$
  $x \geq 0$
  $y \geq 0$

(b) $x + 2y \leq 40$
  $x - 3y \geq 20$
  $x \geq 0$
  $y \geq 0$

(c) $5x + 2y \leq 30$
  $x + y \leq 9$
  $x \geq 0$
  $y \geq 0$

(d) $x + y \geq 5$
  $x + y \leq 20$
  $x \geq 0$
  $y \geq 0$

2. Maximize and minimize (if possible) the quantity

$$z = 5x + 2y$$

subject to the constraints of Problem 1.

3. *Diet Problem.* Katy needs at least 60 units of carbohydrates, 45 units of protein, and 30 units of fat each month. From each pound of Food A, she receives 5 units of carbohydrates, 3 of protein, and 4 of fat. Food B contains 2 units of carbohydrates, 2 units of protein, and 1 unit of fat per pound. If Food A costs $1.30 per pound and Food B costs $0.80 per pound, how many pounds of each food should Katy buy each month to keep costs at a minimum?

4. The ACE Meat Market makes up a combination package of ground beef and ground pork for meat loaf. The ground beef is 75% lean (75% beef, 25% fat) and costs the market 70¢ per pound. The ground pork is 60% lean (60% pork, 40% fat) and costs the market 50¢ per pound. If the meat loaf is to be at least 70% lean, how much ground beef and ground pork should be mixed to keep cost at a minimum?

5. A ski manufacturer makes two types of skies: downhill and cross-country. Using the information given in the table below, how many of each type of ski should be made for a maximum profit to be achieved? What is the maximum profit?

	Downhill	Cross-Country	Maximum Time Available
Manufacturing Time per Ski	2 hours	1 hour	40 hours
Finishing Time per Ski	1 hour	1 hour	32 hours
Profit per Ski	$70	$50	

6. Rework Problem 5 if the manufacturing unit has a maximum of 48 hours available.

Mathematical Questions
From CPA and CMA Exams
(Answers on page 629)

Use the following information to answer Problems 1–3:

CPA Exam—May 1975
The Random Company manufactures two products, Zeta and Beta. Each product must pass through two processing operations. All materials are introduced at the start of Process No. 1. There are no work-in-process inventories. Random may produce either one product exclusively or various combinations of both products subject to the following constraints:

	Process No. 1	Process No. 2	Contribution Margin per Unit
Hours Required to Produce One Unit of:			
Zeta	1 hour	1 hour	$4.00
Beta	2 hours	3 hours	5.25
Total Capacity in Hours per Day	1000 hours	1275 hours	

A shortage of technical labor has limited Beta production to 400 units per day. There are no constraints on the production of Zeta other than the hour constraints in the above schedule. Assume that all relationships between capacity and production are linear, and that all of the above data and relationships are deterministic rather than probabilistic.

1. Given the objective to maximize total contribution margin, what is the production constraint for Process No. 1?
   (a) Zeta + Beta ≤ 1000   (b) Zeta + 2Beta ≤ 1000
   (c) Zeta + Beta ≥ 1000   (d) Zeta + 2Beta ≥ 1000

2. Given the objective to maximize total contribution margin, what is the labor constraint for production of Beta?
   (a) Beta ≤ 400   (b) Beta ≥ 400
   (c) Beta ≤ 425   (d) Beta ≥ 425

3. What is the objective function of the data presented?
   (a) Zeta + 2Beta = $9.25
   (b) ($4.00)Zeta + 3($5.25)Beta = Total contribution margin
   (c) ($4.00)Zeta + ($5.25)Beta = Total contribution margin
   (d) 2($4.00)Zeta + 3($5.25)Beta = Total contribution margin

4. *CPA Exam—November 1976*
   Williamson Manufacturing intends to produce two products, X and Y. Product X requires 6 hours of time on Machine 1 and 12 hours of time on Machine 2. Product Y requires 4 hours of time on Machine 1 and no time on Machine 2. Both machines are available for 24 hours. Assuming that the objective function of the total contribution margin is $2X + $1Y, what product mix will produce the maximum profit?
   (a) No units of Product X and 6 units of Product Y
   (b) 1 unit of Product X and 4 units of Product Y
   (c) 2 units of Product X and 3 units of Product Y
   (d) 4 units of Product X and no units of Product Y

5. *CPA Exam—May 1975*
   Quepea Company manufactures two products, Q and P, in a small building with limited capacity. The selling price, cost data, and production time are given below:

	Product Q	Product P
Selling Price per Unit	$20	$17
Variable Costs of Producing and Selling a Unit	$12	$13
Hours to Produce a Unit	3	1

   Based on this information, the profit maximization objective function for a linear programming solution may be stated as:
   (a) Maximize $20Q + $17P.   (b) Maximize $12Q + $13P.
   (c) Maximize $3Q + $1P.   (d) Maximize $8Q + $4P.

6. *CPA Exam—November 1975*
   Patsy, Inc., manufactures two products, X and Y. Each product must be processed in each of three departments: machining, assembling, and finishing. The hours needed to produce one unit of product per department and the maximum possible hours per department follow:

Department	Production Hours per Unit X	Production Hours per Unit Y	Maximum Capacity in Hours
Machining	2	1	420
Assembling	2	2	500
Finishing	2	3	600

   Other restrictions follow:
   $X \geq 50$ $Y \geq 50$

   The objective function is to maximize profits where profit = $4X + $2Y.

Given the objective and constraints, what is the most profitable number of units of X and Y, respectively, to manufacture?
(a) 150 and 100   (b) 165 and 90
(c) 170 and 80   (d) 200 and 50

7. *CPA Exam—November 1979*
    Milford Company manufactures two models, medium and large. The contribution margin expected is $12 for the medium model and $20 for the large model. The medium model is processed 2 hours in the machining department and 4 hours in the polishing department. The large model is processed 3 hours in the machining department and 6 hours in the polishing department. How would the formula for determining the maximization of total contribution margin be expressed?
    (a) $5X + 10Y$ (b) $6X + 9Y$
    (c) $12X + 20Y$ (d) $12X(2 + 4) + 20Y(3 + 6)$

8. *CMA Exam—December 1979*
    The Elon Co. manufactures two industrial products—X-10 which sells for $90 a unit and Y-12 which sells for $85 a unit. Each product is processed through both of the company's manufacturing departments. The limited availability of labor, material and equipment capacity has restricted the ability of the firm to meet the demand for its products. The production department believes that linear programming can be used to routinize the production schedule for the two products.
    The following data are available to the production department:

	Amount Required per Unit	
	X-10	Y-12
Direct Material: Weekly supply is limited to 1800 pounds at $12.00 per pound	4 lb	2 lb
Direct Labor:		
Department 1—Weekly supply limited to 10 people at 40 hours each at an hourly cost of $6.00	$\frac{2}{3}$ hour	1 hour
Department 2—Weekly supply limited to 15 people at 40 hours each at an hourly rate of $8.00	$1\frac{1}{4}$ hours	1 hour
Machine Time:		
Department 1—Weekly capacity limited to 250 hours	$\frac{1}{2}$ hour	$\frac{1}{2}$ hour
Department 2—Weekly capacity limited to 300 hours	0 hours	1 hour

The overhead costs for Elon are accumulated on a plantwide basis. The overhead is assigned to products on the basis of the number of direct labor hours required to manufacture the product. This base is appropriate for overhead assignment because most of the variable overhead costs vary as a function of labor time. The estimated overhead cost per direct labor hour is:

Variable overhead cost	$ 6.00
Fixed overhead cost	6.00
Total overhead cost per direct labor hour	$12.00

The production department formulated the following equations for the linear programming statement of the problem:

$$A = \text{Number of units of X-10 to be produced}$$
$$B = \text{Number of units of Y-12 to be produced}$$

Objective function to minimize costs:

$$\text{Minimize} \quad Z = 85A + 62B$$

Constraints:

Material	$4A + 2B \leq 1800$ lb
Department 1 labor	$\frac{2}{3}A + 1B \leq 400$ hours
Department 2 labor	$1\frac{1}{4}A + 1B \leq 600$ hours
Nonnegativity	$A \geq 0 \qquad B \geq 0$

(a) The formulation of the linear programming equations as prepared by Elon Co.'s production department is incorrect. Explain what errors have been made in the formulation prepared by the production department.

(b) Formulate and label the proper equations for the linear programming statement of Elon Co.'s production problem.

(c) Explain how linear programming could help Elon Co. determine how large a change in the price of direct materials would have to be to change the optimum production mix of X-10 and Y-12.

Other Articles

Adams, F. Gerard, and James M. Griffin, "Economic Linear Programming Model of the U.S. Petroleum Refining Industry," *J. Amer. Stat. Assoc.* **67** (September 1972), pp. 542–551.

Allman, William P., "An Optimization Approach to Freight Car Allocation Under Time-Mileage Per Diem Rental Rates," *Manage. Sci.,* **18,** 10 (June 1972), pp. B567–B574.

Broaddus, A., "Linear Programming: A New Approach to Bank Portfolio Management," *Fed. Reserve Bank Richmond: Mon. Rev.,* **58,** 11 (November 1972), pp. 3–11.

Cohen, K. J., and F. S. Hammer, "Linear Programming and Optimal Bank Asset Management Decisions," *J. Finan.,* **22** (May 1967), pp. 147–165.

Crandall, Robert H., "A Constrained Choice Model for Student Housing," *Manage. Sci.,* **16,** 2 (October 1969), pp. B112–B120.

Hanssmann, Fred, and Sidney W. Hess, "A Linear Programming Approach to Production and Employment Scheduling," *Manage. Technol.,* **1** (January 1960), pp. 46–51.

Kohn, Robert E., "Application of Linear Programming to a Controversy on Air Pollution Control," *Manage. Sci.,* **17,** 10 (June 1971), pp. B609–B621.

Lee, Sang M., and Edward R. Clayton, "Goal Programming Model for Academic Resource Allocation," *Manage. Sci.,* **18,** 8 (April 1972), pp. B395–B408.

Loucks, Daniel P., Charles S. Revelle, and Walter R. Lynn, "Linear Programming Models for Water Pollution Control," *Manage. Sci.,* **14,** 4 (December 1967), pp. B166–B181.

Thomas, Harold A., Jr., and Roger Revelle, "On the Efficient Use of High Aswan Dam for Hydropower and Irrigation," *Manage. Sci.,* **12,** 8 (April 1966), pp. B296–B311.

Wardle, P. A., "Forest Management and Operations Research: A Linear Programming Study," *Manage. Sci.,* **11,** 10 (August 1965), pp. B260–B270.

4
Linear Programming Part II: The Simplex Method

*This section may be omitted without loss of continuity.

1. Introduction: Slack Variables and Simplex Tableaux

In Chapter 3 we described a geometrical method (using graphs) for solving linear programming problems. Unfortunately, this method is useful only when there are no more than two variables and the number of constraints is small.

If we have a large number of either variables or constraints, it is still true that the optimal solution will be found at a vertex of the set of feasible solutions. In fact, we could find these vertices by writing all the equations corresponding to the inequalities of the problem and then proceeding to solve all possible combinations of these equations. We would of course, have to discard any solutions that are not feasible (because they do not satisfy one or more of the constraints). Then we could evaluate the objective function at the remaining feasible solutions. After all this, we might discover that the problem has no optimal solution after all.

Just how difficult is this procedure? Well, if there were just 4 variables and 7 constraints, we would have to solve all possible combinations of 4 equations chosen from a set of 7 equations—that would be 35 solutions in all. Each of these solutions would then have to be tested for feasibility. So, even for this relatively small number of variables and constraints, the work would be quite tedious. In the real world of applications, it is fairly common to encounter problems with *hundreds* of variables and constraints. Of course, such problems must be solved by computer. Even so, choosing a more efficient problem-solving strategy than the geometrical method might reduce the computer's running time from hours to seconds, or from years to hours in the case of very large problems.

A more systematic approach would involve choosing a solution at one vertex of the feasible set, then moving from there to another vertex at which the objective function has a better value, and continuing in this way until the best possible value is found. One very efficient and popular way of doing this is the subject of the present chapter: the *simplex method*.

In order to apply the simplex method to a maximum problem, we begin with some preliminary steps:

1. **Write the problem in** *standard form.*
2. **Introduce** *slack variables.*
3. **Construct a matrix called the** *simplex tableau.*

Later, we will see how the optimal solution is obtained by applying a sequence of elementary row operations to this matrix.

We go back to Example 6 of Chapter 3 (page 136), where the problem is to maximize

$$P = 3x_1 + 4x_2$$

subject to the constraints

$$2x_1 + 4x_2 \leq 120 \qquad x_1 \geq 0$$
$$2x_1 + 2x_2 \leq 80 \qquad x_2 \geq 0$$

(As we shall see, this problem is in *standard form* for a maximum programming problem.) When we say that $2x_1 + 4x_2 \leq 120$, we mean that there is a number greater than or equal to 0, which we might as well call x_3, such that

$$2x_1 + 4x_2 + x_3 = 120$$

Slack Variable

This number x_3 is a variable. It must be nonnegative since it is the difference between 120 and a number that is less than or equal to 120. We call it a *slack variable* since it "takes up the slack" between the left and right sides of the inequality.

Similarly, when we say that $2x_1 + 2x_2 \leq 80$, we are saying that there is a slack variable x_4 such that

$$2x_1 + 2x_2 + x_4 = 80$$

Further, the objective function $P = 3x_1 + 4x_2$ can be rewritten as

$$-3x_1 - 4x_2 + P = 0$$

In effect, we have now replaced our original system of constraints and objective by a system of three equations in five unknowns:

$$
\begin{array}{llll}
2x_1 + 4x_2 + x_3 & & & = 120 \\
2x_1 + 2x_2 & + x_4 & & = 80 \\
-3x_1 - 4x_2 & & + P & = 0
\end{array}
$$

Here, it is understood that each of the five variables is to be nonnegative. To solve the maximum problem is to find the particular solution (x_1, x_2, x_3, x_4, P) that gives the largest possible value for P. The augmented matrix for this system is

$$
\begin{array}{ccccc}
x_1 & x_2 & x_3 & x_4 & P \\
\end{array}
$$
$$
\left[\begin{array}{ccccc|c}
2 & 4 & 1 & 0 & 0 & 120 \\
2 & 2 & 0 & 1 & 0 & 80 \\
-3 & -4 & 0 & 0 & 1 & 0
\end{array} \right]
$$

This augmented matrix is called the *initial simplex tableau* for the problem. Notice that we have written the name of each variable, $x_1, x_2, \ldots$, etc., above the column in which its coefficients appear.

So far, we have seen this much of the simplex method:

1. Each of the constraints, with the exception of the nonnegativity conditions $(x_1 \geq 0, x_2 \geq 0,$ etc.$)$, is written with a $\leq$ symbol. This is known as the *standard form* for maximum problems. (The standard form for a *minimum* problem will be described later.)
2. The constraints are changed from inequalities to equations by the introduction of extra variables—one for each constraint and all nonnegative—called *slack variables*.

Initial Simplex
Tableau

3. These equations, together with one which describes the objective function, are placed in an augmented matrix called the *initial simplex tableau*. All entries in the last column are required to be nonnegative.

Example 1   The constraints of the following maximum linear programming problem are in standard form. Convert the inequalities into equations by introducing slack variables. Set up the initial simplex tableau using the objective function

$$P = 3x_1 + 2x_2 + x_3$$

$$
\begin{array}{ll}
3x_1 + x_2 + x_3 \le 30 & \qquad x_1 \ge 0 \\
5x_1 + 2x_2 + x_3 \le 24 & \qquad x_2 \ge 0 \\
x_1 + x_2 + 4x_3 \le 20 & \qquad x_3 \ge 0
\end{array}
$$

Solution   For each constraint we introduce a nonnegative slack variable to obtain the following equations:

$$
\begin{array}{llll}
3x_1 + x_2 + x_3 + x_4 = 30 & \quad x_1 \ge 0 & \quad x_4 \ge 0 \\
5x_1 + 2x_2 + x_3 + x_5 = 24 & \quad x_2 \ge 0 & \quad x_5 \ge 0 \\
x_1 + x_2 + 4x_3 + x_6 = 20 & \quad x_3 \ge 0 & \quad x_6 \ge 0
\end{array}
$$

These equations, together with the objective function P, give the initial simplex tableau:

$$
\begin{array}{ccccccc}
x_1 & x_2 & x_3 & x_4 & x_5 & x_6 & P \\
\end{array}
$$

$$
\left[
\begin{array}{ccccccc|c}
3 & 1 & 1 & 1 & 0 & 0 & 0 & 30 \\
5 & 2 & 1 & 0 & 1 & 0 & 0 & 24 \\
1 & 1 & 4 & 0 & 0 & 1 & 0 & 20 \\
-3 & -2 & -1 & 0 & 0 & 0 & 1 & 0
\end{array}
\right]
$$

Exceptional Cases

In the definition of standard form, note that, in this chapter, we also require that all the entries in the last column of the initial simplex tableau be nonnegative. Thus, each of the original constraints must be of the form

$$a_1x_1 + a_2x_2 + \cdots + a_mx_m \le b$$

where b is a nonnegative constant (except, of course, for the constraints on the variables themselves: $x_1 \ge 0$, $x_2 \ge 0, \ldots$).

In practical applications, it is frequently not possible to impose all these conditions. For example, some of the variables may represent quantities that must be allowed to become negative, some of the constraints may have to be equations rather than inequalities, or some of the constants may be negative. We will not attempt to cover these exceptional cases. However, there are techniques for dealing with them, and these may be found in the references at the end of the chapter.

In the next section we give a general description of a matrix operation called *pivoting*. After that, we will discuss *pivoting strategy* as part of the simplex technique; this is the method by which a problem solver (either while doing the problem by hand or in writing the code for a computer solution) decides which pivot operations to use.

Exercise 1
Solutions to Odd-Numbered Problems begin on page 578.

The constraints of each of the following maximum linear programming problems are in standard form. Convert the inequalities into equations by introducing slack variables. Set up the initial simplex tableau using the given objective function.

1. $5x_1 + 2x_2 + x_3 \leq 20$
    $6x_1 + x_2 + 4x_3 \leq 24$
    $x_1 + x_2 + 4x_3 \leq 16$
    $x_1 \geq 0, \quad x_2 \geq 0, \quad x_3 \geq 0$
    $P = 2x_1 + x_2 + 3x_3$

2. $3x_1 + 2x_2 - x_3 \leq 10$
    $x_1 - x_2 + 3x_3 \leq 12$
    $2x_1 + x_2 + x_3 \leq 6$
    $x_1 \geq 0, \quad x_2 \geq 0, \quad x_3 \geq 0$
    $P = 3x_1 + 2x_2 + x_3$

3. $2.2x_1 - 1.8x_2 \leq 5$
    $0.8x_1 + 1.2x_2 \leq 2.5$
    $x_1 + x_2 \leq 0.1$
    $x_1 \geq 0, \quad x_2 \geq 0$
    $P = 3x_1 + 5x_2$

4. $1.2x_1 - 2.1x_2 \leq 0.5$
    $0.3x_1 + 0.4x_2 \leq 1.5$
    $x_1 + x_2 \leq 0.7$
    $x_1 \geq 0, \quad x_2 \geq 0$
    $P = 2x_1 + 3x_2$

5. $x_1 + x_2 + x_3 \leq 50$
    $3x_1 + 2x_2 + x_3 \leq 10$
    $x_1 \geq 0, \quad x_2 \geq 0, \quad x_3 \geq 0$
    $P = 2x_1 + 3x_2 + x_3$

6. $3x_1 + x_2 + x_3 \leq 10$
    $x_1 + x_2 + 3x_3 \leq 5$
    $x_1 \geq 0, \quad x_2 \geq 0, \quad x_3 \geq 0$
    $P = x_1 + 4x_2 + 2x_3$

7. $3x_1 + x_2 + 4x_3 \leq 5$
    $x_1 + x_2 \leq 5$
    $2x_1 - x_2 + x_3 \leq 6$
    $x_1 \geq 0, \quad x_2 \geq 0, \quad x_3 \geq 0$
    $P = 3x_1 + 4x_2 + 2x_3$

8. $2x_1 + x_2 + x_3 \leq 2$
    $x_1 - x_2 \leq 4$
    $2x_1 + x_2 - x_3 \leq 5$
    $x_1 \geq 0, \quad x_2 \geq 0, \quad x_3 \geq 0$
    $P = 2x_1 + x_2 + 3x_3$

2. The Pivot Operation

Before going any further in our discussion of the simplex method, we need to discuss the matrix operation known as *pivoting*. The first thing one does in a pivot operation is to choose a *pivot element*. However, in the present section, the pivot element will be specified in advance; the method of selecting pivot elements in the simplex tableau will be shown in a later section.

Pivoting   To *pivot* a matrix about a given element—called the *pivot element*—is to apply row operations so that the pivot element is replaced by a 1 and all other entries in the same column—called the *pivot column*—become 0's.
     The correct sequence of steps is:
STEP 1:   **In the *pivot row* (where the pivot element appears), divide each entry by the *pivot element* (we assume it is not 0).**
STEP 2:   **Obtain 0's elsewhere in the *pivot column* by performing row operations.**

The following example illustrates a pivot operation.

Example 1 Perform a pivot operation on the matrix given below, where the pivot element is circled, and the pivot row and pivot column are marked by arrows:

$$\rightarrow \begin{bmatrix} \begin{array}{ccccc|c} x_1 & x_2 & x_3 & x_4 & P & \\ 2 & ④ & 1 & 0 & 0 & 120 \\ 2 & 2 & 0 & 1 & 0 & 80 \\ -3 & -4 & 0 & 0 & 1 & 0 \end{array} \end{bmatrix}$$
$$\uparrow$$

(You should recognize this matrix as the initial simplex tableau displayed in the previous section.)

Solution Observe that the entries in columns x_3, x_4, and P form an identity matrix (I_3, to be exact). This makes it easy to solve for x_3, x_4, and P, using the other variables as parameters:

$$
\begin{array}{llll}
2x_1 + 4x_2 + x_3 & = 120 & \text{or} & x_3 = 120 - 2x_1 - 4x_2 \\
2x_1 + 2x_2 + x_4 & = 80 & \text{or} & x_4 = 80 - 2x_1 - 2x_2 \\
-3x_1 - 4x_2 + P & = 0 & \text{or} & P = 3x_1 + 4x_2
\end{array}
$$

For additional emphasis, we write x_3, x_4, and P to the right of the corresponding rows of the tableau as follows:

$$\rightarrow \begin{bmatrix} \begin{array}{ccccc|c} x_1 & x_2 & x_3 & x_4 & P & \\ 2 & ④ & 1 & 0 & 0 & 120 \\ 2 & 2 & 0 & 1 & 0 & 80 \\ -3 & -4 & 0 & 0 & 1 & 0 \end{array} \end{bmatrix} \begin{array}{c} x_3 \\ x_4 \\ P \end{array}$$
$$\uparrow$$

In this matrix, the pivot column is column 2 and the pivot row is row 1. Step 1 of the pivoting procedure tells us to divide row 1 by 4:

$$\begin{bmatrix} \begin{array}{ccccc|c} x_1 & x_2 & x_3 & x_4 & P & \\ \frac{1}{2} & ① & \frac{1}{4} & 0 & 0 & 30 \\ 2 & 2 & 0 & 1 & 0 & 80 \\ -3 & -4 & 0 & 0 & 1 & 0 \end{array} \end{bmatrix}$$

Now, to accomplish Step 2, we multiply row 1 by -2 and add it to row 2; in addition, we multiply row 1 by 4 and add it to row 3. The row operations specified are

$$R_2 = -2r_1 + r_2 \qquad R_3 = 4r_1 + r_3$$

The new matrix looks like this:

$$
\begin{array}{ccccc}
x_1 & x_2 & x_3 & x_4 & P \\
\end{array}
$$

$$
\left[
\begin{array}{ccccc|c}
\frac{1}{2} & \boxed{1} & \frac{1}{4} & 0 & 0 & 30 \\
1 & 0 & -\frac{1}{2} & 1 & 0 & 20 \\
-1 & 0 & 1 & 0 & 1 & 120
\end{array}
\right]
\begin{array}{c}
x_2 \\
x_4 \\
P
\end{array}
$$

This completes the pivot operation, since the pivot column has been replaced by

$$
\begin{array}{c}
1 \\
0 \\
0
\end{array}
$$

Notice that in the above example the identity matrix I_3 now appears in columns 2, 4, and 5, which helps us solve for x_2, x_4, and P in terms of x_1 and x_3:

$$
x_2 = 30 - \tfrac{1}{2}x_1 - \tfrac{1}{4}x_3
$$
$$
x_4 = 20 - x_1 + \tfrac{1}{2}x_3
$$
$$
P = 120 + x_1 - x_3
$$

This may be indicated by writing x_2, x_4, and P to the right of the tableau, as shown above.

Example 2 Perform another pivot operation on

$$
\begin{array}{ccccc}
x_1 & x_2 & x_3 & x_4 & P \\
\end{array}
$$

$$
\rightarrow
\left[
\begin{array}{ccccc|c}
\frac{1}{2} & 1 & \frac{1}{4} & 0 & 0 & 30 \\
\boxed{1} & 0 & -\frac{1}{2} & 1 & 0 & 20 \\
-1 & 0 & 1 & 0 & 1 & 120
\end{array}
\right]
\begin{array}{c}
x_2 \\
x_4 \\
P
\end{array}
$$

$$
\uparrow
$$

where the new pivot element has been circled.

Solution Since the pivot element happens to be a 1 in this case, we skip Step 1. For Step 2, we perform the row operation

$$
R_1 = -\tfrac{1}{2}r_2 + r_1 \qquad R_3 = r_2 + r_3
$$

The result is

$$
\begin{array}{ccccc}
x_1 & x_2 & x_3 & x_4 & P \\
\end{array}
$$

$$
\left[
\begin{array}{ccccc|c}
0 & 1 & \frac{1}{2} & -\frac{1}{2} & 0 & 20 \\
1 & 0 & -\frac{1}{2} & 1 & 0 & 20 \\
0 & 0 & \frac{1}{2} & 1 & 1 & 140
\end{array}
\right]
\begin{array}{c}
x_2 \\
x_1 \\
P
\end{array}
$$

The pivot operation is complete.

Notice that in Example 2 the identity matrix I_3 now appears in columns 1, 2, and 5—with shifted columns, as

$$
\begin{array}{ccc}
0 & 1 & 0 \\
1 & 0 & 0 \\
0 & 0 & 1
\end{array}
$$

We may now solve for x_2, x_1, and P in terms of x_3 and x_4, as indicated on the right of the matrix.

Exercise 2
Solutions to Odd-Numbered Problems begin on page 579.

In Problems 1–5 perform a pivot operation on each augmented matrix. Write the original system of equations and the final system of equations. The pivot element is circled.

1. $x_1\ x_2\ x_3\ x_4$

$$
\begin{bmatrix}
1 & ②& 1 & 0 & \bigm| & 300 \\
3 & 2 & 0 & 1 & \bigm| & 480
\end{bmatrix}
\begin{matrix}
x_3 \\
x_4
\end{matrix}
$$

2. $x_1\ x_2\ x_3\ x_4$

$$
\begin{bmatrix}
1 & 4 & 1 & 0 & \bigm| & 100 \\
2 & ⑤& 0 & 1 & \bigm| & 50
\end{bmatrix}
\begin{matrix}
x_3 \\
x_4
\end{matrix}
$$

3. $x_1\quad x_2\qquad x_3\quad x_4\quad x_5\quad x_6$

$$
\begin{bmatrix}
1 & 2 & 4 & 1 & 0 & 0 & \bigm| & 24 \\
2 & -1 & 1 & 0 & 1 & 0 & \bigm| & 32 \\
3 & ② & 4 & 0 & 0 & 1 & \bigm| & 18
\end{bmatrix}
\begin{matrix}
x_4 \\
x_5 \\
x_6
\end{matrix}
$$

4. $x_1\quad x_2\qquad x_3\quad x_4\quad x_5\quad x_6$

$$
\begin{bmatrix}
1 & ② & 1 & 1 & 0 & 0 & \bigm| & 6 \\
2 & 3 & 1 & 0 & 1 & 0 & \bigm| & 12 \\
1 & -2 & 3 & 0 & 0 & 1 & \bigm| & 0
\end{bmatrix}
\begin{matrix}
x_4 \\
x_5 \\
x_6
\end{matrix}
$$

5. $x_1\quad x_2\quad x_3\quad x_4\quad x_5\quad x_6\quad x_7\quad x_8$

$$
\begin{bmatrix}
-3 & 0 & 1 & 0 & 1 & 0 & 0 & 0 & \bigm| & 20 \\
② & 0 & 0 & 1 & 0 & 1 & 0 & 0 & \bigm| & 24 \\
0 & -3 & 1 & 0 & 0 & 0 & 1 & 0 & \bigm| & 28 \\
0 & -3 & 0 & 1 & 0 & 0 & 0 & 1 & \bigm| & 24
\end{bmatrix}
\begin{matrix}
x_5 \\
x_6 \\
x_7 \\
x_8
\end{matrix}
$$

---

3.   The Simplex Method: Maximization

We are finally ready to state the details of the simplex method for solving a maximum problem in linear programming. This method requires that the problem be in standard form as defined in Section 1, and that the conditions of the problem be placed in an initial simplex tableau with slack variables. We will also require that the constraint column of the tableau contain only nonnegative numbers (although, in general, this requirement may be relaxed by using one of the extensions to the standard simplex method, as detailed in the references at the end of the chapter).

First, let's review the example we used in Sections 1 and 2.

Maximize $P = 3x_1 + 4x_2$ subject to

$$2x_1 + 4x_2 + x_3 \qquad = 120 \qquad x_1 \geq 0 \qquad x_3 \geq 0$$
$$2x_1 + 2x_2 \qquad + x_4 = 80 \qquad x_2 \geq 0 \qquad x_4 \geq 0$$

The initial simplex tableau is

$$
\begin{array}{cccccc}
 & x_1 & x_2 & x_3 & x_4 & P & \\
\left[\begin{array}{ccccc|c}
2 & 4 & 1 & 0 & 0 & 120 \\
2 & 2 & 0 & 1 & 0 & 80 \\
\hline
-3 & -4 & 0 & 0 & 1 & 0
\end{array}\right] & \begin{array}{c} x_3 \\ x_4 \\ P \end{array}
\end{array}
$$

Notice that the bottom row contains the negatives of the coefficients in the objective function and that we have set this row off from the rest of the matrix by a dashed line.

From this point on, the simplex method consists of pivoting from one tableau to another until the optimal solution is found. Two questions remain to be answered:

1. How is the pivot element selected?
2. When does the process end?

<table>
<tr><td>Pivoting
Strategy</td><td>**Pivoting Strategy** **The** *pivoting strategy* **for the simplex method is given by the following rules:**</td></tr>
<tr><td>Pivot Column</td><td>RULE 1: **The** *pivot column* **is selected by locating the smallest negative (i.e., the most negative) entry in the objective row.**</td></tr>
<tr><td>Pivot Row</td><td>RULE 2: **Divide each entry in the last column by the corresponding entry (from the same row) in the pivot column. (Ignore any rows in which the pivot column entry is less than or equal to 0.) The row in which the smallest nonnegative ratio is obtained is the** *pivot row.*</td></tr>
</table>

The *pivot element* **is the entry at the intersection of the pivot row and the pivot column.**

Note that the pivot element is never in the objective row.

In the example we have been using, we select 4 as the pivot element because -4 is the most negative entry in the last row and $120 \div 4 = 30$ is the smallest positive ratio obtainable by dividing an entry in the last column by the corresponding entry in column 2.

$$
\begin{array}{cccccc}
 & x_1 & x_2 & x_3 & x_4 & P & \\
\rightarrow \left[\begin{array}{ccccc|c}
2 & \boxed{4} & 1 & 0 & 0 & 120 \\
2 & 2 & 0 & 1 & 0 & 80 \\
\hline
-3 & -4 & 0 & 0 & 1 & 0
\end{array}\right] & \begin{array}{c} 120 \div 4 = 30 \\ 80 \div 2 = 40 \\ \; \end{array}
\end{array}
$$

$\uparrow$

Now, the reason we choose the most negative entry in the objective row is that it is the negative of the *largest* coefficient in the objective function:

$$P = 3x_1 + 4x_2$$

If we were to set $x_1 = x_2 = 0$, we would obtain $P = 0$ as a first approximation for the profit P. Of course, this is not a very good approximation; it can easily be improved by increasing either x_1 or x_2. But the profit per unit of x_2 is \$4, while the profit per unit of x_1 is only \$3. Thus, it is more effective to increase x_2 than x_1. But what is the largest amount by which x_2 can be increased?

We can answer this question by performing the pivot operation, as we already have in Example 1, Section 2. The matrix becomes

$$
\begin{array}{c}
\begin{array}{ccccccc} x_1 & x_2 & x_3 & x_4 & P & & \end{array} \\
\left[
\begin{array}{ccccc|c}
\frac{1}{2} & \boxed{1} & \frac{1}{4} & 0 & 0 & 30 \\
\hline
1 & 0 & -\frac{1}{2} & 1 & 0 & 20 \\
\hline
-1 & 0 & 1 & 0 & 1 & 120
\end{array}
\right]
\begin{array}{c} x_2 \\ \\ x_4 \\ \\ P \end{array}
\end{array}
$$

and the corresponding equations are

$$
\begin{aligned}
x_2 &= 30 - \tfrac{1}{2}x_1 - \tfrac{1}{4}x_3 \\
x_4 &= 20 - x_1 + \tfrac{1}{2}x_3 \\
P &= 120 + x_1 - x_3
\end{aligned}
$$

This suggests that x_2 can be as large as 30, if we take both x_1 and x_3 to be 0, in which case P will be 120.

So we chose column 2 because we wanted to increase x_2. But why did we choose row 1, rather than row 2, as the pivot row? Let's see what would have happened if we had chosen row 2 as the pivot row. The result would have been

$$
\begin{array}{c}
\begin{array}{ccccc} x_1 & x_2 & x_3 & x_4 & P \end{array} \\
\left[
\begin{array}{ccccc|c}
-2 & 0 & 1 & -2 & 0 & -40 \\
\hline
1 & 1 & 0 & \frac{1}{2} & 0 & 40 \\
\hline
1 & 0 & 0 & 2 & 1 & 160
\end{array}
\right]
\begin{array}{c} x_3 \\ \\ x_2 \\ \\ \end{array}
\end{array}
$$

But this is not acceptable because of the negative number in the last column. (In effect, this matrix tells us that we could get P to be as large as 160, by setting $x_1 = 0$, $x_2 = 40$, and $x_3 = -40$; but this is not a feasible solution because x_3 is supposed to be greater than or equal to 0.)

The reason we get a feasible solution if we choose row 1 to pivot, and an apparent but false solution if we choose row 2, is because the row ratio $(120 \div 4)$ for row 1 is smaller (hence, better) than the row ratio $(80 \div 2)$ for row 2.

So, the reasoning behind the simplex method is fairly complicated, but the process of "moving to a better solution" is made quite easy simply by following the rules. Briefly, the pivoting strategy works like this:

Rule 1 forces us to pivot the variable that will most effectively improve the value of the objective function.

Rule 2 prevents us from making this variable *too large* to be feasible.

Continuing the pivoting procedure on the current version of the simplex tableau we have been discussing, we see that the smallest (in fact, only) negative entry in the objective row is the -1 in column 1. We check the row ratios in the last column:

$$
\rightarrow
\begin{array}{ccccc}
x_1 & x_2 & x_3 & x_4 & P \\
\end{array}
$$

$$
\rightarrow
\left[
\begin{array}{ccccc|c}
\frac{1}{2} & 1 & \frac{1}{4} & 0 & 0 & 30 \\
\textcircled{1} & 0 & -\frac{1}{2} & 1 & 0 & 20 \\
\hline
-1 & 0 & 1 & 0 & 1 & 120
\end{array}
\right]
\begin{array}{l}
30 \div \frac{1}{2} = 60 \\
20 \div 1 = 20 \\
\end{array}
$$

Rule 2 tells us to select the pivot element in row 2. After pivoting (as in Example 2, Section 2), we have

$$
\begin{array}{ccccc}
x_1 & x_2 & x_3 & x_4 & P \\
\end{array}
$$

$$
\left[
\begin{array}{ccccc|c}
0 & 1 & \frac{1}{2} & -\frac{1}{2} & 0 & 20 \\
1 & 0 & -\frac{1}{2} & 1 & 0 & 20 \\
\hline
0 & 0 & \frac{1}{2} & 1 & 1 & 140
\end{array}
\right]
\begin{array}{l}
x_2 \\
x_1 \\
P
\end{array}
$$

Now there are no negative entries in the objective row. Thus, the rules imply that no further pivots can be performed. But this is not surprising because the problem is now solved. In fact, the equation for the objective function is now

$$P = 140 - \tfrac{1}{2}x_3 - x_4$$

The largest possible value for P is 140, which occurs when $x_3 = 0$ and $x_4 = 0$. If we write the equations from the first and second rows, substituting 0 for x_3 and x_4, we have

$$x_2 = 20 - \tfrac{1}{2}x_3 + \tfrac{1}{2}x_4 = 20$$
$$x_1 = 20 + \tfrac{1}{2}x_3 - x_4 = 20$$

In other words, we have found the optimal solution,

$$P = 140 \quad \text{Maximum}$$

which occurs at

$$x_1 = 20 \qquad x_2 = 20$$

This same solution was found earlier in Chapter 3 (page 136) by the geometrical method.

The following should be noted:

1. The column corresponding to the objective function never changes; it is always

$$
\begin{bmatrix}
0 \\
0 \\
\vdots \\
1
\end{bmatrix}
$$

Thus, it is often omitted from the simplex tableau.

2. The columns corresponding to variables that are set equal to 0 (namely, the columns with positive numbers at the bottom) can be deleted from the final

tableau before solving for the other variables. Our final solution for the current problem might therefore appear as

$$
\begin{array}{cc}
x_1 & x_2 \\
\end{array}
$$

$$
\begin{bmatrix}
0 & 1 & 20 \\
1 & 0 & 20 \\
0 & 0 & 140
\end{bmatrix}
\begin{array}{l}
x_2 = 20 \\
x_1 = 20 \\
P = 140
\end{array}
$$

$$(x_3 = x_4 = 0)$$

The column for P has been omitted and the columns for x_3 and x_4 have been deleted.

3. In the current problem, it conveniently turned out that the variables set equal to 0 at the end were the slack variables; they did not appear in the original standard form of the problem and so they could be ignored. You should not always expect this to happen (as the example below illustrates).

Unlike the example above, Example 1 is too complex to be solved by the geometrical method. You will now see how effective the simplex method is in dealing with such problems.

Example 1   Maximize

$$P = 6x_1 + 8x_2 + x_3$$

subject to

$$
\begin{array}{ll}
3x_1 + 5x_2 + 3x_3 \le 20 & x_1 \ge 0 \\
x_1 + 3x_2 + 2x_3 \le 9 & x_2 \ge 0 \\
6x_1 + 2x_2 + 5x_3 \le 30 & x_3 \ge 0
\end{array}
$$

Solution   Note that the problem is in standard form, and the constants 20, 9, and 30 are all greater than or equal to 0. Introducing slack variables x_4, x_5, and x_6, the system becomes

(1)
$$
\begin{array}{lll}
3x_1 + 5x_2 + 3x_3 + x_4 = 20 & x_1 \ge 0 & x_4 \ge 0 \\
x_1 + 3x_2 + 2x_3 + x_5 = 9 & x_2 \ge 0 & x_5 \ge 0 \\
6x_1 + 2x_2 + 5x_3 + x_6 = 30 & x_3 \ge 0 & x_6 \ge 0 \\
-6x_1 - 8x_2 - x_3 + P = 0 &
\end{array}
$$

The pivot column is found by locating the column containing the smallest entry in the last row (-8 in column 2).

The pivot row is obtained by dividing each entry in the last column by the corresponding entry in the pivot column and selecting the smallest nonnegative ratio. Thus, the second row is the pivot row and the pivot element in that row is the circled element 3. The initial simplex tableau is

$$
\begin{array}{ccccccc}
x_1 & x_2 & x_3 & x_4 & x_5 & x_6 & P \\
\end{array}
$$

$$
\begin{bmatrix}
3 & 5 & 3 & 1 & 0 & 0 & 0 & 20 \\
1 & ③ & 2 & 0 & 1 & 0 & 0 & 9 \\
6 & 2 & 5 & 0 & 0 & 1 & 0 & 30 \\
-6 & -8 & -1 & 0 & 0 & 0 & 1 & 0
\end{bmatrix}
\begin{array}{l}
20 \div 5 = 4 \\
9 \div 3 = 3 \\
30 \div 2 = 15
\end{array}
$$

(From now on, we will omit the column for P.)

After pivoting, the new tableau is

$$\rightarrow \begin{bmatrix} \boxed{\frac{4}{3}} & 0 & -\frac{1}{3} & 1 & -\frac{5}{3} & 0 & 5 \\ \frac{1}{3} & 1 & \frac{2}{3} & 0 & \frac{1}{3} & 0 & 3 \\ \frac{16}{3} & 0 & \frac{11}{3} & 0 & -\frac{2}{3} & 1 & 24 \\ \hline -\frac{10}{3} & 0 & \frac{13}{3} & 0 & \frac{8}{3} & 0 & 24 \end{bmatrix} \quad \begin{matrix} 5 \div \frac{4}{3} = 3.75 \\ 3 \div \frac{1}{3} = 9 \\ 24 \div \frac{16}{3} = 4.5 \\ \\ \end{matrix}$$

By the same procedure as before, we determine the next pivot element to be $\frac{4}{3}$, in the upper left corner. After pivoting, we get

$$\rightarrow \begin{bmatrix} 1 & 0 & -\frac{1}{4} & \frac{3}{4} & -\frac{5}{4} & 0 & \frac{15}{4} \\ 0 & 1 & \frac{3}{4} & -\frac{1}{4} & \frac{3}{4} & 0 & \frac{7}{4} \\ 0 & 0 & 5 & -4 & \boxed{6} & 1 & 4 \\ \hline 0 & 0 & \frac{7}{2} & \frac{5}{2} & -\frac{3}{2} & 0 & \frac{73}{2} \end{bmatrix}$$

Since we still observe a negative entry in the last row, we pivot again. (Remember that we ignore rows in which the pivot column contains a negative number—in this case, $-\frac{5}{4}$.) The new tableau is

$$\begin{bmatrix} 1 & 0 & \frac{19}{24} & -\frac{1}{12} & 0 & \frac{5}{24} & \frac{55}{12} \\ 0 & 1 & \frac{1}{8} & \frac{1}{4} & 0 & -\frac{1}{8} & \frac{5}{4} \\ 0 & 0 & \frac{5}{6} & -\frac{2}{3} & 1 & \frac{1}{6} & \frac{2}{3} \\ \hline 0 & 0 & \frac{19}{4} & \frac{3}{2} & 0 & \frac{1}{4} & \frac{75}{2} \end{bmatrix} \begin{matrix} x_1 \\ x_2 \\ x_5 \\ P \end{matrix}$$

This is a final tableau; the last column says that

$$P = \tfrac{75}{2} \qquad x_1 = \tfrac{55}{12} \qquad x_2 = \tfrac{5}{4} \qquad x_3 = 0$$

We see that $x_3 = 0$, because its column contains a number greater than 0 in the last row. We also see that $x_4 = 0$, $x_5 = \frac{2}{3}$, and $x_6 = 0$. These values can be used to check that these are, in fact, solutions of the system of equations (1). ■

Conclusion

So far in our discussion, it has always been possible to continue to choose pivot elements until the problem has been solved. But it may turn out that all the entries in a column of a tableau are 0 or negative at some stage. If this happens, it means that the problem is *unbounded* and a maximum solution does not exist.

For example, consider the tableau

$$\begin{bmatrix} -1 & 1 & 1 & 0 & 2 \\ 1 & -1 & 0 & 1 & 2 \\ \hline -1 & -1 & 0 & 0 & 0 \end{bmatrix}$$

When there are two equal smallest negative entries in the last row, you may choose either column as the pivot column. Suppose we arbitrarily choose column 1 to pivot, and the tableau becomes

$$\left[\begin{array}{cccc|c} 0 & 0 & 1 & 1 & 4 \\ 1 & -1 & 0 & 1 & 2 \\ \hline 0 & -2 & 0 & 1 & 2 \end{array}\right]$$

Now the only negative entry in the last row is in column 2, and it is impossible to choose a pivot element in that column. This implies that the objective function is unbounded. Indeed, it is easy to see that if the only constraints are $-x_1 + x_2 \leq 2$, $x_2 - x_1 \leq 2$, $x_1 \geq 0$, and $x_2 \geq 0$, then $P = x_1 + x_2$ has no maximum.

The flowchart in Figure 1 illustrates the steps to be used in solving maximum linear programming problems. As this flowchart implies, in this book we do not attempt to deal with every possible situation that can occur in real-life applications. In practice, it is often impossible to avoid the difficulties that arise when a problem cannot be placed in the special form discussed in this chapter. An important example is the phenomenon of *cycling*, in which a pivot operation results in a tableau that has already appeared in a previous step. This type of situation can be resolved only by special techniques not covered in this book.

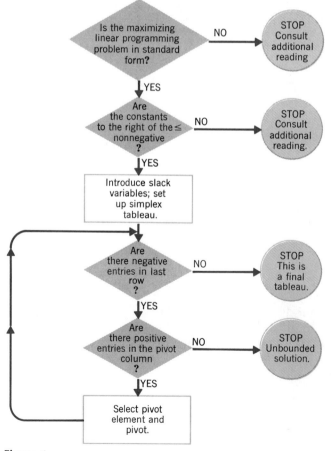

Figure 1

Exercise 3
Solutions to Odd-Numbered Problems begin on page 579.

In Problems 1–6 determine which of the following statements is true about each tableau:

(a) It is the final tableau.

(b) It requires additional pivoting.

(c) It indicates no solution to the problem.

If the answer is (a), write down the solution; if the answer is (b), indicate the pivot element.

1.
$$
\begin{array}{cccc}
x_1 & x_2 & x_3 & x_4 \\
\end{array}
$$
$$
\left[
\begin{array}{cccc|c}
1 & 0 & 1 & -\frac{1}{2} & 20 \\
\frac{1}{2} & 1 & 0 & \frac{1}{4} & 30 \\
\hline
-1 & 0 & 0 & 1 & 120
\end{array}
\right]
\begin{array}{c}
x_3 \\
x_2 \\
\\
\end{array}
$$

2.
$$
\begin{array}{cccc}
x_1 & x_2 & x_3 & x_4 \\
\end{array}
$$
$$
\left[
\begin{array}{cccc|c}
1 & 0 & 1 & -\frac{1}{2} & 20 \\
0 & 1 & -\frac{1}{2} & \frac{1}{2} & 20 \\
\hline
0 & 0 & 1 & \frac{1}{2} & 140
\end{array}
\right]
\begin{array}{c}
x_1 \\
x_2 \\
\\
\end{array}
$$

3.
$$
\begin{array}{cccc}
x_1 & x_2 & x_3 & x_4 \\
\end{array}
$$
$$
\left[
\begin{array}{cccc|c}
0 & \frac{1}{14} & 1 & -\frac{1}{7} & \frac{186}{21} \\
1 & \frac{12}{7} & 0 & \frac{4}{7} & \frac{32}{7} \\
\hline
0 & \frac{12}{7} & 0 & \frac{32}{7} & \frac{256}{7}
\end{array}
\right]
\begin{array}{c}
x_3 \\
x_1 \\
\\
\end{array}
$$

4.
$$
\begin{array}{cccc}
x_1 & x_2 & x_3 & x_4 \\
\end{array}
$$
$$
\left[
\begin{array}{cccc|c}
\frac{1}{4} & \frac{1}{2} & 1 & 0 & 10 \\
\frac{7}{4} & 3 & 0 & 1 & 8 \\
\hline
-8 & -12 & 0 & 0 & 0
\end{array}
\right]
\begin{array}{c}
x_3 \\
x_4 \\
\\
\end{array}
$$

5.
$$
\begin{array}{cccc}
x_1 & x_2 & x_3 & x_4 \\
\end{array}
$$
$$
\left[
\begin{array}{cccc|c}
1 & -2 & 0 & 4 & 24 \\
0 & -2 & 1 & 4 & 36 \\
\hline
5 & -10 & 12 & 4 & 20
\end{array}
\right]
\begin{array}{c}
x_1 \\
x_3 \\
\\
\end{array}
$$

6.
$$
\begin{array}{cccc}
x_1 & x_2 & x_3 & x_4 \\
\end{array}
$$
$$
\left[
\begin{array}{cccc|c}
1 & 3 & 1 & 0 & 30 \\
2 & 1 & 0 & 1 & 12 \\
\hline
-2 & -5 & 0 & 0 & 0
\end{array}
\right]
\begin{array}{c}
x_3 \\
x_4 \\
\\
\end{array}
$$

In Problems 7–17 use the simplex method to solve each maximum linear programming problem.

7. Maximize
$$
P = 5x_1 + 7x_2
$$

subject to
$$
\begin{array}{ll}
2x_1 + 3x_2 \le 12 & x_1 \ge 0 \\
3x_1 + x_2 \le 12 & x_2 \ge 0
\end{array}
$$

8. Maximize

$$P = x_1 + 5x_2$$

subject to

$$2x_1 + x_2 \leq 10 \qquad x_1 \geq 0$$
$$x_1 + 2x_2 \leq 10 \qquad x_2 \geq 0$$

9. Maximize

$$P = 5x_1 + 7x_2$$

subject to

$$x_1 + 2x_2 \leq 2 \qquad x_1 \geq 0$$
$$2x_1 + x_2 \leq 2 \qquad x_2 \geq 0$$

10. Maximize

$$P = 5x_1 + 4x_2$$

subject to

$$x_1 + x_2 \leq 2 \qquad x_1 \geq 0$$
$$2x_1 + 3x_2 \leq 6 \qquad x_2 \geq 0$$

11. Maximize

$$P = 3x_1 + x_2$$

subject to

$$x_1 + x_2 \leq 2 \qquad x_1 \geq 0$$
$$2x_1 + 3x_2 \leq 12 \qquad x_2 \geq 0$$
$$3x_1 + x_2 \leq 12$$

12. Maximize

$$P = 3x_1 + 5x_2$$

subject to

$$2x_1 + x_2 \leq 4 \qquad x_1 \geq 0$$
$$x_1 + 2x_2 \leq 6 \qquad x_2 \geq 0$$

13. Maximize

$$P = 2x_1 + x_2 + x_3$$

subject to

$$-2x_1 + x_2 - 2x_3 \leq 4 \qquad x_1 \geq 0$$
$$x_1 - 2x_2 + x_3 \leq 2 \qquad x_2 \geq 0$$
$$x_3 \geq 0$$

14. Maximize

$$P = 4x_1 + 2x_2 + 5x_3$$

subject to

$$x_1 + 3x_2 + 2x_3 \leq 30 \qquad x_1 \geq 0$$
$$2x_1 + x_2 + 3x_3 \leq 12 \qquad x_2 \geq 0$$
$$x_3 \geq 0$$

15. Maximize

$$P = 2x_1 + x_2 + 3x_3$$

subject to

$$x_1 + 2x_2 + x_3 \leq 25 \qquad x_1 \geq 0$$
$$3x_1 + 2x_2 + 3x_3 \leq 30 \qquad x_2 \geq 0$$
$$x_3 \geq 0$$

16. Maximize

$$P = 6x_1 + 3x_2 + 2x_3$$

subject to

$$2x_1 + 2x_2 + 3x_3 \leq 30 \qquad x_1 \geq 0$$
$$2x_1 + 2x_2 + x_3 \leq 12 \qquad x_2 \geq 0$$
$$x_3 \geq 0$$

17. Maximize

$$P = 2x_1 + 4x_2 + x_3 + x_4$$

subject to

$$2x_1 + x_2 + 2x_3 + 3x_4 \leq 12 \qquad x_1 \geq 0$$
$$2x_2 + x_3 + 2x_4 \leq 20 \qquad x_2 \geq 0$$
$$2x_1 + x_2 + 4x_3 \leq 16 \qquad x_3 \geq 0$$
$$x_4 \geq 0$$

4. The Simplex Method: Dualization and Minimization

So far in this chapter, we have discussed only maximum linear programming problems, in which the optimal solution yields the largest possible value for the objective function. In this section we discuss *minimum* problems, where the smallest possible value is desired. Among a number of techniques for solving such problems is one developed by John Von Neumann and others, in which the solution (if it exists) of a minimum problem is found by solving a related maximum problem called the *dual problem*.

Before constructing the dual problem, the original problem must be placed in *standard form*. For a minimum problem, this means:

Standard Form

1. **All the constraints must be written with $\geq$ signs. (This is just the opposite of the standard form requirement for a maximum problem.)**
2. **The objective function to be minimized must be written with nonnegative coefficients.**

We illustrate by example how to obtain the dual problem.

Example 1 Obtain the dual problem of the minimum problem:
Minimize

$$C = 300x_1 + 480x_2$$

subject to the conditions

$$x_1 + 3x_2 \geq 0.25 \qquad x_1 \geq 0$$
$$2x_1 + 2x_2 \geq 0.45 \qquad x_2 \geq 0$$

Solution Observe that the problem is in standard form. We begin by constructing a special augmented matrix for the coefficients of the constraints of this problem without introducing slack variables. As in a simplex tableau, we place the objective function in the last row. The result is

$$\begin{array}{cc} x_1 & x_2 \end{array}$$
$$\left[\begin{array}{cc|c} 1 & 3 & 0.25 \\ 2 & 2 & 0.45 \\ \hline 300 & 480 & 0 \end{array}\right]$$

Similarly, the special matrix for the maximum problem in Example 5 of Chapter 3 (page 134) would be

$$\left[\begin{array}{cc|c} 1 & 2 & 300 \\ 3 & 2 & 480 \\ \hline 0.25 & 0.45 & 0 \end{array}\right]$$

Observe that this matrix is the transpose of the previous one; that is, the rows of the first matrix (for the minimum problem) are the columns of the second matrix (for the maximum problem). When a maximum and a minimum problem have this relationship, they are called *dual problems* of each other.

——————
Dual Problems

Thus, the dual problem of the given minimum problem is:
Maximize

$$P = 0.25y_1 + 0.45y_2$$

subject to the conditions

$$y_1 + 2y_2 \leq 300 \qquad y_1 \geq 0$$
$$3y_1 + 2y_2 \leq 480 \qquad y_2 \geq 0$$

This duality relationship is significant because of the following principle:

Von Neumann Duality Principle **The optimal solution of a minimum linear programming problem, if the solution exists, has the same value as the optimal solution of the maximum problem that is its dual.**

JOHN von NEUMANN (1903–1957) was born in Budapest, Hungary, but spent most of his life at Princeton University and the Institute for Advanced Study. He developed the theory of games at the age of 25 and is largely responsible for inventing the digital computer. Von Neumann, probably the greatest mathematical genius of this century, had a fantastic capacity for doing mental calculations and possessed a photographic memory. He contributed to quantum mechanics, economics, and computer science, and developed a technique that accelerated the production of the first atomic bomb.

In other words, one way to solve a minimum problem in linear programming is to solve the dual problem. To obtain this dual problem, proceed as follows:

1. **Write the minimum problem in standard form.**
2. **Construct the special matrix from the constraints and the objective function.**
3. **Interchange the rows and columns to form the special matrix of the dual problem.**
4. **Translate this matrix into a maximum problem in standard form.**

Dualization

This process is known as *dualization*. It is illustrated in the next example.

Example 2 Dualize the following problem:
Minimize

$$C = 2x_1 + 3x_2$$

subject to

$$
\begin{array}{ll}
2x_1 + x_2 \geq 6 & x_1 \geq 0 \\
x_1 + 2x_2 \geq 4 & x_2 \geq 0 \\
x_1 + x_2 \geq 5 &
\end{array}
$$

Solution Observe that the constraints are in standard form for minimum linear programming, and the coefficients 2 and 3 in the objective function are greater than or equal to 0. The special matrix is

$$
\left[
\begin{array}{cc|c}
2 & 1 & 6 \\
1 & 2 & 4 \\
1 & 1 & 5 \\
\hline
2 & 3 & 0
\end{array}
\right]
$$

Interchanging rows and columns, we obtain the matrix

$$
\left[
\begin{array}{ccc|c}
2 & 1 & 1 & 2 \\
1 & 2 & 1 & 3 \\
\hline
6 & 4 & 5 & 0
\end{array}
\right]
$$

This is the special matrix form of the following maximum problem:
Maximize

$$P = 6y_1 + 4y_2 + 5y_3$$

subject to

$$
\begin{array}{ll}
2y_1 + y_2 + y_3 \leq 2 & y_1 \geq 0 \\
y_1 + 2y_2 + y_3 \leq 3 & y_2 \geq 0 \\
& y_3 \geq 0
\end{array}
$$

Note that:

1. The variables of the minimum problem have different names (x_1, x_2) from the variables of its dual problem (y_1, y_2, y_3).

2. The minimum problem has three constraints and two variables, while the dual problem has two constraints and three variables. (In general, if a problem has n constraints and k variables, its dual will have k constraints and n variables.)
3. The inequalities defining the constraints are $\geq$ for the minimum problem and $\leq$ for the maximum problem.
4. Since the coefficients in the minimal objective function are positive, the dual problem has nonnegative numbers to the right of the $\leq$ signs.
5. We follow the custom of denoting an objective function by C (for *Cost*) if it is to be minimized, and P (for *Profit*) if it is to be maximized.

Now we will solve the maximum problem by the simplex method and thereby obtain the solution for the minimum problem. We write the initial simplex tableau

$$\begin{array}{ccccc}
y_1 & y_2 & y_3 & u_1 & u_2 \\
\end{array}$$
$$\left[\begin{array}{ccc|cc|c}
② & 1 & 1 & 1 & 0 & 2 \\
1 & 2 & 1 & 0 & 1 & 3 \\
\hline
-6 & -4 & -5 & 0 & 0 & 0
\end{array}\right]\begin{array}{c} u_1 \\ u_2 \\ \\ \end{array}$$

using u_1 and u_2 to represent the slack variables and omitting the column for P. We have drawn an extra vertical line in the tableau to set off the columns of u_1 and u_2. (As you will see, the slack variable columns play a special role in the solution of a dual problem.) Now, using the 2 circled above as a pivot element, we pivot and get

$$\begin{array}{ccccc}
y_1 & y_2 & y_3 & u_1 & u_2 \\
\end{array}$$
$$\left[\begin{array}{ccc|cc|c}
1 & \frac{1}{2} & ②\frac{1}{2} & \frac{1}{2} & 0 & 1 \\
0 & \frac{3}{2} & \frac{1}{2} & -\frac{1}{2} & 1 & 2 \\
\hline
0 & -1 & -2 & 3 & 0 & 6
\end{array}\right]\begin{array}{c} y_1 \\ u_2 \\ \\ \end{array}$$

This time, the entry in row 1, column 3 is the pivot. When we pivot, we obtain

$$\begin{array}{ccccc}
y_1 & y_2 & y_3 & u_1 & u_2 \\
\end{array}$$
$$\left[\begin{array}{ccc|cc|c}
2 & 1 & 1 & 1 & 0 & 2 \\
-1 & 1 & 0 & -1 & 1 & 1 \\
\hline
4 & 1 & 0 & 5 & 0 & 10
\end{array}\right]\begin{array}{c} y_3 \\ u_2 \\ \\ \end{array}$$

Now all the entries in the last row are greater than or equal to 0, so this is a final tableau. We read from it that the solution to the maximum problem is

$$P = 10 \qquad y_1 = 0 \qquad y_2 = 0 \qquad y_3 = 2$$

The duality principle states that the minimum value of the objective function in the original problem is the same as the maximum value in the dual; that is,

$$C = 10$$

But which values of x_1 and x_2 will yield this minimum value? There are some details of the duality principle and its application that we have omitted here;

these concern the relationships between the variables of the original problem and the slack variables used in the solution of the dual problem. As a consequence of these relationships, the entire minimal solution can be read from the right end of the last row of the tableau:

$$x_1 = 5 \qquad x_2 = 0 \qquad C = 10$$

Notice in the solution to Example 2 that the value of x_1 is found at the bottom of the column corresponding to u_1 and x_2 is similarly found in the column corresponding to u_2. In general, the values of the slack variables are not the same as those of the original variables. Observe that here

$$x_1 = 5 \qquad x_2 = 0$$

while

$$u_1 = 0 \qquad u_2 = 1$$

We summarize how to solve a minimum linear programming problem below:

1. **Write the dual (maximum) problem.**
2. **Solve this maximum problem by the simplex method.**
3. **Read the optimal solution for the original problem from the last row of the final simplex tableau. The variables will appear as the last entries in the columns corresponding to the slack variables.**
4. **The minimum value of the objective function (C) will appear in the lower right corner of the final tableau; it is equal to the maximum value of the dual objective function (P).**

Example 3   Minimize

$$C = 6x_1 + 8x_2 + x_3$$

subject to

$$\begin{array}{ll} 3x_1 + 5x_2 + 3x_3 \geq 20 & x_1 \geq 0 \\ x_1 + 3x_2 + 2x_3 \geq 9 & x_2 \geq 0 \\ 6x_1 + 2x_2 + 5x_3 \geq 30 & x_3 \geq 0 \end{array}$$

Solution   The special matrix of this problem is

$$\begin{bmatrix} 3 & 5 & 3 & | & 20 \\ 1 & 3 & 2 & | & 9 \\ 6 & 2 & 5 & | & 30 \\ \hline 6 & 8 & 1 & | & 0 \end{bmatrix}$$

We interchange rows and columns to get

$$\begin{bmatrix} 3 & 1 & 6 & | & 6 \\ 5 & 3 & 2 & | & 8 \\ 3 & 2 & 5 & | & 1 \\ \hline 20 & 9 & 30 & | & 0 \end{bmatrix}$$

The dual problem is:
Maximize

$$P = 20y_1 + 9y_2 + 30y_3$$

subject to

$$
\begin{aligned}
3y_1 + y_2 + 6y_3 &\leq 6 & y_1 &\geq 0 \\
5y_1 + 3y_2 + 2y_3 &\leq 8 & y_2 &\geq 0 \\
3y_1 + 2y_2 + 5y_3 &\leq 1 & y_3 &\geq 0
\end{aligned}
$$

Introducing slack variables u_1, u_2, and u_3, the initial tableau for this problem is

$$
\begin{array}{cccccc}
y_1 & y_2 & y_3 & u_1 & u_2 & u_3 \\
\end{array}
$$
$$
\left[
\begin{array}{ccc|ccc|c}
3 & 1 & 6 & 1 & 0 & 0 & 6 \\
5 & 3 & 2 & 0 & 1 & 0 & 8 \\
3 & 2 & 5 & 0 & 0 & 1 & 1 \\
\hline
-20 & -9 & -30 & 0 & 0 & 0 & 0
\end{array}
\right]
$$

The final tableau (as you may verify) is

$$
\begin{array}{cccccc}
y_1 & y_2 & y_3 & u_1 & u_2 & u_3 \\
\end{array}
$$
$$
\left[
\begin{array}{ccc|ccc|c}
0 & -1 & 1 & 1 & 0 & -1 & 5 \\
0 & -\frac{1}{3} & -\frac{19}{3} & 0 & 1 & -\frac{5}{3} & \frac{19}{3} \\
1 & \frac{2}{3} & \frac{5}{3} & 0 & 0 & \frac{1}{3} & \frac{1}{3} \\
\hline
0 & \frac{13}{3} & \frac{10}{3} & 0 & 0 & \frac{20}{3} & \frac{20}{3}
\end{array}
\right]
\begin{array}{l}
u_1 \\
u_2 \\
y_1 \\
\\
\end{array}
$$

The solution to the maximum problem is

$$P = \tfrac{20}{3} \qquad y_1 = \tfrac{1}{3} \qquad y_2 = 0 \qquad y_3 = 0$$

For the minimum problem, the values of x_1, x_2, and x_3 are read as the last entries in the columns under u_1, u_2, and u_3, respectively. Hence, the solution to the minimum problem is

$$x_1 = 0 \qquad x_2 = 0 \qquad x_3 = \tfrac{20}{3}$$

and the minimum value is $C = \tfrac{20}{3}$. ∎

A final note for this section: If you find that the dual of a minimum problem has an unbounded solution, then the minimum problem has no feasible solution; the solution set of its constraints is empty.

Exercise 4
Solutions to Odd-Numbered Problems begin on page 580.

In Problems 1–4 write the dual problem for each minimum linear programming problem.

1. Minimize

$$C = 2x_1 + 3x_2$$

subject to

$$
\begin{aligned}
x_1 + x_2 &\geq 2 & x_1 &\geq 0 \\
2x_1 + 3x_2 &\geq 6 & x_2 &\geq 0
\end{aligned}
$$

2. Minimize

$$C = 3x_1 + 4x_2$$

subject to

$$2x_1 + x_2 \geq 2 \qquad x_1 \geq 0$$
$$2x_1 + x_2 \geq 6 \qquad x_2 \geq 0$$

3. Minimize

$$C = 3x_1 + x_2 + x_3$$

subject to

$$x_1 + x_2 + x_3 \geq 5 \qquad x_1 \geq 0$$
$$2x_1 + x_2 \qquad \geq 4 \qquad x_2 \geq 0$$
$$\qquad\qquad\qquad\qquad x_3 \geq 0$$

4. Minimize

$$C = 2x_1 + x_2 + x_3$$

subject to

$$2x_1 + x_2 + x_3 \geq 4 \qquad x_1 \geq 0$$
$$x_1 + 2x_2 + x_3 \geq 6 \qquad x_2 \geq 0$$
$$\qquad\qquad\qquad\qquad x_3 \geq 0$$

In Problems 5–9 solve each minimum linear programming problem by using the simplex method.

5. Minimize

$$C = 6x_1 + 3x_2$$

subject to

$$x_1 + x_2 \geq 2 \qquad x_1 \geq 0$$
$$2x_1 + 6x_2 \geq 6 \qquad x_2 \geq 0$$

6. Minimize

$$C = 3x_1 + 4x_2$$

subject to

$$x_1 + x_2 \geq 3 \qquad x_1 \geq 0$$
$$2x_1 + x_2 \geq 4 \qquad x_2 \geq 0$$

7. Minimize

$$C = 6x_1 + 3x_2$$

subject to

$$x_1 + x_2 \geq 4 \qquad x_1 \geq 0$$
$$3x_1 + 4x_2 \geq 12 \qquad x_2 \geq 0$$

8. Minimize

$$C = 2x_1 + 3x_2 + 4x_3$$

subject to

$$x_1 - 2x_2 - 3x_3 \geq -2 \qquad x_1 \geq 0$$
$$x_1 + x_2 + x_3 \geq 2 \qquad x_2 \geq 0$$
$$2x_1 + x_3 \geq 3 \qquad x_3 \geq 0$$

9. Minimize

$$C = x_1 + 2x_2 + x_3$$

subject to

$$x_1 - 3x_2 + 4x_3 \geq 12 \qquad x_1 \geq 0$$
$$3x_1 + x_2 + 2x_3 \geq 10 \qquad x_2 \geq 0$$
$$x_1 - x_2 - x_3 \geq -8 \qquad x_3 \geq 0$$

*5. Applications

The first example is a typical transportation problem.

Example 1
Transportation
Problem

The Red Tomato Company operates two plants for canning their tomatoes and has two warehouses for storing the finished products until they are purchased by retailers. The company wants to arrange its shipments from the plants to the warehouses so that the requirements of the warehouses are met and shipping costs are kept at a minimum. The schedule shown in the table represents the per case shipping costs from plant to warehouse.

		Warehouse A	Warehouse B
Plant	I	$0.25	$0.18
	II	$0.25	$0.14

Each week, Plant I can produce at most 450 cases and Plant II can produce no more than 350 cases of tomatoes. Also, each week, Warehouse A requires at least 300 cases and Warehouse B requires at least 500 cases. If we represent the number of cases shipped from Plant I to Warehouse A by x_1, from Plant I to Warehouse B by x_2, and so on, the above data can be represented by the following table:

		Warehouse A	Warehouse B	Maximum Available
Plant	I	x_1	x_2	450
	II	x_3	x_4	350
Minimum Demand		300	500	

*This section may be omitted without loss of continuity.

The linear programming problem is stated as follows:
Minimize the cost equation

$$C = 0.25x_1 + 0.18x_2 + 0.25x_3 + 0.14x_4$$

subject to

$$
\begin{array}{ll}
x_1 + x_2 \le 450 & x_1 \ge 0 \\
x_3 + x_4 \le 350 & x_2 \ge 0 \\
x_1 + x_3 \ge 300 & x_3 \ge 0 \\
x_2 + x_4 \ge 500 & x_4 \ge 0
\end{array}
$$

To get the problem in standard form, we multiply both sides of the first two inequalities by -1:

$$
\begin{array}{rrrr}
-x_1 - x_2 & & \ge -450 \\
& -x_3 - x_4 & \ge -350 \\
x_1 & + x_3 & \ge 300 \\
x_2 & + x_4 & \ge 500
\end{array}
$$

The special matrix for the minimum problem is

$$
\begin{bmatrix}
-1 & -1 & 0 & 0 & -450 \\
0 & 0 & -1 & -1 & -350 \\
1 & 0 & 1 & 0 & 300 \\
0 & 1 & 0 & 1 & 500 \\
\hline
0.25 & 0.18 & 0.25 & 0.14 & 0
\end{bmatrix}
$$

The dual matrix is

$$
\begin{bmatrix}
-1 & 0 & 1 & 0 & 0.25 \\
-1 & 0 & 0 & 1 & 0.18 \\
0 & -1 & 1 & 0 & 0.25 \\
0 & -1 & 0 & 1 & 0.14 \\
\hline
-450 & -350 & 300 & 500 & 0
\end{bmatrix}
$$

and the dual (maximum) problem is:
Maximize

$$P = -450y_1 - 350y_2 + 300y_3 + 500y_4$$

subject to

$$
\begin{array}{ll}
-y_1 + y_3 \le 0.25 & y_1 \ge 0 \\
-y_1 + y_4 \le 0.18 & y_2 \ge 0 \\
-y_2 + y_3 \le 0.25 & y_3 \ge 0 \\
-y_2 + y_4 \le 0.14 & y_4 \ge 0
\end{array}
$$

Introducing the slack variables u_1, u_2, u_3, and u_4, we construct the initial simplex tableau and proceed to solve the dual problem:

y_1	y_2	y_3	y_4	u_1	u_2	u_3	u_4		
-1	0	1	0	1	0	0	0	0.25	u_1
-1	0	0	1	0	1	0	0	0.18	u_2
0	-1	1	0	0	0	1	0	0.25	u_3
0	-1	0	①	0	0	0	1	0.14	u_4
450	350	-300	-500	0	0	0	0	0	

$\rightarrow$

$\uparrow$

$$
\begin{array}{c}
\begin{array}{cccccccc}
y_1 & y_2 & y_3 & y_4 & u_1 & u_2 & u_3 & u_4
\end{array}\\
\rightarrow
\left[
\begin{array}{cccc|cccc|c}
-1 & 0 & \textcircled{1} & 0 & 1 & 0 & 0 & 0 & 0.25\\
-1 & 1 & 0 & 0 & 0 & 1 & 0 & -1 & 0.04\\
0 & -1 & 1 & 0 & 0 & 0 & 1 & 0 & 0.25\\
0 & -1 & 0 & 1 & 0 & 0 & 0 & 1 & 0.14\\
\hline
450 & -150 & -300 & 0 & 0 & 0 & 0 & 500 & 70
\end{array}
\right]\\
\uparrow
\end{array}
$$

$$
\begin{array}{c}
\begin{array}{cccccccc}
y_1 & y_2 & y_3 & y_4 & u_1 & u_2 & u_3 & u_4
\end{array}\\
\rightarrow
\left[
\begin{array}{cccc|cccc|c}
-1 & 0 & 1 & 0 & 1 & 0 & 0 & 0 & 0.25\\
-1 & \textcircled{1} & 0 & 0 & 0 & 1 & 0 & -1 & 0.04\\
1 & -1 & 0 & 0 & -1 & 0 & 1 & 0 & 0\\
0 & -1 & 0 & 1 & 0 & 0 & 0 & 1 & 0.14\\
\hline
150 & -150 & 0 & 0 & 300 & 0 & 0 & 500 & 145
\end{array}
\right]\\
\uparrow
\end{array}
$$

$$
\begin{array}{cccc|cccc|cc}
y_1 & y_2 & y_3 & y_4 & u_1 & u_2 & u_3 & u_4 & &\\
\left[\begin{array}{cccc}
-1 & 0 & 1 & 0\\
-1 & 1 & 0 & 0\\
0 & 0 & 0 & 0\\
-1 & 0 & 0 & 1\\
\hline
0 & 0 & 0 & 0
\end{array}\right.
&
\left.\begin{array}{cccc}
1 & 0 & 0 & 0\\
0 & 1 & 0 & -1\\
-1 & 1 & 1 & -1\\
0 & 1 & 0 & 0\\
\hline
300 & 150 & 0 & 350
\end{array}\right.
&
\left.\begin{array}{c}
0.25\\
0.04\\
0.04\\
0.18\\
\hline
151
\end{array}\right]
&
\begin{array}{c}
y_3\\
y_2\\
u_3\\
y_4\\
\\
\end{array}
\end{array}
$$

$$
\begin{array}{ccccc}
 & x_1 & x_2 & x_3 & x_4 & C
\end{array}
$$

The final tableau yields the solution to the original minimum problem:

$$
C = \$151 \qquad x_1 = 300 \qquad x_2 = 150 \qquad x_3 = 0 \qquad x_4 = 350
$$

This means Plant I should deliver 300 cases to Warehouse A and 150 cases to Warehouse B; and Plant II should deliver 350 cases to Warehouse B to keep costs at the minimum ($151). ∎

Example 2 Mike's Famous Toy Trucks specializes in making four kinds of toy trucks: a delivery truck, a dump truck, a garbage truck, and a gasoline truck. Three machines— a metal casting machine, a paint spray machine, and a packaging machine—are used in the production of these trucks. The time, in hours, each machine works to make each type of truck and the profit for each truck are given in Table 1. The maximum time available per week for each machine is: metal casting 4000 hours, paint spray 1800 hours, and packaging 1000 hours. How many of each type truck should be produced to maximize profit? Assume that every truck made is sold.

Solution Let x_1, x_2, x_3, and x_4 denote the number of delivery trucks, dump trucks, garbage trucks, and gasoline trucks, respectively, to be made. If P denotes the profit to be maximized, we have the problem:

Table 1

	Metal Casting	Paint Spray	Packaging	Profit
Delivery Truck	2 hours	1 hour	0.5 hour	$0.50
Dump Truck	2.5 hours	1.5 hours	0.5 hour	$1.00
Garbage Truck	2 hours	1 hour	1 hour	$1.50
Gasoline Truck	2 hours	2 hours	1 hour	$2.00

Maximize

$$P = 0.5x_1 + x_2 + 1.5x_3 + 2x_4$$

subject to the conditions

$$2x_1 + 2.5x_2 + 2x_3 + 2x_4 \le 4000 \qquad x_1 \ge 0 \qquad x_3 \ge 0$$
$$x_1 + 1.5x_2 + x_3 + 2x_4 \le 1800 \qquad x_2 \ge 0 \qquad x_4 \ge 0$$
$$0.5x_1 + 0.5x_2 + x_3 + x_4 \le 1000$$

Since this problem is in standard form, we introduce slack variables x_5, x_6, and x_7, write the initial simplex tableau, and solve:

$$\begin{array}{ccccccc}
x_1 & x_2 & x_3 & x_4 & x_5 & x_6 & x_7 \\
\end{array}$$

$$\left[\begin{array}{ccccccc|c}
2 & 2.5 & 2 & 2 & 1 & 0 & 0 & 4000 \\
1 & 1.5 & 1 & \boxed{2} & 0 & 1 & 0 & 1800 \\
0.5 & 0.5 & 1 & 1 & 0 & 0 & 1 & 1000 \\
\hline
-0.5 & -1 & -1.5 & -2 & 0 & 0 & 0 & 0
\end{array}\right]
\begin{array}{c}
x_5 \\ x_6 \\ x_7 \\ \\
\end{array}$$

$$\begin{array}{ccccccc}
x_1 & x_2 & x_3 & x_4 & x_5 & x_6 & x_7 \\
\end{array}$$

$$\left[\begin{array}{ccccccc|c}
1 & 1 & 1 & 0 & 1 & -1 & 0 & 2200 \\
0.5 & 0.75 & 0.5 & 1 & 0 & 0.5 & 0 & 900 \\
0 & -0.25 & \boxed{0.5} & 0 & 0 & -0.5 & 1 & 100 \\
\hline
0.5 & 0.5 & -0.5 & 0 & 0 & 1 & 0 & 1800
\end{array}\right]
\begin{array}{c}
x_5 \\ x_4 \\ x_7 \\ \\
\end{array}$$

$$\begin{array}{ccccccc}
x_1 & x_2 & x_3 & x_4 & x_5 & x_6 & x_7 \\
\end{array}$$

$$\left[\begin{array}{ccccccc|c}
1 & 1.5 & 0 & 0 & 1 & 0 & -2 & 2000 \\
0.5 & 1 & 0 & 1 & 0 & 1 & -1 & 800 \\
0 & -0.5 & 1 & 0 & 0 & -1 & 2 & 200 \\
\hline
0.5 & 0.25 & 0 & 0 & 0 & 0.5 & 1 & 1900
\end{array}\right]
\begin{array}{c}
x_5 \\ x_4 \\ x_3 \\ \\
\end{array}$$

This is a final tableau. The maximum profit is $P = \$1900$, and it is attained for

$$x_1 = 0 \qquad x_2 = 0 \qquad x_3 = 200 \qquad x_4 = 800$$

■

The practical considerations of the situation described in Example 2 are that delivery trucks and dump trucks are too costly to produce or too little profit is being gained from their sale. Since the slack variable x_5 has a value of 2000 for maximum P and since x_5 represents the number of hours the metal casting machine is printing no truck (that is, the time the machine is idle), it may be possible to release this machine for other duties.

Model: Pollution Control

In the pollution control model we presented in Chapter 3, we considered an extremely simplified application. A more realistic version is given in the following model.* In this example we merely indicate the complicated nature of attempting to solve a real-world problem. As a result, the linear programming problem is set up, but no solution is actually given.

There are many pollution sources and five (not one) major pollutants in this larger model. The required pollutant reductions in the St. Louis airshed for the year 1970 are given as follows:

Sulfur dioxide	485,000,000 pounds
Carbon monoxide	1,300,000,000 pounds
Hydrocarbons	280,000,000 pounds
Nitrogen oxides	75,000,000 pounds
Particulate matter	180,000,000 pounds

The model includes a wide variety of possible control methods. Among them are the installation of exhaust and crankcase devices on used as well as new automobiles; the substitution of natural gas for coal; the installation of catalytic oxidation systems to convert sulfur dioxide in the stacks of power plants to salable sulfuric acid; and even the municipal collection of leaves as an alternative to burning.

The most contested control method in the St. Louis airshed has been a restriction on the sulfur content of coal. Consider a particular category of traveling grate stokers that burns 3.1% sulfur coal. Let control method 3 be the substitution of 1.8% sulfur coal for the high-sulfur coal in these stokers. The variable X_3 represents the number of tons of 3.1% sulfur coal replaced with low-sulfur coal.

Total cost of this control method is

$$C = (\$2.50)X_3$$

where \$2.50 is an estimate of the incremental cost of the low-sulfur coal.

Just as the number of barrels of cement controlled by any process was constrained in our simple example (see Chapter 3), so

$$X_3 \leq 200,000$$

where 200,000 tons is the estimate of the quantity of coal that will be burned in this category of traveling grate stokers in 1970.

For every ton of 3.1% sulfur coal replaced by 1.8% sulfur coal, sulfur dioxide emissions are reduced by

$$\left[\left(\begin{array}{c} 0.031 \\ \text{sulfur} \\ \text{content} \end{array} \right) \left(\begin{array}{c} 2000\ \text{lb} \\ \text{per ton} \\ \text{of coal} \end{array} \right) \left(\begin{array}{c} 0.95 \\ \text{complete} \\ \text{burning} \end{array} \right)(2) \right]$$

$$- \left[(0.944) \left(\begin{array}{c} 0.018 \\ \text{sulfur} \\ \text{content} \end{array} \right)(2000\ \text{lb})(0.95)(2) \right] = 53.2\ \text{lb}$$

*Robert E. Kohn, "Application of Linear Programming to a Controversy on Air Pollution Control," *Management Science*, **17**, 10 (June 1971), pp. B609–B621.

where the factor (2) doubles the weight of sulfur burned to get the weight of sulfur dioxide; where the factor (0.944) accounts for the higher BTU content of the low-sulfur coal, which permits 0.944 ton of it to replace 1 ton of the high-sulfur coal; and where (0.95) incorporates an assumption of 95% complete burning. The two expressions within square brackets represent emission of sulfur dioxide from 3.1% and 1.8% sulfur coal, respectively. Thus, we have

$$(53.2)X_3 = \text{Pounds of sulfur dioxide reduced}$$

The remaining pollutant reductions are

$$(0.2)X_3 = \text{Pounds of carbon monoxide reduced}$$
$$(0.1)X_3 = \text{Pounds of hydrocarbons reduced}$$
$$(1.1)X_3 = \text{Pounds of nitrogen oxides reduced}$$
$$(12.2)X_3 = \text{Pounds of particulates reduced}$$

The relatively high reduction in particulates reflects not only the fact that 0.944 ton of the 1.8% sulfur coal is burned in place of 1 ton, but also the lower ash content of the substituted coal. (Reduction coefficients are not always positive; low-sulfur coal in a pulverized coal boiler that is equipped with a high-efficiency electrostatic precipitator can cause an increase in particulate emissions. The presence of less sulfur dioxide in the flue gas reduces the chargeability of the particles so that the benefits of the lower ash and higher BTU content may be offset by the reduced efficiency of the electrostatic precipitator.)

The mathematical programming model for 1970 is shown below. Notice that control methods X_1 and X_2 for the cement industry are included (see Chapter 3), as well as control method X_3. The dots represent the remaining 200–300 control methods.

Minimize $C = \$0.14X_1 + \$0.18X_2 + \$2.50X_3 + \cdots$

subject to

$$
\begin{array}{lllll}
X_1 + & X_2 & & \leq & 2{,}500{,}000 \\
 & & X_3 + \cdots & \leq & 200{,}000 \\
 & & & \vdots & \\
 & & 53.2X_3 + \cdots & \geq & 485{,}000{,}000 \text{ lb of sulfur dioxide} \\
 & & 0.2X_3 + \cdots & \geq & 1{,}300{,}000{,}000 \text{ lb of carbon monoxide} \\
 & & 0.1X_3 + \cdots & \geq & 280{,}000{,}000 \text{ lb of hydrocarbons} \\
 & & 1.1X_3 + \cdots & \geq & 75{,}000{,}000 \text{ lb of nitrogen oxides} \\
1.5X_1 + & 1.8X_2 + & \cdots & \geq & 180{,}000{,}000 \text{ lb of particulates} \\
X_1, & X_2, & X_3, \quad \cdots & \geq & 0
\end{array}
$$

The pollution reduction requirements mentioned above appear in the model. In summing the pollutant reductions contributed by the various control methods, we are assuming that all pounds of any pollutant are homogeneous, regardless of where or when they are emitted. This is a limitation of the model because it is dependent on a close correspondence between a pollutant reduction and a specific concentration measured in parts per million or micrograms per cubic meter of that pollutant in the ambient air.

However, where necessary, meteorological sophistication can be incorporated in the model by selective weighting of those sources that seem to have a greater or lesser proportional effect on air quality than others. When the number of variables is large, it is best to use a computer to obtain a solution.

Model: Ecology

The next model is quoted from an article in *Some Mathematical Models in Biology*,[*] and is presented to illustrate the use of the simplex method in linear programming. This model is an interesting application of linear programming to a bioeconomic situation; it is a good illustration of how the given information must be analyzed, sifted, and interpreted in order to formulate a useful mathematical model.

In the Edwards Plateau country of west Texas the vegetation is easily modified by grazing animals from a mixed vegetation to a dominance of grasses, or forbs, or browse, or various combinations of these. It is common to see in pastures in this area herds of cattle, bands of sheep, and flocks of mohair goats. Whitetail deer and wild turkey are common if there is sufficient browse and mixed vegetation. Catfish will thrive in ponds if there is suitable vegetation cover to prevent siltation. Ranchers sell beef, wool, mutton, mohair and lease deer and turkey hunting and catfishing rights. The relative monetary income values per animal are: cattle, 10.; goats, 1.; sheep, 1. (wool and mutton combined); deer, 0.5; turkey, 0.05; and fish, 0.001. A rancher owns 10 sections of such land which has a maximum carrying capacity of 10 animal units per section per year. The animal unit equivalents for the various species per animal are: cattle, 1.; sheep, 0.2; goats, 0.25; deer, 0.3; and essentially zero for turkeys and fish. To properly organize his operation for livestock production, he has to have at least 20 cattle and at least 20 goats on his ranch. The rancher wants at least some sheep and some deer on his ranch. He can maintain the desired vegetation cover for turkey and fish if he has (a) cattle, sheep, goats, and deer, (b) cattle, sheep, and goats, or (c) cattle, goats, and deer, but no more than 75% of the grazing load (measured in animal units) may be due to cattle and goats combined. Of course, he wants his total stocking rate of all organisms combined to be equal to or less than the carrying capacity of the range. Furthermore, he can put in no more than one pond per section each of which will support no more than 500 fish each, and can harvest no more than 25% of the catfish per pond per year. The requirements and habits of the wild turkey are such that he cannot maintain more than 2 flocks of 10 birds per flock per section and he cannot harvest more than 20% of the population per year. He keeps only castrated male goats for mohair and shears them once each year. His cattle, sheep, and deer harvests which will maintain a given population are respectively about 25, 35, and 15% of the population per year. For simplification, the 35% for sheep includes both wool and mutton.

The first step is to isolate the salient points from this description. They are:

(1) The relative monetary income values per animal are:

Cattle	10
Goats	1
Sheep	1
Deer	0.5
Turkey	0.05
Fish	0.001

[*]G. M. Van Dyne and Kenneth R. Rebman, "Maintaining a Profitable Ecological Balance," in Robert M. Thrall, ed., *Some Mathematical Models in Biology*, University of Michigan, 1967.

(2) There are 10 sections of land, each with a maximum carrying capacity of 10 animal units per year.

(3) Animal unit equivalents for the species are:

Cattle	1
Goats	0.25
Sheep	0.2
Deer	0.3
Turkey	0
Fish	0

(4) The ranch must have at least 20 cattle and 20 goats.

(5) There must be some sheep and some deer.

(6) If there are to be any turkey and fish, there must be

    (a) cattle, sheep and goats

or

    (b) cattle, goats, and deer

(7) Cattle and goats can comprise no more than 75% of the animal units.

(8) Total animal units cannot exceed the carrying capacity.

(9) A maximum of 500 fish per section, with a 25% annual harvest.

(10) A maximum of 20 birds per section, with a 20% annual harvest.

(11) Harvest percentages:

Cattle	25%
Goats	100%
Sheep	35%
Deer	15%

(12) How many individuals of each species should the rancher have in order to maximize annual profit?

The next step is to quantify these conditions.

In the first place the rancher is hoping for an answer that is something like: have 30 cattle, 22 sheep, etc. He will be understandably upset if he is told that to realize a maximum profit, he requires 33.25 cattle and 21.7 sheep. The rancher is certainly anticipating the answer to be in integers. However, any programming problem that imposes integer constraints on the variables is apt to be extremely difficult to solve. Thus, the first simplification is to treat the problem as a continuous programming problem. It may even turn out that all or some of the optimal values of the variables of this problem *are* actually integers. If not, the solution can be rounded to the nearest integer solution. It is important to realize that this rounded solution may *not* be the best integer solution. However, if

p_0 is the maximum profit for the continuous problem
p_1 is the profit obtained by rounding the optimal solution
p_2 is the maximum profit to the integer problem

then clearly $p_1 \leq p_2 \leq p_0$. If $p_0 - p_1$ is very small, the rancher will not care anyway.

The next step is to determine the variables. Since he has 10 parcels of land, each being able to support 6 different species, the first inclination is to use 60 variables $x_{ij}, i = 1 \ldots 6, j = 1 \ldots 10$. Then x_{ij} will represent the number of species i to be placed on parcel j. However, since the conditions for survival are the same in any parcel, it is much simpler to consider the entire 10 parcels as a single unit. Then only 6 variables $x_i, i = 1 \ldots 6$ are needed, where x_i represents the total number of species i. In the final solution, $\frac{1}{10}$ of x_i can be placed in each parcel. (Or other adjustments can be made, at the rancher's preference.) (Note that we cannot just maximize profit over a single parcel. The constraints would require *some* deer on *every* parcel, which is not required in the given problem.)

Thus we define the following 6 variables:

$$\begin{aligned}
x_1&: \quad \text{Number of cattle} \\
x_2&: \quad \text{Number of goats} \\
x_3&: \quad \text{Number of sheep} \\
x_4&: \quad \text{Number of deer} \\
x_5&: \quad \text{Number of turkey} \\
x_6&: \quad \text{Number of fish}
\end{aligned}$$

The conditions then give the following constraints: Condition (2) says the maximum carrying capacity available is 100 units. Condition (3) gives the animal units for each species. Condition (7) gives the constraint:

$$1x_1 + 0.25x_2 \leq 75$$

Condition (8) becomes:

$$1x_1 + 0.25x_2 + 0.2x_3 + 0.3x_4 \leq 100$$

Condition (4) is:

$$\begin{aligned}
x_1 &\geq 20 \\
x_2 &\geq 20
\end{aligned}$$

Condition (5) is:

$$\begin{aligned}
x_3 &\geq \text{"Some"} \\
x_4 &\geq \text{"Some"}
\end{aligned}$$

where "Some" is the minimum number of sheep and deer the rancher wants. Since the rancher is vague about this, let us assume that "Some" = 1. So lower bound constraints are:

$$\begin{aligned}
x_1 &\geq 20 \\
x_2 &\geq 20 \\
x_3 &\geq 1 \\
x_4 &\geq 1
\end{aligned}$$

Now we see that condition (6) is irrelevant. The lower bound constraints guarantee that (6)(a) and (b) will *always* be satisfied. Hence, it will always be possible to have turkey ($x_5 > 0$) and fish ($x_6 > 0$). Conditions (9) and (10) give

$$\begin{aligned}
x_6 &\leq 5000 \\
x_5 &\leq 200
\end{aligned}$$

Finally, it is only needed to calculate the profit. Condition (1) gives profit per animal. Not all animals can be harvested, however. Harvest percentages are given in (9), (10), and (11). The annual profit from each species is:

Cattle $(10)(0.25x_1)$
Goat $(1)(x_2)$
Sheep $(1)(0.35x_3)$
Deer $(0.5)(0.15x_4)$
Turkey $(0.05)(0.20x_5)$
Fish $(0.001)(0.25x_6)$

Thus the rancher's problem is:
Subject to the constraints

$$x_1 + 0.25x_2 \leq 75$$
$$x_1 + 0.25x_2 + 0.2x_3 + 0.3x_4 \leq 100$$
$$x_1 \geq 20$$
$$x_2 \geq 20$$
$$x_3 \geq 1$$
$$x_4 \geq 1$$
$$0 < x_5 \leq 200$$
$$0 < x_6 \leq 5000$$

maximize the objective function

$$z = 2.5x_1 + x_2 + 0.35x_3 + 0.075x_4 + 0.01x_5 + 0.00025x_6$$

[AUTHORS' NOTE: We urge you to consult the original article for the derivation of the solution of this problem.]

For maximum annual profit, the rancher's selection should be:

70	Cattle for a profit of	175.
20	Goats for a profit of	20.
123.5	Sheep for a profit of	43.225
1	Deer for a profit of	0.075
200	Turkeys for a profit of	2.
5000	Fish for a profit of	1.25

giving a profit of 241.55 units.

Of course, the rancher will have to have only 123 sheep, reducing his profit by 0.175. He will not be able to realize any profit on his single deer, which he insisted on having. So his profit is further reduced by 0.075.

Thus, his total profit, with an integer number of species, is 241.30.

Since the *best* integer solution can give no more than 241.55 profit, it is probably not worth finding it. (In fact this is very likely it.)

If the rancher now decides that one deer does not constitute "some," then the problem can be re-done, giving a larger lower bound for x_4.

It only remains to distribute the species over the 10 parcels. If each parcel must have an integer number of species to itself, each parcel will have

7	Cattle
2	Goats
2	Flocks of 10 birds each
1	Pond with 500 fish

Putting an integer number of sheep on each parcel means that only 12 sheep can be on any parcel. This further reduces the profit by 1.05, since only 120 sheep are present. (Now, the total profit is only 240.25, but the *best* integer solution can give a profit no greater than 241.55.)

Note that the 7 cattle, 2 goats, and 12 sheep on each parcel use a total of 9.9 land units. Thus, no single parcel can support the deer. However, the deer can presumably roam over all 10 parcels, in which case there are enough land units to support 3 deer, which are still not enough for a deer "harvest."

Exercise 5
Solutions to Odd-Numbered Problems begin on page 582.

1. *Mixture Problem.* Minimize the cost of preparing the following mixture, which is made up of three foods, I, II, III. Food I costs $2 per unit, Food II costs $1 per unit, and Food III costs $3 per unit. Each unit of Food I contains 2 ounces of protein and 4 ounces of carbohydrate; each unit of Food II has 3 ounces of protein and 2 ounces of carbohydrate; and each unit of Food III has 4 ounces of protein and 2 ounces of carbohydrate. The mixture must contain at least 20 ounces of protein and 15 ounces of carbohydrate.

2. *Mixture Problem.* Nutt's Nut Company has 500 pounds of peanuts, 100 pounds of pecans, and 50 pounds of cashews on hand. They package three types of 5 pound cans of nuts: Can I contains 3 pounds peanuts, 1 pound pecans, and 1 pound cashews; Can II contains 4 pounds peanuts, $\frac{1}{2}$ pound pecans, and $\frac{1}{2}$ pound cashews; and Can III contains 5 pounds peanuts. The selling price for each can is $8 for Can I, $7 for Can II, and $5 for Can III. How many cans of each kind should be made to maximize revenue?

3. *Diet Problem.* A can of cat food, guaranteed by the manufacturer to contain at least 10 units of protein, 20 units of mineral matter, and 6 units of fat, consists of a mixture of four different ingredients. Ingredient A contains 10 units of protein, 2 units of mineral matter, and $\frac{1}{2}$ unit of fat per ounce. Ingredient B contains 1 unit of protein, 40 units of mineral matter, and 3 units of fat per ounce. Ingredient C contains 1 unit of protein, 1 unit of mineral matter, and 6 units of fat per ounce. Ingredient D contains 5 units of protein, 10 units of mineral matter, and 3 units of fat per ounce. The cost of each ingredient is 3¢, 2¢, 1¢, and 4¢ per ounce, respectively. How many ounces of each should be used to minimize the cost of the cat food, while still meeting the guaranteed composition?

4. One of the methods used by the Alexander Company to separate copper, lead, and zinc from ores is the flotation separation process. This process consists of three steps: oiling, mixing, and separation. These steps must be applied for 2, 2, and 1 hour, respectively, to produce 1 unit of copper; 2, 3, and 1 hour, respectively, to produce 1 unit of lead; and 1, 1, and 3 hours, respectively, to produce 1 unit of zinc. The oiling and separation phases of the process can be in oper-

ation for a maximum of 10 hours a day, while the mixing phase can be in operation for a maximum of 11 hours a day. The Alexander Company makes a profit of $45 per unit of copper, $30 per unit lead, and $35 per unit zinc. The demand for these metals is unlimited. How many units of each metal should be produced daily by use of the flotation process to achieve the highest profit?

5. A wood cabinet manufacturer produces cabinets for television consoles, stereo systems, and radios, each of which must be assembled, decorated, and crated. Each television console requires 3 hours to assemble, 5 hours to decorate, and 0.1 hour to crate and returns a profit of $10. Each stereo system requires 10 hours to assemble, 8 hours to decorate, and 0.6 hour to crate and returns a profit of $25. Each radio requires 1 hour to assemble, 1 hour to decorate and 0.1 hour to crate and returns a profit of $3. The manufacturer has 30,000, 40,000, and 120 hours available weekly for assembling, decorating, and crating, respectively. How many units of each product should be manufactured to maximize profit?

Chapter Review

Important Terms

slack variable	**pivot column**
standard form	**simplex method**
initial simplex tableau	**standard form for minimum problem**
pivot operation	**dual problem**
pivot element	**duality principle**
pivot row	**dualization**

True–False Questions
(Answers on page 631)

T F 1. In a maximum problem written in standard form each of the constraints, with the exception of the nonnegativity constraints, are written with a $\leq$ symbol.

T F 2. In a maximum problem written in standard form the slack variables are sometimes negative.

T F 3. Once the pivot element is identified in a tableau, the pivot operation causes the pivot element to become a 1 and causes the remaining entries in the pivot column to become 0's.

T F 4. The pivot element is sometimes in the objective row.

T F 5. To solve a minimum problem, you must first solve its dual, which is a maximum problem.

Fill in the Blanks
(Answers on page 631)

1. The constraints of a maximum problem in standard form are changed from an inequality to an equation by introducing _____ _____ .

2. The pivot _____ is located by selecting the most negative entry in the objective row.

3. For a minimum problem to be in standard form all the constraints must be written with _____ signs.
4. When the rows of the special matrix of a minimum problem are the columns of the special matrix of a maximum problem, we say the problems are

   _____ .

5. The _____ _____ _____ principle states that the optimal solution of a minimum linear programming problem, if it exists, has the same value as the optimal solution of the maximum problem, which is its dual.

Review Exercises
Solutions to Odd-Numbered Problems begin on page 583.

1. Maximize

$$P = 40x_1 + 60x_2 + 50x_3$$

   subject to the constraints

$$2x_1 + 2x_2 + x_3 \leq 8$$
$$x_1 - 4x_2 + 3x_3 \leq 12$$
$$x_1 \geq 0, \quad x_2 \geq 0, \quad x_3 \geq 0$$

2. Maximize

$$P = 2x_1 + 8x_2 + 10x_3 + x_4$$

   subject to the constraints

$$x_1 + 2x_2 + x_3 + x_4 \leq 50$$
$$3x_1 + x_2 + 2x_3 + x_4 \leq 100$$
$$x_1 \geq 0, \quad x_2 \geq 0, \quad x_3 \geq 0, \quad x_4 \geq 0$$

3. Minimize

$$C = 5x_1 + 4x_2 + 3x_3$$

   subject to the constraints

$$x_1 + x_2 + x_3 \geq 100$$
$$2x_1 + x_2 \geq 50$$
$$x_1 \geq 0, \quad x_2 \geq 0, \quad x_3 \geq 0$$

4. Minimize

$$C = 2x_1 + x_2 + 3x_3 + x_4$$

   subject to

$$x_1 + x_2 + x_3 + x_4 \geq 50$$
$$3x_1 + x_2 + 2x_3 + x_4 \geq 100$$
$$x_1 \geq 0, \quad x_2 \geq 0, \quad x_3 \geq 0, \quad x_4 \geq 0$$

5. *Optimal Land Use.* A farmer has 1000 acres of land on which corn, wheat, or soybeans can be grown. Each acre of corn costs $100 for

preparation, requires 7 days of labor, and yields a profit of $30. An acre of wheat costs $120 to prepare, requires 10 days of labor, and yields $40 profit. An acre of soybeans costs $70 to prepare, requires 8 days of labor, and yields $40 profit. If the farmer has $10,000 for preparation, and can count on enough workers to supply 8000 days of labor, how many acres should be devoted to each crop to maximize profits?

Mathematical Questions From CPA Exams (Answers on page 629)

Use the following information to answer Problems 1–4:

CPA Exam—May 1973
The Ball Company manufactures three types of lamps which are labeled A, B, and C. Each lamp is processed in two departments—I and II. Total available man-hours per day for departments I and II are 400 and 600, respectively. No additional labor is available. Time requirements and profit per unit for each lamp type is as follows:

	A	B	C
Man-hours required in Department I	2	3	1
Man-hours required in Department II	4	2	3
Profit per unit (Sales price less all variable costs)	$5	$4	$3

The company has assigned you, as the accounting member of its profit planning committee, to determine the number of types of A, B, and C lamps that it should produce in order to maximize its total profit from the sale of lamps. The following questions relate to a linear programming model that your group has developed.

1. The coefficients of the objective function would be
   (a) 4, 2, 3   (b) 2, 3, 1
   (c) 5, 4, 3   (d) 400, 600

2. The constraints in the model would be
   (a) 2, 3, 1   (b) 5, 4, 3
   (c) 4, 2, 3   (d) 400, 600

3. The constraint imposed by the available man-hours in Department I could be expressed as
   (a) $4X_1 + 2X_2 + 3X_3 \leq 400$ (b) $4X_1 + 2X_2 + 3X_3 \geq 400$
   (c) $2X_1 + 3X_2 + 1X_3 \leq 400$ (d) $2X_1 + 3X_2 + 1X_2 \geq 400$

4. The most types of lamps that would be included in the optimal solution would be
   (a) 2   (b) 1
   (c) 3   (d) 0

5. *CPA Exam—May 1972; January 1979*
   In a system of equations for a linear programming model, what can be done to equalize an inequality such as $3X + 2Y \leq 15$?
   (a) Nothing.   (b) Add a slack variable.
   (c) Add a tableau.   (d) Multiply each element by -1.

Use the following information to answer Problems 6 and 7:

CPA Exam—November 1974
The Golden Hawk Manufacturing Company wants to maximize the profits on products A, B, and C. The contribution margin for each product follows:

Product	Contribution Margin
A	$2
B	$5
C	$4

The production requirements and departmental capacities, by departments, are as follows:

Department	Production Requirements by Product (Hours)		
	A	B	C
Assembling	2	3	2
Painting	1	2	2
Finishing	2	3	1

Department	Departmental Capacity (Total Hours)
Assembling	30,000
Painting	38,000
Finishing	28,000

6. What is the profit maximization formula for the Golden Hawk Company?
   (a) $2A + $5B + $4C = X$ (where X = Profit)
   (b) $5A + 8B + 5C \leq 96,000$
   (c) $2A + $5B + $4C \leq X$ (where X = Profit)
   (d) $2A + $5B + $4C = 96,000$

7. What is the constraint for the Painting Department of the Golden Hawk Company?
   (a) $1A + 2B + 2C \geq 38,000$
   (b) $2A + $5B + $4C \geq 38,000$
   (c) $1A + 2B + 2C \leq 38,000$
   (d) $2A + 3B + 2C \leq 30,000$

8. *CPA Exam—May 1976*
   Watch Corporation manufactures products A, B, and C. The daily production requirements are shown below.

Product	Profit per Unit	Hours Required per Unit per Department		
		Machining	Plating	Polishing
A	$10	1	1	1
B	$20	3	1	2
C	$30	2	3	2
Total Hours per Day per Department		16	12	6

What is Watch's objective function in determining daily production of each unit?

(a) $A + B + C \leq \$60$

(b) $\$3A + \$6B + \$7C = \$60$

(c) $A + B + C \leq$ Profit

(d) $\$10A + \$20B + \$30C =$ Profit

Other Books or Articles

Adams, F. Gerard, and James M. Griffin, "Economic Linear Programming Model of the U.S. Petroleum Refining Industry," *J. Amer. Stat. Assoc.,* **67** (September 1972), pp. 542–551.

Allman, William P., "An Optimization Approach to Freight Car Allocation Under Time-Mileage per Diem Rental Rates," *Manage. Sci.,* **18**, 10 (June 1972), pp. B567–B574.

Aronofsky, J. S., Dutton, J. M., and Tayyabkhan, M. T. *Managerial Planning with Linear Programming,* Wiley, New York, 1978.

Broaddus, A., "Linear Programming: A New Approach to Bank Portfolio Management," *Fed. Reserve Bank Richmond: Mon. Rev.,* **58,** 11 (November 1972), pp. 3–11.

Cohen, K. J., and F. S. Hammer, "Linear Programming and Optimal Bank Asset Management Decisions," *J. Finan.,* **22** (May 1967), pp. 147–165.

Crandall, Robert H., "A Constrained Choice Model for Student Housing," *Manage. Sci.,* **16,** 2 (October 1969), pp. B112–B120.

Dantzig, George B., *Linear Programming and Extensions,* Princeton University Press, Princeton, N.J., 1963.

Ferguson, C. E., *Microeconomic Theory,* Richard D. Irwin, Homewood, Ill., 1969.

Gaber, P. Donald, and Gerald L. Thompson, *Programming and Probability Models in Operations Research,* Brooks/Cole, Monterey, Ca., 1973.

Hanssmann, Fred, and Sidney W. Hess, "A Linear Programming Approach to Production and Employment Scheduling," *Manage. Techn.,* **1** (January 1960), pp. 46–51.

Hillier, S. Fredrick, and Gerald J. Lieberman, *Operations Research,* 2nd ed., Holden-Day, San Francisco, Ca., 1974.

Lee, Sang M., and Edward R. Clayton, "Goal Programming Model for Academic Resource Allocation," *Manage. Sci.,* **18**, 8 (April 1972), pp. B395–B408.

Loucks, Daniel P., Charles S. Revelle, and Walter R. Lynn, "Linear Programming Models for Water Pollution Control," *Manage. Sci.,* **14,** 4 (December 1967), pp. B166–B181.

Murty, K. G., *Linear and Combinatorial Programming,* Wiley, New York, 1976.

Samuelson, Paul, Robert Dorfman, and Robert Solow, *Linear Programming and Economic Analysis,* McGraw-Hill, New York, 1958.

Thomas, Harold A., Jr., and Roger Revelle, "On the Efficient Use of High Aswan Dam for Hydropower and Irrigation," *Manage. Sci.,* **13,** 8 (April 1966), pp. B296–B311.

Wardle, P. A., "Forest Management and Operations Research: A Linear Programming Study," *Manage. Sci.,* **11,** 10 (August 1965), pp. B260–B270.

5

Sets; Counting Techniques

*This section may be omitted without loss of continuity.

1. Sets

Recall from Chapter 1 that a *set* is a collection of objects considered as a whole. The objects of a set S are called *elements* of S, or *members* of S. A set that has no elements, called the *empty set* or *null set,* is denoted by the symbol $\emptyset$.

The elements of a set are not repeated. Thus, we never write $\{3, 2, 2\}$ but rather write $\{3, 2\}$. Also, because a set is a collection of objects considered as a whole, the order in which the elements of a set are listed does not make any difference. Thus, the three sets

$$\{3, 2, 4\} \qquad \{2, 3, 4\} \qquad \{4, 3, 2\}$$

are different listings of the same set. The *elements* of a set distinguish the set—not the order in which the elements are written.

Some other examples of sets are the following:

(a)   Let

$$E = \{\text{All possible outcomes resulting from tossing a coin three times}\}$$

If we let H denote "heads" and T denote "tails," then the set E can also be written as

$$E = \{TTT, HTT, THT, TTH, HHT, HTH, THH, HHH\}$$

where, for instance, THT means the first toss resulted in tails, the second toss in heads, and the third toss in tails.

(b)   Let

$$F = \{\text{Possible arrangements of the digits}\}$$

Some typical elements of F are:

$$1478906532, \qquad 4875326019, \qquad 3214569870$$

The number of elements in F is very large, so listing all of them is impractical. Later on in this chapter we will study a technique to compute the number of elements in F.

Equality of Sets   **Let A and B be two sets. We say that** A *is equal to* B, **written as**

$$A = B$$

if and only if A and B have the same elements.

If two sets A and B are *not equal*, we write

$$A \neq B$$

GEORG F. L. P. CANTOR (1845–1918) was born in St. Petersburg, Russia. His father was a Danish merchant and his mother was a talented artist. The family, which was of Jewish descent converted to Christianity, moved to Frankfurt, Germany in 1856. Cantor was educated at Zurich and the University of Berlin. At Berlin his instructors were the famous mathematicians Kummer, Weierstrauss, and Kronecker. After receiving his Ph.D. degree in 1867, Cantor had an active professional career, but spent it at a mediocre university. At the age of 29 he published his revolutionary paper on the theory of infinite sets, a work that provided a common language for most of mathematics.

Subset   **Let** *A* **and** *B* **be two sets. We say that** *A* *is a subset of B* **or that** *A* *is contained in B,* **written as**

$$A \subseteq B$$

if and only if every element of *A* **is also an element of** *B.*

If a set *A* *is not a subset of a set B,* **we write**

$$A \nsubseteq B$$

When we say that *A* is a subset of *B*, we can also say "there are no elements in set *A* that are not also elements in set *B*." Of course, $A \subseteq B$ if and only if whenever $x \in A$, then $x \in B$ for all *x*. This latter way of interpreting the meaning of $A \subseteq B$ is useful for obtaining various laws that sets obey.

Proper Subset   **Let** *A* **and** *B* **be two sets. We say that** *A* *is a proper subset of B* **or that** *A* *is properly contained in B,* **written as**

$$A \subset B$$

if and only if every element of the set *A* **is also an element of set** *B,* **but there is at least one element in set** *B* **that is** *not* **in set** *A.*

Notice that "*A* is a proper subset of *B*" means that there are *no* elements of *A* that are not also elements of *B*, but there is at least one element of *B* that is not in *A*.

If a set *A* is *not* a proper subset of a set *B*, we write

$$A \not\subset B$$

The following example illustrates some uses of the three relationships, $=$, $\subseteq$, and $\subset$, just defined.

Example 1   Consider three sets *A*, *B*, and *C* given by

$$A = \{1, 2, 3\} \qquad B = \{1, 2, 3, 4, 5\} \qquad C = \{1, 2, 3\}$$

Some of the relationships between pairs of these sets are:
(a) $A = C$ (b) $A \subseteq B$ (c) $A \subseteq C$
(d) $A \subset B$ (e) $C \subseteq A$ ■

In comparing the two definitions of *subset* and *proper subset*, you should notice that if a set *A* is a subset of a set *B*, then either *A* is a proper subset of *B* or else *A* equals *B*. That is,

$$A \subseteq B \text{ if and only if either } A \subset B \text{ or } A = B$$

Also, if A is a proper subset of B, we can infer that A is a subset of B, but A does not equal B. That is,

$$A \subset B \text{ if and only if } A \subseteq B \text{ and } A \neq B$$

The distinction that is made between *subset* and *proper subset* is rather subtle, but quite important.

We can think of the relationship $\subset$ as a refinement of $\subseteq$. On the other hand, the relationship $\subseteq$ is an extension of $\subset$, in the sense that $\subseteq$ may include equality whereas with $\subset$, equality cannot be included.

Because of the way the relationship $\subseteq$ (is a subset of) has been defined, it is easy to see that for any set A, we have

$$\varnothing \subseteq A$$

Since the empty set $\varnothing$ has no elements, there is no element of the set $\varnothing$ that is not also in A.

Also, if A is any nonempty set, that is, any set having at least one element, then

$$\varnothing \subset A$$

In applications, the elements that may be considered are usually limited to some specific all-encompassing set. For example, in discussing students eligible to graduate from Midwestern University, the discussion would be limited to students enrolled at the university.

Universal Set   **The *universal set U* is defined as the set consisting of all elements under consideration.**

Thus, if A is any set and if U is the universal set, then every element in A must be in U (since U consists of all elements under consideration). Hence, we may write

$$A \subseteq U$$

for *any* set A.

It is convenient to represent a set as the interior of a circle. Pairs of sets are usually depicted as interlocking circles enclosed in a rectangle, which represents the universal set. Such diagrams of sets are called *Venn diagrams*. See Figure 1.

Venn Diagram

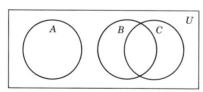

Figure 1

Operations on Sets
Next, we introduce operations that may be performed on sets.

Union of Sets   **Let A and B be any two sets. The *union of A with B*, written as**

$$A \cup B$$

is defined to be the set consisting of those elements either in A or in B or in both A and B. That is,

$$A \cup B = \{x \mid x \in A \text{ or } x \in B\}$$

In the Venn diagram in Figure 2 the shaded area corresponds to $A \cup B$.

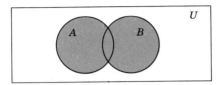

Figure 2

Intersection of Sets **Let A and B be any two sets. The** *intersection of A with B,* **written as**

$$A \cap B$$

is defined as the set consisting of those elements that are both in A and in B. That is,

$$A \cap B = \{x \mid x \in A \text{ and } x \in B\}$$

In other words, to find the intersection of two sets A and B means to find the elements *common* to A and B. In the Venn diagram in Figure 3 the shaded region is $A \cap B$.

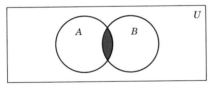

Figure 3

Example 2 For the sets

$$A = \{1, 3, 5\} \qquad B = \{3, 4, 5, 6\} \qquad C = \{6, 7\}$$

find: (a) $A \cup B$ (b) $A \cap B$ (c) $A \cap C$

Solution (a) $A \cup B = \{1, 3, 5\} \cup \{3, 4, 5, 6\} = \{1, 3, 4, 5, 6\}$
  (b) $A \cap B = \{1, 3, 5\} \cap \{3, 4, 5, 6\} = \{3, 5\}$
  (c) $A \cap C = \{1, 3, 5\} \cap \{6, 7\} = \varnothing$ ∎

JOHN VENN (1834–1923), the son of a minister, graduated from Gonville and Caius College in Cambridge, England in 1853, after which he pursued theological interests as a curate in the parishes of London. In addition to his work in logic, he made important contributions to the mathematics of probability. He was an accomplished linguist, a botanist, and a noted mountaineer.

Example 3 Let T be the set of all taxpayers and let S be the set of all people over 65 years of age. Describe $T \cap S$.

Solution $T \cap S$ is the set of all taxpayers who are also over 65 years of age. ■

Disjoint Sets **If two sets A and B have no elements in common, that is, if**

$$A \cap B = \varnothing$$

then A and B are called *disjoint sets.*

Two disjoint sets A and B are illustrated in the Venn diagram in Figure 4. Since the areas corresponding to A and B do not overlap anywhere, $A \cap B$ is empty.

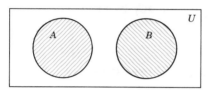

Figure 4

Example 4 Suppose that a die* is tossed. Let A be the set of outcomes in which an even number turns up; let B be the set of outcomes in which an odd number shows. Find $A \cap B$.

Solution $$A = \{2, 4, 6\} \qquad B = \{1, 3, 5\}$$

We note that A and B have no elements in common, since an even number and an odd number cannot occur simultaneously on a single toss of a die. Therefore, $A \cap B = \varnothing$ and the sets A and B are disjoint sets. ■

Suppose we consider all the employees of some company as our universal set U. Let A be the subset of employees who smoke. Then all the nonsmokers will make up some subset of U which is called the *complement* of the set of smokers.

Complement **Let A be any set. The** *complement of A,* **written as**

$$\overline{A} \quad \text{(or } A', \quad \text{or } -A)$$

is defined as the set consisting of elements in the universe U that are not in A. Thus,

$$\overline{A} = \{x \mid x \notin A\}$$

*A *die* (plural *dice*) is a cube with the numbers 1, 2, 3, 4, 5, 6 showing on the six faces.

The shaded region in Figure 5 illustrates the complement, $\bar{A}$.

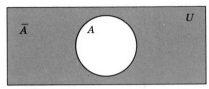

Figure 5

Example 5 Let

$$U = \{a, b, c, d, e, f\} \qquad A = \{a, b, c\} \qquad B = \{a, c, f\}$$

List the elements of the following sets:

(a) $\bar{A}$ (b) $\bar{B}$ (c) $\overline{A \cup B}$

(d) $\bar{A} \cap \bar{B}$ (e) $\overline{A \cap B}$ (f) $\bar{A} \cup \bar{B}$

Solution (a) $\bar{A}$ consists of all the elements in U that are not in A, namely, $\bar{A} = \{d, e, f\}$.

(b) Similarly, $\bar{B} = \{b, d, e\}$.

(c) To determine $\overline{A \cup B}$, we first determine the elements in $A \cup B$:

$$A \cup B = \{a, b, c, f\}$$

The complement of the set $A \cup B$ is then

$$\overline{A \cup B} = \{d, e\}$$

(d) From parts (a) and (b) we find that

$$\bar{A} \cap \bar{B} = \{d, e\}$$

(e) As in part (c), we first determine the elements in $A \cap B$:

$$A \cap B = \{a, c\}$$

Then,

$$\overline{A \cap B} = \{b, d, e, f\}$$

(f) From parts (a) and (b) we find that

$$\bar{A} \cup \bar{B} = \{b, d, e, f\}$$

■

The answers to parts (c) and (d) in Example 5 are the same, and so are the results from parts (e) and (f). This is no coincidence. There are two fundamental formulas involving intersections and unions of complements of sets. They are known as *De Morgan's laws.*

De Morgan's Laws **Let A and B be any two sets.**

(a) $\overline{A \cup B} = \bar{A} \cap \bar{B}$ (b) $\overline{A \cap B} = \bar{A} \cup \bar{B}$

De Morgan's laws state that all we need to do to form the complement of a union (or intersection) of sets is to form the complements of the individual sets and then change the union symbol to an intersection (or the intersection to a union). We shall employ Venn diagrams to verify De Morgan's laws.

(a)   First, we draw two diagrams, as shown in Figure 6.

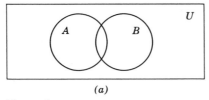
(a)

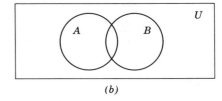
(b)

Figure 6

We will use the diagram on the left for $\bar{A} \cap \bar{B}$ and the one on the right for $\overline{A \cup B}$.

Figure 7 illustrates the completed Venn diagrams of these sets.

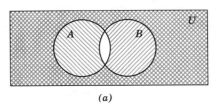
(a)

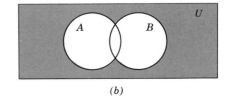
(b)

Figure 7

Thus, in Figure 7(a) $\bar{A} \cap \bar{B}$ is represented by the cross-hatched region and in Figure 7(b) $\overline{A \cup B}$ is represented by the shaded region. Since these regions correspond, this illustrates that the two sets $\bar{A} \cap \bar{B}$ and $\overline{A \cup B}$ are equal.

(b)   This verification is left to you. See Problem 28, part (c).

Example 6   Use a Venn diagram to illustrate
$$A \cup B = (A \cap \bar{B}) \cup (A \cap B) \cup (\bar{A} \cap B)$$

Solution   First, we construct Figure 8.

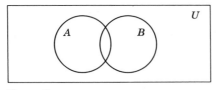

Figure 8

Now, shade the regions $A \cap \bar{B}$, $A \cap B$, and $\bar{A} \cap B$, as shown in Figure 9.

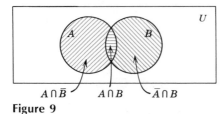

$A \cap \bar{B}$ $A \cap B$ $\bar{A} \cap B$

Figure 9

The three regions together represent the set $A \cup B$. ■

Example 7   Use a Venn diagram to illustrate

$$(A \cup B) \cap C$$

Solution   First we construct Figure 10(a). Then we shade $A \cup B$ and C as in Figure 10(b). The cross-hatched region of Figure 10(b) is the set $(A \cup B) \cap C$.

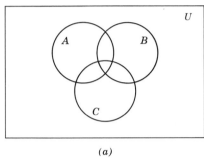 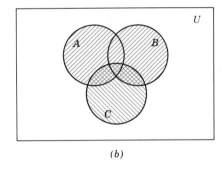

(a)   (b)

Figure 10

■

We close this section with a list of several results we will be using in later chapters:

(a) $A \cup \varnothing = A$ (b) $A \cap \varnothing = \varnothing$ (c) $A \cup \bar{A} = U$
(d) $A \cap \bar{A} = \varnothing$ (e) $\bar{U} = \varnothing$ (f) $\bar{\varnothing} = U$
(g) $(\bar{\bar{A}}) = A$

Exercise 1
Solutions to Odd-Numbered Problems begin on page 584.

In Problems 1–10 replace the asterisk by the symbol(s) $=$, $\subset$, and/or $\subseteq$ to give a true statement. If none of these relationships hold, write "None of these."

1. $\{1, 3, 7\} * \{1, 3\}$ 2. $\{4, 9\} * \{9, 10, 4\}$
3. $\{5, 7\} * \{5, 8\}$ 4. $\{0, 1, 4\} * \{0, 5, 8, 9\}$
5. $\varnothing * \{1, 3\}$ 6. $\{0\} * \{1, 3\}$
7. $\{1, 3\} * \{1, 3, 5, 8\}$ 8. $\{5, 8, 9, 15\} * \{9\}$
9. $\{2, 3\} * \{2, 3, 6, 8, 0\}$ 10. $\{2, 3\} * \{2, 3\}$

11. If $A \subseteq B$ and $B \subseteq C$, what do you conclude? Why?
12. Write down all possible subsets of the set $\{a, b, c\}$.
13. Write down all possible subsets of the set $\{a, b, c, d\}$.
14. If the universal set is the set of people, let A denote the subset of fat people, let B denote the subset of bald people, and let C denote the subset of bald and fat people. Write down several correct relationships involving A, B, and C.

In Problems 15-22, use $A = \{1, 2, 3\}$, $B = \{3, 4, 5, 6\}$, $C = \{3, 5, 7\}$ to evaluate each set.

15. $A \cap B$
16. $A \cap C$
17. $A \cup C$
18. $B \cup C$
19. $(A \cup B) \cap C$
20. $(A \cap B) \cap C$
21. $A \cup (B \cup C)$
22. $(A \cap B) \cup C$

23. If $U = $ Universal set $= \{0, 1, 2, 3, 4, 5, 6, 7, 8, 9\}$ and if $A = \{0, 1, 5, 7\}$, $B = \{2, 3, 5, 8\}$, $C = \{5, 6, 9\}$, find:
    (a) $A \cup B$
    (b) $B \cap C$
    (c) $A \cap B$
    (d) $\overline{A \cap B}$
    (e) $\bar{A} \cap \bar{B}$
    (f) $A \cup (B \cap A)$
    (g) $(C \cap A) \cap (\bar{A})$
    (h) $(A \cap B) \cup (B \cap C)$

24. If $U = $ Universal set $= \{1, 2, 3, 4, 5\}$ and if $A = \{3, 5\}$, $B = \{1, 2, 3\}$, $C = \{2, 3, 4\}$, find:
    (a) $\bar{A} \cap \bar{C}$
    (b) $(A \cup B) \cap C$
    (c) $A \cup (B \cap C)$
    (d) $(A \cup B) \cap (A \cup C)$
    (e) $\overline{A \cap C}$
    (f) $\overline{A \cup B}$
    (g) $\bar{A} \cap \bar{B}$
    (h) $(A \cap B) \cup C$

25. Let

    $U = \{$All letters of the alphabet$\}$
    $A = \{b, c, d\}$ $B = \{c, e, f, g\}$

    List the elements of the sets:
    (a) $A \cup B$
    (b) $A \cap B$
    (c) $\bar{A} \cap \bar{B}$
    (d) $\bar{A} \cup \bar{B}$

26. Let

    $U = \{a, b, c, d, e, f\}$ $A = \{b, c\}$ $B = \{c, d, e\}$

    List the elements of the sets:
    (a) $A \cup B$
    (b) $A \cap B$
    (c) $\bar{A}$
    (d) $\bar{B}$
    (e) $\overline{A \cap B}$
    (f) $\overline{A \cup B}$

27. Use Venn diagrams to illustrate the following sets:
    (a) $\bar{A} \cap B$
    (b) $(\bar{A} \cap \bar{B}) \cup C$
    (c) $A \cap (A \cup B)$
    (d) $A \cup (A \cap B)$
    (e) $(A \cup B) \cap (A \cup C)$
    (f) $A \cup (B \cap C)$
    (g) $A = (A \cap B) \cup (A \cap \bar{B})$
    (h) $B = (A \cap B) \cup (\bar{A} \cap B)$

28. Use Venn diagrams to illustrate the following laws:
    (a) $A \cap (B \cup C) = (A \cap B) \cup (A \cap C)$
       (Distributive law)
    (b) $A \cap (A \cup B) = A$ (Absorption law)
    (c) $\overline{A \cap B} = \bar{A} \cup \bar{B}$ (De Morgan's law)
    (d) $(A \cup B) \cup C = A \cup (B \cup C)$ (Associative law)

In Problems 29-32 use

     $A = \{x | x$ is a customer of IBM$\}$
     $B = \{x | x$ is a secretary employed by IBM$\}$

$$C = \{x \,|\, x \text{ is a computer operator at IBM}\}$$
$$D = \{x \,|\, x \text{ is a stockholder of IBM}\}$$
$$E = \{x \,|\, x \text{ is a member of the Board of Directors of IBM}\}$$

to describe each set.

29. $A \cap E$ 30. $B \cap D$
31. $A \cup D$ 32. $C \cap E$

In Problems 33–36 use

$$U = \{\text{All college students}\}$$
$$M = \{\text{All male students}\}$$
$$S = \{\text{All students who smoke}\}$$

to describe each set.

33. $M \cap S$ 34. $\overline{M}$ 35. $\overline{M} \cap \overline{S}$ 36. $M \cup S$

2. Counting

When you count objects, what you are actually doing is taking each object to be counted and matching each of these objects exactly once to the counting numbers 1, 2, 3, and so on, until *no* objects remain. Even before numbers had names and symbols assigned to them, this method of counting was used. Early cavemen determined how many of their herd of cattle did not return from pasture by using rocks. As each cow left, a rock was placed aside. As each cow returned, a rock was removed from the pile. If rocks remained after all the cows returned, it was then known that some cows were missing. It is important to realize that cavemen were able to do this without developing a language or symbolism for numbers.

We will need some new notation. If A is any set, we will denote by $c(A)$ the number of elements in A. Thus, for example, for the set L of letters in the alphabet,

$$L = \{a, b, c, d, e, f, \ldots, x, y, z\}$$

we write $c(L) = 26$ and say "the number of elements in L is 26."

Also, for the set

$$N = \{1, 2, 3, 4, 5\}$$

we write $c(N) = 5$.

The empty set $\varnothing$ has no elements, and we write

$$c(\varnothing) = 0$$

If the number of elements in a set is zero or a positive integer, we say that the set is *finite*. Otherwise, the set is said to be *infinite*. The area of mathematics that deals with the study of finite sets is called *finite mathematics,* and, as you may have guessed from the title of this text, we will be concerned mainly with finite sets.

Finite
Mathematics

Example 1   A survey of a group of people indicated there were 25 with brown eyes and 15 with black hair. If 10 people had both brown eyes and black hair and 23 people had neither, how many people were interviewed?

Solution   Let A denote the set of people with brown eyes and B the set of people with black hair. Then the data given tell us

$$c(A) = 25 \qquad c(B) = 15 \qquad c(A \cap B) = 10$$

Now, the number of people with either brown eyes or black hair cannot be $c(A) + c(B)$, since those with both would be counted twice. The correct procedure then would be to subtract those with both. That is,

$$c(A \cup B) = c(A) + c(B) - c(A \cap B) = 25 + 15 - 10 = 30$$

The sum of people found either in A or in B and those found neither in A nor in B is the total interviewed. Thus, the number of people interviewed is

$$30 + 23 = 53$$

See Figure 11.

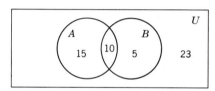

Figure 11

In Example 1 we discovered the following important relationship:

Let A and B be two finite sets. Then

$$c(A \cup B) = c(A) + c(B) - c(A \cap B)$$

Example 2
Consumer Survey   In a survey of 75 consumers, 12 indicated they were going to buy a new car, 18 said they were going to buy a new refrigerator, and 24 said they were going to buy a new stove. Of these, 6 were going to buy both a car and a refrigerator, 4 were going to buy a car and a stove, and 10 were going to buy a stove and refrigerator. One person indicated he was going to buy all three items.
(a)   How many were going to buy none of these items?
(b)   How many were going to buy only a car?
(c)   How many were going to buy only a stove?
(d)   How many were going to buy only a refrigerator?

Solution   Denote the sets of people buying cars, refrigerators, and stoves by C, R, and S, respectively. Then we know from the data given that

$$c(C) = 12 \qquad c(R) = 18 \qquad c(S) = 24$$
$$c(C \cap R) = 6 \qquad c(C \cap S) = 4 \qquad c(S \cap R) = 10$$
$$c(C \cap R \cap S) = 1$$

We use the information given above in the reverse order and put it into a Venn diagram. Thus, beginning with the fact that $c(C \cap R \cap S) = 1$, we place a 1 in that set, as shown in Figure 12(a). Now, $c(C \cap R) = 6$, $c(C \cap S) = 4$, and $c(S \cap R) = 10$. Thus, we place $6 - 1 = 5$ in the proper region (giving a total of 6 in the set $C \cap R$). Similarly, we place 3 and 9 in the proper regions for the sets $C \cap S$ and $S \cap R$. See Figure 12(b). Now, $c(C) = 12$ and 9 of these 12 are already accounted for. Also, $c(R) = 18$ with 15 accounted for and $c(S) = 24$ with 13 accounted for. See Figure 12(c). Finally, the number in $\overline{C \cup R \cup S}$ is the total of 75 less those accounted for in C, R, and S, namely $3 + 5 + 1 + 3 + 3 + 9 + 11 = 35$. Thus,

$$c(\overline{C \cup R \cup S}) = 75 - 35 = 40$$

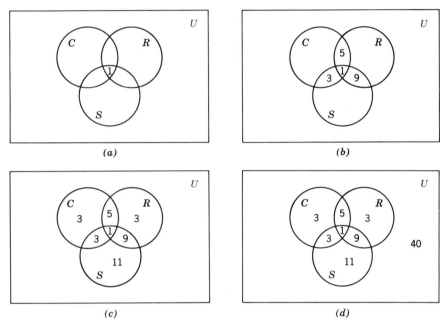

Figure 12

See Figure 12(d). From this figure, we can see that: (a) 40 were going to buy none of the items, (b) 3 were going to buy only a car, (c) 11 were going to buy only a stove, and (d) 3 were going to buy only a refrigerator. ■

Example 3
Demographic
Survey

In a survey of 10,281 people restricted to those who were either black or male or over 18 years of age, the following data were obtained:

Black: 3490
Male: 5822
Over 18: 4722
Black males: 1745
Over 18 and male: 859
Over 18 and black: 1341
Black male over 18: 239

The data are inconsistent. Why?

Solution   We denote the set of people who were black by B, male by M, and over 18 by H. Then we know that

$$c(B) = 3490 \qquad c(M) = 5822 \qquad c(H) = 4722$$
$$c(B \cap M) = 1745 \qquad c(H \cap M) = 859$$
$$c(H \cap B) = 1341 \qquad c(H \cap M \cap B) = 239$$

Since $H \cap M \cap B \neq \varnothing$, we use the Venn diagram shown in Figure 13. This means that

$$239 + 1102 + 620 + 1506 + 3457 + 643 + 2761 = 10{,}328$$

people were interviewed. However, it is given that only 10,281 were interviewed. This means the data are inconsistent.

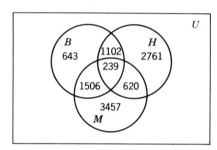

Figure 13

Exercise 2
Solutions to Odd-Numbered Problems begin on page 585.

In Problems 1–4 find the number of elements in each set.

1. $\{1, 3, 5, 7\}$
2. $\{0, 1, 2\}$
3. $\{0, 1, 2, 3, 4, 5, 6, 7, 8, 9\}$
4. $\{2, 4\}$

In Problems 5–10 use the sets $A = \{1, 2, 3, 5\}$ and $B = \{4, 6, 8\}$ to find the number of elements in each set.

5. A
6. B
7. $A \cap B$
8. $A \cup B$
9. $(A \cap B) \cup A$
10. $(B \cap A) \cup B$

In Problems 11–14 use the sets $A = \{1, 3, 6, 8\}$, $B = \{8\}$, and $C = \{8, 10\}$ to find the number of elements in each set.

11. $A \cup (B \cap C)$
12. $A \cup (B \cup C)$
13. $A \cap (B \cap C)$
14. $(A \cap B) \cup C$

15. Find $c(A \cup B)$, given that $c(A) = 4$, $c(B) = 3$, and $c(A \cap B) = 2$.
16. Find $c(A \cup B)$, given that $c(A) = 14$, $c(B) = 11$, and $c(A \cap B) = 6$.
17. Find $c(A \cap B)$, given that $c(A) = 5$, $c(B) = 4$, and $c(A \cup B) = 7$.
18. Find $c(A \cap B)$, given that $c(A) = 8$, $c(B) = 9$, and $c(A \cup B) = 16$.

19. Find $c(A)$, given that $c(B) = 8$, $c(A \cap B) = 4$, and $c(A \cup B) = 14$.
20. Find $c(B)$, given that $c(A) = 10$, $c(A \cap B) = 5$, and $c(A \cup B) = 29$.
21. Motors Incorporated manufactured 325 cars with automatic transmissions, 216 with power steering, and 89 with both these options. How many cars were manufactured if every car has at least one option?
22. Suppose that out of 1500 first-year students at a certain college, 350 are taking history, 300 are taking mathematics, and 270 are taking both history and mathematics. How many first-year students are taking history or mathematics?
23. *Voting Patterns.* In 1948, according to a study made by Berelsa, Lazarfeld, and McPhee, the influence of religion and age on voting in Elmira, New York, was given by the following table:

	Age		
	Below 35	35–54	Over 54
Protestant Voting Republican	82	152	111
Protestant Voting Democratic	42	33	15
Catholic Voting Republican	27	33	7
Catholic Voting Democratic	44	47	33

Find:
(a) The number of voters who are Catholic or Republican or both.
(b) The number of voters who are Catholic or over 54 or both.
(c) The number of Democratic voters below 35 or over 54.

In Problems 24–32 use the data in the figure below to answer each question.

24. How many are in set A?
25. How many are in set B?
26. How many are in A or B?
27. How many are in B or C?
28. How many are in A but not B?
29. How many are in B but not C?
30. How many are in all three?
31. How many are in none?
32. How many are in A and B and C?

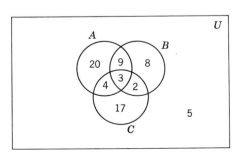

33. The following Venn diagram illustrates the number of seniors (*S*), female students (*F*), and students on the dean's list (*D*) at a small western college. Describe each number.

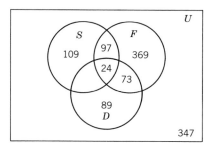

34. At a small midwestern college:

   31   female seniors were on the dean's list
   62   females were on the dean's list who were not seniors
   45   male seniors were on the dean's list
   87   female seniors were not on the dean's list
   96   male seniors were not on the dean's list
   275   females were not seniors and were not on the dean's list
   89   men were on the dean's list who were not seniors
   227   men were not seniors and were not on the dean's list

   (a) How many were seniors?
   (b) How many were females?
   (c) How many were on the dean's list?
   (d) How many were seniors on the dean's list?
   (e) How many were female seniors?
   (f) How many were females on the dean's list?
   (g) How many were students at the college?

35. In a survey of 75 college students, it was found that of the three weekly news magazines *Time*, *Newsweek*, and *U.S. News and World Report*:

   23   read *Time*
   18   read *Newsweek*
   14   read *U.S. News and World Report*
   10   read *Time* and *Newsweek*
   9   read *Time* and *U.S. News and World Report*
   8   read *Newsweek* and *U.S. News and World Report*
   5   read all three

   (a) How many read none of these three magazines?
   (b) How many read *Time* alone?
   (c) How many read *Newsweek* alone?
   (d) How many read *U.S. News and World Report* alone?
   (e) How many read neither *Time* nor *Newsweek*?
   (f) How many read *Time* or *Newsweek* or both?

36. Of the cars sold during the month of July, 90 had air conditioning, 100 had automatic transmissions, and 75 had power steering. Five

cars had all three of these extras. Twenty cars had none of these extras. Twenty cars had only air conditioning; 60 cars had only automatic transmissions; and 30 cars had only power steering. Ten cars had both automatic transmission and power steering.
  (a) How many cars had both power steering and air conditioning?
  (b) How many had both automatic transmission and air conditioning?
  (c) How many had neither power steering nor automatic transmission?
  (d) How many cars were sold in July?
  (e) How many had automatic transmission or air conditioning or both?

37. A staff member at a large engineering school was presenting data to show that the students there received a liberal education as well as a scientific one. "Look at our record," she said. "Out of one senior class of 500 students, 281 are taking English, 196 are taking English and History, 87 are taking History and a foreign language, 143 are taking a foreign language and English, and 36 are taking all of these." She was fired. Why?

38. *Blood Classification.* Blood is classified as being either Rh-positive or Rh-negative and according to type. If blood contains an A antigen, it is type A; if it has a B antigen, it is type B; if it has both A and B antigens, it is type AB; and if it has neither antigen, it is type O. Use a Venn diagram to illustrate these possibilities. How many different possibilities are there?

39. A survey of 52 families from a suburb of Chicago indicated that there was a total of 241 children below the age of 18. Of these, 109 were male; 132 were below the age of 11; 143 had played Little League; and 69 males were below the age of 11. If 45 females under 11 had played Little League and 30 males under 11 had played Little League, how many children over 11 and under 18 had played Little League?

3. Permutations

In this section and the next, we discuss two general types of counting problems that can be solved by employing formulas. These two types of problems are called *permutation problems* and *combination problems* (see Section 4).

Before discussing the nature of a permutation, we shall introduce a useful shorthand notation—the *factorial symbol.*

Factorial **The symbol $n!$, read as "n factorial," means**

$$0! = 1 \qquad 1! = 1 \qquad n! = n(n-1)(n-2)\cdots(3)(2)(1), \quad n \geq 1$$

Thus, to compute $n!$, we find the product of all consecutive integers from 1 to n inclusive. For example,

$$4! = (4)(3)(2)(1) = 24 \qquad 3! = (3)(2)(1) = 6$$

A formula we shall find useful is

$$(n + 1)! = (n + 1) \cdot n!$$

For example, since $5! = 5 \cdot 4!$,

$$\frac{5!}{4!} = \frac{5 \cdot 4!}{4!} = 5$$

We begin the study of permutations by considering the following problem.

Example 1   In traveling from New York to Los Angeles, Mr. Doody wishes to stop over in Chicago. If he has 5 different routes to choose from in driving from New York to Chicago and has 3 routes to choose from in driving from Chicago to Los Angeles, in how many ways can Mr. Doody travel from New York to Los Angeles?

Solution   The task of traveling from New York to Los Angeles is composed of two consecutive operations:

Drive from New York to Chicago Operation 1		Drive from Chicago to Los Angeles Operation 2

In Figure 14, we see that following each of the 5 routes from New York to Chicago there are 3 routes from Chicago to Los Angeles. Thus, in all, there are $5 \cdot 3 = 15$ different routes.

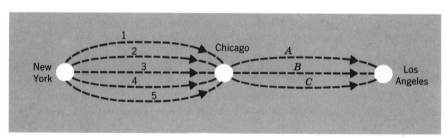

Figure 14

These 15 different routes can be enumerated as

1A, 1B, 1C   2A, 2B, 2C   3A, 3B, 3C   4A, 4B, 4C   5A, 5B, 5C

■

Tree Diagram   Example 1 can also be worked by using a *tree diagram*. See Figure 15.

In general, this leads to the following principle:

Principle of Counting   **If we can perform a first task in p different ways, a second task in q different ways, a third task in r different ways, . . . , then the total act of performing the first task followed by performing the second task, and so on, can be done in $p \cdot q \cdot r \cdot \cdots$ ways.**

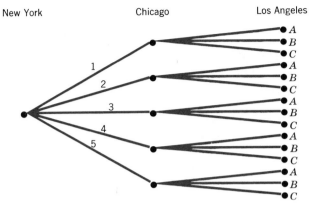

Figure 15

Example 2   In a city election, there are 4 candidates for mayor, 3 candidates for vice-mayor, 6 candidates for treasurer, and 2 for secretary. In how many ways can these four offices be filled?

Solution   The task of filling an office can be divided into four consecutive operations:

| Select a mayor | Select a vice-mayor | Select a treasurer | Select a secretary |

Corresponding to each of the 4 possible mayors, there are 3 vice-mayors. These two offices can be filled in 4 • 3 = 12 different ways. Also, corresponding to each of these 12 possibilities, we have 6 different choices for treasurer—giving 12 • 6 = 72 different possibilities. Finally, to each of these 72 possibilities there can correspond 2 choices for secretary. Thus, all told, these offices can be filled in 4 • 3 • 6 • 2 = 144 different ways. A partial illustration is given by the tree diagram in Figure 16.

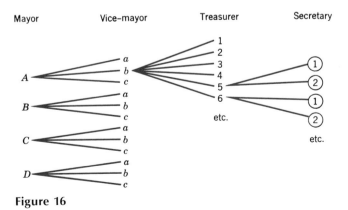

Figure 16

Example 3   (a)   From how many different batting orders must the manager of a baseball
Batting Orders   team (nine players) select?
                    (b)   If the manager adheres to the rule that the pitcher always bats last and the

star home run hitter is always cleanup (fourth), then from how many possibilities must the manager select?

Solution (a) In the first slot, any of the 9 players can be chosen. In the second slot, any one of the remaining 8 can be chosen; and so on, so that there are

$$9 \cdot 8 \cdot 7 \cdot 6 \cdot 5 \cdot 4 \cdot 3 \cdot 2 \cdot 1 = 9! = 362{,}880$$

possible batting orders.

(b) The first position can be filled in any one of 7 ways, the second in any of 6 ways, the third in any of 5 ways, the fourth has been designated, the fifth in any of 4 ways, . . . , so that here there are

$$7 \cdot 6 \cdot 5 \cdot 4 \cdot 3 \cdot 2 \cdot 1 = 7! = 5040$$

different batting orders of 9 players after 2 have been designated.

Example 4 Suppose we are setting up a code of 3 letter words and have 6 different letters, a, b, c, d, e, and f, from which to choose. If the code must not repeat any letter more than once, and if such words as abc and bac are considered different, how many different words can be formed?

Solution We solve the problem by using the principle of counting. In selecting a first letter, we have 6 choices. Since whatever letter is chosen cannot be repeated, we have 5 choices available for the second letter and 4 for the last letter. In all, then, there are $6 \cdot 5 \cdot 4 = 120$ words of 3 letters that can be formed. See Figure 17 for a partial tree diagram of this solution.

Observe two important features of the above two examples: First, no item is repeated (that is, replacements were not allowed). Second, order is important (for example, abc and bac are different words). When these two characteristics appear in a counting problem, it is called a *permutation*.

Permutation **The number of** *permutations of n different things taken r at a time,* **denoted by** $P(n, r)$**, means the number of all possible different arrangements of** r **things chosen from** n **different things, in which order is important.**

Let's look for a general formula for $P(n, r)$. We want to find the number of all possible different arrangements of r quantities that are chosen from n different quantities in which no item is repeated and order is important. The first entry can be filled by any one of the n possibilities, the second by any one of the remaining $(n - 1)$, the third by any one of the now remaining $(n - 2)$, and so on. Since there are r positions to be filled, the number of possibilities is

$$P(n, r) = \underbrace{n(n - 1)(n - 2) \cdots}_{r \text{ factors}}$$

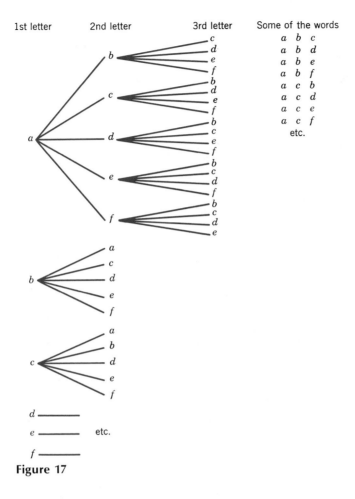

1st letter   2nd letter   3rd letter   Some of the words

Figure 17

For example, if $n = 6$ and $r = 2$,
$$P(6, 2) = \underbrace{6 \cdot 5}_{2 \text{ factors}} = 30$$

Other examples are
$$P(7, 3) = \underbrace{7 \cdot 6 \cdot 5}_{3 \text{ factors}} = 210 \qquad P(5, 5) = \underbrace{5 \cdot 4 \cdot 3 \cdot 2 \cdot 1}_{5 \text{ factors}} = 5! = 120$$

To obtain the last factor in the expression for $P(n, r)$, we observe the following pattern:

First factor is n
Second factor is $n - 1$
Third factor is $n - 2$
$\vdots$
rth factor is $n - (r - 1) = n - r + 1$

The number of different arrangements of r objects chosen from n objects in which

1. **The n objects are all different**
2. **No object is repeated more than once in an arrangement**
3. **Order is important**

is given by the formula

$$P(n, r) = n(n - 1) \cdots (n - r + 1)$$

Multiplying the right side by 1 in the form of $(n - r)!/(n - r)!$, we obtain

$$P(n, r) = n(n - 1)(n - 2) \bullet \cdots \bullet (n - r + 1)\frac{(n - r)!}{(n - r)!}$$

Thus, since $n(n - 1)(n - 2) \bullet \cdots \bullet (n - r + 1)(n - r)! = n!$, we get the following useful formula for $P(n, r)$:

$$P(n, r) = \frac{n!}{(n - r)!}$$

Example 5 A station wagon has 9 seats in it. In how many different ways can 5 people be seated?

Solution The first person can choose any one of the 9 seats. The second person can then choose from any of the 8 seats left. The third from 7 seats, the fourth from 6, and the fifth from 5 seats. Thus, in all, there are

$$9 \bullet 8 \bullet 7 \bullet 6 \bullet 5 = 15,120$$

different seating arrangements.

In Example 5, we observe that the properties of a permutation are satisfied: the 9 seats are all different, no seat is taken more than once, and order is important. We conclude that Example 5 is asking for the number of permutations of 9 seats taken 5 at a time. That is,

$$P(9, 5) = 9 \bullet 8 \bullet 7 \bullet 6 \bullet 5 = 15,120$$

Suppose that, instead, there were 9 people to be seated in the 9 passenger station wagon. In this case, the number of possible arrangements is

$$P(9, 9) = 9 \bullet 8 \bullet 7 \bullet 6 \bullet 5 \bullet 4 \bullet 3 \bullet 2 \bullet 1 = 9! = 362,880$$

In general, the number of permutations of n different objects taken n at a time is

$$P(n, n) = n!$$

Exercise 3
Solutions to Odd-Numbered Problems begin on page 586.

In Problems 1–16 evaluate each expression.

1. $\dfrac{5!}{2!}$ 2. $\dfrac{8!}{2!}$ 3. $\dfrac{6!}{3!}$ 4. $\dfrac{9!}{3!}$

5. $\dfrac{10!}{8!}$

6. $\dfrac{11!}{9!}$

7. $\dfrac{9!}{8!}$

8. $\dfrac{10!}{9!}$

9. $\dfrac{8!}{2!6!}$

10. $\dfrac{9!}{3!6!}$

11. $P(7, 2)$

12. $P(5, 1)$

13. $P(8, 1)$

14. $P(6, 6)$

15. $P(5, 0)$

16. $P(6, 4)$

17. A woman has 4 blouses and 5 skirts. How many different outfits can she wear?

18. XYZ Company wants to build a complex consisting of a factory, office building, and warehouse. If the building contractor has 3 different kinds of factories, 2 different office buildings, and 4 different warehouses, how many models must be built to show all possibilities to XYZ Company?

19. Cars Incorporated has 3 different car models and 6 color schemes. If you are one of the dealers, how many cars must you display to show each possibility?

20. A man has 3 pairs of shoes, 8 pairs of socks, 4 pairs of slacks, and 9 sweaters. How many outfits can he wear?

21. There are 14 teachers in a Math Department. A student is asked to indicate her favorite and her least favorite. In how many ways is this possible?

22. A house has 3 doors and 12 windows. In how many ways can a burglar rob the house by entering through a window and exiting through a door?

23. Using the digits 1, 2, 3, and 4, how many different 4 digit numbers can be formed?

24. On a math test there are 10 multiple-choice questions with 4 possible answers and 15 true–false questions. In how many possible ways can the 25 questions be answered?

25. Five different Mathematics books, 3 different Physics books, and 2 different Computer Science books are to be arranged on a student's desk. The student wants the books to be grouped by subject matter. How many arrangements are possible?

26. An automobile manufacturer produces 3 different models. Models *A* and *B* can come in any of 3 body styles; Model *C* can come in only 2 body styles. Each car also comes in either black or green. How many distinguishable car types are there? [*Hint:* Use a tree diagram.]

27. How many basketball games are played in the Big Ten, if every team plays every other team twice?

4. Combinations

Up to this point, we have been concerned with the order in which *n* distinct objects can be rearranged without repeating. However, in many cases, order is not important. For example, in a draw poker hand, the order in which you receive the cards is not important—all that matters is what cards are received. That is, with poker hands, we are concerned with the *combination* of the cards—not the particular order of the cards.

To further emphasize the role that order plays in a counting problem, suppose we have 4 letters, *a, b, c, d,* and wish to choose 2 of them without repeating any letter more than once. If order is important, then we have $P(4, 2) = 4 \cdot 3 = 12$ possible arrangements, namely,

$$ab, ac, ad \qquad bc, bd, cd \qquad ba, ca, da \qquad cb, db, dc$$

If order is not a consideration, we have only 6 selections, namely,

$$ab, ac, ad, bc, bd, cd$$

The latter counting problem is typical of a *combination problem.*

Combination **The number of** *combinations of n different things taken r at a time,* **denoted by** $C(n, r)$**, is defined to be the number of all possible selections of r objects chosen from n objects, neglecting the order of selection.**

In order to obtain a formula for $C(n, r)$, we observe that we have *n* different things taken *r* at a time. Since each of these combinations has *r* objects, each can be permuted in *r*! different ways. Thus, by the principle of counting, there are

$$r! \cdot C(n, r)$$

different arrangements of *n* things taken *r* at a time. But this is just the number of permutations of *n* things taken *r* at a time. Hence,

$$r!C(n, r) = P(n, r)$$

$$C(n, r) = \frac{P(n, r)}{r!} = \frac{n!}{r!(n - r)!}$$

The number of different arrangements of r objects chosen from n objects in which

1. **The n objects are all different**
2. **No object is repeated**
3. **Order is not important**

is given by the formula

$$C(n, r) = \frac{n!}{r!(n - r)!}$$

Example 1 Compute the following numbers:
(a) $C(50, 2)$ (b) $C(7, 5)$ (c) $C(7, 7)$ (d) $C(7, 0)$

Solution (a) $C(50, 2) = \dfrac{50!}{2!(50 - 2)!} = \dfrac{50!}{2!48!} = 1225$

(b) $C(7, 5) = \dfrac{7!}{5!(7 - 5)!} = \dfrac{7!}{5!2!} = 21$

(c) $C(7, 7) = \dfrac{7!}{7!(7 - 7)!} = \dfrac{7!}{7!0!} = 1$

(d) $C(7, 0) = \dfrac{7!}{0!(7 - 0)!} = \dfrac{7!}{0!7!} = 1$ ∎

Example 2 From a deck of 52 cards, a hand of 5 cards is dealt. How many different hands are possible?

Solution If the order of receipt of the cards is considered, there are

$$52 \cdot 51 \cdot 50 \cdot 49 \cdot 48$$

different hands. But order is not important. Thus, since corresponding to each hand of 5 cards there are 5! different arrangements, we see that the number of different hands without regard to order is

$$\frac{52 \cdot 51 \cdot 50 \cdot 49 \cdot 48}{5!} = 2{,}598{,}960$$

Of course, we can also arrive at this result by recognizing that the number of different hands is $C(52, 5)$. That is,

$$C(52, 5) = \frac{52!}{5!47!} = \frac{52 \cdot 51 \cdot 50 \cdot 49 \cdot 48}{5 \cdot 4 \cdot 3 \cdot 2 \cdot 1}$$

$$= 2{,}598{,}960$$ ∎

Example 3 A sociologist needs a sample of 12 welfare recipients located in a large metropolitan area. He divides the city into 4 areas—northwest, northeast, southwest, southeast. Each section contains 25 welfare recipients. The sociologist may select the 12 recipients in any way he wants—all from the same area, 2 from the southwest area and 10 from the northwest area, and so on. How many different groups of 12 recipients are there?

Solution Since order of selection is not important and since the selection is of 12 things from a possible $4 \cdot 25 = 100$ things, there are $C(100, 12)$ different groups. That is,

$$C(100, 12) = \frac{100!}{12!88!}$$ ∎

Example 4 From 5 faculty members and 4 students, a committee of 4 is to be chosen which includes 2 students and 2 faculty members. In how many ways can this be done?

Solution The faculty members can be chosen in $C(5, 2)$ ways. The students can be chosen in $C(4, 2)$ ways. By the principle of counting, there are then

$$C(5, 2) \cdot C(4, 2) = \frac{5!}{2!3!} \cdot \frac{4!}{2!2!} = 10 \cdot 6 = 60 \text{ different ways}$$ ∎

Pascal Triangle

Binomial
Coefficient

Sometimes the notation $\binom{n}{r}$, read as "n things taken r at a time" is used in place of $C(n, r)$. Here, $\binom{n}{r}$ is called the *binomial coefficient*. A triangular display of $\binom{n}{r}$ for $n = 0$ to $n = 6$ is given in Figure 18. This triangular display is called a *Pascal triangle*.

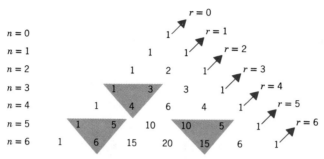

Figure 18

For example, $\binom{5}{2} = 10$, is found in the row marked $n = 5$ and on the diagonal marked $r = 2$.

In the Pascal triangle, successive entries can be obtained by adding the two nearest entries in the row above it. The shaded triangles in Figure 18 illustrate this. For example, $10 + 5 = 15$, etc.

The Pascal triangle, as the figure indicates, is symmetric. That is, when n is even, the largest entry occurs in the middle, and corresponding entries on either side are equal. When n is odd, there are two equal middle entries with corresponding equal entries on either side.

Exercise 4

Solutions to Odd-Numbered Problems begin on page 586.

In Problems 1–8 find the value of each expression.

1. $C(6, 4)$
2. $C(5, 4)$
3. $C(7, 2)$
4. $C(8, 7)$
5. $\binom{5}{1}$
6. $\binom{8}{1}$
7. $\binom{8}{6}$
8. $\binom{8}{4}$

9. In how many ways can a committee of 3 senators be selected from a group of 8 senators?
10. In how many ways can a committee of 4 representatives be selected from a group of 9 representatives?
11. A Math Department is allowed to tenure 4 of 17 eligible teachers. In how many ways can the selection for tenure be made?
12. How many different hands are possible in a bridge game? (A bridge hand consists of 13 cards dealt from a deck of 52 cards.)
13. There are 25 students in the Math Club. How many ways can 3 officers be selected?

BLAISE PASCAL (1623–1662) is most well-known for his creation of a theory of probability. He constructed the first computer, and later in life became interested in theology, contributing several literary masterpieces in this area.

14. How many different relay teams of 4 persons can be chosen from a group of 10 runners?

15. A basketball team has 6 players who play at guard (2 of 5 starting positions). How many different teams are possible, assuming the remaining 3 positions are filled and it is not possible to distinguish a left guard from a right guard?

16. On a basketball team of 12 players, 2 play only at center, 3 play only at guard, and the rest play at forward (5 men on a team: 2 forwards, 2 guards, and 1 center). How many different teams are possible, assuming it is not possible to distinguish left and right guards and left and right forwards?

17. The Student Affairs Committee has 3 faculty, 2 administration members, and 5 students on it. In how many ways can a subcommittee of 1 faculty, 1 administration member, and 2 students be formed?

18. Of 1352 stocks traded in 1 day on the New York Stock Exchange, 641 advanced, 234 declined, and the remainder were unchanged. In how many ways can this happen?

19. How many different ways can an offensive football team be formed from a squad that consists of 20 linemen, 3 quarterbacks, 8 halfbacks, and 4 fullbacks? This football team must have 1 quarterback, 2 halfbacks, 1 fullback, and 7 linemen.

20. How many different ways can a baseball team be made up from a squad of 15 players, if 3 players are used only as pitchers and the remaining players can be placed at any position except pitcher (9 players on a team)?

21. A little girl has 1 penny, 1 nickel, 1 dime, 1 quarter, and 1 half dollar in her purse. If she pulls out 3 coins, how many different sums are possible?

5. Further Counting Problems

In this section we give some counting examples that will be helpful in our discussion of probability in the next chapter.

The first example deals with a coin-tossing experiment in which a coin is tossed a fixed number of times. There are exactly two possible outcomes on each trial or toss (heads, H, or tails, T). For instance, in tossing a coin three times, one possible outcome is HTH—heads on the first toss, tails on the second toss, and heads on the third toss.

Example 1   Suppose an experiment consists of tossing a coin 8 times.
(a) How many different outcomes are possible?
(b) How many different outcomes have exactly 3 tails?
(c) How many outcomes have at most 2 tails?
(d) How many outcomes have at least 3 tails?

Solution   (a) Each outcome of the experiment consists of a sequence of eight letters H or T, where the first letter records the result of the first toss, the second letter the result of the second toss, and so forth. Thus, the process can be visualized as filling an empty box at each toss:

| 1st toss | T | | | | | | | |

| 2nd toss | T | H | | | | | | |

| 3rd toss | T | H | H | | | | | |

$\vdots$ $\qquad$ $\vdots$

| 8th toss | T | H | H | H | T | H | H | T |

Since each box can be filled in two ways, by the principle of counting, the sequence of eight boxes can be filled in

$$\underbrace{2 \cdot 2 \cdot 2 \cdot \ldots \cdot 2}_{8 \text{ factors}} = 2^8 = 256 \text{ ways}$$

Thus, there are $2^8 = 256$ different possible outcomes.

(b) Any sequence that contains exactly 3 T's must contain 5 H's. A particular outcome is determined as soon as we decide where to place the T's in the eight boxes. The three boxes to receive the T's can be selected from the eight boxes in $C(8, 3)$ different ways. So the number of outcomes with exactly 3 tails is

$$C(8, 3) = \frac{8!}{3!5!} = 8 \cdot 7 = 56$$

(c) The outcomes with at most 2 tails correspond to the sequences with 0, 1, or 2 T, and they are:

$\quad$ 0 T: $\quad$ One outcome is possible, namely $HHHHHHHH$.
$\quad$ 1 T: $\quad$ This outcome is determined by selecting one box out of eight in which to place the single T. This can be done in $C(8, 1) =$ 8 ways.
$\quad$ 2 T: $\quad$ This outcome is determined by selecting two boxes out of eight in which to place the 2 T's. This can be done in $C(8, 2) = 28$ ways.

Thus, the number of outcomes with at most 2 tails is just the sum of all these outcomes, which is $1 + 8 + 28 = 37$ ways.

(d) The outcomes with at least 3 tails are the results with 3, 4, 5, 6, 7, or 8 tails. The total number of such outcomes is

$$C(8, 3) + C(8, 4) + C(8, 5) + C(8, 6) + C(8, 7) + C(8, 8)$$

But there is a simpler way of obtaining the answer. If we start with the total number of outcomes obtained in part (a) and subtract the number of outcomes of at most 2 tails obtained in part (c), we get the number of outcomes with at least 3 tails:

$$256 - 37 = 219 \text{ ways}$$

Example 2 An urn contains 8 white balls and 4 red balls. Four balls are selected. In how many ways can the 4 balls be drawn from the total of 12 balls:
(a) If the color is not considered?
(b) If 3 balls are white and 1 is red?
(c) If all 4 balls are white?
(d) If all 4 balls are red?

Solution (a) Since order is not important, this experiment is simply a selection of 4 balls out of 12. There are $C(12, 4)$ possible ways to select the balls, that is,

$$C(12, 4) = \frac{12!}{4!8!} = \frac{12 \cdot 11 \cdot 10 \cdot 9}{4 \cdot 3 \cdot 2 \cdot 1} = 495 \text{ ways}$$

(b) The desired answer involves two operations: first, the selection of 3 white balls from 8; and second, the selection of 1 red ball from 4:

Select 3 white balls Operation 1	Select 1 red ball Operation 2

The first operation can be performed in $C(8, 3)$ ways; the second operation can be performed in $C(4, 1)$ ways. By the principle of counting, the answer is

$$C(8, 3) \cdot C(4, 1) = \frac{8!}{3!5!} \cdot \frac{4!}{1!3!} = 224$$

(c) Since all 4 balls must be selected from the 8 that are white, the answer is

$$C(8, 4) = \frac{8!}{4!4!} = \frac{8 \cdot 7 \cdot 6 \cdot 5}{4 \cdot 3 \cdot 2 \cdot 1} = 70 \text{ ways}$$

(d) Since the 4 red balls must be selected from 4 red balls, the answer is 1 way. ∎

We conclude this section with counting problems that are a variation on permutations. Recall that a permutation problem requires that the objects be distinct. Many problems, however, contain duplications of an object—that is, some of the objects are repeated. Although counting problems of this type are not, strictly speaking, permutations, they bear a close resemblance to permutation problems.

The next few examples illustrate how to find the number of different arrangements of n objects taken n at a time when:

1. Some of the n objects are the same (repeated)
2. Order is important

Example 3 How many different 3 letter words (real or imaginary) can be formed from the letters in each word?

(a) MAD   (b) DAD

Solution (a) The word MAD contains 3 different letters, order is important, and no letter is repeated. The number of different words is a permutation of 3 things taken 3 at a time, or

$$P(3,3) = 3! = 6$$

The six different words are

MAD	MDA	AMD
DAM	DMA	ADM

(b) The word DAD contains 3 letters, and, if all were different [as in part (a)], the answer would be $P(3,3) = 3!$ different words. However, there are 2 D's, which we cannot distinguish, so that 3! must be too large. [For example, if in part (a) we set M = D, then MAD and DAM are the same.] If N is the number of different arrangements of DAD, and we think of the D's as different letters, say D_1 and D_2, the number of different arrangements of D_1AD_2 is $2!N$. But we have treated all letters as distinct so that

$$2!N = 3!$$
$$N = \frac{3!}{2!} = 3$$

The three different arrangements are DAD, DDA, and ADD.   ◼

Reasoning as in Example 3, we can state the following general result:

The number of distinct permutations of n things of which n_1 are of one kind, n_2 of a second kind, ..., n_k of a kth kind, is

$$\frac{n!}{n_1! \cdot n_2! \cdot \cdots \cdot n_k!}$$

Example 4   How many different vertical arrangements are possible for 10 flags, if 2 are white, 3 are red, and 5 are blue.

Solution   Here we want the different arrangements of 10 objects, which are not all different. Following the example above, we have

$$\frac{10!}{2!3!5!} = \frac{10 \cdot 9 \cdot 8 \cdot 7 \cdot \cancel{6} \cdot \cancel{5!}}{2 \cdot \cancel{3} \cdot \cancel{2} \cdot \cancel{5!}} = 2520 \text{ different arrangements}$$

◼

Example 5   How many different 11 letter words (real or imaginary) can be formed from the word below?

MISSISSIPPI

Solution   Here we want the number of distinct 11 letter words with 4 I's, 4 S's, 2 P's, and 1

M, so that the total number of 11 letter words is

$$\frac{11!}{2!4!4!} = \frac{39,916,800}{1152} = 34,650$$

■

Example 6 A sorority house has 3 bedrooms and 10 students. One bedroom has 3 beds, the second has 2 beds, and the third has 5 beds. In how many different ways can the students be assigned rooms?

Solution The number of different ways the 10 students can be assigned is

$$\frac{10!}{2!3!5!} = 2520 \text{ different ways}$$

■

Exercise 5
Solutions to Odd-Numbered Problems begin on page 587.

1. An experiment consists of tossing a coin ten times.
   (a) How many different outcomes are possible?
   (b) How many different outcomes have exactly 4 heads?
   (c) How many outcomes have at most 2 heads?
   (d) How many outcomes have at least 3 heads?
2. An experiment consists of tossing a coin six times.
   (a) How many different outcomes are possible?
   (b) How many outcomes have exactly 3 heads?
   (c) How many different outcomes have at least 2 heads?
   (d) How many outcomes have 4 heads or 5 heads?
3. An urn contains 7 white balls and 3 red balls. Three balls are selected. In how many ways can the 3 balls be drawn from the total of 10 balls:
   (a) If the color is not considered?
   (b) If 2 balls are white and 1 is red?
   (c) If all 3 balls are white?
   (d) If all 3 balls are red?
4. An urn contains 15 red balls and 10 white balls. Five balls are selected. In how many ways can the 5 balls be drawn from the total of 25 balls:
   (a) If the color is not considered?
   (b) If all balls are red?
   (c) If 3 balls are red and 2 are white?
   (d) If at least 4 are red balls?
5. In the World Series the American League team (*A*) and the National League team (*N*) play until one team wins four games. If the sequence of winners is designated by letters (for example, *NAAAA* means the National League team won the first game and the American League team won the next four), how many different sequences are possible?

6. How many different ways can 3 red, 4 yellow, and 5 blue bulbs be arranged in a string of Christmas tree lights with 12 sockets?

7. In how many ways can 3 apple trees, 4 peach trees, and 2 plum trees be arranged along a fence line if one does not distinguish between trees of the same kind?

8. How many different 8 letter words (real or imaginary) can be formed from the letters in the word ECONOMICS?

9. How many different 11 letter words (real or imaginary) can be formed from the letters in the word MATHEMATICS?

10. The United States Senate has 100 members. Suppose it is desired to place each senator on exactly 1 of 7 possible committees. The first committee has 22 members, the second has 13, the third has 10, the fourth has 5, the fifth has 16, and the sixth and seventh have 17 apiece. In how many ways can these committees be formed?

11. In how many ways can 10 children be placed on 3 teams of 3, 3, and 4 members?

12. A group of 9 people is going to be split into committees of 4, 3, and 2 people. How many committees can be formed if:
    (a) A person can serve on any number of committees?
    (b) No person can serve on more than one committee?

13. A group consists of 5 men and 8 women. A committee of 4 is to be formed from this group, and policy dictates that at least 1 woman be on this committee.
    (a) How many different committees can be formed that contain exactly 1 man?
    (b) How many committees can be formed that contain exactly 2 women?
    (c) How many committees can be formed that contain at least 1 man?

*6.   The Binomial Theorem

The binomial theorem deals with the problem of expanding an expression of the form $(x + y)^n$, where n is a positive integer.

Expressions such as $(x + y)^2$ and $(x + y)^3$ are not too difficult to expand. For example,

$$(x + y)^2 = x^2 + 2xy + y^2 \qquad (x + y)^3 = x^3 + 3x^2y + 3xy^2 + y^3$$

However, expanding expressions such as $(x + y)^6$ or $(x + y)^8$ by the normal process of multiplication would be tedious and time-consuming. As it turns out, we can use the binomial theorem, which depends on some properties of combinations.

Recall that

$$C(n, r) = \binom{n}{r} = \frac{n!}{r!(n - r)!}$$

*This section may be omitted without loss of continuity.

Then, for example, the expression

$$(x + y)^2 = x^2 + 2xy + y^2$$

can be written as

$$(x + y)^2 = \binom{2}{0}x^2 + \binom{2}{1}xy + \binom{2}{2}y^2$$

The expansion of $(x + y)^3$ can be written as

$$(x + y)^3 = x^3 + 3x^2y + 3xy^2 + y^3 = \binom{3}{0}x^3 + \binom{3}{1}x^2y + \binom{3}{2}xy^2 + \binom{3}{3}y^3$$

In general, we have the binomial theorem.

Binomial Theorem **If n is a positive integer,**

$$(x + y)^n = \binom{n}{0}x^n + \binom{n}{1}x^{n-1}y + \binom{n}{2}x^{n-2}y^2 + \cdots + \binom{n}{k}x^{n-k}y^k$$

(1)

$$+ \cdots + \binom{n}{n}y^n$$

Observe that the powers of x begin at n and decrease by 1, while the powers of y begin with 0 and increase by 1. Also, the coefficient of y^k is always $\binom{n}{k}$.

Example 1 Expand $(x + y)^6$ using the binomial theorem.

Solution

$$(x + y)^6 = \binom{6}{0}x^6 + \binom{6}{1}x^5y + \binom{6}{2}x^4y^2 + \binom{6}{3}x^3y^3$$

$$+ \binom{6}{4}x^2y^4 + \binom{6}{5}xy^5 + \binom{6}{6}y^6$$

$$= x^6 + 6x^5y + 15x^4y^2 + 20x^3y^3 + 15x^2y^4 + 6xy^5 + y^6$$

Note that the coefficients in the expansion of $(x + y)^6$ are the entries in the Pascal triangle for $n = 6$. (See Figure 18, page 218.)

Example 2 Find the coefficient of y^4 in the expansion of $(x + y)^7$.

Solution The coefficient of y^4 is

$$\binom{7}{4} = \frac{7 \cdot 6 \cdot 5}{3 \cdot 2 \cdot 1} = 35$$

Example 3 Expand $(x + 2y)^4$ using the binomial theorem.

Solution
$$(x + 2y)^4 = \binom{4}{0}x^4 + \binom{4}{1}x^3(2y) + \binom{4}{2}x^2(2y)^2$$
$$+ \binom{4}{3}x(2y)^3 + \binom{4}{4}(2y)^4$$
$$= x^4 + 8x^3y + 24x^2y^2 + 32xy^3 + 16y^4$$

Example 4 Show that
$$\binom{n}{0} + \binom{n}{1} + \binom{n}{2} + \cdots + \binom{n}{n} = 2^n$$

Solution Since the binomial theorem is valid for all values of x and y, we may set $x = y = 1$ in (1). This gives
$$(1 + 1)^n = \binom{n}{0} + \binom{n}{1} + \binom{n}{2} + \cdots + \binom{n}{n}$$

The result obtained in Example 4 can be used to count the number of subsets of a set with n elements. This is so since $\binom{n}{0}$ gives the number of subsets with 0 elements, $\binom{n}{1}$ gives the number of subsets with 1 element, $\binom{n}{2}$ is the number of subsets with 2 elements, and so on.

Example 5 Determine the number of subsets of a set with 6 elements.

Solution The total number of subsets of a set with 6 elements is $2^6 = 64$.

Exercise 6
Solutions to Odd-Numbered Problems begin on page 587.

In Problems 1–6 use the binomial theorem to expand each expression.

1. $(x + y)^5$
2. $(x + y)^4$
3. $(x + 3y)^3$
4. $(2x + y)^3$
5. $(2x - y)^4$
6. $(x - y)^4$

7. What is the coefficient of y^3 in the expansion of $(x + y)^5$?
8. What is the coefficient of y^6 in the expansion of $(x + y)^8$?
9. What is the coefficient of x^8 in the expansion of $(x + 3)^{10}$?
10. What is the coefficient of x^3 in the expansion of $(x + 2)^5$?
11. How many different subsets can be chosen from a set with 5 elements?
12. How many different subsets can be chosen from a set of 50 elements?

Chapter Review

Important Terms

set
empty set
equal sets
subset (⊆)
proper subset (⊂)
universal set
Venn diagram
union (∪)
intersection (∩)
disjoint sets

complement
De Morgan's laws
finite sets
factorial
tree diagram
principle of counting
permutation
combination
Pascal triangle
***binomial theorem**

True–False Questions
(Answers on page 631)

T F 1. If $A \cup B = A \cap B$, then $A = B$.
T F 2. If A and B are disjoint sets, then $c(A \cup B) = c(A) + c(B)$.
T F 3. The number of permutations of 4 different objects taken 4 at a time is 12.
T F 4. $C(5, 3) = 20$
T F 5. In the binomial expansion of $(x + 1)^5$, the coefficient of x^3 is 3^5.

Fill in the Blanks
(Answers on page 631)

1. Two sets that have no elements in common are called _____.
2. The number of different arrangements of r objects from n objects in which (a) the n objects are different, (b) no object is repeated more than once in an arrangement, and (c) order is important is called a _____.
3. If in Problem 2 above, condition (c) is replaced by "order is not important," we have a _____.
4. A triangular display of combinations is called the _____ triangle.
5. The combinations $\binom{n}{r}$ are sometimes called _____ _____.

Review Exercises
Solutions to Odd-Numbered Problems begin on page 587.

In Problems 1–16 replace the asterisk by the symbol(s) ∈, ⊂, ⊆, and/or = to give a true statement. If none of these relationships hold, write "None of these."

1. $0 * \varnothing$
2. $\{0\} * \{1, 0, 3\}$
3. $\{5, 6\} \cap \{2, 6\} * \{8\}$
4. $\{2, 3\} \cup \{3, 4\} * \{3\}$
5. $\{8, 9\} * \{9, 10, 11\}$
6. $1 * \{1, 3, 5\} \cap \{3, 4\}$
7. $5 * \{0, 5\}$
8. $\varnothing * \{1, 2, 3\}$
9. $\varnothing * \{1, 2\} \cap \{3, 4, 5\}$
10. $\{2, 3\} * \{3, 4\}$
11. $\{1, 2\} * \{1\} \cup \{3\}$
12. $5 * \{1\} \cup \{2, 3\}$
13. $\{4, 5\} \cap \{5, 6\} * \{4, 5\}$
14. $\{6, 8\} * \{8, 9, 10\}$
15. $\{6, 7, 8\} \cap \{8\} * \{6\}$
16. $4 * \{6, 8\} \cap \{4, 8\}$

*From optional section.

17. For the sets

$$A = \{1, 3, 5, 6, 8\} \qquad B = \{2, 3, 6, 7\} \qquad C = \{6, 8, 9\}$$

find:
(a) $(A \cap B) \cup C$ (b) $(A \cap B) \cap C$ (c) $(A \cup B) \cap B$

18. For the sets $U = $ Universal set $= \{1, 2, 3, 4, 5, 6, 7\}$ and

$$A = \{1, 3, 5, 6\} \qquad B = \{2, 3, 6, 7\} \qquad C = \{4, 6, 7\}$$

find:
(a) $\overline{A \cap B}$ (b) $(B \cap C) \cap A$ (c) $\overline{B} \cup \overline{A}$

19. If A and B are sets and if $c(A) = 24$, $c(A \cup B) = 33$, $c(B) = 12$, find $c(A \cap B)$.

20. During June, Colleen's Motors sold 75 cars with air conditioning, 95 with power steering, and 100 with automatic transmission. Twenty cars had all three options, 10 cars had none of these options, and 10 cars were sold that had only air conditioning. In addition, 50 cars had both automatic transmission and power steering, and 60 cars had both automatic transmission and air conditioning.
(a) How many cars were sold in June?
(b) How many cars had only power steering?

21. In a survey of 125 college students, it was found that of three newspapers, the *Wall Street Journal*, *New York Times*, and *Chicago Tribune*:

    60 read the *Chicago Tribune*
    40 read the *New York Times*
    15 read the *Wall Street Journal*
    25 read the *Chicago Tribune* and *New York Times*
     8 read the *New York Times* and *Wall Street Journal*
     3 read the *Chicago Tribune* and *Wall Street Journal*
     1 read all three

(a) How many read none of these papers?
(b) How many read only the *Chicago Tribune*?
(c) How many read neither the *Chicago Tribune* nor the *New York Times*?

22. If $U = $ Universal set $= \{1, 2, 3, 4, 5\}$ and $B = \{1, 4, 5\}$, find all sets A for which $A \cap B = \{1\}$.

23. Compute $P(6, 3)$.

24. Compute $C(6, 2)$.

25. In how many different ways can a committee of 3 people be formed from a group of 5 people?

26. In how many different ways can 4 people line up?

27. In how many different ways can 3 books be placed on a shelf?

28. In how many different ways can 3 people be seated in 4 chairs?

29. How many house styles are possible if a contractor offers 3 choices of roof designs, 4 choices of window designs, and 6 choices of brick?

30. How many different answers are possible in a true–false test consisting of 10 questions?

31. You are to set up a code of 2 digit words using the digits 1, 2, 3, 4

without using any digit more than once. What is the maximum number of words in such a language? If the words 12 and 21, for example, designate the same word, how many words are possible?

32. You are to set up a code of 3 digit words using the digits 1, 2, 3, 4, 5, 6 without using any digit more than once in the same word. What is the maximum number of words in such a language? If the words 124, 142, etc., designate the same word, how many different words are possible?

33. A small town consists of a north side and a south side. The north side has 16 houses and the south side has 10 houses. A pollster is asked to visit 4 houses on the north side and 3 on the south side. In how many ways can this be done?

34. *Program Selection.* A ceremony is to include 7 speeches and 6 musical selections.
    (a) How many programs are possible?
    (b) How many programs are possible if speeches and musical selections are to be alternated?

35. There are 7 boys and 6 girls willing to serve on a committee. How many 7 member committees are possible if a committee is to contain:
    (a) 3 boys and 4 girls?
    (b) At least one member of each sex?

36. Colleen's Ice Cream Parlor offers 31 different flavors to choose from, and specializes in double dip cones.
    (a) How many different cones are there to choose from if you may select the same flavor for each dip?
    (b) How many different cones are there to choose from if you cannot repeat any flavor? Assume that a cone with vanilla on top of chocolate is different from a cone with chocolate on top of vanilla.
    (c) How many different cones are there if you consider any cone having chocolate on top and vanilla on the bottom the same as having vanilla on top and chocolate on the bottom?

37. A person has 4 History, 5 English, and 6 Mathematics books. How many ways can they be arranged on a shelf if books of the same subject must be together?

38. Five people are to line up for a group photograph. If 2 of them refuse to stand next to each other, in how many ways can the photograph be taken?

39. The figure below indicates the locations of two houses, *A* and *B*, in

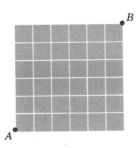

a city, where the lines represent streets. A person at *A* wishes to reach *B* and can only travel in two directions, to the right and up. How many different paths are there from *A* to *B*?

40. *Selecting a Route.* A cab driver picks up a passenger at point *A* (see the figure below) whose destination is point *B*. After completing the trip, the driver is to proceed to the garage at point *C*. If the cab must travel to the right or up, how many different routes are there from *A* to *C*?

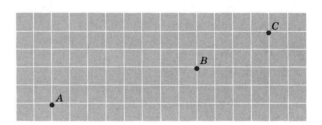

41. In how many ways can we choose three words, one each from five 3 letter words, six 4 letter words, and eight 5 letter words?

42. A newborn child can be given 1, 2, or 3 names. In how many ways can a child be named if we can choose from 100 names?

43. In how many ways can 5 girls and 3 boys be divided into 2 teams of 4 if each team is to include at least 1 boy?

44. A meeting is to be addressed by 5 speakers, *A, B, C, D, E.* In how many ways can the speakers be ordered if *B* must not precede *A*?

45. What is the answer to Problem 44 if *B* is to speak immediately after *A*?

46. *License Plate Numbers.* An automobile license number contains 1 or 2 letters followed by a 4 digit number. Compute the maximum number of different licenses.

47. How many different words (real or imaginary) can be formed using the letters in the word ELEVEN?

Other Articles

Benson, Oliver, "The Use of Mathematics in the Study of Political Science," paper presented to a symposium sponsored by The American Academy on Political and Social Science, Philadelphia (June 1963).

Riker, William H., "Voting and the Summations of Preferences," *Amer. Political Sci. Rev.,* **55** (1961), pp. 900–911.

Rudestam, Kjell Erik, and Bruce John Morrison, "Student Attitudes Regarding the Temporary Closing of a Major University," *Amer. Psychol.,* **26,** 5 (May 1971), pp. 519–525.

Slapley, L. S., and M. Shubik, "A Method for Evaluating the Distribution of Power in a Committee System," *Amer. Political Sci. Rev.,* **48** (1954), pp. 787ff.

6
Introduction to Probability

1. Introduction

Probability theory is a part of mathematics that is useful for discovering and investigating the *regular* features of *random events*. Although it is not really possible to give a precise and simple definition of what is meant by the words *random* and *regular,* we hope that the explanation and the examples given below will help you understand these concepts.

Certain phenomena in the real world may be considered *chance phenomena*. These phenomena do not always produce the same observed outcome, and the outcome of any given observation of the phenomena may not be predictable. But they have a long-range behavior known as *statistical regularity*.

In some cases, we are familiar enough with the phenomenon under investigation to feel justified in making *exact* predictions with respect to the result of each individual observation. For example, if you want to know the time and place of a solar eclipse, you may not hesitate to predict an exact time, based on astronomical data.

However, in many cases our knowledge is not precise enough to allow exact predictions in particular situations. Some examples of such cases, called *random events,* are:

(a) Tossing a fair coin gives a result that is either a head or a tail. For any one throw, we cannot predict the result, although it is obvious that it is determined by definite causes (such as the initial velocity of the coin, the initial angle of throw, and the surface on which the coin rests). Even though some of these causes can be controlled, we cannot predetermine the result of any particular toss. Thus, the result of tossing a coin is a *random event.*

(b) In a series of throws with an ordinary die, each throw yields as its result one of the numbers 1, 2, 3, 4, 5, or 6. Thus, the result of throwing a die is a *random event.*

(c) The sex of a newborn baby is either male or female. However, the sex of a newborn baby cannot be predicted in any particular case. This, too, is an example of a *random event.*

The above examples demonstrate that in studying a sequence of random experiments, it is not possible to forecast individual results. These are subject to irregular, random fluctuations that cannot be exactly predicted. However, if the number of observations is large, that is, if we deal with a *mass phenomenon,* some regularity appears.

In Example (a), we cannot predict the result of any particular toss of the coin. However, if we perform a long sequence of tosses, we notice that the number of times heads occurs is approximately equal to the number of times tails appears. That is, it seems *reasonable* to say that in any toss of this fair coin, a head or a tail is *equally likely* to occur. As a result, we might *assign a probability* of $\frac{1}{2}$ for obtaining a head (or tail) on a particular toss.

For Example (b), the appearance of any particular face of the die is a random event. However, if we perform a long series of tosses, any face is as *equally likely* to occur as any other, provided the die is fair. Here, we might *assign a probability* of $\frac{1}{6}$ for obtaining a particular face.

For Example (c), our intuition tells us that a boy baby and a girl baby are *equally likely* to occur. If we follow this reasoning, we might *assign a probability* of $\frac{1}{2}$ to having a boy baby. However, if we consult the data found in Table 1, we see that it might be more accurate to *assign a probability* of .512 to having a boy baby.

Table 1

Year of C Birth	Number of Births		Total Number of Births $b + g$	Ratio of Births	
	Boys b	Girls g		$\dfrac{b}{b + g}$	$\dfrac{g}{b + g}$
1960	1,863,000	1,768,000	3,631,000	.513	.487
1961	1,960,000	1,863,000	3,823,000	.513	.487
1962	2,005,000	1,908,000	3,913,000	.512	.488
1963	2,034,000	1,931,000	3,965,000	.513	.487
1964	2,090,000	1,988,000	4,078,000	.513	.488
1965	2,103,000	2,001,000	4,104,000	.512	.488
1966	2,162,000	2,056,000	4,218,000	.513	.487
1967	2,207,000	2,101,000	4,308,000	.512	.488
1968	2,179,000	2,076,000	4,255,000	.512	.488
1969	2,174,000	2,071,000	4,245,000	.512	.488
1970	2,180,000	2,078,000	4,258,000	.512	.488
Totals	22,957,000	21,841,000	44,798,000	.512	.488

The examples below illustrate some of the kinds of problems we shall encounter and solve in this chapter.

Example 1 A fair die is thrown. With what probability will the face 5 occur?

Example 2 A fair coin is tossed. If it comes up heads (H), a fair die is rolled and the experiment is finished. If the coin comes up tails (T), the coin is tossed again and the experiment is finished. With what probability will the situation heads first, 5 second, occur?

Example 3 A room contains 50 people. With what probability will at least 2 of them have the same birthday?

Example 4 A factory produces light bulbs of which 80% are not defective. A sample of 6 bulbs is taken. With what probability will 3 or more of them be defective?

Example 5 Two dice are rolled. If they are fair, with what probability will the total be 11? If one is "loaded" in a certain way, what is the probability of an 11?

Example 6 A group of 1200 people includes 50 who qualify for an executive position and 500 females. Furthermore, suppose 35 females qualify. With what probability will a person chosen at random be both qualified and female?

◼

Other questions that can be answered by using probability theory are given below. This chapter will not enable you to solve such problems. They are listed here merely as illustrations of the power of probability theory. Consult the references found at the end of this chapter if you wish to pursue a deeper study of probability theory.

Example 7 Consider a telephone exchange with a finite number of lines. Suppose that the exchange is constructed in such a way that an incoming call that finds all the lines busy does not wait, but is lost. This is called an *exchange without waiting lines*. The most important problem to be solved *before* the exchange is constructed is to determine for any time t, the probability of finding all the lines busy at time t.

◼

Example 8 People arrive at random times at a ticket counter to be served by an attendant, lining up on queue if others are waiting. Given information about the rate of arrival and the length of time an attendant requires to serve each customer, how much of the time is the attendant idle? How much of the time is the line more than 15 persons long? What would be the effect of adding another attendant? If the people are not allowed to wait in line but must go elswhere, what percentage of arrivals go unanswered? The same questions can be asked about gas stations, toll booths on roads, hospital beds, and so on.

◼

Example 9 The following problem occurs quite often in physics and biology and was formulated by Galton in 1874 in his study of the diappearance of family lines: Given that a man of a known family has a probability of $p_0, p_1, p_2, \ldots$ of producing 0, 1, 2 male offspring, what is the probability that the family will eventually die out?

◼

Example 10 Suppose that an infectious disease is spread by contact, that a susceptible person has a chance of catching it with each contact with an infected person, but that one becomes immune after having had the disease and can no longer transmit it. Some of the questions we would like answered are: How many susceptibles will be left when the number of infected is 0? How long will the epidemic last? For a given community, what is the probability that the disease will die out?

◼

Exercise 1

1. Consult the United States census from 1970–1980 and construct a table similar to Table 1. What probability would you assign to the birth of a boy baby based on these data?

2. Pick a page at random in your telephone directory and list the last digit of every number. Are all digits used equally often?

3. Toss a die six times and record the face shown. Denote this number by x (x can take the values 1, 2, 3, 4, 5, 6). Repeat the experiment 20 more times and tabulate the results. Do you observe any regularity?

4. *Buffon Needle Problem.* Suppose a needle is dropped at random onto a floor that is marked with parallel lines 6 inches apart. Suppose the needle is 4 inches long. With what probability does the needle fall between the two lines? Perform the experiment 20 times and record the number of times the needle rests completely within the two lines. An illustration is provided below and a solution may be found in *Mathematics in the Modern World.**

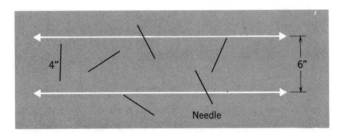

5. *Gambler's Ruin Problem.* Conduct the following experiment with a classmate. Assume that you have $90 and your classmate has $10. Flip a fair coin. If you lose, you give your classmate $1, and if you win, your classmate gives you $1. The game ends when one of you loses all your money. Can you guess how long the game will last? Can you guess who has the better chance of winning? (A solution to this problem can be found in Chapter 8.)

6. *Birthday Problem.* Conduct the following experiment in your class. Find out how many students would bet that no 2 students have the same birthday. List the birthdays of all the students and determine whether any 2 have the same birthday. Would you have won or lost the bet? (See page 257 for a table that provides a rationale for betting one way or the other.)

7. *Chevalier de Mere's Problem.* Which of the following random events do you think is more likely to occur?
    (a)   To obtain a 1 on at least one die in a simultaneous throw of four fair dice
    (b)   To obtain at least one pair of 1's in a series of 24 throws of a pair of fair dice.
    (See Problem 23, page 273.)

**Mathematics in the Modern World,* Readings from *Scientific American,* W. H. Freeman, San Francisco, 1968, pp. 169ff.

8. Pick an editorial from your daily newspaper that contains at least 1000 words. List the number of times each letter of the alphabet is used. Based on this, what probability might you assign to the occurrence of a letter in an editorial?

2. Sample Spaces and Assignment of Probabilities

In studying probability we are concerned with experiments, real or conceptual, and their outcomes. In this study we try to formulate in a precise manner a mathematical theory that closely resembles the experiment in question. The first stage of development of a mathematical theory is the building of what is termed a *mathematical model*. This model is then used as a predictor of outcomes of the experiment. The purpose of this section is to learn how a *probabilistic model* can be constructed.

Probabilistic Model

We begin by writing down the associated *sample space* of an experiment; that is, we write down all outcomes that can occur as a result of the experiment.

For example, if the experiment consists of flipping a coin, we would ordinarily agree that the only possible outcomes are heads, H, and tails, T. Therefore, a sample space for the experiment is the set $\{H, T\}$.

Example 1 Consider an experiment in which, for the sake of simplicity, one die is green and the other is red. When the 2 dice are rolled, the set of outcomes consists of all the different ways that the dice may come to rest. This is referred to as a set of all *logical possibilities*. This experiment can be displayed in two different ways. One way is to use a tree diagram, as shown in Figure 1.

Outcome

Another way is to let g and r denote, respectively, the number that comes up on the green die and the red die. Then an *outcome* can be represented by an ordered pair (g, r), where both g and r can assume all values of a set S whose members are 1, 2, 3, 4, 5, 6. Thus, a sample space S of this experiment is the set

$$S = \{(g, r) \mid 1 \leq g \leq 6, \quad 1 \leq r \leq 6\}$$

Also, notice that the number of elements in S is 36, which is found by applying the principle of counting, namely, $6 \cdot 6 = 36$. Figure 2 illustrates a graphical representation for S.

■

Sample space A *sample space* S**, associated with a real or conceptual experiment, is the set of all logical possibilities that can occur as a result of the experiment. Each element of a sample space S is called an** *outcome*.

CHEVALIER DE MERE (1607–1684), a philosopher and a man of letters, was a prominent figure at the court of Louis XIV. A French knight, de Mere was an ardent dice gambler and tried to become rich by this game. He was constantly thinking of various complicated rules that he hoped would help him reach his goal. He knew and corresponded with almost all leading mathematicians of his time, including Pascal, seeking their assistance.

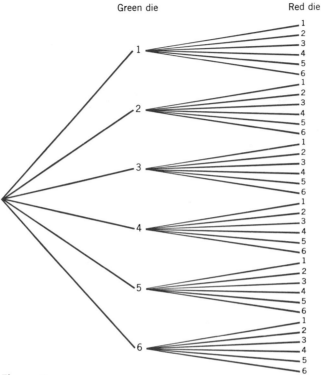

Figure 1

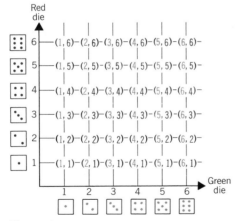

Figure 2

The theory of probability begins as soon as a sample space has been specified. The sample space of an experiment plays the same role as the universal set in set theory for all questions concerning the experiment.

In this book, we confine our attention to those cases for which the sample space is finite, that is, to those situations in which it is possible to have only a finite number of outcomes.

Notice that in our definition we say *a* sample space, rather than *the* sample space, since an experiment can be described in many different ways. In general, it is a safe guide to include as much detail as possible in the description of the outcomes of the experiment in order to answer all pertinent questions concerning the result of the experiment.

Example 2 Consider the set of all different types of families with 3 children. Describe the sample space for the experiment of drawing one family from the set of all possible 3 child families.

Solution One way of describing the sample space is by denoting the number of girls in the family. The only possibilities are members of the set

$$\{0, 1, 2, 3\}$$

That is, a 3 child family can have 0, 1, 2, or 3 girls.

This sample space has four outcomes. A disadvantage of describing the experiment using this sample space is that a question such as "Was the second child a girl?" cannot be answered. Thus, this method of classifying the outcomes may be too coarse, since it may not provide enough wanted information.

Another way of describing the sample space is by first defining B and G as "Boy" and "Girl," respectively. Then the sample space might be given as

$$\{BBB, BBG, BGB, BGG, GBB, GBG, GGB, GGG\}$$

where BBB means first child is a boy, second child is a boy, third child is a boy; and so on. This experiment can be depicted by the tree diagram in Figure 3. Notice that the experiment has eight possible outcomes.

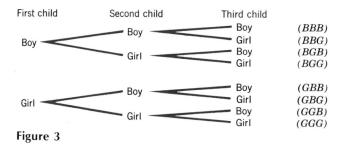

Figure 3

The advantage of the second type of classification of the sample space in Example 2 is that each outcome of the experiment corresponds to exactly one element in the sample space.

Event; Simple Event **An** *event* **is a subset of the sample space. If an event has exactly one element, that is, consists of only one outcome, it is called a** *simple event.*

Every event can be written as the union of simple events. For example, consider the sample space of Example 2. The event E that the family consists of exactly 2 boys is

$$E = \{BBG, BGB, GBB\}$$

The event E is the union of the three simple events $\{BBG\}$, $\{BGB\}$, $\{GBB\}$. That is,

$$E = \{BBG\} \cup \{BGB\} \cup \{GBB\}$$

Since a sample space S is also an event, we can express a sample space S as the union of simple events. Thus, if the sample space S consists of n outcomes,

$$S = \{e_1, e_2, \ldots, e_n\}$$

then

$$S = \{e_1\} \cup \{e_2\} \cup \cdots \cup \{e_n\}$$

Example 3   In the experiment of Example 1, involving a green die and a red die, let A be the event that the green die comes up less than or equal to 3 and the red die is 5, and let B be the event that the green die is 2 and the red die is 5 or 6. Describe the event A or B.

Solution $$A = \{(g, r) \,|\, g \leq 3, \quad r = 5\} \qquad B = \{(g, r) \,|\, g = 2, \quad r = 5, 6\}$$
$$\quad = \{(1, 5), (2, 5), (3, 5)\} \qquad\qquad = \{(2, 5), (2, 6)\}$$

Clearly, A has three members and B has two members. The event A or B is merely the union of A with B. Thus,

$$A \cup B = \{(1, 5), (2, 5), (3, 5), (2, 6)\}$$

That is, the event A or B has four members. [Of course, the event A and B, namely, $A \cap B$, has one member, $(2, 5)$.]   ■

We are now in a position to formulate a definition for the probability of a simple event of a sample space.

(1)   Probability of a Simple Event   **Let S denote a sample space. To each simple event $\{e\}$ of S, we assign a real number, $P(e)$, called the** *probability of the simple event* $\{e\}$, **which has the two properties:**

(I) $P(e) \geq 0$ **for all simple events $\{e\}$ in S**
(II)   **The sum of the probabilities of all the simple events of S equals** 1

If the sample space S is given by

$$S = \{e_1, e_2, \ldots, e_n\}$$

then

$$\text{(I)} \quad P(e_1) \geq 0, \quad P(e_2) \geq 0, \quad \ldots, \quad P(e_n) \geq 0$$
$$\text{(II)} \quad P(e_1) + P(e_2) + \cdots + P(e_n) = 1$$

The real number assigned to the simple event $\{e\}$ is *completely arbitrary* within the framework of the above restrictions. For example, let a die be thrown. A sample space S is then

$$S = \{1, 2, 3, 4, 5, 6\}$$

There are six simple events in S: $\{1\}, \{2\}, \{3\}, \{4\}, \{5\}, \{6\}$. Either of the following two assignments of probabilities is acceptable.

(a)
$$\begin{array}{lll} P(1) = \tfrac{1}{6} & P(2) = \tfrac{1}{6} & P(3) = \tfrac{1}{6} \\ P(4) = \tfrac{1}{6} & P(5) = \tfrac{1}{6} & P(6) = \tfrac{1}{6} \end{array}$$

This choice is in agreement with the definition, since the probability of each simple event is nonnegative and their sum is 1. This is an example of a "fair" die in which each simple event is equally likely to occur.

(b)
$$\begin{array}{lll} P(1) = 0 & P(2) = 0 & P(3) = \tfrac{1}{3} \\ P(4) = \tfrac{2}{3} & P(5) = 0 & P(6) = 0 \end{array}$$

This choice is also acceptable, even though it is unnatural. It implies that the die is "loaded," since only a 3 or a 4 appears and a 4 is twice as likely to occur as a 3.

Example 4   A coin is weighted so that heads $\{H\}$ is five times more likely to occur than tails $\{T\}$. What probability should we assign to heads? To tails?

Solution   Let x denote the probability that tails occurs. Then,

$$P(T) = x \qquad \text{and} \qquad P(H) = 5x$$

Since the sum of the probabilities of all the simple events equals 1, we must have

$$P(H) + P(T) = 5x + x = 1$$
$$6x = 1$$
$$x = \tfrac{1}{6}$$

Thus, we assign the probabilities

$$P(H) = \tfrac{5}{6} \qquad P(T) = \tfrac{1}{6}$$

■

Suppose probabilities have been assigned to each simple event of S. We now raise the question, "What is the probability of an event?" Let S be a sample space and let E be any event of S. It is clear that either $E = \varnothing$ or E is a simple event or E is the union of two or more simple events.

(2)   Probability of an Event   **If $E = \varnothing$, we define the** *probability of* $\varnothing$ **to be**

$$P(\varnothing) = 0$$

In this case, the event $E = \varnothing$ is said to be *impossible.*

If E is simple, (1) is applicable.

If E is the union of r simple events $\{e_{i_1}\}$, $\{e_{i_2}\}$, ..., $\{e_{i_r}\}$, we define the *probability* of E **to be**

$$P(E) = P(e_{i_1}) + P(e_{i_2}) + \cdots + P(e_{i_r})$$

In particular, if the sample space S is given by

$$S = \{e_1, e_2, \ldots, e_n\}$$

we must have

$$P(S) = P(e_1) + \cdots + P(e_n) = 1$$

Thus, the probability of S, the sample space, is 1.

Example 5 Let 2 coins be tossed. A sample space S is

$$S = \{HH, TH, HT, TT\}$$

This can be depicted in two ways. See Figure 4.

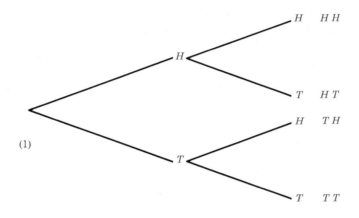

(1)

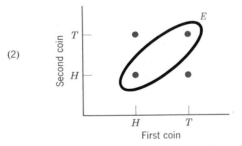

(2)

$E =$ same result on both tosses $= \{HH, TT\}$

Figure 4

Let E be the event that they are both heads or both tails. Compute the probability for event E with the following two assignments of probabilities:

(a) $P(HH) = P(TH) = P(HT) = P(TT) = \frac{1}{4}$
(b) $P(HH) = \frac{1}{9}$, $P(TH) = \frac{2}{9}$, $P(HT) = \frac{2}{9}$, $P(TT) = \frac{4}{9}$

Solution   The event E is $\{HH, TT\}$.

(a) $P(E) = P(HH) + P(TT) = \frac{1}{4} + \frac{1}{4} = \frac{1}{2}$
(b) $P(E) = P(HH) + P(TT) = \frac{1}{9} + \frac{4}{9} = \frac{5}{9}$

■

The fact that we obtained different probabilities for the same event in Example 5 is not unexpected, since it results from our original assignment of probabilities to the simple events of the experiment. Any assignment that conforms to the restrictions given in (1) is mathematically correct. The question of which assignment should be made is not a mathematical question, but is one that depends on the real-world situation to which the theory is applied. In this example the coins were fair in case (a) and were loaded in case (b).

Now that we have introduced the concepts of sample space, event, and probability of events, we introduce the idea of a *probabilistic model*.

To construct a *probabilistic model* **we need to do the following:**
(a)   List all possible outcomes of the experiment under investigation; that is, give a sample space or, if this is not easy to do, determine the number of simple events in the sample space.
(b)   Assign to each simple event a probability $P(e)$ such that (1) is satisfied.

Example 6   A fair coin is tossed. If it comes up heads, H, a fair die is rolled and the experiment is finished; if it comes up tails, T, the coin is tossed once more. Describe a probabilistic model for this experiment.

Solution   All the possible outcomes of this experiment are

$$S: \quad H1, \ H2, \ H3, \ H4, \ H5, \ H6, \ \ TT, \ TH$$

where $H1$ indicates heads for the coin and then 1 for the die, and so on. See Figure 5 for the tree diagram.

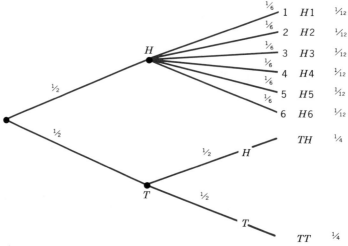

Figure 5

To these eight possible outcomes we assign the following probabilities:

$$P(H1) = P(H2) = P(H3) = P(H4) = P(H5) = P(H6) = \tfrac{1}{12}$$
$$P(TH) = P(TT) = \tfrac{1}{4}$$

The above discussion constitutes a model, called a *probabilistic* or *stochastic model,* for the experiment.   ■

Example 7   For the model described in Example 6, let E be the event

$$E = \{H2, H4, TH\}$$

The probability of the event E is

$$P(E) = P(H2) + P(H4) + P(TH)$$
$$= \tfrac{1}{12} + \tfrac{1}{12} + \tfrac{1}{4} = \tfrac{5}{12}$$ ■

Exercise 2
Solutions to Odd-Numbered Problems begin on page 588.

In Problems 1–4 describe the sample space associated with each random experiment. List the elements in each sample space.

1. Tossing a coin three times
2. Tossing 3 coins once
3. Tossing a coin two times and then a die
4. Tossing a coin and then a die

In Problems 5–12 use the spinners pictured below to list the elements in the sample space associated with each experiment described.

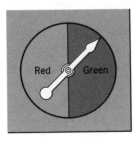 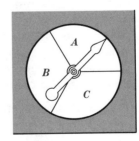 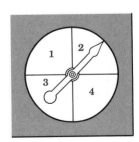

5.   First Spinner 1 is spun and then Spinner 2 is spun.
6.   First Spinner 3 is spun and then Spinner 1 is spun.
7.   Spinner 1 is spun twice.
8.   Spinner 3 is spun twice.
9.   Spinner 2 is spun twice and then Spinner 3 is spun.
10.   Spinner 3 is spun once and then Spinner 2 is spun twice.
11.   Spinners 1, 2, 3 are each spun once in this order.
12.   Spinners 3, 2, 1 are each spun once in this order.

In Problems 13–18 count the elements in the sample space associated with each random experiment.

13. Tossing a coin four times
14. Tossing a coin five times
15. Tossing 3 dice
16. Tossing 2 dice and then a coin
17. Selecting 2 cards (without replacement) from an ordinary deck of 52 cards*
18. Selecting 3 cards (without replacement) from an ordinary deck of 52 cards*

In Problems 19–22 consider the experiment of tossing a coin twice. The table lists six possible assignments of probabilities for this experiment:

Simple Event		Sample Space			
		HH	HT	TH	TT
Assignments	1	$\frac{1}{4}$	$\frac{1}{4}$	$\frac{1}{4}$	$\frac{1}{4}$
	2	0	0	0	1
	3	$\frac{3}{16}$	$\frac{5}{16}$	$\frac{5}{16}$	$\frac{3}{16}$
	4	$\frac{1}{2}$	$\frac{1}{2}$	$-\frac{1}{2}$	$\frac{1}{2}$
	5	$\frac{1}{8}$	$\frac{1}{4}$	$\frac{1}{4}$	$\frac{1}{8}$
	6	$\frac{1}{9}$	$\frac{2}{9}$	$\frac{2}{9}$	$\frac{4}{9}$

Answer the following questions.

19. Which of the assignments of probabilities satisfy the restrictions in (1)?
20. Which of the assignments should be used if the coin is known to be fair?
21. Which of the assignments of probabilities should be used if the coin is known to always come up tails?
22. What assignment of probabilities should be used if tails is twice as likely as heads to occur?

In Problems 23–26 assign valid probabilities to the simple events of each random experiment.

23. Tossing a fair coin twice
24. Tossing a fair coin three times
25. Tossing a fair die and then a fair coin
26. Tossing a fair die and then 2 fair coins

*An ordinary *deck of cards* has 52 cards. There are four suits of 13 cards each. The suits are called *clubs* (black), *diamonds* (red), *hearts* (red), and *spades* (black). In each suit the 13 cards are labeled A (ace), 2, 3, 4, 5, 6, 7, 8, 9, 10, J (jack), Q (queen), and K (king).

In Problems 27–32 the random experiment consists of tossing a fair coin four times.

27. List the elements of the sample space and assign probabilities to each simple event.
28. Write the elements of the event, "The first two tosses are heads."
29. Write the elements of the event, "The last three tosses are tails."
30. Write the elements of the event, "Exactly three tosses come up tails."
31. Write the elements of the event, "The number of heads exceeds 1 but is fewer than 4."
32. Write the elements of the event, "The first two tosses are heads and the second two are tails."

In Problems 33–38 the random experiment consists of tossing 2 fair dice. Construct a probabilistic model for this experiment and find the probability of each given event.

33. $A = \{(1, 2), (2, 1)\}$
34. $B = \{(1, 5), (2, 4), (3, 3), (4, 2), (5, 1)\}$
35. $C = \{(1, 4), (2, 4), (3, 4), (4, 4)\}$
36. $D = \{(1, 2), (2, 1), (2, 4), (4, 2), (3, 6), (6, 3)\}$
37. $E = \{(1, 1), (2, 2), (3, 3), (4, 4), (5, 5), (6, 6)\}$
38. $F = \{(6, 6)\}$

In Problems 39–44 the random experiment consists of tossing a fair die and then a fair coin. Construct a probabilistic model for this experiment and find the probability of each given event.

39. A: The coin comes up heads
40. B: The die comes up 1
41. C: The die does *not* come up 1
42. D: The die comes up 5 or 6
43. E: The die comes up 3, 4, or 5
44. F: The coin comes up heads and the die comes up a number less than 4

45. In Example 5, if the events E, F, G are defined as

$$E: \quad \text{At least 1 head}$$
$$F: \quad \text{Exactly 1 tail}$$
$$G: \quad \text{Tails on both tosses}$$

find $P(E)$, $P(F)$, $P(G)$ for the two given assignments of probabilities.

46. If the events E and F are defined as

$$E: \quad \text{Common stocks are a good buy}$$
$$F: \quad \text{Corporate bonds are a good buy}$$

state in words the meaning of:

(a) $P(E \cup F)$ (b) $P(\bar{E})$ (c) $P(\bar{E} \cap \bar{F})$
(d) $P(E \cup \bar{F})$ (e) $P(\bar{E} \cup F)$ (f) $P(\bar{E} \cap F)$

47. *T-maze.* In a T-maze a mouse may turn to the right (*R*) and receive
     a mild shock, or to the left (*L*) and get a piece of cheese. Its behav-
     ior in making such "choices" is studied by psychologists. Suppose a
     mouse runs a T-maze three times. List the set of all possible out-
     comes and assign valid probabilities to each simple event. Find the
     probability of each of the following events:
     (a) *E*:   Run to the right two consecutive times
     (b) *F*:   Never run to the right
     (c) *G*:   Run to the left on the first trial
     (d) *H*:   Run to the right on the second trial

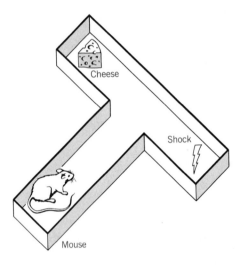

48. A marketing study reveals two major rival companies, *G* and *H*, and
     four minor firms, *a, b, c, d*, who always ally themselves with one of
     the two major companies on prices. Free competition results if a
     major company is backed by two smaller ones. Construct a sample
     space and list the events that maintain free competition.

49. A red die and a green die are tossed. If *r* denotes the result on the
     red die and *g* the result on the green die, give verbal descriptions of
     the following algebraically described events:
     (a) $r = 3g$ (b) $r - g = 1$ (c) $r \leq g$
     (d) $r + g = 8$ (e) $g = r^2$ (f) $r = g$
     Graph each of these events using Figure 2 as a backdrop.

50. Let $S = \{e_1, e_2, e_3, e_4, e_5, e_6, e_7\}$ be a given sample space. Let the
     probabilities assigned to the simple events be given as follows:

     $$P(e_1) = P(e_2) = P(e_6)$$
     $$P(e_3) = 2P(e_4) = \tfrac{1}{2}P(e_1)$$
     $$P(e_5) = \tfrac{1}{2}P(e_7) = \tfrac{1}{4}P(e_1)$$

     (a) Find $P(e_1)$, $P(e_2)$, $P(e_3)$, $P(e_4)$, $P(e_5)$, $P(e_6)$, $P(e_7)$.
     (b) If $A = \{e_1, e_2\}$, $B = \{e_2, e_3, e_4\}$, $C = \{e_5, e_6, e_7\}$, and $D =$
          $\{e_1, e_5, e_6\}$, find $P(A)$, $P(B)$, $P(C)$, $P(D)$, $P(A \cup B)$, $P(A \cap D)$,
          $P(D \cap B)$, and $P(A \cap \bar{B})$.

51. Three cars, C_1, C_2, C_3, are in a race. If the probability of C_1 winning is p, that is, $P(C_1) = p$, and $P(C_1) = \frac{1}{2}P(C_2)$ and $P(C_3) = \frac{1}{2}P(C_2)$, find $P(C_1)$, $P(C_2)$, and $P(C_3)$. Also, find $P(C_1 \cup C_2)$ and $P(C_1 \cup C_3)$.

52. Consider an experiment with a loaded die such that the probability of any of the faces appearing in a toss is equal to that face times the probability that a 1 will occur. That is, $P(6) = 6 \cdot P(1)$, $P(5) = 5 \cdot P(1)$, and so on.
    (a) Describe the sample space.
    (b) Find $P(1)$, $P(2)$, $P(3)$, $P(4)$, $P(5)$, and $P(6)$.
    (c) Let the events A, B, and C be described as

    A: Even-numbered face
    B: Odd-numbered face
    C: Prime number on face (2, 3, 5 are prime)

    Find $P(A)$, $P(B)$, $P(C)$, $P(A \cup B)$, and $P(A \cup \bar{C})$.

3. Properties of the Probability of an Event

In this section, we state and prove results involving the probability of an event after the probabilistic model has been determined. The main tool we employ is set theory.

Mutually Exclusive Events **Two or more events of a sample space S are said to be** *mutually exclusive* **if and only if they have no simple events in common.**

That is, if we treat the events as sets, they are disjoint.

The following result gives us a way of computing probabilities for mutually exclusive events.

Let E and F be two events of a sample space S. If E and F are mutually exclusive, that is, if $E \cap F = \varnothing$, then the probability of the event E or F is the sum of their probabilities, namely,

(1)
$$P(E \cup F) = P(E) + P(F)$$

Since E and F can be written as a union of simple events in which no simple event of E appears in F and no simple event of F appears in E, the result follows.

Example 1 In the experiment of tossing 2 fair dice, what is the probability of obtaining either a sum of 7 or a sum of 11?

Solution Let E and F be the events

E: Sum is 7 F: Sum is 11

Since the dice are fair,

$$P(E) = \tfrac{6}{36} \qquad P(F) = \tfrac{2}{36}$$

The two events E and F are mutually exclusive. Therefore, by (1), the probability that the sum is 7 or 11 is

$$P(E \cup F) = P(E) + P(F) = \tfrac{6}{36} + \tfrac{2}{36} = \tfrac{8}{36} = \tfrac{2}{9}$$

The probability of any simple event of a sample space S is nonnegative. Furthermore, since any event E of S is the union of simple events in S, and since $P(S) = 1$, it is easy to see that

$$0 \le P(E) \le 1$$

To summarize, the probability of an event E of a sample space S has the following three properties:

(I)   *Positiveness:* $0 \le P(E) \le 1$ **for every event E of S**
(II)   *Certainty:* $P(S) = 1$
(III)   *Union:* $P(E \cup F) = P(E) + P(F)$ **for any two events E and F of S for which** $E \cap F = \emptyset$

The following result, called the *additive rule,* provides a technique for finding the probability of the union of two events when they are not disjoint.

Additive Rule   **For any two events E and F of a sample space S,**

$$P(E \cup F) = P(E) + P(F) - P(E \cap F)$$

Proof
From Example 6 in Section 1, Chapter 5 (page 200), we have

$$E \cup F = (E \cap \bar{F}) \cup (E \cap F) \cup (\bar{E} \cap F)$$

Since $E \cap \bar{F}$, $E \cap F$, and $\bar{E} \cap F$ are pairwise disjoint, we can use property (III) to write

(2) $$P(E \cup F) = P(E \cap \bar{F}) + P(E \cap F) + P(\bar{E} \cap F)$$

We may write the sets E and F in the form

$$E = (E \cap F) \cup (E \cap \bar{F})$$
$$F = (E \cap F) \cup (\bar{E} \cap F)$$

Since $E \cap F$ and $E \cap \bar{F}$ are disjoint and $E \cap F$ and $\bar{E} \cap F$ are disjoint, we have

(3) $$P(E) = P(E \cap F) + P(E \cap \bar{F})$$
$$P(F) = P(E \cap F) + P(\bar{E} \cap F)$$

Combining the results in (2) and (3), we get

$$P(E \cup F) = P(E) + P(F) - P(E \cap F)$$

Example 2 Consider the two events

E: A shopper spends at least $40 for food
F: A shopper spends at least $15 for meat

Because of recent studies, we might assign

$$P(E) = .56 \qquad P(F) = .63$$

Suppose the probability that a shopper spends at least $40 for food and $15 for meat is .33. What is the probability that a shopper spends at least $40 for food or at least $15 for meat?

Solution Since we are looking for the probability of $E \cup F$, we use the additive rule and find that

$$P(E \cup F) = P(E) + P(F) - P(E \cap F)$$
$$= .56 + .63 - .33 = .86 \qquad ■$$

Sometimes a Venn diagram is helpful. A Venn diagram depicting the information of Example 2 is given in Figure 6. From this figure, we conclude that the probability of the event E, but not F, is .23 and that the probability of neither E nor F is .14.

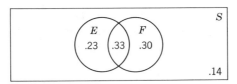

Figure 6

Example 3 In an experiment with 2 fair dice, consider the events

E: The sum of the faces is 8
F: Doubles are thrown

What is the probability of obtaining E or F?

Solution
$$E = \{(2,6), (3,5), (4,4), (5,3), (6,2)\}$$
$$F = \{(1,1), (2,2), (3,3), (4,4), (5,5), (6,6)\}$$
$$E \cap F = \{(4,4)\}$$

Also,

$$P(E) = \tfrac{5}{36} \qquad P(F) = \tfrac{6}{36} \qquad P(E \cap F) = \tfrac{1}{36}$$

Thus, the probability of E or F is

$$P(E \cup F) = \tfrac{5}{36} + \tfrac{6}{36} - \tfrac{1}{36} = \tfrac{10}{36} = \tfrac{5}{18} \qquad ■$$

Let E be an event of a sample space. The complement of E is then the event "Not E" in S. The next result gives a relationship between their probabilities.

Let E be an event of a sample space S. Then

(4)
$$P(\overline{E}) = 1 - P(E)$$

where $\overline{E}$ is the complement of E.

Proof
We know that
$$S = E \cup \overline{E} \qquad E \cap \overline{E} = \varnothing$$
Since E and $\overline{E}$ are mutually exclusive,
$$P(S) = P(E) + P(\overline{E})$$
Now, we apply property (II), setting $P(S) = 1$. It follows that
$$P(\overline{E}) = 1 - P(E)$$

This result gives us a tool for finding the probability that an event does not occur if we know the probability that it does occur. Thus, the probability $P(\overline{E})$ that E does not occur is obtained by subtracting from 1 the probability $P(E)$ that E does occur.

Example 4 In a study of people over 40 with an MBA degree, it is reasonable to assign a probability of .756 that such a person will have annual earnings in excess of $15,000. The probability that such a person will not have earnings in excess of $15,000 is

$$1 - .756 = .244$$

Example 5 In an experiment using 2 fair dice find:
(a)   The probability that the sum of the faces is less than or equal to 7
(b)   The probability that the sum of the faces is greater than 7

Solution   (a)   The number of simple events in the event E described is 21. The number of simple events of the sample space S is 36. Thus, because the dice are fair,
$$P(E) = \tfrac{21}{36} = \tfrac{7}{12}$$
(b)   We need to find $P(\overline{E})$. From (4)
$$P(\overline{E}) = 1 - P(E) = 1 - \tfrac{7}{12} = \tfrac{5}{12}$$
That is, the probability that the sum of the faces is greater than 7 is $\tfrac{5}{12}$.

Odds

Odds   In many instances, the probability of an event may be expressed as *odds*—either *odds for* an event or *odds against* an event.

If E is an event:

The *odds for E* **are** $\dfrac{P(E)}{P(\bar{E})}$ **or** $P(E)$ to $P(\bar{E})$

The *odds against E* **are** $\dfrac{P(\bar{E})}{P(E)}$ **or** $P(\bar{E})$ to $P(E)$

Example 6   The probability of the event

$$E: \quad \text{It will rain}$$

is .3. The odds for rain are

$$\frac{.3}{.7} \quad \text{or} \quad 3 \text{ to } 7$$

The odds against rain are

$$\frac{.7}{.3} \quad \text{or} \quad 7 \text{ to } 3$$

∎

To obtain the probability of the event E when either the odds for E or the odds against E are known, we use the following formulas:

If the odds for E are a to b, then

$$P(E) = \frac{a}{a + b}$$

If the odds against E are a to b, then

$$P(E) = \frac{b}{a + b}$$

Example 7   (a)   The odds for a Republican victory in the Presidential election are 7 to 5. What is the probability that a Republican victory occurs?
(b)   The odds against the Chicago Cubs winning the league pennant are 200 to 1.* What is the probability that the Cubs win the pennant?

Solution   (a)   The event E is "A Republican victory occurs." The odds for E are 7 to 5. Thus,

$$P(E) = \frac{7}{7 + 5} = \frac{7}{12} \approx .583$$

*Las Vegas odds for the 1982 season.

(b) The event F is "The Cubs win the pennant." The odds against F are 200 to 1. Thus,

$$P(F) = \frac{1}{200 + 1} = \frac{1}{201} \approx .00498$$

Exercise 3
Solutions to Odd-Numbered Problems begin on page 589.

In Problems 1-6 find the probability of the indicated event when $P(A) = .20$ and $P(B) = .30$.

1. $P(\bar{A})$
2. $P(\bar{B})$
3. $P(A \cup B)$ if A, B are mutually exclusive
4. $P(A \cap B)$ if A, B are mutually exclusive
5. $P(A \cup B)$ if $P(A \cap B) = .15$
6. $P(A \cap B)$ if $P(A \cup B) = .40$

7. In tossing 2 fair dice, are the events "Sum is 2" and "Sum is 12" mutually exclusive? What is the probability of obtaining either a 2 or a 12?

8. In tossing 2 fair dice, are the events "Sum is 6" and "Sum is 8" mutually exclusive? What is the probability of obtaining either a 6 or an 8?

9. The Chicago Bulls basketball team has a probability of winning of .65. What is their probability of losing?

10. The Chicago Black Hawks hockey team has a probability of winning of .6 and a probability of losing of .25. What is the probability of a tie?

11. Jill needs to pass both Mathematics and English in order to graduate. She estimates her probability of passing Mathematics at .4 and English at .6, and she estimates her probability of passing at least one of them at .8. What is her probability of passing both courses?

12. After midterm exams, the student in Problem 11 reassesses her probability of passing Mathematics to .7. She feels her probability of passing at least one of these courses is still .8, but she has only a probability of .1 of passing both courses. If her probability of passing English is less than .4, she will drop English. Should she drop English? Why?

13. Let A and B be events of a sample space S and let $P(A) = .5$, $P(B) = .3$, and $P(A \cap B) = .1$. Find the probabilities for each of the following events:
   (a) A or B (b) A but not B
   (c) B but not A (d) Neither A nor B

14. If A and B represent two mutually exclusive events such that $P(A) = .35$ and $P(B) = .50$, find each of the following:

(a) $P(A \cup B)$ (b) $P(\overline{A \cup B})$ (c) $P(\overline{B})$

(d) $P(\overline{A})$ (e) $P(A \cap B)$

15. At the Milex tune-up, brake repair shop, the manager has found that a car will require a tune-up with probability .6, a brake job with probability .1, and both with probability .02.
    (a) What is the probability that a car requires either a tune-up or a brake job?
    (b) What is the probability that a car requires a tune-up but not a brake job?
    (c) What is the probability that a car requires neither type of repair?

16. A factory needs two raw materials, say E and F. The probability of not having an adequate supply of material E is .06, whereas the probability of not having an adequate supply of material F is .04. A study shows that the probability of a shortage of both E and F is .02. What is the probability of the factory being short of either material E or F?

17. In a survey of the number of TV sets in a house, the following probability table was constructed:

Number of TV Sets	0	1	2	3	4 or more
Probability	.05	.24	.33	.21	.17

Find the probability of a house having:
(a) 1 or 2 TV sets   (b) 1 or more TV sets
(c) 3 or fewer TV sets   (d) 3 or more TV sets
(e) Less than 2 TV sets   (f) Less than 1 TV set
(g) 1, 2, or 3 TV sets   (h) 2 or more TV sets

18. Through observation it has been determined that the probability for a given number of people waiting in line at a particular check-out register of a supermarket is:

Number Waiting in Line	0	1	2	3	4 or more
Probability	.10	.15	.20	.24	.31

Find the probability of:
(a) At most 2 people in line
(b) At least 2 people in line
(c) At least 1 person in line

In Problems 21–24 determine the probability of E for the given odds.

19. 3 to 1 for E
20. 4 to 1 against E
21. 7 to 5 against E
22. 2 to 9 for E
23. 1 to 1 for E (even)
24. 50 to 1 for E

In Problems 25–28 determine the odds for and against each event for the given probability.

25. $P(E) = .7$ 26. $P(H) = \frac{1}{3}$ 27. $P(F) = \frac{4}{5}$ 28. $P(G) = .01$

29. If 2 fair dice are thrown, what are the odds of obtaining a 7? An 11? A 7 or 11?

30. If the odds for event A are 1 to 5 and the odds for event B are 1 to 3, what are the odds for the event A or B, assuming the event A and B is impossible?

31. In a track contest, the odds that A will win are 1 to 2 and the odds that B will win are 2 to 3. Find the probability and the odds that A or B wins the race, assuming a tie is impossible.

32. It has been estimated that in 70% of the fatal accidents involving two cars, at least one of the drivers is drunk. If you hear of a two-car fatal accident, what odds should you give a friend for the event that at least one of the drivers is drunk?

*33. Generalize the additive rule by showing that the probability of the occurrence of at least one of the three events A, B, C is given by

$$P(A \cup B \cup C) = P(A) + P(B) + P(C)$$
$$- P(A \cap B) - P(A \cap C) - P(B \cap C)$$
$$+ P(A \cap B \cap C)$$

4. Probability of Equally Likely Events

Equally Likely Events

So far, we have seen that in some cases it is reasonable to assign the same probability to each simple event of the sample space. Such events are termed *equally likely events*.

Equally likely events occur when items are selected randomly. For example, in randomly selecting 1 person from a group of 10, the probability of selecting a particular individual is $\frac{1}{10}$. If a card is chosen randomly from a deck of 52 cards, the probability of drawing a particular card is $\frac{1}{52}$. In general, if a sample space S has n equally likely simple events, the probability assigned to each simple event is $\frac{1}{n}$.

(1) **Let a sample space S be given by**

$$S = \{e_1, e_2, \ldots, e_n\}$$

Suppose each of the simple events $\{e_1\}, \ldots, \{e_n\}$ are equally likely to occur. If E is the union of m of these n simple events, then

$$P(E) = \frac{m}{n}$$

Proof
Since the simple events $e_1, \ldots, e_n$ are equally likely, we know that

(2) $$P(e_1) = \cdots = P(e_n)$$

Since

$$S = \{e_1\} \cup \cdots \cup \{e_n\}$$

we have

(3)
$$P(S) = P(e_1) + \cdots + P(e_n) = 1$$

To satisfy both (2) and (3) we must have

$$P(e_1) = P(e_2) = \cdots = P(e_n) = \frac{1}{n}$$

Now, for the event E of S, in which the m events have been reordered for convenience, we have

$$E = \{e_1\} \cup \cdots \cup \{e_m\}$$

Thus,

$$P(E) = P(e_1) + \cdots + P(e_m) = \underbrace{\frac{1}{n} + \cdots + \frac{1}{n}}_{m \text{ times}} = \frac{m}{n}$$

The above result is sometimes stated in the following way:

If an experiment has n equally likely outcomes, among which the event E occurs m times, then the probability of event E, written as $P(E)$, is m/n. That is,

$$P(E) = \frac{\text{Number of possible ways the event } E \text{ can take place}}{\text{Number of all logical possibilities}} = \frac{m}{n}$$

If the fact that the event E has occurred is termed a *success*, then

(4)
$$P(E) = \frac{\text{Number of successes}}{\text{Number of all logical possibilities}} = \frac{m}{n}$$

Event E not occurring is referred to as a *failure*.

Thus, to compute the probability of an event E in which the outcomes are equally likely, count the number $c(E)$ of simple events in E, and divide by the total number $c(S)$ of simple events in the sample space. Then,

$$P(E) = \frac{c(E)}{c(S)}$$

Statement (1) is often used to define *probability*. Using this definition, the properties (I), (II), and (III) previously stated in Section 3 are still valid.

Suppose an experiment resulted in no successes at all. By (1), we have

(5)
$$P(\text{Success}) = \frac{0}{n} = 0$$

If the experiment resulted in all events in the sample space being successes, then $m = n$, and

$$P(\text{Success}) = \frac{m}{n} = \frac{n}{n} = 1$$

From this result and (5), we see that

$$0 \leq P(\text{Success}) \leq 1$$

Suppose E is an event with m successes in a sample space S of n elements. Then

$$P(E) = \frac{m}{n}$$

Now $\bar{E}$ contains $n - m$ elements. Hence,

$$P(\bar{E}) = \frac{(n - m)}{n} = \frac{n}{n} - \frac{m}{n} = 1 - \frac{m}{n} = 1 - P(E)$$

Example 1 In an experiment with 2 dice, we present the following in terms of events:
(a) The sum of the faces is 3.
(b) The sum of the faces is 7.
(c) The sum of the faces is 7 or 3.
(d) The sum of the faces is 7 and 3.
Find the probability of these events, assuming the dice are fair.

Solution (a) The sum of the faces is 3 if and only if the outcome is the event $A = \{(1, 2), (2, 1)\}$. Since $c(A) = 2$ and $c(S) = 36$, we have

$$P(A) = \frac{2}{36} = \frac{1}{18}$$

(b) The sum of the faces is 7 if and only if the outcome is a member of the event $B = \{(1, 6), (2, 5), (3, 4), (4, 3), (5, 2), (6, 1)\}$. Since $c(B) = 6$, we have

$$P(B) = \frac{6}{36} = \frac{1}{6}$$

(c) The sum of the faces is 7 or 3 if and only if the outcome is a member of $A \cup B$, as defined in parts (a) and (b).

$$A \cup B = \{(2, 1), (1, 2), (1, 6), (2, 5), (3, 4), (4, 3), (5, 2), (6, 1)\}$$

Since $c(A \cup B) = 8$,

$$P(A \cup B) = \frac{8}{36} = \frac{2}{9}$$

(d) The sum of the faces is 3 and 7 if and only if the outcome is a member of $A \cap B$. Since $A \cap B = \emptyset$, the event is impossible. That is, $P(A \cap B) = 0$. ∎

Example 2 An interesting problem in which formula (4) is used is the so-called *birthday problem*. In general, the problem is to find the probability that in a group of r people there are at least 2 people who have the same birthday (the same month and day of the year).

Solution To solve the problem, let us first determine the number of simple events in the sample space. There are 365 possibilities for each person's birthday (we exclude

February 29 for simplicity). Since there are r people in the group, there are 365^r possibilities for the birthdays. [For 1 person in the group, there are 365 days on which his or her birthday can fall; for 2 people, there are $(365)(365) = 365^2$ pairs of days; and, in general, using the principle of counting, for r people there are 365^r possibilities.]

Next, we assume a person is no more likely to be born on one day than another, so that we assign the probability $1/365^r$ to each simple event.

We wish to find the probability that at least 2 people have the same birthday. It is difficult to count the elements in this set; it is much easier to count the elements of the event

$$E: \text{ No 2 people have the same birthday}$$

Notice that the event $\bar{E}$ is that at least 2 people have the same birthday. To find the probability of E, we proceed as follows: Choose 1 person at random. There are 365 possibilities for his or her birthday. Choose a second person. There are 364 possibilities for this birthday, if no 2 people are to have the same birthday. Choose a third person. There are 363 possibilities left for this birthday. Finally, we arrive at the rth person. There are $365 - (r - 1)$ possibilities left for this birthday. By the principle of counting, the total number of possibilities is $365 \cdot 364 \cdot 363 \cdot \cdots \cdot (365 - r + 1)$.

Hence, the probability of event E is

$$P(E) = \frac{365 \cdot 364 \cdot 363 \cdot \cdots \cdot (365 - r + 1)}{365^r}$$

The probability of 2 or more people having the same birthday is then $P(\bar{E}) = 1 - P(E)$. ■

The table below gives the probabilities for 2 or more people having the same birthday for some values of r. Notice that the probability is better than $\frac{1}{2}$ for any group of 23 or more people.

		Number of People														
	5	10	15	20	21	22	23	24	25	30	40	50	60	70	80	90
Probability That 2 or More Have Same Birthday	.027	.117	.253	.411	.444	.476	.507	.538	.569	.706	.891	.970	.994	.99916	.99991	.99999

Examples Using Counting Techniques
The next two examples utilize counting techniques developed in the previous chapter. They may be omitted without loss of continuity.

Example 3 A box contains 12 light bulbs of which 5 are defective. All bulbs look alike and have equal probability of being chosen. Three light bulbs are picked at random.
(a) What is the probability that all 3 are defective?
(b) What is the probability that at least 2 are defective?

Solution   (a)   The number of elements in the sample space S is equal to the number of combinations of 12 light bulbs taken 3 at a time, namely,

$$\binom{12}{3} = \frac{12!}{3!9!} = 220$$

Define E as the event, "3 bulbs are defective." Then E can occur in $\binom{5}{3}$ ways, that is, the number of ways in which 3 defective bulbs can be chosen from 5 defective ones. The probability $P(E)$ is

$$P(E) = \frac{\binom{5}{3}}{\binom{12}{3}} = \frac{\frac{5!}{3!2!}}{220} = \frac{10}{220} = .04545$$

(b)   What is the probability of the event F: At least 2 are defective? The event F is equivalent to asking for the probability of selecting either 2 or 3 defective bulbs. Thus,

$$P(F) = \frac{\binom{5}{2}\binom{7}{1}}{\binom{12}{3}} + P(E) = \frac{70}{220} + \frac{10}{220} = .36364$$

∎

Example 4   Find the probability of obtaining (a) a straight and (b) a flush in a poker hand. (A poker hand is a set of 5 cards chosen at random from a deck of 52 cards.*)

Solution   (a)   A straight consists of 5 consecutive cards, not all of the same suit. The sample space contains $\binom{52}{5}$ simple events, each equally likely to occur. Now, for the straight 4, 5, 6, 7, 8, the 4 can be drawn in 4 different ways, as can the 5, the 6, the 7, and the 8, for a total of 4^5 ways. There are a total of 10 different kinds of straights $(A, 2, 3, 4, 5)$, $(2, 3, 4, 5, 6)$, . . . , $(9, 10, J, Q, K)$, and $(10, J, Q, K, A)$. Thus, all together, there are $10 \cdot 4^5$ straights. However, among these are the straight flushes (36 straights all in one suit) and the four royal flushes (straight flushes consisting of 10, J, Q, K, A), which should not be included in the straight category. Thus, there are

$$10 \cdot 4^5 - 36 - 4 = 10{,}240 - 40 = 10{,}200 \text{ straights}$$

The probability of drawing a straight is therefore

$$\frac{10{,}200}{\binom{52}{5}} = .0039$$

(b)   A flush consists of 5 cards in a single suit. The number of ways of obtaining a flush in a given suit is $\binom{13}{5} = 1287$, and there are four different suits, for a total of $4(1287) = 5148$ flushes. However, straight flushes (36) and the four royal flushes should not be included in the flush category. Thus, there are

$$5148 - 36 - 4 = 5108 \text{ flushes}$$

*See the footnote on page 244.

The probability of drawing a flush is therefore

$$\frac{5108}{\binom{52}{5}} = .0020$$

∎

Exercise 4
Solutions to Odd-Numbered Problems begin on page 590.

In Problems 1–10 a card is drawn at random from a regular deck of 52 cards (see the footnote on page 244). Calculate the probability of each event.

1. The ace of hearts is drawn.
2. An ace is drawn.
3. A spade is drawn.
4. A red card is drawn.
5. A picture card (J, Q, K) is drawn.
6. A number card (A, 2, 3, 4, 5, 6, 7, 8, 9, 10) is drawn.
7. A card with a number less than 6 is drawn (count A as 1).
8. A card with a value of 10 or higher is drawn.
9. A card that is not an ace is drawn.
10. A card that is either a queen or king of any suit is drawn.

In Problems 11–18 a ball is picked at random from a box containing 3 white, 5 red, 8 blue, and 7 green balls. Find the probability of each event.

11. White ball is picked.
12. Blue ball is picked.
13. Green ball is picked.
14. Red ball is picked.
15. White or red ball is picked.
16. Green or blue ball is picked.
17. Neither red nor green ball is picked.
18. Red or white or blue ball is picked.

19. In a throw of 2 fair dice, what is the probability that the number on one die is double the number on the other?
20. In a throw of 2 fair dice, what is the probability that one die gives a 5 and the other die a number less than 5?
21. From a sales force of 150 people, 1 person will be chosen to attend a special sales meeting. If 52 are single, 72 are college graduates, and, of the 52 who are single, $\frac{3}{4}$ are college graduates, what is the probability that a salesperson selected at random will be neither single nor a college graduate?
22. In an election, two amendments were proposed. The results indicate that of 1000 people eligible to cast a ballot, 480 voted in favor

of Amendment I, 390 voted for Amendment II, 120 voted for both, and 100 approved of neither. If an eligible voter is selected at random (that is, any one is as likely to be chosen as another), compute the following probabilities:

(a) The voter is in favor of I, but not II.

(b) The voter is in favor of II, but not I.

23. What is the probability that, in a group of 3 people, at least 2 were born in the same month (disregard day and year)?

24. What is the probability that, in a group of 6 people, at least 2 were born in the same month (disregard day and year)?

25. A box contains 100 slips of paper numbered from 1 to 100. If 3 slips are drawn in succession with replacement, what is the probability that at least 2 of them have the same number?

26. If, in Problem 25, 10 slips are drawn with replacement, what is the probability that at least 2 of them have the same number?

27. Use a calculator and the idea behind Example 2 to find the approximate probability that 2 or more United States Senators have the same birthday. (There are 100 Senators.)

28. Follow the directions of Problem 27 for the House of Representatives. (There are more than 365 Representatives.)

29. Through a mix-up on the production line, 6 defective refrigerators were shipped out with 44 good ones. If 5 are selected at random, what is the probability that all 5 are defective? What is the probability that at least 2 of them are defective?

30. In a shipment of 50 transformers, 10 are known to be defective. If 30 transformers are picked at random, what is the probability that all 30 are nondefective? Assume that all transformers look alike and have an equal probability of being chosen.

31. Five cards are dealt at random from a regular deck of 52 playing cards. Find the probability that:

(a) All are hearts.

(b) Exactly 4 are spades.

(c) Exactly 2 are clubs.

32. *Bridge.* In a game of bridge, find the probability that a hand of 13 cards consists of 5 spades, 4 hearts, 3 diamonds, and 1 club.

33. *Poker.* Find the probability of obtaining each of the following poker hands:

(a) Royal flush (10, J, Q, K, A in a single suit)

(b) Straight flush (5 cards in sequence in a single suit, but not a royal flush)

*(c) Four of a kind (4 cards of the same face value)

*(d) Full house (one pair and one triple of the same face values)

*(e) Straight or better

*34. *Elevator Problem.*† An elevator starts with 5 passengers and stops at 8 floors. Find the probability that no 2 passengers leave at the same floor. Assume that all arrangements of discharging the passengers have the same probability.

†William Feller, *An Introduction to Probability Theory and Its Applications,* 3rd ed., Wiley, New York, 1968.

5.   Conditional Probability

In this section we introduce *conditional probability*. Recall that whenever we compute the probability of an event we do it relative to the entire sample space in question. Thus, when we ask for the probability $P(E)$ of the event E, this probability $P(E)$ represents an appraisal of the likelihood that a chance experiment will produce an outcome in the set E relative to a sample space S.

However, sometimes we would like to compute the probability of an event E of a sample space relative to another event F of the same sample space. That is, if we have *prior* information that the outcome must be in a set F, this information should be used to reappraise the likelihood that the outcome will also be in E. This reappraised probability is denoted by $P(E \mid F)$, and is read as the *conditional probability of E given F*.

Let's discuss some examples to illustrate the above and then state the definition.

Example 1   Consider the experiment of flipping 2 fair coins. As we have previously seen, the sample space S is

$$S = \{HH, HT, TH, TT\}$$

Figure 7 illustrates the sample space and, for convenience, the probability of each event.

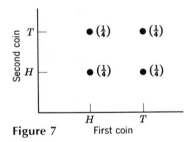

Figure 7   First coin

Suppose the experiment is performed by another person and we have no knowledge of the result, but we are informed that at least 1 tail was tossed. This information means the outcome HH could not have occurred. But the remaining outcomes HT, TH, TT are still possible. How does this alter the probabilities of the remaining outcomes?

For instance, we might be interested in calculating the probability of the event $\{TT\}$. The three simple events $\{TH\}, \{HT\}, \{TT\}$ were each assigned the probability $\frac{1}{4}$ *before* we knew the information that at least 1 tail occurred, so it is not reasonable to assign them this same probability now. Since only three outcomes are now possible, we assign to each of them the probability $\frac{1}{3}$. See Figure 8.

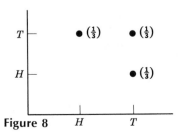

Figure 8   H   T

Example 2   Consider the experiment of drawing a single card from a deck of 52 playing cards. We are interested in the event E consisting of the outcome that a black ace is drawn. Since we may assume that there are 52 equally likely possible outcomes and there are 2 black aces in the deck, we have

$$P(E) = \frac{2}{52}$$

However, suppose a card is drawn and we are informed that it is a spade. How should this information be used to *reappraise* the likelihood of the event E?

Solution   Clearly, since the event F "A spade has been drawn" has occurred, the event "Not spade" is no longer possible. Hence, the sample space has changed from 52 playing cards to 13 spade cards, and the number of black aces that can be drawn has been reduced to 1. Therefore, we must compute the probability of event E relative to the new sample space F. This probability is denoted by $P(E|F)$ and has the value

$$P(E|F) = \frac{1}{13}$$

∎

Let's analyze the situation in Example 2 more carefully. The event E is "A black ace is drawn." We have computed the probability of event E knowing event F has occurred. This means we are computing a probability relative to a *new sample space* F. That is, F is treated as the universal set. We should only consider that part of E that is included in F; that is, we consider $E \cap F$. See Figure 9.

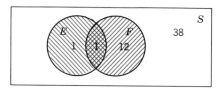

Figure 9

Thus, the probability of E given F is the ratio of the number of entries in $E \cap F$ to the number of entries in F. Since $P(E \cap F) = \frac{1}{52}$ and $P(F) = \frac{13}{52}$, then

$$P(E|F) = \frac{\frac{1}{52}}{\frac{13}{52}} = \frac{1}{13}$$

Conditional Probability   **Let E and F be events of a sample space S and suppose $P(F) > 0$. The** *conditional probability of event E assuming the event F*, **denoted by $P(E|F)$, is defined as**

(1)
$$P(E|F) = \frac{P(E \cap F)}{P(F)}$$

Example 3   Suppose a population of 1000 people includes 70 accountants and 520 females. Let E be the event "A person is an accountant." Let F be the event "A person is female." Then

$$P(E) = \frac{70}{1000} = .07 \qquad P(F) = \frac{520}{1000} = .52$$

Instead of studying the entire population, we may want to investigate the female subpopulation and ask for the probability that a female chosen at random is also an accountant. If there are 40 females who are accountants, the ratio $\frac{40}{520}$ represents the conditional probability of the event E (accountant) assuming the event F (the person chosen is female). In symbols, we would write

$$P(E \mid F) = \frac{40}{520} = \frac{1}{13}$$

Figure 10 illustrates that in computing $P(E \mid F)$ in Example 3, we form the ratio of the numbers of those entries in E and in F with the numbers that are in F.

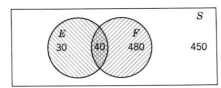

Figure 10

Alternately, using the definition of conditional probability, we see that

$$P(E \cap F) = \frac{40}{1000} \qquad P(F) = \frac{520}{1000}$$

$$P(E \mid F) = \frac{\frac{40}{1000}}{\frac{520}{1000}} = \frac{40}{520} = \frac{1}{13}$$

In the definition of conditional probability, if we replace F by S, the sample space, we get

$$P(E \mid S) = \frac{P(E \cap S)}{P(S)}$$

But $E \cap S = E$ and $P(S) = 1$. This reduces to

$$P(E \mid S) = P(E)$$

as expected.

The symbol $P(E \mid F)$ is usually read as "the probability of E given F."

Example 4   Consider a 3 child family* for which the sample space S is

$$S = \{BBB, BBG, BGB, BGG, GBB, GBG, GGB, GGG\}$$

*Refer to Example 2 in Section 2 (page 238).

We assume each simple event is equally likely, so that each is assigned a probability of $\frac{1}{8}$. Let E be the event, "The family has exactly 2 boys" and let F be the event, "The first child is a boy." What is the probability that the family has 2 boys, given that the first child is a boy?

Solution We want to find $P(E|F)$. The events E and F are

$$E = \{BBG, BGB, GBB\} \qquad F = \{BBB, BBG, BGB, BGG\}$$

Clearly, $E \cap F = \{BBG, BGB\}$, so we have

$$P(E \cap F) = \tfrac{1}{4} \qquad P(F) = \tfrac{1}{2}$$

$$P(E|F) = \frac{P(E \cap F)}{P(F)} = \frac{\tfrac{1}{4}}{\tfrac{1}{2}} = \frac{1}{2}$$

Example 5 Motors Incorporated has two plants to manufacture cars. Plant I manufactures 80% of the cars and Plant II manufactures 20%. At Plant I, 85 out of every 100 cars are rated standard quality or better. At Plant II, only 65 out of every 100 cars are rated standard quality or better. We would like to find the answers to the following questions:

(a) What is the probability that a customer obtains a standard quality car if he buys a car from Motors Inc.?

(b) What is the probability that the car came from Plant I if it is known that the car is of standard quality?

Solution Let the events A, B, C, and D be defined as follows:

A: The car purchased is of standard quality
B: The car is of standard quality and came from Plant I
C: The car is of standard quality and came from Plant II
D: The car came from Plant I

As a preliminary step, we make the following computations: The percentage of cars that are both manufactured in Plant I and of standard quality is 85% of 80%, which is equal to 68%. Similarly, the percentage of cars manufactured in Plant II and of standard quality is 65% of 20%, which is equal to 13%.

(a) We have

$$P(B) = .68 \qquad P(C) = .13$$

Since $B \cap C = \emptyset$,

$$P(A) = P(B \cup C) = P(B) + P(C) = .68 + .13 = .81$$

Thus, a total of 81% of the cars are of standard quality.

(b) We need to compute $P(D|A)$. Since $D \cap A = B$, we have

$$P(D|A) = \frac{P(D \cap A)}{P(A)} = \frac{P(B)}{P(A)} = \frac{.68}{.81} = .8395$$

If in formula (1), we multiply both sides of the equation by $P(F)$, we obtain the

Product Rule   following useful relationship, which is referred to as the *product rule:*

$$P(E \cap F) = P(F) \bullet P(E|F)$$

The next example illustrates how the product rule is used to compute the probability of an event which is itself a sequence of two events.

Example 6   Two cards are drawn at random (without replacement) from a standard deck of 52 cards. What is the probability that the first card is black and the second is red?

Solution   We seek the probability of an event which is a sequence of two events, namely,

E: The first card is black
F: The second card is red

Since there are 52 cards in the deck, of which 26 are black,

$$P(E) = \frac{26}{52} = \frac{1}{2}$$

If E occurred, that means that there are only 51 cards left in the deck, of which 26 are red, so

$$P(F|E) = \frac{26}{51}$$

By the product rule,

$$P(F \cap E) = P(E) \bullet P(F|E) = \frac{1}{2} \bullet \frac{26}{51} = \frac{13}{51}$$

Exercise 5
Solutions to Odd-Numbered Problems begin on page 590.

In Problems 1–12 use the table below to obtain probabilities for events in a sample space S.

Read the following directly from the table:

	E	F	G	Totals
H	.10	.06	.08	.24
I	.30	.14	.32	.76
Totals	.40	.20	.40	1.00

1. $P(E)$	2. $P(G)$	3. $P(H)$	4. $P(I)$
5. $P(E \cap H)$	6. $P(E \cap I)$	7. $P(G \cap H)$	8. $P(G \cap I)$

In Problems 9–12 use equation (1) and the appropriate values from the above table to compute the conditional probability.

| 9. $P(E|H)$ | 10. $P(E|I)$ | 11. $P(G|H)$ | 12. $P(G|I)$ |

13. If E and F are events with $P(E) = .4$, $P(F) = .2$, and $P(E \cap F) = .1$, find the probability of E given F. Find $P(F|E)$.

14. If E and F are events with $P(E) = .6$, $P(F) = .5$, and $P(E \cap F) = .3$, find the probability of E given F. Find $P(F|E)$.

15. If E and F are events with $P(E \cap F) = .1$ and $P(E|F) = .2$, find $P(F)$.

16. If E and F are events with $P(E \cap F) = .2$ and $P(E|F) = .5$, find $P(F)$.

17. A card is drawn at random from a regular deck of 52 cards. What is the probability that:
    (a) The card is a red ace?
    (b) The card is a red ace if it is known an ace was picked?
    (c) The card is a red ace if it is known a red card was picked?

18. A card is drawn at random from a regular deck of 52 cards. What is the probability that:
    (a) The card is a black jack?
    (b) The card is a black jack if it is known a jack was picked?
    (c) The card is a black jack if it is known a black card was picked?

19. A recent poll of residents in a certain community revealed the following information about voting preferences:

	Democrat	Republican	Independent
Male	50	40	30
Female	60	30	25

Events M, F, D, R, and I are defined as follows:

M: Resident is male
F: Resident is female
D: Resident is a Democrat
R: Resident is a Republican
I: Resident is an Independent

Find:
    (a) $P(F|I)$ (b) $P(R|F)$ (c) $P(M|D)$
    (d) $P(D|M)$ (e) $P(M|R \cup I)$ (f) $P(I|M)$

20. Let E be the event, "A person is an executive" and let F be the event, "A person earns over \$25,000 per year." State in words what is expressed by each of the following probabilities:
    (a) $P(E|F)$ (b) $P(F|E)$ (c) $P(\bar{E}|\bar{F})$ (d) $P(\bar{E}|F)$

21. For a 3 child family, find the probability of exactly 2 girls, given that the first child is a girl.

22. For a 3 child family, find the probability of exactly 1 girl, given that the first child is a boy.

23. A fair coin is tossed four successive times. Find the probability of obtaining 4 heads. Does the probability change if we are told that the second throw resulted in a head?

24. A pair of fair dice is thrown and we are told that at least one of them shows a 2. If we know this, what is the probability that the total is 7?

25. In a small town, it is known that 25% of the families have no chil-

dren, 25% have 1 child, 18% have 2 children, 16% have 3 children, 8% have 4 children, and 8% have 5 or more children. Find the probability that a family has more than 2 children if it is known that it has at least 1 child.

26. A sequence of 2 cards is drawn from an ordinary deck of 52 cards (without replacement). What is the probability that the first card is red and the second is black?

*27. In a sample survey, it is found that 35% of the men and 70% of the women are under 160 pounds. Assume that 50% of the sample are men. If a person is selected at random and this person is under 160 pounds, what is the probability that this person is a woman?

*28. If the probability that a married man will vote in a given election is .50, the probability that a married woman will vote in the election is .60, and the probability that a woman will vote in the election, given that her husband votes is .90, find:

(a) The probability that a husband and wife will both vote in the elections

(b) The probability that a married man will vote in the election, given that at least one member of the married couple will vote

*29. Of the first-year students in a certain college, it is known that 40% attended private secondary schools and 60% attended public schools. The registrar reports that 30% of all students who attended private schools maintain an A average in their first year at college and that 24% of all first-year students had an A average. At the end of the year, one student is chosen at random from the class. If the student has an A average, what is the conditional probability that the student attended a private school? [*Hint:* Use a Venn diagram.]

30. In a rural area in the north, registered Republicans outnumber registered Democrats by 3 to 1. In a recent election, all Democrats voted for the Democratic candidate and enough Republicans also voted for the Democratic candidate so that the Democrat won by a ratio of 5 to 4. If a voter is selected at random, what is the probability he or she is Republican? What is the probability a voter is Republican, if it is known that he or she voted for the Democratic candidate?

*31. If E and F are two events with $P(E) > 0$ and $P(F) > 0$, show that

$$P(F) \cdot P(E|F) = P(E) \cdot P(F|E) \cdot$$

*32. Show that $P(E|E) = 1$ when $P(E) \neq 0$.

*33. Show that $P(E|F) + P(\bar{E}|F) = 1$.

6. Independent Events

One of the most important concepts in probability is that of independence. In this section we define what is meant by two events being *independent*. First, however, we try to develop an intuitive idea of the meaning of independent events.

Example 1 Consider a group of 36 students. Suppose that E and F are two properties that each student either has or does not have. For example, the events E and F might be

$$E: \quad \text{Student has blue eyes}$$
$$F: \quad \text{Student is a male}$$

With regard to these two properties, suppose it is found that the 36 students are distributed as follows:

	Blue Eyes E	Not Blue Eyes $\overline{E}$	Totals
Male, F	6	6	12
Female, $\overline{F}$	12	12	24
Totals	18	18	36

If we choose a student at random, the probabilities corresponding to the events E and F are

$$P(E) = \frac{18}{36} = \frac{1}{2}$$

$$P(F) = \frac{12}{36} = \frac{1}{3}$$

$$P(E \cap F) = \frac{6}{36} = \frac{1}{6}$$

$$P(E \mid F) = \frac{P(E \cap F)}{P(F)} = \frac{\frac{1}{6}}{\frac{1}{3}} = \frac{1}{2} = P(E)$$ ∎

In Example 1, the probability of E given F equals the probability of E. This situation can be described by saying that the information that the event F has occurred does not affect the probability of the event E. If this is the case, we say that E *is independent of F*.

Independent Events **Let E and F be two events of a sample space S with $P(F) > 0$. The** *event E is independent of the event F* **if and only if**

$$P(E \mid F) = P(E)$$

In Problem 31, Exercise 5, you were asked to show that

(1) $$P(F) \cdot P(E \mid F) = P(E) \cdot P(F \mid E)$$

provided $P(E) > 0$ and $P(F) > 0$. If E is independent of F, then we know that $P(E \mid F) = P(E)$. Substituting this into (1), we find that

$$P(F \mid E) = P(F)$$

That is, the event F is independent of E.

Thus, if two events E and F have positive probabilities and if the event E is independent of F, then F is also independent of E. In this case, E and F are called *independent events.*

We also have the following result concerning independent events:

Two events E and F of a sample space S are independent events if an only if

(2) $$P(E \cap F) = P(E) \bullet P(F)$$

That is, the probability of E and F is equal to the product of the probability of E and the probability of F.

Proof
If E and F are independent events, then

$$P(E|F) = \frac{P(E \cap F)}{P(F)} \qquad \text{and} \qquad P(E|F) = P(E)$$

Thus,

$$\frac{P(E \cap F)}{P(F)} = P(E) \qquad \text{or} \qquad P(E \cap F) = P(E) \bullet P(F)$$

Conversely, if $P(E \cap F) = P(E) \bullet P(F)$, then

$$P(E|F) = \frac{P(E \cap F)}{P(F)} = \frac{P(E) \bullet P(F)}{P(F)} = P(E)$$

That is, E and F are independent events.

This result is used to verify whether two events are independent.

Example 2 Suppose a red die and a green die are thrown. Let event E be "Throw a 5 with the red die," and let event F be "Throw a 6 with the green die."

Solution In this experiment, the events E and F are

$$E = \{(5, 1), (5, 2), (5, 3), (5, 4), (5, 5), (5, 6)\}$$
$$F = \{(1, 6), (2, 6), (3, 6), (4, 6), (5, 6), (6, 6)\}$$

and

$$P(E) = \frac{1}{6} \qquad P(F) = \frac{1}{6}$$

Also, the event E and F is

$$E \cap F = \{(5, 6)\}$$

so that

$$P(E \cap F) = \frac{1}{36}$$

Since $P(E) \bullet P(F) = \frac{1}{6} \bullet \frac{1}{6} = \frac{1}{36} = P(E \cap F)$, E and F are independent events. ■

Example 3   For the data in the T-maze problem (Problem 47, Exercise 2), show that the events E and G are not independent, but that the events G and H are independent, where E, G, and H are defined as before:

> E: Run to the right two consecutive times
> G: Run to the left on the first trial
> H: Run to the right on the second trial

Solution   The events E and G are

$$E = \{RRL, LRR, RRR\}$$
$$G = \{LLL, LLR, LRL, LRR\}$$

The sample space S has eight elements so that

$$P(E) = \frac{3}{8} \qquad P(G) = \frac{1}{2}$$

Also, the event E *and* G is

$$E \cap G = \{LRR\}$$

and

$$P(E \cap G) = \frac{1}{8}$$

Since $P(E \cap G) \neq P(E) \bullet P(G)$, the events E and G are not independent. Thus, running to the right two consecutive times and running to the left on the first trial are dependent.

Next, the event H is

$$H = \{RRL, RRR, LRL, LRR\}$$

and

$$P(H) = \frac{1}{2}$$

The event G *and* H and its probability are

$$G \cap H = \{LRL, LRR\} \qquad P(G \cap H) = \frac{1}{4}$$

Since $P(G \cap H) = P(G) \bullet P(H)$, the events G and H are independent. Thus, running to the left on the first trial and running to the right on the second trial are independent events. ■

Example 3 illustrates that the question of whether two events are independent can be answered simply by determining whether formula (2) is satisfied. Although we may often suspect two events E and F of being independent, our intuition must be checked by computing $P(E)$, $P(F)$, and $P(E \cap F)$ and determining whether $P(E \cap F) = P(E) \cdot P(F)$.

The following steps summarize the procedure to use to check for events E and F being independent:

1. Compute the probability of event E.
2. Compute the probability of event F.
3. Compute the probability of the event E and F, $P(E \cap F)$.
4. If $P(E \cap F) = P(E) \cdot P(F)$, the events are independent.
   If $P(E \cap F) \neq P(E) \cdot P(F)$, the events are not independent.

For some probabilistic models, an assumption of independence is made. In such instances when two events are independent, formula (2) may be used to compute the probability that both events occur. The following example illustrates such a situation.

Example 4 In a group of seeds, $\frac{1}{4}$ of which should produce white plants, the best germination that can be obtained is 75%. If one seed is planted, what is the probability that it will grow into a white plant?

Solution Let G and W be the events

$$G: \text{ The plant will grow}$$
$$W: \text{ The seed will produce a white plant}$$

Assume that W does not depend on G and vice versa, so that W and G are independent events.

Then, the probability that the plant grows and is white, namely, $P(W \cap G)$ is

$$P(W \cap G) = P(W) \cdot P(G) = \frac{1}{4} \cdot \frac{3}{4} = \frac{3}{16}$$

A white plant will grow 3 out of 16 times.

■

There is a danger that mutually exclusive events and independent events may be confused. A source of this confusion is the common expression. "They have nothing to do with each other." This expression provides a description of independence when applied to everyday events; but when it is applied to sets, it suggests nonoverlapping. Nonoverlapping sets are mutually exclusive but are not necessarily independent. See Problem 17 in Exercise 6.

Exercise 6
Solutions to Odd-Numbered Problems begin on page 591.

1. If E and F are independent events and if $P(E) = .3$ and $P(F) = .5$, find $P(E \cap F)$.
2. If E and F are independent events and if $P(E) = .6$ and $P(E \cap F) = .3$, find $P(F)$.
3. If E and F are independent events, find $P(F)$ if $P(E) = .2$ and $P(E \cup F) = .3$.

4. If E and F are independent events, find $P(E)$ if $P(F) = .3$ and $P(E \cup F) = .6$.

5. If $P(E) = .3$, $P(F) = .2$, and $P(E \cup F) = .4$, what is $P(E|F)$? Are E and F independent?

6. If $P(E) = .4$, $P(F) = .6$, and $P(E \cup F) = .7$, what is $P(E|F)$? Are E and F independent?

7. A fair die is rolled. Let E be the event "1, 2, or 3 is rolled" and let F be the event "3, 4, or 5 is rolled." Are E and F independent?

8. A loaded die is rolled. The probabilities for this die are $P(1) = P(2) = P(4) = P(5) = \frac{1}{8}$ and $P(3) = P(6) = \frac{1}{4}$. Are the events defined in Problem 7 independent in this case?

9. For a 3 child family, let E be the event "The family has at most 1 boy" and let F be the event "The family has children of each sex." Are E and F independent events?

10. For a 2 child family, are the events E and F as defined in Problem 9 independent?

11. A first card is drawn at random from a regular deck of 52 cards and is then put back in the deck. A second card is drawn. What is the probability that:
    (a) The first card is a club?
    (b) The second card is a heart, given that the first is a club?
    (c) The first card is a club and the second is heart?

12. For the situation described in Problem 11, what is the probability that:
    (a) The first card is an ace?
    (b) The second card is a king, given that the first card is an ace?
    (c) The first card is an ace and the second is a king?

13. In the T-maze problem (Problem 47, Exercise 2), are the two events E and F independent?

14. Define the events E and F to be

    > E: A head turns up on the first throw of a fair coin
    > F: A tail turns up on the second throw of a fair coin

    Show that E and F are independent events.

15. A die is loaded so that

    $$P(1) = P(2) = P(3) = \frac{1}{4}$$

    $$P(4) = P(5) = P(6) = \frac{1}{12}$$

    If $A = \{1, 2\}$, $B = \{2, 3\}$, $C = \{1, 3\}$, show that any pair of these events is independent.

16. In a survey of 100 people, categorized as drinkers or nondrinkers, with or without a liver ailment, the following data were obtained:

	F Liver Ailment	$\bar{F}$ No Liver Ailment
Drinkers, E	52	18
Nondrinkers, $\bar{E}$	8	22

(a) Are the events E and F independent?
(b) Are the events $\bar{E}$ and $\bar{F}$ independent?
(c) Are the events E and $\bar{F}$ independent?

17. Give an example of two events that are:
    (a) Independent, but not mutually exclusive (disjoint)
    (b) Not independent, but mutually exclusive (disjoint)
    (c) Not independent and not mutually exclusive (disjoint)

18. Show that whenever two events are both independent and mutually exclusive, then at least one of them is impossible.

19. Let E be any event. If F is an impossible event, show that E and F are independent.

*20. Show that if E and F are independent events, so are $\bar{E}$ and F.
    [*Hint:* Use De Morgan's law.]

*21. Show that if E and F are independent events and if $P(E) \neq 0$, $P(F) \neq 0$, then E and F are not mutually exclusive.

*22. Three events E, F, and G are *independent* if any two of them are independent and

$$P(E \cap F \cap G) = P(E) \cdot P(F) \cdot P(G)$$

Use this definition to determine whether the events E, F, and G defined below for the experiment of tossing 2 fair dice are independent.

> E: The first die shows a 6
> F: The second die shows a 3
> G: The sum on the 2 dice is 7

*23. *Chevalier de Mere's Problem.* Solve Problem 7 in Exercise 1 (page 235). [*Hint:* Part (a) $P(\text{No 1's are obtained}) = \frac{5^4}{6^4} = \frac{625}{1296} = .4823$. Part (b) The probability of not obtaining a double 1 on any given toss is $\frac{35}{36}$. Thus, $P(\text{No double 1's are obtained}) = (\frac{35}{36})^{24} = .509$.]

*24. A woman has 10 keys but only 1 fits her door. She tries them successively (without replacement). Find the probability that a key fits in exactly 5 tries.†

7. Bayes' Formula

In this section we consider experiments with sample spaces that can be divided or partitioned into two (or more) mutually exclusive events. This study involves a further application of conditional probabilities and leads us to the famous formula of Thomas Bayes, first published in 1763.

†William Feller, *An Introduction to Probability Theory and Its Applications*, 3rd ed., Wiley, New York, 1968.

THOMAS BAYES (1702–1761), born in London, was the son of a Presbyterian minister. Bayes, who was also ordained and began his ministry by assisting his father, was elected a Fellow of the Royal Society in 1742. He published several theological papers, but is most famous for his paper on probability, which was published after his death by a friend who found it among his effects. This work is noteworthy because it is the first discussion of inductive inference in precise quantitive form.

We begin by considering the following example.

Example 1 Given two urns, I and II, suppose Urn I contains 4 black and 7 white balls. Urn II contains 3 black, 1 white, and 4 yellow balls. We select an urn at random and then draw a ball. What is the probability that we obtain a black ball?

Solution Let U_I and U_{II} stand for the events "Urn I is chosen" and "Urn II is chosen," respectively. Similarly, let B, W, Y stand for the event that "A black," "A white," or "A yellow ball is chosen," respectively.

$$P(U_I) = P(U_{II}) = \frac{1}{2}$$

$$P(B|U_I) = \frac{4}{11} \qquad P(B|U_{II}) = \frac{3}{8}$$

The event B can be written as

$$B = (B \cap U_I) \cup (B \cap U_{II})$$

Since $B \cap U_I$ and $B \cap U_{II}$ are disjoint, we add their probabilities. Then

$$P(B) = P(B \cap U_I) + P(B \cap U_{II})$$

Using the definition of conditional probability, we have

$$P(B|U_I) = \frac{P(B \cap U_I)}{P(U_I)} \qquad\qquad P(B|U_{II}) = \frac{P(B \cap U_{II})}{P(U_{II})}$$

$$P(B \cap U_I) = P(U_I) \cdot P(B|U_I) \qquad P(B \cap U_{II}) = P(U_{II}) \cdot P(B|U_{II})$$

Thus,

$$P(B) = P(U_I) \cdot P(B|U_I) + P(U_{II}) \cdot P(B|U_{II})$$

$$= \frac{1}{2} \cdot \frac{4}{11} + \frac{1}{2} \cdot \frac{3}{8} = \frac{65}{176} = .369$$

A solution to Example 1 can be depicted using a tree diagram, as shown in Figure 11.

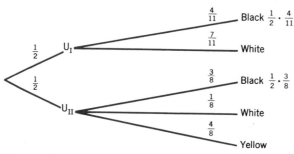

Figure 11

Suppose A_1 and A_2 are two nonempty, mutually exclusive events of a sample space S and the union of A_1 and A_2 is S; that is,

$$A_1 \neq \varnothing \qquad A_2 \neq \varnothing \qquad A_1 \cap A_2 = \varnothing \qquad S = A_1 \cup A_2$$

Partition   In this case, we say that A_1 and A_2 form a *partition* of S. See Figure 12.

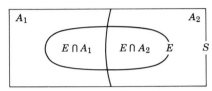

Figure 12

Now, if we let E be any event in S, we may write the set E in the form

$$E = (E \cap A_1) \cup (E \cap A_2)$$

The sets $E \cap A_1$ and $E \cap A_2$ are disjoint, since

$$(E \cap A_1) \cap (E \cap A_2) = (E \cap E) \cap (A_1 \cap A_2) = E \cap \varnothing = \varnothing$$

Using the definition for conditional probability, the probability of E is therefore

(1)
$$\begin{aligned} P(E) &= P(E \cap A_1) + P(E \cap A_2) \\ &= P(A_1) \cdot P(E|A_1) + P(A_2) \cdot P(E|A_2) \end{aligned}$$

The above formula is used to find the probability of an event E of a sample space when the sample space is partitioned into two sets A_1 and A_2.

Example 2   Of the applicants to a medical school, it is felt that 80% are eligible to enter and 20% are not. To aid in the selection process, an admissions test is administered which is designed so that an eligible candidate will pass 90% of the time, while an ineligible candidate will pass only 30% of the time. What is the probability that an applicant for admission will pass the admissions test?

Solution   The sample space S consists of the applicants for admission, and S can be partitioned into the following two events:

$$A_1\text{:   Eligible applicant} \qquad A_2\text{:   Ineligible applicant}$$

These two events are disjoint, and their union is S. The event E is

$$E\text{:   Applicant passes admissions test}$$

Now,

$$\begin{aligned} P(A_1) &= .8 & P(A_2) &= .2 \\ P(E|A_1) &= .9 & P(E|A_2) &= .3 \end{aligned}$$

Using formula (1), we have

$$P(E) = P(A_1) \cdot P(E|A_1) + P(A_2) \cdot P(E|A_2) = (.8)(.9) + (.2)(.3) = .78$$

Thus, the probability that an applicant will pass the admissions test is .78.

If we partition a sample space S into three sets A_1, A_2, and A_3 so that

$$S = A_1 \cup A_2 \cup A_3$$

$$A_1 \cap A_2 = \emptyset \qquad A_2 \cap A_3 = \emptyset \qquad A_1 \cap A_3 = \emptyset$$

$$A_1 \neq \emptyset \qquad A_2 \neq \emptyset \qquad A_3 \neq \emptyset$$

we may write any set E in S in the form

$$E = (E \cap A_1) \cup (E \cap A_2) \cup (E \cap A_3)$$

The probability of event E is

(2)
$$\begin{aligned} P(E) &= P(E \cap A_1) + P(E \cap A_2) + P(E \cap A_3) \\ &= P(A_1) \cdot P(E|A_1) + P(A_2) \cdot P(E|A_2) + P(A_3) \cdot P(E|A_3) \end{aligned}$$

since $E \cap A_1$, $E \cap A_2$, and $E \cap A_3$ are disjoint. See Figure 13.

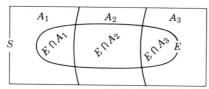

Figure 13

Formula (2) is used to find the probability of an event E of a sample space when the sample space is partitioned into three sets A_1, A_2, and A_3.

Example 3 Three machines, I, II, and III, manufacture .4, .5, and .1 of the total production in a plant, respectively. The percentage of defective items produced by I, II, and III is 2%, 4%, and 1%, respectively. For an item chosen at random, what is the probability that it is defective?

Solution In this example, the sample space S is partitioned into three events A_1, A_2, and A_3 defined as follows:

A_1: Item produced by Machine I
A_2: Item produced by Machine II
A_3: Item produced by Machine III

Clearly, the events A_1, A_2, and A_3 are mutually exclusive, and their union is S. Define the event E in S to be

E: Item is defective

Now,

$$P(A_1) = .4 \qquad P(A_2) = .5 \qquad P(A_3) = .1$$
$$P(E|A_1) = .02 \qquad P(E|A_2) = .04 \qquad P(E|A_3) = .01$$

Thus, using formula (2), we see that

$$\begin{aligned} P(E) &= (.4)(.02) + (.5)(.04) + (.1)(.01) \\ &= .008 + .020 + .001 = .029 \end{aligned}$$

Figure 14 gives a tree diagram solution to Example 3.

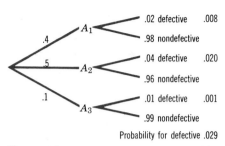

Figure 14

To generalize formulas (1) and (2) to a sample space S partitioned into n sets, we first introduce the following definition:

Partition **A sample space S is** *partitioned* **into n subsets $A_1, A_2, \ldots, A_n$, provided:**
(a) The intersection of any two of the subsets is empty.
(b) Each subset is nonempty.
(c) $A_1 \cup A_2 \cup \cdots \cup A_n = S$

Let S be a sample space and let $A_1, A_2, A_3, \ldots, A_n$ be n events that form a partition of the set S. If E is any event in S, then

$$E = (E \cap A_1) \cup (E \cap A_2) \cup \cdots \cup (E \cap A_n)$$

Clearly, $E \cap A_1, E \cap A_2, \ldots, E \cap A_n$ are mutually exclusive events. Hence,

(3) $$P(E) = P(E \cap A_1) + P(E \cap A_2) + \cdots + P(E \cap A_n)$$

In (3), replace $P(E \cap A_1), P(E \cap A_2), \ldots, P(E \cap A_n)$ using the definition of conditional probability. Then we obtain the formula

(4) $$P(E) = P(A_1) \cdot P(E|A_1) + P(A_2) \cdot P(E|A_2) + \cdots + P(A_n) \cdot P(E|A_n)$$

Example 4 In Example 2, suppose an applicant passes the admissions test. What is the probability that he or she was among those eligible; that is, what is the probability $P(A_1|E)$?

Solution By the definition of conditional probability,

$$P(A_1|E) = \frac{P(A_1 \cap E)}{P(E)} = \frac{P(A_1) \cdot P(E|A_1)}{P(E)}$$

But $P(E)$ is given by (4) when $n = 2$ or by (1). Thus,

(5) $$P(A_1|E) = \frac{P(A_1) \cdot P(E|A_1)}{P(A_1) \cdot P(E|A_1) + P(A_2) \cdot P(E|A_2)}$$

Using the information supplied in Example 2, we find

$$P(A_1|E) = \frac{(.8)(.9)}{.78} = \frac{.72}{.78} = .923$$

The admissions test is a reasonably effective device. Less than 8% of the students passing the test are ineligible.

∎

Equation (5) is a special case of *Bayes' formula* when the sample space is partitioned into two sets A_1 and A_2. The general formula is given next.

Bayes' Formula **Let S be a sample space partitioned into n events, $A_1, \ldots, A_n$. Let E be any event of S for which $P(E) > 0$. The probability of the event A_j ($j = 1, 2, \ldots, n$), given the event E, is**

(6)
$$P(A_j | E) = \frac{P(A_j) \cdot P(E|A_j)}{P(E)}$$

$$= \frac{P(A_j) \cdot P(E|A_j)}{P(A_1) \cdot P(E|A_1) + P(A_2) \cdot P(E|A_2) + \cdots + P(A_n) \cdot P(E|A_n)}$$

The proof is left as an exercise (see Problem 32, Exercise 7).

The following example illustrates a use for Bayes' formula when the sample space S is partitioned into three events.

Example 5 Motors Incorporated has three plants, I, II, and III. Plant I produces 35% of the car output, Plant II produces 20%, and Plant III produces the remaining 45%. One percent of the output of Plant I is defective, as is 1.8% of the output of Plant II, and 2% of the output of Plant III. The annual total output of Motors Incorporated is 1,000,000 cars. A car is chosen at random from the annual output and it is found to be defective. What is the probability that it came from Plant I? Plant II? Plant III?

Solution To answer these questions, let's define the following events:

E: Car is defective
A_1: Car produced by Plant I
A_2: Car produced by Plant II
A_3: Car produced by Plant III

Also, $P(A_1|E)$ indicates the probability that a car is produced by Plant I, given that it was defective; $P(A_2|E)$ and $P(A_3|E)$ are similarly defined. To find these probabilities, we proceed as follows.

From the data given in the problem, we can determine the following:

(7)
$$
\begin{array}{ll}
P(A_1) = .35 & P(E|A_1) = .010 \\
P(A_2) = .20 & P(E|A_2) = .018 \\
P(A_3) = .45 & P(E|A_3) = .020
\end{array}
$$

Now,

$A_1 \cap E$ is the event "Produced by Plant I and is defective"
$A_2 \cap E$ is the event "Produced by Plant II and is defective"
$A_3 \cap E$ is the event "Produced by Plant III and is defective"

From the definition of conditional probability, we find

$$P(A_1 \cap E) = P(A_1) \cdot P(E|A_1) = (.35)(.010) = .0035$$
$$P(A_2 \cap E) = P(A_2) \cdot P(E|A_2) = (.20)(.018) = .0036$$
$$P(A_3 \cap E) = P(A_3) \cdot P(E|A_3) = (.45)(.020) = .0090$$

Since $E = (A_1 \cap E) \cup (A_2 \cap E) \cup (A_3 \cap E)$, we have

$$P(E) = P(A_1 \cap E) + P(A_2 \cap E) + P(A_3 \cap E)$$
$$= .0035 + .0036 + .0090$$
$$= .0161$$

Thus, the probability that a defective car is chosen is .0161.

Given that the car chosen is defective, the probability that it came from Plant I is $P(A_1|E)$, from Plant II is $P(A_2|E)$, and from Plant III is $P(A_3|E)$. To compute these probabilities, we use Bayes' formula:

$$P(A_1|E) = \frac{P(A_1) \cdot P(E|A_1)}{P(A_1) \cdot P(E|A_1) + P(A_2) \cdot P(E|A_2) + P(A_3) \cdot P(E|A_3)}$$

$$= \frac{P(A_1) \cdot P(E|A_1)}{P(E)} = \frac{(.35)(.01)}{.0161} = .217$$

(8)

$$P(A_2|E) = \frac{P(A_2) \cdot P(E|A_2)}{P(E)} = \frac{.0036}{.0161} = .224$$

$$P(A_3|E) = \frac{P(A_3) \cdot P(E|A_3)}{P(E)} = \frac{.0090}{.0161} = .559 \qquad \blacksquare$$

Compare the probabilities in (7) with those in (8). The probabilities $P(E|A_1)$, $P(E|A_2)$, and $P(E|A_3)$ are probabilities of a defective car being produced by one of the plants *before* it is chosen and examined. This is what we refer to as *a priori probability*—that is, "before-the-fact" probability. The probabilities $P(A_1|E)$, $P(A_2|E)$, and $P(A_3|E)$ are probabilities of a defective car being produced by one of the plants *after* we have examined it and found it to be defective. This is referred to as *a posteriori probability,* or "after-the-fact" probability. Thus, Bayes' formula gives us a technique for computing *a posteriori probabilities.*

a priori Probability

a posteriori Probability

For example, before a car is chosen, the probability of choosing a defective car assuming it was from Plant I is .01. After it is known that a defective car was chosen, the probability that it came from Plant I is .217.

Example 6   The residents of a community are examined for cancer. The examination results are classified as postive (+), if a malignancy is suspected, and as negative (−), if there are no indications of a malignancy. If a person has cancer, the probability of a suspected malignancy is .98; and the probability of reporting cancer where none existed is .15. If 5% of the community has cancer, what is the probability of a person not having cancer if the examination is positive?

Solution   Let us define the following events:

A_1:   Person has cancer
A_2:   Person does not have cancer
E: Examination is positive

We want to know the probability of a person not having cancer if it is known that the examination is positive; that is, we wish to find $P(A_2|E)$. Now,

$$P(A_1) = .05 \qquad P(A_2) = .95$$
$$P(E|A_1) = .98 \qquad P(E|A_2) = .15$$

Using Bayes' formula, we get

$$P(A_2|E) = \frac{P(A_2) \cdot P(E|A_2)}{P(A_1) \cdot P(E|A_1) + P(A_2) \cdot P(E|A_2)}$$
$$= \frac{(.95)(.15)}{(.05)(.98) + (.95)(.15)} = .744$$

Thus, even if the examination is positive, the person examined is more likely not to have cancer than to have cancer. The reason the test is designed this way is that it is better for a healthy person to be examined more thoroughly, than for someone with cancer to go undetected. ■

Example 7 The manager of a car repair shop knows from past experience that when a call is received from a person whose car will not start, the probabilities for various troubles (assuming no two can occur simultaneously) are as follows:

Event	Trouble	Probability
A_1:	Flooded	.3
A_2:	Battery cable loose	.2
A_3:	Points bad	.1
A_4:	Out of gas	.3
A_5:	Something else	.1

The manager also knows that if the person will hold the gas pedal down and try to start the car, the probability that it will start (E) is

$$P(E|A_1) = .9 \qquad P(E|A_2) = 0 \qquad P(E|A_3) = .2$$
$$P(E|A_4) = 0 \qquad P(E|A_5) = .2$$

(a) If a person has called and is instructed to "hold the pedal down . . . ," what is the probability that the car will start?

(b) If the car does start after holding the pedal down, what is the probability that the car was flooded?

Solution (a) We need to compute $P(E)$. Using formula (4) for $n = 5$ (the sample space is partitioned into five disjoint sets), we have

$$P(E) = P(A_1) \cdot P(E|A_1) + P(A_2) \cdot P(E|A_2) + P(A_3) \cdot P(E|A_3)$$
$$\quad + P(A_4) \cdot P(E|A_4) + P(A_5) \cdot P(E|A_5)$$
$$= (.3)(.9) + (.2)(0) + (.1)(.2) + (.3)(0) + (.1)(.2)$$
$$= .27 + .02 + .02 = .31$$

(b) We use Bayes' formula to compute the *a posteriori* probability $P(A_1|E)$:

$$P(A_1|E) = \frac{P(A_1) \cdot P(E|A_1)}{P(E)} = \frac{(.3)(.9)}{.31} = \frac{.27}{.31} = .87$$

Thus, the probability that the car is flooded, after it is known that holding down the pedal started the car, is .87.

■

When the probability of each event of the partition is equally likely,

$$P(A_1) = P(A_2) = \cdots = P(A_n)$$

we obtain a special case of Bayes' formula:

(9)
$$P(A_j|E) = \frac{P(E|A_j)}{P(E|A_1) + P(E|A_2) + \cdots + P(E|A_n)}$$

Let's return to Example 5 and assume that $P(A_1) = P(A_2) = P(A_3)$, so that the three plants' share of the total production is the same. In this case, it is easier to use (9) to obtain the probability that a car is produced at Plant I, given that it was defective:

$$P(A_1|E) = \frac{P(E|A_1)}{P(E|A_1) + P(E|A_2) + P(E|A_3)}$$

$$= \frac{.010}{.010 + .018 + .020}$$

$$= \frac{.010}{.048} = \frac{5}{24} = .208$$

Exercise 7
Solutions to Odd-Numbered Problems begin on page 592.

In Problems 1–6 find the indicated probabilities by referring to the following tree diagram:

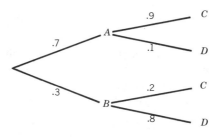

1. $P(C)$
2. $P(D)$
3. $P(C|A)$
4. $P(D|A)$
5. $P(C|D)$
6. $P(D|C)$

In Problems 7–12 find the indicated probabilities by referring to the following tree diagram and using Bayes' formula:

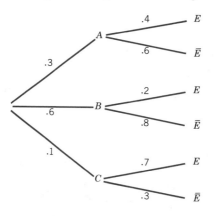

7. $P(A|E)$
8. $P(B|\bar{E})$
9. $P(C|E)$
10. $P(A|\bar{E})$
11. $P(B|E)$
12. $P(C|\bar{E})$

13. Events A_1 and A_2 form a partition of a sample space S with $P(A_1) = .3$ and $P(A_2) = .7$. If E is an event in S with $P(E|A_1) = .01$ and $P(E|A_2) = .02$, compute $P(E)$.

14. Events A_1 and A_2 form a partition of a sample space S with $P(A_1) = .4$ and $P(A_2) = .6$. If E is an event in S with $P(E|A_1) = .03$ and $P(E|A_2) = .01$, compute $P(E)$.

15. Events A_1, A_2, and A_3 form a partition of a sample space S with $P(A_1) = .5$, $P(A_2) = .3$, and $P(A_3) = .2$. If E is an event in S with $P(E|A_1) = .01$, $P(E|A_2) = .03$, and $P(E|A_3) = .02$, compute $P(E)$.

16. Events A_1, A_2, and A_3 form a partition of a sample space S with $P(A_1) = .3$, $P(A_2) = .3$, and $P(A_3) = .4$. If E is an event in S with $P(E|A_1) = .01$, $P(E|A_2) = .02$, and $P(E|A_3) = .02$, compute $P(E)$.

17. Use the information in Problem 13 to find $P(A_1|E)$ and $P(A_2|E)$.

18. Use the information in Problem 14 to find $P(A_1|E)$ and $P(A_2|E)$.

19. Use the information in Problem 15 to find $P(A_1|E)$, $P(A_2|E)$, and $P(A_3|E)$.

20. Use the information in Problem 16 to find $P(A_1|E)$, $P(A_2|E)$, and $P(A_3|E)$.

21. In Example 3 (page 276), suppose it is known that a defective item was produced. Find the probability that it came from Machine I; from Machine II; from Machine III.

22. In Example 5 (page 278), suppose $P(A_1) = P(A_2) = P(A_3) = \frac{1}{3}$. Find $P(A_2|E)$ and $P(A_3|E)$.

23. In Example 7 (page 280), compute the *a posteriori* probabilities $P(A_2|E)$, $P(A_3|E)$, $P(A_4|E)$, and $P(A_5|E)$.

24. In Example 6 (page 279), compute $P(A_1|E)$.

25. Three urns contain colored balls as follows:

Urn	Red, R	White, W	Blue, B
I	5	6	5
II	3	4	9
III	7	5	4

One urn is chosen at random and a ball is withdrawn. The ball is red. What is the probability that it came from Urn I? From Urn II? From Urn III? [*Hint:* Define the events E: Ball selected is red, U_I: Urn I selected, U_{II}: Urn II selected, and U_{III}: Urn III selected. Determine $P(U_I|E)$, $P(U_{II}|E)$, and $P(U_{III}|E)$ by using Bayes' formula.]

26. Suppose that if a person with tuberculosis is given a TB screening, the probability that his or her condition will be detected is .90. If a person without tuberculosis is given a TB screening, the probability that he or she will be diagnosed incorrectly as having tuberculosis is .3. Suppose, further, that 11% of the adult residents of a certain city have tuberculosis. If one of these adults is diagnosed as having tuberculosis based on the screening, what is the probability that he or she actually has tuberculosis? Interpret your result.

27. Cars are being produced by two factories, I and II, but Factory I produces twice as many cars as Factory II in a given time. Factory I is known to produce 2% defectives and Factory II produces 1% defectives. A car is examined and found to be defective. What are the *a priori* and *a posteriori* probabilities that the car was produced by Factory I?

28. An absent-minded nurse is to give Mr. Brown a pill each day. The probability that the nurse forgets to administer the pill is $\frac{2}{3}$. If he receives the pill, the probability that Brown will die is $\frac{1}{3}$. If he does not get his pill, the probability that he will die is $\frac{3}{4}$. Mr. Brown died. What is the probability that the nurse forgot to give Brown the pill?

29. An oil well is to be drilled in a certain location. The soil there is either rock (probability .53), clay (probability .21), or sand. If it is rock, a geological test gives a positive result with 35% accuracy; if it is clay, this test gives a positive result with 48% accuracy; and if it is sand, the test gives a positive result with 75% accuracy. Given that the test is positive, what is the probability that the soil is rock? What is the probability that the soil is clay? What is the probability that the soil is sand?

30. A geologist is using seismographs to test for oil. It is found that if oil is present, the test gives a positive result 95% of the time, and if oil is not present, the test gives a positive result 2% of the time. Finally, oil is discovered in 1% of the cases tested. If the test shows positive, what is the probability that oil is present?

31. *Political Polls.* In conducting a political poll, a pollster divides the United States into four sections: Northeast (N), containing 40% of the population; South (S), containing 10% of the population; Midwest (M), containing 25% of the population; and West (W), containing 25% of the population. From the poll, it is found that in the next election 40% of the people in the Northeast say they will vote for Republicans, in the South 56% will vote Republican, in the Midwest 48% will vote Republican, and in the West 52% will vote Republican. What is the probability that a person chosen at random will vote Republican? Assuming a person votes Republican, what is the probability that he or she is from the Northeast?

*32. Prove Bayes' formula (6).

8. The Binomial Probability Model

In this section we study practical situations that can be interpreted by using a simple probabilistic model, called the *binomial probability model*. The model was first studied by J. Bernoulli about 1700 and, for this reason, the model is sometimes referred to as a *Bernoulli trial*.

The binomial probability model is a sequence of trials, each of which consists of repetition of a single experiment. We assume the outcome of one experiment does not affect the outcome of any other one; that is, we assume the trials to be independent. Furthermore, we assume that there are only two possible outcomes for each trial and label them *S*, for *Success*, and *F*, for *Failure*. This is a rather simple experiment and it may be classified completely in terms of a single number *p*, the probability of success. The probability of success, $p = P(S)$, remains the same from trial to trial. In addition, since there are only two outcomes in each trial, the probability of failure must be $1 - p$, and we write

$$q = 1 - p = P(F)$$

Any random experiment for which the binomial probability model is appropriate is called a *Bernoulli trial*.

Bernoulli Trial **Repeated trials of a random experiment are called** *Bernoulli trials* **if:**
(a) There are only two possible outcomes *S* **and** *F* **in each trial.**
(b) The probabilities of the outcomes *S* **and** *F* **do not change from trial to trial.**
(c) The trials are independent.

Many real-world situations have the characteristics of the binomial probability model. For example, in repeatedly running a subject through a T-maze, we may label a turn to the left by *S* and a turn to the right by *F*. The assumption of independence of each trial is equivalent to presuming the subject has no memory.

In opinion polls, one person's response is independent of any other person's response, and we may designate the answer "Yes" by an *S* and any other answer ("No" or "Don't know") by an *F*.

In testing TV's, we have a sequence of independent trials (each test of a particular TV is a trial) and we label a nondefective TV with an *S* and a defective one with an *F*.

When a sequence of experiments has more than two outcomes in each trial, we can convert it to a Bernoulli trial by considering the occurrence of an event *E* as a success and that of the event $\bar{E}$ as a failure. In this case,

$$p = P(S) = P(E) \qquad \text{and} \qquad q = P(F) = P(\bar{E})$$

JAMES (JACQUES) BERNOULLI (1654–1705) was a member of a family of famous Swiss mathematicians. At the insistence of his father, he studied theology. Later, he refused a church appointment and began lecturing on experimental physics at the University of Basel. Thanks to Bernoulli's contributions, probability theory was raised to the status of a science. In 1713, his book *Ars Conjectardi* was published in Latin by his nephew Nicholas Bernoulli, who also was a mathematician.

Consider a Bernoulli trial that consists of six stages, or six trials. One path, or one particular outcome, might appear as *FSSSFS*. Since we are assuming that the trials are independent, the probability of this particular outcome would be

$$q \cdot p \cdot p \cdot p \cdot q \cdot p = q \cdot p^3 \cdot q \cdot p = p^4 \cdot q^2$$

The probability of a different outcome, such as *SFSFSS*, is also equal to $p^4 q^2$. The same is true for any outcome that has *exactly* the same number of *S*'s and *F*'s, regardless of their order. To analyze these trials in a systematic way, let's consider tree diagrams for the cases of 2 and 3 trials. See Figure 15.

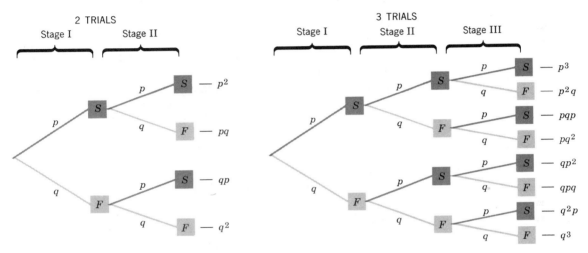

Figure 15

Several observations should be made with regard to the two tree diagrams shown in Figure 15. First, notice that if we sum the probabilities at the conclusion of the last trial of each experiment, we find that

$$p^2 + pq + qp + q^2 = p^2 + 2pq + q^2 = (p + q)^2$$
$$p^3 + p^2q + pqp + pq^2 + qp^2 + qpq + q^2p + q^3$$
$$= p^3 + 3p^2q + 3pq^2 + q^3 = (p + q)^3$$

In general, with an experiment involving n trials, the sum of the probabilities after the nth trial is $(p + q)^n$.

Second, notice that in a sequence of n independent trials with two outcomes, any sequence that contains k successes and $n - k$ failures has probability $p^k q^{n-k}$. To find the probability of obtaining exactly k successes in n trials, we must find the number of sequences having k successes. This number is obtained by noting that the k successes can appear in any k of the n trials; thus, the number of such sequences must be equal to the number of combinations of k objects that can be taken from a set of n objects, or $\binom{n}{k}$. If we multiply this number by the probability for obtaining this sequence, we obtain the following result:

In a Bernoulli trial the probability of exactly k successes in n trials is given by

(1)
$$b(n, k; p) = \binom{n}{k} p^k \cdot q^{n-k} = \frac{n!}{k!(n-k)!} p^k \cdot q^{n-k}$$

where $q = 1 - p$.

Binomial Probability

The symbol $b(n, k; p)$, which represents the probability of exactly k successes in n trials, is called a *binomial probability*.

Example 1 A common example of a Bernoulli trial is a coin-flipping experiment:

1. There are exactly two possible mutually exclusive outcomes on each trial or toss (heads or tails).
2. The probability of a particular outcome (say, H) remains constant from trial to trial (toss to toss).
3. The outcome on any trial (toss) is independent of the outcome on any other trial (toss).

We would like to compute the probability of obtaining exactly 1 tail in six tosses of a fair coin.

Solution Let S denote the simple event "Tail shows" and let F denote the simple event "Head shows." Using Formula (1) in which $k = 1$, $n = 6$, and $p = \frac{1}{2} = P(S)$, we obtain

$$P(\text{Exactly one success}) = b\left(6, 1; \frac{1}{2}\right) = \binom{6}{1}\left(\frac{1}{2}\right)^1\left(\frac{1}{2}\right)^{6-1}$$

$$= \frac{6}{64} \approx .0938 \qquad \blacksquare$$

It is not always necessary to compute binomial probabilities, because many values have been tabulated. Table 1 (page 528) lists the values of the binomial probability $b(n, k; p)$ for $n = 2, 3, \ldots, 20$ and $p = .05, .10, .15, .20, .25, .30, .35, .40, .45,$ and $.50$. One section of Table 1, giving values for $n = 7$, is shown here:

n	k	.05	.10	.15	.20	.25	.30	.35	.40	.45	.50
7	0	.6983	.4783	.3206	.2097	.1335	.0824	.0490	.0280	.0152	.0078
	1	.2573	.3720	.3960	.3670	.3115	.2471	.1848	.1306	.0872	.0547
	2	.0406	.1240	.2097	.2753	.3115	.3177	.2985	.2613	.2140	.1641
	3	.0036	.0230	.0617	.1147	.1730	.2269	.2679	.2903	.2918	.2734
	4	.0002	.0026	.0109	.0287	.0577	.0972	.1442	.1935	.2388	.2734
	5	.0000	.0002	.0012	.0043	.0115	.0250	.0466	.0774	.1172	.1641
	6	.0000	.0000	.0001	.0004	.0013	.0036	.0084	.0172	.0320	.0547
	7	.0000	.0000	.0000	.0000	.0001	.0002	.0006	.0016	.0037	.0078

For instance, $b(7, 3; .35)$ is the circled entry in the table. If a situation requires some other choice of p, more extensive tables should be used or the computation should be done using formula (1). For large n, a different model must be used. We will take this up in Chapter 19.

Notice in Table 1 that there are no probabilities listed for $p > .50$. The reason for this (see Problem 44, Exercise 8) is that

$$b(n, k; p) = b(n, n - k; 1 - p)$$

For example, if $n = 6$, $k = 2$, and $p = .7$, then

$$b(6, 2; .7) = b(6, 4; .3) = .0595$$

In the next example, as in many other applications, it is necessary to compute the probability not of exactly k successes, but of *at least* or *at most* k successes. To obtain such probabilities we have to compute all the individual probabilities and add them.

Example 2   A machine produces light bulbs to meet certain specifications, and 80% of the bulbs produced meet these specifications. A sample of 6 bulbs is taken from the machine's production. What is the probability that 3 or more of them fail to meet the specifications?

Solution   In this example we are looking for the probability of the event

A: At least 3 fail to meet specifications

But this event is just the union of the mutually exclusive events "Exactly 3 failures," "Exactly 4 failures," "Exactly 5 failures," and "Exactly 6 failures." Hence, we use formula (1) for $n = 6$ and $k = 3, 4, 5$, and 6. Since the probability of failure is .20, we have

$$P(\text{Exactly 3 failures}) = b(6, 3; .20) = .0819$$
$$P(\text{Exactly 4 failures}) = b(6, 4; .20) = .0154$$
$$P(\text{Exactly 5 failures}) = b(6, 5; .20) = .0015$$
$$P(\text{Exactly 6 failures}) = b(6, 6; .20) = .0001$$

Therefore,

$$P(\text{At least 3 failures}) = P(A) = .0819 + .0154 + .0015 + .0001$$
$$= .0989$$

Another way of getting this answer is to compute the probability of the complementary event

E: Less than 3 failures

Then,

$$P(E) = P(\text{Exactly 2 failures}) + P(\text{Exactly 1 failure}) + P(\text{Exactly 0 failures})$$
$$= b(6, 2; .20) + b(6, 1; .20) + b(6, 0; .20)$$
$$= .2458 + .3932 + .2621 = .9011$$

As a result,

$$P(\text{At least 3 failures}) = 1 - P(E) = 1 - .9011 = .0989$$

Example 3   A man claims to be able to distinguish between two kinds of wine with 90% accuracy and presents his claim to an agency interested in promoting the consumption of one of the two kinds of wine. The following experiment is conducted to check his claim. The man is to taste the two types of wine and distinguish between them. This is to be done 9 times with a 3 minute break after each taste. It is agreed that if the man is correct at least 6 out of the 9 times, he will be hired.

The main questions to be asked are, on the one hand, whether the above procedure gives sufficient protection to the hiring agency against a person guessing and, on the other hand, whether the man is given sufficient chance to be hired if he is really a wine connoisseur.

Solution To answer the first question, let's assume that the man is guessing. Then in each trial he has probability $\frac{1}{2}$ of identifying the wine correctly. Let k be the number of correct identifications. Let's compute the binomial probability for $k = 6, 7, 8, 9$, to find the likelihood of the man being hired while guessing:

$$b\left(9, 6; \frac{1}{2}\right) + b\left(9, 7; \frac{1}{2}\right) + b\left(9, 8; \frac{1}{2}\right) + b\left(9, 9; \frac{1}{2}\right)$$

$$= .1641 + .0703 + .0176 + .0020 = .2540$$

Thus, there is a likelihood of .254 that he will pass if he is just guessing.

To answer the second question in the case where the claim is true, we need to find the sum of the probabilities $b(9, k; .90)$ for $k = 6, 7, 8, 9$:

$$b(9, 6; .90) + b(9, 7; .90) + b(9, 8; .90) + b(9, 9; .90)$$
$$= b(9, 3; .10) + b(9, 2; .10) + b(9, 1; .10) + b(9, 0; .10)$$
$$= .0446 + .1722 + .3874 + .3874 = .9916$$

◼

Notice that the test in Example 3 is fair to the man, since it practically assures him the position if his claim is true. However, the company may not like the test because 25% of the time a person who guesses will pass the test.

Model: Testing a Serum or Vaccine*

Suppose that the normal rate of infection of a certain disease in cattle is 25%. To test a newly discovered serum, healthy animals are injected with it. How can we evaluate the result of the experiment?

For an absolutely worthless serum, the probability that exactly k of n test animals remain free from infection may be equated to $b(n, k; .75)$. For $k = n = 10$, this probability is about $b(10, 10; .75) = .056$. Thus, if out of 10 test animals none catches infection, this may be taken as an indication that the serum has had an effect, although it is not conclusive proof. Notice that, without serum, the probability that out of 17 animals at most 1 catches infection is $b(17, 0; .25) + b(17, 1; .25) = .0501$. Therefore, there is *stronger evidence* in favor of the serum if out of 17 test animals at most 1 gets infected than if out of 10 all remain healthy. For $n = 23$ the probability of at most 2 animals catching infection is about .0492, and thus, at most 2 failures out of 23 is again better evidence for the serum than at most 1 out of 17 or 0 out of 10.

*P. V. Sukhatme and V. G. Panse, "Size of Experiments for Testing Sera or Vaccines," *Indiana Journal of Veterinary Science and Animal Husbandry,* **13** (1943), pp. 75–82.

Exercise 8
Solutions to Odd-Numbered Problems begin on page 593.

In Problems 1–8 use Table 1 (page 528) to compute each binomial probability.

1. $b(7, 5; .30)$
2. $b(8, 6; .40)$
3. $b(15, 8; .70)$
4. $b(8, 5; .60)$
5. $b(15, 10; \frac{1}{2})$
6. $b(12, 6; .90)$
7. $b(15, 3; .3) + b(15, 2; .3) + b(15, 1; .3) + b(15, 0; .3)$
8. $b(8, 6; .4) + b(8, 7; .4) + b(8, 8; .4)$

In Problems 9–14 use formula (1), page 286, and a calculator to compute each binomial probability.

9. $n = 3, \quad k = 2, \quad p = \frac{1}{3}$
10. $n = 3, \quad k = 1, \quad p = \frac{1}{3}$
11. $n = 3, \quad k = 0, \quad p = \frac{1}{6}$
12. $n = 3, \quad k = 3, \quad p = \frac{1}{6}$
13. $n = 5, \quad k = 3, \quad p = \frac{2}{3}$
14. $n = 5, \quad k = 0, \quad p = \frac{2}{3}$

Problems 15–20 deal with binomial probabilities. Use Table 1 (page 528) to solve each problem.

15. Find the probability of obtaining exactly 6 successes in 10 trials when the probability of success is .3.
16. Find the probability of obtaining exactly 5 successes in 9 trials when the probability of success is .2.
17. Find the probability of obtaining exactly 9 successes in 12 trials when the probability of success is .8.
18. Find the probability of obtaining exactly 8 successes in 15 trials when the probability of success is .75.
19. Find the probability of obtaining at least 5 successes in 8 trials when the probability of success is .25.
20. Find the probability of obtaining at most 3 successes in 7 trials when the probability of success is .15.

In Problems 21–26 a fair coin is tossed eight times.

21. What is the probability of obtaining exactly 1 head?
22. What is the probability of obtaining exactly 2 heads?
23. What is the probability of obtaining at least 5 tails?
24. What is the probability of obtaining at most 2 tails?
25. What is the probability of obtaining exactly 2 heads if it is known that at least 1 head appeared?
26. What is the probability of obtaining exactly 3 tails if it is known that at least 1 tail appeared?
27. What is the probability of obtaining 7's exactly two times in 5 rolls of 2 fair dice?
28. What is the probability of obtaining 11's exactly three times in 7 rolls of 2 fair dice?
29. Suppose that 5% of the items produced by a factory are defective. If 8 items are chosen at random, what is the probability that:
    (a) Exactly 1 is defective?   (b) Exactly 2 are defective?
    (c) At least 1 is defective?   (d) Less than 3 are defective?

30. Suppose that 60% of the voters intend to vote for a conservative candidate. What is the probability that a survey polling 8 people reveals that 3 or fewer intend to vote for a conservative candidate?

31. Assuming all sex distributions to be equally probable, what is the probability that a family with exactly 6 children will have 3 boys and 3 girls?

32. What is the probability that in a family of 7 children:
    (a) 4 will be girls?
    (b) At least 2 are girls?
    (c) At least 2 and not more than 4 are girls?

33. An experiment is performed four times, with 2 possible outcomes F (Failure) and S (Success) with probabilities $\frac{1}{4}$ and $\frac{3}{4}$, respectively.
    (a) Draw the tree diagram describing the experiment.
    (b) Calculate the probability of exactly 2 successes and 2 failures by using the tree diagram from part (a).
    (c) Verify your answer to part (b) by using formula (1) and Table 1.

34. For a baseball player with a .250 batting average, what is the probability that the player will have at least 2 hits in four times at bat? What is the probability of a least 1 hit in four times at bat?

35. If the probability of hitting a target is $\frac{1}{5}$ and 10 shots are fired independently, what is the probability of the target being hit at least twice?

36. A television manufacturer tests a random sample of 15 picture tubes to determine whether any are defective. The probability that a picture tube is defective has been found from past experience to be .05.
    (a) What is the probability that there are no defective tubes in the sample?
    (b) What is the probability that more than 2 of the tubes are defective?

37. In a 15 item true–false examination, what is the probability that a student who guesses on each question will get at least 10 correct answers? If another student has .8 probability of correctly answering each question, what is the probability that this student will answer at least 12 questions correctly?

38. Opinion polls based on small samples often yield misleading results. Suppose 65% of the people in a city are opposed to a bond issue and the others favor it. If 7 people are asked for their opinion, what is the probability that a majority of them will favor the bond issue?

39. A supposed coffee connoisseur claims she can distinguish between a cup of instant coffee and a cup of percolator coffee 75% of the time. You give her 6 cups of coffee and tell her that you will grant her claim if she correctly identifies at least 5 of the 6 cups.
    (a) What are her chances of having her claim granted if she is in fact only guessing?
    (b) What are her chances of having her claim rejected when in fact she really does have the ability she claims?

*40. How many times should a fair coin be flipped in order to have the probability of at least 1 head appearing to be greater than .98?

*41. What is the probability that the birthdays of 6 people fall in 2 calendar months, leaving exactly 10 months free? (Assume independent and equal probabilities for all months.)

*42. A book of 500 pages contains 500 misprints. Estimate the chance that a given page contains at least 3 misprints.

*43. In a Bernoulli trial with $p = \frac{1}{3}$, for what least value of n does the probability of exactly 2 successes have its only maximum value?

*44. Prove the identity

$$b(n, k; p) = b(n, n - k; 1 - p)$$

Chapter Review

Important Terms

random event
probabilistic model
outcome
sample space
event
simple event
mutually exclusive
additive rule
odds for
odds against
equally likely

success
failure
conditional probability
product rule
independent events
Bayes' formula
partition
a priori **probability**
a posteriori **probability**
binomial probability
Bernoulli trial

True–False Questions (Answers on page 631)

T F 1. If the odds for an event E are 2 to 1, then $P(E) = \frac{2}{3}$.

T F 2. The conditional probability of E given F is

$$P(E \mid F) = \frac{P(E \cap F)}{P(E)}$$

T F 3. If two events in a sample space have no simple events in common, they are said to be *independent*.

T F 4. Bayes' formula is useful for computing *a posteriori* probability.

T F 5. In tossing a fair coin 100 times, the probability that exactly 50 heads occurs is $\frac{1}{2}$.

Fill in the Blanks (Answers on page 631)

1. If $P(E) = .6$, the odds _____ E are 3 to 2.

2. When each simple event in a sample space is assigned the same probability, the events are termed _____ _____.

3. If two events in a sample space have no simple events in common, they are said to be _____ _____.

4. The formula

$$P(A_1 \mid E) = \frac{P(A_1) \cdot P(E \mid A_1)}{P(E)}$$

is called _____ _____.

5. Repeated trials of a random experiment are called *Bernoulli trials* if:
   (a) There are two possible outcomes in each trial.
   (b) The probabilities of these outcomes are the same from trial to trial.

   (c) The trials are _____.

Review Exercises
Solutions to Odd-Numbered Problems begin on page 594.

1. A survey of families with 2 children is made, and the sexes of the children are recorded. Describe the sample space and draw a tree diagram of this random experiment.
2. A fair coin is tossed three times.
   (a) Construct a probabilistic model corresponding to this experiment.
   (b) Find the probabilities of the following events:
      (i)   The first toss is *T*.
      (ii) The first toss is *H*.
      (iii) Either the first toss is *T* or the third toss is *H*.
      (iv) At least one of the tosses is *H*.
      (v)   There are at least two *T*'s.
      (vi) No tosses are *H*.
3. An urn contains 3 white marbles, 2 yellow marbles, 4 red marbles, and 5 blue marbles. Two marbles are picked at random. What is the probability that:
   (a) Both are blue?
   (b) Exactly 1 is blue?
   (c) At least 1 is blue?
4. Let *A* and *B* be events with $P(A) = .3$, $P(B) = .5$, and $P(A \cap B) = .2$. Find the probability that:
   (a) *A* or *B* happens.
   (b) *A* does not happen.
   (c) Neither *A* nor *B* happens.
   (d) Either *A* does not happen or *B* does not happen.
5. Jones lives at *O* (see the figure). He owns 5 gas stations located 4 blocks away (dots). Each afternoon he checks on one of his gas stations. He starts at *O*. At each intersection he flips a fair coin. If it shows heads, he will head North (N); otherwise, he will head toward the East (E). What is the probability that he will end up at gas station *G* before coming to one of the other stations?

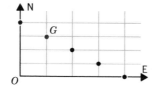

6. Consider the experiment of spinning the spinner in the figure below three times. (Assume the spinner cannot fall on a line.)

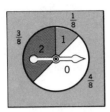

(a) Are all outcomes equally likely?
(b) If not, which of the outcomes has the highest probability?
(c) Let F be the event, "Each digit will occur exactly once." Find $P(F)$.

7. If E and F are events with $P(E \cup F) = \frac{5}{8}$, $P(E \cap F) = \frac{1}{3}$, and $P(E) = \frac{1}{2}$, find:
(a) $P(\overline{E})$ (b) $P(F)$ (c) $P(\overline{F})$

8. If E and F represent mutually exclusive events, $P(E) = .30$, and $P(F) = .45$, find each of the following probabilities:
(a) $P(\overline{E})$ (b) $P(\overline{F})$ (c) $P(E \cap F)$
(d) $P(E \cup F)$ (e) $P(\overline{E \cap F})$ (f) $P(\overline{E \cup F})$
(g) $P(\overline{E} \cup \overline{F})$ (h) $P(\overline{E} \cap \overline{F})$

9. Three envelopes are addressed for three secret letters written in invisible ink. A secretary randomly places each of the letters in an envelope and mails them. What is the probability that at least one person receives the correct letter?

10. What are the odds in favor of a 5 when a fair die is thrown?

11. A better is willing to give 7 to 6 odds that the Bears will win the NFL title. What is the probability of the Bears winning?

12. A biased coin is such that the probability of heads (H) is $\frac{1}{4}$ and the probability of tails (T) is $\frac{3}{4}$. Show that in flipping this coin twice the events E and F defined below are independent.

E: A head turns up in the first throw
F: A tail turns up in the second throw

13. The records of Midwestern University show that in one semester, 38% of the students failed Mathematics, 27% of the students failed Physics, and 9% of the students failed Mathematics and Physics. A student is selected at random.
(a) If a student failed Physics, what is the probability that he or she failed Mathematics?
(b) If a student failed Mathematics, what is the probability that he or she failed Physics?
(c) What is the probability that he or she failed Mathematics or Physics?

14. The table on page 294 indicates a survey conducted by a deodorant producer:

	Like the Deodorant	Did Not Like the Deodorant	No Opinion
Group I	180	60	20
Group II	110	85	12
Group III	55	65	7

Let the events E, F, G, H, and K be defined as follows:

E: Customer likes the deodorant
F: Customer does not like the deodorant
G: Customer is from Group I
H: Customer is from Group II
K: Customer is from Group III

Find:

(a) $P(E|G)$ (b) $P(G|E)$ (c) $P(H|E)$
(d) $P(K|E)$ (e) $P(F|G)$ (f) $P(G|F)$
(g) $P(H|F)$ (h) $P(K|F)$

15. In a certain population of people, 25% are blue-eyed and 75% are brown-eyed. Also, 10% of the blue-eyed people are left-handed and 5% of the brown-eyed people are left-handed.

(a) What is the probability that a person chosen at random is blue-eyed and left-handed?

(b) What is the probability that a person chosen at random is left-handed?

(c) What is the probability that a person is blue-eyed, given that the person is left-handed?

16. Three machines in a factory, A_1, A_2, A_3, produce 55%, 30% and 15% of total production, respectively. The percentage of defective output of these machines is 1%, 2% and 3%, respectively. An item is chosen at random and it is defective. What is the probability that it came from machine A_1? From A_2? From A_3?

17. A lung cancer test has been found to have the following reliability. The test can detect 85% of the people who have cancer and does not detect 15% of these people. Among the noncancerous group it detects 92% of the people not having cancer, whereas 8% of this group are detected erroneously as having lung cancer. Statistics show that about 1.8% of the population have cancer. Suppose an individual is given the test for lung cancer and it detects the disease. What is the probability that the person actually has cancer?

18. A pair of fair dice is thrown three times. What is the probability that on the first toss the sum of the 2 dice is even, on the second toss the sum is less than 6, and on the third toss the sum is 7?

19. Find the probability of throwing an 11 at least three times in five throws of a pair of fair dice.

20. Management believes that 1 out of 5 people watching a television advertisement about their new product will purchase the product. Five people who watched the advertisement are picked at random.

What is the probability that 0, 1, 2, 3, 4, or 5 of these people will purchase the product?

21. Suppose that the probability of a player hitting a home run is $\frac{1}{20}$. In five tries, what is the probability that the player hits at least 1 home run?

22. In a 12 item true-false examination:
    (a) What is the probability that a student will obtain all correct answers by chance if he or she is guessing?
    (b) If 7 correct answers constitute a passing grade, what is the probability that he or she will pass?
    (c) What are the odds in favor of passing?

Mathematical Questions
From Actuary Exams (Answers on page 629)

1. *Actuary Exam—Part I*
   If P and Q are events having positive probability in the sample space S such that $P \cap Q = \varnothing$, then all of the following pairs are independent EXCEPT:
   (a) $\varnothing$ and P (b) P and Q (c) P and S
   (d) P and $P \cap Q$ (e) $\varnothing$ and the complement of P

2. *Actuary Exam—Part I*
   A box contains 12 varieties of candy and exactly 2 pieces of each variety. If 12 pieces of candy are selected at random, what is the probability that a given variety is represented?

   (a) $\dfrac{2^{12}}{(12!)^2}$ (b) $\dfrac{2^{12}}{24!}$ (c) $\dfrac{2^{12}}{\binom{24}{12}}$ (d) $\dfrac{11}{46}$ (e) $\dfrac{35}{46}$

3. *Actuary Exam—Part II*
   What is the probability that a 3 card hand drawn at random and without replacement from an ordinary deck consists entirely of black cards?

   (a) $\frac{1}{17}$ (b) $\frac{2}{17}$ (c) $\frac{1}{8}$ (d) $\frac{3}{17}$ (e) $\frac{4}{17}$

4. *Actuary Exam—Part II*
   Events S and T are independent with $\Pr(S) < \Pr(T)$, $\Pr(S \cap T) = \frac{6}{25}$, and $\Pr(S|T) + \Pr(T|S) = 1$. What is $\Pr(S)$?

   (a) $\frac{1}{25}$ (b) $\frac{1}{5}$ (c) $\frac{6}{25}$ (d) $\frac{2}{5}$ (e) $\frac{3}{5}$

5. *Actuary Exam—Part II*
   What is the least number of independent times that an unbiased die must be thrown to make the probability that all throws do not give the same result greater than .999?

   (a) 3   (b) 4   (c) 5   (d) 6   (e) 7

6. *Actuary Exam—Part II*
   In a group of 20,000 men and 10,000 women, 6% of the men and 3% of the women have a certain affliction. What is the probability that an afflicted member of the group is a man?

   (a) $\frac{3}{5}$ (b) $\frac{2}{3}$ (c) $\frac{3}{4}$ (d) $\frac{4}{5}$ (e) $\frac{8}{9}$

7. *Actuary Exam—Part II*
   An unbiased die is thrown two independent times. Given that the first throw resulted in an even number, what is the probability that the sum obtained is 8?

   (a) $\frac{5}{36}$ (b) $\frac{1}{6}$ (c) $\frac{4}{21}$ (d) $\frac{7}{36}$ (e) $\frac{1}{3}$

8. *Actuary Exam—Part II*
   If the events S and T have equal probability and are independent with $\Pr(S \cap T) = p > 0$, then $\Pr(S) =$

   (a) $\sqrt{p}$ (b) p^2 (c) $\dfrac{p}{2}$ (d) p (e) $2p$

9. *Actuary Exam—Part II*
   What is the probability that 10 independent tosses of an unbiased coin result in no fewer than 1 head and no more than 9 heads?

   (a) $\left(\dfrac{1}{2}\right)^9$ (b) $1 - 11\left(\dfrac{1}{2}\right)^9$ (c) $1 - 11\left(\dfrac{1}{2}\right)^{10}$ (d) $1 - \left(\dfrac{1}{2}\right)^9$

   (e) $1 - \left(\dfrac{1}{2}\right)^{10}$

10. *Actuary Exam—Part II*
    The probability that both S and T occur, the probability that S occurs and T does not, and the probability that T occurs and S does not are all equal to p. What is the probability that either S or T occurs?

    (a) p (b) $2p$ (c) $3p$ (d) $3p^2$ (e) p^3

11. *Actuary Exam—Part II*
    What is the probability that a bridge hand contains 1 card of each denomination (i.e., 1 ace, 1 king, 1 queen, . . . , 1 three, 1 two)?

    (a) $\dfrac{13!}{13^{13}}$ (b) $\dfrac{4^{13}}{\binom{52}{13}}$ (c) $\dfrac{\binom{52}{4}}{\binom{52}{13}}$ (d) $\left(\dfrac{1}{13}\right)^{13}$ (e) $\dfrac{13^4}{\binom{52}{13}}$

Other Books or Articles

Deutsch, Karl W., and William G. Madow, "A Note on the Appearance of Wisdom in Large Bureaucratic Organizations," *Behav. Sci.*, **6** (1961), pp. 72–78.

Gelfand, Alan E., and Herbert Solomon, "Modeling Jury Verdicts in the American Legal System," *J. Amer. Stat. Assoc.*, **69** (March 1974), pp. 32–37.

Horvath, Frank S., and John E. Reid, "The Reliability of Polygraph Examiner Diagnosis of Truth and Deception," *J. Crim. Law, Criminol. Police Sci.*, **62,** 2 (1971), pp. 276–281.

Mizrahi, A. and M. Sullivan, *Mathematics for Business and Social Science,* 3rd Ed., Wiley, New York, 1983.

Mosteller, F., and D. L. Wallace, *Inference and Disputed Authorship: The Federalist*, Addison-Wesley, Reading, Mass., 1964.

Mosteller, F., and D. L. Wallace, "Deciding Authorship," in Judith M. Tanur, ed., *Statistics: A Guide to the Unknown,* Holden-Day, San Francisco, 1972, pp. 164–175.

Overall, John E., and Clyde M. Williams, "Conditional Probability Program for Diagnosis of Thyroid Function," *J. Amer. Med. Assoc.*, **183,** 5 (February 2, 1963), pp. 307–313.

Pascal, Gerald R., and Barbara Suttell, "Testing the Claims of a Graphologist," *J. Pers.*, **16** (1947), pp. 192–197.

Smith, Paul F., "Measuring Risk on Consumer Installment Credit," *Manage. Sci.*, **11,** 2 (November 1964), pp. 327–340.

Warner, Homer R., Alan F. Toronto, L. George Veasey, and Robert Stephenson, "A Mathematical Approach to Medical Diagnosis," *J. Amer. Med. Assoc.*, **177,** 3 (July 22, 1961), pp. 177–183.

7
Decision Theory

1. Expectation

An important concept, which had its origin in gambling and to which probability can be applied, is *expected value*. For instance, gamblers are quite concerned with the *expectation*, or *expected value*, of a game. Suppose, for example, 1000 tickets are sold to raffle off a television set worth $300. Out of the 1000 tickets, one ticket is worth $300 and the remaining 999 are worth $0. The *expected (average) value* of a ticket is

$$E = \frac{\$300 + \$0 + \cdots + \$0}{1000}$$

$$= \$300 \cdot \frac{1}{1000} + \$0 \cdot \frac{1}{1000} + \cdots + \$0 \cdot \frac{1}{1000} = \frac{\$300}{1000} = \$0.30$$

If the raffle is to be nonprofit to all participants, the charge for each ticket should be $0.30.

As another example of expectation, suppose that you are to receive $3.00 each time you obtain 2 heads on a single toss of 2 coins and $0 otherwise. Then the *expected value* is

$$E = \$3.00 \cdot \tfrac{1}{4} + \$0 \cdot \tfrac{3}{4} = \$0.75$$

This means that you should be willing to pay $0.75 each time you toss the coins if the game is to be a fair one. We arrive at the expected value E by multiplying the amount earned for a given result of the toss times the probability for that loss to occur, and adding all the products.

Another example is a game consisting of flipping a single coin. If a head shows, the player loses $1; but if a tail shows, the player wins $2. Thus, half the time the player loses $1 and the other half the player wins $2. The expected value E of the game is

$$E = \$2 \cdot \tfrac{1}{2} + (-\$1) \cdot \tfrac{1}{2} = \tfrac{1}{2} = \$0.50$$

The player is expected to win an average of $0.50 on each play.

In each of the above examples, we have assigned a *payoff* to each outcome in the sample space. For example, in the raffle problem a payoff of $300 is assigned to the outcome of winning (probability $\frac{1}{1000}$), and $0 is assigned to the outcome of losing (probability $\frac{999}{1000}$).

In the second example, the outcome *HH* is assigned a payoff of $3.00, and the outcomes *HT*, *TH*, and *TT* are assigned $0.

Finally, in the last example, the outcome *H* is assigned a payoff of $-$1 and the outcome *T* a payoff of $2.

In each experiment, we not only assign a probability to each outcome, but we also assign a payoff or number to each outcome. These examples lead us to the following definition.

Expected Value **If an experiment has n outcomes that are assigned the** *payoffs* $m_1, m_2, \ldots, m_n$ **occurring with probabilities** $p_1, p_2, \ldots, p_n$, **respectively, then the** *expected value* **is given by**

$$E = m_1 \cdot p_1 + m_2 \cdot p_2 + \cdots + m_n \cdot p_n$$

Suppose an experiment consists of a sample space $S = \{e_1, e_2, \ldots, e_n\}$, corresponding probabilities $p_1, p_2, \ldots, p_n$, and corresponding payoffs $m_1, m_2, \ldots, m_n$. Then it is sometimes convenient to summarize the data of the experiment by listing the outcomes, probabilities, and payoffs in tabular form, as shown:

Outcome	e_1	e_2	e_3	$\cdots$	e_n
Probability	p_1	p_2	p_3	$\cdots$	p_n
Payoff	m_1	m_2	m_3	$\cdots$	m_n

The expected value E of this experiment is

$$E = m_1 \cdot p_1 + m_2 \cdot p_2 + \cdots + m_n \cdot p_n$$

The term *expected value* should not be interpreted as the value that will necessarily occur on a single trial. It is the *average* gain per game in a long series of games.

In gambling, for instance, E is interpreted as the averge winnings expected for the player in the long run. If E is positive, we say that the game is favorable to the player; if $E = 0$, we say the game is fair; and if E is negative, we say the game is unfavorable to the player.

When the payoff assigned to an outcome of an experiment is positive, it can be interpreted as a profit, winnings, or gain. When it is negative, it represents losses, penalties, or deficits.

Example 1 Consider the experiment of rolling a fair die. The player recovers an amount of dollars equal to the number of dots on the face that turns up, except when face 5 or 6 turns up, in which case the player will lose $5 or $6, respectively. What is the expected value of the game?

Solution Since all faces are equally likely to occur, we assign a probability of $\frac{1}{6}$ to each of them. The payoffs for the outcomes 1, 2, 3, 4, 5, 6 are, respectively, $1, $2, $3, $4, $-5, $-6. In tabular form, we have the following:

Outcome	1	2	3	4	5	6
Probability	$\frac{1}{6}$	$\frac{1}{6}$	$\frac{1}{6}$	$\frac{1}{6}$	$\frac{1}{6}$	$\frac{1}{6}$
Payoff	$1	$2	$3	$4	$-5	$-6

The expected value of the game is

$$E = \$1 \cdot \tfrac{1}{6} + \$2 \cdot \tfrac{1}{6} + \$3 \cdot \tfrac{1}{6} + \$4 \cdot \tfrac{1}{6} + (-\$5) \cdot \tfrac{1}{6} + (-\$6) \cdot \tfrac{1}{6}$$
$$= -\$\tfrac{1}{6} = -16.7¢$$

The player would expect to lose an average of 16.7¢ on each throw. ∎

Example 2 An oil company may bid for only one of two contracts for oil drilling in two different areas, I and II. It is estimated that a profit of $300,000 would be realized from the first field and $400,000 from the second field. Legal and other costs of bidding for the first oil field are $2500 and for the second are $5000. The probability of discovering oil in the first field is .60 and in the second is .70. The question is which oil field should the company bid for; that is, for which oil field is the expectation larger?

Solution In the first field, the company expects to discover oil .6 of the time at a gain of $300,000. Thus, it would not discover oil .4 of the time at a loss of $2500. The expectation E_I is therefore

$$E_I = (\$300,000)(.6) + (-\$2500)(.4) = \$179,000$$

Similarly, for the second field, the expectation E_{II} is

$$E_{II} = (\$400,000)(.7) + (-\$5000)(.3) = \$278,500$$

Since the expected value for the second field exceeds that for the first, the oil company should bid on the second field. ■

Example 3 A laboratory contains 10 electron microscopes, of which 2 are defective. If all microscopes are equally likely to be chosen and if 4 are chosen, what is the expected number of defective microscopes?

Solution The sample of 4 microscopes can contain 0, 1, or 2 defective microscopes. The probability p_0 that none in the sample is defective is

$$p_0 = \frac{\binom{2}{0}\binom{8}{4}}{\binom{10}{4}} = \frac{1}{3}$$

Similarly, the probabilities p_1 and p_2 for 1 and 2 defective microscopes are

$$p_1 = \frac{\binom{2}{1}\binom{8}{3}}{\binom{10}{4}} = \frac{8}{15} \quad \text{and} \quad p_2 = \frac{\binom{2}{2}\binom{8}{2}}{\binom{10}{4}} = \frac{2}{15}$$

Since we are interested in determining the expected number of defective microscopes, we assign a payoff of 0 to the outcome "0 defectives are selected," a payoff of 1 to the outcome "1 defective is chosen," and a payoff of 2 to the outcome "2 defectives are chosen." The expected value E is

$$E = 0 \cdot p_0 + 1 \cdot p_1 + 2 \cdot p_2 = \frac{8}{15} + \frac{4}{15} = \frac{4}{5}$$

Of course, we cannot have $\frac{4}{5}$ of a defective microscope. However, we can interpret this to mean that in the long run such a sample will average just under one defective microscope. ■

Expected Value for Bernoulli Trials

We close this section with a formula for computing expected value in Bernoulli trials.

In a Bernoulli trial, if there are n trials and p is the probability for success, then for any single trial, the expected value E is

$$E = 1 \cdot p + 0 \cdot (1 - p) = p$$

For n such trials, the expected value is

$$E = np$$

Thus, we have the following result:

In a Bernoulli process with n trials, the expected value E for a success is

$$E = np$$

where p is the probability for success.

Example 4 illustrates the usefulness of this result.

Example 4   In flipping a fair coin five times, there are 6 possible outcomes: 0 tails, 1 tail, 2 tails, 3 tails, 4 tails, or 5 tails, each with the respective probabilities

$$\binom{5}{0}\left(\frac{1}{2}\right)^5, \quad \binom{5}{1}\left(\frac{1}{2}\right)^5, \quad \binom{5}{2}\left(\frac{1}{2}\right)^5, \quad \binom{5}{3}\left(\frac{1}{2}\right)^5, \quad \binom{5}{4}\left(\frac{1}{2}\right)^5, \quad \binom{5}{5}\left(\frac{1}{2}\right)^5$$

The expected number of tails is

$$E = 0 \cdot \binom{5}{0}\left(\frac{1}{2}\right)^5 + 1 \cdot \binom{5}{1}\left(\frac{1}{2}\right)^5 + 2 \cdot \binom{5}{2}\left(\frac{1}{2}\right)^5$$

$$+ 3 \cdot \binom{5}{3}\left(\frac{1}{2}\right)^5 + 4 \cdot \binom{5}{4}\left(\frac{1}{2}\right)^5 + 5 \cdot \binom{5}{5}\left(\frac{1}{2}\right)^5 = \frac{5}{2}$$

Clearly, using the result $E = np$ is much easier, since for $n = 5$ and $p = \frac{1}{2}$, we obtain $E = (5)(\frac{1}{2}) = \frac{5}{2}$. ■

Example 5   In a true–false test with 100 questions, what is the expected number of correct answers if a person guesses on each question?

Solution   This is an example of a Bernoulli trial. The probability for success (a correct answer) when guessing is $p = \frac{1}{2}$. Since there are $n = 100$ questions, the expected number of correct answers is

$$E = np = (100)(\tfrac{1}{2}) = 50$$

■

Exercise 1
Solutions to Odd-Numbered Problems begin on page 595.

1. For the data given below, compute the expected value.

Outcome	e_1	e_2	e_3	e_4
Probability	.4	.2	.1	.3
Payoff	2	3	−2	0

2. For the data below, compute the expected value.

Outcome	e_1	e_2	e_3	e_4
Probability	$\frac{1}{3}$	$\frac{1}{6}$	$\frac{1}{4}$	$\frac{1}{4}$
Payoff	1	0	4	−2

3. Attendance at a football game in a certain city results in the following pattern. If it is extremely cold, the attendance will be 35,000; if it is cold, it will be 40,000; if it is moderate, 48,000; and if it is warm, 60,000. If the probabilities for extremely cold, cold, moderate, and warm are .08, .42, .42, and .08, respectively, how many fans are expected to attend the game?

4. A player rolls a fair die and receives a number of dollars equal to the number of dots appearing on the face of the die. What is the least the player should expect to pay in order to play the game?

5. Mary will win $8 if she draws an ace from a set of 10 different cards from ace to 10. How much should she pay for one draw?

6. Thirteen playing cards, ace through king, are placed randomly with faces down on a table. The prize for guessing correctly the value of any given card is $1. What would be a fair price to pay for a guess?

7. David gets $10 if he throws a double on a single throw of a pair of dice. How much should he pay for a throw?

8. You pay a $1 to toss 2 coins. If you toss 2 heads, you get $2 (including your $1); if you toss only 1 head, you get back your $1; and if you toss no heads, you lose your $1. Is this a fair game to play?

9. *Raffles.* In a raffle, 1000 tickets are being sold at 60¢ each. The first prize is $100, and there are three second prizes of $50 each. By how much does the price of a ticket exceed its expected value?

10. *Raffles.* In a raffle, 1000 tickets are being sold at 60¢ each. The first prize is $100. There are two second prizes of $50 each, and five third prizes of $10 each (there are eight prizes in all). Laura buys one ticket. How much more than the expected value of the ticket does she pay?

11. A fair coin is tossed three times, and a player wins $3 if 3 tails occur, wins $2 if 2 tails occur, and loses $3 if no tails occur. If 1 tail occurs, no one wins.
    (a) What is the expected value of the game?
    (b) Is the game fair?
    (c) If the answer to part (b) is "No," how much should the player win or lose for a toss of exactly 1 tail to make the game fair?

12. Colleen bets $1 on a 2 digit number. She wins $75 if she draws her number from the set of all 2 digit numbers, {00, 01, 02, . . . , 99}; otherwise, she loses her $1.
    (a) Is this game fair to the player?
    (b) How much is Colleen expected to lose in a game?

13. Two teams, A and B, have played each other 14 times. Team A won 9 games, and team B won 5 games. They will play again next week. Bob offers to bet $6 on team A while you bet $4 on team B. The winner gets the $10. Is the bet fair to you in view of the past records of the two teams? Explain your answer.

14. A department store wants to sell 11 purses that cost them $41 each and 32 purses that cost them $9 each. If all purses are wrapped in 43 identical boxes and if each customer picks a box randomly, find:
    (a) Each customer's expectation
    (b) The department store's expected profit if it charges $13 for each box.

15. Caryl draws a card from a deck of 52 cards. She receives 40¢ for a heart, 50¢ for an ace, and 90¢ for the ace of hearts. If the cost of a draw is 15¢, should she play the game? Explain.

16. *Family Size.* The following data give information about family size in the United States for a household in which the wife resides and the male head of household is in the 30–34 age bracket:

Number of Children	0	1	2	3
Proportion of Families	10.2%	15.9%	31.8%	42.1%

A family is chosen at random. Find the expected number of children in the family.

17. Assume that the odds for a certain race horse to win are 7 to 5. If a better receives $5 when the horse wins, how much should he pay when the horse loses to make the game fair?

18. In roulette, there are 38 equally likely possibilities: the numbers 1–36, 0, and 00 (double zero). See the figure. What is the expected

value for a gambler who bets $1 on number 15 if she wins $35 each time the number 15 turns up and loses $1 if any other number turns up? If the gambler plays the number 15 for 200 consecutive times, what is the total expected gain?

19. *Site Selection.* A company operating a chain of supermarkets plans to open a new store in one of two locations. They conducted a survey of the two locations and estimated that the first location will show an annual profit of $15,000 if it is successful and a $3000 loss otherwise. For the second location, the estimated annual profit is $20,000 if successful and a $6000 loss results otherwise. The probability of success at each location is $\frac{1}{2}$. What location should the management decide on in order to maximize its expected profit?

20. For Problem 19 assume the probability of success at the first location is $\frac{2}{3}$ and at the second location is $\frac{1}{3}$. What location should be chosen?

21. Find the number of times the face 5 is expected to occur in a sequence of 2000 throws of a fair die.

22. What is the expected number of tails that will turn up if a fair coin is tossed 582 times?

23. A certain kind of light bulb has been found to have .02 probability of being defective. A shop owner receives 500 light bulbs of this kind. How many of these bulbs are expected to be defective?

24. A student enrolled in a Math course has .9 probability of passing the course. In a class of 20 students, how many would you expect to fail the Math course?

25. *Drug Reaction.* A doctor has found that the probability that a patient who is given a certain drug will have unfavorable reactions to the drug is .002. If a group of 500 patients is going to be given the drug, how many of them does the doctor expect to have unfavorable reactions?

26. A true–false test consisting of 30 questions is scored by subtracting the number of wrong answers from the number of right ones. Find the expected number of correct answers of a student who just guesses on each question. What will the test score be?

*27. A coin is weighted so that $P(H) = \frac{1}{4}$ and $P(T) = \frac{3}{4}$. Find the expected number of tosses of the coin required in order to obtain either a head or 4 tails.

*28. A box contains 3 defective bulbs and 9 good bulbs. If 5 bulbs are drawn from the box without replacement, what is the expected number of defective bulbs?

*29. Prove that if the payoff assigned to each outcome of an experiment with expected value E is multiplied by a constant k, the expected value of the new experiment is $k \cdot E$. Similarly, if to the payoff for each outcome, we add the same constant k, prove the expected value of the new game is $E + k$.

2. Applications to Operations Research

The field of *operations research,* the science of making optimal or best decisions, has experienced remarkable growth and development since the 1940's. The purpose of this section is to introduce you to some examples from operations research that utilize the concept of expectation.

Example 1
Market
Assessment

A national car rental agency rents cars for $16 per day (gasoline and mileage are additional expenses to the customer). The daily cost per car (for example, lease costs and overhead) is $6 per day. The daily profit to the company is $10 per car if the car is rented, and the company incurs a daily loss of $6 per car if the car is not rented. The daily profit depends on two factors: the demand for cars and the number of cars the company has available to rent. Previous rental records show that the daily demand is:

Number of Customers	8	9	10	11	12
Probability	.10	.10	.30	.30	.20

Find the expected number of customers and determine the optimal number of cars the company should have available for rental. (This is the number that yields the largest expected profit.)

Solution
The expected number of customers is

$$8(.1) + 9(.1) + 10(.3) + 11(.3) + 12(.2) = 10.4$$

If 10.4 customers are expected, how many cars should be on hand? Surely, the number should not exceed 11, since fewer than 11 customers are expected. However, the number may not be the integer closest to 10.4, since costs play a major role in the determination of profit. We need to compute the expected profit for each possible number of cars. The largest expected profit will tell us how many cars to have on hand.

For example, if there are 10 cars available, the expected profit for 8, 9, or 10 customers is

$$68(.1) + 84(.1) + 100(.8) = \$95.20$$

We obtain the entry 68(.1) by noting that the 10 cars cost the company $60, and 8 cars rented with probability .10 bring in $128, for a profit of $68. Similarly, we obtain the entry 84(.1) by noting that the 10 cars cost the company $60, and 9 cars rented with probability .10 bring in $144, for a profit of $84. The entry 100(.8) is obtained since for 10 or more customers, (probability .3 + .3 + .2 = .8) the profit is 10 × $16 − $60 = $100.

The table lists the expected profit for 8–12 cars. Clearly, the optimal stock size is 11 cars, since this number of cars maximizes expected profit.

Number of Cars	8	9	10	11	12
Expected Profit	$80.00	$88.40	$95.20	$97.20	$94.40

Example 2
Quality
Control

A factory produces electronic components, and each component must be tested. If the component is good, it will allow the passage of current; if the component is defective, it will block the passage of current. Let p denote the probability that a component is good. See Figure 1.

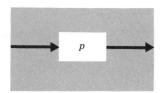

Figure 1

With this system of testing, a large number of components requires an equal number of tests. This increases the production cost of the electronic components since it requires one test per component. To reduce the number of tests, a quality control engineer proposes, instead, a new testing procedure: Connect the components pairwise in series, as shown in Figure 2.

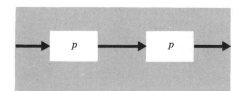

Figure 2

If the current passes two components in series, then both components are good and only one test was required. The probability that two components are good is p^2. If the current does not pass, they must be sent individually to the quality control department, where each component is tested separately. In this case, three tests are required. The probability that three tests are needed is $1 - p^2$ (1 minus probability of success p^2). The expected number of tests for a pair of components is

$$E = 1 \cdot p^2 + 3 \cdot (1 - p^2) = p^2 + 3 - 3p^2 = 3 - 2p^2$$

The number of tests saved for a pair is

$$2 - (3 - 2p^2) = 2p^2 - 1$$

The number of tests saved per component is

$$\frac{2p^2 - 1}{2} = p^2 - \frac{1}{2} \text{ tests}$$

The greater the probability p that the component is good, the greater the saving. For example, if p is almost 1, we have a saving of almost $1 - \frac{1}{2}$ or $\frac{1}{2}$, which is 50% of the original number of tests needed. Of course, if p is small, say less than .7, we do not save anything since $(.7)^2 - \frac{1}{2}$ is less than 0, and we are wasting tests. ■

If the reliability of the components manufactured in Example 2 is very high, it might even be advisable to make larger groups. Suppose three components are connected in series. See Figure 3.

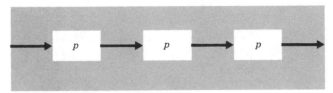

Figure 3

For individual testing, we need three tests. For group testing, we have

1   test needed with probability p^3
4   tests needed with probability $1 - p^3$

The expected number of tests is

$$E = 1 \cdot p^3 + 4 \cdot (1 - p^3) = 4 - 3p^3 \text{ tests}$$

The number of tests saved per component is

$$\frac{3p^3 - 1}{3} = p^3 - \frac{1}{3} \text{ tests}$$

In a similar way we can show that if the components are arranged in groups of four connected in series, then the number of tests saved per component is

$$p^4 - \frac{1}{4} \text{ tests}$$

In general, for groups of n, the number of tests saved per component is

$$p^n - \frac{1}{n} \text{ tests}$$

Notice from the above formula that as n, the group size, gets very large, the number of tests saved per component gets very, very small.

To determine the optimal group size for $p = .9$, we refer to Table 1. From the

Table 1

Group Size	Expected Tests Saved per Component $p = .9$	Percent Saving
2	$p^2 - \frac{1}{2} = .81 - .50 = .31$	31
3	$p^3 - \frac{1}{3} = .729 - .333 = .396$	39.6
4	$p^4 - \frac{1}{4} = .6561 - .25 = .4061$	40.61
5	$p^5 - \frac{1}{5} = .59049 - .2 = .39049$	39.05
6	$p^6 - \frac{1}{6} = .531 - .167 = .364$	36.4
7	$p^7 - \frac{1}{7} = .478 - .143 = .335$	33.5
8	$p^8 - \frac{1}{8} = .430 - .125 = .305$	30.5

table, we can see that the optimal group size is 4, resulting in a substantial saving of approximately 41%.

We also note that larger group sizes do not increase savings.

Example 3 A $75,000 oil detector is lowered under the sea to detect oil fields, and it becomes detached from the ship. If the instrument is not found within 24 hours, it will crack under the pressure of the sea. It is assumed that a skin diver will find it with probability .85, but it costs $500 to hire him. How many skin divers should be hired?

Solution Let's assume that x skin divers are hired. The probability that they will fail to discover the instrument is $.15^x$. Thus, the instrument will be found with probability $1 - .15^x$.

The expected gain from hiring the skin divers is

$$\$75{,}000(1 - .15^x) = \$75{,}000 - \$75{,}000(.15^x)$$

while the cost for hiring them is

$$\$500 \cdot x$$

Thus, the expected net gain, denoted by $E(x)$, is

$$E(x) = \$75{,}000 - \$75{,}000(.15^x) - \$500x$$

The problem is then to choose x so that $E(x)$ is maximum.

We begin by evaluating $E(x)$ for various values of x:

$$E(1) = \$75{,}000 - \$75{,}000(.15^1) - \$500(1) = \$63{,}250.00$$
$$E(2) = \$75{,}000 - \$75{,}000(.15^2) - \$500(2) = \$72{,}312.50$$
$$E(3) = \$75{,}000 - \$75{,}000(.15^3) - \$500(3) = \$73{,}246.88$$
$$E(4) = \$75{,}000 - \$75{,}000(.15^4) - \$500(4) = \$72{,}962.03$$
$$E(5) = \$75{,}000 - \$75{,}000(.15^5) - \$500(5) = \$72{,}494.31$$
$$E(6) = \$75{,}000 - \$75{,}000(.15^6) - \$500(6) = \$71{,}999.15$$

Thus, the expected net gain is optimal when 3 divers are hired. Notice that hiring additional skin divers does not necessarily increase expected net gain. In fact, the expected net gain declines if more than 3 divers are hired. ∎

Exercise 2
Solutions to Odd-Numbered Problems begin on page 596.

1. *Market Assessment.* A car agency has fixed costs of $8 per car per day and the revenue for each car rented is $14 per day. The daily demand is given in the table:

Number of Customers	7	8	9	10	11
Probability	.10	.20	.40	.20	.10

Find the expected number of customers. Determine the optimal number of cars the company should have on hand each day. What is the expected profit in this case?

2. In Example 2 in this section, suppose $p = .8$. Show that the optimal group size is 3.

3. In Example 2 in this section, suppose $p = .95$. Show that the optimal group size is 5.

4. In Example 2 in this section, suppose $p = .99$. Compute savings for group sizes 10, 11, and 12, and thus show that 11 is the optimal group size. Determine the percent saving.

5. In Example 3 in this section, suppose the probability of the skin divers discovering the instrument is .95. Find:
   (a)   An equation expressing the net expected gain
   (b)   The number x of skin divers that maximizes the net gain

Chapter Review

Important Terms
expectation
expected value
payoff

Review Exercises
Solutions to Odd-Numbered Problems begin on page 596.

1. In a certain game, a player has the probability $\frac{1}{7}$ of winning a prize worth $89.99 and the probability $\frac{1}{3}$ of winning another prize worth $49.99. What is the expected cost of the game for the player?

2. Frank pays 70¢ to play a certain game. He draws 2 balls (together) from a bag containing 2 red balls and 4 green balls. He receives $1 for each red ball that he draws. If he draws no red balls, he loses his 70¢. Has he paid too much? By how much?

3. In a lottery, 1000 tickets are sold at 25¢ each. There are three cash prizes: $100, $50, and $30. Alice buys five tickets.
   (a)   What would have been a fair price for a ticket?
   (b)   How much extra did Alice pay?

4. The figure below shows a spinning game for which a person pays $0.30 to purchase an opportunity to spin the dial. The numbers in the figure indicate the amount of payoff and its corresponding probability. Find the expected value of this game. Is the game fair?

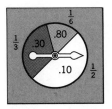

5. Consider the three boxes in the figure below. The game is played in two stages. The first stage is to choose a ball from Box A. If the result is a ball marked I, then we go to Box I, and select a ball from there. If the ball is marked II, then we select a ball from Box II. The number drawn on the second stage is the gain. Find the expected value of this game.

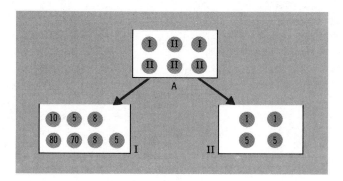

6. What is the expected number of heads that will turn up if a biased coin, $P(H) = \frac{1}{4}$, is tossed 200 times?

7. *European Roulette.* A European roulette wheel has only 37 compartments, 18 red, 18 black, and 1 green. A player will be paid $2 (including his $1 bet) if he picks correctly the color of the compartment in which the ball finally rests. Otherwise, he loses $1. Is the game fair to the player? Explain.

8. *The Blood Testing Problem.** A group of 1000 people are subjected to a blood test that can be administered in two ways: (1) each person can be tested separately (in this case 1000 tests are required) or (2) the blood samples of 30 people can be pooled and analyzed together. If we use the second way and the test is negative, then one test suffices for 30 people. If the test is positive, each of the 30 people can then be tested separately, and, in all, 30 + 1 tests are required for the 30 people. Assume the probability p that the test is positive is the same for all people and that the people to be tested are independent.
   (a) What is the probability that the test for a pooled sample of 30 people will be positive?
   (b) What is the expected number of tests necessary under plan (2)?

Mathematical Questions From CPA Exams (Answers on page 629)

1. *CPA Exam—May 1975*
The Stat Company wants more information on the demand for its products. The following data are relevant:

*William Feller, *An Introduction to Probability Theory and Its Applications,* 3rd ed., Wiley, New York, 1968, pp. 239–240.

Units Demanded	Probability of Unit Demand	Total Cost of Units Demanded
0	.10	$0
1	.15	1.00
2	.20	2.00
3	.40	3.00
4	.10	4.00
5	.05	5.00

What is the total expected value or payoff with perfect information?
(a) $2.40   (b) $7.40   (c) $9.00   (d) $9.15

2. *CPA Exam—May 1976*
Your client wants your advice on which of two alternatives he should choose. One alternative is to sell an investment now for $10,000. Another alternative is to hold the investment 3 days after which he can sell it for a certain selling price based on the following probabilities:

Selling Price	Probability
$5,000	.4
$8,000	.2
$12,000	.3
$30,000	.1

Using probability theory, which of the following is the most reasonable statement?
(a)   Hold the investment 3 days because the expected value of holding exceeds the current selling price.
(b)   Hold the investment 3 days because of the chance of getting $30,000 for it.
(c)   Sell the investment now because the current selling price exceeds the expected value of holding.
(d)   Sell the investment now because there is a 60% chance that the selling price will fall in 3 days.

3. *CPA Exam—November 1975*
Your client, a charity, is planning a carnival to raise money. The charity has permission from the local authorities to have games of chance. For one of these games, the player draws 1 card from a standard deck of 52 cards. If the player draws a jack of hearts, jack of diamonds, or jack of spades, he is paid $6.50. If he draws any card of clubs, he is paid $2.50. Assume X equals the price your client should charge per draw so that the long-run expected value of this game is zero. Which one of the following equations should be used to determine that price?

(a) $\frac{3}{52}(6.50 - X) + \frac{13}{52}(2.50 - X) = X$

(b) $\frac{3}{52}(6.50 - X) + \frac{13}{52}(2.50 - X) = \frac{36}{52}X$

(c) $\dfrac{3}{52}(6.50) + \dfrac{13}{52}(2.50) = \dfrac{36}{52}X$

(d) $6.50 - 2.50 = \dfrac{36}{52}X$

4. *CPA Exam—May 1979*

The Polly Company wishes to determine the amount of safety stock that it should maintain for Product D that will result in the lowest cost.

The following information is available:

Stockout cost	$80 per occurrence
Carrying cost of safety stock	$2 per unit
Number of purchase orders	5 per year

The available options open to Polly are as follows:

Units of Safety Stock	Probability of Running Out of Safety Stock
10	50%
20	40%
30	30%
40	20%
50	10%
55	5%

The number of units of safety stock that will result in the lowest cost are:

(a) 20   (b) 40   (c) 50   (d) 55

Other Books

Dyer, J. S. and Shapiro, R. D., *Management Science/Operations Research: Cases and Readings,* 1982, Wiley, New York, 1982.

Gaver, D. P., and G. L. Thompson, *Programming and Probability Models in Operations Research,* Brooks/Cole, Monterey, Ca., 1973.

Hillier, F. S., and G. J. Lieberman, *Operations Research,* 2nd ed. Holden-Day, San Francisco, Ca., 1974.

Mizrahi, A., and M. Sullivan, *Mathematics for Business and Social Science,* 3rd ed., Wiley, New York, 1983.

8
Markov Chains

*This section may be omitted without loss of continuity.

1. An Introduction to Markov Chains

In Chapter 6 we introduced Bernoulli trials. In discussing Bernoulli trials, we made the assumption that the outcome of each experiment is *independent* of the outcome of any previous experiment.

Here, we will discuss another type of probabilistic model, called a *Markov chain*. The Markov chain model can be used to characterize a series of experiments in which the outcome of each experiment will depend only on the outcome of the immediately preceding experiment and not on other prior experiments.

This type of process has proven to have application to many of the sciences, as we will illustrate in our examples and exercises. First, let's discuss one such application, and then we will introduce some of the theory behind it.

Consider the maze consisting of four connecting rooms shown in Figure 1. The rooms are numbered 1, 2, 3, 4 for convenience and each room contains pulsating lights of a different color. The experiment consists of releasing a mouse in a particular room and observing its behavior.

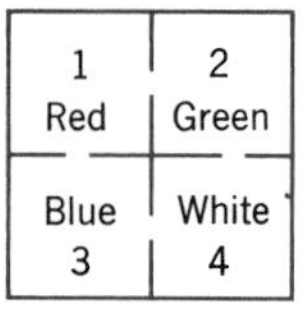

1 Red	2 Green
Blue 3	White 4

Figure 1

Initial State

Initial Probability Distribution

The system is composed of the mouse and the maze, and the experiment begins when the mouse is placed in a room. This is called the *initial state*. We assign an initial probability to each possible initial state. For example, in our experiment, if we decide the selection of the initial state should be made in an equally likely way, the *initial probability distribution* is the row vector $A^{(0)} = (\frac{1}{4} \ \frac{1}{4} \ \frac{1}{4} \ \frac{1}{4})$. If we decide to always begin the experiment by placing the mouse in room 1, the initial probability distribution is $A^{(0)} = (1 \ 0 \ 0 \ 0)$.

The experiment consists of observing at regular fixed intervals of time the position and movement of the mouse. For example, if the mouse is placed initially in room 1, after a fixed time it may be in state 1, state 2, or state 3. It could not have moved to state 4 since the maze does not contain a passage from 1 to 4. We assume an observation is made whenever a movement occurs or after a fixed time interval, whichever comes first.

Since it is not possible to determine exactly the movement of the mouse (because it is random in character), we will use probabilistic terms to describe it. The mouse's behavior at a specific instant of time will depend on where it is and how it arrived there. For example, due to the pulsating lights, the probability p_{12} that the mouse moves from state 1 to state 2 might be $p_{12} = \frac{1}{2}$, while the probabilities of moving from state 1 to either 1 or 3 might be $p_{11} = p_{13} = \frac{1}{4}$ each. We make the assumption that the state of the mouse on a given observation de-

---

ANDREI ANDREEVICH MARKOV (1856–1922), an outstanding Russian mathematician, developed the modern theory of stochastic processes. Markov studied and taught at the University of St. Petersburg and was a member of the Soviet Academy of Sciences.

pends only on the state occupied in the preceding observation. (This is equivalent to the assumption that the mouse has no memory.)

At a given observation, the mouse can be in any of four states. Suppose we assign probabilities for moving from one state to another. We can then conveniently display these probabilities in a matrix, called the *transition matrix*. If p_{ij} is the probability of moving from state i to state j, then $P = [p_{ij}]$ is the *transition matrix* for the experiment.

In our example, there are four states, so the transition matrix $P = [p_{ij}]$ is a 4×4 matrix.

Transition Matrix (margin note)

In general, a *Markov chain* is a sequence of n experiments in which each experiment has m possible outcomes $E_1, E_2, \ldots, E_m$ and the probability that a particular outcome occurs depends only on the outcome of the preceding experiment.

Suppose, then, that we are given a sequence of experiments and, as a result of each experiment, there can be only one outcome out of a finite number of m mutually exclusive events. Let's call each outcome a *state* and denote all the possible states by $E_1, E_2, E_3, \ldots, E_m$. Of course, any one of these states can occur in any one of the n trials of the experiment. We shall use the notation $E_j^{(n)}$ for $1 \le j \le m$ to indicate that the experiment is in the state E_j in the nth trial. The *transition probability*, denoted by p_{ij}, is the probability that the experiment moves into the state E_j from the state E_i. That is, p_{ij} is a conditional probability which can be expressed as

Transition Probability (margin note)

$$p_{ij} = P(E_j | E_i)$$

The subscripts i and j of p_{ij} can assume any integer between 1 and m. If we let the first subscript stand for a row and the second for a column, the transition probabilities can be arranged in a *matrix P of transition probabilities*, with all entries being nonnegative and less than or equal to 1. That is,

$$P = \begin{bmatrix} p_{11} & p_{12} & \cdots & p_{1m} \\ p_{21} & p_{22} & \cdots & p_{2m} \\ \vdots & \vdots & & \vdots \\ p_{m1} & p_{m2} & \cdots & p_{mm} \end{bmatrix}$$

Each entry of P represents the transition probability for moving from one state to another. The entry p_{24}, for instance, stands for the probability of moving from the state E_2 to the state E_4; whereas, p_{42} represents the probability of moving from state E_4 to the state E_2. Since the probability for a subsequent state depends only on the preceding state, once the transition matrix P is determined, the probability of the outcomes for all successive stages can be found, provided the *initial probability distribution* $A^{(0)}$ is known. Of course, $A^{(0)}$ is a row vector of the form

$$A^{(0)} = [p_1^{(0)} \quad p_2^{(0)} \quad \cdots \quad p_m^{(0)}]$$

This is the probability of being in a particular state when the experiment begins.

It should be clear that a transition matrix P is a square matrix with entries that are always nonnegative. The sum of the entries in every row is 1. Similarly, the initial probability distribution is a row vector, with entries that are nonnegative, and the sum of the entries is 1. In general, any matrix M with entries that are nonnegative and in which the sum of the entries in every row is 1, is called a

---
Stochastic Matrix

stochastic matrix or a *probability matrix*. Thus, a transition matrix is a square stochastic matrix, while an initial probability distribution is a stochastic row vector.

Example 1 Look at the maze in Figure 1. Suppose we assign the following transition probabilities:

$$\text{From room 1 to } \begin{pmatrix} 1 & 2 & 3 & 4 \\ \frac{1}{3} & \frac{1}{3} & \frac{1}{3} & 0 \end{pmatrix}$$

Here, the mouse starts in room 1, and $\frac{1}{3}$ of the time it remains there during the time interval of observation, $\frac{1}{3}$ of the time it enters room 2, and $\frac{1}{3}$ of the time it enters room 3. Since it cannot go to room 4 directly from room 1, the probability assignment is 0. Similarly, the transition probabilities in moving from room 2, room 3, and room 4 may be given as follows:

$$\text{From room 2 to } \begin{pmatrix} 1 & 2 & 3 & 4 \\ \frac{1}{3} & \frac{1}{3} & 0 & \frac{1}{3} \end{pmatrix} \qquad \text{From room 3 to } \begin{pmatrix} 1 & 2 & 3 & 4 \\ \frac{1}{3} & 0 & \frac{1}{3} & \frac{1}{3} \end{pmatrix}$$

$$\text{From room 4 to } \begin{pmatrix} 1 & 2 & 3 & 4 \\ 0 & \frac{1}{3} & \frac{1}{3} & \frac{1}{3} \end{pmatrix}$$

Find the transition matrix P. If the initial placement of the mouse is in room 4, find the initial probability distribution. What are the probabilities of being in each room after two observations?

Solution The transition matrix P is

$$P = [p_{ij}] = \begin{array}{c} \\ 1 \\ 2 \\ 3 \\ 4 \end{array} \begin{array}{c} \begin{array}{cccc} 1 & 2 & 3 & 4 \end{array} \\ \begin{bmatrix} \frac{1}{3} & \frac{1}{3} & \frac{1}{3} & 0 \\ \frac{1}{3} & \frac{1}{3} & 0 & \frac{1}{3} \\ \frac{1}{3} & 0 & \frac{1}{3} & \frac{1}{3} \\ 0 & \frac{1}{3} & \frac{1}{3} & \frac{1}{3} \end{bmatrix} \end{array}$$

Next, since the initial placement of the mouse is in room 4, the initial probability distribution is

$$A^{(0)} = [p_1^{(0)} \quad p_2^{(0)} \quad p_3^{(0)} \quad p_4^{(0)}] = [0 \quad 0 \quad 0 \quad 1]$$

To answer the last question, we use a tree diagram. See Figure 2. The numbers in each square refer to the room occupied. From this tree diagram we deduce, for example, that the mouse will be in state 1 after two observations with probability

$$p_{41}^{(2)} = \frac{1}{3} \cdot \frac{1}{3} + \frac{1}{3} \cdot \frac{1}{3} = \frac{2}{9}$$

Similarly,

$$p_{42}^{(2)} = \frac{1}{3} \cdot \frac{1}{3} + \frac{1}{3} \cdot \frac{1}{3} = \frac{2}{9}$$

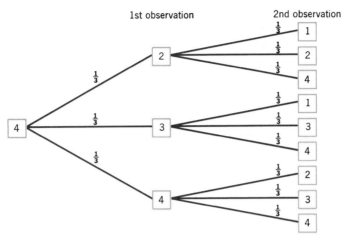

1st observation   2nd observation

Figure 2

$$p_{43}^{(2)} = \frac{1}{3} \cdot \frac{1}{3} + \frac{1}{3} \cdot \frac{1}{3} = \frac{2}{9}$$

(1)

$$p_{44}^{(2)} = \frac{1}{3} \cdot \frac{1}{3} + \frac{1}{3} \cdot \frac{1}{3} + \frac{1}{3} \cdot \frac{1}{3} = \frac{1}{3}$$

∎

The technique used above to compute the probabilities of being in a given state after k observations is cumbersome and tedious. A fundamental property of Markov chains is the availability of the following straightforward technique.

In a Markov chain the probability distribution after k observations is

(2)
$$A^{(k)} = A^{(0)}P^k = A^{(k-1)}P$$

where P^k is the kth power of the transition matrix P and $A^{(0)}$ is the initial probability distribution.

Example 2   For the data in Example 1, find the probability distribution after two observations.

Solution   We square the transition matrix P, obtaining

$$P^2 = \begin{bmatrix} \frac{1}{3} & \frac{2}{9} & \frac{2}{9} & \frac{2}{9} \\ \frac{2}{9} & \frac{1}{3} & \frac{2}{9} & \frac{2}{9} \\ \frac{2}{9} & \frac{2}{9} & \frac{1}{3} & \frac{2}{9} \\ \frac{2}{9} & \frac{2}{9} & \frac{2}{9} & \frac{1}{3} \end{bmatrix}$$

Notice that the four results in (1) appear in row 4 of P^2. The probability distribution after two observations, namely $A^{(2)}$, is

$$A^{(2)} = A^{(0)}P^2 = [\frac{2}{9} \quad \frac{2}{9} \quad \frac{2}{9} \quad \frac{1}{3}]$$

The interpretation of $A^{(2)}$ is that after two observations, the probability that the mouse is in room 1 is $\frac{2}{9}$, room 2 is $\frac{2}{9}$, room 3 is $\frac{2}{9}$, and room 4 is $\frac{1}{3}$. This, of course, agrees with our previous result. ∎

Example 3
Population
Movement

Suppose that the city of Glenwood is experiencing a movement of its population to the suburbs. At present, 85% of the total population lives in the city and 15% lives in the suburbs. But each year 7% of the city people move to the suburbs, while only 1% of the suburb people move back to the city. Assuming that the total population (city and suburbs together) remains constant, what percent of the total will remain in the city after 5 years?

Solution

This problem can be expressed as a sequence of experiments in which each experiment measures the proportion of people in the city and the proportion of people in the suburbs.

In the $(n + 1)$st year, these proportions will depend for their value only on the proportions in the nth year and not on the proportions found in earlier years. Thus, we have an experiment that can be represented as a Markov chain.

The initial probability distribution for this system is

$$\begin{array}{cc} \text{City} & \text{Suburbs} \\ A^{(0)} = [.85 & .15] \end{array}$$

That is, initially, 85% of the people reside in the city and 15% in the suburbs.
The transition matrix P is

$$P = \begin{array}{c} \\ \text{City} \\ \text{Suburbs} \end{array} \begin{array}{cc} \text{City} & \text{Suburbs} \\ \begin{bmatrix} .93 & .07 \\ .01 & .99 \end{bmatrix} \end{array}$$

That is, each year 7% of the city people move to the suburbs (so that 93% remain in the city) and 1% of the suburb people move to the city (so that 99% remain in the suburbs).

To find the probability distribution after 5 years, we need to compute $A^{(5)}$:

$$A^{(1)} = A^{(0)}P = [.85 \quad .15]\begin{bmatrix} .93 & .07 \\ .01 & .99 \end{bmatrix} = [.792 \quad .208]$$

$$A^{(2)} = A^{(1)}P = [.792 \quad .208]\begin{bmatrix} .93 & .07 \\ .01 & .99 \end{bmatrix} = [.73864 \quad .26136]$$

$$A^{(3)} = A^{(2)}P = [.73864 \quad .26136]\begin{bmatrix} .93 & .07 \\ .01 & .99 \end{bmatrix} = [.68955 \quad .31045]$$

$$A^{(4)} = A^{(3)}P = [.68955 \quad .31045]\begin{bmatrix} .93 & .07 \\ .01 & .99 \end{bmatrix} = [.64439 \quad .35561]$$

$$A^{(5)} = A^{(4)}P = [.64439 \quad .35561]\begin{bmatrix} .93 & .07 \\ .01 & .99 \end{bmatrix} = [.60284 \quad .39716]$$

Thus, by property (2), the probability distribution after 5 years is

$$A^{(5)} = A^{(0)}P^5 = A^{(4)}P = [.60284 \quad .39716]$$

Thus, after 5 years, 60.28% of the residents live in the city and 39.72% live in the suburbs.

∎

This example leads us to inquire whether the situation in Glenwood ever stabilizes; that is, after a certain number of years is an equilibrium reached? Also, does the equilibrium state depend on the initial state or are they independent? This type of problem is dealt with in the next section.

Exercise 1
Solutions to Odd-Numbered Problems begin on page 597.

1. Explain why the matrix below cannot be a stochastic matrix.

$$\begin{bmatrix} 0 & 1 & 0 \\ \frac{1}{3} & \frac{1}{3} & \frac{1}{3} \\ \frac{1}{2} & -\frac{1}{2} & \frac{1}{2} \end{bmatrix}$$

2. Explain why the matrix below cannot be the transition matrix for a Markov chain.

$$\begin{bmatrix} 1 & \frac{1}{2} & \frac{1}{3} & \frac{1}{4} \\ 0 & 1 & 0 & 0 \\ 0 & \frac{1}{2} & \frac{1}{2} & 0 \\ 1 & 0 & 0 & 0 \end{bmatrix}$$

3. Consider a Markov chain with transition matrix

$$\begin{array}{cc} & \text{State 1} \quad \text{State 2} \end{array}$$
$$\begin{array}{c} \text{State 1} \\ \text{State 2} \end{array} \begin{bmatrix} \frac{1}{3} & \frac{2}{3} \\ \frac{1}{4} & \frac{3}{4} \end{bmatrix}$$

   (a) What does the entry $\frac{2}{3}$ in this matrix represent?
   (b) Assuming that the system is initially in state 1, find the probability distribution one observation later.
   (c) Assuming that the system is initially in state 2, find the probability distribution one observation later.
   (d) Draw a tree diagram to find the probability distribution two observations later.

4. Consider a Markov chain with transition matrix

$$\begin{array}{cc} & \text{State 1} \quad \text{State 2} \end{array}$$
$$\begin{array}{c} \text{State 1} \\ \text{State 2} \end{array} \begin{bmatrix} .3 & .7 \\ .4 & .6 \end{bmatrix}$$

   (a) What does the entry .4 in the matrix represent?
   (b) Assuming that the system is initially in state 1, find the probability distribution two observations later.
   (c) Assuming that the system is initially in state 2, find the probability distribution two observations later.

5. Consider the transition matrix of Problem 4. If the initial probability distribution is [.25   .75], what is the probability distribution after two observations?

6. Consider a Markov chain with transition matrix

$$P = \begin{bmatrix} .7 & .2 & .1 \\ .6 & .2 & .2 \\ .4 & .1 & .5 \end{bmatrix}$$

If the initial distribution is [.25   .25   .5], what is the probability distribution in the next observation?

7. Find the values of a, b, and c that will make the following matrix a transition matrix for a Markov chain:

$$\begin{bmatrix} .2 & a & .4 \\ b & .6 & .2 \\ 0 & c & 0 \end{bmatrix}$$

8. In the maze of Figure 1, if the initial probability distribution is $A^{(0)} = [\tfrac{1}{2}\ \ 0\ \ \tfrac{1}{2}\ \ 0]$, find the probability distribution after two observations.

9. In Example 3, if the initial probability distribution for Glenwood is $A^{(0)} = [.7\ \ .3]$, what is the population distribution after 5 years?

10. A new rapid transit system has just been installed. It is anticipated that each week 90% of the commuters who used the rapid transit will continue to do so. Of those who travelled by car, 20% will begin to use the rapid transit instead.
    (a) Explain why the above is a Markov chain.
    (b) Set up the 2×2 stochastic matrix P with columns and rows labeled R (rapid transit) and C (car) to display these transitions.
    (c) Compute P^2 and P^3.

11. The voting pattern for a certain group of cities is such that 60% of the Democratic (D) mayors were succeeded by Democrats and 40% by Republicans (R). Also, 30% of the Republican mayors were succeeded by Democrats and 70% by Republicans.
    (a) Explain why the above is a Markov chain.
    (b) Set up the 2×2 stochastic matrix P with columns and rows labeled D and R to display these transitions.
    (c) Compute P^2 and P^3.

12. Consider the maze with nine rooms shown in the figure. The system consists of the maze and a mouse. We assume that the following learning pattern exists: If the mouse is in room 1, 2, 3, 4, or 5, it

moves with equal probability to any room that the maze permits; if it is in room 8, it moves directly to room 9; if it is in room 6, 7, or 9, it remains in that room.

(a)   Explain why the above experiment is a Markov chain.

(b)   Construct the transition matrix P.

13.   *Market Penetration.*   A company is promoting a certain product, say Brand X wine. The result of this is that 75% of the people drinking Brand X wine over any given period of 1 month, continue to drink it the next month; of those people drinking other brands of wine in the period of 1 month, 35% change over to the promoted wine the next month. We would like to know what fraction of wine drinkers will drink Brand X after 2 months if 50% drink Brand X wine now.

14.   A professor either walks or drives to a university. He never drives 2 days in a row, but if he walks one day, he is just as likely to walk the next day as to drive his car. Show that this forms a Markov chain and give the transition matrix.

15.   Suppose that, during the year 1980, 45% of the drivers in a certain metropolitan area had Travelers automobile insurance, 30% had General American insurance, and 25% were insured by some other companies. Suppose also that a year later: (*1*) of those who had been insured by Travelers in 1980, 92% continued to be insured by Travelers, but 8% had switched their insurance to General American; (*2*) of those who had been insured by General American in 1980, 90% continued to be insured by General American, but 4% had switched to Travelers and 6% had switched to some other companies; (*3*) of those who had been insured by some other companies in 1980, 82% continued but 10% had switched to Travelers, and 8% had switched to General American. Using these data, answer the following questions:

(a)   What percentage of drivers in the metropolitan area were insured by Travelers and General American in 1981?

(b)   If these trends continued for one more year, what percentage of the drivers were insured by Travelers and General American in 1982?

*16.   If A is a transition matrix, what about A^2? A^3? What do you conjecture about A^n?

*17.   Let

$$A = \begin{bmatrix} a_{11} & a_{12} \\ a_{21} & a_{22} \end{bmatrix}$$

be a transition matrix and

$$u = [u_1 \quad u_2]$$

be a stochastic row vector. Prove that uA is a stochastic vector.

*18.   Let A and B be two stochastic matrices for which AB is defined. Prove that AB is stochastic.

2. Regular Markov Chains

Another fundamental property of a Markov chain is that sometimes we can obtain the transition probabilities after a large number of observations in a straightforward manner. When this is possible, questions involving the nature of long-run probability distributions can be answered with relative ease. In this section, we investigate the condition under which a Markov chain leads to an *equilibrium*, or *steady-state*, situation and give techniques for finding this *equilibrium distribution*.

We begin the discussion by referring to Problem 13 in Exercise 1. The transition matrix is

$$P = \begin{array}{c} \\ \text{Brand } X, E_1 \\ \text{Other brands, } E_2 \end{array} \begin{array}{cc} \overset{\displaystyle \text{Brand } X}{\underset{E_1}{}} & \overset{\displaystyle \text{Other brands}}{\underset{E_2}{}} \\ \begin{bmatrix} .75 & .25 \\ .35 & .65 \end{bmatrix} \end{array}$$

The tree diagram depicting this experiment is given in Figure 3.

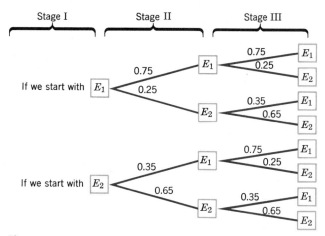

Figure 3

The probability $p_{11}^{(2)}$ of proceeding from E_1 to E_1 in two stages is

$$p_{11}^{(2)} = (.75)(.75) + (.25)(.35) = .65$$

The probability $p_{12}^{(2)}$ from E_1 to E_2 in two stages is

$$p_{12}^{(2)} = (.75)(.25) + (.25)(.65) = .35$$

The probability $p_{21}^{(2)}$ from E_2 to E_1 in two stages is

$$p_{21}^{(2)} = (.35)(.75) + (.65)(.35) = .49$$

The probability $p_{22}^{(2)}$ from E_2 to E_2 in two stages is

$$p_{22}^{(2)} = (.35)(.25) + (.65)(.65) = .51$$

If we square the matrix P, we obtain

$$P^2 = \begin{bmatrix} (.75)(.75) + (.25)(.35) & (.75)(.25) + (.25)(.65) \\ (.35)(.75) + (.65)(.35) & (.35)(.25) + (.65)(.65) \end{bmatrix}$$

$$= \begin{bmatrix} .65 & .35 \\ .49 & .51 \end{bmatrix} = \begin{bmatrix} p_{11}^{(2)} & p_{12}^{(2)} \\ p_{21}^{(2)} & p_{22}^{(2)} \end{bmatrix}$$

Thus, the *square* of the transition matrix gives the probabilities for moving from one state to another state in *two* stages. To see that this is true in general, recall that the entry p_{ij} of P stands for the transition probability of passing from state E_i to E_j in *one* step. However, we would like to find the probability of passing from the state E_i to the state E_j in exactly n steps. For $n = 1$, the original matrix P provides the answer; for $n = 2$, we square the matrix P, obtaining

$$P^2 = \begin{bmatrix} p_{11} \cdot p_{11} + p_{12} \cdot p_{21} & p_{11} \cdot p_{12} + p_{12} \cdot p_{22} \\ p_{21} \cdot p_{11} + p_{22} \cdot p_{21} & p_{21} \cdot p_{12} + p_{22} \cdot p_{22} \end{bmatrix} = \begin{bmatrix} p_{11}^{(2)} & p_{12}^{(2)} \\ p_{21}^{(2)} & p_{22}^{(2)} \end{bmatrix}$$

We observe that the entries in P^2 are the probabilities that an experiment that is in the state E_i will pass to the state E_j after the second trial. For instance,

$$p_{11}^{(2)} = p_{11} \cdot p_{11} + p_{12} \cdot p_{21}$$

is the probability of starting in state E_1 and then passing to state E_1 or to state E_2 and finally passing back to state E_1. See Figure 4.

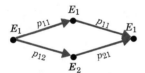

Figure 4

A similar interpretation can be given to the other entries of P^2. It seems, then, that the answer to the question as to what are the probabilities of passing from a state E_i to a state E_j in two steps can be found in the entries of P^2. Similarly, the probabilities of passing from E_i to E_j in n steps are given by the entries of P^n.

If P is the transition matrix of a Markov chain, then the entry $p_{ij}^{(n)}$ of P^n (nth power of P) gives the probability for passing from state E_i to state E_j in n stages, for any i or j.

In studying Markov chains, one question of particular interest is whether, after a given number of stages of a Markov process, the transition matrix approaches a steady, or equilibrium, state. We will find out that, under certain conditions, an equilibrium state is attained which is unique, and which depends only on the transition matrix and not on the initial probability distribution of the states (the distribution when the process begins).

Example 1 Again, let's return to Problem 13 of Exercise 1. For the data supplied, what will be the distribution of the wine drinkers in the long run?

Solution Some of the powers of the transition matrix P are given below.

$$P = \begin{bmatrix} .7500 & .2500 \\ .3500 & .6500 \end{bmatrix} \qquad P^7 = \begin{bmatrix} .5840 & .4159 \\ .5823 & .4176 \end{bmatrix}$$

$$P^2 = \begin{bmatrix} .6500 & .3500 \\ .4900 & .5100 \end{bmatrix} \qquad P^8 = \begin{bmatrix} .5836 & .4163 \\ .5829 & .4170 \end{bmatrix}$$

$$P^3 = \begin{bmatrix} .6100 & .3900 \\ .5460 & .4540 \end{bmatrix} \qquad P^9 = \begin{bmatrix} .5834 & .4165 \\ .5831 & .4168 \end{bmatrix}$$

$$P^4 = \begin{bmatrix} .5940 & .4060 \\ .5683 & .4316 \end{bmatrix} \qquad P^{10} = \begin{bmatrix} .5833 & .4166 \\ .5832 & .4167 \end{bmatrix}$$

$$P^5 = \begin{bmatrix} .5876 & .4124 \\ .5773 & .4226 \end{bmatrix} \qquad P^{11} = \begin{bmatrix} .5833 & .4166 \\ .5833 & .4166 \end{bmatrix} \leftarrow \text{No change, so we stop here}$$

$$P^6 = \begin{bmatrix} .5850 & .4149 \\ .5809 & .4190 \end{bmatrix} \qquad P^{12} = \begin{bmatrix} .5833 & .4166 \\ .5833 & .4166 \end{bmatrix}$$

Thus, in the long run, 58.33% will be drinking Brand X wine. ■

Notice an interesting fact about P^n in Example 1. The entries in P^n stay the same after P^{11}. Thus, as we increase n, the matrix P^n reaches a point of equilibrium where its entries are stabilized. The entries, of course, as stated earlier, are the probabilities that the process moves from one state to another in n steps.

We do not always have to raise the transition matrix P to a certain nth power to obtain these probabilities. In some cases, we can take a short cut. Once again, let's return to Example 1 and perform the following computation:

$$[.5833 \quad .4166] \begin{bmatrix} .75 & .25 \\ .35 & .65 \end{bmatrix} = [.5833 \quad .4166]$$

The product of a row vector (taken from the matrix P^{12}) and the original matrix P results in the same row vector. Such a vector is called a *fixed vector* and shows the *equilibrium state* of the process.

Fixed Probability Vector **A probability row vector t, satisfying the equation**

(1) $$tP = t$$

is called a *fixed probability vector for the transition matrix P.*

Equation (1) tells us that the distribution of states tends toward or approaches the vector **t**, which is independent of the original distribution. Hence, **t** is sometimes called the *equilibrium distribution* since, once this distribution is reached, it will be maintained. In the previous example, the fixed vector **t** was obtained

Equilibrium
Distribution

after raising the transition matrix to the 12th power. Note that n does not have to be 12 in all cases and, in fact, it may happen that no finite value of n gives the fixed vector $\mathbf{t}$ as the rows of P^n.

Also, note that the equilibrium distribution is not usually reached by looking at only a few powers of P. The fixed probability vector $\mathbf{t}$ is most easily found by using the method described below.

Example 2   Find the fixed probability vector for Example 3 in Section 1.

Solution   Let $\mathbf{t} = [t_1 \quad t_2]$ be the desired fixed probability vector. Then $t_1 + t_2 = 1$ and

$$[t_1 \quad t_2]\begin{bmatrix} .93 & .07 \\ .01 & .99 \end{bmatrix} = [t_1 \quad t_2]$$

Or,

$$[.93t_1 + .01t_2 \quad .07t_1 + .99t_2] = [t_1 \quad t_2]$$

Equating corresponding entries yields the following system of two equations in two unknowns

$$.93t_1 + .01t_2 = t_1$$
$$.07t_1 + .99t_2 = t_2$$

Or,

$$-.07t_1 + .01t_2 = 0$$
$$.07t_1 - .01t_2 = 0$$

As it stands this system has infinitely many solutions. However, when we include the equation

$$t_1 + t_2 = 1$$

the resulting system is

$$-.07t_1 + .01t_2 = 0$$
$$.07t_1 - .01t_2 = 0$$
$$t_1 + t_2 = 1$$

which will have a unique solution, namely

$$t_1 = \tfrac{1}{8} \qquad t_2 = \tfrac{7}{8}$$

In obtaining the fixed probability vector $[\tfrac{1}{8} \quad \tfrac{7}{8}]$, we learn that in the long run, $\tfrac{1}{8}$ of the population will move to the city from the suburbs and $\tfrac{7}{8}$ will move to the suburbs from the city.   ∎

Example 3   Find the fixed probability vector $\mathbf{t}$ of the transition matrix

$$P = \begin{bmatrix} \tfrac{1}{2} & 0 & \tfrac{1}{2} \\ 0 & 1 & 0 \\ \tfrac{1}{3} & \tfrac{1}{3} & \tfrac{1}{3} \end{bmatrix}$$

Solution   Let $[t_1 \quad t_2 \quad t_3]$ be the fixed vector. Then $t_1 + t_2 + t_3 = 1$ and

$$[t_1 \quad t_2 \quad t_3] \begin{bmatrix} \frac{1}{2} & 0 & \frac{1}{2} \\ 0 & 1 & 0 \\ \frac{1}{3} & \frac{1}{3} & \frac{1}{3} \end{bmatrix} = [t_1 \quad t_2 \quad t_3]$$

$$\tfrac{1}{2}t_1 + 0 \cdot t_2 + \tfrac{1}{3}t_3 = t_1$$
$$0 \cdot t_1 + 1 \cdot t_2 + \tfrac{1}{3}t_3 = t_2$$
$$\tfrac{1}{2}t_1 + 0 \cdot t_2 + \tfrac{1}{3}t_3 = t_3$$

or equivalently,

$$-3t_1 + 2t_3 = 0$$
$$t_3 = 0$$
$$3t_1 - 4t_3 = 0$$

Since $[t_1 \quad t_2 \quad t_3]$ is a fixed probability vector, we have $t_1 + t_2 + t_3 = 1$. Thus, we obtain the following system of equations:

$$t_1 + t_2 + t_3 = 1$$
$$-3t_1 + 2t_3 = 0$$
$$t_3 = 0$$
$$3t_1 - 4t_3 = 0$$

The solution of this system is

$$\mathbf{t} = [t_1 \quad t_2 \quad t_3] = [0 \quad 1 \quad 0]$$

■

Until now, we have only discussed a way for finding the equilibrium state of a Markov chain, but we have not indicated how you can tell which Markov chains have equilibrium states and which do not. At this point, we consider a particularly nice kind of Markov chain, one with long-run behavior that is very regular.

Regular Markov Chain   **A Markov chain is said to be *regular* if for some power of its transition matrix P, all of the entries are positive.**

Example 4   The transition matrix

$$P = \begin{bmatrix} \frac{1}{2} & \frac{1}{2} \\ 1 & 0 \end{bmatrix}$$

is regular since the square of P, namely,

$$P^2 = \begin{bmatrix} \frac{3}{4} & \frac{3}{4} \\ \frac{1}{2} & \frac{1}{2} \end{bmatrix}$$

has only positive entries.

■

Example 5 The matrix

$$P = \begin{bmatrix} 1 & 0 \\ \frac{3}{4} & \frac{1}{4} \end{bmatrix}$$

is not regular since every power of P will always have $p_{12} = 0$.
The matrix

$$\begin{bmatrix} 0 & 1 \\ 1 & 0 \end{bmatrix}$$

is another example of a transition matrix that is not regular. ∎

A regular Markov chain has the property that all possible states or outcomes will occur sooner or later. From the above example and the definition of a regular Markov chain, we conjecture the following result:

Let P be a transition matrix of a regular Markov chain. Then:

(a) P **has a unique, fixed probability vector t, with entries that are all positive.**

(b) **The matrices** P^n **approach a matrix** T**, as** n **gets large. That is,**

$$P^n \to T \quad \text{(as } n \text{ gets very large)}$$

and the rows of T **are all identical and equal to the fixed probability vector t.**

(c) **If q is any probability row vector, then**

$$qP^n \to t \quad \text{(as } n \text{ gets very large)}$$

Models using Markov chains equip the researcher with a technique for finding the long-run behavior that is typical of many sequential experiments. The researcher hopes that no matter how the process begins it will settle down to some stable and, hopefully, predictable behavior. Such stable long-run behaviors that are independent of the initial state are not always possible. However, as the above result points out, when the Markov chain is regular, stable long-run behaviors are established and can be predicted.

Example 6
Consumer Loyalty
Consider a certain community in a well-defined area with three grocery stores, I, II, and III. Within this community (we assume that the population is fixed) there always exists a shift of customers from one grocery store to another. A study was made on January 1, and it was found that $\frac{1}{4}$ of the population shopped at Store I, $\frac{1}{3}$ at Store II, and $\frac{5}{12}$ at Store III. Each month Store I retains 90% of its customers and loses 10% of them to Store II. Store II retains 5% of its customers and loses 85% of them to Store I and 10% of them to Store III. Store III retains 40% of its

customers and loses 50% of them to Store I and 10% to Store II. The transition matrix P is

$$P = \begin{array}{c} \\ \text{I} \\ \text{II} \\ \text{III} \end{array} \begin{array}{ccc} \text{I} & \text{II} & \text{III} \\ \begin{bmatrix} .90 & .10 & 0 \\ .85 & .05 & .10 \\ .50 & .10 & .40 \end{bmatrix} \end{array}$$

We would like to answer the following questions:
(a) What proportion of customers will each store retain by February 1?
(b) By March 1?
(c) Assuming the same pattern continues, what will be the long-run distribution of customers among the three stores?

Solution (a) To answer the first question, we note that the initial probability distribution is $A^{(0)} = [\frac{1}{4} \quad \frac{1}{3} \quad \frac{5}{12}]$. By February 1, the probability distribution is

$$A^{(1)} = A^{(0)}P = [\frac{1}{4} \quad \frac{1}{3} \quad \frac{5}{12}] \begin{bmatrix} .90 & .10 & .00 \\ .85 & .05 & .10 \\ .50 & .10 & .40 \end{bmatrix} = [.7167 \quad .0833 \quad .2000]$$

(b) To find the probability distribution after 2 months (March 1), we compute $A^{(2)}$:

$$A^{(2)} = A^{(0)}P^2 = [\frac{1}{4} \quad \frac{1}{3} \quad \frac{5}{12}] \begin{bmatrix} .895 & .095 & .010 \\ .857 & .098 & .045 \\ .735 & .095 & .170 \end{bmatrix} = [.8155 \quad .0956 \quad .0882]$$

(c) To find the long-run distribution we determine the fixed probability vector $\mathbf{t}$ of the regular transition matrix P. Let $\mathbf{t} = [t_1 \quad t_2 \quad t_3]$, where $t_1 + t_2 + t_3 = 1$. Then

$$[t_1 \quad t_2 \quad t_3] \begin{bmatrix} .90 & .10 & .00 \\ .85 & .05 & .10 \\ .50 & .10 & .40 \end{bmatrix} = [t_1 \quad t_2 \quad t_3]$$

$$[t_1 \quad t_2 \quad t_3] = [.8889 \quad .0952 \quad .0159]$$

Thus, in the long run Store I will have about 88.9% of all customers, Store II will have 9.5%, and Store III will have 1.6%

■

Example 7
Spread of Rumor

A United States Senator has determined whether to vote Yes or No on an important bill pending in Congress and conveys this decision to an aide. The aide then passes this news on to another individual, who passes it on to a friend, and so on, each time to a new individual. Assume p is the probability that any one person passes on the information opposite to the way he heard it. Then $1 - p$ is the probability a person passes on the information the same way he heard it. With what probability will the nth person receive the information as a Yes vote?

Solution This situation is another example of a Markov chain model. Although it is not intuitively obvious, we shall find the answer is independent of p.

To obtain the transition matrix, we observe that two stages are possible: Yes or No vote. The transition from a Yes to a No or from a No to a Yes occurs with probability p. The transition from Yes to Yes or from No to No occurs with probability $1 - p$. Thus, the transition matrix P is

$$\begin{array}{cc} & \begin{array}{cc} \text{Yes} & \quad \text{No} \end{array} \\ \begin{array}{c} \text{Yes} \\ \text{No} \end{array} & \begin{bmatrix} 1 - p & p \\ p & 1 - p \end{bmatrix} \end{array}$$

The probability that the nth person will receive the information in one state or the other is given by successive powers of the matrix P, that is, by the matrices P^n. In fact, the answer in this case rapidly approaches $t_1 = \frac{1}{2}$, $t_2 = \frac{1}{2}$, after any considerable number of people are involved. This can easily be shown by verifying that the fixed probability vector is $[\frac{1}{2} \quad \frac{1}{2}]$. Hence, no matter what the Senator's initial decision is, eventually (after enough information exchange), half the people hear that the Senator is going to vote Yes and half hear that the Senator is going to vote No.

■

An interesting interpretation of this result is to successive voting situations in Congress. If we substitute the probability of a member changing his or her mind for that of spreading the rumor, we arrive at a possible model for explaining the standard parliamentary device of minority delaying actions.

Model: Social Mobility*

This model is based on an article by S. J. Prais, Department of Applied Economics, University of Cambridge.

In the example, the following assumptions are made:

1. Class is treated as if it related only to the male side of the family line. This is largely because in these studies social class is measured by the occupation of the father.
2. The influence of one's ancestors in determining one's class is transmitted entirely through one's father so that, if the influence of one's father has been taken into account, then the total influence of one's ancestors is accounted for.

A social transition matrix representing England in 1949 is given in Table 1.

The element in the ith row and jth column of this matrix, denoted by p_{ij}, gives the proportion of fathers in the ith social class whose sons move into the jth social class. Furthermore, it is supposed that if there is uncertainty in the tracing of a family line through time, then p_{ij} represents the probability of transition by a family from class i into class j in the interval of one generation. For example, p_{42} indicates that .039 of the sons of fathers in class 4 (lower grade supervisory and nonmanual) move into class 2 (managerial and executive). The equilibrium

*S. J. Prais, "Measuring Social Mobility," *Journal of the Royal Statistical Society,* **118** (1955), pp. 55–66.

Table 1
The Social Transition Matrix for England, 1949

	1	2	3	4	5	6	7
1. Professional and high administrative	.388	.146	.202	.062	.140	.047	.015
2. Managerial and executive	.107	.267	.227	.120	.206	.053	.020
3. Higher grade supervisory and nonmanual	.035	.101	.188	.191	.357	.067	.061
4. Lower grade supervisory and nonmanual	.021	.039	.112	.212	.430	.124	.062
5. Skilled manual and routine nonmanual	.009	.024	.075	.123	.473	.171	.125
6. Semi-skilled manual	.000	.013	.041	.088	.391	.312	.155
7. Unskilled manual	.000	.008	.036	.083	.364	.235	.274

probability vector for the matrix in Table 1 was found by Prais to be

$$[.023 \quad .042 \quad .088 \quad .127 \quad .409 \quad .182 \quad .129]$$

Prais compared the above result with the actual data and obtained the figures listed in Table 2.

Table 2
Actual and Equilibrium Distributions of the Social Classes in England

	Actual Distribution		Equilibrium Distribution (3)
Class	Fathers (1)	Sons (2)	
1. Professional	.037	.029	.023
2. Managerial	.043	.046	.042
3. Higher grade nonmanual	.098	.094	.088
4. Lower grade nonmanual	.148	.131	.127
5. Skilled manual	.432	.409	.409
6. Semi-skilled manual	.131	.170	.182
7. Unskilled manual	.111	.121	.129

The equilibrium distribution depends only on the structural propensities of the society and not on the distribution of the population among the classes found at any instant. The equilibrium distribution is also independent of the unit of time in which the elements of P are measured. Suppose, for example, that observations were taken showing the relationship between the social status of grandson and grandfather. Every element of the transition matrix would then be different, since it would refer to a transition during a period of two generations instead of one generation. However, the equilibrium distribution corresponding to such a matrix would be unchanged. For, if the matrix relating the status of sons to fathers is P, that relating those of grandsons to grandfathers will be P^2 (provided, of course, that nothing has happened to change the characteristics of the society in the period considered), and when these matrices are raised to the nth power, they obviously tend to the same value as n gets very large.

Suppose we would like to compute the average number of periods spent in a social class. Let s_j be the number of families in class j in the current generation. Of these, the number $s_j \cdot p_{jj}$ is the expected number that remain in the jth class in the next generation; the number $s_j \cdot p_{jj}^2$ is the expected number that remain in the jth class in the third generation; and so on. Hence, the total time t spent in the jth class by the s_j families at present in that class is expected to be

$$t = s_j + s_j \cdot p_{jj} + s_j \cdot p_{jj}^2 + \cdots$$

Dividing by s_j, we find the average time t_j spent by a family in that class:

$$t_j = 1 + p_{jj} + p_{jj}^2 + \cdots$$

Since the jth class is an arbitrary class, the general formula is

$$T = I + P + P^2 + \cdots = [I - P]^{-1}$$

where T is the given average time, P is the social transition matrix, and I is the corresponding identity matrix.

Exercise 2
Solutions to Odd-Numbered Problems begin on page 598.

In Problems 1–6 determine which of the given matrices are regular. For those that are, find the fixed probability vector.

1. $\begin{bmatrix} \frac{1}{2} & \frac{1}{2} \\ 1 & 0 \end{bmatrix}$

2. $\begin{bmatrix} \frac{1}{2} & \frac{1}{2} \\ 0 & 1 \end{bmatrix}$

3. $\begin{bmatrix} 0 & 1 \\ \frac{1}{4} & \frac{3}{4} \end{bmatrix}$

4. $\begin{bmatrix} \frac{1}{3} & \frac{2}{3} \\ 1 & 0 \end{bmatrix}$

5. $\begin{bmatrix} 1 & 0 & 0 \\ \frac{1}{4} & \frac{1}{2} & \frac{1}{4} \\ 0 & 1 & 0 \end{bmatrix}$

6. $\begin{bmatrix} \frac{1}{4} & \frac{3}{4} & 0 \\ \frac{1}{2} & 0 & \frac{1}{2} \\ 0 & 1 & 0 \end{bmatrix}$

7. Show that the transition matrix P of Example 7 has a fixed probability vector $[\frac{1}{2} \quad \frac{1}{2}]$.

8. Verify the result we obtained in Example 6, part (c).

9. *Consumer Loyalty.* A grocer stocks his store with three types of detergents, A, B, C. When Brand A is sold out, the probability is .7 that he stocks up with Brand A again. When he sells out Brand B, the probability is .8 that he will stock up again with Brand B. Finally, when he sells out Brand C, the probability is .6 that he will stock up with Brand C again. When he switches to another detergent, he does so with equal probability for the remaining two brands. Find the transition matrix. In the long run, how does he stock up with detergents?

10. *Consumer Loyalty.* A housewife buys three kinds of cereal: A, B, C. She never buys the same cereal in successive weeks. If she buys Cereal A, then the next week she buys Cereal B. However, if she buys either B or C, then the next week she is three times as likely to buy A as the other brand. Find the transition matrix. In the long run, how often does she buy each of the three brands?

11. *Voting Loyalty.* In England, of the sons of members of the Conservative party, 70% vote Conservative and the rest vote Labor. Of

the sons of Laborites, 50% vote Labor, 40% vote Conservative, and 10% vote Socialist. Of the sons of Socialists, 40% vote Socialist, 40% vote Labor, and 20% vote Conservative. What is the probability that the grandson of a Laborite will vote Socialist? What is the membership distribution in the long run?

12. If $[\frac{1}{3} \ \ 0 \ \ \frac{1}{3} \ \ \frac{1}{3}]$ is a fixed probability vector of a matrix P, can P be regular?

13. *Family Traits.* The probabilities that a blonde mother will have a blonde, brunette, or redheaded daughter are .6, .2 and .2, respectively. The probabilities that a brunette mother will have a blonde, brunette, or redheaded daughter are .1, .7, and .2, respectively. And the probabilities that a redheaded mother will have a blonde, brunette, or redheaded daughter are .4, .2, and .4, respectively. What is the probability that a blonde woman is the grandmother of a brunette? If the population of women is now 50% brunettes, 30% blondes, and the rest redheads, what will the distribution be:
(a) After two generations?
(b) In the long run?

14. *Education Tends.* Use the data given in the table and assume that the indicated trends continue in order to answer the questions below.

		Maximum Education Children Achieve		
		College	H.S.	E.S.
Highest Educational Level of Parents	College	80%	18%	2%
	High School	40%	50%	10%
	Elementary School	20%	60%	20%

(a) What is the transition matrix?
(b) What is the probability that a grandchild of a college graduate is a college graduate?
(c) What is the probability that the grandchild of a high school graduate only finishes elementary school?
(d) If at present 30%, 40%, and 30% of the population are college, high school, and elementary school graduates, respectively, what will be the distribution of the grandchildren of the present population?
(e) What will the long-run distribution be?

3. Absorbing Markov Chains

We have already seen examples of transition matrices in our presentation of Markov chains in which there are states that are impossible to leave. Such states are called *absorbing*. For instance, in Problem 12 in Exercise 1, room 9 is absorbing since once room 9 is reached, the probability of leaving it and passing to some different room is 0. Similarly, rooms 6 and 7 are absorbing states since it is impossible to leave these rooms once they have been reached.

Absorbing State; Absorbing Chain **In a Markov chain, if p_{ij} denotes the probability of going from state E_i to state E_j, then E_i is called an** *absorbing state* **if $p_{ii} = 1$. A Markov chain is said to be an** *absorbing chain* **if and only if it contains at least one absorbing state and it is possible to go from** *any* **nonabsorbing state to an absorbing state in one or more stages.**

Thus, an absorbing state will capture the process and will not allow any state to pass from it.

In general, chains described by stochastic matrices can oscillate indefinitely from state to state in such a way that they exhibit no long-term trend. One such example is a Markov process chain having the nonregular matrix

$$\begin{bmatrix} 0 & 1 \\ 1 & 0 \end{bmatrix}$$

as its transition matrix. The idea of introducing absorbing states is to reduce the degree of oscillation since when an absorbing state is reached, the process no longer changes. That is, absorbing chain matrices exhibit a long-term trend. Furthermore, we can determine this trend using a simple computational technique.

When working with an absorbing Markov chain, it is convenient to rearrange the states so that the absorbing states come first and then the nonabsorbing states follow.

$$\begin{bmatrix} \overbrace{\text{Absorbing}} & \vdots & \overbrace{\text{Nonabsorbing}} \\ & \vdots & \end{bmatrix}$$

Once this rearrangement takes place, the transition matrix can be subdivided into four submatrices:

$$\begin{bmatrix} \overbrace{\text{Absorbing}} & & \overbrace{\text{Nonabsorbing}} \\ I & \vdots & 0 \\ \hline S & \vdots & Q \end{bmatrix}$$

Here, I is an identity matrix, $\mathbf{0}$ denotes a matrix having all 0 entries, and the matrices S and Q are the two submatrices corresponding to the absorbing and nonabsorbing states. For example, the absorbing transition matrix

$$\begin{array}{c} \begin{array}{ccccc} E_1 & E_2 & E_3 & E_4 & E_5 \end{array} \\ \begin{array}{c} E_1 \\ E_2 \\ E_3 \\ E_4 \\ E_5 \end{array} \begin{bmatrix} 0 & .5 & 0 & 0 & .5 \\ 0 & 0 & .9 & 0 & .1 \\ 0 & 0 & 0 & .7 & .3 \\ 0 & 0 & 0 & 1 & 0 \\ 0 & 0 & 0 & 0 & 1 \end{bmatrix} \end{array}$$

is first rearranged to get

$$
\begin{array}{c}
 \\
E_4 \\
E_5 \\
E_1 \\
E_2 \\
E_3
\end{array}
\begin{array}{c}
\begin{array}{ccccc} E_4 & E_5 & E_1 & E_2 & E_3 \end{array} \\
\begin{bmatrix}
1 & 0 & 0 & 0 & 0 \\
0 & 1 & 0 & 0 & 0 \\
0 & .5 & 0 & .5 & 0 \\
0 & .1 & 0 & 0 & .9 \\
.7 & .3 & 0 & 0 & 0
\end{bmatrix}
\end{array}
$$

Then the partitioned matrix is

$$
\left[
\begin{array}{cc|ccc}
1 & 0 & 0 & 0 & 0 \\
0 & 1 & 0 & 0 & 0 \\
\hline
0 & .5 & 0 & .5 & 0 \\
0 & .1 & 0 & 0 & .9 \\
.7 & .3 & 0 & 0 & 0
\end{array}
\right]
$$

Here,

$$
S = \begin{bmatrix} 0 & .5 \\ 0 & .1 \\ .7 & .3 \end{bmatrix}
\qquad
Q = \begin{bmatrix} 0 & .5 & 0 \\ 0 & 0 & .9 \\ 0 & 0 & 0 \end{bmatrix}
$$

Example 1 Consider the Markov chains with P_1 and P_2 as their transition matrices:

$$
P_1 =
\begin{array}{c}
E_1 \\ E_2 \\ E_3 \\ E_4
\end{array}
\begin{array}{c}
\begin{array}{cccc} E_1 & E_2 & E_3 & E_4 \end{array} \\
\begin{bmatrix}
.4 & .2 & .4 & 0 \\
0 & 1 & 0 & 0 \\
.1 & 0 & .5 & .4 \\
.1 & 0 & .3 & .6
\end{bmatrix}
\end{array}
\qquad
P_2 =
\begin{array}{c}
E_1 \\ E_2 \\ E_3
\end{array}
\begin{array}{c}
\begin{array}{ccc} E_1 & E_2 & E_3 \end{array} \\
\begin{bmatrix}
1 & 0 & 0 \\
0 & \frac{1}{4} & \frac{3}{4} \\
0 & \frac{1}{3} & \frac{2}{3}
\end{bmatrix}
\end{array}
$$

Test to see whether either or both are absorbing chains.

Solution The chain having P_1 as its transition matrix is absorbing since the second state is an absorbing state and it is possible to pass from each of the other states to the second. Specifically, it is possible to pass from the first state directly to the second state and from either the third or the fourth state to the first state and then to the second. On the other hand, the matrix P_2 is an example of a nonabsorbing matrix since it is impossible to go from the nonabsorbing state E_2 to the absorbing state E_1. ■

Gambler's Ruin Problem

Consider the following game involving two players; this is sometimes called the *gambler's ruin problem*. Player I has $3 and player II has $2. They flip a fair coin; if it is a head, Player I pays Player II $1, and if it is a tail, Player II pays Player I $1. The total amount of money in the game is, of course, $5. We would like to know how long the game will last, that is, how long it will take for one of the players to go broke or win all the money. (This game can easily be generalized by assuming that Player I has M dollars and Player II has N dollars.)

In this experiment, how much money a player has after any given flip of the coin depends only on how much he had after the previous flip and will not depend (directly) on how much he had in the preceding stages of the game. This experiment can thus be represented by a *Markov chain*.

For the *gambler's ruin* problem, the game does not have to involve flipping a coin. That is, the probability that Player I wins may not equal the probability that Player II wins. Also, questions can be raised as to what happens if the stakes are doubled, how long the game can be expected to last, and so on.

Suppose the coin being flipped is fair so that a probability of $\frac{1}{2}$ is assigned to each event. The states are the amounts of money each player has at each stage of the game. Each player can increase or decrease the amount of money he has by only $1 at a time.

The transition matrix P is then of the following form:

$$
P = \begin{array}{c} \\ 0 \\ 1 \\ 2 \\ 3 \\ 4 \\ 5 \end{array}
\begin{array}{cccccc}
0 & 1 & 2 & 3 & 4 & 5 \\
\left[\begin{array}{cccccc}
1 & 0 & 0 & 0 & 0 & 0 \\
\frac{1}{2} & 0 & \frac{1}{2} & 0 & 0 & 0 \\
0 & \frac{1}{2} & 0 & \frac{1}{2} & 0 & 0 \\
0 & 0 & \frac{1}{2} & 0 & \frac{1}{2} & 0 \\
0 & 0 & 0 & \frac{1}{2} & 0 & \frac{1}{2} \\
0 & 0 & 0 & 0 & 0 & 1
\end{array}\right]
\end{array}
$$

Notice that p_{00} is the probability of having $0 given that a player has started with $0. This is a sure event, since, once a player is in state 0, he stays there forever (he is broke). Similarly p_{55} represents the probability of having $5, given that a player started with $5, which is again a sure event (the player has won all the money).

With regard to this problem, the following questions are of interest:

(a) Given that one gambler is in a nonabsorbing state, what is the expected number of times that he will hold between $1 and $4 inclusive before the termination of the game? That is, on the average, how many times will the process be in nonabsorbing states?
(b) What is the expected length of the process (game)?
(c) What is the probability that an absorbing state is reached (that is, that one gambler will eventually be wiped out)?

To answer the above questions, let's look at the transition matrix P. Rearrange this matrix so that the two absorbing states will appear in the first 2 rows:

$$
P = \begin{array}{c} \\ 0 \\ 5 \\ 1 \\ 2 \\ 3 \\ 4 \end{array}
\begin{array}{cccccc}
0 & 5 & 1 & 2 & 3 & 4 \\
\left[\begin{array}{cc:cccc}
1 & 0 & 0 & 0 & 0 & 0 \\
0 & 1 & 0 & 0 & 0 & 0 \\ \hdashline
\frac{1}{2} & 0 & 0 & \frac{1}{2} & 0 & 0 \\
0 & 0 & \frac{1}{2} & 0 & \frac{1}{2} & 0 \\
0 & 0 & 0 & \frac{1}{2} & 0 & \frac{1}{2} \\
0 & \frac{1}{2} & 0 & 0 & \frac{1}{2} & 0
\end{array}\right]
\end{array}
$$

If we let I_2, **0**, S, and Q denote the matrices

$$I_2 = \begin{bmatrix} 1 & 0 \\ 0 & 1 \end{bmatrix} \qquad \mathbf{0} = \begin{bmatrix} 0 & 0 & 0 & 0 \\ 0 & 0 & 0 & 0 \end{bmatrix}$$

$$S = \begin{bmatrix} \frac{1}{2} & 0 \\ 0 & 0 \\ 0 & 0 \\ 0 & \frac{1}{2} \end{bmatrix} \qquad Q = \begin{bmatrix} 0 & \frac{1}{2} & 0 & 0 \\ \frac{1}{2} & 0 & \frac{1}{2} & 0 \\ 0 & \frac{1}{2} & 0 & \frac{1}{2} \\ 0 & 0 & \frac{1}{2} & 0 \end{bmatrix}$$

we can rewrite the matrix P in shorthand notation as

$$P = \left[\begin{array}{c|c} I_2 & \mathbf{0} \\ \hline S & Q \end{array} \right]$$

Note that the above technique can be applied to any matrix representing an absorbing Markov chain. If r of the states are absorbing, the transition matrix P can be written as

$$P = \left[\begin{array}{c|c} I_r & \mathbf{0} \\ \hline S & Q \end{array} \right]$$

where I_r is the $r \times r$ identity matrix, **0** is the zero matrix of dimension $r \times s$, S is of dimension $s \times r$, and Q is of dimension $s \times s$.

In order to answer the questions raised about the data of the gambler's ruin problem, we need the following result:

For an absorbing Markov chain that has a transition matrix P of the form

$$P = \left[\begin{array}{c|c} I_r & \mathbf{0} \\ \hline S & Q \end{array} \right]$$

where S is of dimension $s \times r$ and Q is of dimension $s \times s$, define the matrix T as

(1)
$$T = [I_s - Q]^{-1}$$

The entries of T give the expected number of times the process is in each nonabsorbing state, provided the process began in a nonabsorbing state.

Fundamental Matrix

The matrix T given in (1) is called the *fundamental matrix* of an absorbing Markov chain.

In the gambler's ruin problem, the fundamental matrix T is

$$T = \left[\begin{bmatrix} 1 & 0 & 0 & 0 \\ 0 & 1 & 0 & 0 \\ 0 & 0 & 1 & 0 \\ 0 & 0 & 0 & 1 \end{bmatrix} - \begin{bmatrix} 0 & \frac{1}{2} & 0 & 0 \\ \frac{1}{2} & 0 & \frac{1}{2} & 0 \\ 0 & \frac{1}{2} & 0 & \frac{1}{2} \\ 0 & 0 & \frac{1}{2} & 0 \end{bmatrix} \right]^{-1} = \begin{array}{c} \\ 1 \\ 2 \\ 3 \\ 4 \end{array} \begin{array}{cccc} 1 & 2 & 3 & 4 \\ \begin{bmatrix} 1.6 & 1.2 & .8 & .4 \\ 1.2 & 2.4 & 1.6 & .8 \\ .8 & 1.6 & 2.4 & 1.2 \\ .4 & .8 & 1.2 & 1.6 \end{bmatrix} \end{array}$$

This provides the answers to question (a). The entry .8 in row 3, column 1, indicates that .8 is the expected number of times the player will have \$1 if he started with \$3. In the fundamental matrix T, the column headings indicate present money, while the row headings indicate money started with.

The expected number of steps before absorption for each nonabsorbing state is found by adding the entries in the corresponding row of the fundamental matrix T.

To answer question (b), we again look at the fundamental matrix T. The expected number of games before absorption (when one of the players wins or loses all the money) can be found by adding the entries in each row of T. Thus, if a player starts with \$3, the expected number of games before absorption is

$$.8 + 1.6 + 2.4 + 1.2 = 6.0$$

If a player starts with \$1, the expected number of games before absorption is

$$1.6 + 1.2 + .8 + .4 = 4.0$$

To answer question (c), we find the product of the matrices T and S:

$$T \cdot S = \begin{bmatrix} 1.6 & 1.2 & .8 & .4 \\ 1.2 & 2.4 & 1.6 & .8 \\ .8 & 1.6 & 2.4 & 1.2 \\ .4 & .8 & 1.2 & 1.6 \end{bmatrix} \begin{bmatrix} \frac{1}{2} & 0 \\ 0 & 0 \\ 0 & 0 \\ 0 & \frac{1}{2} \end{bmatrix} = \begin{array}{c} \\ 1 \\ 2 \\ 3 \\ 4 \end{array} \begin{array}{c} \begin{array}{cc} 0 & 5 \end{array} \\ \begin{bmatrix} .8 & .2 \\ .6 & .4 \\ .4 & .6 \\ .2 & .8 \end{bmatrix} \end{array}$$

The entry in row 3, column 2, indicates the probability is .6 that the player starting with \$3 will win all the money. The entry in row 2, column 1, indicates the probability is .6 that a player starting with \$2 will lose all his money.

The entries in $T \cdot S = [p_{ir}]$ represent the probability that an absorbing state is reached if it starts in a nonabsorbing state i. The index r represents the number of absorbing states.

The above techniques are applicable in general to any transition matrix P of an absorbing Markov chain. Also, note the similarity between the fundamental matrix T of an absorbing Markov chain and the matrix T of the social mobility model (page 333), which gives the average time spent in a social class.

In the gambler's ruin problem, we assumed Player I started with \$3 and Player II with \$2. Furthermore, we assumed the probability of Player I winning \$1 was .5.

Table 3

Probability That Player Wins	Amount of Units Player I Starts with	Amount of Units Player II Starts with	Probability That Player I Goes Broke	Expected Length of Game	Expected Gain of Player I
.50	9	1	.1	9	0
.50	90	10	.1	900	0
.50	900	100	.1	90,000	0
.50	8000	2000	.2	16,000,000	0
.45	9	1	.210	11	−1.1
.45	90	10	.866	765.6	−76.6
.45	99	1	.182	171.8	−17.2
.40	90	10	.983	441.3	−88.3
.40	99	1	.333	161.7	−32.3

Table 3 gives probabilities for ruin and expected length for other kinds of betting situations for which the bet is 1 unit.

Suppose, for example, that Player I starts with $90 and Player II with $10, with Player I having a probability of .45 of winning (the game being unfavorable to Player I). If at each trial, the stake is $1, Table 3 shows that the probability is .866 that Player I is ruined. If the same game is played for a stake of $10, the probability that Player I is ruined drops to .210. Thus, the effect of raising the stakes even in unfavorable games is very pronounced.

Exercise 3
Solutions to Odd-Numbered Problems begin on page 599.

In Problems 1–6 state which of the given matrices are absorbing Markov chains.

1. $\begin{bmatrix} 0 & 1 \\ \frac{1}{4} & \frac{3}{4} \end{bmatrix}$

2. $\begin{bmatrix} 1 & 0 \\ \frac{1}{3} & \frac{2}{3} \end{bmatrix}$

3. $\begin{bmatrix} 1 & 0 & 0 \\ \frac{1}{8} & \frac{5}{8} & \frac{2}{8} \\ 0 & 0 & 1 \end{bmatrix}$

4. $\begin{bmatrix} 0 & 0 & 1 \\ 1 & 0 & 0 \\ 0 & 1 & 0 \end{bmatrix}$

5. $\begin{bmatrix} 0 & 1 & 0 & 0 \\ 1 & 0 & 0 & 0 \\ 0 & 0 & 1 & 0 \\ \frac{1}{4} & 0 & \frac{3}{4} & 0 \end{bmatrix}$

6. $\begin{bmatrix} \frac{1}{3} & \frac{1}{3} & 0 & \frac{1}{3} \\ 0 & \frac{1}{4} & \frac{1}{2} & \frac{1}{4} \\ 0 & 0 & 1 & 0 \\ 0 & \frac{1}{2} & 0 & \frac{1}{2} \end{bmatrix}$

7. Find the fundamental matrix T of the absorbing Markov chain in Problem 3. Also, find S and $T \cdot S$.
8. Follow the directions of Problem 7 for the matrix in Problem 6.
9. Suppose that for a certain absorbing Markov chain the fundamental matrix T is found to be

$$
\begin{array}{c c c c}
 & \$1 & \$2 & \$3 \\
\$1 & \begin{bmatrix} 1.5 & .5 & .8 \\ \$2 & 1.2 & 2.3 & .6 \\ \$3 & .3 & 1.8 & 2.1 \end{bmatrix}
\end{array}
$$

(a) What is the expected number of times a person will have $3 given that he started with $1? With $2?
(b) If a player starts with $3, how many games can he expect to play before absorption?

10. For the data in Problem 9, suppose that we are given the following matrix S:

$$
S = \begin{bmatrix} \frac{1}{2} & 0 \\ 0 & 0 \\ 0 & \frac{1}{2} \end{bmatrix}
$$

What is the probability that the player will be absorbed if he started with $3?

11. *Gambler's Ruin Problem.* A person repeatedly bets $1 each day. If he wins, he wins $1 (he receives his bet of $1 plus winnings of $1). He stops playing when he goes broke, or when he accumulates $3. His probability of winning is .4 and of losing is .6. What is the probability of eventually accumulating $3 if he starts with $1? With $2?

12. The following data were obtained from the admissions office of a 2-year junior college. Of the first-year class (*F*), 75% became sophomores (*S*) the next year and 25% dropped out (*D*). Of those who were sophomores during a particular year, 90% graduated (*G*) by the following year and 10% dropped out.
    (a) Set up a Markov chain with states *D*, *F*, *G*, and *S* which describes the situation.
    (b) How many are absorbing?
    (c) Determine the matrix *T*.
    (d) Determine the probability that an entering first-year student will eventually graduate.

13. *Gambler's Ruin Problem.* Marsha wants to purchase a $4000 used car, but only has $1000 available. Not wishing to finance the purchase, she makes a series of wagers in which the winnings equal whatever is bet. The probability of winning is .4 and the probability of losing is .6. In a daring strategy Marsha decides to bet all her money or at least enough to obtain $4000 until she loses everything or has $4000. That is, if she has $1000, she bets $1000; if she has $2000, she bets $2000.
    (a) What is the expected number of wagers placed before the game ends?
    (b) What is the probability that Marsha is wiped out?
    (c) What is the probability that Marsha wins the amount needed to purchase the car?

14. Answer the questions in Problem 13 if the probability of winning is .5.

15. Answer the questions in Problem 13 if the probability of winning is .6.

16. Three armored cars, *A*, *B*, and *C*, are engaged in a three-way battle. Armored car *A* has probability $\frac{1}{3}$ of destroying its target, *B* has probability $\frac{1}{2}$ of destroying its target, and *C* has probability $\frac{1}{6}$ of destroying its target. The armored cars fire at the same time and each fires at the strongest opponent not yet destroyed. Using as states the surviving cars at any round, set up a Markov chain and answer the following questions:
    (a) How many states are in this chain?
    (b) How many are absorbing?
    (c) Find the expected number of rounds fired.
    (d) Find the probability that *A* survives.

*4. An Application to Genetics

Most of this section is based on the work of Gregor Mendel. The Mendelian theory of genetics states that many traits of an offspring are determined by the genes of the parents. Each parent has a pair of genes and the basic assumption of Mendel's theory is that the offspring inherits one gene from each parent in a random, independent way.

Dominant
Recessive

Homozygous
Heterozygous

In the most simple cases genes are of two types: *dominant,* denoted by A, and *recessive,* denoted by a. There are four possible pairings of the two types of genes: AA, Aa, aA, and aa. However, genetically, the two genotypes Aa and aA are the same. An individual having the genotype AA is called *dominant* or *homozygous;* an individual with the genotype Aa is called *hybrid* or *heterozygous;* and one with the genotype aa is called *recessive.*

Let's consider some of the possibilities. If both parents are dominant (homozygous), their offspring must be dominant (homozygous); if both parents are recessive, their offspring are recessive; and if one parent is dominant (homozygous) and one recessive, their offspring are hybrid (heterozygous).

If one parent is dominant (AA) and the other is hybrid (Aa), the offspring must get a dominant gene A from the dominant parent and either a dominant gene A or a recessive gene a from the hybrid parent. In this case, the probability is $\frac{1}{2}$ that the offspring will be dominant (AA) and the probability is $\frac{1}{2}$ that the offspring will be hybrid (Aa).

Similarly, if one parent is recessive (aa) and the other is hybrid (Aa), the probability is $\frac{1}{2}$ that the offspring will be recessive (aa) and is $\frac{1}{2}$ that the offspring will be hybrid (Aa).

If both parents are hybrid (heterozygous), the offspring have equal probability of getting a dominant gene or recessive gene from each parent. Thus, the probability that the offspring will be dominant (homozygous) is $\frac{1}{4}$; recessive, $\frac{1}{4}$; and hybrid (heterozygous), $\frac{1}{2}$. See Figure 5.

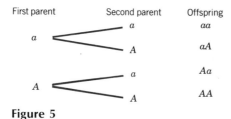

First parent   Second parent   Offspring

a — a → aa
a — A → aA

A — a → Aa
A — A → AA

Figure 5

Example 1 Suppose we start with one parent whose genotype is unknown and another whose genotype is known, say hybrid (heterozygous). Their offspring is mated with a person whose genotype is hybrid (heterozygous). This mating procedure is continued. In the long run, what is the genotype of the offspring?

GREGOR JOHANN MENDEL (1822–1884), an Austrian monk, discovered the first laws of heredity and thereby laid the foundation for the science of genetics. For many years, Mendel taught science in the technical high school at Brunn, Austria, without a teacher's license. The reason—he failed the *biology* portion of the license examination!

*This section may be omitted without loss of continuity.

Solution   Since the genotype of an offspring depends solely on the genotype of the parents, such a mating process is an example of a Markov chain. Label the possible states in the process by D (dominant), H (hybrid), and R (recessive). The transition matrix P is

(1)
$$
\begin{array}{c}
\begin{array}{ccc} D & H & R \end{array} \\
P = \begin{array}{c} D \\ H \\ R \end{array}\left[\begin{array}{ccc} \frac{1}{2} & \frac{1}{2} & 0 \\ \frac{1}{4} & \frac{1}{2} & \frac{1}{4} \\ 0 & \frac{1}{2} & \frac{1}{2} \end{array}\right]
\end{array}
$$

The entries of P are obtained as follows: The first row $[\frac{1}{2} \ \frac{1}{2} \ 0]$ of P gives the probabilities that the offspring will be D, H, R, respectively, when the unknown parent is dominant (AA); the second row $[\frac{1}{4} \ \frac{1}{2} \ \frac{1}{4}]$ of P gives the probabilities that the offspring will be D, H, R, respectively, when the unknown parent is hybrid (Aa); the third row $[0 \ \frac{1}{2} \ \frac{1}{2}]$ of P gives probabilities that the offspring will be D, H, R, respectively, when the unknown parent is recessive (aa).

Now, P is regular since the entries of P^2 are all positive:

$$
P^2 = \left[\begin{array}{ccc} \frac{3}{8} & \frac{1}{2} & \frac{1}{8} \\ \frac{1}{4} & \frac{1}{2} & \frac{1}{4} \\ \frac{1}{8} & \frac{1}{2} & \frac{3}{8} \end{array}\right]
$$

The fixed probability vector of P is found to be

(2)
$$
\mathbf{t} = [\tfrac{1}{4} \ \tfrac{1}{2} \ \tfrac{1}{4}]
$$

Thus, in the long run, no matter what the genotype of the unknown parent, the probability that the genotype of the offspring will be dominant (homozygous) is $\frac{1}{4}$; hybrid (heterozygous), $\frac{1}{2}$; and recessive, $\frac{1}{4}$. ∎

Example 2
Brother–
Sister Mating
Problem

In the so-called *brother–sister mating model,* two individuals are mated, and, from among their direct descendants, two individuals of opposite sex are selected at random. These are mated, and the process continues indefinitely. With three possible genotypes, AA, Aa, aa, for each parent, we have to distinguish six combinations of offspring as follows:

$$
\begin{array}{lll}
E_1: \ AA \times AA & E_2: \ AA \times Aa & E_3: \ Aa \times Aa \\
E_4: \ Aa \times aa & E_5: \ aa \times aa & E_6: \ AA \times aa
\end{array}
$$

where, for example, $E_4: \ Aa \times aa$ indicates the mating of a hybrid (Aa) with a recessive (aa). The transition matrix for this experiment is

(3)
$$
\begin{array}{c}
\begin{array}{cccccc} E_1 & E_2 & E_3 & E_4 & E_5 & E_6 \end{array} \\
\begin{array}{c} E_1 \\ E_2 \\ E_3 \\ E_4 \\ E_5 \\ E_6 \end{array}\left[\begin{array}{cccccc}
1 & 0 & 0 & 0 & 0 & 0 \\
\frac{1}{4} & \frac{1}{2} & \frac{1}{4} & 0 & 0 & 0 \\
\frac{1}{16} & \frac{1}{4} & \frac{1}{4} & \frac{1}{4} & \frac{1}{16} & \frac{1}{8} \\
0 & 0 & \frac{1}{4} & \frac{1}{2} & \frac{1}{4} & 0 \\
0 & 0 & 0 & 0 & 1 & 0 \\
0 & 0 & 1 & 0 & 0 & 0
\end{array}\right]
\end{array}
$$

We obtain the entries in (3) using the following reasoning: States E_1 and E_5 both have 1 on the diagonal and 0 for all other elements in the same row, since crossing two dominants (homozygous) always yields a dominant (homozygous); likewise, crossing two recessives always yields a recessive. When the process is in one of the other states, say row E_3, we have

$$E_3: \quad Aa \times Aa \qquad P(AA) = \tfrac{1}{4} \qquad P(aA) = \tfrac{1}{2} \qquad P(aa) = \tfrac{1}{4}$$

$$\begin{aligned}
E_1: & \quad AA \times AA & \tfrac{1}{4} \times \tfrac{1}{4} = \tfrac{1}{16} \\
E_2: & \quad AA \times Aa & 2 \times \tfrac{1}{4} \times \tfrac{1}{2} = \tfrac{1}{4} \\
E_3: & \quad Aa \times Aa & \tfrac{1}{2} \times \tfrac{1}{2} = \tfrac{1}{4} \\
E_4: & \quad Aa \times aa & 2 \times \tfrac{1}{2} \times \tfrac{1}{4} = \tfrac{1}{4} \\
E_5: & \quad aa \times aa & \tfrac{1}{4} \times \tfrac{1}{4} = \tfrac{1}{16} \\
E_6: & \quad AA \times aa & 2 \times \tfrac{1}{4} \times \tfrac{1}{4} = \tfrac{1}{8}
\end{aligned}$$

The process described above is an example of an absorbing Markov chain. The states E_1 and E_5 are absorbing states.

Now, let's perform the same calculations for the transition matrix in (3) as we did for the gambler's ruin problem in Section 3. The transition matrix P is rewritten as follows:

$$P = \begin{array}{c} \\ E_1 \\ E_5 \\ E_2 \\ E_3 \\ E_4 \\ E_6 \end{array}
\begin{array}{c} \begin{array}{cccccc} E_1 & E_5 & E_2 & E_3 & E_4 & E_6 \end{array} \\
\left[\begin{array}{cc|cccc}
1 & 0 & 0 & 0 & 0 & 0 \\
0 & 1 & 0 & 0 & 0 & 0 \\ \hline
\tfrac{1}{4} & 0 & \tfrac{1}{2} & \tfrac{1}{4} & 0 & 0 \\
\tfrac{1}{16} & \tfrac{1}{16} & \tfrac{1}{4} & \tfrac{1}{4} & \tfrac{1}{4} & \tfrac{1}{8} \\
0 & \tfrac{1}{4} & 0 & \tfrac{1}{4} & \tfrac{1}{2} & 0 \\
0 & 0 & 0 & 1 & 0 & 0
\end{array} \right] \end{array}
= \left[\begin{array}{c|c} I_2 & \mathbf{0} \\ \hline S & Q \end{array} \right]$$

where the matrices I_2, $\mathbf{0}$, S, and Q are

$$I_2 = \begin{bmatrix} 1 & 0 \\ 0 & 1 \end{bmatrix} \qquad \mathbf{0} = \begin{bmatrix} 0 & 0 & 0 & 0 \\ 0 & 0 & 0 & 0 \end{bmatrix}$$

$$S = \begin{bmatrix} \tfrac{1}{4} & 0 \\ \tfrac{1}{16} & \tfrac{1}{16} \\ 0 & \tfrac{1}{4} \\ 0 & 0 \end{bmatrix} \qquad Q = \begin{bmatrix} \tfrac{1}{2} & \tfrac{1}{4} & 0 & 0 \\ \tfrac{1}{4} & \tfrac{1}{4} & \tfrac{1}{4} & \tfrac{1}{8} \\ 0 & \tfrac{1}{4} & \tfrac{1}{2} & 0 \\ 0 & 1 & 0 & 0 \end{bmatrix}$$

The fundamental matrix T is

$$T = [I_4 - Q]^{-1} = \begin{array}{c} \\ E_2 \\ E_3 \\ E_4 \\ E_6 \end{array}
\begin{array}{c} \begin{array}{cccc} E_2 & E_3 & E_4 & E_6 \end{array} \\
\left[\begin{array}{cccc}
\tfrac{8}{3} & \tfrac{4}{3} & \tfrac{2}{3} & \tfrac{1}{6} \\
\tfrac{4}{3} & \tfrac{8}{3} & \tfrac{4}{3} & \tfrac{1}{3} \\
\tfrac{2}{3} & \tfrac{4}{3} & \tfrac{8}{3} & \tfrac{1}{6} \\
\tfrac{4}{3} & \tfrac{8}{3} & \tfrac{4}{3} & \tfrac{4}{3}
\end{array} \right] \end{array}$$

The product of the fundamental matrix and S is

$$
T \cdot S =
\begin{bmatrix}
\frac{8}{3} & \frac{4}{3} & \frac{2}{3} & \frac{1}{6} \\
\frac{4}{3} & \frac{8}{3} & \frac{4}{3} & \frac{1}{3} \\
\frac{2}{3} & \frac{4}{3} & \frac{8}{3} & \frac{1}{6} \\
\frac{4}{3} & \frac{8}{3} & \frac{4}{3} & \frac{4}{3}
\end{bmatrix}
\begin{bmatrix}
\frac{1}{4} & 0 \\
\frac{1}{16} & \frac{1}{16} \\
0 & \frac{1}{4} \\
0 & 0
\end{bmatrix}
=
\begin{array}{c}
 \\ E_2 \\ E_3 \\ E_4 \\ E_6
\end{array}
\begin{matrix}
E_1 & E_5 \\
\begin{bmatrix}
\frac{3}{4} & \frac{1}{4} \\
\frac{1}{2} & \frac{1}{2} \\
\frac{1}{4} & \frac{3}{4} \\
\frac{1}{2} & \frac{1}{2}
\end{bmatrix}
\end{matrix}
$$

Genetically, the matrix $T \cdot S$ can be interpreted to mean that after a large number of inbred matings, a person is either in state E_1 or state E_5. That is, only pure genotypes remain, while the mixed genotype (hybrid heterozygous) will disappear. Notice also that if one starts in the state E_4: $Aa \times aa$, which has 3 recessive genes and 1 dominant gene, the probability for ending up in the state E_1: $AA \times AA$ is $\frac{1}{4}$, which is the ratio of dominant genes to total genes.

From the fundamental matrix, we can find the expected number of generations needed to pass from a nonabsorbing state to either absorbing state. Thus, the expected number of generations needed to pass from E_3 to either E_1 or E_5 is

$$
\frac{4}{3} + \frac{8}{3} + \frac{4}{3} + \frac{1}{3} = \frac{17}{3} = 5\frac{2}{3}
$$

■

Finally, consider a genetic experiment in which a large population is randomly mated. We assume that males and females have the same proportion of each genotype and that male and female offspring are equally likely to occur. It would seem a logical conclusion of Mendel's law that after a large number of matings, the recessive genotype must disappear. However, the mere fact that recessive genotypes continue to exist implies that this is not the case. This seeming discrepancy in the theory was resolved early in the twentieth century, by the famous mathematician G. H. Hardy who proved that the proportion of genotypes in a population stabilizes after one generation.*

Exercise 4
Solutions to Odd-Numbered Problems begin on page 600.

1. In Example 1, prove that the fixed probability vector **t** for the transition matrix P of (1) is given by (2).
2. *Mating Problem.* In Example 1, suppose the known genotype is dominant (homozygous) and each offspring is mated with a person having a dominant (homozygous) genotype.
   (a) Find the transition matrix P.
   (b) Find the fixed probability vector. Interpret the answer.

G. H. HARDY (1877–1947), an English mathematician, is credited with the discovery in 1908 of the Hardy–Weinberg law in genetics. He published many brilliant articles in number theory as well.

*G. H. Hardy, "Mendelian Proportions in a Mixed Population," *Science*, N.S. **28** (1908), pp. 49–50.

(c) Find the fundamental matrix T.

(d) What is the expected number of generations needed to pass from each nonabsorbing stage?

3. Answer the same questions given in Problem 2 if the known genotype is recessive.

Chapter Review

Markov chain
initial state
initial probability distribution
transition matrix
transition probability
stochastic matrix
regular Markov chain

fixed probability vector
equilibrium state
equilibrium distribution
absorbing state
absorbing Markov chain
fundamental matrix

Review Exercises

Solutions to Odd-Numbered Problems begin on page 600.

1. Find the fixed probability vector of:

(a) $\begin{bmatrix} \frac{1}{4} & \frac{3}{4} \\ \frac{1}{2} & \frac{1}{2} \end{bmatrix}$

(b) $\begin{bmatrix} \frac{1}{3} & \frac{2}{3} \\ \frac{2}{3} & \frac{1}{3} \end{bmatrix}$

2. Define and explain in words the meaning of a *regular stochastic matrix*. Give an example of such a matrix and of a matrix that is not regular.

3. *Customer Loyalty.* Three beer distributors, A, B, and C, each presently holds $\frac{1}{3}$ of the beer market. Each wants to increase its share of the market, and to do so, each introduces a new brand. During the next year, it is learned that:

(a) A keeps 50% of its business and loses 20% to B and 30% to C.

(b) B keeps 40% of its business and loses 40% to A and 20% to C.

(c) C keeps 25% of its business and loses 50% to A and 25% to B.

Assuming this trend continues, after 2 years what share of the market does each distributor have? In the long-run, what is each distributor's share?

4. If the current share of the market for each beer distributor A, B, and C in Problem 3, is A: 25%, B: 25%, C: 50%, and the market trend is the same, answer the same questions.

5. A representative of a book publishing company has to cover three universities, U_1, U_2, and U_3. She never sells at the same university in successive months. If she sells at University U_1, then the next month she sells at U_2. However, if she sells at either U_2 or U_3, then the next month she is three times as likely to sell at U_1 as at the other university. In the long run, how often does she sell at each of the universities?

6. *Family Traits*: Assume that the probability of a fat father having a fat son is .7 and that of a skinny father having a skinny son is .4. What is the probability of a fat father being the great grandfather of a fat great grandson? In the long run, what will be the distribution? Does it depend on the initial physical state of the fathers?

7. *Gambler's Ruin Problem.* Suppose a man has $2, which he is going to bet $1 at a time until he either loses all his money or he wins $5. Assume he wins with a probability of .45 and he loses with a probability of .55. Construct the transition probability for this game and answer the questions as stated on page 337 in Section 3. *Hint:* The fundamental matrix T of the transition matrix P is

$$T = \begin{bmatrix} 1.584282 & 1.062331 & .635281 & .285876 \\ 1.298405 & 2.360736 & 1.411736 & .635281 \\ .94899 & 1.725454 & 2.360736 & 1.062331 \\ .52194 & .949000 & 1.298405 & 1.584281 \end{bmatrix}$$

Other Books and Articles

Bourne, Larry S., "Physical Adjustment Process and Land Use Succession: A Conceptual Review and Central City Example," *Econ. Geogr.* **47** (1971), pp. 1–15.

Bower, Gordon H., "Application of a Model to Paired-Associate Learning," *Psychometrika,* **26,** 3 (September 1961), pp. 255–280.

Cohen, Bernard P., "A Probability Model for Conformity," *Sociometry,* **21** (1958), pp. 69–81.

Cohen, Bernard P., *Conflict and Conformity: A Probability Model and Its Application.* MIT Press, Cambridge, Mass., 1963.

Cyert, R. M., H. J. Davidson, and G. L. Thompson, "Estimation of the Allowance for Doubtful Accounts by Markov Chains," *Manage. Sci.,* **8,** 3 (April 1962), pp. 287–303.

Hampton, P., "Regional Economic Development in New Zealand," *J. Reg. Sci.,* **8,** 1 (1968), pp. 41–51.

Hoffman, Hans, "Markov Chains in Ethiopia," in Paul Kay, ed., *Explorations in Mathematical Anthropology,* MIT Press, Cambridge, Mass., 1971.

Hunter, Albert, "Community Change: A Stochastic Analysis of Chicago's Local Communities, 1930–1960," *Amer. J. Sociol.,* **79** (January 1974), pp. 923–947.

Kemeny, John G., and J. Laurie Snell, *Mathematical Models in the Social Sciences,* Blaisdell, New York, 1962.

Mosimann, J., *Elementary Probability for the Biological Sciences,* Prentice-Hall, Englewood Cliffs, N.J., 1968.

9
Applications to Games of Strategy

1. Introduction

Game theory, as a branch of mathematics, is a relatively new field. It is concerned with the analysis of human behavior in conflicts of interest. In other words, game theory gives mathematical expression to the strategies of opposing players and offers techniques for choosing the best possible strategy. In most parlor games, it is relatively easy to define winning and losing and, on this basis, to quantify the best strategy for each player. However, game theory is not merely a tool for the gambler, so that he or she can take advantage of the odds, nor is it merely a method for winning games like tic-tac-toe, matching pennies, or the Italian game called *Morra* (described in Section 3).

Gottfried Wilhelm von Leibniz is generally recognized as being the first to see the relationship between games of strategy and the theory of social behavior. For example, when union and management sit down at the bargaining table to discuss contracts, each has definite strategies open to him. Each will bluff, persuade, and try to discover the other's strategy, while at the same time trying to prevent the discovery of his own. If enough information is known, results from the theory of games can determine what is the best possible rational behavior or the best possible strategy for each player. Another application of game theory can be made to politics. If two people are vying for the same political office, each has open to him various campaign strategies. If it is possible to determine the impact of alternate strategies on the voters, the theory of games can be used to find the best strategy (usually the one that gains the most votes, while losing the least votes). Thus, game theory can be used in certain situations of conflict to indicate how people should behave to achieve certain goals. Of course, game theory does not tell us how people actually behave. Game theory is the study, then, of rational behavior in conflict situations.

Two-Person Game **Any conflict or competition between two people is called a** *two-person game.*

Let's consider some examples of two-person games.

Example 1 In a game similar to matching pennies, Player I picks heads or tails and Player II attempts to guess the choice. Player I will pay Player II $3 if both choose heads; Player I will pay Player II $2 if both choose tails. If Player II guesses incorrectly, he will pay Player I $5.

∎

We use Example 1 to illustrate some terminology. First, since two players are involved, this is a two-person game. Next, notice that no matter what outcome occurs (*HH, HT, TH, TT*), whatever is lost (or gained) by Player I is gained (or Zero-Sum Games lost) by Player II. Such games are called *two-person zero-sum games.*

GOTTFRIED WILHELM von LEIBNIZ (1646–1716) is credited with the development of differential and integral calculus. He was a philosopher, lawyer, theologian, and historian and wrote in several languages. His later years were clouded by a controversy over who first discovered calculus, Leibniz or Newton. In fact, both men should be credited since each discovered calculus by different means.

If we denote the gains of Player I by positive entries and his losses by negative entries, we can display this game in a 2×2 matrix as

$$\begin{array}{cc} & H \quad\ \ T \\ \begin{array}{c} H \\ T \end{array} & \begin{bmatrix} -3 & 5 \\ 5 & -2 \end{bmatrix} \end{array}$$

Payoff
Game Matrix

Each entry a_{ij} of a matrix game is termed a *payoff* and the matrix is called the *game matrix* or *payoff matrix*.

Conversely, any $m \times n$ matrix $A = [a_{ij}]$ can be regarded as the game matrix for a two-person zero-sum game in which Player I chooses any one of the m rows of A and simultaneously Player II chooses any one of the n columns of A. The entry in the row and column chosen is the payoff.

We will assume that the game is played repeatedly, and that the problem facing each player is what choice he should make so that he gains the most benefit. Thus, Player I wishes to maximize his winnings and Player II wishes to minimize his losses. By a strategy of Player I for a given matrix game A, we mean the decision by Player I to select rows of A in some manner.

Example 2

Consider a two-person zero-sum game given by the matrix

$$\begin{bmatrix} 3 & 6 \\ -2 & -3 \end{bmatrix}$$

in which the entries denote the winnings of Player I. The game consists of Player I choosing a row and Player II simultaneously choosing a column, with the intersection of row and column giving the payoff for this play in the game. For example, if Player I chooses row 1 and Player II chooses column 2, then Player I wins $6; if Player I chooses row 2 and Player II chooses column 1, then Player I loses $2.

It is immediately evident from the matrix that this particular game is biased in favor of Player I, who will always choose row 1 since he cannot lose by doing so. Similarly, Player II, recognizing that Player I will choose row 1 will always choose column 1, since his losses are then minimized.

Best Strategy

Thus, the *best strategy* for Player I is row 1 and the *best strategy* for Player II is column 1. When both players employ their best strategy, the result is that Player I wins $3. This amount is called the *value* of the game. Notice that the payoff $3 is the minimum of the entries in its row and is the maximum of the entries in its column.

Strictly Determined Game **A game defined by a matrix is said to be** *strictly determined* **if and only if there is an entry of the matrix that is the smallest element in its row and is also the largest element in its column. This entry is then called a** *saddle point* **and is the** *value* **of the game.**

Fair Game

If a game has a positive value, the game favors Player I. If a game has a negative value, the game favors Player II. Any game with a value of 0 is termed a *fair game*.

Pure Strategy

If a matrix game has a saddle point, it can be shown that the row containing the saddle point is the best strategy for Player I and the column containing the saddle point is the best strategy for Player II. This is why such games are called *strictly determined games*. Such games are also called games of *pure strategy*.

Of course, a matrix may have more than one saddle point, in which case each player has more than one best strategy available. However, the value of the game is always the same no matter how many saddle points the matrix may have. See Problem 12 in Exercise 1.

Example 3   Determine whether the game defined by the matrix below is strictly determined.

$$\begin{bmatrix} 3 & 0 & -2 & -1 \\ 2 & -3 & 0 & -1 \\ 4 & 2 & 1 & 0 \end{bmatrix}$$

Solution   First, we look at each row and find the smallest entry in each row:

$$\text{Row 1:} \quad -2 \qquad \text{Row 2:} \quad -3 \qquad \text{Row 3:} \quad 0$$

Next, we check to see if any of the above elements are also the largest in their column. The element -2 in row 1 is not the largest entry in column 3; the element -3 in row 2 is not the largest entry in column 2; however, the element 0 in row 3 is the largest entry in column 4. Thus, this game is strictly determined. Its value is 0 so the game is fair.

∎

The game of Example 3 is represented by a 3×4 matrix. This means that Player I has 3 strategies open to him, while Player II can choose from 4 strategies.

Example 4   Two franchising firms, Alpha Products and Omega Industries, are each planning to add an outlet in a certain city. It is possible for the site to be located either in the center of the city or in a large suburb of the city. If both firms decide to build in the center of the city, Alpha Products will show an annual profit of $1000 more than the profit of Omega Industries. If both firms decide to locate their outlet in the suburb, then it is determined that Alpha Products' profit will be $2000 less than the profit of Omega Industries. If Alpha locates in the suburb and Omega in the city, then Alpha will show a profit of $4000 more than Omega. Finally, if Alpha locates in the city and Omega in the suburb, then Alpha will have a profit of $3000 less than Omega's. Is there a best site for each firm to locate its franchise? In this case, by *best site* we mean the one that produces the most competition against the other firm—not the site that produces the highest gross sales. Of course, someone else may well have a different interpretation of what constitutes the best site.

Solution   If we assign rows as Alpha strategies and columns as Omega strategies and if we use positive entries to denote the gain of Alpha over Omega and negative entries for the gain of Omega over Alpha, then the matrix game for this situation is

Omega

$$\text{Alpha} \quad \begin{array}{cc} & \begin{array}{cc} \text{City} & \text{Suburb} \end{array} \\ \begin{array}{c} \text{City} \\ \text{Suburb} \end{array} & \begin{bmatrix} 1 & -3 \\ 4 & -2 \end{bmatrix} \end{array}$$

where the entries are in thousands of dollars.

This game is strictly determined and the saddle point is -2, which is the value of the game. Thus, if both firms locate in the suburb, this results in the best competition. This is so since Omega will always choose to locate in the suburb, guaranteeing a larger profit than Alpha. This being the case, Alpha, in order to minimize this larger profit of Omega, must always choose the suburb. Of course, the game is not fair since it is favorable to Omega. ∎

Exercise 1
Solutions to Odd-Numbered Problems begin on page 601.

In Problems 1–4 write the matrix game that corresponds to each two-person conflict situation.

1. Tami and Laura simultaneously each show one or two fingers. If they show the same number of fingers, Tami pays Laura one dime. If they show a different number of fingers, Laura pays Tami one dime.
2. Tami and Laura simultaneously each show one or two fingers. If the total number of fingers shown is even, Tami pays Laura that number of dimes. If the total number of fingers shown is odd, Laura pays Tami that number of dimes.
3. Tami and Laura, simultaneously and independently, each write down one of the numbers 1, 4, or 7. If the sum of the numbers is even, Tami pays Laura that number of dimes. If the sum of the numbers is odd, Laura pays Tami that number of dimes.
4. Tami and Laura, simultaneously and independently, each write down one of the numbers 3, 6, or 8. If the sum of the numbers is even, Tami pays Laura that number of dimes. If the sum of the numbers is odd, Laura pays Tami that number of dimes.

In Problems 5–14 determine which of the two-person, zero-sum games are strictly determined. For those that are, find the value of the game. All entries are the winnings of Player I, who plays rows.

5. $\begin{bmatrix} -1 & 2 \\ -3 & 6 \end{bmatrix}$ 6. $\begin{bmatrix} 4 & 0 \\ 0 & -1 \end{bmatrix}$

7. $\begin{bmatrix} 4 & 2 \\ 3 & 1 \end{bmatrix}$ 8. $\begin{bmatrix} -6 & -1 \\ 0 & 0 \end{bmatrix}$

9. $\begin{bmatrix} 2 & 0 & -1 \\ 3 & 6 & 0 \\ 1 & 3 & 7 \end{bmatrix}$ 10. $\begin{bmatrix} 2 & 3 & -2 \\ -2 & 0 & 4 \\ 0 & -3 & -2 \end{bmatrix}$

11. $\begin{bmatrix} 1 & 0 & 3 \\ -1 & 2 & 1 \\ 2 & 2 & 3 \end{bmatrix}$ 12. $\begin{bmatrix} 1 & -3 & -2 \\ 2 & 5 & 4 \\ 2 & 3 & 2 \end{bmatrix}$

13. $\begin{bmatrix} 6 & 4 & -2 & 0 \\ -1 & 7 & 5 & 2 \\ 1 & 0 & 4 & 4 \end{bmatrix}$ 14. $\begin{bmatrix} 8 & 6 & 4 & 0 \\ -1 & 6 & 5 & -2 \\ 0 & 1 & 3 & 3 \end{bmatrix}$

15. For what values of a is the matrix below strictly determined?

$$\begin{bmatrix} a & 8 & 3 \\ 0 & a & -9 \\ -5 & 5 & a \end{bmatrix}$$

16. Show that the matrix below is strictly determined for any choice of a, b, or c.

$$\begin{bmatrix} a & a \\ b & c \end{bmatrix}$$

*17. Find necessary and sufficient conditions for the matrix below to be strictly determined.

$$\begin{bmatrix} a & 0 \\ 0 & b \end{bmatrix}$$

2. Mixed Strategies

Example 1   Consider a two-person zero-sum game given by the matrix

$$\begin{bmatrix} 6 & 0 \\ -2 & 3 \end{bmatrix}$$

in which the entries denote the winnings of Player I. Is this game strictly determined? If so, find its value.

Solution   We find that the smallest entry in each row is

Row 1: 0   Row 2: -2

The entry 0 in row 1 is not the largest element in its column; similarly, the entry -2 in row 2 is not the largest element in its column. Thus, this game is not strictly determined.

■

At this stage, we would like to stress the point that a matrix game is not usually played just once. With this in mind, Player I in Example 1 might decide always to play row 1 since he may win $6 at best and win $0 at worst. Does this mean he should always employ this strategy? If he does, Player II would catch on and begin to choose column 2 since this strategy limits his losses to $0. However, after awhile, Player I would probably start choosing row 2 to obtain a payoff of $3. Thus, in a nonstrictly determined game, it would be advisable for the players to *mix* their strategies rather than to use the same one all the time. That is, a random selection is desirable. Indeed, to make certain that the other player does not discover the pattern of moves, it may be best not to have any pattern at all. For instance, Player I may elect to play row 1 in 40% of the plays (that is, with probability .4), while Player II elects to play column 2 in 80% of the plays (that is, with probability .8). This idea of mixing strategies is important and useful in game theory. Games in which each player's strategies are *mixed* are termed *mixed-strategy games.*

Mixed-Strategy Games

Suppose we know the probability for each player to choose a certain strategy. What meaning can be given to the term *payoff of a game* if mixed strategies are used? Since the payoff has been defined for a pair of pure strategies and in a mixed-strategy situation we do not know which strategy is being used, it is not possible to define a payoff for a single game. However, in the long run, we do know how often each strategy is being used, and we can use this information to compute the *expected payoff* of the game.

Expected Payoff

In Example 1, if Player I chooses row 1 in 50% of the plays and row 2 in 50% of the plays, and if Player II chooses column 1 in 30% of the plays and column 2 in 70% of the plays, the expected payoff of the game can be computed. For example, the strategy of row 1, column 1, is chosen $(.5)(.3) = .15$ of the time. This strategy has a payoff of $6, so that the expected payoff will be $(\$6)(.15) = \$0.90$. Table 1 summarizes the entire process. Thus, the expected payoff E of this game, when the given strategies are employed, is $1.65, which makes the game favorable to Player I.

Table 1

Strategy	Payoff	Probability	Expected Payoff
Row 1—Column 1	6	.15	$0.90
Row 2—Column 1	−2	.15	−0.30
Row 1—Column 2	0	.35	0.00
Row 2—Column 2	3	.35	1.05
Totals		1.00	$1.65

If we look very carefully at the above derivation, we get a clue as to how the expected payoff of a game that is not strictly determined should be defined.

Let's consider a game defined by the 2×2 matrix

$$A = \begin{bmatrix} a_{11} & a_{12} \\ a_{21} & a_{22} \end{bmatrix}$$

Let the strategy for Player I, who plays rows, be denoted by the row vector $P = (p_1 \quad p_2)$ and the strategy for Player II, who plays columns, be denoted by the column vector

$$Q = \begin{bmatrix} q_1 \\ q_2 \end{bmatrix}$$

The probability that Player I wins the amount a_{11} is $p_1 q_1$. Similarly, the probabilities that he wins the amounts a_{12}, a_{21}, and a_{22} are $p_1 q_2$, $p_2 q_1$, and $p_2 q_2$, respectively. If we denote by $E(P, Q)$ the expectation of Player I, that is, the expected value of the amount he wins when he uses strategy P and Player II uses strategy Q, then

$$E(P, Q) = p_1 q_1 a_{11} + p_1 q_2 a_{12} + p_2 q_1 a_{21} + p_2 q_2 a_{22}$$

Using matrix notation, the above can be expressed as

$$E(P, Q) = PAQ$$

In general, if A is an $m \times n$ matrix game, we are led to the following definition:

Expected Payoff   The *expected payoff* E **of a two-person zero-sum game, defined by the matrix A, in which the row vector P and column vector Q define the respective strategy probabilities of Player I and Player II is**

$$E = PAQ$$

If a matrix game $A = [a_{ij}]$ of dimension $m \times n$ is strictly determined, then one of the entries is a saddle point. This saddle point can always be placed in the first row and first column by simply rearranging and renumbering the rows and columns of A. The value of the game is then a_{11}, and P and Q are vectors of the form

$$P = [1 \ \ 0 \ \ 0 \ \ 0 \ \ 0 \ \ \cdots \ \ 0] \qquad Q = \begin{bmatrix} 1 \\ 0 \\ \vdots \\ 0 \end{bmatrix}$$

where P is of dimension $1 \times m$ and Q is of dimension $n \times 1$.

Example 2   Find the expected payoff of the matrix game

$$\begin{bmatrix} 3 & -1 \\ -2 & 1 \\ 1 & 0 \end{bmatrix}$$

if Player I and Player II decide on the strategies

$$P = \begin{bmatrix} \frac{1}{3} & \frac{1}{3} & \frac{1}{3} \end{bmatrix} \qquad Q = \begin{bmatrix} \frac{1}{3} \\ \frac{2}{3} \end{bmatrix}$$

Solution   The expected payoff E of this game is

$$E = P \cdot \begin{bmatrix} 3 & -1 \\ -2 & 1 \\ 1 & 0 \end{bmatrix} \cdot Q = \begin{bmatrix} \frac{1}{3} & \frac{1}{3} & \frac{1}{3} \end{bmatrix} \begin{bmatrix} 3 & -1 \\ -2 & 1 \\ 1 & 0 \end{bmatrix} \begin{bmatrix} \frac{1}{3} \\ \frac{2}{3} \end{bmatrix}$$

$$= \begin{bmatrix} \frac{2}{3} & 0 \end{bmatrix} \begin{bmatrix} \frac{1}{3} \\ \frac{2}{3} \end{bmatrix} = \frac{2}{9}$$

Thus, the game is biased in favor of Player I and has an expected payoff of $\frac{2}{9}$. ∎

Most games are not strictly determined. That is, most games do not give rise to best pure strategies for each player. Examples of games that are not strictly determined are matching pennies (see Example 1, Section 1), bridge, poker, and so on. In the next two sections, we discuss techniques for finding optimal strategies for games that are not strictly determined.

Exercise 2

Solutions to Odd-Numbered Problems begin on page 602.

1. For the game of Example 1, find the expected payoff E if Player I chooses row 1 in 30% of the plays and Player II chooses column 1 in 40% of the plays.

2. For the game of Example 2, find the expected payoff E if Player I chooses row 1 with probability .3 and row 2 with probability .4, while Player II chooses column 1 half the time.

In Problems 3–6 find the expected payoff of the game $\begin{bmatrix} 4 & 0 \\ 2 & 3 \end{bmatrix}$ for the given strategies.

3. $P = [\frac{1}{2} \ \frac{1}{2}]; \quad Q = \begin{bmatrix} \frac{1}{2} \\ \frac{1}{2} \end{bmatrix}$

4. $P = [\frac{1}{2} \ \frac{1}{2}]; \quad Q = \begin{bmatrix} \frac{3}{4} \\ \frac{1}{4} \end{bmatrix}$

5. $P = [\frac{1}{4} \ \frac{3}{4}]; \quad Q = \begin{bmatrix} \frac{1}{2} \\ \frac{1}{2} \end{bmatrix}$

6. $P = [0 \ 1]; \quad Q = \begin{bmatrix} 0 \\ 1 \end{bmatrix}$

In Problems 7–10 find the expected payoff of each game.

7. $\begin{bmatrix} 4 & 0 \\ -3 & 6 \end{bmatrix}; \quad P = [\frac{2}{3} \ \frac{1}{3}]; \quad Q = \begin{bmatrix} \frac{1}{3} \\ \frac{2}{3} \end{bmatrix}$

8. $\begin{bmatrix} 1 & -1 \\ -2 & 3 \end{bmatrix}; \quad P = [\frac{1}{4} \ \frac{3}{4}]; \quad Q = \begin{bmatrix} \frac{1}{3} \\ \frac{2}{3} \end{bmatrix}$

9. $\begin{bmatrix} 1 & 0 & 0 \\ 0 & 1 & 0 \\ 0 & 0 & 1 \end{bmatrix}; \quad P = [\frac{1}{3} \ \frac{1}{3} \ \frac{1}{3}]; \quad Q = \begin{bmatrix} \frac{1}{3} \\ \frac{1}{3} \\ \frac{1}{3} \end{bmatrix}$

10. $\begin{bmatrix} 4 & -1 & 0 \\ 2 & 3 & 1 \end{bmatrix}; \quad P = [\frac{1}{3} \ \frac{2}{3}]; \quad Q = \begin{bmatrix} \frac{2}{3} \\ \frac{1}{6} \\ \frac{1}{6} \end{bmatrix}$

*11. Show that in a 2 × 2 game

$$\begin{bmatrix} a_{11} & a_{12} \\ a_{21} & a_{22} \end{bmatrix}$$

the only games that are not strictly determined are those for which either

(a) $a_{11} > a_{12}, \quad a_{11} > a_{21}, \quad a_{21} < a_{22}, \quad a_{12} < a_{22}$

or

(b) $a_{11} < a_{12}, \quad a_{11} < a_{21}, \quad a_{21} > a_{22}, \quad a_{12} > a_{22}$

Also show that all others are strictly determined.

3. Optimal Strategy in Two-Person Zero-Sum Games with 2 × 2 Matrices

We have already seen that the best strategy for two-person zero-sum games that are strictly determined is found in the row and column containing the saddle point. Suppose the game is not strictly determined so that the conditions given in Problem 11, Exercise 2, are satisfied.

In 1927, John von Neumann, along with E. Borel, initiated research in the theory of games and proved that, even in nonstrictly determined games, there is a single course of action that represents the best strategy. In practice, this means that in order to avoid always using a single strategy, a player in a game may instead choose plays randomly according to a fixed probability. This has the effect of making it impossible for the opponent to know what the player will do, since even the player will not know until the final moment. That is, by selecting a strategy randomly according to the laws of probability, the actual strategy chosen at any one time cannot even be known to the one choosing it.

For example, in the Italian game of *Morra* each player shows 1, 2, or 3 fingers and simultaneously calls out his guess as to what the sum of his and his opponent's fingers is. It can be shown that if he guesses 4 fingers each time and varies his own moves so that every twelve times he shows 1 finger five times, 2 fingers four times, and 3 fingers three times, he will, at worst, break even (in the long run).

Example 1 Consider the nonstrictly determined game

$$\begin{bmatrix} 1 & -1 \\ -2 & 3 \end{bmatrix}$$

in which Player I plays rows and Player II plays columns. Determine the optimal strategy for each player.

Solution If Player I chooses row 1 with probability p, then he must choose row 2 with probability $1 - p$. If Player II chooses column 1, Player I then expects to earn

(1)
$$E_I = p + (-2)(1 - p) = 3p - 2$$

Similarly, if Player II chooses column 2, Player I expects to earn

(2)
$$E_I = (-1)p + 3(1 - p) = -4p + 3$$

We graph these using E_I as the vertical axis and p as the horizontal axis. See Figure 1(a).

Player I wants to maximize his expected earning so he should maximize the minimum expected gain. This occurs when the two lines intersect, since for any other choice of p one or the other of the two expected earnings is less. Thus, solving equations (1) and (2) simultaneously, we obtain

$$3p - 2 = -4p + 3$$
$$7p = 5$$
$$p = \tfrac{5}{7}$$

EMIL BOREL (1871–1956) was a prominent French mathematician. In his book, *Le Hasard,* he described the penetration of probabilistic methods into physics, biology, and other branches of science as well as the relationship between probability theory and other branches of mathematics. His pioneering work helped launch the field of measure theory on which the modern notions of length, area, and probability rest. He was a member of the Chamber of Deputies and served as the Minister of the Navy.

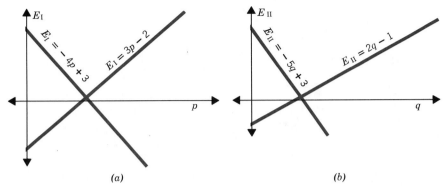

Figure 1

The optimal strategy for Player I is therefore

$$P = [\tfrac{5}{7} \quad \tfrac{2}{7}]$$

Similarly, suppose Player II chooses column 1 with probability q (and therefore column 2 with probability $1 - q$). If Player I chooses row 1, Player II's expected earnings are

$$E_{\text{II}} = q + (-1)(1 - q) = 2q - 1$$

If Player I chooses row 2, Player II's expected earnings are

$$E_{\text{II}} = (-2)(q) + 3(1 - q) = -5q + 3$$

The optimal strategy for Player II occurs when

$$2q - 1 = -5q + 3$$
$$7q = 4$$
$$q = \tfrac{4}{7}$$

See Figure 1(b). The optimal strategy for Player II is

$$Q = \begin{bmatrix} \tfrac{4}{7} \\ \tfrac{3}{7} \end{bmatrix}$$

The expected payoff E corresponding to these optimal strategies is

$$E = PAQ = [\tfrac{5}{7} \quad \tfrac{2}{7}] \begin{bmatrix} 1 & -1 \\ -2 & 3 \end{bmatrix} \begin{bmatrix} \tfrac{4}{7} \\ \tfrac{3}{7} \end{bmatrix} = \tfrac{1}{7}$$

Now, consider a two-person zero-sum game given by the 2×2 matrix

$$A = \begin{bmatrix} a_{11} & a_{12} \\ a_{21} & a_{22} \end{bmatrix}$$

in which Player I chooses row strategies and Player II chooses column strategies.
Using the method illustrated above, it can be shown that the optimal strategy for Player I is given by $P = [p_1 \quad p_2]$, where

(3)
$$p_1 = \frac{a_{22} - a_{21}}{a_{11} + a_{22} - a_{12} - a_{21}} \qquad p_2 = \frac{a_{11} - a_{12}}{a_{11} + a_{22} - a_{12} - a_{21}}$$

with $a_{11} + a_{22} - a_{12} - a_{21} \neq 0$. Notice that $p_1 + p_2 = 1$, which must be the case. Similarly, the optimal strategy for Player II is given by $Q = \begin{bmatrix} q_1 \\ q_2 \end{bmatrix}$, where

(4)
$$q_1 = \frac{a_{22} - a_{12}}{a_{11} + a_{22} - a_{12} - a_{21}} \qquad q_2 = \frac{a_{11} - a_{21}}{a_{11} + a_{22} - a_{12} - a_{21}}$$

with $a_{11} + a_{22} - a_{12} - a_{21} \neq 0$, and $q_1 + q_2 = 1$. The expected payoff E of the game corresponding to these optimal strategies is

$$E = PAQ = \frac{a_{11} \cdot a_{22} - a_{12} \cdot a_{21}}{a_{11} + a_{22} - a_{12} - a_{21}}$$

Value of a Game

When optimal strategies are used, the expected payoff E of the game is called the *value V of the game.*

Example 2   For the game matrix

$$\begin{bmatrix} 1 & -1 \\ -2 & 3 \end{bmatrix}$$

determine the optimal strategies for Player I and Player II, and find the value of the game.

Solution   Using formula (3), we have

$$p_1 = \frac{3 - (-2)}{1 + 3 - (-1) - (-2)} = \frac{5}{7}$$

$$p_2 = \frac{1 - (-1)}{1 + 3 - (-1) - (-2)} = \frac{2}{7}$$

Thus, Player I's optimal strategy is to select row 1 with probability $\frac{5}{7}$ and row 2 with probability $\frac{2}{7}$. Also, by (4), Player II's optimal strategy is

$$q_1 = \frac{3 - (-1)}{1 + 3 - (-1) - (-2)} = \frac{4}{7}$$

$$q_2 = \frac{1 - (-2)}{1 + 3 - (-1) - (-2)} = \frac{3}{7}$$

Player II's optimal strategy is to select column 1 with probability $\frac{4}{7}$ and column 2 with probability $\frac{3}{7}$. The value V of the game is

$$V = \frac{1 \cdot 3 - (-1)(-2)}{1 + 3 - (-1) - (-2)} = \frac{1}{7}$$

Thus, in the long run, the game is favorable to Player I.   ◼

The results obtained in Example 2 are in agreement with those obtained earlier using the graphical technique.

Example 3   Find the optimal strategy for each player, and determine the value of the game given by the matrix

$$\begin{bmatrix} 6 & 0 \\ -2 & 3 \end{bmatrix}$$

Solution Using the graphical technique or formulas (3) and (4), we find Player I's optimal strategy to be

$$p_1 = \tfrac{5}{11} \qquad p_2 = \tfrac{6}{11}$$

Player II's optimal strategy is

$$q_1 = \tfrac{3}{11} \qquad q_2 = \tfrac{8}{11}$$

The value V of the game is

$$V = 1.64$$

Thus, the game favors Player I, whose optimal strategy is $[\tfrac{5}{11} \quad \tfrac{6}{11}]$. ■

Example 4 In a presidential campaign, there are two candidates, a Democrat (D) and a Republican (R), and two types of issues, domestic issues and foreign issues. The units assigned to each candidate's strategy are given in the table. We assume that positive entries indicate a strength for the democratic candidate, while negative entries indicate a weakness. We also assume that a strength of one candidate equals a weakness of the other so that the game is zero-sum. The question is, what is the best strategy for each candidate? What is the value of the game?

		Republican	
		Domestic	Foreign
Democrat	Domestic	4	−2
	Foreign	−1	3

Solution Notice first that this game is not strictly determined. If D chooses to always play his strongest hand (foreign issues), then R will counter with domestic issues, in which case D would also talk about domestic issues, in which case, etc., etc. There is no *single* strategy either can use. We compute that the optimal strategy for the Democrat is

$$p_1 = \frac{3 - (-1)}{4 + 3 - (-2) - (-1)} = \frac{4}{10} = .4 \qquad p_2 = \frac{4 - (-2)}{10} = .6$$

The optimal strategy for the Republican is

$$q_1 = \frac{3 - (-2)}{10} = .5 \qquad q_2 = \frac{4 - (-1)}{10} = .5$$

Thus, the best strategy for the Democrat is to spend 40% of his time on domestic issues and 60% on foreign issues, while the Republican should divide his time evenly between the two issues.

The value of the game is

$$V = \frac{3 \cdot 4 - (-1)(-2)}{10} = \frac{10}{10} = 1.0$$

Thus, no matter what the Republican does, the Democrat gains at least 1.0 unit by employing his best strategy. ■

Example 5
War Game

In a naval battle, attacking bomber planes are trying to sink ships in a fleet protected by an aircraft carrier with fighter planes. The bombers can attack either high or low, with a low attack giving more accurate results. Similarly, the aircraft carrier can send its fighters at high altitudes or low altitudes to search for the bombers. If the bombers avoid the fighters, credit the bombers with 8 points; if the bombers and fighters meet, credit the bombers with -2 points. Also, credit the bombers with 3 additional points for flying low (since this results in more accurate bombing). Find optimal strategies for the bombers and the fighters. What is the value of the game?

Solution

First, we set up the game matrix. Designate the bombers as playing rows and the fighters as playing columns. Also, each entry of the matrix will denote winnings of the bombers. Then the game matrix is

$$
\begin{array}{c}
\\
\\
\text{Bombers}
\end{array}
\begin{array}{cc}
 & \text{Fighters} \\
 & \begin{array}{cc}\text{Low} & \text{High}\end{array} \\
\begin{array}{c}\text{Low}\\ \text{High}\end{array} &
\begin{bmatrix} 1 & 11 \\ 8 & -2 \end{bmatrix}
\end{array}
$$

The reason for a 1 in row 1, column 1, is that -2 points are credited for the planes meeting, but 3 additional points are credited to the bombers for a low flight.

Next, using formulas (3) and (4), the optimal strategies for the bombers $[p_1 \ p_2]$ and for the fighters $[\begin{smallmatrix}q_1\\q_2\end{smallmatrix}]$ are

$$
p_1 = \frac{-10}{-20} = \frac{1}{2} \qquad p_2 = \frac{-10}{-20} = \frac{1}{2}
$$

$$
q_1 = \frac{-13}{-20} = \frac{13}{20} \qquad q_2 = \frac{-7}{-20} = \frac{7}{20}
$$

The value V of the game is

$$
V = \frac{-2 - 88}{-20} = \frac{-90}{-20} = 4.5
$$

Thus, the game is favorable to the bombers, if both players employ their optimal strategies.

The bombers can decide whether to fly high or low by flipping a fair coin and flying high whenever heads appears. The fighters can decide whether to fly high or low by using an urn with 13 black balls and 7 white balls. Each day, a ball should be selected at random and then replaced. If the ball is black, they will go low; if it is white, they will go high.

Exercise 3
Solutions to Odd-Numbered Problems begin on page 602.

In Problems 1–6 find the optimal strategy for each player and determine the value of each 2 × 2 game by using graphical techniques. Check your answers by using formulas (3) and (4).

1. $\begin{bmatrix} 1 & 2 \\ 4 & 1 \end{bmatrix}$

2. $\begin{bmatrix} 2 & 4 \\ 3 & -2 \end{bmatrix}$

3. $\begin{bmatrix} -3 & 2 \\ 1 & 0 \end{bmatrix}$

4. $\begin{bmatrix} 3 & -2 \\ -1 & 2 \end{bmatrix}$

5. $\begin{bmatrix} 2 & -1 \\ -1 & 4 \end{bmatrix}$

6. $\begin{bmatrix} 5 & 4 \\ -3 & 7 \end{bmatrix}$

7. In Example 4, suppose the candidates are assigned the following weights for each issue:

		Republican	
		Domestic	Foreign
Democrat	Domestic	4	−1
	Foreign	0	3

What is each candidate's best strategy? What is the value of the game and whom does it favor?

8. *War Game.* For the situation described in Example 5, credit the bomber with 4 points for avoiding the fighters and with −6 points for meeting the fighters. Also, grant the bombers 2 additional points for flying low. What are the optimal strategies and the value of the game? Give instructions to the fighters and bombers as to how they should decide whether to fly high or low.

9. A spy can leave an airport through two exits, one a relatively deserted exit and the other an exit heavily used by the public. His opponent, having been notified of the spy's presence in the airport, must guess which exit he will use. If the spy and opponent meet at the deserted exit, the spy will be killed; if the two meet at the heavily used exit, the spy will be arrested. Assign a payoff of 30 points to the spy if he avoids his opponent by using the deserted exit and of 10 points to the spy if he avoids his opponent by using the busy exit. Assign a payoff of −100 points to the spy if he is killed and −2 points if he is arrested. What are the optimal strategies and the value of the game?

*10. Prove formulas (3) and (4).

*11. In the matrix game

$$\begin{bmatrix} a_{11} & a_{12} \\ a_{21} & a_{22} \end{bmatrix}$$

what can be said if $a_{11} + a_{22} - a_{12} - a_{21} = 0$?

4. Optimal Strategy in Other Two-Person Zero-Sum Games Using Geometric Methods

So far we have only discussed how to find optimal strategies for two-person zero-sum games that can be represented by 2 × 2 matrices. In this section, we shall give techniques for finding optimal strategies when the matrix is not 2 × 2.

We begin with the following definition.

Dominant Row; Recessive Row **If a matrix A contains a row r^* with entries that are all less than or equal to the corresponding entries in some other row r, then row r is said to *dominate* row r^* and r^* is said to be *recessive*.**

Example 1 In the matrix

$$A = \begin{bmatrix} -6 & -3 & 2 & 2 \\ -2 & 0 & 3 & 2 \\ 5 & -2 & 4 & 0 \end{bmatrix}$$

row 1 is dominated by row 2, since each entry in row 1 is less than or equal to its corresponding entry in row 2; that is,

$$-6 < -2 \qquad -3 < 0 \qquad 2 < 3 \qquad 2 = 2$$

■

If the matrix A of Example 1 were a game in which the entries represent winnings for Player I and if Player I chooses rows, it is clear that Player I would always choose row 2 over row 1, since the values in row 2 always give greater benefit to him than those in row 1. Thus, as far as the matrix representation of

Reduced Matrix this game is concerned, we could represent it by the *reduced matrix*

$$\begin{bmatrix} -2 & 0 & 3 & 2 \\ 5 & -2 & 4 & 0 \end{bmatrix}$$

in which row 1 of matrix A is eliminated since it would never be chosen.

Dominant Column; Recessive Column **If a matrix A contains a column c^* with entries that are all greater than or equal to the corresponding entries in some other column c, then column c is said to *dominate* column c^* and c^* is said to be *recessive*.**

Example 2 In the matrix

$$A = \begin{bmatrix} -6 & 2 & 4 \\ 4 & 4 & 2 \\ 1 & 3 & -1 \end{bmatrix}$$

column 1 dominates column 2, since each entry in column 2 is greater than or equal to its corresponding entry in column 1; that is,

$$2 > -6 \qquad 4 = 4 \qquad 3 > 1$$

■

If the matrix A in Example 2 were a game in which the entries denote winnings for Player I and if Player II chooses columns, it is clear that Player II would always prefer column 1 over column 2, since the smaller entries indicate lower losses. For this reason, column 2 can be eliminated from matrix A, and instead the reduced matrix below may be used:

$$\begin{bmatrix} -6 & 4 \\ 4 & 2 \\ 1 & -1 \end{bmatrix}$$

Example 3   By eliminating recessive rows and columns, find the reduced form of the matrix

$$A = \begin{bmatrix} -6 & -4 & 2 \\ 2 & -1 & 2 \\ -3 & 4 & 4 \end{bmatrix}$$

Solution   First we look at the rows of the matrix A. Notice that each entry in row 3 is greater than or equal to each entry in row 1. Thus, row 1 is recessive and can be eliminated. The new matrix is

$$\begin{bmatrix} 2 & -1 & 2 \\ -3 & 4 & 4 \end{bmatrix}$$

Neither row 1 nor row 2 in the new matrix is recessive, so we now consider the columns. Notice that the entries of column 3 are greater than or equal to the corresponding entries in either column 1 or column 2. Thus, column 3 is recessive. The reduced matrix is

$$\begin{bmatrix} 2 & -1 \\ -3 & 4 \end{bmatrix}$$

The above example shows how a 3×3 matrix game can sometimes be reduced to a 2×2 matrix by eliminating recessive rows and recessive columns.

Example 4   Find the optimal strategy for each player, and find the value of the two-person, zero-sum game

$$\begin{bmatrix} -6 & -4 & 2 \\ 2 & -1 & 2 \\ -3 & 4 & 4 \end{bmatrix}$$

in which the entries denote the winnings of Player I, who chooses rows, and in which each player has three possible strategies.

Solution   By eliminating recessive rows and columns, this matrix reduces to

$$\begin{bmatrix} 2 & -1 \\ -3 & 4 \end{bmatrix}$$

Using formulas (3) and (4) on pages 359 and 360, we find that the optimal strategy for Player I is

$$p_1 = \tfrac{7}{10} \qquad p_2 = \tfrac{3}{10}$$

and the optimal strategy for Player II is

$$q_1 = \tfrac{5}{10} \qquad q_2 = \tfrac{5}{10}$$

The value of the game is

$$V = \tfrac{5}{10}$$

Thus, the game given in this example is favorable to Player I, and his best strategy is to choose row 2 in 70% of the plays and row 3 in 30% of the plays (row 1 is recessive).

■

2 × m or m × 2 Matrix Games

Suppose we now consider two-person zero-sum games with matrix representations that are $2 \times m$ or $m \times 2$ ($m > 2$) matrices that are not strictly determined and that contain no recessive rows or columns. For a $2 \times m$ matrix game, Player I has two strategies and Player II has m strategies; for an $m \times 2$ matrix game, Player I has m strategies and Player II has 2 strategies.

We begin with the following example to illustrate how to find optimal strategies.

Example 5 Find the optimal strategy for each player in the 2×3 game

$$\begin{bmatrix} 4 & -1 & 0 \\ -1 & 4 & 2 \end{bmatrix}$$

in which entries denote winnings for Player I. What is the value of this game?

Solution In the above game, Player I has two strategies and Player II has three strategies. Suppose p is the probability that Player I plays row 1. Then $1 - p$ is the probability that row 2 is played. Now let's compute the expected earnings of Player I in terms of p.

If Player II elects to play column 1, then the expected earnings E_I of Player I are equal to $4p - 1 \cdot (1 - p)$, or

$$\text{①} \quad E_I = 5p - 1$$

Similarly, if Player II selects column 2 or column 3, the expected earnings for Player I are, respectively,

$$\text{②} \quad E_I = 4 - 5p \qquad \text{③} \quad E_I = 2 - 2p$$

Next, we graph each of these three straight lines measuring E_I along the y-axis and p along the x-axis, and we look at the situation from Player II's point of view. Player II wants to make Player I's earnings as small as possible, since then he maximizes his own earnings. Thus, Player II will always choose the lowest strategy (line), since the height of each line measures winnings of Player I. In other words, Player II's best strategy lies along the darkened line in Figure 2.

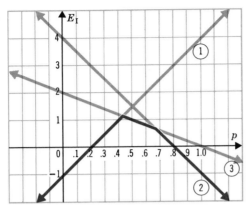

Figure 2

Player I, realizing this, will choose the value of p that yields the most earnings for him. This value occurs at the intersection of the lines

$$\text{①}\; E_I = 5p - 1 \qquad \text{③}\; E_I = 2 - 2p$$

Their intersection is the point

$$p = \tfrac{3}{7} \qquad E_I = \tfrac{8}{7}$$

Thus, the optimal strategy for Player I is to choose row 1 in $\tfrac{3}{7}$ of the plays and row 2 in $\tfrac{4}{7}$ of the plays. The value of the game in this case is $\tfrac{8}{7}$.

To find the optimal strategy for Player II, notice that Player I's optimal strategy comes from earnings calculated by using columns 1 and 3 of the matrix game. The matrix that results by eliminating column 2 from the matrix is

$$\begin{bmatrix} 4 & 0 \\ -1 & 2 \end{bmatrix}$$

The optimal strategy for Player II can now be found by formula (4), page 360. It is

$$q_1 = \tfrac{2}{7} \qquad q_2 = 0 \qquad q_3 = \tfrac{5}{7}$$

Thus, Player II's strategy is to play column 1 in $\tfrac{2}{7}$ of the plays and column 3 in $\tfrac{5}{7}$ of the plays. Since column 2 is eliminated, it is never played. ∎

Example 6 Find the optimal strategy for each player in the 5×2 matrix game

$$\begin{bmatrix} -2 & 2 \\ -1 & 1 \\ 2 & 0 \\ 3 & -1 \\ 4 & -2 \end{bmatrix}$$

in which the entries denote winnings for Player I. What is the value of this game?

Solution Here, Player II has two strategies. Let q be the probability that he chooses column 1, so that $1 - q$ is the probability that he chooses column 2. Player I's earnings E_I are then

   ① $E_I = -2q + 2(1 - q)$ ② $E_I = -q + (1 - q)$ ③ $E_I = 2q$
          $= -4q + 2$ $= -2q + 1$

   ④ $E_I = 3q - (1 - q)$ ⑤ $E_I = 4q - 2(1 - q)$
          $= 4q - 1$ $= 6q - 2$

for rows 1–5, respectively. We graph these five linear equations in Figure 3.

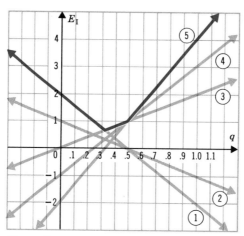

Figure 3

Player I may select any of the five strategies represented by the lines in Figure 3. Since the height of each line represents his earnings, he will employ strategies that carry him along the darkened line in Figure 3.

But Player II wants the earnings of Player I to be as small as possible. This occurs at the intersection of ① and ③. This point is $q = \frac{1}{3}$, $E_I = \frac{2}{3}$. Thus, the optimal strategy for Player II is to choose column 1 in $\frac{1}{3}$ of the plays and column 2 in $\frac{2}{3}$ of the plays. The value of the game is $\frac{2}{3}$, and it is favorable to Player I.

Now, to find Player I's optimal strategy, we notice that Player II's optimal strategy comes from lines ① and ③. If we eliminate rows 2, 4, and 5 from the matrix above, we obtain the matrix

$$\begin{bmatrix} -2 & 2 \\ 2 & 0 \end{bmatrix}$$

Applying formula (3), page 359, Player I's optimal strategy is

$$p_1 = \frac{-2}{-6} = \frac{1}{3} \qquad p_3 = \frac{-4}{-6} = \frac{2}{3}$$

The following is an example from a paper by J. D. Williams.*

*J. D. Williams, *La Strategie dans les Actions Humaines,* Dunod, Paris, 1956.

Example 7
Investment
Problem

An investor plans to invest $10,000 during a period of international uncertainty as to whether there will be peace, a continuation of the cold war, or an actual war. Her investment can be made in government bonds, armament stocks, or industrial stocks. The game is a struggle between the investor and nature. The matrix below gives the rates of interest for each player's strategy.

		Hot war	Cold war	Peace
	Government bonds	2	3	3.2
Investor	Armament stocks	18	6	−2
	Industrial stocks	2	7	12

Calculate the investor's optimal strategy.

Solution

First we look at the matrix to see if there is any row dominance or column dominance. Notice that row 3 dominates row 1 so that the reduced matrix for this game is

	Hot war	Cold war	Peace
Armament stocks	18	6	−2
Industrial stocks	2	7	12

This is a 2×3 matrix that can be solved by the graphing method. The optimal strategy for the investor is

$$p_1 = 0 \qquad p_2 = \tfrac{5}{17} \qquad p_3 = \tfrac{12}{17}$$

The value of the game is $V = 6.7$

Thus, the investor is assured of a return of at least 6.7% when she invests $\tfrac{5}{17} = 29\%$ in armament stocks and $\tfrac{12}{17} = 71\%$ in industrial stocks. In the event of a hot war, the return is

$$18(\tfrac{5}{17}) + 2(\tfrac{12}{17}) = 6.7\%$$

In the event of a cold war, the return is

$$6(\tfrac{5}{17}) + 7(\tfrac{12}{17}) = 6.7\%$$

In the event of peace, the return is

$$(-2)(\tfrac{5}{17}) + 12(\tfrac{12}{17}) = 7.9\%$$

■

Example 8
War Game

General White's army and the enemy are each trying to occupy three hills. General White has three regiments and the enemy has two regiments. A hill is occupied when one force has more regiments present than the other force; if both try to occupy a hill with the same number of regiments, a draw results. How should the troops be deployed to gain maximum advantage?

Solution

We denote the three strategies available to General White as follows:

3:   All three regiments used together to attack one hill.
2,1:   Two regiments used together and one used by itself to attack two hills.
1,1,1:   All three regiments used separately to attack three hills.

White's opponent has two strategies available, namely:

2: The two regiments used together to defend one hill.
1,1: The two regiments used separately to defend two of the hills.

White will play rows, and the entries in the game matrix will denote White's expected winnings based on the rule that when White takes a hill, he earns 1 point; when a draw results, he earns 0 points; and when he is defeated, he loses 1 point. Also, for each division that is overpowered, 1 point is earned. Table 2 shows the points won (or lost) by General White for all possible deployments of his regiments. Notice that the order of deployment is quite important.

Table 2

	2,0,0	0,2,0	0,0,2	1,1,0	1,0,1	0,1,1
3,0,0	3	0	0	1	1	−1
0,3,0	0	3	0	1	−1	1
0,0,3	0	0	3	−1	1	1
2,1,0	1	−1	1	2	2	0
2,0,1	1	1	−1	2	2	0
1,2,0	−1	1	1	2	0	2
0,2,1	1	1	−1	2	0	2
1,0,2	−1	1	1	0	2	2
0,1,2	1	−1	1	0	2	2
1,1,1	0	0	0	1	1	1

For example, if White deploys his regiments as 3,0,0 and his opponent uses the deployment 2,0,0, then White captures Hill I, winning 1 point, and overpowers two regiments, winning 2 points, for a total score of 3 points. If White uses 0,2,1 and his opponent uses 0,1,1, then Hill I is a standoff, White wins Hill II and overpowers one regiment, and Hill III is a draw. Here, White has a total score of 2 points.

To determine the game matrix, we proceed as follows: If White uses a 3 deployment and his enemy uses a 2 deployment, then White expects to score 3 points $\frac{1}{3}$ of the time and score 0 points $\frac{2}{3}$ of the time. We assign an expected payoff to White of $3 \cdot \frac{1}{3} + 0 \cdot \frac{2}{3} = 1$ point in this case. If White uses a 2,1 deployment and his enemy uses a 1,1 deployment, then White expects to gain 2 points $\frac{2}{3}$ of the time and 0 points $\frac{1}{3}$ of the time for an expected payoff of $\frac{4}{3}$ points. The game matrix can be written as

$$
\begin{array}{c}
 \\
 \\
 \\
\text{White} \\
 \\
 \\
\end{array}
\begin{array}{c}
\text{Enemy} \\
\begin{array}{cc}
2 & 1,1
\end{array} \\
\begin{array}{c}
3 \\
2,1 \\
1,1,1
\end{array}
\begin{bmatrix}
1 & \frac{1}{3} \\
\frac{1}{3} & \frac{4}{3} \\
0 & 1
\end{bmatrix}
\end{array}
$$

Notice that this matrix can be reduced, since row 2 dominates row 3. The reduced matrix is

$$
\begin{array}{cc}
 & \text{Enemy} \\
 & \begin{array}{cc} 2 & 1,1 \end{array}
\end{array}
$$

$$
\text{White}\ \begin{array}{c} 3 \\ 2,1 \end{array} \begin{bmatrix} 1 & \frac{1}{3} \\ \frac{1}{3} & \frac{4}{3} \end{bmatrix}
$$

This matrix is not strictly determined. The optimal (mixed) strategy for General White is

$$
p_1 = \frac{1}{\frac{7}{3} - \frac{2}{3}} = .6 \qquad p_2 = \frac{\frac{2}{3}}{\frac{5}{3}} = .4 \qquad p_3 = 0
$$

The optimal strategy for the enemy is

$$
q_1 = \frac{1}{\frac{5}{3}} = .6 \qquad q_2 = \frac{\frac{2}{3}}{\frac{5}{3}} = .4
$$

The value of the game is

$$
V = \frac{\frac{4}{3} - \frac{1}{9}}{\frac{5}{3}} = \frac{\frac{11}{9}}{\frac{5}{3}} = \frac{11}{15}
$$

The game is favorable to General White, who should deploy his troops in a 3 strategy 60% of the time and in a 2,1 strategy 40% of the time. Since no one hill is more likely to be chosen for attack than any other, it follows that each hill should be attacked by all three regiments 20% of the time. Furthermore, for the 2,1 deployment, each possible selection of the hills to receive 0,1, or 2 regiments (6 in all) will be used $\frac{.40}{6} = 6.67\%$ of the time.

■

We close this section by pointing out that any game theory problem can be converted to a linear programming problem and then the simplex method may be applied. If you are interested in studying this relationship, see the references at the end of this chapter.

Model: Cultural Anthropology

In 1960, Davenport* published an analysis of the behavior of Jamaican fishermen. Each fishing crew is confronted with a three-choice decision of fishing in the inside banks, the outside banks, or a combination of inside–outside banks. Fairly reliable estimates can be made of the quantity and quality of fish caught in these three areas under the two conditions that current is present, or not present.

If we take the village as a whole as one player and the environment as another player, we have the components for a two-person zero-sum game, in which the village has three strategies (inside, inside–outside, outside) and the environment has two strategies (current, no current). Davenport computed an estimate of income claimed by the fishermen using each of the alternatives. This estimate is

*E. Davenport, "Jamaican Fishing: A Game Theory Analysis in Papers on Caribbean Anthropology," Yale University Publication in Anthropology, Nos. 57–64, 1960.

given in matrix form by

		Environment	
		Current	No current
	Inside	17.3	11.5
Village	Inside–Outside	5.2	17.0
	Outside	−4.4	20.6

(1)

Here the environment has two strategies. Let q be the probability of current, so that $1 - q$ is the probability of no current. If E_I represents the villagers' expected earnings, then

① $E_I = 17.3q + 11.5(1 - q)$
$= 5.8q + 11.5$

② $E_I = 5.2q + 17(1 - q)$
$= -11.8q + 17$

③ $E_I = -4.4q + 20.6(1 - q)$
$= -25q + 20.6$

Figure 4 shows that the optimal strategy of the environment comes from the intersection of lines ① and ②.

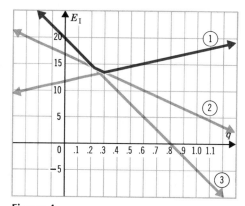

Figure 4

Computing this intersection, we obtain

$$q = .31 \quad \text{and} \quad 1 - q = .69$$

To obtain the optimal strategy of the village, we note that the optimal strategy of the environment comes from lines ① and ②. If we eliminate row 3 from the matrix in (1), we find

$$\begin{bmatrix} 17.3 & 11.5 \\ 5.2 & 17.0 \end{bmatrix}$$

Applying formula (3), page 359, the village's optimal strategy is

$$p_1 = \frac{17.0 - 5.2}{34.3 - 16.7} = \frac{11.8}{17.6} = .67 \qquad p_2 = \frac{5.8}{17.6} = .33$$

Table 3 compares the observed frequency of strategy usage as compared with the optimal usage as predicted by the game.

Table 3

	Observed	Predicted
Outside	0	0
Inside	.69	.67
Inside–Outside	.31	.33
Current	.25	.31
No Current	.75	.69

Exercise 4
Solutions to Odd-Numbered Problems begin on page 603.

1. Find the optimal strategy for each player in the following games, where Player I plays rows and entries denote winnings of Player I. What is the value of each game?

   (a) $\begin{bmatrix} 8 & 3 & 8 \\ 6 & 5 & 4 \\ -2 & 4 & 1 \end{bmatrix}$

   (b) $\begin{bmatrix} 2 & 1 & 0 & 6 \\ 3 & -2 & 1 & 2 \end{bmatrix}$

   (c) $\begin{bmatrix} 6 & -4 & 2 & -3 \\ -4 & 6 & -5 & 7 \end{bmatrix}$

   (d) $\begin{bmatrix} 4 & -5 & 5 \\ -6 & 3 & 3 \\ 2 & -6 & 3 \end{bmatrix}$

   (e) $\begin{bmatrix} 1 & 3 & 0 \\ 0 & -3 & 1 \\ 0 & 4 & 1 \\ -2 & 1 & 1 \end{bmatrix}$

   (f) $\begin{bmatrix} 4 & 3 & -1 \\ 1 & 1 & 4 \\ 1 & 0 & 2 \end{bmatrix}$

2. Find optimal strategies for both players in each of the following games. What is the value of each game? Player I plays rows and the entries denote his winnings.

   (a) $\begin{bmatrix} 3 & -1 & 0 \\ -2 & 1 & -1 \end{bmatrix}$

   (b) $\begin{bmatrix} -1 & 1 \\ 5 & -3 \\ 1 & -2 \\ -2 & 5 \end{bmatrix}$

   (c) $\begin{bmatrix} 3 & -2 & 2 \\ -1 & 1 & 0 \end{bmatrix}$

   (d) $\begin{bmatrix} -5 & -4 & -3 & 2 & 3 \\ 3 & 2 & 1 & -2 & -4 \end{bmatrix}$

   (e) $\begin{bmatrix} 6 & -4 \\ 4 & -3 \\ 1 & 0 \\ -3 & 2 \\ -5 & 4 \end{bmatrix}$

3. In a department store, one area (A) is usually very crowded and the other area (B) is usually relatively empty. The store employs two detectives and has closed-circuit television (T) to control pilferage. The television covers A and B and the detectives can be in either area A or area B or watching the television (T). The matrix below gives an estimate of the probability for the detectives to find and arrest a thief:

Thief

		A	B
	TT	.51	.75
	AA	.64	.36
	BB	.19	.91
Detectives	TA	.58	.60
	TB	.37	.85
	AB	.56	.76

Here, TT means both detectives are at the television, TA means the first detective is at the television and the second is in area A, and so on. Find the optimal strategy for the thief and the detectives. What is the value of the game?

4. *Effectiveness of Antibiotics.* This problem is adapted from J. D. Williams.* Three antibiotics, A_1, A_2, and A_3, and five types of bacilli, M_1, M_1, M_3, M_4, and M_5, are involved in a study of the effectiveness of antibiotics on bacilli, with A_1 having a probability .3 of destroying M_1, and so on, as given below. Without knowing the proportion in which these germs are distributed during an epidemic, in what ratio should the antibiotics be mixed to have the greatest probability of being effective?

Bacilli

		M_1	M_2	M_3	M_4	M_5
	A_1	.3	.4	.5	1	0
Antibiotics	A_2	.2	.3	.6	0	1
	A_3	.1	.5	.3	.1	0

5. Two-Person Nonzero-Sum Games

So far we have only been concerned with two-person games in which the winnings of Player I are equal to the losses of Player II, and vice versa; that is, we have considered only zero-sum games. In this section we shall discuss the situation in which the play can result in a gain for both players, or a loss for both players, or a gain for one not equal to the loss of the other. Such games between two players are called *two-person nonzero-sum games.*

Cooperative
Games
We divide the class of two-person nonzero-sum games into two categories: (1) *cooperative* games in which preplay communication between the players

*J. D. Williams, *La Strategie dans les Actions Humaines*, Dunod, Paris, 1956.

Noncooperative
Games can occur or preplay binding contracts are used, and (2) *noncooperative games* in which no sharing of information and no communication between the players takes place.

For two-person nonzero-sum games, we use two matrices A and B to describe the payoff for a given strategy. Here, the matrix A represents the gains of Player I and matrix B represents the gains of Player II. If Player I chooses to play row i and Player II plays column j, then the element a_{ij} in the matrix A gives the payoff to Player I and the entry b_{ij} in the matrix B gives the payoff to Player II.

Example 1 In a two-person nonzero-sum game, the matrices A and B below give the payoffs of Player I and Player II, respectively:

$$\text{Player I} \qquad\qquad \text{Player II}$$
$$A = \begin{bmatrix} 2 & -1 & 3 \\ 1 & 4 & -3 \end{bmatrix} \qquad B = \begin{bmatrix} 1 & 0 & 5 \\ -2 & 6 & -3 \end{bmatrix}$$

Player I has two strategies and Player II has three strategies. If Player I plays row 1 and Player II plays column 3, then Player I wins 3 and Player II wins 5. ■

Example 2
Prisoners'
Dilemma
Two prisoners who have committed a crime together are separated for questioning by the District Attorney, who claims to have enough evidence to convict them. Each has the choice of squealing or not squealing on the other. If only one of them confesses, he will receive a suspended sentence, while the other will be sentenced to 10 years in jail. However, if both confess, they will each get 6 years in jail. If neither confesses, each will receive a sentence of 2 years. We assume the prisoners cannot communicate with each other. Describe payoff matrices A and B for these prisoners.

Solution Before writing the matrices, let's assign a value to each decision. If one confesses and the other does not, then the one who confessed has done quite well for himself while the one who did not confess has done very poorly. We assign a high value of 10 for confessing and a low value of 0 for not confessing. If both confess, the jail terms are not as severe as when one confesses and the other does not. We assign a value of 3 to this situation. Finally, if neither confesses, the jail terms are quite lenient for each, so we assign a value of 7 for this occurrence.

Based on this assignment of values for the possible situations, the payoff matrices A and B are

$$A = \begin{matrix} & \text{Confess} & \text{Not confess} \\ \text{Confess} & \\ \text{Not confess} \end{matrix} \begin{bmatrix} 3 & 10 \\ 0 & 7 \end{bmatrix}$$

$$B = \begin{matrix} & \text{Confess} & \text{Not confess} \\ \text{Confess} & \\ \text{Not confess} \end{matrix} \begin{bmatrix} 3 & 0 \\ 10 & 7 \end{bmatrix}$$

in which the entries of A are those of Prisoner I, who plays rows, and the entries of B are those of Prisoner II, who plays columns. ■

At this point, we confine our discussion to noncooperative games. In a manner quite similar to that of Section 1, we can define a *saddle point* for nonzero-sum games.

In a nonzero-sum game, let A and B denote payoff matrices in which A is the payoff matrix for Player I, who plays rows, and B is the payoff matrix for Player II, who plays columns. If each entry in the ith row of matrix A is greater than or equal to corresponding entries in the other rows of A and if each entry in the jth column of matrix B is greater than or equal to the corresponding entries in the other columns of B, then the *saddle pair* for this game is a_{ij} and b_{ij}.

Saddle Pair

For example, in the prisoner's dilemma of Example 2, each entry in row 1 of matrix A exceeds the corresponding entry of row 2. Thus, Player I would always choose to play row 1. Also, each entry in column 1 of matrix B exceeds the corresponding entry in column 2, so that Player II would always choose column 1. (Remember that the entries in matrix B denote payoffs for Player II, so that he wishes to maximize these values if he can.) Thus, row 1 and column 1 give a saddle pair for this game.

Notice that this saddle pair (both prisoners confess) is not the *best* choice each prisoner could have made. Clearly, if neither one confesses, they (as a team) do much better. However, without cooperation and communication, the choice of confessing is the best strategy *to their knowledge*.

Just as in two-person zero-sum games, it turns out that two-person nonzero-sum games do not always possess a saddle pair. When a saddle pair exists, then a pure strategy also exists. When we try to determine an optimal strategy for two-person, nonzero-sum games, we encounter one of the more important complications of such games. For zero-sum games, we considered the notion of an expected payoff and then, in some sense, each player is found to have an optimal strategy that maximizes his expected payoff. However, this approach will not hold in general for nonzero-sum games. In fact, it is difficult to establish that any kind of optimal strategy is really optimal in a mathematical sense.

Let's now turn our attention to two-person, nonzero-sum games in which cooperation takes place.

In the prisoner's dilemma example we saw that without cooperation each prisoner finds it to his advantage to confess. In doing so, each prisoner maximizes his own position while at the same time minimizing the other prisoner's position. The dilemma occurs since each prisoner thinks it is to his personal disadvantage to choose the strategy that is most advantageous from a cooperative point of view. The only way for the prisoners to reach the attractive strategy of both not confessing, which is not maximal individual strategy, is through cooperation in the form of prior communication and agreement, which can somehow be enforced through means not described in the game matrix.

As a final note, we do not want to give you the impression that our discussion of nonzero-sum games is complete. As a matter of fact, nonzero-sum games are much too complicated to be discussed in any detail here. There are many unsolved problems in this area involving both the nature of play and possible applications. You can find many game theoretical analyses of bargaining, arbitration, and fair divisions of property as well as applications to the fields of antitrust law, international law, and international relations in the references listed at the end of this chapter.

Chapter Review

Important Terms

two-person game
zero-sum game
payoff
game matrix
strategy
best strategy
value
strictly determined
saddle point
fair game
pure strategy
mixed strategy

expected payoff
optimal strategy
dominant row
recessive row
reduced matrix
dominant column
recessive column
two-person nonzero-sum games
cooperative games
noncooperative games
saddle pair

Review Exercises
Solutions to Odd-Numbered Problems begin on page 605.

1. Determine which of the following two-person zero-sum games are strictly determined. For those that are, find the value of the game.

(a) $\begin{bmatrix} 5 & 3 \\ 2 & 4 \end{bmatrix}$

(b) $\begin{bmatrix} 29 & 15 \\ 79 & 3 \end{bmatrix}$

(c) $\begin{bmatrix} 50 & 75 \\ 30 & 15 \end{bmatrix}$

(d) $\begin{bmatrix} 7 & 14 \\ 9 & 13 \end{bmatrix}$

(e) $\begin{bmatrix} 0 & 2 & 4 \\ 4 & 6 & 10 \\ 16 & 14 & 12 \end{bmatrix}$

2. Find the expected payoff of the game below for the given strategies:

$$\begin{bmatrix} -1 & 1 \\ 1 & -1 \end{bmatrix}$$

(a) $P = \begin{bmatrix} \frac{1}{3} & \frac{2}{3} \end{bmatrix}; \quad Q = \begin{bmatrix} 1 \\ 0 \end{bmatrix}$

(b) $P = \begin{bmatrix} 0 & 1 \end{bmatrix}; \quad Q = \begin{bmatrix} \frac{1}{2} \\ \frac{1}{2} \end{bmatrix}$

(c) $P = \begin{bmatrix} \frac{1}{2} & \frac{1}{2} \end{bmatrix}; \quad Q = \begin{bmatrix} \frac{1}{2} \\ \frac{1}{2} \end{bmatrix}$

3. Show that if a 2 × 2 or 2 × 3 matrix game has a saddle point, then either one row dominates the other or one column dominates another column.

4. Give an example to show that the result of Problem 3 is not true for 3 × 3 matrix games.

5. Find the optimal strategy for each player in the following games. Assume Player I plays rows and entries denote winnings of Player I. What is the value of each game?

(a) $\begin{bmatrix} 4 & 6 & 3 \\ 1 & 2 & 5 \end{bmatrix}$

(b) $\begin{bmatrix} 1 & 6 \\ 5 & 2 \\ 7 & 4 \end{bmatrix}$

(c) $\begin{bmatrix} 2 & 1 \\ 4 & 0 \\ 3 & 4 \end{bmatrix}$

(d) $\begin{bmatrix} 0 & 3 & 2 \\ 4 & 2 & 3 \end{bmatrix}$

6. *Retail Discounting.* Consider a neighborhood in which there are only two competitive stores handling two different, but similar, brands of spark plugs. In ordinary circumstances each retailer pays $0.60 for each plug and sells it for $1.00. However, from time to time, the manufacturers have incentive plans in which they sell the plugs to the retailers for $0.40, provided that the retailer will sell them for $0.70. Each month the retailers must decide, independently of one another, what the selling price for the spark plugs should be. From previous sales patterns, each retailer observes the following pattern: At the usual price, each sells 1000 plugs per month; if one retailer discounts the price and the other does not, the discount store will sell 2000 plugs each month and the other will sell only 300 plugs; if both stores discount the price, they will each sell 1300 plugs per month. Set up the game matrix for this problem. In your opinion, how should each store manager proceed?

Other Books or Articles

Bennion, Edward G., "Capital Budgeting and Game Theory," *Harv. Bus. Rev.,* **34,** 6 (November–December 1956), pp. 115–123.

Blackett, D. W., "Some Blotto Games," *Nav. Res. Logist. Q.,* **1** (1954), pp. 55–60.

Buchler, Ira, and Hugo Nutini, *Game Theory in the Behavioral Sciences,* University of Pittsburg Press, 1969.

Caywood, T. E., and C. J. Thomas, "Applications of Game Theory in Fighter versus Bomber Combat," *Oper. Res.,* **3** (1955), pp. 402–411.

Friedman, Lawrence, "Game-Theory Models in the Allocation of Advertising Expenditures," *Oper. Res.,* **6** (1958), pp. 699–709.

Gould, Peter R., "Man Against His Environment: A Game Theoretic Framework," *Ann. Assoc. Amer. Geogr.,* **53,** 3 (September 1963), pp. 290–297.

Haywood, O. G., Jr., "Military Decision and the Mathematical Theory of Games," *Air Univ. Q. Rev.,* **4** (1950), pp. 17–30.

Haywood, O. G., Jr., "Military Decision and Game Theory," *Oper. Res.,* **2,** 4 (November 1954), pp. 365–385.

Jones, A. J., *Game Theory: Mathematical Models of Conflict,* Wiley, New York, 1980.

Kaplan, Martin, and Nicholas Katzenbach, *The Political Foundations of International Law,* Wiley, New York, 1961.

Luce, R. Duncan, and Howard Raiffa, *Games and Decisions,* Wiley, New York, 1957.

Luce, R. Duncan, and Arnold A. Rogow, "A Game Theoretic Analysis of Congressional Power Distributions for a Stable Two-Party System," *Behav. Sci.,* **1,** 2 (April 1956), pp. 83–95.

McClintock, C. G., and D. M. Messick, "Empirical Approaches to Game Theory and Bargaining: A Bibliography," *Gen. Syst.,* **11** (1966), pp. 229–238.

Mathematics in the Modern World, readings from *Scientific American,* Freeman, San Francisco, 1968, pp. 300–312.

Rapoport, Anatol, and Albert M. Chammah, "Sex Differences in Factors Contributing to the Level of Cooperation in the Prisoner's Dilemma Game," *J. Pers. Soc. Psychol.,* **2,** 6 (December 1965), pp. 831–838.

Shapley, L. S., and Martin Shubik, "A Method for Evaluating the Distribution of Power in a Committee System," *Amer. Polit. Sci. Rev.,* **48,** 3 (September 1954), pp. 787–792.

Shubik, Martin, "The Uses of Game Theory in Management," *Manage. Sci.,* **2** (1955), pp. 40–54.

Thie, P. R., *An Introduction to Linear Programming and Game Theory,* Wiley, New York, 1979.

10
Statistics

1. Introductory Remarks

Statistics is the science of collecting, organizing, analyzing, and interpreting numerical facts. By making observations, statisticians obtain *data* in the form of measurements or counts. The *organization of data* involves the presentation of the collected measurements or counts in a form suitable for determining logical conclusions. Usually, tables or graphs are used to represent the collected data. The *analysis of data* is the process of extracting, from given measurements or counts, related and relevant information from which a brief numerical description can be formulated. In this process we use concepts known as the *mean, median, range, variance,* and *standard deviation.* By *interpretation of data* we mean the art of drawing conclusions from the analysis of the data. This involves the formulation of predictions concerning a large collection of objects based on the information available from a small collection of similar objects.

In collecting data concerning varied characteristics, it is often impossible or impractical to observe an entire group. Instead of examining an entire group, called the *population,* a small segment, called the *sample,* is chosen. It would be difficult, for example, to question all cigarette smokers in order to study the effects of smoking. Therefore, appropriate samples of smokers are usually selected for questioning.

The method of selecting the sample is extremely important if we want the results to be reliable. All members of the population under investigation should have an equal probability of being selected; otherwise, a *biased sample* could result. For example, if we want to study the relationship between smoking cigarettes and lung cancer, we cannot choose a sample of smokers who all live in the same location. The individuals chosen might have dozens of characteristics peculiar to their area, which would give a false impression with regard to all smokers.

As another example, suppose we want to study the effects of drugs on youths. If we decide to choose a sample from a group of students at a specific university or from a group of youths in a ghetto, we will get a biased sample, since university students and ghetto youths may be heavy users of drugs. It would be more appropriate to arrange the sample so that all members of the population under investigation have an equal probability of being selected.

Samples collected in such a way that each selection is equally likely to be chosen are called *random samples.* Of course, there are many random samples that can be chosen from a population. By combining the results of more than one random sample of a population, it is possible to obtain a more accurate representation of the population.

If a sample is representative of a population, important conclusions about the population can often be inferred from analysis of the sample. The phase of statistics dealing with conditions under which such inference is valid is called *inductive statistics* or *statistical inference.* Since such inference cannot be absolutely certain, the language of probability is often used in stating conclusions. Thus, when a meteorologist makes a forecast, weather data collected over a large region are studied, and based on this study, the weather forecast is given in terms of chances. A typical forecast might be "There is a 20% possibility for rain tomorrow."

To summarize, in statistics we are interested in four principles: gathering data or information, organizing it, analyzing it, and interpreting it.

Margin notes:
Organization of Data

Analysis of Data

Population

Sample

Random Sample

Inductive Statistics

In gathering data or in choosing a random sample it is important to:

1. Describe the method for choosing the sample clearly and carefully.
2. Choose the sample so that it is random, that is, so that it is dependable and not subject to personal choice or bias.

Example 1   Suppose television tubes on an assembly line pass an inspection, and suppose it is desired to test on the average one out of four tubes. If the test is to be performed in a random fashion, how should the inspection proceed?

Solution   To remove any personal choice on the part of the inspector, 2 fair coins can be flipped. Then, whenever 2 tails appear (probability $\frac{1}{4}$), the inspector can select a tube for testing.   ■

Exercise 1
Solutions to Odd-Numbered Problems begin on page 606.

In Problems 1–6 list some possible ways to choose random samples for each study.

1. A study to determine opinion about a certain television program
2. A study to detect defective radio resistors
3. A study of the opinions of people toward Medicare
4. A study to determine opinions about an election of a United States president
5. A study of the number of savings accounts per family in the United States
6. A national study of the monthly budget for a family of 4

7. The following is an example of a biased sample: In a study of political party preferences, poorly dressed interviewers obtained a significantly greater proportion of answers favoring Democratic party candidates in their samples than did their well-dressed and wealthier-looking counterparts. Give two more examples of biased samples.
8. In a study of the number of savings acounts per family, a sample of accounts totaling less than $10,000 was taken, and, from the owners of these accounts, information about the total number of accounts owned by all family members was obtained. Criticize this sample.
9. It is customary for news reporters to sample the opinions of a few people to find out how the population at large feels about the events of the day. A reporter questions people on a downtown street corner. Is there anything wrong with such an approach?
10. In 1936 the Literary Digest conducted a poll to predict the presidential election. Based on their poll they predicted the election of Landon over Roosevelt. In the actual election, Roosevelt won. The sample was taken by drawing the mailing list from telephone directories and lists of car owners. What was wrong with the sample?

2. Organization of Data

Quite often a study results in a collection of large masses of data. If the data are to be understood and, at the same time, effective, they must be summarized in some manner. Two methods of presenting data are in common use. One method involves a summarized presentation of the numbers themselves according to order in a tabular form; the other involves presenting the quantitative data in pictorial form, such as by using graphs or diagrams.

Example 1 Suppose a random sample of 71 children from a group of 10,000 indicate their weight measurements, as shown in Table 1:

Table 1
Weight Measurements of 71 Students, in Pounds

69	71	71	55	52	55	58	58	58	62	67	94
82	94	95	89	89	104	93	93	58	62	67	62
94	85	92	75	75	79	75	82	94	105	115	104
105	109	94	92	89	85	85	89	95	92	105	71
72	72	79	79	85	72	79	119	89	72	72	69
79	79	69	93	85	93	79	85	85	69	79	

Certain information available from the sample becomes more evident once the data are ordered according to some scheme. If the 71 measurements are written in order of magnitude, we obtain Table 2:

Table 2

52	55	55	58	58	58	58	62	62	62	67	67
69	69	69	69	71	71	71	72	72	72	72	72
75	75	75	79	79	79	79	79	79	79	79	82
82	85	85	85	85	85	85	85	89	89	89	89
89	92	92	92	93	93	93	93	94	94	94	94
94	95	95	104	104	105	105	105	109	115	119	

Frequency Table The data in Table 2 can be presented in a so-called *frequency table*. This is done as follows: Tally marks are used to record the occurrence of the respective scores. Then the *frequency f* with which each score occurs can be determined. In doing this, further information may become evident. See Table 3.

Table 3

Score	Tally	Frequency, f	Score	Tally	Frequency, f
119	/	1	82	//	2
115	/	1	79	//// ///	8
109	/	1	75	///	3
105	///	3	72	////	5
104	//	2	71	///	3
95	//	2	69	////	4
94	////	5	67	//	2
93	////	4	62	///	3
92	///	3	58	////	4
89	////	5	55	//	2
85	//// //	7	52	/	1

Line Chart   A graph representation of the same data may be presented in a *line chart,* which is obtained in the following way: If we let the vertical axis denote the frequency *f* and the horizontal axis denote the score data, we obtain the graph shown in Figure 1.

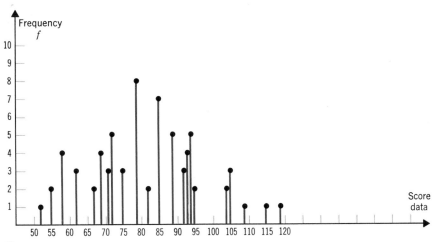

Figure 1

In studying data, a distinction should be made as to whether the data are *discrete* or *continuous.*

Variable; Continuous Variable; Discrete Variable   **A measurable characteristic is called a** *variable.* **If a variable can assume any real value between certain limits, it is called a** *continuous variable.* **It is called a** *discrete variable* **if it can assume only a finite set of values or as many values as there are whole numbers.**

Examples of continuous variables are weight, height, length, time, etc. Examples of discrete variables are the number of votes a candidate gets, number of cars sold, etc.

Example 2   A random sample of 71 children from a group of 10,000 indicate their weight measurements, as shown in Table 4 (these are the data from Table 2, but measured more accurately).

Table 4

52.30	55.61	55.71	58.01	58.41	58.51	58.91	62.33	62.50	62.71
67.13	67.23	69.51	69.67	69.80	69.82	71.34	71.65	71.83	72.15
72.22	72.41	72.59	72.67	75.11	75.71	75.82	79.03	79.06	79.09
79.15	79.28	79.32	79.51	79.62	82.32	82.61	85.09	85.13	85.25
85.31	85.41	85.51	85.58	89.21	89.32	89.49	89.61	89.78	92.41
92.63	92.89	93.05	93.19	93.28	93.91	94.17	94.28	94.31	94.52
94.71	95.32	95.51	104.31	104.71	105.21	105.37	105.71	109.34	115.71
119.38									

The data in Table 4 illustrate an example of a continuous variable, whereas the data given in Table 1 are discrete. The difference is in the accuracy of the measuring device.

■

Raw Data   The data in Table 4 are ordered, but are still considered to be *raw data* because they have not yet been subjected to any kind of statistical treatment. To begin to classify the raw data, two decisions must be made:

1. We have to decide on the *number of classes* into which the data are to be grouped.
2. We must decide on the *range of values* each class is to cover.

In grouping any data, experience indicates that we should seldom use fewer than six classes or more than twenty. This is, of course, not a firm rule and there are exceptions to it.

The size of each class depends to a large extent on the nature of the data, and above all, on the actual number of items within each class. For the data in Table 4, the smallest value is 52.30 and the largest value is 119.38. In order to use all the data, we have to cover the interval from 52.30 to 119.38.

Range   **The *range* of a set of numbers is the difference between the largest and the smallest value in the data under consideration. Thus,**

$$\text{Range} = (\text{Largest value}) - (\text{Smallest value})$$

For the weight measurements of Example 2, the range is

$$119.38 - 52.30 = 67.08$$

Histogram
Class Interval
Class Limit   Now, we would like to present the data in Table 4 in the form of a graph called a *histogram*. To do this, we must first determine the *class intervals* and the *class limits*. The class intervals for our data will be obtained by dividing the range into equal intervals. Tables 5 and 6 show the use of two different class intervals—one of size 5 and the other of size 10. In choosing intervals of size 5 and 10, we will be able to cover all the scores.

Lower Class Limit
Upper Class Limit   The intervals given in column 2 of Tables 5 and 6 are called *class intervals*. Numbers such as 49.995–59.995 are called *class limits*: 49.995 is the *lower class limit* and 59.995 is the *upper class limit* for the class interval. To avoid confusion, we will always use one decimal place more for class limits than appears in the raw data. Thus, for our data, we choose the class intervals 114.995–119.995, 109.995–114.995, and so on, so that each score could be assigned to one and only one class interval.

Notice that once raw data are converted to grouped data, it is impossible to retrieve or recover the original data from the frequency table. The best we can do is to choose the midpoint of each class interval as a representative for each class. In Table 5, for example, the actual scores of 105.21, 105.37, 105.71, and 109.34 are viewed as being represented by the midpoint of the class interval 104.995–109.995, namely, 107.500.

Table 5

Class	Class Interval	Tally	Frequency
14	114.995–119.995	//	2
13	109.995–114.995		0
12	104.995–109.995	////	4
11	99.995–104.995	//	2
10	94.995– 99.995	//	2
9	89.995– 94.995	7HL 7HL //	12
8	84.995– 89.995	7HL 7HL //	12
7	79.995– 84.995	//	2
6	74.995– 79.995	7HL 7HL /	11
5	69.995– 74.995	7HL ///	8
4	64.995– 69.995	7HL /	6
3	59.995– 64.995	///	3
2	54.995– 59.995	7HL /	6
1	49.995– 54.995	/	1

Table 6

Class	Class Interval	Tally	Frequency
7	109.995–119.995	//	2
6	99.995–109.995	7HL /	6
5	89.995– 99.995	7HL 7HL ////	14
4	79.995– 89.995	7HL 7HL ////	14
3	69.995– 79.995	7HL 7HL 7HL ////	19
2	59.995– 69.995	//// ////	9
1	49.995– 59.995	7HL //	7

To build a histogram for the data in Table 6, we construct a set of rectangles having as a base the size of the class interval and as height the frequency of occurrence of data in that particular interval. The center of the base is the midpoint of each class interval. See Figure 2.

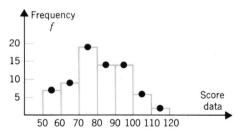

Figure 2

If we connect all the midpoints of the tops of the rectangles in Figure 2, we obtain a line graph called a *frequency polygon*. (In order not to leave the graph hanging, we always connect it to the horizontal axis on both sides.) See Figure 3 on page 388.

Frequency
Polygon

Sometimes it is more useful to learn how many cases fall below (or above) a certain value. For the data of Table 6, we may want to know how many students had weights less than 99.995 or less than 69.995 (or how many had weights more

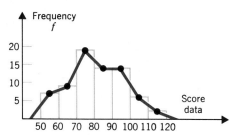

Figure 3

than 59.995 or more than 99.995). If this is the case, we can convert the data as follows: Start at the lowest class interval (49.995–59.995) and note how many scores are below the upper limit of this interval. The number is 7. So we write 7 in the column labelled cf of Table 7 in the row for 49.995–59.995. Next, we ask how many scores fall below the upper limit of the next class interval (59.995–69.995); that is, how many scores are below 69.995? The answer is $7 + 9 = 16$. The process is continued upward. The top entry of the last column should agree with the total number of scores in the sample. The numbers in this column are called the *cumulative (less than) frequencies*.

Cumulative Frequency

Table 7

Class Interval	Tally	f	cf
109.995–119.995	//	2	71
99.995–109.995	₮₮₭ /	6	69
89.995– 99.995	₮₮₭ ₮₮₭ ////	14	63
79.995– 89.995	₮₮₭ ₮₮₭ ////	14	49
69.995– 79.995	₮₮₭ ₮₮₭ ₮₮₭ ////	19	35
59.995– 69.995	₮₮₭ ////	9	16
49.995– 59.995	₮₮₭ //	7	7

Cumulative Frequency Distribution

The graph in which the horizontal axis represents class intervals and the vertical axis represents cumulative frequencies is called the *cumulative (less than) frequency distribution*. See Figure 4 for the cumulative frequency distribution for the data from Table 7. Notice that the points obtained are connected by lines in order to aid interpretation of the graph.

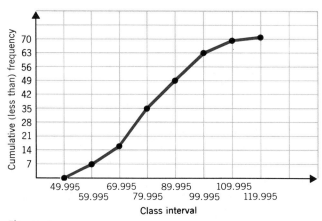

Figure 4

In a similar manner, the *cumulative (more than) frequency distribution* can be obtained.

Exercise 2
Solutions to Odd-Numbered Problems begin on page 606.

1. Consider the data given in the table.

Votes Cast	Number of Precincts
600–649	1
550–599	9
500–549	26
450–499	48
400–449	67
350–399	104
300–349	150
250–299	190
200–249	120
150–199	33
100–149	4
50–99	1
	Total: 753

Distribution of Cleveland Voting Precincts according to total vote cast for governor.
SOURCE: *Ohio Election Statistics,* 1932, pp. 218–242.

With reference to this table, determine the following:
(a) The lower limit of the fifth class
(b) The upper limit of the fourth class
(c) The midpoint of the fifth class
(d) The size of the fifth interval
(e) The frequency of the third class
(f) The class interval having the largest frequency
(g) The number of precincts with less than 600 votes
(h) Construct the histogram
(i) Construct the frequency polygon

2. The following scores were made on a 60 item test:

25	30	34	37	41	42	46	49	53
26	31	34	37	41	42	46	50	53
28	31	35	37	41	43	47	51	54
29	32	36	38	41	44	48	52	54
30	33	36	39	41	44	48	52	55
30	33	37	40	42	45	48	52	

(a) Set up a frequency table for the above data. What is the range?
(b) Draw a line chart for the data.

(c) Draw a histogram for the data using a class interval of size 2.
(d) Draw the frequency polygon for this histogram.
(e) Find the cumulative (less than) frequencies.
(f) Draw the cumulative (less than) frequency distribution.
(g) Find the cumulative (more than) frequencies.
(h) Draw the cumulative (more than) frequency distribution.

3. For Table 5 in the text:
   (a) Draw a line chart.
   (b) Draw a histogram.
   (c) Draw the frequency polygon.
   (d) Find the cumulative (less than) frequencies.
   (e) Draw the cumulative (less than) frequency distribution.

4. *Commercial Bank Earnings.* According to the *Fortune Directory* (June 15, 1967), the following are the earnings of the 50 largest commercial banks in the United States (as percentage of capital funds for the year 1966):

12.2	9.9	11.2	12.5	9.8
11.5	11.8	11.1	12.3	10.1
11.4	9.2	12.8	9.8	12.6
9.9	10.2	12.6	14.4	10.9
10.2	10.3	11.6	10.2	13.1
10.4	10.9	8.4	14.6	13.4
12.3	11.4	9.2	12.8	11.0
11.2	10.9	10.1	10.9	12.9
11.2	13.2	10.2	16.0	13.6
10.9	11.4	11.6	11.7	13.0

Answer the same questions as in Problem 2, using a class interval of 0.5 beginning with 8.05.

5. *Number of Physicians.* The following are the number of physicians per 100,000 population in 110 selected large American cities in 1962 (*Statistical Abstract of the United States,* 1967):

131	245	145	129	155	232	256	204	296	222
185	166	198	127	153	230	175	161	240	169
169	158	116	171	111	152	126	140	218	142
141	116	176	127	156	185	207	218	153	128
176	162	100	138	129	211	178	198	132	289
165	129	137	78	146	148	145	146	161	119
119	116	245	137	95	169	131	156	136	122
194	113	184	132	172	91	110	188	185	144
105	166	154	108	144	202	212	190	165	128
131	157	115	153	127	224	171	154	149	112
134	190	130	192	123	224	131	190	136	123

Answer the same questions as in Problem 2, using a class interval of 10 beginning with 70.5.

3. Analysis of Data

3.1 Measures of Central Tendency

Average   The idea of taking an *average* is familiar to practically everyone. Quite often we hear people talk about average salary, average height, average grade, average family, and so on. However, the idea of averages is so commonly used that it should not surprise you to learn that several kinds of averages have been introduced in statistics.

Averages are called *measures of central tendency*. The three most common measures of central tendency are the *arithmetic mean, median,* and *mode.*

Mean   **The** *arithmetic mean,* **or** *mean,* **of a set of real numbers** $x_1, x_2, \ldots, x_n$ **is denoted by** $\overline{X}$ **and is defined as**

(1)
$$\overline{X} = \frac{x_1 + x_2 + \cdots + x_n}{n}$$

Example 1   The grades of a student on eight examinations were $70, 65, 69, 85, 94, 62, 79,$ and 100. Find the mean.

Solution   The mean of this set of grades is

$$\overline{X} = \frac{70 + 65 + 69 + 85 + 94 + 62 + 79 + 100}{8} = 78$$

In this example, $n = 8$ and the mean grade is 78.

An interesting fact about the mean is that the sum of deviations of each item from the mean is zero. In Example 1, the deviation of each score from the mean $\overline{X} = 78$ is $(100 - 78)$, $(94 - 78)$, $(85 - 78)$, $(79 - 78)$, $(70 - 78)$, $(69 - 78)$, $(65 - 78)$, and $(62 - 78)$. Table 8 lists each score, the mean, and the deviation from the mean. If we add up the deviations from the mean, we obtain a sum of zero.

Table 8

Score	Mean	Deviation from Mean
100	78	22
94	78	16
85	78	7
79	78	1
70	78	−8
69	78	−9
65	78	−13
62	78	−16
		Sum of Deviations: 0

For any group of data, the following result is true:

The sum of the deviations from the mean is zero.

As a matter of fact, we could have defined the mean as that real number for which the sum of the deviations is zero.

Another interesting fact about the mean is that if Y is any guessed or assumed mean (which may be any real number) and if we let d_j denote the deviation of each item of the data from the assumed mean, $(d_j = x_j - Y)$, then the actual mean is

(2)
$$\overline{X} = Y + \frac{d_1 + d_2 + \cdots + d_n}{n}$$

Consider Example 1. We know that the actual mean is 78. Suppose we had guessed the mean to be 52. Then, using formula (2), we obtain

$$\overline{X} = 52 + \frac{\begin{aligned}(100 - 52) + (94 - 52) + (85 - 52) + (79 - 52)\\ + (70 - 52) + (69 - 52) + (65 - 52) + (62 - 52)\end{aligned}}{8}$$

$$= 52 + 26 = 78$$

which agrees with what we have already found.

The purpose of introducing equation (2) to find the mean is that, if the numbers to be added in finding the mean are large, (2) can simplify the computation.

A method for computing the mean for grouped data given in a frequency table is illustrated here by the use of an example.

Example 2 Find the mean for the grouped data given in Table 6, page 387.

Table 9 displays the information needed to complete the example.

Table 9

Class Interval	f_i	m_i	$f_i m_i$
109.995–119.995	2	115	230
99.995–109.995	6	105	630
89.995– 99.995	14	95	1330
79.995– 89.995	14	85	1190
69.995– 79.995	19	75	1425
59.995– 69.995	9	65	585
49.995– 59.995	7	55	385
$n = 71$			5775 = Sum of $f_i m_i$

1. Take the midpoint (m_i) of each of the intervals as a reference point and enter the result in column 3. For example, the midpoint of the interval 79.995–89.995 is 85.
2. Next, multiply the entry in column 3 by the frequency f_i for that class interval and enter the product in column 4, which is labeled $f_i m_i$.
3. Add the entries in column 4.

The mean is then computed by dividing the sum by the number of entries. That is,

(3)

$$\overline{X} = \frac{\Sigma f_i m_i}{n}$$

where

Σ means to add up the entries
f_i = Number of entries in the ith class interval
m_i = Midpoint of ith class interval
n = Number of items

Now we can use the data in Table 9 and equation (3) to find the mean:

$$\overline{X} = \frac{5775}{71} = 81.3$$

When data grouped, the original data are lost due to grouping. As a result, the number obtained by using equation (3) is only an approximation to the actual mean. The reason for this is that using (3) amounts to computing the weighted average midpoint of a class interval (weighted by the frequency of scores in that interval) and therefore cannot be a computation for $\overline{X}$ exactly.

Median **The** *median* **of a set of real numbers arranged in order of magnitude is the middle value if the number of items is odd, and it is the arithmetic mean of the two middle values if the number of items is even.**

Example 3 (a) The group of data 2, 2, 3, 4, 5, 7, 7, 7, 11 has median 5.
(b) The group of data 2, 2, 3, 3, 4, 5, 7, 7, 7, 11 has median 4.5, since

$$\frac{4 + 5}{2} = 4.5$$

To find the median for the grouped data in Table 6, page 387, we proceed as follows: The median is that point in the data that will have 50% of the cases above it and 50% below it. Now, 50% of 71 cases is 35.5 cases, so we are interested in finding the point in the distribution with 35 cases above it and 35 below it.

We start by counting up from the bottom until we come as close to 35 cases as possible, but not exceeding it. This brings us through the interval 69.995–79.995. Thus, the median must lie in the interval 79.995–89.995. Now, the median will

Interpolation
Factor

equal the lower limit of the interval 79.995–89.995, namely 79.995, plus an *interpolation factor*. The interpolation factor is determined as follows:

1. Count the number p of entries or fractional entries needed to reach the median (in our example, the number is 0.5).

2. If the frequency for the interval is q, divide the interval into q parts.
3. The interpolation factor I is

$$I = \frac{p}{q} \cdot i$$

where

p = Number of entries needed to reach the median
q = Number of entries in the interval
i = Size of the interval

The median M is then given by

$$M = (\text{Lower limit of interval}) + (\text{Interpolation factor})$$

For the data of Table 6, the median M is

$$M = 79.995 + \frac{0.5}{14} \cdot 10 = 80.352$$

Again, keep in mind that this median is an approximation to the actual median, since it is obtained from grouped data. If we go back to the original data listed in Table 4, we obtain $M = 82.32$.

Centile Point   The median is sometimes called the *centile point* and is denoted by C_{50} to indicate that 50% of the data are below it and 50% are above it. Similarly, we can find C_{25}, or the first quartile, and C_{75}, or the third quartile.

For the data in Table 9, C_{25} is formed by first finding the class interval containing the tally equal to 25% of all the tallies. Thus, the tally corresponding to C_{25} is found in the class interval 69.995–79.995, since

$$25\% \text{ of } 71 = 17.75$$

and 16 tallies lie in the first two class intervals. Using the interpolation factor, we find that

$$C_{25} = 69.995 + (1.75) \frac{1}{19} (10) = 69.995 + 0.921 = 70.916$$

Mode   The *mode* of a set of real numbers is the value that occurs with the greatest frequency exceeding a frequency of 1.

The mode does not necessarily exist, and if it does, it is not always unique. For the data in Table 3, page 384, the mode is 79 (8 is the highest frequency).

Example 4   The group of data 2, 3, 4, 5, 7, 15 has no mode.

∎

Example 5   The group of data 2, 2, 2, 3, 3, 7, 7, 7, 11, 15 has two modes 2 and 7, and is called *bimodal*.

Bimodal

∎

When data have been listed in a frequency table, the mode is defined as the midpoint of the interval consisting of the largest number of cases. For example, the mode for the data in Table 6, page 387, is 75 (the midpoint of the interval 69.995–79.995).

Of the three measures of central tendency considered so far, the mean is the most important, the most reliable, and the one most frequently used. The reason for this is that it is easy to understand, easy to compute, and uses all the data in the collection. If two samples are chosen from the same population, the two means corresponding to the two samples will not generally differ by as much as the two medians of these samples.

The second most reliable measure is the median. It, too, is easy to understand and easy to compute. One advantage of the median over the mean is that it is independent of extreme values.

Exercise 3.1
Solutions to Odd-Numbered Problems begin on page 610.

In Problems 1–6 compute the mean, median, and mode of the given raw data.

1. 21, 25, 43, 36
2. 16, 18, 24, 30
3. 55, 55, 80, 92, 70
4. 65, 82, 82, 95, 70
5. 62, 71, 83, 90, 75
6. 48, 65, 80, 92, 80

7. If an investor purchased 50 shares of IBM stock at $155 per share, 90 shares at $190 per share, 120 shares at $210 per share, and another 75 shares at $255 per share, what is the average cost per share?

8. If a farmer sells 120 bushels of corn at $2 per bushel, 80 bushels at $2.10 per bushel, 150 bushels at $1.90 per bushel, and 120 bushels at $2.20 per bushel, what is the average income per bushel?

9. The annual salaries of five faculty members in the Mathematics Department at a large university are $14,000, $15,000, $16,000, $16,500, and $35,000. Compute the mean and median. Which measure describes the situation more realistically? If you were among the four lowest-paid members, which measure would you use to describe the situation? What if you were the one making $35,000?

10. For the grouped data in Table 5, page 387, compute the mean, median, and mode.

11. The distribution of the weekly earnings of 1155 secretaries in May 1978 in the Chicago metropolitan area is summarized in the table. Find the mean salary and the median salary.

Weekly Earnings	Number of Secretaries
Under $100	25
$100–$125	55
$125–$150	325
$150–$175	410
$175–$200	215
$200–$225	75
Over $225	50

12. For the data given in Problems 2, 4, and 5 in Exercise 2 (page 389), find the mean, median, and mode.

13. Find C_{75} and C_{40} for the grouped data in Tables 5 and 6.

14. In a labor/management wage negotiation in which the laborers are the lowest paid of the workers in the company, which measure of central tendency would labor tend to use as an argument for more pay? Which would management use? Why?

15. For the data given in Problem 1 in Exercise 2 (page 389), find the mean, using an assumed mean.

*16. In a frequency table, the score x_1 appears f_1 times, the score x_2 appears f_2 times, . . . , and the score x_n appears f_n times. Show that the mean $\bar{X}$ is given by the formula

$$\bar{X} = \frac{x_1 \cdot f_1 + x_2 \cdot f_2 + \cdots + x_n \cdot f_n}{f_1 + f_2 + \cdots + f_n}$$

3.2 Measures of Dispersion

We begin with an example.

Example 6   Consider the following sets of scores:

$$S_1: \quad 4, 6, 8, 10, 12, 14, 16$$
$$S_2: \quad 4, 7, 9, 10, 11, 13, 16$$

Notice that the mean of S_1 and S_2 is 10, and the median of S_1 and S_2 is 10. The scores in each set are different, but those in S_2 seem to be more closely clustered around 10 than those in S_1.

■

We need a statistical measure to indicate the extent to which the scores in Example 6 are spread out. Such measures are called *measures of dispersion*.

Range   The simplest measure of dispersion is the *range,* which we have already defined as the difference between the largest value and the smallest value. For S_1 and S_2 the range is $16 - 4 = 12$. We can see that the range is a poor measure of dispersion since it depends only on two measures and tells us nothing about the rest of the scores.

Deviation from the Mean   Another measure of dispersion is the *deviation from the mean.* Recall that this measure is characterized by the fact that if the deviations from the mean of each score are all added up, the result is zero. Because of this, it is not widely used as a measure of dispersion.

We need a measure that will give us an idea of how much deviation is involved without having these deviations add up to zero. By squaring each deviation from the mean, adding them, and dividing by the number of scores, we obtain an average squared deviation, which is called the *variance* of the set of scores. The formula for the variance, which is denoted by σ^2, is*

Variance

*The Greek letter sigma.

$$\sigma^2 = \frac{(x_1 - \overline{X})^2 + (x_2 - \overline{X})^2 + \cdots + (x_n - \overline{X})^2}{n}$$

where $\overline{X}$ is the mean of the scores $x_1, x_2, \ldots, x_n$ and n is the number of scores.

In order to apply this measure in practical situations (for instance, if our data represent dollars, we cannot talk about "squared dollars"), we use the square root of the variance. This is called the *standard deviation* of a set of scores. The standard deviation is denoted by σ and is given by the formula

Standard
Deviation

$$\sigma = \sqrt{\frac{(x_1 - \overline{X})^2 + (x_2 - \overline{X})^2 + \cdots + (x_n - \overline{X})^2}{n}}$$

where $\overline{X}$ and the x_i's are defined the same way as for the variance.

For the data in Example 6, the standard deviation for S_1 is

$$\sigma = \sqrt{\frac{36 + 16 + 4 + 0 + 4 + 16 + 36}{7}} = \sqrt{\frac{112}{7}} = \sqrt{16} = 4$$

and the standard deviation for S_2 is

$$\sigma = \sqrt{\frac{36 + 9 + 1 + 0 + 1 + 9 + 36}{7}} = \sqrt{\frac{92}{7}} = \sqrt{13.14} = 3.625$$

The fact that the standard deviation of the set S_2 is less than that for the set S_1 is an indication that the scores of S_2 are more clustered around the mean than those of S_1.

Example 7   Find the standard deviation for the data

$$100, 90, 90, 85, 80, 75, 75, 75, 70, 70, 65, 65, 60, 40, 40, 40$$

Solution   The mean is

$$\overline{X} = \frac{100 + 2 \cdot 90 + 85 + 80 + 3 \cdot 75 + 2 \cdot 70 + 2 \cdot 65 + 60 + 3 \cdot 40}{16} = 70$$

The deviations from the mean and their squares are given in Table 10 on page 398. The standard deviation is

$$\sigma = \sqrt{\frac{4950}{16}} = \frac{70.4}{4} = 17.6$$

■

Example 8   Find the standard deviation for the data

$$80, 80, 80, 80, 75, 75, 75, 75, 70, 70, 65, 65, 60, 60, 55, 55$$

Solution   Here the mean is $\overline{X} = 70$ for the 16 scores. Table 11 gives the deviations from the mean and their squares. The standard deviation is

$$\sigma = \sqrt{\frac{1200}{16}} = \sqrt{75} = 8.7$$

■

Table 10

Scores x	Deviation from the Mean $x - \bar{X}$	Deviation Squared $(x - \bar{X})^2$
100	30	900
90	20	400
90	20	400
85	15	225
80	10	100
75	5	25
75	5	25
75	5	25
70	0	0
70	0	0
65	−5	25
65	−5	25
60	−10	100
40	−30	900
40	−30	900
40	−30	900
Mean = 70 n = 16	Sum = 0	Sum = 4950

Table 11

Scores x	Deviation from the Mean $x - \bar{X}$	Deviation Squared $(x - \bar{X})^2$
80	10	100
80	10	100
80	10	100
80	10	100
75	5	25
75	5	25
75	5	25
75	5	25
70	0	0
70	0	0
65	−5	25
65	−5	25
60	−10	100
60	−10	100
55	−15	225
55	−15	225
Mean = 70 n = 16	Sum = 0	Sum = 1200

These two examples show that although the samples have the same mean, 70, and the same sample size, 16, the scores in the first set deviate further from the mean than do the scores in the second set.

In general, a relatively small standard deviation indicates that the measures tend to cluster close to the mean, and a relatively high standard deviation shows that the measures are widely scattered from the mean.

To find the standard deviation for grouped data we use the formula

$$\sigma = \sqrt{\frac{(x_1 - \bar{X})^2 \cdot f_1 + (x_2 - \bar{X})^2 \cdot f_2 + \cdots + (x_n - \bar{X})^2 \cdot f_n}{n}}$$

where $x_1, x_2, \ldots, x_n$ are the class midpoints; $f_1, f_2, \ldots, f_n$ are the respective frequencies; n is the sum of the frequencies, that is, $n = f_1 + f_2 + \cdots + f_n$; and $\bar{X}$ is the mean.

Example 9   Find the standard deviation for the grouped data given in Table 9, page 392.

Solution   We have already found that the mean for the grouped data is

$$\bar{X} = 81.3$$

The class midpoints are 55, 65, 75, 85, 95, 105, and 115. The deviations of the mean from the class midpoints, their squares, and the products of the squares by the respective frequencies are listed in Table 12. The standard deviation is

$$\sigma = \sqrt{\frac{16{,}447.99}{71}} = \sqrt{231.66} = 15.22$$

■

Table 12

Class Midpoint	f_i	$x_i - \bar{X}$	$(x_i - \bar{X})^2$	$(x_i - \bar{X})^2 \cdot f_i$
115	2	33.7	1,135.69	2,271.38
105	6	23.7	561.69	3,370.14
95	14	13.7	187.69	2,627.66
85	14	3.7	13.69	191.66
75	19	−6.3	39.69	754.11
65	9	−16.3	265.69	2,391.21
55	7	−26.3	691.69	4,841.83
Sum	71			16,447.99

A little computation shows that the sum of the deviations of the approximate mean from the class midpoints is not exactly zero. This is because we are using only an approximation to the mean, since we cannot compute the exact mean for grouped data.

Exercise 3.2
Solutions to Odd-Numbered Problems begin on page 611.

In Problems 1–6 compute the standard deviation for the given raw data.

1. 4, 5, 9, 9, 10, 14, 25
2. 6, 8, 10, 10, 11, 12, 18
3. 62, 58, 70, 70
4. 55, 65, 80, 80, 90
5. 85, 75, 62, 78, 100
6. 92, 82, 75, 75, 82

7. The lifetimes of six light bulbs are 968, 893, 769, 845, 922, and 815 hours. Calculate the mean lifetime and the standard deviation.

8. A group of 25 applicants for admission to Midwestern University made the following scores on the quantitative part of an aptitude test:

591	570	425	472	555
490	415	479	517	570
606	614	542	607	441
502	506	603	488	460
550	551	420	590	482

Find the mean and standard deviation of these scores.

9. Find the standard deviation for the data given in Problem 1, Exercise 2 (page 389).

10. Find the standard deviation for the grouped data given in Table 5 (page 387).

4. Normal Distribution

Frequency polygons or frequency distributions can assume almost any shape or form, depending on the data. However, the data obtained from many experiments often follow a common pattern which has been thoroughly investigated. For example, heights of people, weights of people, test scores, and coin tossing all lead to data which have the same kind of frequency distribution. This distribution is referred to as the *normal distribution* or the *Gaussian distribution*. Because it occurs so often in practical situations, it is generally regarded as the most important distribution, and much statistical theory is based on it. The graph of the normal distribution, called the *normal curve*, is the bell-shaped curve shown in Figure 5.

Normal Distribution

Normal Curve

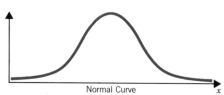

Normal Curve x

Figure 5

Some properties of the normal curve are listed below.

1. Normal curves are bell-shaped and are symmetrical with respect to a vertical line. See Figure 6.
2. The mean is at the center. See Figure 6.

CARL FRIEDRICH GAUSS (1777–1855), sometimes called the "prince of mathematicians," made profound contributions to number theory, the theory of functions, probability and statistics. He discovered a way to calculate the orbits of asteroids, made basic discoveries in electromagnetic theory, and invented a telegraph.

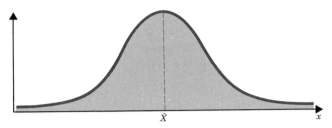

Figure 6

3. Irrespective of the shape, the area enclosed by the curve and the x-axis is always equal to 1. See the shaded region in Figure 6.
4. The probability that an outcome of a normally distributed experiment is between a and b equals the area under the associated normal curve from x = a to x = b. See the shaded region in Figure 7.

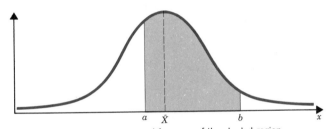

Probability between a and b = area of the shaded region.

Figure 7

It is also important to recognize that, in theory, the normal curve will never touch the x-axis, but will extend to infinity in either direction. In addition, every normal distribution has its mean, median, and mode at the same point.

5. The standard deviation of a normal distribution plays a major role in describing the area under the normal curve. As shown in Figure 8, the standard deviation is related to the area under the normal curve as follows:
    (a) Within 1 standard deviation (from $\bar{X} - \sigma$ to $\bar{X} + \sigma$) is about 68.27% of the total area under the curve

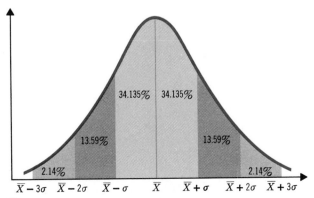

Figure 8

(b) Within 2 standard deviations (from $\bar{X} - 2\sigma$ to $\bar{X} + 2\sigma$) is about 95.45% of the total area under the curve

(c) Within 3 standard deviations (from $\bar{X} - 3\sigma$ to $\bar{X} + 3\sigma$) is about 99.73% of the total area under the curve

Example 1 At Jefferson High School, the average IQ score of the 1200 students is 100, with a standard deviation of 15. The IQ scores have a normal distribution.

(a) How many students will have an IQ between 85 and 115?
(b) How many students will have an IQ between 70 and 130?
(c) How many students will have an IQ between 55 and 145?
(d) How many students will have an IQ under 55 or over 145?
(e) How many students will have an IQ over 145?

Solution (a) Since we are assuming that the IQ scores have a normal distribution, we know that the mean is 100. Since the standard deviation σ is 15, then 1σ either side of the mean is from 85 and 115. By property 5(a) we know that 68.27% of 1200, or

$$(.6827)(1200) = 819 \text{ students}$$

have IQ's between 85 and 115.

(b) The scores from 70 to 130 extend 2σ ($= 30$) either side of the mean. By property 5(b) we know that 95.45% of 1200, or

$$(.9545)(1200) = 1145 \text{ students}$$

have IQ's between 70 and 130.

(c) The scores from 55 to 145 extend 3σ ($= 45$) either side of the mean. By property 5(c) we know that 99.73% of 1200, or

$$(.9973)(1200) = 1197 \text{ students}$$

have IQ's between 55 and 145.

(d) There are about 3 students ($1200 - 1197$) who have scores that are not between 55 and 145.

(e) About 1 or 2 of them are above 145.

See Figure 9.

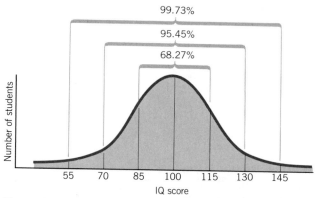

Figure 9

A normal distribution curve is completely determined by $\bar{X}$ and σ. Hence, different normal distributions of data with different means and standard deviations give rise to different shapes of the normal curve. Figure 10 indicates how the normal curve changes when the standard deviation changes. For the sake of clarity, we assume all data have mean 0.

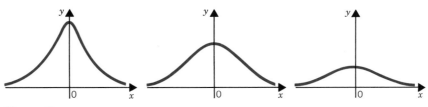

Figure 10

As the standard deviation increases, the normal curve flattens out. A flatter curve indicates a greater likelihood for the outcomes to be spread out. A sharper curve indicates that the outcomes are more likely to be close to the mean.

It would be a hopeless task to attempt to set up separate tables of normal curve areas for every conceivable value of $\bar{X}$ and σ. Fortunately, we are able to transform all the observations to one table—the table corresponding to the so-called *standard normal curve,* which is the normal curve for which $\bar{X} = 0$ and $\sigma = 1$. This can be achieved by introducing new score data, called *Z-scores,* defined as

Standard Normal Curve

Z-Score

(1)
$$Z = \frac{\text{Distance between } x \text{ and } \bar{X}}{\text{Standard deviation}} = \frac{x - \bar{X}}{\sigma}$$

where

$x = $ Old score data
$\bar{X} = $ Mean of the old data
$\sigma = $ Standard deviation of the old data

Standard Score

The new score data defined by (1) will always have a *zero mean* and a *unit standard deviation.* Such data are said to be expressed in *standard units* or *standard scores.* By expressing data in terms of standard units, it becomes possible to make a comparison of distributions. Furthermore, as for all normal curves, the total area under a standard normal curve is equal to 1.

Example 2 On a test, 80 is the mean and 7 is the standard deviation. What is the Z-score of a score of:
(a) 88?   (b)   62?
Interpret your results.

Solution (a)   Here, 88 is the regular score. Using (1) with $x = 88$, $\bar{X} = 80$, $\sigma = 7$, we get

$$Z = \frac{x - \bar{X}}{\sigma} = \frac{88 - 80}{7} = \frac{8}{7} = 1.1429$$

(b)   Here, 62 is the regular score. Using (1) with $x = 62$, $\bar{X} = 80$, and $\sigma = 7$, we get

$$Z = \frac{62 - 80}{7} = \frac{-18}{7} = -2.5714$$

The Z-score of 1.1429 tells us that the original score of 88 is 1.1429 standard deviations *above* the mean. See Figure 11. The Z-score of -2.5714 tells us that the original score of 62 is 2.5714 standard deviations *below* the mean. A negative Z-score always means that the score is below the mean. See Figure 11.

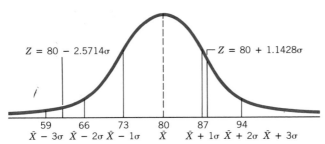

$Z = 80 - 2.5714\sigma$ $Z = 80 + 1.1428\sigma$

59	66	73	80	87	94
$\bar{X} - 3\sigma$	$\bar{X} - 2\sigma$	$\bar{X} - 1\sigma$	$\bar{X}$	$\bar{X} + 1\sigma$	$\bar{X} + 2\sigma$ $\bar{X} + 3\sigma$

Figure 11

The curve in Figure 8 with mean $\bar{X} = 0$ and standard deviation $\sigma = 1$ is the standard normal curve. For this curve, the areas between $Z = -1$ and 1, $Z = -2$ and 2, $Z = -3$ and 3 are equal, respectively, to 68.27%, 95.45%, and 99.73% of the total area under the curve, which is 1. To find the areas cut off between other points, we proceed as in the following example.

Example 3   Suppose, to begin with, we consider the standard normal curve illustrated in Figure 12. We wish to find the proportion of the area, or the proportion of cases, included between the two points 0.6 and 1.86 units from the mean.

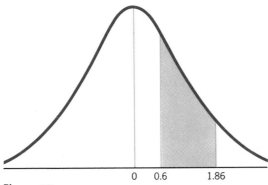

0   0.6   1.86

Figure 12

Solution   This problem is worked by using a *normal curve table,* Table 2 on page 533. We
Normal Curve Table   begin by checking the table to find the area of the curve cut off between the

mean and a point equivalent to a standard score of 0.6 from the mean. This value appears in the second column of the table next to 0.6 and is found to be 0.2257. Next, we continue down the table in the left-hand column until we come to a standard score of 1.8. By looking across the row to the column below 0.06 (column 8), we find that 0.4686 of the area is included between the mean and this point. Then the area of the curve between these two points is the difference between the two areas, 0.4686 − 0.2257, which is 0.2429. We can then state that approximately 24.29% of the cases fall between 0.6 and 1.86, or that *the probability of a score falling between these two points is about .2429.*

In the next example, we take two points that are on different sides of the mean.

Example 4   We want to determine what proportion of the area of the normal curve falls between a standard score of −0.39 and one of 1.86 for the standard normal curve given in Figure 13.

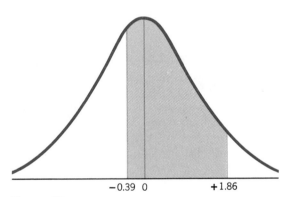

−0.39 0   +1.86

Figure 13

Solution   There are no values for negative standard scores in Table 2. Because of the symmetry of normal curves, equal standard scores, whether positive or negative, give equal areas when taken from the mean. From Table 2, we find that a standard score of −0.39 cuts off an area of 0.1517 between it and the mean. A standard score of 1.86 includes 0.4686 of the area of the curve between it and the mean. The area included between both points is then equal to the sum of these two areas, 0.1517 + 0.4686, which is 0.6203. Thus, approximately 62.03% of the area is between −0.39 and 1.86. In other words, the probability of a score falling between these two points is about .6203.

Example 5   A student receives a grade of 82 on a final examination in Biology for which the mean is 73 and the standard deviation is 9. In his final examination in Sociology for which the mean grade is 81 and the standard deviation is 15, he receives an 89. In which examination is his relative standing higher?

Solution　In their present form, these distributions are not comparable, since they have different means and, more important, different standard deviations. In order to compare the data, we transform the data to standard scores. For the Biology test data, the new score data for the student's examination score is

$$Z = \frac{82 - 73}{9} = \frac{9}{9} = 1$$

For the Sociology test data, the new score data for the student's examination score is

$$Z = \frac{89 - 81}{15} = \frac{8}{15} = 0.533$$

This means the student's score in the Biology exam is 1 standard unit above the mean, while his score in the Sociology exam is 0.533 standard unit above the mean. Hence, his *relative standing* is higher in Biology.

The Normal Curve as an Approximation to the Binomial Distribution

We start with an example.

Example 6　Consider an experiment in which a fair coin is tossed ten times. Find the frequency distribution for the probability of tossing a head.

Solution　The probability for obtaining exactly k heads is given by a binomial distribution $b(10, k; \frac{1}{2})$. Thus, from Table 1 on page 528, we obtain the distribution given in Table 13. If we graph this frequency distribution, we obtain the line chart shown in Figure 14. When we connect the tops of the lines of the line chart, we obtain a *normal curve*, as shown.

Table 13

No. of Heads	Probability $b(10, k; \frac{1}{2})$
0	.0010
1	.0098
2	.0439
3	.1172
4	.2051
5	.2461
6	.2051
7	.1172
8	.0439
9	.0098
10	.0010

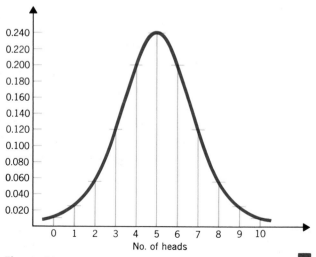

No. of heads

Figure 14

This particular distribution for $n = 10$ and $p = \frac{1}{2}$ is not a result of the choice of n or p. As a matter of fact, the line chart for any binomial probability $b(n, k; p)$ will give a normal curve. You should verify this for the cases in which $n = 15$, $p = .3$, and $n = 8$, $p = \frac{3}{4}$.

Probabilities associated with binomial experiments are readily obtainable from the formula $b(n, k; p)$ of the binomial distribution or from Table 1 on page 528 when n is small. If n is not listed in any available table, we can compute the binomial probabilities by an approximating procedure using a normal curve. It turns out that the standard normal distribution provides a very good approximation to the binomial distribution when n is large or p is close to $\frac{1}{2}$.

In Chapter 7, Section 1, we have shown that the mean $\bar{X}$ for the binomial distribution is given by $\bar{X} = np$. Moreover, it can be shown that the standard deviation is $\sigma = \sqrt{npq}$.

Example 7   A company manufactures 60,000 pencils each day. Quality control studies have shown that, on the average, 4% of the pencils are defective. A random sample of 500 pencils is selected from each day's production and tested. What is the probability that in the sample there are:
(a)   At least 12 and no more than 24 defective pencils?
(b)   32 or more defective pencils?

Solution   (a)   Since $n = 500$ is very large, it is appropriate to use a normal curve approximation for the binomial distribution. Thus, with $n = 500$ and $p = .04$,

$$\bar{X} = np = 500(.04) = 20 \qquad \sigma = \sqrt{npq} = \sqrt{500(.04)(.96)} \approx 4.38$$

To find the approximate probability of the number of defective pencils in a sample being at least 12 and no more than 24, we find the area under a normal curve from $x = 12$ to $x = 24$. See Figure 15. Areas A_1 and A_2 are found as follows:

$$Z_1 = \frac{x - \bar{X}}{\sigma} = \frac{12 - 20}{4.38} = -1.83 \qquad A_1 = 0.4664$$

$$Z_2 = \frac{x - \bar{X}}{\sigma} = \frac{24 - 20}{4.38} = 0.91 \qquad A_2 = 0.3186$$

$$\text{Total area} = A_1 + A_2 = 0.4664 + 0.3186 = 0.785$$

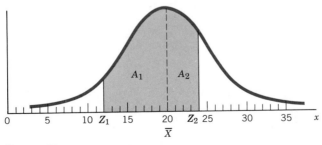

Figure 15

Thus, the approximate probability of the number of defective pencils in the sample being at least 12 and not more than 24 is .785

(b) We want to find the area A_2 indicated in Figure 16. We know that the area to the right of the mean is 0.5, and if we subtract the area A_1 from 0.5, we will obtain A_2. Therefore, we find the area A_1:

$$Z = \frac{x - \overline{X}}{\sigma} = \frac{32 - 20}{4.38} = 2.74 \qquad A_1 = 0.4969$$

Then,

$$A_2 = 0.5 - A_1 = 0.5 - 0.4969 = 0.0031$$

Thus, the approximate probability of finding 32 or more defective pencils in the sample is .0031

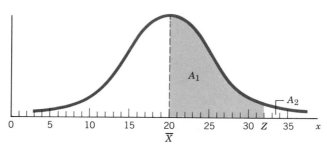

Figure 16

Exercise 4
Solutions to Odd-Numbered Problems begin on page 612.

In Problems 1–4 determine $\overline{X}$ and σ by inspection.

1.

2.
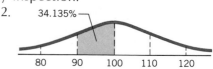

3.
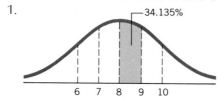

4.
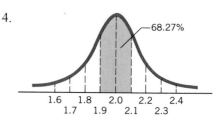
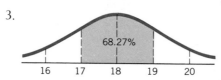

5. Given a normal distribution with a mean of 13.1 and a standard deviation of 9.3, find the Z-score equivalent of the following scores in the distribution:

7, 9, 13, 15, 29, 37, 41

6. Given a normal distribution with a mean of 15.2 and a standard deviation of 5.1, find the Z-score equivalent of the following scores in the distribution:

$$8, 9, 15, 16, 22, 23, 25$$

In Problems 7–10 use Table 2, page 533, to find each area of the shaded region under the standard normal curve.

7.
−0.5

8.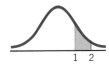
1 2

9.
1.5

10.
−0.5 0 0.5

11. Given the following Z-scores on a standard normal distribution, find the area from the mean to each score.
    (a) 0.89   (b) 1.10   (c) 2.50   (d) 3.00
    (e) −0.75   (f) −2.31   (g) 0.80   (h) 3.03

12. An instructor assigns grades in an examination according to the following procedure:

    A   if score exceeds $\bar{X} + 1.6\sigma$
    B   if score is between $\bar{X} + 0.6\sigma$ and $\bar{X} + 1.6\sigma$
    C   if score is between $\bar{X} - 0.3\sigma$ and $\bar{X} + 0.6\sigma$
    D   if score is between $\bar{X} - 1.4\sigma$ and $\bar{X} - 0.3\sigma$
    F   if score is below $\bar{X} - 1.4\sigma$

    What percentage of each grade does this instructor give, assuming that the scores are normally distributed?

13. The average height of 2000 women in a random sample is 64 inches. The standard deviation is 2 inches. The heights have a normal distribution.
    (a) How many women are between 62 and 66 inches tall?
    (b) How many women are between 60 and 68 inches tall?
    (c) How many women are between 58 and 70 inches tall?

14. Corn flakes come in a box that says it holds a mean weight of 16 ounces of cereal. The standard deviation is 0.1 ounce. Suppose that the manufacturer packages 600,000 boxes with weights that have a normal distribution.
    (a) How many boxes weigh between 15.9 and 16.1 ounces?
    (b) How many boxes weigh between 15.8 and 16.2 ounces?
    (c) How many boxes weigh between 15.7 and 16.3 ounces?
    (d) How many boxes weigh under 15.7 or over 16.3 ounces?
    (e) How many boxes weigh under 15.7 ounces?

15. The weight of 100 college students closely follows a normal distribution with a mean of 130 pounds and a standard deviation of 5.2 pounds.
    (a) How many of these students would you expect to weigh at least 142 pounds?
    (b) What range of weights would you expect to include the middle 70% of the students in this group?

16. *Life Expectancy of Clothing.*   If the average life of a certain make of clothing is 40 months with standard deviation of 7 months, what percentage of these clothes can be expected to last from 28 months to 42 months? Assume that clothing lifetime follows a normal distribution.

17. *Life Expectancy of Shoes.*   Records show that the average life expectancy of a pair of shoes is 2.2 years with a standard deviation of 1.7 years. A manufacturer guarantees that shoes lasting less than a year are replaced free. For every 1000 shoes sold, how many shoes should the manufacturer expect to replace free?

18. The attendance over a weekly period of time at a movie theater is normally distributed with a mean of 10,000 and a standard deviation of 1000 persons. Find:
    (a) The number in the lowest 70% of the attendance figures
    (b) The percentage of attendance figures that falls between 8500 and 11,000 persons
    (c) The percentage of attendance figures that differs from the mean by 1500 persons or more

19. Caryl, Mary, and Kathleen are vying for a position as secretary. Caryl, who is tested with Group I, gets a score of 76 on her test; Mary, who is tested with Group II, gets a score of 89; and Kathleen, who is tested with Group III, gets a score of 21. If the average score for Group I is 82, for Group II is 93, and for Group III is 24, and if the standard deviation for each group is 7, 2, and 9, respectively, which person has the highest relative standing?

20. In Mathematics 135, the average final grade is 75.0 and the standard deviation is 10.0. The professor's grade distribution shows that 15 students with grades from 68.0 to 82.0 received C's. Assuming the grades follow a normal distribution, how many students are in Mathematics 135?

21. Draw the line chart and frequency curve for the probability of a head in an experiment in which a biased coin is tossed fifteen times and the probability that a head occurs is .3. [*Hint:*   Find $b(15, k; .30)$ for $k = 0, 1, \ldots, 15$, by using Table 1, page 528.]

22. Follow the same directions as in Problem 21 for an experiment in which a biased coin is tossed eight times and the probability that heads appears is $\frac{3}{4}$.

In Problems 23–28 suppose a binomial experiment consists of 750 trials and the probability of success for each trial is .4. Then

$$\bar{X} = np = 300 \qquad \text{and} \qquad \sigma = \sqrt{npq} = \sqrt{(750)(.4)(.6)} \approx 13$$

Approximate the probability of obtaining the number of successes indicated by using a normal curve.

23. 285–315   24. 280–320
25. 300 or more   26. 300 or less
27. 325 or more   28. 275 or less

5. Chi-Square Distribution

In studying experiments of chance, a discrepancy usually exists between the observed frequencies of occurrence of an event and the expected frequencies. Consider the following examples.

Example 1 A coin is tossed 100 times, and the observed results are 65 heads and 35 tails. Can we assume (hypothesize) that this distribution of 65 heads and 35 tails does not differ from what we would expect by chance, namely, 50 heads and 50 tails? The results are listed in the table. Here, O denotes the observed frequency and E denotes the expected frequency.

	H	T	Totals
O	65	35	100
E	50	50	100

■

Example 2 A die is tossed 60 times. The results are listed in the table, where O denotes the observed frequency, and E denotes the expected, theoretical, or hypothetical frequency.

	\multicolumn{6}{c}{Outcome}	

	Outcome						
	1	2	3	4	5	6	Totals
O	11	8	12	9	11	9	60
E	10	10	10	10	10	10	60

■

Example 3
Sex Ratios in Rats

A sample of 50 rats includes 38 males and 12 females. Is this sample consistent with the assumption (hypothesis) that the sex ratio in the population is 1 to 1 (that is, Probability of male = Probability of female = $\frac{1}{2}$)? See the observed and expected results listed in the table.

	Male	Female	Totals
O	38	12	50
E	25	25	50

■

From the above three examples and from previous discussions, we see that we would like to be able to guess (hypothesize) how data for a given problem will be distributed, and then to accumulate and examine data to see how well the hypothesis predicted the actual pattern of data. This is called *hypothesis testing*.

The technique that we shall be using to implement this procedure is called the *chi-square distribution*. This distribution will enable us to determine whether a certain distribution differs from some predetermined theoretical distribution. For Examples 1 and 2, we have a distribution based on the toss of a coin and the roll of a die. We can determine whether our observed frequencies differ from the frequencies that we would expect if our distribution follows a stated theoretical distribution in the following way.

Let's return to Example 1. In this example we expect each of the outcomes to occur half the time. That is, our hypothesis is that the coin is fair so that each face will turn up half the time. Notice in the table given in Example 1 that the sum of the observed frequencies equals the sum of the expected frequencies. Also, it is important to note that we must use all the data; that is, if no head appears, this fact must also be taken into account.

We test our hypothesis by using the measure χ^2, called *chi-square*, which is obtained from the general formula

$$\chi^2 = \frac{(O_1 - E_1)^2}{E_1} + \frac{(O_2 - E_2)^2}{E_2} + \cdots + \frac{(O_n - E_n)^2}{E_n}$$

where O_i is the ith observed frequency, E_i is the corresponding expected frequency, and n is the number of possible outcomes.

For our example, χ^2 is found to be 9, since

$$\chi^2 = \frac{(65 - 50)^2}{50} + \frac{(35 - 50)^2}{50} = 9$$

If the results of tossing the coin had corresponded exactly to the expected frequently, that is, if there had been no deviation of the observed frequencies from the expected frequencies (so that instead of $O_1 = 65$ and $O_2 = 35$, we would have $O_1 = 50$ and $O_2 = 50$), then we would have calculated χ^2 to be

$$\chi^2 = \frac{(50 - 50)^2}{50} + \frac{(50 - 50)^2}{50} = 0$$

Thus, in the case of an experiment agreeing completely with the theoretical frequencies, the measure χ^2 will equal 0. Similarly, the more the observed frequencies deviate from the theoretical, the larger the measure χ^2 will be.

Example 4   For the data given in Example 2, compute χ^2.

Solution   To find χ^2, we use the data from the table in Example 2 and rearrange it as shown in Table 14. Thus, we determine that $\chi^2 = 1.2$ for this experiment.

For the above example, notice that the smallest value for χ^2 is 0. The next value for χ^2 occurs when, for example, the face 1 is observed to occur 9 times, the face

Table 14

Face	O	E	$O - E$	$(O - E)^2$	$\dfrac{(O - E)^2}{E}$
1	11	10	1	1	$\frac{1}{10}$
2	8	10	-2	4	$\frac{4}{10}$
3	12	10	2	4	$\frac{4}{10}$
4	9	10	-1	1	$\frac{1}{10}$
5	11	10	1	1	$\frac{1}{10}$
6	9	10	-1	1	$\frac{1}{10}$
Totals	60	60			$\frac{12}{10} = 1.2$

2 occurs 11 times, and the others occur 10 times each. In this case,

$$\chi^2 = \frac{(9 - 10)^2}{10} + \frac{(11 - 10)^2}{10} + \frac{(10 - 10)^2}{10} + \frac{(10 - 10)^2}{10}$$

$$+ \frac{(10 - 10)^2}{10} + \frac{(10 - 10)^2}{10} = \frac{1}{10} + \frac{1}{10} = 0.2$$

If an experiment like the one mentioned above is repeated many times, each time under the same hypothesis, and each time the measure χ^2 is calculated, we obtain a set of values for χ^2. If we graph these values, we obtain a frequency curve of χ^2. See Figure 17.

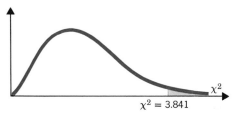

$$\chi^2 = 3.841$$

Figure 17

In Figure 17 we marked a point corresponding to $\chi^2 = 3.841$. This point divides the area under the curve into two parts. The shaded area to the right of the point contains 5% of the total area and the area on the left contains 95% of the total area. The 5% shaded area is called the *critical region*. Any result of χ^2 that lies in this 5% shaded area is said to be *significant;* otherwise, it is *not significant.* The 5% is called the *significance level*. The notation $\chi^2_{0.05} = 3.841$ is used to indicate that 5% of the possible occurrences of χ^2 lie to the right of the point.

For the data of Example 1, the computed value of χ^2 is 9. Should we reject our hypothesis that the coin is fair at a 5% level of significance? Since $\chi^2 = 9$ is much larger than 3.841, we *reject our hypothesis* that the coin is fair at a 5% level of significance. That is, we can be fairly confident (with probability .95) that these results are different from those produced by chance alone. In other words, we suspect the coin is loaded.

Table 3, page 534, gives various levels of significance for the measure χ^2. This table enables us to evaluate the approximate significance of the measure χ^2.

Degrees of Freedom

Contingency Table

Notice that the first column of Table 3 is headed by the letter ν.* This is the number of *degrees of freedom,* which the χ^2 distribution depends on.

The degree of freedom is determined as follows: Organize the data of the experiment in tabular form, called a *contingency table,* as we did in Examples 1, 2, and 3. The degrees of freedom for these experiments are 1, 5, and 1, respectively. In Examples 1 and 3 there are only two possible choices. Therefore, once we know how many heads (or tails) have come up or how many males (or females) there are, the number of the other choice is determined. Hence, there is 1 degree of freedom. In Example 2 there are six possibilities. Once five places in the table are known, the sixth is determined; that is, there are 5 degrees of freedom.

Return to Table 3. For $\nu = 4$ the value of χ^2 for a 30% significant level is 4.878, which means that for 4 degrees of freedom, the probability of obtaining a value of χ^2 greater than or equal to 4.878 is 0.30 (30% significant level).

Figure 18 shows the graphs of the χ^2 distribution for $\nu = 1, 3, 5,$ and 15.

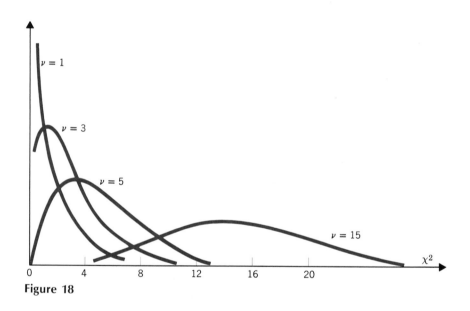

Figure 18

To summarize, in testing a hypothesis:

1. **Find the degrees of freedom.**
2. **Determine the value χ^2.**

There is evidence against the hypothesis at the p level if χ^2 exceeds the tabulated value of χ_p^2 for the determined degrees of freedom.

Example 5
Hereditary Variations

In searching for hereditary variations in the garden plant *Coleus,* Boye and Rife* employed self-pollination of plants that had previously been propagated vege-

*The Greek letter nu.

*C. L. Boye and D. C. Rife, *Journal of Heredity,* **29** (1938), p. 55.

tatively. In the latter case, no variations due to segregation are observed. With self-pollination, one case resulted in 787 plants, of which 207 bore leaves with green-purple pattern and 580 had purple leaves. These observed frequencies are not exactly in the ratio 3 to 1 as is expected. Is there evidence against the hypothesis of 3 to 1?

Solution   First, construct the contingency table:

	Purple	Pattern
O	580	207
E	590.25	196.75

The expected frequency is found by noting that $\frac{3}{4}$ of the 787 plants should be purple and $\frac{1}{4}$ of the 787 plants should have a pattern. The degree of freedom is 1 since once we learn that 580 plants have purple leaves, then 207 must have patterned leaves.

Next, we compute χ^2, obtaining

$$\chi^2 = \frac{(580 - 590.25)^2}{590.25} + \frac{(207 - 196.75)^2}{196.75} = 0.712$$

Consulting Table 3, we find that $\chi^2 = 0.712$ falls between levels of significance of 30% and 50%. This means that the observed frequencies will occur more than 30% of the time by chance alone when the expected ratio is 3 to 1. Thus, there is no significant evidence against the hypothesis.

Example 6
Smoking vs.
Nonsmoking

In an experiment to study the effect of smoking, a sample of 500 people were selected randomly, of which 300 were smokers and 200 were nonsmokers. After 10 years, 40 smokers and 10 nonsmokers had died. Is there evidence to substantiate the hypothesis that the death rate of smokers and nonsmokers is the same?

Solution   The table below summarizes the information given in the problem. The degree of freedom is 1.

	Died	Survived	Totals
Smokers	40	260	300
Nonsmokers	10	190	200
Totals	50	450	500

To obtain the expected frequencies, we note that 50 out of the total group of 500 died; that is, the probability of death is $\frac{50}{500} = .10$, and hence the probability of survival is $1 - .10 = .90$. Under the hypothesis, we assume that the probability of death for smokers and nonsmokers is the same, namely, .10. Similarly, the probability of survival for smokers and nonsmokers is assumed the same, namely, .90. Using this information we can construct the contingency table:

	Smokers Died	Nonsmokers Died	Smokers Survived	Nonsmokers Survived
O	40	10	260	190
E	$(.10)(300) = 30$	$(.10)(200) = 20$	$(.90)(300) = 270$	$(.90)(200) = 180$

The measure χ^2 is

$$\chi^2 = \frac{(40-30)^2}{30} + \frac{(10-20)^2}{20} + \frac{(260-270)^2}{270} + \frac{(190-180)^2}{180}$$

$$= \frac{10}{3} + 5 + \frac{10}{27} + \frac{5}{9} = 9.26$$

With 1 degree of freedom, the value of χ^2 at the 1% level of significance equals 6.635. Since $9.26 > 6.635$, we reject the hypothesis that there is no difference in the death rate between smokers and nonsmokers.

∎

Exercise 5
Solutions to Odd-Numbered Problems begin on page 613.

1. *Drinking Age.* A nationwide sample of 2500 college students was asked to agree or disagree with the statement: "The drinking age should be lowered to 18 years old." The responses of the two sexes were tabulated as follows:

	Disagree	Agree
Males	540	710
Females	380	870

Is there significant evidence at the 5% level against the hypothesis that males and females are likely to give the same answer?

2. *Marital Happiness.* A study to determine the relationship between level of education and marital happiness disclosed the following results:

	Marital Happiness	
	Above Average	Below Average
Completed High School	140	60
Completed College	160	40

(a) What is the value of χ^2 for this problem?

(b) At the 2% level, does this study indicate a significant difference in marital happiness between the two educational levels?

(c) What about at the 5% level?

3. *Color Preference.* The following experiment attempts to determine whether there is a difference in color preference between infants of each sex. An infant is simultaneously offered two identical toys— one red and one yellow. The color which the infant first reaches for is recorded as a preference. The results for 200 infants are shown below. At the 5% significance level, is a color preference indicated? State the computed value of χ^2.

	Preference	
	Red	Yellow
Boys	60	50
Girls	60	30

4. Five pennies were tossed 75 times, with the following results:

5 heads,	0 tails	1
4 heads,	1 tail	6
3 heads,	2 tails	15
2 heads,	3 tails	35
1 head,	4 tails	16
0 heads,	5 tails	2

Are the results different from what would be expected by chance?

5. *Testing Vaccine.* As a test for a cold vaccine, 100 subjects were inoculated, 50 with the cold vaccine and 50 with a dummy shot. The results showed that of those inoculated with the vaccine, 16 came down with a cold and, of those inoculated with the dummy shot, 20 came down with a cold. Is there promise here at the 5% level for a vaccine to cure colds?

6. In a random sample of 500 housewives, 60% showed a preference for Tide and 40% for Ivory Flakes. Is there evidence against the hypothesis at the 5% level that 50% of all housewives prefer Tide over Ivory Flakes?

7. A random survey of 1000 people of which 450 are male is taken and it is found that 40 males are color-blind and 10 females are color-blind. Is there evidence against the hypothesis at the 5% level that males and females are equally likely to be color-blind?

8. A plant is self-pollinated and produces 400 offspring, 317 of which have white flowers and 83 of which have colored flowers. Using χ^2, determine whether this segregation best fits a ratio of 3 to 1 or a ratio of 13 to 3.

9. *Crossing Sweet Peas.* Punnet* reported the following observations of a dehybrid cross in sweet peas, which produce four basic types of offspring: If the plants are self-pollinated, we should expect the off-

*R. C. Punnett, *Journal of Genetics,* **13** (1923), p. 101.

spring in a ratio of 9 bright, tendril; to 3 bright, acacia; to 3 dull, tendril; to 1 dull, acacia. These give expected frequencies of $\frac{9}{16}$, $\frac{3}{16}$, $\frac{3}{16}$, and $\frac{1}{16}$, respectively. For the observed frequencies listed in the table, is there evidence against the hypothesis of 9:3:3:1 at the 5% significance level?

Class	Observed Frequency
Bright, Tendril	847
Bright, Acacia	298
Dull, Tendril	300
Dull, Acacia	49

Chapter Review

Important Terms

population
sample
biased sample
random sample
inductive statistics
frequency table
line chart
continuous variable
discrete variable
histogram
class interval
upper class limit
lower class limit
frequency polygon
cumulative (less than) frequency
cumulative (more than) frequency
measure of central tendency
mean
median
mode

deviation from the mean
interpolation factor
centile point
bimodal
measure of dispersion
range
variance
standard deviation
normal distribution
normal curve, bell-shaped curve
standard normal curve
Z-score
standard score
normal curve table
chi-square distribution
hypothesis testing
critical region
significance level
degrees of freedom
contingency table

Review Exercises
Solutions to Odd-Numbered Problems begin on page 615.

1. The following scores were made on a math exam:

80	99	82	21	100	55	80	26	78	52
12	73	20	44	72	63	19	85	33	66
78	42	87	90	30	10	48	75	83	77
63	85	69	80	14	87	66	52	17	60
74	70	73	95	89	14	92	8	100	72

12
Matrix Applications to Directed Graphs

1. Introduction

Many situations that occur in psychology, sociology, and business are of a combinatorial nature and can be interpreted by using techniques found in a relatively new area of mathematics called *graph theory*. In this chapter, we present a brief introduction and explain some of the more elementary results of graph theory and their applications.

We will only be able to proceed as far with each topic as is necessary to introduce you to the types of problems and to some of the techniques used to solve them. The associated theory is demonstrated through examples.

Before giving a formal definition of a graph, we point out that the term *graph* has two quite different meanings. One definition of a graph is the one we studied in Chapter 1 and used in Chapter 3 when we graphed straight lines and linear inequalities.

In this chapter a *graph* will mean a collection of points (called *vertices*) with one or more curves or lines (called *edges*) connecting a pair of points. For a given pair of vertices, our concern is not what the edge looks like, but rather whether the two vertices have an edge joining them.

Graphs may be used to interpret many situations. For example, in team competition, two teams are pitted against each other. If eight teams, *A*, *B*, *C*, *D*, *E*, *F*, *G*, *H*, all belong to the same league, then after a few matches have taken place, we might have the situation that

A	has played *D*, *G*, *H*
B	has played *C*, *F*
C	has played *B*, *G*, *H*
D	has played *A*
E	has not played
F	has played *B*
G	has played *A*, *C*
H	has played *A*, *C*

We can illustrate this situation by a diagram in which dots represent the teams *A*, *B*, *C*, *D*, *E*, *F*, *G*, *H*, and a line joining two dots indicates these two teams have played. Such a geometric design is called a *graph*. The points *A*, *B*, *C*, *D*, *E*, *F*, *G*, *H* are *vertices* and the lines *AD*, *CB*, and so on, are called *edges*. See Figure 1.

<table><tr><td>Vertices</td></tr><tr><td>Edges</td></tr></table>

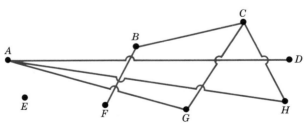

Figure 1

Notice that a "hook" is used to indicate that the line joining *B* and *F* does not meet the lines joining *AD*, *AH*, and *AG*.

Graph A *graph* **is a collection of a finite number of** vertices $P_1, P_2, P_3, \ldots, P_n$ **together with a finite number of** edges P_iP_j **joining a pair of vertices** P_i **and** P_j.

A pair of vertices may have more than one edge joining them. Also, a vertex may have no edge joining it. (The team E in Figure 1 is an example of such a vertex.) An edge may join a vertex to itself. (Such an edge is called a *loop*.)

Loop

Finally, it is understood that edges are not ordered, so that the edge P_iP_j and the edge P_jP_i are identical.

In depicting graphs we may denote the edges by either a line or a curve, whichever is more convenient.

Figure 2 illustrates some graphs. Notice that the graph in part (a) has an edge from vertex A back to A. This is a loop. Also, the graph in part (d) has two different edges joining the vertices A and C.

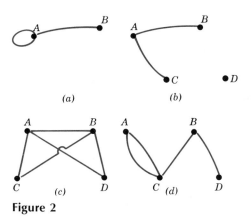

Figure 2

Figure 2(a) is a graph with two vertices A and B and two edges AA and AB; part (b) is a graph with four vertices A, B, C, D and two edges AB, AC; part (c) is a graph with four vertices A, B, C, D and five edges AB, AC, AD, BC, BD; and part (d) is a graph with four vertices A, B, C, D and four edges AC, AC, BC, BD.

Let's return to the team competition depicted by the graph in Figure 1. This graph shows which teams have played by using edges to join pairs of vertices. However, we are usually more interested in who won rather than who played. Thus, if we are told that

A won over G, H and lost to D
B won over C, F
C won over G and lost to B, H
D won over A
E has not played
F lost to B
G lost to A, C
H won over C and lost to A

we can use a directed edge with the arrow pointing toward the loser to illustrate this information. This is an example of a *directed graph,* or *digraph*. See Figure 3.

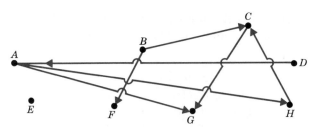

Figure 3

At this point, we will define the ideas we have just presented more precisely.

Digraph   A *directed graph,* **or** *digraph,* **is a collection of a finite number of vertices** $P_1, P_2, \ldots, P_n$ **together with a finite number of directed edges** P_iP_j **in which** $i \neq j$.

Notice that since the edges are now directed, the directed edge P_iP_j (depicted by an arrow from P_i pointing toward P_j) is different from the directed edge P_jP_i. Also, in a digraph, it is not possible to have a loop since we do not allow directed edges from a vertex back to itself. Some examples of directed graphs are given in Figure 4.

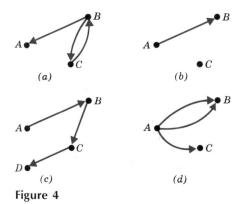

Figure 4

Figure 4(a) is a directed graph with vertices A, B, C and three directed edges BA, BC, CB; part (b) is a directed graph with vertices A, B, C and one directed edge AB; part (c) is a directed graph with vertices A, B, C, D and three directed edges AB, BC, CD; and part (d) is a directed graph with vertices A, B, C and three directed edges AB, AB, AC.

Usually, we shall denote a directed edge AB by $A \rightarrow B$. Also, if AB and BA are two directed edges in a digraph, we will write $A \leftrightarrow B$.

In order to analyze the information given in a digraph and draw conclusions about the situation depicted, we use a matrix to represent the information given in a digraph. This allows us to take full advantage of computers for tedious computations.

To determine the matrix representation of a digraph, we use a square matrix in which the entry in row A column B is the number of directed edges from A to B.

For example, the digraphs in Figure 4 have the following matrix representations:

$$
\begin{array}{c c} & \begin{array}{c c c} A & B & C \end{array} \\ \begin{array}{c} A \\ B \\ C \end{array} & \left[\begin{array}{c c c} 0 & 0 & 0 \\ 1 & 0 & 1 \\ 0 & 1 & 0 \end{array}\right] \end{array}
\qquad
\begin{array}{c c} & \begin{array}{c c c} A & B & C \end{array} \\ \begin{array}{c} A \\ B \\ C \end{array} & \left[\begin{array}{c c c} 0 & 1 & 0 \\ 0 & 0 & 0 \\ 0 & 0 & 0 \end{array}\right] \end{array}
$$

$$(a) \qquad\qquad\qquad (b)$$

$$
\begin{array}{c c} & \begin{array}{c c c c} A & B & C & D \end{array} \\ \begin{array}{c} A \\ B \\ C \\ D \end{array} & \left[\begin{array}{c c c c} 0 & 1 & 0 & 0 \\ 0 & 0 & 1 & 0 \\ 0 & 0 & 0 & 1 \\ 0 & 0 & 0 & 0 \end{array}\right] \end{array}
\qquad
\begin{array}{c c} & \begin{array}{c c c} A & B & C \end{array} \\ \begin{array}{c} A \\ B \\ C \end{array} & \left[\begin{array}{c c c} 0 & 2 & 1 \\ 0 & 0 & 0 \\ 0 & 0 & 0 \end{array}\right] \end{array}
$$

$$(c) \qquad\qquad\qquad (d)$$

Systems or organizations (such as highway systems, networks for telephone communication, political parties) with components (the cities in a highway system, the homes in a telephone network, the people in a political party) that are related in pairs can often be depicted by a directed graph. In this chapter, we shall study four general types of organizational structures: dominance, perfect communication, business communication, and cliques. We give a brief description of each type here, and we will discuss them further in Sections 2–5.

Dominance

Here we study organizations of people in which we assume that for every pair of people one of them either dominates (has influence over) or is dominated by (is influenced by) the other. If we use a vertex to represent a person and an edge to represent dominance or influence so that AB or $A \to B$ means A has influence over B, then organizations with this property can be illustrated with a directed graph, called a *dominance digraph*.

Such a situation occurs in round-robin tournaments in which each team must play every other team once and no ties are allowed. This means, of course, that for every pair of teams, one wins and the other loses. For example, in Figure 5, we have a group of four teams, A, B, C, D, in which

> Team A has won over B and C
> Team B has won over C, D
> Team C has won over D
> Team D has won over A

where $A \to B$ indicates A has won over B.

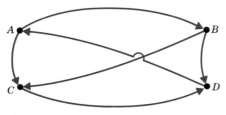

Figure 5

The matrix representation for this digraph is

$$
\begin{array}{c@{\ }c@{\ }c@{\ }c@{\ }c}
 & A & B & C & D \\
\begin{array}{c}A\\B\\C\\D\end{array} &
\left[\begin{array}{cccc}
0 & 1 & 1 & 0 \\
0 & 0 & 1 & 1 \\
0 & 0 & 0 & 1 \\
1 & 0 & 0 & 0
\end{array}\right]
\end{array}
$$

Other situations that give rise to a *dominance digraph* occur in large groups in which an investigation of every pair of people reveals the dominant or influential one. For example, in a group of four people, *A, B, C, D*, we might write all possible pairings and determine which in each pair is the dominant one. The following table illustrates this:

Pair	AB	AC	AD	BC	BD	CD
Dominant One	A	A	D	C	B	D

A dominance digraph can be used to represent this situation if, by $A \to B$, we mean *A* dominates *B* in the pairing *AB*. See Figure 6.

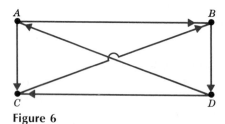

Figure 6

The matrix representation for the digraph in Figure 6 is

$$
\begin{array}{c@{\ }c@{\ }c@{\ }c@{\ }c}
 & A & B & C & D \\
\begin{array}{c}A\\B\\C\\D\end{array} &
\left[\begin{array}{cccc}
0 & 1 & 1 & 0 \\
0 & 0 & 0 & 1 \\
0 & 1 & 0 & 0 \\
1 & 0 & 1 & 0
\end{array}\right]
\end{array}
$$

Every situation that gives rise to a dominance digraph has the properties that

1. **For every pair of vertices, either $A \to B$ or $B \to A$, but not both.**
2. **An edge $A \to B$ may not occur more than once.**

Incidence Matrix

This means the matrix representation of a dominance digraph has entries that are either 0's or 1's. Such matrices are called *incidence matrices*. Moreover, in a dominance digraph, if *A* dominates *B*, then *B* cannot dominate *A*. Thus, if *M* =

Asymmetric
Matrix

(a_{ij}) is the incidence matrix for a dominance digraph, then $a_{ij} = 0$ implies $a_{ji} = 1$ and $a_{ij} = 1$ implies $a_{ji} = 0, i \neq j$. Such an incidence matrix is said to be *asymmetric*.

The matrix representation of a dominance digraph is always an asymmetric incidence matrix.

Perfect Communication

Here we study collections of towns connected by highways or collections of homes connected by telephone links. That is, we will study collections with the properties that

1. **If $A \rightarrow B$, then $B \rightarrow A$.**
2. **The edge $A \rightarrow B$ may occur more than once.**

Such situations occur in long-distance telephone communications among cities in which we assume a city does not directly have a long-distance line to itself. We also assume that if City A is connected by a direct line to City B, then City B is also connected to City A. Of course, A and B may be connected by more than one line.

For example, suppose three cities, A, B, C, have long-distance telephone lines connected in the following way:

A is connected with B by two different lines
B is connected to C by one line

If $A \leftrightarrow B$ denotes a telephone line between A and B, we can use a *perfect communication digraph* to represent this situation. See Figure 7.

Figure 7

The matrix representation for the digraph in Figure 7 is

$$
\begin{array}{c@{}c}
 & \begin{array}{ccc} A & B & C \end{array} \\
\begin{array}{c} A \\ B \\ C \end{array} &
\left[\begin{array}{ccc}
0 & 2 & 0 \\
2 & 0 & 1 \\
0 & 1 & 0
\end{array} \right]
\end{array}
$$

Symmetric Matrix

Thus, in a perfect communication diagram, if A communicates with B, then B will communicate with A. If $M = (a_{ij})$ is the matrix representation of a perfect communication diagram, then $a_{ij} = a_{ji}$. Such matrices are called *symmetric*.

It is characteristic of a perfect communication digraph that its matrix representation is symmetric.

Business Communication

The business communication digraph in Figure 8 illustrates a situation in which A, B, C, D, and E are officials of a business structure, and the double arrow $\leftrightarrow$ indicates a communication relationship between them. For example, $\leftrightarrow$ might mean memos are exchanged.

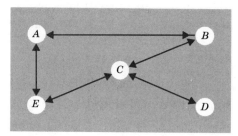

Figure 8

The matrix representation for the digraph in Figure 8 is

$$
\begin{array}{c c}
& \begin{array}{c c c c c} A & B & C & D & E \end{array} \\
\begin{array}{c} A \\ B \\ C \\ D \\ E \end{array} &
\left[\begin{array}{c c c c c}
0 & 1 & 0 & 0 & 1 \\
1 & 0 & 1 & 0 & 0 \\
0 & 1 & 0 & 1 & 1 \\
0 & 0 & 1 & 0 & 0 \\
1 & 0 & 1 & 0 & 0
\end{array}\right]
\end{array}
$$

Business communication digraphs have the following properties:

1. $A \rightarrow B$, if $B \rightarrow A$.
2. **No pair of vertices is joined by more than one edge.**

It is characteristic of the matrix representing a business communication digraph that it is a symmetric incidence matrix.

Cliques

In a group of people, relationships such as "is a friend of" or "communicates with" may exist. It is clear that in a large group, person A may be a friend of B, while B is not a friend of A. Also, A and C may have no communication between each other at all; while B and C may be mutual friends or have mutual communication. A *clique* is the largest collection of three or more individuals with the property that any two of them are mutual friends.

For example, suppose that in a group of four people, A, B, C, D, we find that A

likes B, C; B likes C, D; C likes B, D; and D likes B, C. If we use the directed edge AB or $A \rightarrow B$ to denote A likes B, then this situation can be illustrated by the *friendship digraph* in Figure 9.

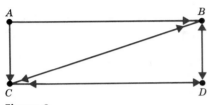

Figure 9

Notice that $\{B, C, D\}$ form a clique since they are mutual friends. The matrix representation of the digraph in Figure 9 is

$$
\begin{array}{c c}
 & \begin{array}{cccc} A & B & C & D \end{array} \\
\begin{array}{c} A \\ B \\ C \\ D \end{array} &
\left[\begin{array}{cccc}
0 & 1 & 1 & 0 \\
0 & 0 & 1 & 1 \\
0 & 1 & 0 & 1 \\
0 & 1 & 1 & 0
\end{array} \right]
\end{array}
$$

The matrix representation of any friendship digraph is an incidence matrix.

Exercise 1

Solutions to Odd-Numbered Problems begin on page 619.

For the matrix given in Problems 1–8, draw the corresponding directed graph. List all the models (that is, dominance, perfect communication, business communication, friendship) that each matrix could represent.

1. $\begin{bmatrix} 0 & 1 \\ 1 & 0 \end{bmatrix}$

2. $\begin{bmatrix} 1 & 0 \\ 1 & 1 \end{bmatrix}$

3. $\begin{bmatrix} 0 & 0 & 1 \\ 1 & 0 & 1 \\ 0 & 0 & 0 \end{bmatrix}$

4. $\begin{bmatrix} 0 & 1 & 0 \\ 1 & 0 & 1 \\ 0 & 1 & 0 \end{bmatrix}$

5. $\begin{bmatrix} 0 & 1 & 1 & 1 \\ 0 & 0 & 1 & 1 \\ 0 & 0 & 0 & 1 \\ 0 & 0 & 0 & 0 \end{bmatrix}$

6. $\begin{bmatrix} 0 & 1 & 0 & 0 \\ 1 & 0 & 1 & 0 \\ 0 & 0 & 0 & 0 \\ 1 & 0 & 1 & 0 \end{bmatrix}$

7. $\begin{bmatrix} 0 & 2 & 1 & 0 \\ 2 & 0 & 0 & 0 \\ 1 & 0 & 0 & 1 \\ 0 & 0 & 1 & 0 \end{bmatrix}$

8. $\begin{bmatrix} 0 & 2 & 0 & 1 \\ 2 & 0 & 2 & 0 \\ 0 & 2 & 0 & 0 \\ 1 & 0 & 0 & 0 \end{bmatrix}$

For each digraph in Problems 9–14, write the corresponding matrices. List all the models (that is, dominance, perfect communication, business, friendship) that each could represent.

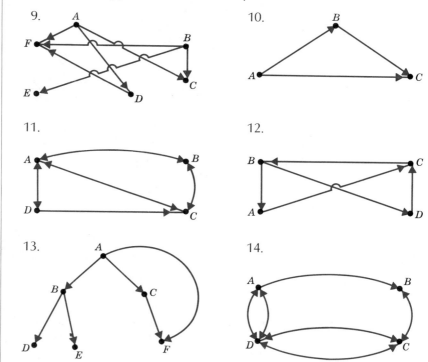

9.

10.

11.

12.

13.

14.

15. Four people, A, B, C, D, live in an apartment building. If A hears a piece of gossip, he will pass it on to B and D; B passes gossip on to C; C passes gossip on to A; D never gossips. Write a directed graph for this situation. What is the matrix representation? Is this situation an example of a dominance, communication, or friendship digraph?

2. Dominance Model

A common sociological relationship is the dominance relationship, where, as we mentioned in Section 1, we assume that in every pair of people one dominates or is dominated by the other.

For example, suppose a sociologist wishes to determine the influence generated by each person in a street gang on the other members of the gang. As a first step, the sociologist might pair off the members of the gang and determine which one in each pair has influence over the other. Although there are obvious drawbacks to this procedure, it seems reasonable to assume that in every one-on-one situation, one person will have influence or will dominate the other. The results of this survey can be represented by a digraph in which $A \rightarrow B$ means B is influenced by A or A dominates B. Notice that in this model, if A dominates B, then B cannot dominate A.

Example 1 A gang consisting of five members, A, B, C, D, E, is interviewed by a sociologist in the manner described above and the resulting dominance digraph is shown in Figure 10.

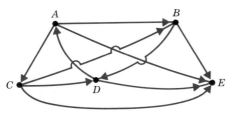

Figure 10

The incidence matrix for this situation is

$$
M = \begin{array}{c} \\ A \\ B \\ C \\ D \\ E \end{array}
\begin{array}{c}
\begin{array}{ccccc} A & B & C & D & E \end{array} \\
\left[\begin{array}{ccccc}
0 & 1 & 1 & 0 & 1 \\
0 & 0 & 0 & 1 & 1 \\
0 & 1 & 0 & 1 & 1 \\
1 & 0 & 0 & 0 & 1 \\
0 & 0 & 0 & 0 & 0
\end{array}\right]
\end{array}
$$

We notice from either the digraph or the matrix that member A dominates B, C, and E; B dominates D and E; C dominates B, D, and E; D dominates A and E; and E dominates no one.

■

By adding the entries in a row, we obtain the number of *one-stage dominances* of each person. In Example 1, A dominates three people in one stage; C also dominates three people in one stage. Any person who dominates everyone in one stage is called a *consensus leader* of the group.

Consensus Leader

If there is no person that dominates everyone in one stage, as in Example 1, we look for the person who dominates the most people in one stage, and call this individual a *leader*. In our example, there are two people, A and C, who dominate the most people in one stage. Which one should be designated as leader?

Two-Stage Dominance

To answer this, we introduce the notion of *two-stage dominance*. Notice that A dominates B and B dominates D. Here, A does not dominate D; however, since $A \rightarrow B$ and $B \rightarrow D$, we say that A has two-stage dominance (or two-stage influence) over D. In this case, we write $A \rightarrow B \rightarrow D$ to indicate A dominates D in two stages. Because of this concept, in the case of a tie for the most number of one-stage dominances, we agree that a person who dominates the most people in one or two stages will be designated as a *leader* of the group.

Leader

Note that there is no transitive property for dominance. That is, if A dominates B and B dominates C, it may or may not follow that A dominates C.

But how can the number of two-stage dominances of one individual be determined? As we shall see, the square (M^2) of the incidence matrix M plays a major role. For the incidence matrix of Example 1,

$$M^2 = \begin{bmatrix} 0 & 1 & 0 & 2 & 2 \\ 1 & 0 & 0 & 0 & 1 \\ 1 & 0 & 0 & 1 & 2 \\ 0 & 1 & 1 & 0 & 1 \\ 0 & 0 & 0 & 0 & 0 \end{bmatrix}$$

How should the matrix M^2 be interpreted?

From the incidence matrix M, we see that A dominates C and C dominates B so that A has two-stage dominance over B, as the matrix M^2 indicates. Similarly, C dominates D and D dominates A, so C has two-stage dominance over A, as M^2 indicates. The entry "2" in row A, column D indicates A has two-stage dominance over D in two ways, namely $A \rightarrow B \rightarrow D$ and $A \rightarrow C \rightarrow D$. Thus:

The square of an incidence matrix gives the number of two-stage dominances for each entry.

If we add the matrices M and M^2, the total number of ways that people can be dominated by A in either one or two stages is the sum of the entries in row A, while the sum of the entries in column A gives the total number of ways people can dominate A in one or two stages:

$$M + M^2 = \begin{array}{c} \\ A \\ B \\ C \\ D \\ E \end{array} \begin{array}{ccccc} A & B & C & D & E \\ \begin{bmatrix} 0 & 2 & 1 & 2 & 3 \\ 1 & 0 & 0 & 1 & 2 \\ 1 & 1 & 0 & 2 & 3 \\ 1 & 1 & 1 & 0 & 2 \\ 0 & 0 & 0 & 0 & 0 \end{bmatrix} \end{array}$$

We see that A can dominate in 8 ways in one or two stages; B can dominate in 4 ways in one or two stages; C can dominate in 7 ways in one or two stages; D can dominate in 5 ways in one or two stages; and E dominates no one in one or two stages. Also, A can be dominated in 3 ways; B can be dominated in 4 ways; C in 2 ways; D in 5 ways; and E in 10 ways, each in one or two stages.

Now, if we go back to the question of who the leader of the gang is (recall that A and C each dominated four people in one stage), we might call A the leader since A dominates the most people in one or two stages.

If we want more information in order to make a determination, we can cube the incidence matrix M, obtaining the matrix M^3, namely,

$$M^3 = \begin{bmatrix} 2 & 0 & 0 & 1 & 3 \\ 0 & 1 & 1 & 0 & 1 \\ 1 & 1 & 1 & 0 & 2 \\ 0 & 1 & 0 & 2 & 2 \\ 0 & 0 & 0 & 0 & 0 \end{bmatrix}$$

This gives us the number of three-stage dominances in the group. The matrix M^4 gives the number of four-stage dominances, and so on.

In general, we state the following result:

In an incidence matrix M of dimension $n \times n$, suppose the kth power of M is:

(1)
$$M^k = [a_{ij}] = \begin{array}{c} 1 \\ 2 \\ \vdots \\ n \end{array} \begin{bmatrix} a_{11} & a_{12} & \cdots & a_{1n} \\ a_{21} & a_{22} & \cdots & a_{2n} \\ \vdots & \vdots & & \vdots \\ a_{n1} & a_{n2} & \cdots & a_{nn} \end{bmatrix} \begin{array}{c} 1 \quad 2 \quad \cdots \quad n \end{array}$$

The entry in row i column j, a_{ij}, is the number of k-stage *dominances* **of person i over person j.**

For example, the matrix M^3 on page 458 indicates that person A has three-stage dominance over person E in exactly 3 ways, namely, $A \rightarrow B \rightarrow D \rightarrow E$, $A \rightarrow C \rightarrow B \rightarrow E$, and $A \rightarrow C \rightarrow D \rightarrow E$. Notice that $A \rightarrow B \rightarrow E \rightarrow E$ is not a three-stage dominance.

Let M be an incidence matrix of dimension $n \times n$. The sum of the entries in the ith row of the matrix

(2)
$$M + M^2 + \cdots + M^k$$

gives the total number of ways the ith person can dominate in one, two, . . . , up to k stages.

Example 2   In a group of three people, A, B, C, suppose we know that B dominates A, A dominates C, and C dominates B. Find a digraph illustrating this situation. Write the incidence matrix and find the number of two-stage influences. Find the leader. Is there a consensus leader? Find the total number of ways to dominate each person in one or two stages.

Solution   The digraph is given in Figure 11.

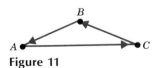

Figure 11

The incidence matrix M is

$$M = \begin{array}{c} A \\ B \\ C \end{array} \begin{bmatrix} 0 & 0 & 1 \\ 1 & 0 & 0 \\ 0 & 1 & 0 \end{bmatrix} \begin{array}{c} A \quad B \quad C \end{array}$$

Since no row of M has entries that sum to 2, there is no consensus leader. Also, the square of M is

$$M^2 = \begin{array}{c} \\ A \\ B \\ C \end{array} \begin{array}{ccc} A & B & C \\ \begin{bmatrix} 0 & 1 & 0 \\ 0 & 0 & 1 \\ 1 & 0 & 0 \end{bmatrix} \end{array}$$

The sum $M + M^2$ is

$$M + M^2 = \begin{array}{c} \\ A \\ B \\ C \end{array} \begin{array}{ccc} A & B & C \\ \begin{bmatrix} 0 & 1 & 1 \\ 1 & 0 & 1 \\ 1 & 1 & 0 \end{bmatrix} \end{array}$$

A is a leader since A dominates two people in one or two stages; similarly, B and C also dominate two people in one or two stages. Here we have an example of the paradoxical situation of three people, all of whom could be designated as leaders. ■

Let's turn to a somewhat similar application of dominance—to tournaments. A *tournament* consists of teams $A, B, C, \ldots$ in which every pair of teams plays each other once, and one of the teams wins while the other loses (no ties are allowed). If A wins over B, we will write $A \to B$. Thus, tournaments can be represented by dominance digraphs.

Example 3 A tournament involving five teams, A, B, C, D, E, ended up as

$$A \to B, \quad A \to C, \quad B \to C, \quad B \to D, \quad B \to E,$$
$$C \to D, \quad D \to A, \quad E \to A, \quad E \to C, \quad E \to D$$

Draw a digraph for this situation. Find the incidence matrix. Who should be declared winner of the tournament?

Solution The digraph is given in Figure 12.

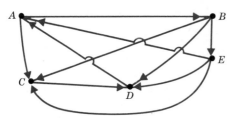

Figure 12

The incidence matrix is

$$M = \begin{array}{c} \\ A \\ B \\ C \\ D \\ E \end{array} \begin{array}{ccccc} A & B & C & D & E \\ \begin{bmatrix} 0 & 1 & 1 & 0 & 0 \\ 0 & 0 & 1 & 1 & 1 \\ 0 & 0 & 0 & 1 & 0 \\ 1 & 0 & 0 & 0 & 0 \\ 1 & 0 & 1 & 1 & 0 \end{bmatrix} \end{array}$$

The number of games each team won is the sum of the entries of their row. Thus, team A won 2 games, B won 3, C won 1, D won 1, and E won 3. Since there is a tie for first between teams B and E, there is no clear winner.

To see which team should be declared the winner, we might look at the matrix M^2 to determine the number of two-stage wins for each team:

$$M^2 = \begin{array}{c} \\ A \\ B \\ C \\ D \\ E \end{array} \begin{array}{c} \begin{array}{ccccc} A & B & C & D & E \end{array} \\ \left[\begin{array}{ccccc|c} 0 & 0 & 1 & 2 & 1 & 4 \\ 2 & 0 & 1 & 2 & 0 & 5 \\ 1 & 0 & 0 & 0 & 0 & 1 \\ 0 & 1 & 1 & 0 & 0 & 2 \\ 1 & 1 & 1 & 1 & 0 & 4 \end{array} \right] \end{array}$$

Team B has a total of 5 two-stage wins, while team E has a total of 4 two-stage wins. Also, team A has a total of 4 two-stage wins and team D has only 2. Thus, we might award the top prize to team B, followed by team E, team A, team D, and, lastly, team C.

■

With regard to dominance digraphs, the following result is quite interesting:

In a dominance digraph, the person who dominates the most people in one stage will also dominate everyone, except himself, in one or two stages.

Paired Comparison
Another situation that leads to a dominance digraph is that of a *paired comparison*. In making paired comparisons, a woman is asked to select her favorite flavor of ice cream or favorite color, etc., through a pairing of all flavors or colors and selecting the one she favors better of the two. Since in every possible pair, one is chosen over the other and this is done for all possible pairs, this situation can be depicted as a dominance digraph. See Problem 12 in Exercise 2.

Exercise 2
Solutions to Odd-Numbered Problems begin on page 620.

In Problems 1–8 determine which of the given matrices can be interpreted as a dominance matrix. For those that can be so interpreted, find the matrix representing two-stage dominance and find the total number each person dominates in one or two stages.

1. $\begin{bmatrix} 0 & 1 \\ 1 & 0 \end{bmatrix}$

2. $\begin{bmatrix} 0 & 1 \\ 0 & 0 \end{bmatrix}$

3. $\begin{bmatrix} 0 & 1 & 1 \\ 0 & 0 & 0 \\ 0 & 1 & 0 \end{bmatrix}$

4. $\begin{bmatrix} 0 & 1 & 1 \\ 0 & 0 & 0 \\ 0 & 1 & 1 \end{bmatrix}$

5. $\begin{bmatrix} 0 & 0 & 0 \\ 1 & 0 & 1 \\ 1 & 0 & 0 \end{bmatrix}$

6. $\begin{bmatrix} 0 & 0 & 0 \\ 1 & 0 & 1 \\ 1 & 0 & 0 \end{bmatrix}$

7. $\begin{bmatrix} 0 & 1 & 1 & 0 \\ 0 & 0 & 1 & 0 \\ 0 & 0 & 0 & 1 \\ 1 & 1 & 0 & 0 \end{bmatrix}$.

8. $\begin{bmatrix} 0 & 0 & 1 & 1 \\ 1 & 0 & 0 & 1 \\ 0 & 1 & 0 & 0 \\ 0 & 0 & 1 & 0 \end{bmatrix}$

9. For the dominance matrix

$$M = \begin{array}{c} \\ A \\ B \\ C \end{array} \begin{array}{ccc} A & B & C \\ \begin{bmatrix} 0 & 1 & 1 \\ 0 & 0 & 1 \\ 0 & 0 & 0 \end{bmatrix} \end{array}$$

find the two-stage dominances and interpret your answer. Interpret $M + M^2$.

10. For the dominance digraph below, write the incidence matrix. Find the two-stage dominances. What total number are dominated in one or two stages by A, B, and C?

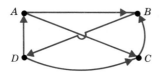

11. *Tournament.* In a basketball tournament composed of seven teams, the final standings showed that

Team	Won	Lost
A	4	2
B	4	2
C	4	2
D	3	3
E	3	3
F	2	4
G	1	5

It is known that

A	beat D, E, F, G
B	beat A, C, D, F
C	beat A, E, F, G
D	beat C, F, G
E	beat B, D, G
F	beat E, G
G	beat B

Who should be declared the winner?

12. *Paired Comparisons.* In trying to determine the flavor of ice cream Mr. Polansky likes best, a survey team decides to use paired comparisons. The questionnaire establishes that Polansky would choose Vanilla over Neapolitan, Pecan, Fudge Ripple and Cherry.

Chocolate was preferred over Vanilla, Strawberry, Neapolitan, and Fudge Ripple. Strawberry was chosen over Vanilla, Pecan, Fudge Ripple, and Cherry. Pecan won out over Chocolate, Neapolitan, and Cherry. Fudge Ripple was preferred to Pecan and Cherry; Neapolitan was preferred over Fudge Ripple, Cherry, and Strawberry. Finally, Cherry was chosen over Chocolate. What flavor does Mr. Polansky like best?

*13. It has been established among the countries in Southeast Asia that the following relationships exist: In a war between any two, say A and B, either A defeats B or B defeats A. Prove that there is a strongest country, S, in the sense that either S can defeat any other country X or S can defeat a country Y which can defeat X. Also show that there is a weakest country W in the sense that if X is any other country, then either X can defeat W or X can defeat a country Y which can defeat W.

*14. In a closed community, suppose:
  (a) No one hates himself/herself.
  (b) Given any two people, A and B, either A hates B or B hates A but not both.
  Prove that there is a person P in this community such that if X is any other person, then either X hates P or X hates Y who hates P.

3. Perfect Communication Model

As an example of a perfect communication model, consider a group of cities A, B, C, . . . , and a mode of communication between them such as highways or long-distance telephone lines. In such a model, if City A communicates with City B, then by necessity, City B communicates with City A. Two cities may or may not communicate with each other, but there may be more than one line connecting two cities. A communication relationship between two cities will be denoted by a double arrow. Thus, the double arrow between A and B, namely, $A \leftrightarrow B$, indicates that City A communicates with City B and vice versa. The matrix representation for such a situation will be a *symmetric matrix*. However, it will not usually be an incidence matrix, since we allow for more than one edge connecting two vertices. The following example illustrates this.

Example 1 Connecting four cities, there exist direct telephone lines as depicted in the directed graph in Figure 13. The number of lines directly connecting A with B is

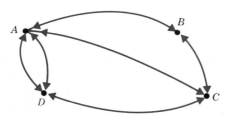

Figure 13

one; directly connecting A with C is one; directly connecting A with D is two; and one line connects B with C and D with C. If we use a 0 to denote the number of connections of a city with itself, we can represent the digraph of direct connections by the matrix

$$
\begin{array}{c c} & \begin{array}{cccc} A & B & C & D \end{array} \\ \begin{array}{c} A \\ B \\ C \\ D \end{array} & \left[\begin{array}{cccc} 0 & 1 & 1 & 2 \\ 1 & 0 & 1 & 0 \\ 1 & 1 & 0 & 1 \\ 2 & 0 & 1 & 0 \end{array}\right] \end{array}
$$

The significance of the matrix M^2 is that it tells the number of lines of communication between two cities that pass through exactly one other city:

$$
M^2 = \begin{bmatrix} 6 & 1 & 3 & 1 \\ 1 & 2 & 1 & 3 \\ 3 & 1 & 3 & 2 \\ 1 & 3 & 2 & 5 \end{bmatrix}
$$

The entries given in M^2 can be verified by looking at Figure 13.

Thus, the matrix M^2 tells us that there are three different ways that A can communicate with C in two stages. The ways are $A \rightarrow B \rightarrow C$, $A \rightarrow D \rightarrow C$, $A \rightarrow D \rightarrow C$.

The matrix M^3 gives the number of lines of communication between two cities that pass through exactly two other cities.

■

Example 2   A perfect communication matrix showing telephone lines connecting the homes of three people is

$$
\begin{array}{c c} & \begin{array}{ccc} A & B & C \end{array} \\ M = \begin{array}{c} A \\ B \\ C \end{array} & \left[\begin{array}{ccc} 0 & 1 & 1 \\ 1 & 0 & 1 \\ 1 & 1 & 0 \end{array}\right] \end{array}
$$

The square of the matrix M is

$$
\begin{array}{c c} & \begin{array}{ccc} A & B & C \end{array} \\ M^2 = \begin{array}{c} A \\ B \\ C \end{array} & \left[\begin{array}{ccc} 2 & 1 & 1 \\ 1 & 2 & 1 \\ 1 & 1 & 2 \end{array}\right] \end{array}
$$

This matrix illustrates the number of two-stage communication lines between pairs of homes in the group. The 2's on the diagonal indicate that there are two ways for A to get information back to himself through one other person (in this case, through B and also through C). The 1's indicate the number of ways, for example, B can communicate with A through one other person (in this case, C).

The matrix M^3 will give the number of three-stage communication lines between pairs of homes. The values along the diagonal are of importance since they give the number of ways a person in one home can get information back to himself through two other homes (*feedback information*). In this example, we see that A has two ways of obtaining feedback information, namely $A \to B \to C \to A$ or $A \to C \to B \to A$.

$$M^3 = \begin{array}{c} A \\ B \\ C \end{array} \overset{\begin{array}{ccc} A & B & C \end{array}}{\begin{bmatrix} 2 & 3 & 3 \\ 3 & 2 & 3 \\ 3 & 3 & 2 \end{bmatrix}}$$

To find out how many ways A, for example, can obtain two-stage or three-stage feedback, we look at the values in the diagonal of the matrix $M + M^2 + M^3$:

$$M + M^2 + M^3 = \begin{array}{c} A \\ B \\ C \end{array} \overset{\begin{array}{ccc} A & B & C \end{array}}{\begin{bmatrix} 4 & 5 & 5 \\ 5 & 4 & 5 \\ 5 & 5 & 4 \end{bmatrix}}$$

Thus, A has four ways to get such feedback. The 5 in row A, column B, indicates the total number of ways for A to communicate with B using one stage, two stages, or three stages.

Exercise 3
Solutions to Odd-Numbered Problems begin on page 621.

In Problems 1–8 determine which of the given matrices can be interpreted as perfect communication matrices. For those that can be so interpreted, find the two-stage communication lines.

1. $\begin{bmatrix} 0 & 1 \\ 1 & 0 \end{bmatrix}$

2. $\begin{bmatrix} 0 & 2 \\ 2 & 0 \end{bmatrix}$

3. $\begin{bmatrix} 1 & 1 & 1 \\ 1 & 1 & 1 \\ 1 & 1 & 1 \end{bmatrix}$

4. $\begin{bmatrix} 0 & 0 & 1 \\ 1 & 0 & 1 \\ 1 & 1 & 0 \end{bmatrix}$

5. $\begin{bmatrix} 0 & 1 & 0 \\ 1 & 0 & 1 \\ 0 & 1 & 0 \end{bmatrix}$

6. $\begin{bmatrix} 0 & 2 & 1 \\ 2 & 0 & 1 \\ 1 & 1 & 0 \end{bmatrix}$

7. $\begin{bmatrix} 0 & 2 & 1 & 0 \\ 2 & 0 & 0 & 1 \\ 1 & 0 & 0 & 0 \\ 0 & 1 & 0 & 0 \end{bmatrix}$

8. $\begin{bmatrix} 0 & 1 & 0 & 1 \\ 1 & 0 & 2 & 1 \\ 0 & 2 & 0 & 0 \\ 1 & 1 & 0 & 0 \end{bmatrix}$

9. For the communication network between three cities shown in the digraph below, write a matrix M describing the number of lines

connecting two cities without passing through another city. Obtain M^2 and interpret this result.

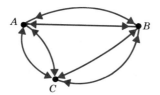

10. For the data in Problem 9, find the number of ways that city A can communicate with itself through one other city. What are the total number of ways City A can communicate with City C using no other cities or one other city?

11. Write a communication matrix for the group Mike, Danny, and Katy if Katy communicates with Mike and Danny, and Mike communicates with Danny. Find the total number of ways Katy can communicate with Mike through no other person or one other person. In how many ways can Mike get one-stage feedback information?

4. Business Communication Model*

In this section we discuss a special class of business communication models dealing with relationships that arise in the world of business.

Consider a mode of communication among a finite number of officials A, B, C, . . . , in a business structure that obeys the following assumptions:

1. **If official A communicates with B, then by necessity B communicates with A. We will use $A \leftrightarrow B$ to indicate this.**
2. **No official communicates with himself/herself.**
3. **Two officials may or may not communicate at all.**
4. **The matrix representation is always an incidence matrix.**

Assumption 4 makes the business communication model different from the perfect communication model discussed in Section 3. (Why?)

Even though we are confining ourselves to a business situation, similar situations arise in the areas of mutual influence, two-way communication, and reciprocated sociometric choice.

Example 1 Figure 14 depicts the internal communication digraph as it exists in an organization headed by five officials, who are denoted by A, B, C, D, and E.

*Adapted from F. Harary, and I. C. Ross, "Identification of the Liaison Persons of an Organization Using the Structure Matrix," *Management Science,* **1** (1955).

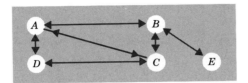

Figure 14

The double arrow from A to B, for example, denotes a communication relationship between A and B. No arrow indicates no such relationship between two officials. For instance, there is no communication relationship between B and D. However, we can reach D from B if we go through C or A; that is, there is a *path* from B to D, namely, $B \to C \to D$ or $B \to A \to D$. Also, for example, we can use the path $A \to B \to E$ to go from A to E. ∎

Path **In general, a** *path* **joining two people** P_1 **and** P_2 **is a collection of arrows and vertices of the form**

$$P_1 \to P_3 \to P_4 \to P_5 \to \cdots \to P_2$$

in which no person is repeated.

For example, in Figure 14,

$$A \to B \to C \to A \to D$$

is *not* a path from A to D, since A has been repeated. Another example from Figure 14 that is *not* a path is

$$E \to B \to C \to B \to A$$

since B is repeated. However, $E \to B \to A$ is a path from E to A.

Connected Digraph **A digraph is said to be** *connected* **if there is a path between every two officials.**

Disconnected Digraph   Figure 14 is an example of a connected digraph; Figure 15 is a *disconnected digraph*. We obtain this by simply deleting B and all arrows connected to B from Figure 14.

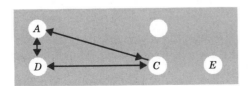

Figure 15

Liaison Official   A *liaison official* in a connected digraph is an official whose removal from the digraph results in a disconnected graph. Officials in an organization which appear as liaison officials in the digraph of the organization structure may be viewed as having special static and dynamic properties. From the static point of view, a liaison official is crucial because his or her removal destroys the connected unity of the organization. This is why an organization is most vulnerable at such official positions. From the dynamic point of view, a liaison official is crucial because he or she cannot be replaced by some other official. For example, if a liaison official is a "bottleneck," the organization will suffer; if he or she is very efficient, the organization may operate well.

If we follow the convention adopted thus far to construct the matrix representation of the digraph in Figure 14, we obtain the incidence matrix

(1)
$$M = \begin{array}{c} \\ A \\ B \\ C \\ D \\ E \end{array} \begin{array}{c} \begin{array}{ccccc} A & B & C & D & E \end{array} \\ \left[\begin{array}{ccccc} 0 & 1 & 1 & 1 & 0 \\ 1 & 0 & 1 & 0 & 1 \\ 1 & 1 & 0 & 1 & 0 \\ 1 & 0 & 1 & 0 & 0 \\ 0 & 1 & 0 & 0 & 0 \end{array}\right] \end{array}$$

The 0's along the diagonal indicate that no official can communicate with himself/herself.

From (1) on page 459, we know that a nonzero entry in row i, column j of the kth power of the incidence matrix M implies that we can go from person P_i to person P_j using k stages. However, as we have seen, a connection from P_i to P_j may not be a path. But if we eliminate all repeated vertices from this connection, we then have a path from P_i to P_j.

Recall that the square of the incidence matrix M gives the number of two-stage connections between vertices. Clearly, in a connected digraph, every official must have two-way communication with at least one other person so that he or she will be able to get feedback in two stages. That is, the diagonal entries of M^2 will be nonzero for a business communication digraph. For example, for the connected digraph of Figure 14, the square of the incidence matrix M is

$$M^2 = \begin{array}{c} \\ A \\ B \\ C \\ D \\ E \end{array} \begin{array}{c} \begin{array}{ccccc} A & B & C & D & E \end{array} \\ \left[\begin{array}{ccccc} 3 & 1 & 2 & 1 & 1 \\ 1 & 3 & 1 & 2 & 0 \\ 2 & 1 & 3 & 1 & 1 \\ 1 & 2 & 1 & 2 & 0 \\ 1 & 0 & 1 & 0 & 1 \end{array}\right] \end{array}$$

Referring to (2) on page 459 and applying this result to business communication digraphs, we can state the following result, which serves as a test for determining whether a graph is connected or disconnected:

(2)   **The graph of a relationship obeying assumptions 1, 2, 3, and 4 involving n officials is disconnected if and only if the corresponding incidence matrix M of the graph has the property that**

$$M + M^2 + M^3 + \cdots + M^{n-1}$$

has one or more 0 entries.

Example 2   Determine by computation with matrices whether the graph in Figure 14 (page 467) is connected. (Actually, in elementary examples such as pictured in Figure 14, it is easy for us to see that the digraph is connected. However, the analysis of more complicated problems is often done by computer; and, since a computer does not have eyes to see, it is necessary for a computer to determine the connectedness of a digraph by some other method, such as matrix computation.)

Solution   First of all, there are five officials in the organization, so we must find

$$M + M^2 + M^3 + M^4$$

where M is given in (1). A little computation with the assistance of a computer yields

$$M + M^2 + M^3 + M^4 = \begin{bmatrix} 23 & 18 & 23 & 16 & 8 \\ 18 & 20 & 18 & 16 & 6 \\ 23 & 18 & 23 & 16 & 8 \\ 16 & 16 & 16 & 14 & 4 \\ 8 & 6 & 8 & 4 & 4 \end{bmatrix}$$

Since no 0 entry appears, the graph in Figure 14 is connected, as we expected. ∎

Example 3   Determine whether the graph in Figure 15 (page 467) is connected.

Solution   The incidence matrix N for the graph in Figure 15 is

$$N = \begin{array}{c} \\ A \\ C \\ D \\ E \end{array} \begin{array}{c} \begin{array}{cccc} A & C & D & E \end{array} \\ \begin{bmatrix} 0 & 1 & 1 & 0 \\ 1 & 0 & 1 & 0 \\ 1 & 1 & 0 & 0 \\ 0 & 0 & 0 & 0 \end{bmatrix} \end{array}$$

Since the graph contains four officials, we look at the matrix $N + N^2 + N^3$. It is easy to verify that this matrix contains all 0 entries in the last row. Thus, the graph in Figure 15 is disconnected, as we expected. ∎

Recall that a liaison official is a person that, if removed, causes a connected digraph to become a disconnected digraph. Let's see how the result (2) helps us to determine whether an official is a liaison person.

To determine whether a person P from among n officials is a liaison official, delete from the incidence matrix M the column and the row corresponding to P. Call the deleted matrix N. Then the graph obtained by deleting P is disconnected if

$$N + N^2 + N^3 + \cdots + N^{n-2}$$

contains one or more 0 entries. In this case, P is a liaison official.

For the graph of Figure 15, with five officials, the person E is not a liaison official, since if E is removed, we still have a connected graph. We can verify this by using the result (2). Delete from the incidence matrix M in (1) the row and the column corresponding to E. We get the deleted matrix:

$$N = \begin{array}{c} \\ A \\ B \\ C \\ D \end{array} \begin{array}{cccc} A & B & C & D \\ \begin{bmatrix} 0 & 1 & 1 & 1 \\ 1 & 0 & 1 & 0 \\ 1 & 1 & 0 & 1 \\ 1 & 0 & 1 & 0 \end{bmatrix} \end{array}$$

You should be able to verify that $N + N^2 + N^3$ contains no 0 entries, thus showing that E is not a liaison official.

Exercise 4
Solutions to Odd-Numbered Problems begin on page 621.

1. For the business communication digraph below, construct the incidence matrix corresponding to the digraph.
   (a) Is the graph disconnected?
   (b) Which officials are liaison officials?

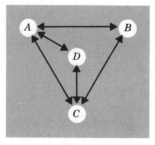

2. For the business communication digraph below, answer the same questions as in Problem 1.

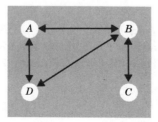

3. In what way is the digraph below different from the one in Problem 2 above?

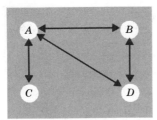

4. Write the incidence matrix for the business communication digraph below and use it to find all liaison officials.

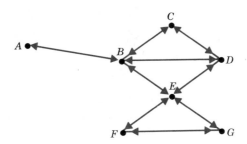

5. (a) Give the digraph corresponding to the following business communication matrix:

$$M = \begin{bmatrix} 0 & 1 & 0 & 1 \\ 1 & 0 & 1 & 0 \\ 0 & 1 & 0 & 1 \\ 1 & 0 & 1 & 0 \end{bmatrix}$$

    (b) Which of the officials are liaison officials?

6. Consider five people, A, B, C, D, E, some of whom gossip with each other. The incidence matrix representing this situation is given below, where the entry 1 means gossiping takes place and 0 means it does not:

$$\begin{array}{c} \\ A \\ B \\ C \\ D \\ E \end{array} \begin{array}{c} \begin{array}{ccccc} A & B & C & D & E \end{array} \\ \begin{bmatrix} 0 & 1 & 0 & 1 & 1 \\ 1 & 0 & 0 & 1 & 0 \\ 0 & 0 & 0 & 1 & 1 \\ 1 & 1 & 1 & 0 & 1 \\ 1 & 0 & 1 & 1 & 0 \end{bmatrix} \end{array}$$

If person E moves out of the neighborhood, is it possible for a rumor to spread among the remaining four people?

5. Clique Model*

So far, we have discussed several digraphs used in social science and business applications, two of which are the dominance digraph and the business communication digraph. Recall that in a dominance digraph, we assume that for every pair of people one always dominates the other so that the incidence matrix representation is *asymmetric*. That is, if A dominates B, then B cannot dominate A. In a business communication matrix, we assume that if A communicates with B, then B communicates with A, so that the incidence matrix representation is *symmetric*. In this section, we discuss social situations in which the matrix representations are incidence matrices, but they are not necessarily asymmetric or symmetric. Since the relationship of friendship is one that is usually neither symmetric nor asymmetric, we represent such situations by *friendship digraphs*.

Friendship Digraph

For example, in a group of five people, A, B, C, D, E, the relationship "is friendly to" might result in the following situation:

> A is friendly to B, C, D, E
> B is friendly to A, C, D
> C is friendly to A, B, D, E
> D is friendly to B, C, E
> E is friendly to A, B, C, D

The friendship digraph representing this situation is given in Figure 16, in which an arrow → denotes the relationship "is friendly to" and a double arrow ↔ denotes mutual friends.

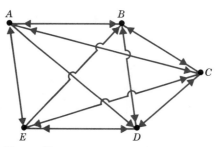

Figure 16

In analyzing the friendship digraph in Figure 16, we find that certain subsets of the group are mutual friends. For example {A, B, C} are mutual friends, as are {C, D, E}, {B, C, D}, and {A, C, E}. Each of these is an example of a *clique*.

Clique A *clique* is a subset of a group of people with the following three properties:

1. **There must be at least three people in the subset.**
2. **Any two people in the subset are mutual friends.**
3. **The subset is maximal in the sense that it cannot be enlarged by adding another person and still satisfy property 2.**

*Adapted from R. Duncan Luce, and Albert D. Perry, "A Method of Matrix Analysis of Group Structure," *Psychometrika*, **14** (1949), pp. 94–116.

Thus, even though two people are mutual friends, they do not form a clique since every clique must have at least three members. Furthermore, if three people are mutual friends and if each one is a mutual friend of a fourth person, the three do not form a clique, since they do not form the *largest* collection of mutual friends.

Using the procedure of the previous sections, the incidence matrix M of the group structure given in Figure 16 is

$$M = \begin{array}{c} \\ A \\ B \\ C \\ D \\ E \end{array} \begin{array}{c} \begin{array}{ccccc} A & B & C & D & E \end{array} \\ \begin{bmatrix} 0 & 1 & 1 & 1 & 1 \\ 1 & 0 & 1 & 1 & 0 \\ 1 & 1 & 0 & 1 & 1 \\ 0 & 1 & 1 & 0 & 1 \\ 1 & 1 & 1 & 1 & 0 \end{bmatrix} \end{array}$$

This incidence matrix M is not asymmetric nor is it symmetric. However, if we limit ourselves to the pairs connected by a double arrow $\leftrightarrow$, namely

$$A \leftrightarrow B, \quad A \leftrightarrow C, \quad A \leftrightarrow E, \quad C \leftrightarrow E,$$
$$B \leftrightarrow C, \quad B \leftrightarrow D, \quad C \leftrightarrow D, \quad D \leftrightarrow E$$

the resulting matrix representing this situation, denoted by S, is

$$S = \begin{array}{c} \\ A \\ B \\ C \\ D \\ E \end{array} \begin{array}{c} \begin{array}{ccccc} A & B & C & D & E \end{array} \\ \begin{bmatrix} 0 & 1 & 1 & 0 & 1 \\ 1 & 0 & 1 & 1 & 0 \\ 1 & 1 & 0 & 1 & 1 \\ 0 & 1 & 1 & 0 & 1 \\ 1 & 0 & 1 & 1 & 0 \end{bmatrix} \end{array}$$

Clearly, the matrix S is a symmetric matrix.

In general, the matrix S obtained from M by eliminating unidirectional arrows is called the *symmetric matrix S associated with the matrix M.* That is, if two people are mutual friends, the entry 1 appears in their respective row and column in S; otherwise, a 0 appears.

To find cliques in a group, we examine the entries in the matrix S^3. The reason for this is that the entries along the diagonal of S^3 give the number of three-stage relations between a person and himself. Since a person cannot be a friend to himself, a nonzero diagonal entry indicates that a relationship from a person back to himself through two others exists.

We proceed to state without proof a result we will use to determine cliques in a group.

Symmetric Matrix S

(1) Let M be the incidence matrix representation of a friendship digraph and let $S = [s_{ij}]$ be the symmetric matrix associated with M. Let $s_{ij}^{(3)}$ denote the entry in row i, column j of matrix S^3.

(a) If $s_{ii}^{(3)}$ is positive, the person P_i belongs to at least one clique.
(b) If $s_{ii}^{(3)} = 0$, the person P_i belongs to no clique.

If the number of individuals in the group to be analyzed is large, then it is difficult to find cliques by inspection. Therefore, we find cliques using matrix techniques but let computers do any necessary calculations.

Example 1   Consider a group of four people, A, B, C, D, whose incidence matrix is

$$M = \begin{array}{c} \\ A \\ B \\ C \\ D \end{array} \overset{\begin{array}{cccc} A & B & C & D \end{array}}{\begin{bmatrix} 0 & 1 & 0 & 0 \\ 1 & 0 & 1 & 0 \\ 1 & 0 & 0 & 1 \\ 0 & 0 & 1 & 0 \end{bmatrix}}$$

Analyze the group structure.

Solution   Here, of course, A is friendly to B, B is friendly to A and C, C is friendly to A and D, and D is friendly to C. The symmetric matrix S associated with M is

$$S = \begin{array}{c} \\ A \\ B \\ C \\ D \end{array} \overset{\begin{array}{cccc} A & B & C & D \end{array}}{\begin{bmatrix} 0 & 1 & 0 & 0 \\ 1 & 0 & 0 & 0 \\ 0 & 0 & 0 & 1 \\ 0 & 0 & 1 & 0 \end{bmatrix}}$$

The cube of S is

$$S^3 = \begin{array}{c} \\ A \\ B \\ C \\ D \end{array} \overset{\begin{array}{cccc} A & B & C & D \end{array}}{\begin{bmatrix} 0 & 1 & 0 & 0 \\ 1 & 0 & 0 & 0 \\ 0 & 0 & 0 & 1 \\ 0 & 0 & 1 & 0 \end{bmatrix}}$$

Since the diagonal entries are 0, this group contains no clique.   ∎

You should verify that $\{B, C, D\}$ in Figure 9, page 455, form a clique by using (1).

The next result gives us some information regarding the size and number of cliques in a group.

Let $S = [s_{ij}]$ be the symmetric matrix associated with a friendship digraph. Suppose a person P_i belongs to exactly one clique. Then P_i is a member of one clique with k members if and only if the diagonal entry $s_{ii}^{(3)}$ in S^3 is

$$s_{ii}^{(3)} = (k - 1)(k - 2)$$

For example, in a group of four people, a clique of either three or four members can result. Suppose a person belongs to exactly one clique. If the corresponding diagonal entry in S^3 is $(3 - 1)(3 - 2) = 2$, the person belongs to one clique of three members. If the diagonal entry is $(4 - 1)(4 - 2) = 6$, the person belongs to one clique of four members. If the diagonal entry is 0, the person belongs to no clique. If the diagonal entry is neither 0, 2, nor 6, the person belongs to more than one clique.

In a group of five people, the only possible sizes for a clique are three, four, or five members. Suppose a person belongs to exactly one clique. Then

$$(3 - 1)(3 - 2) = 2$$
$$(4 - 1)(4 - 2) = 6$$
$$(5 - 1)(5 - 2) = 12$$

If the diagonal entry is 2, the person belongs to one clique of three members. If the diagonal entry is 6, the person belongs to one clique of four members. If it is 12, the person belongs to one clique of five members. If the diagonal entry is 0, the person belongs to no clique. If the diagonal entry is neither 0, 2, 6, nor 12, the person belongs to more than one clique.

Example 2 Consider a group of ten people and let the relationship be one of friendship. The matrix M that describes the friendship relationship is given by

$$
M = \begin{array}{c} \\ 1 \\ 2 \\ 3 \\ 4 \\ 5 \\ 6 \\ 7 \\ 8 \\ 9 \\ 10 \end{array}
\begin{array}{c} \begin{array}{cccccccccc} 1 & 2 & 3 & 4 & 5 & 6 & 7 & 8 & 9 & 10 \end{array} \\
\begin{bmatrix}
0 & 0 & 1 & 1 & 1 & 0 & 0 & 0 & 0 & 1 \\
0 & 0 & 0 & 0 & 0 & 1 & 0 & 0 & 1 & 0 \\
1 & 0 & 0 & 1 & 0 & 0 & 0 & 0 & 0 & 0 \\
1 & 0 & 1 & 0 & 0 & 1 & 0 & 0 & 1 & 1 \\
1 & 0 & 0 & 0 & 0 & 0 & 0 & 0 & 0 & 0 \\
0 & 1 & 0 & 0 & 0 & 0 & 1 & 0 & 0 & 0 \\
0 & 1 & 0 & 0 & 0 & 1 & 0 & 0 & 0 & 0 \\
0 & 0 & 0 & 0 & 1 & 0 & 0 & 0 & 1 & 0 \\
0 & 0 & 0 & 1 & 1 & 0 & 0 & 1 & 0 & 0 \\
1 & 0 & 1 & 0 & 0 & 0 & 1 & 0 & 0 & 0
\end{bmatrix}
\end{array}
$$

Analyze the group structure.

Solution The symmetric matrix S associated with M is

$$
S = \begin{array}{c} \\ 1 \\ 2 \\ 3 \\ 4 \\ 5 \\ 6 \\ 7 \\ 8 \\ 9 \\ 10 \end{array}
\begin{array}{c} \begin{array}{cccccccccc} 1 & 2 & 3 & 4 & 5 & 6 & 7 & 8 & 9 & 10 \end{array} \\
\begin{bmatrix}
0 & 0 & 1 & 1 & 1 & 0 & 0 & 0 & 0 & 1 \\
0 & 0 & 0 & 0 & 0 & 1 & 0 & 0 & 0 & 0 \\
1 & 0 & 0 & 1 & 0 & 0 & 0 & 0 & 0 & 0 \\
1 & 0 & 1 & 0 & 0 & 0 & 0 & 0 & 1 & 0 \\
1 & 0 & 0 & 0 & 0 & 0 & 0 & 0 & 0 & 0 \\
0 & 1 & 0 & 0 & 0 & 0 & 1 & 0 & 0 & 0 \\
0 & 0 & 0 & 0 & 0 & 1 & 0 & 0 & 0 & 0 \\
0 & 0 & 0 & 0 & 0 & 0 & 0 & 0 & 1 & 0 \\
0 & 0 & 0 & 1 & 0 & 0 & 0 & 1 & 0 & 0 \\
1 & 0 & 0 & 0 & 0 & 0 & 0 & 0 & 0 & 0
\end{bmatrix}
\end{array}
$$

Next, using a computer, we find the matrix S^3 to be

$$
S^3 = \begin{array}{c} \\ 1 \\ 2 \\ 3 \\ 4 \\ 5 \\ 6 \\ 7 \\ 8 \\ 9 \\ 10 \end{array}
\begin{array}{cccccccccc}
1 & 2 & 3 & 4 & 5 & 6 & 7 & 8 & 9 & 10 \\
\hline
2 & 0 & 5 & 6 & 4 & 0 & 0 & 1 & 1 & 4 \\
0 & 0 & 0 & 0 & 0 & 2 & 0 & 0 & 0 & 0 \\
5 & 0 & 2 & 4 & 1 & 0 & 0 & 1 & 1 & 1 \\
6 & 0 & 4 & 2 & 1 & 0 & 0 & 0 & 4 & 1 \\
4 & 0 & 1 & 1 & 0 & 0 & 0 & 0 & 1 & 0 \\
0 & 2 & 0 & 0 & 0 & 0 & 2 & 0 & 0 & 0 \\
0 & 0 & 0 & 0 & 0 & 2 & 0 & 0 & 0 & 0 \\
1 & 0 & 1 & 0 & 0 & 0 & 0 & 0 & 2 & 0 \\
1 & 0 & 1 & 4 & 1 & 0 & 0 & 2 & 0 & 1 \\
4 & 0 & 1 & 1 & 0 & 0 & 0 & 0 & 1 & 0
\end{array}
$$

By consulting the diagonal of S^3, we determine that persons 2, 5, 6, 7, 8, 9, and 10 belong to no clique, since a 0 appears in their respective row and column. Those people whose diagonal entries are nonzero, namely persons 1, 3, and 4, belong to at least one clique.

To find the composition and number of the cliques, we compute the values of $(k - 1)(k - 2)$ for $k = 3, 4, 5, 6, 7, 8, 9, 10$.

Number of Members of Clique	$(k - 1)(k - 2)$
3	2
4	6
5	12
6	20
7	30
8	42
9	56
10	72

The entry 2 in row 1, column 1; row 3, column 3; and row 4, column 4 tells us that these three belong to exactly one clique.

■

Example 3 Analyze the group structure given by the digraph in Figure 16, page 472.

Solution The incidence matrix M and the symmetric matrix S associated with M were given earlier. The cube of S is

$$
S^3 = \begin{array}{c} \\ A \\ B \\ C \\ D \\ E \end{array}
\begin{array}{ccccc}
A & B & C & D & E \\
\hline
4 & 8 & 8 & 4 & 8 \\
8 & 4 & 8 & 8 & 4 \\
8 & 8 & 8 & 8 & 8 \\
4 & 8 & 8 & 4 & 8 \\
8 & 4 & 8 & 8 & 4
\end{array}
$$

Clearly, each person in the group belongs to at least one clique since their diagonal entries are positive. Our problem is to determine the composition and number of cliques. Since none of the diagonal entries equals 2, 6, or 12, each person must belong to more than one clique.

To determine how many cliques each person belongs to, we proceed as follows: Consider person A whose diagonal entry in S^3 is 4. Using only addition and the numbers 2, 6, and 12, how can a 4 be arrived at? Clearly, the only possible way is $2 + 2 = 4$. This means person A belongs to exactly two cliques, each containing three people. Similarly, persons B, D, and E belong to two cliques, each containing three people.

The diagonal entry 8 in S^3 can only be obtained from 2, 6, and 12 by $2 + 2 + 2 + 2$ or $2 + 6$. Thus, person C belongs to four cliques of three people each ($2 + 2 + 2 + 2$) or else to two cliques where one contains three people and the other contains four people. Since no one else in the group belongs to a clique of four people, person C must belong to four cliques of three people each.

Consulting the matrix S, we determine that the composition of the four cliques are: $\{A, B, C\}$, $\{A, C, E\}$, $\{B, C, D\}$, and $\{C, D, E\}$. ■

A more precise technique for identifying cliques can be found in the article by Harary and Ross listed in the references at the end of this chapter.

Exercise 5
Solutions to Odd-Numbered Problems begin on page 622.

1. Analyze the structure of a group whose incidence matrix is

$$
\begin{array}{c}
 \\ A \\ B \\ C \\ D \\ E
\end{array}
\begin{array}{c}
\begin{array}{ccccc} A & B & C & D & E \end{array} \\
\left[\begin{array}{ccccc}
0 & 0 & 1 & 1 & 1 \\
1 & 0 & 1 & 1 & 1 \\
1 & 1 & 0 & 1 & 1 \\
1 & 1 & 1 & 0 & 1 \\
0 & 1 & 1 & 1 & 0
\end{array} \right]
\end{array}
$$

2. Analyze the structure of a group whose incidence matrix is

$$
\begin{array}{c}
 \\ 1 \\ 2 \\ 3 \\ 4 \\ 5 \\ 6
\end{array}
\begin{array}{c}
\begin{array}{cccccc} 1 & 2 & 3 & 4 & 5 & 6 \end{array} \\
\left[\begin{array}{cccccc}
0 & 1 & 1 & 1 & 1 & 0 \\
1 & 0 & 1 & 1 & 1 & 1 \\
1 & 1 & 0 & 1 & 1 & 1 \\
1 & 1 & 1 & 0 & 1 & 1 \\
1 & 0 & 0 & 0 & 0 & 0 \\
0 & 1 & 0 & 1 & 1 & 0
\end{array} \right]
\end{array}
$$

3. Analyze the structure of a group whose incidence matrix is

$$
M = \begin{array}{c} \\ 1 \\ 2 \\ 3 \\ 4 \\ 5 \\ 6 \\ 7 \end{array}
\begin{array}{c}
\begin{array}{ccccccc} 1 & 2 & 3 & 4 & 5 & 6 & 7 \end{array} \\
\left[\begin{array}{ccccccc}
0 & 1 & 1 & 0 & 1 & 0 & 1 \\
1 & 0 & 1 & 0 & 0 & 0 & 0 \\
1 & 1 & 0 & 1 & 1 & 0 & 0 \\
0 & 0 & 1 & 0 & 1 & 1 & 1 \\
1 & 0 & 1 & 1 & 0 & 1 & 1 \\
0 & 0 & 1 & 1 & 1 & 0 & 1 \\
1 & 1 & 0 & 1 & 1 & 1 & 0
\end{array}\right]
\end{array}
$$

The cube of the associated matrix S of M is

$$
S^3 = \begin{array}{c} \\ 1 \\ 2 \\ 3 \\ 4 \\ 5 \\ 6 \\ 7 \end{array}
\begin{array}{c}
\begin{array}{ccccccc} 1 & 2 & 3 & 4 & 5 & 6 & 7 \end{array} \\
\left[\begin{array}{ccccccc}
6 & 6 & 10 & 7 & 12 & 6 & 11 \\
6 & 2 & 6 & 4 & 4 & 4 & 4 \\
10 & 6 & 6 & 11 & 12 & 6 & 7 \\
7 & 4 & 11 & 8 & 12 & 9 & 12 \\
12 & 4 & 12 & 12 & 12 & 11 & 12 \\
6 & 4 & 6 & 9 & 11 & 6 & 9 \\
11 & 4 & 7 & 12 & 12 & 9 & 8
\end{array}\right]
\end{array}
$$

4. Analyze the structure of a group whose incidence matrix is

$$
M = \begin{array}{c} \\ 1 \\ 2 \\ 3 \\ 4 \\ 5 \\ 6 \\ 7 \end{array}
\begin{array}{c}
\begin{array}{ccccccc} 1 & 2 & 3 & 4 & 5 & 6 & 7 \end{array} \\
\left[\begin{array}{ccccccc}
0 & 1 & 1 & 0 & 1 & 0 & 1 \\
1 & 0 & 1 & 0 & 0 & 1 & 0 \\
1 & 1 & 0 & 1 & 1 & 0 & 0 \\
0 & 0 & 1 & 0 & 1 & 1 & 1 \\
0 & 0 & 1 & 1 & 0 & 1 & 1 \\
0 & 0 & 0 & 1 & 1 & 0 & 1 \\
0 & 0 & 1 & 1 & 1 & 1 & 0
\end{array}\right]
\end{array}
$$

The cube of the associated matrix S of M is

$$
S^3 = \begin{array}{c} \\ 1 \\ 2 \\ 3 \\ 4 \\ 5 \\ 6 \\ 7 \end{array}
\begin{array}{c}
\begin{array}{ccccccc} 1 & 2 & 3 & 4 & 5 & 6 & 7 \end{array} \\
\left[\begin{array}{ccccccc}
2 & 3 & 5 & 2 & 2 & 2 & 2 \\
3 & 2 & 5 & 2 & 2 & 2 & 2 \\
5 & 5 & 4 & 9 & 9 & 4 & 4 \\
2 & 2 & 9 & 8 & 9 & 9 & 9 \\
2 & 2 & 9 & 9 & 8 & 9 & 9 \\
2 & 2 & 4 & 9 & 9 & 6 & 7 \\
2 & 2 & 4 & 9 & 9 & 7 & 6
\end{array}\right]
\end{array}
$$

Chapter Review

Important
Terms

graph
vertices
edges
loop
directed graph
digraph
dominance digraph
incidence matrix
asymmetric matrix
perfect communication
   digraph
symmetric matrix
business communication
   digraph

friendship digraph
consensus leader
two-stage dominance
leader
***k*-stage dominance**
paired comparison
perfect communication matrix
feedback information
path
connected digraph
disconnected graph
liaison official

Review Exercises
Solutions to Odd-Numbered Problems begin on page 622.

1. For the matrices below, find the corresponding directed graph. Determine which are incidence matrices and list all the models they could represent.

(a) $\begin{bmatrix} 0 & 1 & 0 \\ 0 & 0 & 1 \\ 0 & 1 & 0 \end{bmatrix}$
(b) $\begin{bmatrix} 0 & 1 & 2 \\ 1 & 0 & 0 \\ 2 & 0 & 0 \end{bmatrix}$
(c) $\begin{bmatrix} 0 & 1 & 1 \\ 0 & 0 & 0 \\ 0 & 1 & 0 \end{bmatrix}$

2. For those that are dominance situations in Problem 1, find the two-stage dominance relationships and find the number of people each person dominates in one or two stages.

3. *Tournament.* In a five-team round-robin tournament, the final standings were

	Won	Lost
A	3	1
B	3	1
Team C	2	2
D	2	2
E	0	4

If

A	beat B, C, E
B	beat C, D, E
C	beat D, E
D	beat A, E
E	beat no one

who should be declared the winner? Give reasons!

4. How many ways can City A communicate with City B through one other city for the situation below? Give reasons!

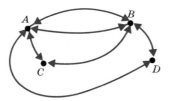

5. Which are liaison officials for the business situation below?

$$M = \begin{array}{c} \\ A \\ B \\ C \\ D \end{array} \begin{array}{cccc} A & B & C & D \\ \begin{bmatrix} 0 & 1 & 0 & 1 \\ 1 & 0 & 1 & 0 \\ 0 & 1 & 0 & 1 \\ 1 & 0 & 1 & 0 \end{bmatrix} \end{array}$$

6. For the communication network shown below, write the matrix A describing the number of lines connecting two cities without passing through another city.

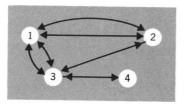

7. Analyze the group structure of the matrix M:

$$M = \begin{bmatrix} 0 & 1 & 1 & 1 \\ 1 & 0 & 0 & 1 \\ 1 & 0 & 0 & 1 \\ 1 & 1 & 1 & 0 \end{bmatrix}$$

(a) Find S and S^3.
(b) Find all cliques, if there are any.

Other Articles

Beltrami, E. J., and L. D. Bodin, "Networks and Vehicle Routing for Municipal Waste Collection," *Networks,* **4** (1973), pp. 65–94.

Doreian, Patrick, "Interaction under Conditions of Crisis: Applications of Graph Theory to International Relations," *Peace Res. Soc. (Int.) Pap.,* **11** (1969), pp. 89–107.

Festinger, L., "The Analysis of Sociograms Using Matrix Algebra," *Human Relations,* **2** (1949), pp. 153–158.

Guetzkow, Harold, and Herbert A. Simon, "The Impact of Certain Communication Nets upon Organization and Performance in Task-Oriented Groups," *Manage. Sci.,* **1,** 3–4 (April–July 1955), pp. 233–250.

Harary, Frank, "Status and Contrastatus," *Sociometry,* (1959), pp. 23–43.

Harary, Frank, and Ian C. Ross, "A Procedure for Clique Determination Using the Group Matrix," *Sociometry,* (1957), pp. 205–215.

Hart, Jeffrey, "Structures of Influence and Cooperation-Conflict," *Int. Interact.,* **1** (1974), pp. 141–162.

Hart, Jeffrey, "Symmetry and Polarization in the European International System, 1870–1879: A Methodological Study," *J. Peace Res.,* **11** (1974), pp. 229–244.

Healy, Brian, and Arthur Stein, "The Balance of Power in International History: Theory and Reality," *J. Conflict Resolut.,* **17,** 1 (March 1973), pp. 33–61.

Leavitt, Harold J., "Some Effects of Certain Communication Patterns on Group Performance," *J. Abnorm. Soc. Psychol.,* **46** (1951), pp. 38–50.

Saaty, Thomas L., "A Model for the Control of Arms," *Oper. Res.,* **12** (September–October 1964), pp. 586–609.

Stoffers, Karl E., "Scheduling of Traffic Lights—A New Approach," *Transp. Res.,* **2** (1968), pp. 199–234.

Zajonc, Robert B., and Eugene Burnstein, "The Learning of Balanced and Unbalanced Social Structures," *J. Pers.,* **33,** 2 (June 1965), pp. 153–163.

13

Logic

1. Introduction

In this chapter, we survey many of the fundamental concepts found in the area of mathematics called *logic*. There are several reasons for studying logic. Two of the more important ones are (*1*) to gain proficiency in correct mathematical reasoning and (*2*) to apply the tool of logic to practical situations.

In mathematics, the words "not," "or," "if . . . , then . . . ," "if and only if," and so on, are used extensively. A knowledge of the exact meaning of these words is necessary before we can make precise the laws of inference and deduction that are constantly used in mathematics. The study of logic will enable you to gain a basic understanding of what constitutes a mathematical argument. This will eliminate common errors made in mathematical, as well as nonmathematical, arguments.

In the last two sections of this chapter, we use the concepts of logic to study practical applications in the area of life insurance and elementary electrical circuits.

We hope this chapter will give you some indication of the usefulness of logic in uncovering ambiguities and non sequiturs. Furthermore, we hope this chapter offers evidence in favor of Church's remark that "the value of logic . . . is not that it supports a particular system, but that the process of logical organization of any system (empiricist or otherwise) serves to test its internal consistency, to verify its logical adequacy to its declared purpose, and to isolate and clarify the assumptions on which it rests."*

2. Propositions

Let's first consider the development of language. Any developed language, such as English, is composed of various words and phrases with distinct functions. These special words and phrases have a bearing on the truth or falsity of the assertion in which they occur.

English sentences are usually classified as belonging to one of four categories: (*1*) declarative, (*2*) interrogative, (*3*) exclamatory, and (*4*) imperative. We assume that you can easily recognize these categories, and this ability will be required in the study of logic. We will deal mainly with *declarative sentences*.

Proposition   **A *proposition* is a declarative sentence that can be meaningfully classified as either true or false.**

Example 1   The price of corn in Chicago rose on June 16, 1982.
   This is a proposition, although few of us can say whether it is true or false. ■

---

*Church, *Introduction to Mathematical Logic,* Vol. 1, Princeton University Press, Princeton, N.J., 1956, p. 55.

BERTRAND RUSSELL (1872–1970) was a British philosopher and mathematician as well as a noted social reformer. In his principal work, he developed symbolic logic and applied it to mathematics and philosophy.

Example 2   The earth is round.

This sentence records a possible fact about reality and is a proposition. Some people would classify this proposition as true and others as false, depending on their interpretation of the word *round*. Thus, we see that the classification of propositions as true or false is an idealization. Actually, the truth values of propositions fluctuate as we sharpen our interpretation of the words they contain. ∎

Example 3   What is the exchange rate from United States dollars to German marks?

This is not a proposition—it is a question. ∎

Example 4   The prices of most stocks on the New York Stock Exchange rose during the period 1929–1931.

Although we know this to be a false statement, it is a proposition. ∎

We conclude that the classification of propositions into the two categories, true and false, rests on the ideal assumption that the meanings of the words assumed in the propositions are perfectly clear. We shall see that this idealism can be avoided when we encounter propositions in mathematics and use the symbolism of mathematical logic.

Example 5   Consider the proposition "Jones is handsome and Smith is selfish." This sentence is obtained by joining the two propositions "Jones is handsome" "Smith is selfish" by the word "and." ∎

Compound Proposition; Connectives   **The combination of two or more propositions is called a** *compound proposition*. **The words used to combine the propositions of a compound proposition are called** *connectives.*

Some examples of connectives are: *or; and; if . . . , then; if and only if.*

Conjunction   **Let** p **and** q **denote any propositions. The compound proposition** p *and* q **is called the** *conjunction of* p *and* q, **and is denoted symbolically by**

$$p \wedge q$$

We define the statement $p \wedge q$ **to be true when both** p **and** q **are true and to be false otherwise.**

Example 6   Consider the two statements

p: Washington, D.C., is the capital of the United States.
q: Hawaii is the fiftieth state of the United States.

The conjunction of p and q is

$p \wedge q$: Washington, D.C., is the capital of the United States and Hawaii is the fiftieth state of the United States.

Since both p and q are true statements, we conclude that the compound statement $p \wedge q$ is true.

■

Example 7 Consider the two statements

p: Washington, D.C., is the capital of the United States.
q: Vermont is the largest of the fifty states.

The compound proposition $p \wedge q$ is

$p \wedge q$: Washington, D.C., is the capital of the United States and Vermont is the largest of the fifty states.

Since the statement q is false, the compound statement $p \wedge q$ is false—even though p is true.

■

Inclusive Disjunction **Let p and q be any propositions. The compound proposition p or q is called the** *inclusive disjunction of p and q* **and is denoted symbolically by**

$$p \vee q$$

We define the compound proposition $p \vee q$ to be true if both p and q are true, if p is true and q is false, or if p is false and q is true. The compound proposition $p \vee q$ is false if both p and q are false.

Example 8 Consider the propositions

p: XYZ Company is the largest producer of nails in the world.
q: Mines Ltd. has three uranium mines in Nevada.

The compound proposition $p \vee q$ is

$p \vee q$: XYZ Company is the largest producer of nails in the world or Mines Ltd. has three uranium mines in Nevada.

■

Exclusive Disjunction **Let p and q be any propositions. The** *exclusive disjunction of p and q,* **read as p or q, is denoted symbolically by**

$$p \veebar q$$

We define the compound proposition $p \veebar q$ to be true whenever p is true and q is false, and whenever p is false and q is true. The compound proposition $p \veebar q$ is false whenever p is false and q is false or whenever p is true and q is true.

Thus, in the English language, "or" is a connective that can be used in two different ways. The correct meaning is usually apparent from the context in which it is used. However, to remain precise, we shall distinguish between the two meanings of "or."

Example 9 Consider the propositions

> p: XYZ Company earned \$3.20 per share in 1980.
> q: XYZ Company paid a dividend of \$1.20 per share in 1980.

The inclusive disjunction of p and q is

> $p \lor q$: XYZ Company earned \$3.20 per share in 1980 or XYZ Company paid a dividend of \$1.20 per share in 1980, or both.

The exclusive disjunction of p and q is

> $p \underline{\lor} q$: XYZ Company earned \$3.20 per share in 1980 or XYZ Company paid a dividend of \$1.20 per share in 1980, but *not* both.

∎

Example 10 Consider the compound proposition

> p: This weekend I will date Caryl or Mary.

The use of the connective "or" is not clear here. If the "or" means inclusive disjunction, then at least one and possibly both girls will be dated. If the "or" means exclusive disjunction, then only one girl will be dated.

∎

Negation **If p is any proposition, the** *negation of p,* **denoted by**

$$\sim p$$

and read as *not p,* **is that proposition for which:**

1. **If p is true, then $\sim p$ is false.**
2. **If p is false, then $\sim p$ is true.**

Law of
Contradiction

This definition implies that the *law of contradiction* from classical logic holds. This law states that a proposition p and its negation $\sim p$ cannot both be true.

Example 11 Consider the proposition

> p: One share of XYZ Company is worth \$85.

The negation of p is

> $\sim p$: One share of XYZ Company is not worth \$85.

The statement "One share of XYZ Company is worth \$80" is *not* a correct negation of p.

∎

Quantifier   A *quantifier* is a word or phrase telling how many (*quant*). The quantifiers "each," "every," "any," and "all" are interchangeable.

Example 12   The following propositions all have the same meaning:

> *p*: All people are intelligent.
> *q*: Every person is intelligent.
> *r*: Each person is intelligent.
> *s*: Any person is intelligent.

■

The quantifiers "some" and "there exists" are interchangeable.

Example 13   The negation of the proposition

> *p*: All people are intelligent.

is

> ~*p*: Some people are not intelligent.
> ~*p*: There exists a person who is not intelligent.

The negation of

> *q*: There is a person who is not intelligent.
> *q*: Some people are not intelligent.

is

> ~*q*: All people are intelligent.

■

Exercise 2
Solutions to Odd-Numbered Problems begin on page 622.

In Problems 1–8 determine which are propositions.

1. The cost of shell egg futures was up on June 18, 1980.
2. The gross national product exceeded one billion dollars in 1935.
3. What a portfolio!
4. Why did you buy XYZ Company stock?
5. The earnings of XYZ Company doubled last year.
6. Where is the new mine of Mines Ltd?
7. Jones is guilty of murder in the first degree.
8. What a hit!

In Problems 9–16 negate each proposition.

9. A fox is an animal.
10. The outlook for bonds is not good.
11. I am buying stocks and bonds.

12. Mike is selling his apartment building and his business.
13. No one wants to buy my house.
14. Everyone has at least one television set.
15. Some people have no car.
16. Jones is permitted not to see that all votes are not counted.

In Problems 17–24 let p denote "John is an economics major" and let q denote "John is a sociology minor." State each proposition as a simple sentence.

17. $p \lor q$
18. $p \veebar q$
19. $p \land q$
20. $\sim p$
21. $\sim p \lor \sim p$
22. $\sim(\sim q)$
23. $\sim p \lor q$
24. $\sim p \land q$

3. Truth Tables

Truth Value

For a given proposition p we are interested in determining whether the proposition is true or false; that is, we seek the *truth value of p*. If we denote "true" by "T" and "false" by "F," we can construct a *truth table* that diagrams the truth value of a compound proposition for all possible cases.

For example, consider the conjunction of any two propositions p and q. Recall that $p \land q$ is false if either p is false or q is false, or if both p and q are false. There are four truth value possibilities for the compound statement:

1. p is true and q is true.
2. p is true and q is false.
3. p is false and q is true.
4. p is false and q is false.

The four truth value cases for $p \land q$ are listed in Table 1. For convenience, the possibilities for p and for q will always be listed in the order they appear in Table 1.

The truth values of $\sim p$ are given in Table 2.

Using the previous definitions of inclusive disjunction and exclusive disjunction, we obtain truth tables for $p \lor q$ and $p \veebar q$. See Table 3.

Table 1

	p	q	$p \land q$
Case 1	T	T	T
Case 2	T	F	F
Case 3	F	T	F
Case 4	F	F	F

Table 2

p	$\sim p$
T	F
F	T

Table 3

p	q	$p \lor q$	$p \veebar q$
T	T	T	F
T	F	T	T
F	T	T	T
F	F	F	F

In addition to using the connectives $\lor$, $\land$, $\veebar$ separately to form compound propositions, we can use them together to form more complex assertions. Let's denote by $P(p, q, \ldots)$ a compound proposition, where $p, q, \ldots$ are the components making the compound proposition. The truth value of a compound proposition depends exclusively on the truth values of its components; that is, the truth value of a compound proposition is known once the truth values of its components are known.

For example, the truth table for $(p \vee q) \underline{\vee} (\sim p)$, which involves two components p and q, is given in Table 4.

Table 4

p	q	$p \vee q$	$\sim p$	$(p \vee q) \underline{\vee} (\sim p)$
T	T	T	F	T
T	F	T	F	T
F	T	T	T	F
F	F	F	T	T

Observe that the first columns of the table are for the component propositions $p, q, \ldots$ and that there are enough rows in the table to allow for all possible combinations of T and F (for two components p and q, 4 rows are necessary; for three components $p, q,$ and r, 8 rows would be necessary; and for n components, 2^n rows would be necessary).

Table 4 has five columns, and each column corresponds to a stage in constructing the compound proposition. Notice that each stage depends on its predecessors. The first two columns and the last one are of interest to us and the middle columns are just intermediate stages leading to the final result. To obtain these stages it is necessary to analyze the compound proposition very carefully.

First construct the skeleton of the truth table to correspond to the given proposition:

p	q	$p \vee q$	$\sim p$	$(p \vee q) \underline{\vee} (\sim p)$
T	T			
T	F			
F	T			
F	F			

Observe that the compound proposition is written on the top row to the right of its components and that there is a column under each component or connective. Truth values are then entered in the truth table, one step at a time:

Stage 1

p	q	$p \vee q$	$\sim p$	$(p \vee q) \underline{\vee} (\sim p)$
T	T	T		
T	F	T		
F	T	T		
F	F	F		

Stage 2

p	q	$p \vee q$	$\sim p$	$(p \vee q) \underline{\vee} (\sim p)$
T	T	T	F	
T	F	T	F	
F	T	T	T	
F	F	F	T	

Stage 3

p	q	$p \vee q$	$\sim p$	$(p \vee q) \underline{\vee} (\sim p)$
T	T	T	F	T
T	F	T	F	T
F	T	T	T	F
F	F	F	T	T

The truth table of the compound proposition then consists of the original columns under p and q and the fifth column entered into the table, namely the last stage.

Example 1   Determine the truth table for $(p \vee \sim q) \wedge p$. Notice that the component parts of this proposition are p, $\sim q$, and $p \vee \sim q$. The truth table is given below:

p	q	$\sim q$	$p \vee \sim q$	$(p \vee \sim q) \wedge p$
T	T	F	T	T
T	F	T	T	T
F	T	F	F	F
F	F	T	T	F

Example 2   Determine the truth table for $\sim(p \vee q) \vee (\sim p \wedge \sim q)$. (It is understood that the first negation symbol only negates $p \vee q$ and is not intended to negate the entire expression.) The truth table is given below:

p	q	$\sim p$	$\sim q$	$p \vee q$	$\sim(p \vee q)$	$(\sim p \wedge \sim q)$	$\sim(p \vee q) \vee (\sim p \wedge \sim q)$
T	T	F	F	T	F	F	F
T	F	F	T	T	F	F	F
F	T	T	F	T	F	F	F
F	F	T	T	F	T	T	T

The following is an example of a truth table involving three components, p, q, and r.

Example 3 Determine the truth table for $p \wedge (q \vee r)$. The truth table is given below:

p	q	r	$q \vee r$	$p \wedge (q \vee r)$
T	T	T	T	T
T	T	F	T	T
T	F	T	T	T
T	F	F	F	F
F	T	T	T	F
F	T	F	T	F
F	F	T	T	F
F	F	F	F	F

Very often, two propositions stated in different ways have the same meaning. For example, in law, to say that "Jones has a duty to Smith to paint his house" is the same as saying that "it ought to be the case Jones does paint the house for Smith."

Logically Equivalent **If two propositions a and b have the same truth values in every possible case, the propositions are called** *logically equivalent.* **This situation is denoted by $a \equiv b$.**

Example 4 Show that $\sim(p \wedge q)$ is logically equivalent to $\sim p \vee \sim q$.

Solution First, construct the truth table as shown below.

1	2	3	4	5	6	7
p	q	$p \wedge q$	$\sim(p \wedge q)$	$\sim p$	$\sim q$	$\sim p \vee \sim q$
T	T	T	F	F	F	F
T	F	F	T	F	T	T
F	T	F	T	T	F	T
F	F	F	T	T	T	T

Notice that the entries in columns 4 and 7 of the truth table are the same. Hence, the two propositions are logically equivalent.

Example 5 Show that $\sim p \wedge \sim q$ is logically equivalent to $\sim(p \vee q)$.

Solution First, construct the truth table as shown. The entries in the last two columns are the same, so the two propositions are logically equivalent.

p	q	$p \lor q$	$\sim p$	$\sim q$	$\sim p \land \sim q$	$\sim(p \lor q)$
T	T	T	F	F	F	F
T	F	T	F	T	F	F
F	T	T	T	F	F	F
F	F	F	T	T	T	T

Now that the idea of logically equivalent propositions has been introduced, we can discuss various identities or properties that will be used later in this chapter. That is, certain combinations of statements and connectives will turn out to have the *same* truth values as other combinations of statements and connectives.

Idempotent Laws

For any proposition p,

$$p \land p \equiv p \qquad p \lor p \equiv p$$

Thus, $p \land p \equiv p$ means that the compound statement p *and* p is logically equivalent to p. Similarly, p *or* p is logically equivalent to p.

Associative Laws

For any three propositions p, q, r,

$$(p \land q) \land r \equiv p \land (q \land r) \qquad (p \lor q) \lor r \equiv p \lor (q \lor r)$$

The sentence $(p \land q) \land r \equiv p \land (q \land r)$ means that given a compound statement composed of three propositions connected by *and*, changing the position of parentheses does not change the statement. (The same is true of the word *or*.)

Commutative Laws

For any two propositions p and q,

$$p \land q \equiv q \land p \qquad p \lor q \equiv q \lor p$$

The sentence $p \land q \equiv q \land p$ means that the compound proposition p *and* q is equivalent to the compound proposition q *and* p. The commutative law tells us that when two propositions are compounded by using the connectives *or* or *and*, the order in which the propositions appear does not affect the truth value of the compound proposition.

For example, for the two statements

p: Jones is attractive.
q: Jones is intelligent.

the truth values of the compound propositions

$p \land q$: Jones is attractive and Jones is intelligent.
$q \land p$: Jones is intelligent and Jones is attractive.

are the same.

Of course, the same remarks are also valid for the connective *or*.

Distributive Laws

For any three propositions p, q, r,

$$p \vee (q \wedge r) \equiv (p \vee q) \wedge (p \vee r)$$
$$p \wedge (r \vee q) \equiv (p \wedge r) \vee (p \wedge q)$$

The sentence $p \vee (q \wedge r) \equiv (p \vee q) \wedge (p \vee r)$ means that p or (q and r) is the same as (p or q) and (p or r). Also, $p \wedge (r \vee q) \equiv (p \wedge r) \vee (p \wedge q)$ means that the compound proposition p and (r or q) is equivalent to the compound proposition (p and r) or (p and q).

For example, consider the three propositions

p: Jones is attractive.
q: Jones is intelligent.
r: Jones is humble.

The significance of the first distributive law, namely,

$$p \vee (q \wedge r) \equiv (p \vee q) \wedge (p \vee r)$$

is that the two statements below are equivalent:

1. Jones is attractive or (Jones is intelligent and humble).
2. (Jones is attractive or intelligent) and (Jones is attractive or humble).

De Morgan's Laws

For any two propositions p and q,

$$\sim(p \vee q) \equiv \sim p \wedge \sim q \qquad \sim(p \wedge q) \equiv \sim p \vee \sim q$$

That is, the negation of p or q is logically equivalent to the negation of p and the negation of q. Moreover, the negation of p and q is logically equivalent to the negation of p or the negation of q. The truth tables given in Examples 4 and 5 diagram De Morgan's laws.

De Morgan's laws are useful for finding the negation of compound statements.

Example 6   Negate the compound statements:
(a)   The first child is a girl and the second child is a boy.
(b)   Tonight I will study or I will go bowling.

Solution   (a)   To begin, we let p and q represent the components:

p: The first child is a girl.
q: The second child is a boy.

We want to negate the statement $p \wedge q$; that is, we want to find $\sim(p \wedge q)$.

AUGUSTUS DE MORGAN (1806–1871), British mathematician and logician, was born in Madura, India, the son of a British army officer. He was graduated from Trinity College in Cambridge, England in 1827, but was denied a teaching position there for refusing to subscribe to religious tests. He was, however, appointed to a mathematics professorship at the newly opened University of London. He is best known for his work *Formal Logic*, which appeared in 1847. He also wrote papers on the foundations of algebra, philosophy of mathematical methods, and probability, as well as several successful elementary textbooks.

By De Morgan's law,

$$\sim(p \wedge q) \equiv \sim p \vee \sim q$$

Thus, the negation is

The first child is not a girl or the second child is not a boy.

(b) As above, we begin by representing p and q as

$$p: \text{ I will study.}$$
$$q: \text{ I will go bowling.}$$

We want to negate the statement $p \vee q$. By De Morgan's law,

$$\sim(p \vee q) \equiv \sim p \wedge \sim q$$

Hence, the negation is

Tonight I will not study and I shall not go bowling.

Absorption Laws

For any two propositions p and q,

$$p \vee (p \wedge q) \equiv p \qquad p \wedge (p \vee q) \equiv p$$

The sentence $p \vee (p \wedge q) \equiv p$ means that p or (p and q) is logically equivalent to p. Also, $p \wedge (p \vee q) \equiv p$ means that p and (p or q) is logically equivalent to p.

Example 7 Prove the distributive law, $p \vee (q \wedge r) \equiv (p \vee q) \wedge (p \vee r)$.

Solution Since the entries in the last two columns of the truth table below are the same, the two propositions are logically equivalent.

p	q	r	$q \wedge r$	$p \vee q$	$p \vee r$	$p \vee (q \wedge r)$	$(p \vee q) \wedge (p \vee r)$
T	T	T	T	T	T	T	T
T	T	F	F	T	T	T	T
T	F	T	F	T	T	T	T
T	F	F	F	T	T	T	T
F	T	T	T	T	T	T	T
F	T	F	F	T	F	F	F
F	F	T	F	F	T	F	F
F	F	F	F	F	F	F	F

Example 8   Prove the idempotent law, $p \wedge p \equiv p$.

Solution   The truth table is

p	$p \wedge p$
T	T
F	F

■

The construction of truth tables for the rest of the laws are left as exercises.

Exercise 3
Solutions to Odd-Numbered Problems begin on page 623.

In Problems 1–16 construct a truth table for each compound proposition.

1. $p \vee \sim q$
2. $\sim p \vee \sim q$
3. $\sim p \wedge \sim q$
4. $\sim p \wedge q$
5. $\sim(\sim p \wedge q)$
6. $(p \vee \sim q) \wedge \sim p$
7. $\sim(\sim p \vee \sim q)$
8. $(p \vee \sim q) \wedge (q \wedge \sim p)$
9. $(p \vee \sim q) \wedge p$
10. $p \wedge (q \vee \sim q)$
11. $(p \veebar q) \wedge (p \wedge \sim q)$
12. $(p \wedge \sim q) \vee (q \wedge \sim p)$
13. $(p \wedge q) \vee (\sim p \wedge \sim q)$
14. $(p \wedge q) \vee (p \wedge r)$
15. $(p \wedge \sim q) \veebar r$
16. $(\sim p \vee q) \wedge \sim r$

In Problems 17–22 construct a truth table for each law.

17. Idempotent laws
18. Commutative laws
19. Associative laws
20. Distributive laws
21. Absorption laws
22. De Morgan's laws

In Problems 23–26 show that the given propositions are logically equivalent.

23. $p \wedge (\sim q \vee q)$ and p
24. $p \vee (q \wedge \sim q)$ and p
25. $\sim(\sim p)$ and p
26. $p \wedge q$ and $q \wedge p$

In Problems 27–30 construct a truth table for each proposition.

27. $p \wedge (q \wedge \sim p)$
28. $(p \wedge q) \vee p$
29. $[(p \wedge q) \vee (\sim p \wedge \sim q)] \wedge p$
30. $(\sim p \wedge \sim q \wedge r) \vee (p \wedge q \wedge r)$

In Problems 31–33 use the propositions

p: Smith is an exconvict.
q: Smith is rehabilitated.

to give examples, using English sentences, of each law.

31. Idempotent laws
32. Commutative laws
33. De Morgan's laws

In Problems 34–36 use De Morgan's laws to negate each compound statement.

34. Mike can hit the ball well and he can pitch strikes.
35. Katy is a good volley ball player and is not conceited.
36. The baby is crying or talking all the time.

4. Implications

Consider the following compound proposition: "If I get an A in Math, then I will continue to study." The above sentence states a condition under which I shall continue to study.

Another example of such a proposition is: "If today is Sunday, then tomorrow is Monday."

Such propositions occur quite frequently in mathematics, and an understanding of their nature is extremely important.

Implication; Conditional Connective   **If p and q are any two propositions, then we call the proposition**

$$\textit{If } p, \textit{ then } q$$

an *implication* **and the connective** *If—then—* **the** *conditional connective.*

We denote the conditional connective symbolically by $\Rightarrow$ **and the implication by** $p \Rightarrow q$ **(read as** *If p, then q***).**

Hypothesis
Conclusion

In the above, p **is called the** *hypothesis* **and** q **is called the** *conclusion.*
The conditional $p \Rightarrow q$ **can also be read as follows:**

1. p **implies** q.
2. p **is sufficient for** q.
3. p **only if** q.
4. q **is necessary for** p.

In order to arrive at a truth table for implication we consider the following situation. Suppose we make the statement

If XYZ common stock reaches $90 per share, it will be sold.

When is the statement true and when is it false? Clearly, if XYZ stock reaches $90 per share and it is not sold, the implication is false. It is also clear that if XYZ stock reaches $90 per share and it is sold, the implication is true. In other words, if the hypothesis and conclusion are both true, the implication is true; if the hypothesis is true and the conclusion false, the implication is false.

But what happens when the hypothesis is false? In this case, we claim the implication is not subject to verification and we arbitrarily say that the implication is true (mainly because we cannot say it is false). The truth table for implication is given in Table 5.

Table 5

p	q	$p \Rightarrow q$
T	T	T
T	F	F
F	T	T
F	F	T

We shall say that a compound proposition has been expressed symbolically if each component sentence has been replaced by an appropriate symbol.

For example, denoting "I study" and "I shall pass" by a and b, respectively, the proposition "If I study, then I shall pass," is written as $a \Rightarrow b$. This proposition can also be read as "A sufficient condition for passing is to study."

To understand "implication" better, look at an implication as if it is a conditional promise. If the promise is broken, the implication is false; otherwise, it is true. For this reason, the only circumstances under which the implication $p \Rightarrow q$ is false is when p is true and q is false.

Example 1 Consider the implication

If you are guilty, then you will go to jail.

If you are guilty and you do go to jail, the promise is not broken. Hence, the implication is true. If you are guilty and you do not go to jail, the promise is broken. Hence, the implication is false. If you are not guilty, the promise is not tested and therefore it is not broken; hence, the implication is true.

■

The word *then* in an implication merely serves to separate the conclusion from the hypothesis—it could be, and usually is, omitted.

The implication $p \Rightarrow q$ is, in essence, a part of the language we developed thus far. If we construct the truth table of $\sim p \vee q$, we find out that $\sim p \vee q$ is logically equivalent to $p \Rightarrow q$, that is,

$$\sim p \vee q \equiv p \Rightarrow q$$

See Table 6.

Table 6

p	q	$\sim p$	$\sim p \vee q$	$p \Rightarrow q$
T	T	F	T	T
T	F	F	F	F
F	T	T	T	T
F	F	T	T	T

Suppose we start with the implication $p \Rightarrow q$ and then interchange the roles of p and q, obtaining the implication, "If q, then p."

Converse   **The implication** *If q, then p* **is called the** *converse* **of the implication** *If p, then q.*

Example 2   If we let p and q stand for propositions, then $q \Rightarrow p$ is the converse of $p \Rightarrow q$.

■

Let's consider the truth tables for the implication $p \Rightarrow q$ and its converse $q \Rightarrow p$ simultaneously. See Table 7.

Table 7

p	q	$p \Rightarrow q$	$q \Rightarrow p$
T	T	T	T
T	F	F	T
F	T	T	F
F	F	T	T

Notice that $p \Rightarrow q$ and $q \Rightarrow p$ are not equivalent. That is, the fact that an implication is true tells us nothing about the truth of its converse. As an illustration, consider the following example.

Example 3   Consider the statements

p: You are a murderer.
q: You are in jail.

The implication $p \Rightarrow q$ states that

If you are a murderer, then you are in jail.

The converse of this implication, namely, $q \Rightarrow p$, states that

If you are in jail, then you are a murderer.

To say that all murderers are in jail is not the same as saying that everyone who is in jail is a murderer.

■

This example illustrates that the truth of an implication does not imply the truth of its converse. Many of the most common fallacies in thinking arise from confusing an implication with its converse.

Contrapositive   **The implication** *If not q, then not p,* **written as** $\sim q \Rightarrow \sim p$**, is called the** *contrapositive* **of the implication** $p \Rightarrow q$**.**

Example 4   Consider the statements

p: You are a murderer.
q: You are in jail.

The implication $p \Rightarrow q$ states that "If you are a murderer, then you are in jail." The contrapositive of $p \Rightarrow q$, namely, $\sim q \Rightarrow \sim p$, is "If you are not in jail, then you are not a murderer."

■

Inverse **The implication** *If not p, then not q,* **written as** $\sim p \Rightarrow \sim q$, **is called the** *inverse* **of the implication** *If p, then q.*

Example 5 Consider the statements

p: You are a murderer.
q: You are in jail.

The implication $p \Rightarrow q$ states that "If you are a murderer, then you are in jail." The inverse of $p \Rightarrow q$, namely, $\sim p \Rightarrow \sim q$, is "If you are not a murderer, then you are not in jail."

■

Example 6 The truth table for $p \Rightarrow q$, $q \Rightarrow p$, $\sim p \Rightarrow \sim q$, and $\sim q \Rightarrow \sim p$ is given in Table 8.

Table 8

State-ments		Impli-cation	Con-verse			Inverse	Contra-positive
p	q	$p \Rightarrow q$	$q \Rightarrow p$	$\sim p$	$\sim q$	$\sim p \Rightarrow \sim q$	$\sim q \Rightarrow \sim p$
T	T	T	T	F	F	T	T
T	F	F	T	F	T	T	F
F	T	T	F	T	F	F	T
F	F	T	T	T	T	T	T

Notice that the entries under Implication and Contrapositive are the same; also, the entries under Converse and Inverse are the same. Hence, we conclude that

$$p \Rightarrow q \equiv \sim q \Rightarrow \sim p \qquad q \Rightarrow p \equiv \sim p \Rightarrow \sim q$$

Thus, we have shown that an implication and its contrapositive are logically equivalent. Also, the converse and inverse of an implication are logically equivalent.

■

Exercise 4
Solutions to Odd-Numbered Problems begin on page 625.

In Problems 1–12 write the converse, contrapositive, and inverse of each statement.

1. $\sim p \Rightarrow q$ 2. $\sim p \Rightarrow \sim q$ 3. $\sim q \Rightarrow \sim p$ 4. $p \Rightarrow \sim q$

THE BICONDITIONAL CONNECTIVE

5. If it is raining, the grass is wet.
6. It is raining if it is cloudy.
7. It is raining or it is cloudy.
8. If it is not cloudy, then it is not raining.
9. A necessary condition for rain is that it be cloudy.
10. A sufficient condition for rain is that it be cloudy.
11. Rain is sufficient for it to be cloudy.
12. Rain is necessary for it to be cloudy.

13. Give a verbal sentence that describes
    (a) $p \Rightarrow q$ (b) $q \Rightarrow p$ (c) $\sim p \Rightarrow q$
    using the components

p: Jack studies psychology.
q: Mary studies sociology.

5. The Biconditional Connective

Consider the statement "q, *only if p*." In general, this can be reworded in the form

If q, then p.

For example, consider the propositions

p: The youth is handsome.
q: The youth is intelligent.

The compound proposition "The youth is intelligent only if the youth is handsome" means that the only time the youth is intelligent is when the youth is handsome. Another way of saying this is to say that if the youth is intelligent, then the youth is handsome. Thus, it should be clear that

Only if p, then q (or q only if p).

and

If q, then p.

are equivalent. However, it is already known that

If q, then p.
If not p, then not q.

are equivalent.

Hence, the three compound statements

Only if p, then q.
If q, then p.
If not p, then not q.

are equivalent to each other.

Thus, we have another rule for forming the converse of the implication "If p then q." That is, to form the converse of "If p, then q," replace "If" by "Only if."

Biconditional Connective   **The connective** *if and only if* **is called the** *biconditional connective* **and is denoted by** $\Leftrightarrow$. **If** p **and** q **are two propositions for which**

$$p \Rightarrow q \quad \text{and} \quad q \Rightarrow p$$

then we say p *if and only if* q **and we write**

$$p \Leftrightarrow q$$

The statement $\Leftrightarrow$ may be read as "p if and only if q," or as "p is equivalent to q," or as "p implies q, and q implies p," or as "p is necessary and sufficient for q." An abbreviation for $p \Leftrightarrow q$ is "p iff q," read as "p if and only if q."

We can restate the definition of the biconditional connective by using the truth table in Table 9.

Table 9

p	q	$p \Rightarrow q$	$q \Rightarrow p$	$(p \Rightarrow q) \wedge (q \Rightarrow p)$	$p \Leftrightarrow q$
T	T	T	T	T	T
T	F	F	T	F	F
F	T	T	F	F	F
F	F	T	T	T	T

Example 1   Let p and q denote the statements

p: Smith is a murderer.
q: Smith is in jail.

Then "A necessary condition for Smith to be in jail is that Smith be a murderer" is equivalent to

If Smith is in jail, then Smith is a murderer.

Also, "A sufficient condition for Smith to be in jail is that Smith be a murderer" is equivalent to

If Smith is a murderer, then Smith is in jail.

Notice that the statements "If Smith is a murderer, Smith is in jail," "If Smith is not in jail, then Smith is not a murderer," and "Only if Smith is in jail is Smith a murderer" are equivalent.

Also, assuming the two implications $p \Rightarrow q$ and $q \Rightarrow p$ are both correct from a practical point of view, then we conclude that a necessary and sufficient condition for Smith to be in jail is that Smith is a murderer. In this case, we say

Smith is in jail if and only if Smith is a murderer.

■

The truth table for the biconditional connective $\Leftrightarrow$ for two statements p and q is illustrated by the truth table given in Table 9. The statement $p \Leftrightarrow q$ is true whenever p and q are both true or both false; $p \Leftrightarrow q$ is false otherwise.

Exercise 5
Solutions to Odd-Numbered Problems begin on page 625.

In Problems 1–10 construct a truth table for each statement.

1. $\sim p \lor (p \land q)$
2. $\sim p \land (p \lor q)$
3. $p \lor (\sim p \land q)$
4. $(p \lor q) \land \sim q$
5. $\sim p \Rightarrow q$
6. $(p \lor q) \Rightarrow p$
7. $\sim p \lor p$
8. $p \land \sim p$
9. $p \land (p \Rightarrow q)$
10. $p \lor (p \Rightarrow q)$

In Problems 11–14 prove that the following only have truth value T.

11. $p \land (q \land r) \Leftrightarrow (p \land q) \land r$
12. $p \lor (q \lor r) \Leftrightarrow (p \lor q) \lor r$
13. $p \land (p \lor q) \Leftrightarrow p$
14. $p \lor (p \land q) \Leftrightarrow p$

In Problems 15–20 let p be "The examination is hard" and q be "The grades are low." Write each symbolically.

15. If the examination is hard, the grades are low.
16. The examination is not hard nor are the grades low.
17. The grades are not low, and the examination is not hard.
18. The examination is not hard and the grades are low.
19. The grades are low only if the examination is hard.
20. The grades are low if the examination is hard.

6. Tautologies and Arguments

In Section 3 we saw how it is possible to obtain compound propositions from simple propositions by using connectives. By using symbols of grouping, such as parentheses and brackets, we can form more complicated propositions. We denote by $P(p, q, \ldots)$ a compound proposition, where $p, q, \ldots$ are the components making the compound proposition. Some examples of such propositions are

$$\sim (p \land q) \qquad \sim p \land \sim q \qquad p \land \sim q \qquad (p \land \sim q) \lor (\sim p \land q)$$

Ordinarily, when we write a compound proposition, we cannot be certain of the truth of that proposition unless we know the truth or falsity of the component propositions. There are certain compound propositions that are true regardless of the truth or falsity of the component propositions. Compound propositions which have this characteristic are called *tautologies*.

Tautology   **A** *tautology* **is a compound proposition** $P(p, q, \ldots)$ **that is always true.**

Examples of tautologies are

$$p \lor \sim p \qquad p \Rightarrow (p \lor q)$$

Tables 10 and 11 show the truth tables of these tautologies.

Table 10

p	$\sim p$	$p \vee \sim p$
T	F	T
F	T	T

Table 11

p	q	$p \vee q$	$p \Rightarrow (p \vee q)$
T	T	T	T
T	F	T	T
F	T	T	T
F	F	F	T

Let $P(p, q, \ldots)$ represent a compound composition. Now, if we substitute for p a proposition h that is logically equivalent to p, we obtain a compound proposition $P(h, q, \ldots)$ that is logically equivalent to $P(p, q, \ldots)$. This is a reasonable assumption since the truth of $P(p, q, \ldots)$ depends on the truth of the component propositions $p, q, \ldots$ and h *is true whenever p is true* and h *is false whenever p is false*. This leads us to assert the law of substitution.

Law of Substitution

If $h \equiv p$ and we substitute h for p in the compound proposition $P(p, q, \ldots)$, then

$$P(p, q, \ldots) \equiv P(h, q, \ldots)$$

This principle can be used to obtain new tautologies. If we have a tautology and substitute for some of the component propositions other propositions that are logically equivalent to them, we obtain a new tautology.

Argument   **By** *argument* **or** *proof,* **we mean the assertion that a certain statement (called the** *conclusion*) **follows from certain other statements (called** *premises* **or** *hypotheses*). **An argument is** *valid* **if and only if the conjunction of the premises implies (yields, has as a consequence) the conclusion; if an argument is** *false* **(that is,** *not valid*), **it is called a** *fallacy.*

Valid Conclusions   Valid arguments give rise to what are called *valid conclusions*. Valid arguments
True Conclusion   together with a true premise give rise to *true conclusions*. A valid argument does not necessarily lead to a true conclusion.

It is important to realize that the truth of the conclusion is irrelevant as a test for the validity of the argument. A true conclusion does not necessarily mean a valid argument has been given. For example, sometimes students will do a problem and make several errors but accidentally arrive at the right answer. This is an example of an invalid argument giving rise to a true conclusion.

We are now in a position to discuss how to determine whether a given implication is true or false. Until this time, we were concerned with the various truth values that could be assigned to the implication

If p, then q.

for all possible truth values of p and q. Now we shall discuss how to demonstrate that a statement q is true whenever p is true. This will then show that the implication $p \Rightarrow q$ is true. Of course, if q is false whenever p is true, then the implication $p \Rightarrow q$ is false.

We shall limit our discussion to two types: direct proof and indirect proof.

Direct Proof   In a *direct proof* we go through a chain of propositions, beginning with the hypotheses and leading to the desired conclusion.

Example 1   Suppose it is true that

Either John obeys the law or John is punished

and

John was not punished.

We would like to prove that

John obeyed the law.

Solution   A valid argument in the form of a direct proof can be given as follows:

Let p and q denote the propositions

p: John obeys the law.
q: John is punished.

We can write the premise as

$$p \vee q \quad \text{and} \quad \sim q$$

Since $\sim q$ is true then, by the law of contradiction (see page 487), q is false. Since $p \vee q$ is true, either p is true or q is true. Thus, p must be true.   ■

More examples of direct proof are given later, but before we look at them, let's discuss two laws of logic that are quite useful in a direct proof.

Law of Detachment

If the implication

$$p \Rightarrow q$$

is true, and if p is true, then q must be true.

See Table 5, page 498, for an illustration of this law.

Law of Syllogisms

Let p, q, r be three propositions. If

$$p \Rightarrow q \quad \text{and} \quad q \Rightarrow r$$

are both true, then

$$p \Rightarrow r$$

is true.

Table 12 illustrates this law.

Table 12

p	q	r	$p \Rightarrow q$	$q \Rightarrow r$	$p \Rightarrow r$	$(p \Rightarrow q) \wedge (q \Rightarrow r)$	$(p \Rightarrow q) \wedge (q \Rightarrow r) \Rightarrow (p \Rightarrow r)$
T	T	T	T	T	T	T	T
T	T	F	T	F	F	F	T
T	F	T	F	T	T	F	T
T	F	F	F	T	F	F	T
F	T	T	T	T	T	T	T
F	T	F	T	F	T	F	T
F	F	T	T	T	T	T	T
F	F	F	T	T	T	T	T

Example 2 Suppose it is true that

It is snowing.

and

If it is warm, then it is not snowing.

and

If it is not warm, then I cannot go swimming.

We want to prove that

I cannot go swimming.

is a true statement.

Solution We give a valid argument for this as a direct proof. Let p, q, r represent the statements

p: It is snowing.
q: It is warm.
r: I can go swimming.

Our premise is that the propositions

$$p \qquad q \Rightarrow \sim p \qquad \sim q \Rightarrow \sim r$$

are true. We want to prove that

$$\sim r$$

is true. Since $q \Rightarrow \sim p$ is true, its contrapositive

$$p \Rightarrow \sim q$$

is also true. Using the law of syllogisms, since $p \Rightarrow \sim q$ and $\sim q \Rightarrow \sim r$, we see that

$$p \Rightarrow \sim r$$

But we know p is true. By the law of detachment, $\sim r$ is true. That is, I cannot go swimming.

■

Example 3 Suppose it is true that

If Dan comes, so will Bill.

and

If Sandy will not come, then Bill will not come.

We want to show that

If Dan comes, then Sandy will come.

Solution Let p, q, r denote the propositions

p: Dan comes.
q: Bill will come.
r: Sandy will come.

Then we know that

$$p \Rightarrow q \qquad \sim r \Rightarrow \sim q$$

Since $\sim r \Rightarrow \sim q$ is true, then $q \Rightarrow r$ is also true. Thus,

$$p \Rightarrow q \qquad q \Rightarrow r$$

By the law of syllogisms, it is true that

$$p \Rightarrow r$$

That is, if Dan comes, then Sandy will come.

■

Example 4 Suppose it is true that

If I enjoy studying, then I will study.

and

I will do my homework or I will not study.

and

I will not do my homework.

We want to show that

I do not enjoy studying.

Solution Let p, q, r denote the three propositions

p: I enjoy studying.
q: I will study.
r: I will do my homework.

Then we know that

$$\sim r \qquad r \lor \sim q \qquad p \Rightarrow q$$

are true. We want to prove that $\sim p$ is true. Since $\sim r$ is true, then r is false. Also, either r or $\sim q$ is true. Thus, $\sim q$ is true. Since $p \Rightarrow q$, we have

$$\sim q \Rightarrow \sim p$$

is true. Hence, $\sim p$ must be true.

■

The above are all examples of proving statements by means of a direct proof. Notice that this technique is essentially one of proceeding by means of the laws of logic from the premise to the desired conclusion.

Indirect Proof

Suppose we want to show that $p \Rightarrow q$; in other words, the conclusion q is true whenever p is true. To prove that q is true by the method of an *indirect proof,* we simply show that $\sim q$ is false. This can be done by first assuming $\sim q$ is true and then showing that this assumption, when combined with other statements of the premise, leads to a logical contradiction.

The following two examples illustrate indirect proof.

Example 5 Prove the result of Example 1 using an indirect proof.

Solution Since we wish to prove that p is true, we shall make the assumption that p is false or that $\sim p$ is true, hoping that this leads to a contradiction—since, if it does, then p must be true.

We accept that

$$\sim p \qquad \sim q \qquad p \lor q$$

are true. Either p is true or q is true. But both p and q are false. This is impossible. Thus, we have reached a contradiction, which means that p must be true.

■

Example 6 Suppose that it is true that

If I am lazy, then I do not study.

and

I study or I enjoy myself.

and

I do not enjoy myself.

Prove that

I am not lazy.

Solution Let p, q, r be the statements

> p: I am lazy.
> q: I study.
> r: I enjoy myself.

Then, we know that

$$\sim r \qquad p \Rightarrow \sim q \qquad q \vee r$$

are true.

We want to show that $\sim p$ is true. If we use an indirect proof, then we assume that p is true. Since p is true and $p \Rightarrow \sim q$ is true, then $\sim q$ is true. Thus, q is false. Also, r is false. But either q or r is true. This is impossible. This contradiction means that the assumption that p is true is a false one. Thus, $\sim p$ is true. ∎

Model: Life Insurance*

The following problem was first studied by Edmund C. Berkeley in 1936 and was solved by the use of principles of logic. His employer, the Prudential Life Insurance Company, had the procedure that when any policyholder requested a change in the schedule of premium payments, one of two rules was involved as company policy. The question was raised as to whether these two rules were logically equivalent. That is, did both rules give rise to the same payment arrangements or did the use of one rule over the other give different payment arrangements?

Berkeley was of the opinion that the two rules, in some instances, gave different directions to the policyholder. An example of a typical clause found in one of the rules was: If a policyholder was making premium payments several times a year with one of the payments falling due on the policy anniversary and if he requested the schedule be changed to one annual payment on the anniversary date, and if his payments were in full up to a date not the anniversary date and if he made this request more than 2 months after the issue date and if his request also came within 2 months after the policy anniversary date, then a certain action was to be taken!

Berkeley replaced this complicated part of one of the rules by the compound proposition

$$p \wedge q \wedge r \wedge s \wedge t \Rightarrow A$$

where p, q, r, s, t are the five statements and A is the action called for. By doing the same with all parts of both rules and by using the laws of logic, Berkeley was able to demonstrate an inconsistency of application of one rule over the other. In fact, there turned out to be four situations in which contradictory actions occurred.

As a result of Berkeley's effort, Prudential replaced the two cumbersome rules by a simple one.

Since this incident, similar situations involving a maze of if's, and's, but's, and implications, particularly in the areas of legal contracts between corporations, have been checked for accuracy and consistency (to eliminate loopholes, etc.) by the use of logic.

*John E. Pfeiffer, "Symbolic Logic," *Scientific American* (December 1960).

Exercise 6
Solutions to Odd-Numbered Problems begin on page 626.

Prove the statements in Problems 1–4 first by using a direct proof and then by using an indirect proof.

1. When it rains, John does not go to school. John is going to school. Show that it is not raining.
2. If I do not go to work, I will go fishing. I will not go fishing. Show that I shall go to work.
3. If Smith is elected president, Kuntz will be elected secretary. If Kuntz is elected secretary, then Brown will not be elected treasurer. Smith is elected president. Show that Brown is not elected treasurer.
4. Either Katy is a good girl or Mike is a good boy. If Danny cries, then Katy is not a good girl. Mike is not a good boy. Does Danny cry?

In Problems 5–7 determine whether the arguments are valid.

5. Hypothesis: When students study, they receive good grades. These students do not study.
   Conclusion: These students do not receive good grades.
6. Hypothesis: If Danny is affluent, he is either a snob or a hypocrite. Danny is a snob and is not a hypocrite.
   Conclusion: Danny is not affluent.
7. Hypothesis: If Tami studies, she will not fail this course. If she does not play with her dolls too often, she will study. Tami failed the course.
   Conclusion: She played with her dolls too often.

7. Application to Switching Networks

By a switching network we mean a collection of wires capable of carrying an electric current, combined with various switches capable of creating gaps in the wire. Switching networks are widely used in digital computers.

The simplest kind of network is a single wire capable of transmitting currents from one end A to the other end B. See Figure 1(a). If we add a switch to this wire, we obtain the network of Figure 1(b).

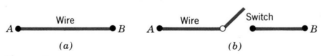

Figure 1

This switch admits only two possibilities—it is either open (O), in which case current does not flow; or else it is closed (C), in which case current will flow. Thus, we have a situation very much like the one we had with propositions. That is, a proposition is either true (T) or false (F); a switch is either closed (C) or open (O).

Now, suppose we represent switches by p, q, and so on, and let's analyze some very elementary networks. Consider the network of Figure 2.

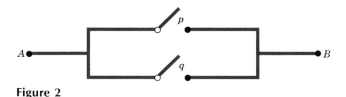

Figure 2

This network has two switches, p and q, placed in *parallel*. Suppose the question is asked, "When does current flow from A to B?" It is clear that if either p or q or both are closed, then current flows from A to B; but if p and q are both open, then current does not flow. The values given in column 3 of Table 13 indicate this. Notice that these values are merely the inclusive disjunction $p \vee q$.

Parallel Network

Thus, the truth values of $p \vee q$ will tell us whether current flows in a *parallel network*.

Table 13

1	2	3
p	q	
C	C	C
C	O	C
O	C	C
O	O	O

Series Network

Another type of network commonly encountered is the *series network*. See Figure 3. Here, we discover that current flows from A to B only if both p and q are closed, and current will not flow if either p or q or both are open. The values are given in Table 14. Notice that the values in column 3 are those of the conjunction of p and q, namely, $p \wedge q$. That is, for a series network, if $p \wedge q$ is true, current flows; whereas if $p \wedge q$ is false, current does not flow.

Table 14

1	2	3
p	q	
C	C	C
C	O	O
O	C	O
O	O	O

$A \bullet\!\!\!-\!\!\!-\!\!\!-\!\!\!\circ\!\!\diagup^{p}\!\!\bullet\!\!\!-\!\!\!-\!\!\!-\!\!\!\circ\!\!\diagup^{q}\!\!\bullet\!\!\!-\!\!\!-\!\bullet B$

Figure 3

Next, let's interpret the network in Figure 4. The question is asked, "When does current flow from A to B?" To answer this, we want to find the truth value of $r \vee (p \wedge q)$, since p and q are in series ($p \wedge q$) and r is in parallel with $p \wedge q$. The answer is given in Table 15.

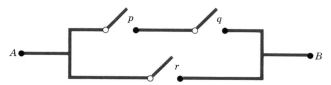

Figure 4

Table 15

1	2	3	4	5
p	q	r	$p \wedge q$	$r \vee (p \wedge q)$
C	C	C	C	C
C	C	O	C	C
C	O	C	O	C
C	O	O	O	O
O	C	C	O	C
O	C	O	O	O
O	O	C	O	C
O	O	O	O	O

By looking at column 5, we see that current flows from A to B only under the following conditions:

1. p closed, q closed, r closed
2. p closed, q closed, r open
3. p closed, q open, r closed
4. p open, q closed, r closed
5. p open, q open, r closed

In this problem, suppose we had demanded that whenever p was closed, r was open and whenever p was open, r was closed. This means that

$$r \equiv {\sim}p$$

Under these circumstances, current flows from A to B depending on the truth value of

$${\sim}p \vee (p \wedge q)$$

Instead of constructing a truth table to get the answer, let's use some of the laws developed earlier to simplify the compound statement ${\sim}p \vee (p \wedge q)$. Then, using the distributive law,

$${\sim}p \vee (p \wedge q) \equiv ({\sim}p \vee p) \wedge ({\sim}p \vee q)$$

Since $\sim p \vee p$ is always true, the above reduces to

$$\sim p \vee (p \wedge q) \equiv \sim p \vee q$$

In other words, the network of Figure 4 with $r \equiv \sim p$, is equivalent to the network given in Figure 5.

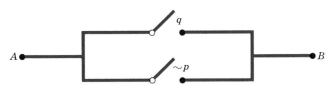

Figure 5

Example 1   For the network of Figure 6, determine when the current flows from A to B. Also, write a network equivalent to it with fewer switches in it.

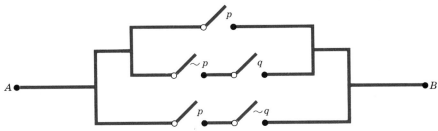

Figure 6

Solution   Current flows from A to B whenever the truth value of

$$(p \wedge \sim q) \vee [p \vee (\sim p \wedge q)]$$

is C. Let's first simplify the expression in the brackets:

$$p \vee (\sim p \wedge q) \equiv (p \vee \sim p) \wedge (p \vee q) \equiv p \vee q$$

Then, using this fact, we have

$$
\begin{aligned}
(p \wedge \sim q) \vee [p \vee (\sim p \wedge q)] &\equiv (p \wedge \sim q) \vee (p \vee q) \\
&\equiv [(p \wedge \sim q) \vee p] \vee q \\
&\equiv p \vee q
\end{aligned}
$$

Thus, the complicated network of Figure 6 is equivalent to a network of two switches p and q placed in parallel. Also, current flows from A to B in the network of Figure 6 if:

1. p is closed, q is closed.
2. p is open, q is closed.
3. p is closed, q is open.   ■

A network in which current always flows no matter what position the switches are in is a tautology; a network in which current never flows is the negation of a tautology.

Exercise 7
Solutions to Odd-Numbered Problems begin on page 627.

In Problems 1-4 determine when current flows from A to B in each circuit by using a truth table.

1.

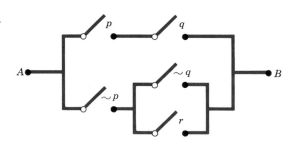

2.

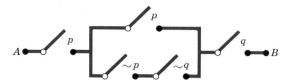

3.

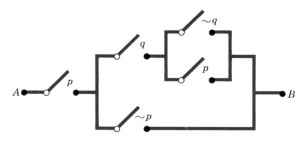

4.

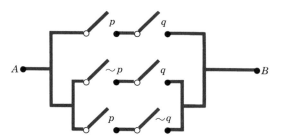

In Problems 5-8 construct a network corresponding to each proposition.

5. $(\sim p \vee \sim q) \wedge (p \wedge q)$ 6. $(p \vee \sim q) \wedge \sim p$
7. $\sim(p \vee q) \wedge \sim p$ 8. $(\sim p \vee q) \wedge (\sim p \wedge \sim q)$

9. For the networks in Problems 5-8, design simpler networks having the same properties.
10. Construct a network with the switches p and q for which current flows from A to B whenever:
    (a) p is open, q is open.
    (b) p is closed, q is open.

11. Design a circuit so that a light can be turned on (current flows) or off (current does not flow) from any of two switches p and q.
12. Design a network in which current always flows.
13. Design a network in which current never flows.

Chapter Review

Important Terms

proposition
connective
conjunction ($\wedge$)
inclusive disjunction ($\vee$)
exclusive disjunction ($\underline{\vee}$)
negation
law of contradiction
quantifier
truth value
logically equivalent ($\equiv$)
idempotent laws
associative laws
commutative laws
distributive laws
De Morgan's laws
absorption laws
implication ($\Rightarrow$)
conditional connective ($\Rightarrow$)

hypothesis conclusion
sufficient condition
necessary condition
converse
contrapositive
inverse
biconditional connective ($\Leftrightarrow$)
tautology
law of substitution
argument
fallacy
direct proof
law of detachment
law of syllogisms
indirect proof
circuit
parallel network
series network

Review Exercises
Solutions to Odd-Numbered Problems begin on page 628.

In Problems 1–4 circle each correct answer; some questions may have more than one correct answer.

1. Which of the following negate the statement below?

   p: All people are rich.

   (a) Some people are rich.
   (b) Some people are poor.
   (c) Some people are not rich.
   (d) No person is rich.

2. Which of the following negate the statement below?

   p: It is either hot or humid.

   (a) It is neither hot nor humid.
   (b) Either it is not hot or it is not humid.
   (c) It is not hot and it is not humid.
   (d) It is hot, but not humid.

3. Which of the following statements are logically equivalent to the statement below?

$$(\sim p \lor q) \land r$$

(a) $(p \Rightarrow q) \land r$ (b) $\sim p \lor (q \land r)$
(c) $(\sim p \Rightarrow q) \land r$ (d) $(\sim p \lor r) \land (q \land r)$

4. Which of the following statements are logically equivalent to the statement below?

$$p \land \sim q$$

(a) $\sim q \land p$ (b) $p \lor q$
(c) $\sim p \lor q$ (d) $q \Rightarrow \sim p$

In Problems 5 to 8 negate each proposition.

5. Some people are rich.
6. All people are rich.
7. Danny is not tall and Mary is short.
8. Neither Mike nor Katy are big.

In Problems 9–12 construct a truth table for each compound proposition.

9. $(p \land q) \lor \sim p$ 10. $(p \lor q)r \land p$
11. $\sim p \lor (p \lor \sim q)$ 12. $\sim p \Rightarrow (p \lor q)$

In Problems 13–15 let p stand for "I will pass the course" and let q stand for "I will do homework regularly." Put each statement into symbolic form.

13. I will pass the course, if I do homework regularly.
14. Passing this course is a sufficient condition for me to do homework regularly.
15. I will pass this course if and only if I do homework regularly.

16. Write the converse, contrapositive, and inverse of the statement

If it is not sunny, it is cold.

17. Prove the following by the use of direct proof: If I do not paint the house, I will go bowling. I will not go bowling. Show that I will paint the house.
18. Using reasons from logic, give a valid argument to answer the question, "Is Katy a good girl?" Given that:
     (a) Mike is a bad boy or Danny is crying.
     (b) If Katy is a good girl, then Mike is not a bad boy.
     (c) Danny is not crying.
19. Determine whether the following are logically equivalent:

$$\sim p \lor q \qquad p \Rightarrow q$$

20. Determine whether the two statements below are logically equivalent:

$$(p \Rightarrow q) \land (\sim q \lor p) \qquad p \Leftrightarrow q$$

Other Articles

Hohfeld, W. N., *Fundamental Legal Conceptions as Applied in Judicial Reasoning and Other Essays,* Walter Wheeler Cook, ed., Yale University Press, New Haven, 1919.

Hohn, Franz, "Some Mathematical Aspects of Switching," *The American Mathematical Monthly,* **62** (1955), pp. 75–90.

Appendix
Functions

In many applications, a correspondence often exists between two sets of numbers. For example, the revenue R resulting from the sale of x items selling for $10 each is $R = 10x$. If we know how many items have been sold, we can then find the revenue R by using the rule $R = 10x$. This is an example of a function.

Very simply, a *function f* is a rule that associates to any given number x a single number $f(x)$, read "f of x." Here, $f(x)$ is the number that results when x is given; $f(x)$ does not mean f times x.

For example, the function f that associates the square of a number to the given number x is

$$f(x) = x^2$$

Independent
Variable
Dependent
Variable

The given number x is called the *independent variable,* and the number associated to it by the function is called the *dependent variable* since it depends on x for its value. We shall usually denote this dependent variable by y and write

$$y = f(x)$$

Example 1   For the function

$$y = f(x) = 4x^2 - 5$$

find the value of the dependent variable $y = f(x)$ when the independent variable x equals 3.

Solution   The value of the dependent variable when $x = 3$ is

$$y = f(3) = 4 \cdot 3^2 - 5 = 4 \cdot 9 - 5 = 36 - 5 = 31$$

∎

Let's look at one more example before defining a function formally.

Example 2   Suppose a man standing on the moon throws a rock 20 meters (almost 22 yards) up and starts a stopwatch just as the rock begins to fall back down. Let x represent the number of seconds shown on the stopwatch, and let y represent the height (in meters) of the rock above the surface of the moon. Then there is a correspondence between the time and the height, that is, between the numbers x and the numbers y. When the time is 0, the rock is at its highest point of 20 meters; therefore, $x = 0$ corresponds to $y = 20$. But to what heights do the numbers $x = 1$, $x = 2.5$, and $x = 5$ correspond?

Solution   To find approximate answers to these questions without actually sending someone to the moon, we may use the following formula:

$$y = 20 - 0.8x^2$$

The height corresponding to $x = 1$ is found when we replace the letter x in the formula by the number 1, as follows:

$$y = 20 - 0.8(1)^2 = 19.2$$

Thus, when the stopwatch shows 1 second, the rock is still 19.2 meters above the surface of the moon. Similarly, when $x = 2.5$, the height is

$$y = 20 - 0.8(2.5)^2 = 15$$

When $x = 5$, the height is

$$y = 20 - 0.8(5)^2 = 0$$

and the rock has again reached the surface of the moon. (If you think that the rock falls to the moon more slowly than it would fall to the earth, you are right.) ∎

An important point made by this example is that if X is the set of times from 0 to 5 seconds and Y is the set of heights from 0 to 20 meters, then each element of X corresponds to one and only one element of Y. The correspondence $y = 20 - 0.8x^2$ is called a *function from X into Y*.

Function; Domain; Range   **Let X and Y be two sets of numbers. A *function* from X into Y is a correspondence that associates with each element of X a unique element of Y. The set X is called the *domain* of the function. For each element x in X, the corresponding element y in Y is called the *value* of the function at x, or the *image* of x. The set of all images of the elements of the domain is called the *range* of the function.**

Since there may be elements in Y that are the image of no x in X, it follows that the range of a function is a subset of Y.

Functions are often denoted by letters such as f, F, g, G, and so on. Thus, if f is a function from X into Y, then for each number x in X the corresponding image in the set Y is designated by the symbol $f(x)$ and is read "f of x." We refer to $f(x)$ as the *value of f at the number x*. For example, in the case of the falling rock, we may designate the function by the letter H (to remind us of the word *height*). Then for each x in X, $H(x)$ designates the value of H at x, that is, $H(x)$ designates the height of the rock at time x. In symbols, we write

$$H(x) = 20 - 0.8x^2$$

How do we designate the value of H at the times $x = 1$, $x = \frac{5}{4}$, $x = \sqrt{2}$? These are the heights $H(1)$, $H(\frac{5}{4})$, $H(\sqrt{2})$, and they may be computed by using the formula as follows:

$$H(1) = 20 - 0.8(1)^2 = 19.2$$
$$H(\tfrac{5}{4}) = 20 - 0.8(\tfrac{5}{4})^2 = 18.75$$
$$H(\sqrt{2}) = 20 - 0.8(\sqrt{2})^2 = 18.4$$

The expression $H(1) = 19.2$ is read as "the value of H at 1 is 19.2," or "19.2 meters corresponds to the time 1 second."

Sometimes it is helpful to visualize a function as an apparatus that manipulates numbers; the domain is the input for the apparatus and the range is the output. We can call such an apparatus an *input–output machine*. See Figure 1.

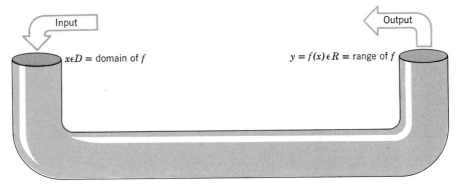

Figure 1

The only restrictions on an input–output machine are:

1. It only accepts numbers from the domain of f, that is, it only accepts numbers for which there is an output.

2. For each input there is exactly one output (which may be repeated for different inputs).

We can also consider a function as a set of *ordered pairs* (x, y) in which no different pairs have the same first element. The set of all first elements is the *domain* and the set of all second elements is the *range* of the function. Thus, there is associated with each element x in the domain a unique element y in the range. An advantage of expressing a function (or any correspondence) as a set of ordered pairs is that we can then graph the set of pairs to make a "picture" of the function.

Example 3   Determine whether the correspondences below are functions:
(a) $y = x^2$ (b) $x = y^2$
Graph each of them.

Solution   (a)   Some of the ordered pairs (x, y) in this set are

$$(2, 2^2) = (2, 4) \quad (0, 0^2) = (0, 0) \quad (-2, (-2)^2) = (-2, 4) \quad (\tfrac{1}{2}, (\tfrac{1}{2})^2) = (\tfrac{1}{2}, \tfrac{1}{4})$$

In this set no two different pairs have the same *first* element (even though there are different pairs that have the same *second* element). This set is the squaring function, which associates with each real number x the value x^2.

(b)   The ordered pairs (x, y) for which $x = y^2$ do not represent a function because there are ordered pairs with the same first number but different second numbers. For example, $(1, 1)$ and $(1, -1)$ are ordered pairs obeying the relationship $x = y^2$ with the same first number, but different second numbers.

To graph $y = x^2$, we set up a table that provides several points on the graph:

x	0	1	2	3	-1	-2	-3
y	0	1	4	9	1	4	9

In Figure 2 we list these points and, connecting them with a smooth curve, we obtain the graph (a *parabola*).

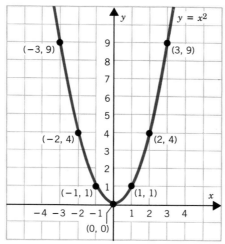

Figure 2

To graph $x = y^2$, we do the same:

x	0	1	1	4	4
y	0	1	-1	2	-2

Figure 3 shows the graph of $x = y^2$.

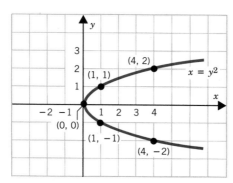

Figure 3

To summarize, we have determined that a function f associates with real numbers x other real numbers y, and we now agree to use the notation

$$y = f(x)$$

to denote the rule that associates x and y. The set of all ordered pairs (x, y), where $y = f(x)$ is the *ordinate* and x is the *abscissa,* is called the *graph* of the function f.

Graph

Regardless of whether a function is described by a formula, by some rule, or by other means, it will always have a graph. However, not every collection of points is the graph of a function. In fact, a graph provides a visual technique for determining whether a collection of ordered pairs is a function. *If any vertical line intersects the graph in more than one point, the graph is not that of a function.* Compare Figures 2 and 3.

Example 4   Find the domain of the function

$$f(x) = \sqrt{1 - x}$$

Solution   To find the domain of f, we ask the question, "What are the numbers x for which we can compute $\sqrt{1 - x}$?" Now, we know it is impossible (in the set of real numbers) to find the square root of a negative number. Thus, only those x for which

$$1 - x \geq 0 \qquad \text{or} \qquad x \leq 1$$

can be in the domain. Hence, the domain of f is the set

$$\{x \mid x \leq 1\}$$

■

Example 5   Find the domain of the function

$$y = f(x) = 20x + 100$$

Graph this function.

Solution   For what real numbers x is it possible to compute $20x + 100$? That is, "When can we add 100 to twenty times a number?" The answer is, "Always." Thus, the domain of f is the set of real numbers.

The graph of this function consists of all points (x, y) for which $y = 20x + 100$. See Figure 4.

■

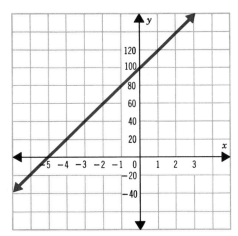

Figure 4

Example 6 Suppose the function f of Example 5 represents the total expense of production in a factory in which overhead is $100 and the cost for each item manufactured is $20. In this situation, x represents the number of items produced. What is the domain of f? What is the graph of f?

Solution Since the variable x now represents the number of items produced and since it is only meaningful to use nonnegative integers to represent the number of items produced, the domain of this function must be the set

$$\{0, 1, 2, 3 \ldots\}$$

Now, when the variable x is 0, 1, 2, 3, . . . , the variable y is

$$f(0) = 20 \cdot 0 + 100 = 100$$
$$f(1) = 20 \cdot 1 + 100 = 120$$
$$f(2) = 20 \cdot 2 + 100 = 140$$
And so forth.

The graph is given in Figure 5.

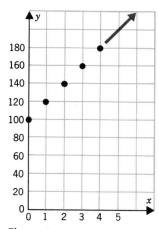

Figure 5

We will find that many times practical considerations alter the domain and/or range of the function. Observe that in Example 5 the function may assume any value, whereas in Example 6 the function may assume only nonnegative integer values. The domain of the function in Example 5 is referred to as *continuous,* while the domain of the function in Example 6 is called *discrete.* Time is an example of a variable that is measured continuously; the number of people in a given age bracket must be measured discretely.

A Exercises
Solutions to Odd-Numbered Problems begin on page 628.

1. For the function $f(x) = 3x - 2$, find:
   (a) $f(3)$ (c) $f(0)$ (e) $f(x + h)$
   (b) $f(-2)$ (d) $f(x + 2)$ (f) $f(1/x)$

2. For the function $f(x) = 3x^2 + 1$, find:
   (a) $f(1)$ (c) $f(0)$ (e) $f(x + h)$
   (b) $f(-2)$ (d) $f(x + 4)$ (f) $f(1/x)$

In Problems 3–14 determine whether the correspondence determines a function $y = f(x)$.

3. $y = x^2 + 2x + 1$ 4. $y = x^3 - 3x$

5. $y = \dfrac{2}{x}$ 6. $y = \dfrac{3}{x - 4}$

7. $y^2 = 1 - x^2$ 8. $y = \pm\sqrt{1 - 2x}$
9. $x^2 + y = 1$ 10. $x + y^2 = 1$
11. $x^2y^2 = 5$ 12. $x^2y = 4$
13. $y = (x - 2)^2$ 14. $y = \sqrt{x^2}$

In Problems 15–24 find the domain of the function f.

15. $f(x) = 3x + 5$ 16. $f(x) = x^2 + 1$
17. $f(x) = \sqrt{x - 1}$ 18. $f(x) = \sqrt{2x + 5}$
19. $f(x) = \sqrt{x^2 + 4}$ 20. $f(x) = \sqrt{x^2 - 4}$

21. $f(x) = \dfrac{2x}{x - 2}$ 22. $f(x) = \dfrac{x^2}{x^2 - 4}$

23. $f(x) = \sqrt{3/x}$ 24. $f(x) = \dfrac{3x^2}{x^4 + 1}$

25. *Falling Rocks on Jupiter.* If a rock falls from a height of 20 meters on the planet Jupiter, then its height H after x seconds is approximately

$$H(x) = 20 - 13x^2$$

   (a) What is the height of the rock when $x = 1$ second? When $x = 1.1$? When $x = 1.2$? When $x = 1.3$?
   (b) When does the rock strike the ground?

26. *Falling Rocks on Earth.* If a rock falls from a height of 20 meters here on the earth, the height H after x seconds is approximately

$$H(x) = 20 - 4.9x^2$$

Use this function to answer all parts of Problem 25.

Tables

Table 1
Binomial Probabilities $b(n,k;p)$

n	k	.05	.10	.15	.20	.25	.30	.35	.40	.45	.50
1	0	.9500	.9000	.8500	.8000	.7500	.7000	.6500	.6000	.5500	.5000
	1	.0500	.1000	.1500	.2000	.2500	.3000	.3500	.4000	.4500	.5000
2	0	.9025	.8100	.7225	.6400	.5625	.4900	.4225	.3600	.3025	.2500
	1	.0950	.1800	.2550	.3200	.3750	.4200	.4550	.4800	.4950	.5000
	2	.0025	.0100	.0225	.0400	.0625	.0900	.1225	.1600	.2025	.2500
3	0	.8574	.7290	.6141	.5120	.4219	.3430	.2746	.2160	.1664	.1250
	1	.1354	.2430	.3251	.3840	.4219	.4410	.4436	.4320	.4084	.3750
	2	.0071	.0270	.0574	.0960	.1406	.1890	.2389	.2880	.3341	.3750
	3	.0001	.0010	.0034	.0080	.0156	.0270	.0429	.0640	.0911	.1250
4	0	.8145	.6561	.5220	.4096	.3164	.2401	.1785	.1296	.0915	.0625
	1	.1715	.2916	.3685	.4096	.4219	.4116	.3845	.3456	.2995	.2500
	2	.0135	.0486	.0975	.1536	.2109	.2646	.3105	.3456	.3675	.3750
	3	.0005	.0036	.0115	.0256	.0469	.0756	.1115	.1536	.2005	.2500
	4	.0000	.0001	.0005	.0016	.0039	.0081	.0150	.0256	.0410	.0625
5	0	.7738	.5905	.4437	.3277	.2373	.1681	.1160	.0778	.0503	.0312
	1	.2036	.3280	.3915	.4096	.3955	.3602	.3124	.2592	.2059	.1562
	2	.0214	.0729	.1382	.2048	.2637	.3087	.3364	.3456	.3369	.3125
	3	.0011	.0081	.0244	.0512	.0879	.1323	.1811	.2304	.2757	.3125
	4	.0000	.0004	.0022	.0064	.0146	.0284	.0488	.0768	.1128	.1562
	5	.0000	.0000	.0001	.0003	.0010	.0024	.0053	.0102	.0185	.0312
6	0	.7351	.5314	.3771	.2621	.1780	.1176	.0754	.0467	.0277	.0156
	1	.2321	.3543	.3993	.3932	.3560	.3025	.2437	.1866	.1359	.0938
	2	.0305	.0984	.1762	.2458	.2966	.3241	.3280	.3110	.2780	.2344
	3	.0021	.0146	.0415	.0819	.1318	.1852	.2355	.2765	.3032	.3125
	4	.0001	.0012	.0055	.0154	.0330	.0595	.0951	.1382	.1861	.2344
	5	.0000	.0001	.0004	.0015	.0044	.0102	.0205	.0369	.0609	.0938
	6	.0000	.0000	.0000	.0001	.0002	.0007	.0018	.0041	.0083	.0156
7	0	.6983	.4783	.3206	.2097	.1335	.0824	.0490	.0280	.0152	.0078
	1	.2573	.3720	.3960	.3670	.3115	.2471	.1848	.1306	.0872	.0547
	2	.0406	.1240	.2097	.2753	.3115	.3177	.2985	.2613	.2140	.1641
	3	.0036	.0230	.0617	.1147	.1730	.2269	.2679	.2903	.2918	.2734
	4	.0002	.0026	.0109	.0287	.0577	.0972	.1442	.1935	.2388	.2734
	5	.0000	.0002	.0012	.0043	.0115	.0250	.0466	.0774	.1172	.1641
	6	.0000	.0000	.0001	.0004	.0013	.0036	.0084	.0172	.0320	.0547
	7	.0000	.0000	.0000	.0000	.0001	.0002	.0006	.0016	.0037	.0078
8	0	.6634	.4305	.2725	.1678	.1001	.0576	.0319	.0168	.0084	.0039
	1	.2793	.3826	.3847	.3355	.2670	.1977	.1373	.0896	.0548	.0312
	2	.0515	.1488	.2376	.2936	.3115	.2965	.2587	.2090	.1569	.1094
	3	.0054	.0331	.0839	.1468	.2076	.2541	.2786	.2787	.2568	.2188
	4	.0004	.0046	.0185	.0459	.0865	.1361	.1875	.2322	.2627	.2734
	5	.0000	.0004	.0026	.0092	.0231	.0467	.0808	.1239	.1719	.2188
	6	.0000	.0000	.0002	.0011	.0038	.0100	.0217	.0413	.0703	.1094
	7	.0000	.0000	.0000	.0001	.0004	.0012	.0033	.0079	.0164	.0312
	8	.0000	.0000	.0000	.0000	.0000	.0001	.0002	.0007	.0017	.0039

Table 1   **(continued)**

n	k	.05	.10	.15	.20	.25	.30	.35	.40	.45	.50
9	0	.6302	.3874	.2316	.1342	.0751	.0404	.0207	.0101	.0046	.0020
	1	.2985	.3874	.3679	.3020	.2253	.1556	.1004	.0605	.0339	.0176
	2	.0629	.1722	.2597	.3020	.3003	.2668	.2162	.1612	.1110	.0703
	3	.0077	.0446	.1069	.1762	.2336	.2668	.2716	.2508	.2119	.1641
	4	.0006	.0074	.0283	.0661	.1168	.1715	.2194	.2508	.2600	.2461
	5	.0000	.0008	.0050	.0165	.0389	.0735	.1181	.1672	.2128	.2461
	6	.0000	.0001	.0006	.0028	.0087	.0210	.0424	.0743	.1160	.1641
	7	.0000	.0000	.0000	.0003	.0012	.0039	.0098	.0212	.0407	.0703
	8	.0000	.0000	.0000	.0000	.0001	.0004	.0013	.0035	.0083	.0176
	9	.0000	.0000	.0000	.0000	.0000	.0000	.0001	.0003	.0008	.0020
10	0	.5987	.3487	.1969	.1074	.0563	.0282	.0135	.0060	.0025	.0010
	1	.3151	.3874	.3474	.2684	.1877	.1211	.0725	.0403	.0207	.0098
	2	.0746	.1937	.2759	.3020	.2816	.2335	.1757	.1209	.0763	.0439
	3	.0105	.0574	.1298	.2013	.2503	.2668	.2522	.2150	.1665	.1172
	4	.0010	.0112	.0401	.0881	.1460	.2001	.2377	.2508	.2384	.2051
	5	.0001	.0015	.0085	.0264	.0584	.1029	.1536	.2007	.2340	.2461
	6	.0000	.0001	.0012	.0055	.0162	.0368	.0689	.1115	.1596	.2051
	7	.0000	.0000	.0001	.0008	.0031	.0090	.0212	.0425	.0746	.1172
	8	.0000	.0000	.0000	.0001	.0004	.0014	.0043	.0106	.0229	.0439
	9	.0000	.0000	.0000	.0000	.0000	.0001	.0005	.0016	.0042	.0098
	10	.0000	.0000	.0000	.0000	.0000	.0000	.0000	.0001	.0003	.0010
11	0	.5688	.3138	.1673	.0859	.0422	.0198	.0088	.0036	.0014	.0005
	1	.3293	.3835	.3248	.2362	.1549	.0932	.0518	.0266	.0125	.0054
	2	.0867	.2131	.2866	.2953	.2581	.1998	.1395	.0887	.0513	.0269
	3	.0137	.0710	.1517	.2215	.2581	.2568	.2254	.1774	.1259	.0806
	4	.0014	.0158	.0536	.1107	.1721	.2201	.2428	.2365	.2060	.1611
	5	.0001	.0025	.0132	.0388	.0803	.1321	.1830	.2207	.2360	.2256
	6	.0000	.0003	.0023	.0097	.0268	.0566	.0985	.1471	.1931	.2256
	7	.0000	.0000	.0003	.0017	.0064	.0173	.0379	.0701	.1128	.1611
	8	.0000	.0000	.0000	.0002	.0011	.0037	.0102	.0234	.0462	.0806
	9	.0000	.0000	.0000	.0000	.0001	.0005	.0018	.0052	.0126	.0269
	10	.0000	.0000	.0000	.0000	.0000	.0000	.0002	.0007	.0021	.0054
	11	.0000	.0000	.0000	.0000	.0000	.0000	.0000	.0000	.0002	.0005
12	0	.5404	.2824	.1422	.0687	.0317	.0138	.0057	.0022	.0008	.0002
	1	.3413	.3766	.3012	.2062	.1267	.0712	.0368	.0174	.0075	.0029
	2	.0988	.2301	.2924	.2835	.2323	.1678	.1088	.0639	.0339	.0161
	3	.0173	.0852	.1720	.2362	.2581	.2397	.1954	.1419	.0923	.0537
	4	.0021	.0213	.0683	.1329	.1936	.2311	.2367	.2128	.1700	.1208
	5	.0002	.0038	.0193	.0532	.1032	.1585	.2039	.2270	.2225	.1934
	6	.0000	.0005	.0040	.0155	.0401	.0792	.1281	.1766	.2124	.2256
	7	.0000	.0000	.0006	.0033	.0115	.0291	.0591	.1009	.1489	.1934
	8	.0000	.0000	.0001	.0005	.0024	.0078	.0199	.0420	.0762	.1208
	9	.0000	.0000	.0000	.0001	.0004	.0015	.0048	.0125	.0277	.0537
	10	.0000	.0000	.0000	.0000	.0000	.0002	.0008	.0025	.0068	.0161
	11	.0000	.0000	.0000	.0000	.0000	.0000	.0001	.0003	.0010	.0029
	12	.0000	.0000	.0000	.0000	.0000	.0000	.0000	.0000	.0001	.0002

Table 1 (continued)

n	k	.05	.10	.15	.20	.25	.30	.35	.40	.45	.50
13	0	.5133	.2542	.1209	.0550	.0238	.0097	.0037	.0013	.0004	.0001
	1	.3512	.3672	.2774	.1787	.1029	.0540	.0259	.0113	.0045	.0016
	2	.1109	.2448	.2937	.2680	.2059	.1388	.0836	.0453	.0220	.0095
	3	.0214	.0997	.1900	.2457	.2517	.2181	.1651	.1107	.0660	.0349
	4	.0028	.0277	.0838	.1535	.2097	.2337	.2222	.1845	.1350	.0873
	5	.0003	.0055	.0266	.0691	.1258	.1803	.2154	.2214	.1989	.1571
	6	.0000	.0008	.0063	.0230	.0559	.1030	.1546	.1968	.2169	.2095
	7	.0000	.0001	.0011	.0058	.0186	.0442	.0833	.1312	.1775	.2095
	8	.0000	.0000	.0001	.0011	.0047	.0142	.0336	.0656	.1089	.1571
	9	.0000	.0000	.0000	.0001	.0009	.0034	.0101	.0243	.0495	.0873
	10	.0000	.0000	.0000	.0000	.0001	.0006	.0022	.0065	.0162	.0349
	11	.0000	.0000	.0000	.0000	.0000	.0001	.0003	.0012	.0036	.0095
	12	.0000	.0000	.0000	.0000	.0000	.0000	.0000	.0001	.0005	.0016
	13	.0000	.0000	.0000	.0000	.0000	.0000	.0000	.0000	.0000	.0001
14	0	.4877	.2288	.1028	.0440	.0178	.0068	.0024	.0008	.0002	.0001
	1	.3593	.3559	.2539	.1539	.0832	.0407	.0181	.0073	.0027	.0009
	2	.1229	.2570	.2912	.2501	.1802	.1134	.0634	.0317	.0141	.0056
	3	.0259	.1142	.2056	.2501	.2402	.1943	.1366	.0845	.0462	.0222
	4	.0037	.0349	.0998	.1720	.2202	.2290	.2022	.1549	.1040	.0611
	5	.0004	.0078	.0352	.0860	.1468	.1963	.2178	.2066	.1701	.1222
	6	.0000	.0013	.0093	.0322	.0734	.1262	.1759	.2066	.2088	.1833
	7	.0000	.0002	.0019	.0092	.0280	.0618	.1082	.1574	.1952	.2095
	8	.0000	.0000	.0003	.0020	.0082	.0232	.0510	.0918	.1398	.1833
	9	.0000	.0000	.0000	.0003	.0018	.0066	.0183	.0408	.0762	.1222
	10	.0000	.0000	.0000	.0000	.0003	.0014	.0049	.0136	.0312	.0611
	11	.0000	.0000	.0000	.0000	.0000	.0002	.0010	.0033	.0093	.0222
	12	.0000	.0000	.0000	.0000	.0000	.0000	.0001	.0005	.0019	.0056
	13	.0000	.0000	.0000	.0000	.0000	.0000	.0000	.0001	.0002	.0009
	14	.0000	.0000	.0000	.0000	.0000	.0000	.0000	.0000	.0000	.0001
15	0	.4633	.2059	.0874	.0352	.0134	.0047	.0016	.0005	.0001	.0000
	1	.3658	.3432	.2312	.1329	.0668	.0305	.0126	.0047	.0016	.0005
	2	.1348	.2669	.2856	.2309	.1559	.0916	.0476	.0219	.0090	.0032
	3	.0307	.1285	.2184	.2501	.2252	.1700	.1110	.0634	.0318	.0139
	4	.0049	.0428	.1156	.1876	.2252	.2186	.1792	.1268	.0780	.0417
	5	.0006	.0105	.0449	.1032	.1651	.2061	.2123	.1859	.1404	.0916
	6	.0000	.0019	.0132	.0430	.0917	.1472	.1906	.2066	.1914	.1527
	7	.0000	.0003	.0030	.0138	.0393	.0811	.1319	.1771	.2013	.1964
	8	.0000	.0000	.0005	.0035	.0131	.0348	.0710	.1181	.1647	.1964
	9	.0000	.0000	.0001	.0007	.0034	.0116	.0298	.0612	.1048	.1527
	10	.0000	.0000	.0000	.0001	.0007	.0030	.0096	.0245	.0515	.0916
	11	.0000	.0000	.0000	.0000	.0001	.0006	.0024	.0074	.0191	.0417
	12	.0000	.0000	.0000	.0000	.0000	.0001	.0004	.0016	.0052	.0139
	13	.0000	.0000	.0000	.0000	.0000	.0000	.0001	.0003	.0010	.0032
	14	.0000	.0000	.0000	.0000	.0000	.0000	.0000	.0000	.0001	.0005
	15	.0000	.0000	.0000	.0000	.0000	.0000	.0000	.0000	.0000	.0000

Table 1   (continued)

n	k	.05	.10	.15	.20	.25	.30	.35	.40	.45	.50
16	0	.4401	.1853	.0743	.0281	.0100	.0033	.0010	.0003	.0001	.0000
	1	.3706	.3294	.2097	.1126	.0535	.0228	.0087	.0030	.0009	.0002
	2	.1463	.2745	.2775	.2111	.1336	.0732	.0353	.0150	.0056	.0018
	3	.0359	.1423	.2285	.2463	.2079	.1465	.0888	.0468	.0215	.0085
	4	.0061	.0514	.1311	.2001	.2252	.2040	.1553	.1014	.0572	.0278
	5	.0008	.0137	.0555	.1201	.1802	.2099	.2008	.1623	.1123	.0667
	6	.0001	.0028	.0180	.0550	.1101	.1649	.1982	.1983	.1684	.1222
	7	.0000	.0004	.0045	.0197	.0524	.1010	.1524	.1889	.1969	.1746
	8	.0000	.0001	.0009	.0055	.0197	.0487	.0923	.1417	.1812	.1964
	9	.0000	.0000	.0001	.0012	.0058	.0185	.0442	.0840	.1318	.1746
	10	.0000	.0000	.0000	.0002	.0014	.0056	.0167	.0392	.0755	.1222
	11	.0000	.0000	.0000	.0000	.0002	.0013	.0049	.0142	.0337	.0667
	12	.0000	.0000	.0000	.0000	.0000	.0002	.0011	.0040	.0115	.0278
	13	.0000	.0000	.0000	.0000	.0000	.0000	.0002	.0008	.0029	.0085
	14	.0000	.0000	.0000	.0000	.0000	.0000	.0000	.0001	.0005	.0018
	15	.0000	.0000	.0000	.0000	.0000	.0000	.0000	.0000	.0001	.0002
	16	.0000	.0000	.0000	.0000	.0000	.0000	.0000	.0000	.0000	.0000
17	0	.4181	.1668	.0631	.0225	.0075	.0023	.0007	.0002	.0000	.0000
	1	.3741	.3150	.1893	.0957	.0426	.0169	.0060	.0019	.0005	.0001
	2	.1575	.2800	.2673	.1914	.1136	.0581	.0260	.0102	.0035	.0010
	3	.0415	.1556	.2359	.2393	.1893	.1245	.0701	.0341	.0144	.0052
	4	.0076	.0605	.1457	.2093	.2209	.1868	.1320	.0796	.0411	.0182
	5	.0010	.0175	.0668	.1361	.1914	.2081	.1849	.1379	.0875	.0472
	6	.0001	.0039	.0236	.0680	.1276	.1784	.1991	.1839	.1432	.0944
	7	.0000	.0007	.0065	.0267	.0668	.1201	.1685	.1927	.1841	.1484
	8	.0000	.0001	.0014	.0084	.0279	.0644	.1134	.1606	.1883	.1855
	9	.0000	.0000	.0003	.0021	.0093	.0276	.0611	.1070	.1540	.1855
	10	.0000	.0000	.0000	.0004	.0025	.0095	.0263	.0571	.1008	.1484
	11	.0000	.0000	.0000	.0001	.0005	.0026	.0090	.0242	.0525	.0944
	12	.0000	.0000	.0000	.0000	.0001	.0006	.0024	.0081	.0215	.0472
	13	.0000	.0000	.0000	.0000	.0000	.0001	.0005	.0021	.0068	.0182
	14	.0000	.0000	.0000	.0000	.0000	.0000	.0001	.0004	.0016	.0052
	15	.0000	.0000	.0000	.0000	.0000	.0000	.0000	.0001	.0003	.0010
	16	.0000	.0000	.0000	.0000	.0000	.0000	.0000	.0000	.0000	.0001
	17	.0000	.0000	.0000	.0000	.0000	.0000	.0000	.0000	.0000	.0000
18	0	.3972	.1501	.0536	.0180	.0056	.0016	.0004	.0001	.0000	.0000
	1	.3763	.3002	.1704	.0811	.0338	.0126	.0042	.0012	.0003	.0001
	2	.1683	.2835	.2556	.1723	.0958	.0458	.0190	.0069	.0022	.0006
	3	.0473	.1680	.2406	.2297	.1704	.1046	.0547	.0246	.0095	.0031
	4	.0093	.0700	.1592	.2153	.2130	.1681	.1104	.0614	.0291	.0117
	5	.0014	.0218	.0787	.1507	.1988	.2017	.1664	.1146	.0666	.0327
	6	.0002	.0052	.0301	.0816	.1436	.1873	.1941	.1655	.1181	.0708
	7	.0000	.0010	.0091	.0350	.0820	.1376	.1792	.1892	.1657	.1214
	8	.0000	.0002	.0022	.0120	.0376	.0811	.1327	.1734	.1864	.1669
	9	.0000	.0000	.0004	.0033	.0139	.0386	.0794	.1284	.1694	.1855
	10	.0000	.0000	.0001	.0008	.0042	.0149	.0385	.0771	.1248	.1669
	11	.0000	.0000	.0000	.0001	.0010	.0046	.0151	.0374	.0742	.1214
	12	.0000	.0000	.0000	.0000	.0002	.0012	.0047	.0145	.0354	.0708
	13	.0000	.0000	.0000	.0000	.0000	.0002	.0012	.0045	.0134	.0327
	14	.0000	.0000	.0000	.0000	.0000	.0000	.0002	.0011	.0039	.0117
	15	.0000	.0000	.0000	.0000	.0000	.0000	.0000	.0002	.0009	.0031
	16	.0000	.0000	.0000	.0000	.0000	.0000	.0000	.0000	.0001	.0006
	17	.0000	.0000	.0000	.0000	.0000	.0000	.0000	.0000	.0000	.0001
	18	.0000	.0000	.0000	.0000	.0000	.0000	.0000	.0000	.0000	.0000

Table 1   **(continued)**

n	k	.05	.10	.15	.20	.25	.30	.35	.40	.45	.50
19	0	.3774	.1351	.0456	.0144	.0042	.0011	.0003	.0001	.0000	.0000
	1	.3774	.2852	.1529	.0685	.0268	.0093	.0029	.0008	.0002	.0000
	2	.1787	.2852	.2428	.1540	.0803	.0358	.0138	.0046	.0013	.0003
	3	.0533	.1796	.2428	.2182	.1517	.0869	.0422	.0175	.0062	.0018
	4	.0112	.0798	.1714	.2182	.2023	.1491	.0909	.0467	.0203	.0074
	5	.0018	.0266	.0907	.1636	.2023	.1916	.1468	.0933	.0497	.0222
	6	.0002	.0069	.0374	.0955	.1574	.1916	.1844	.1451	.0949	.1518
	7	.0000	.0014	.0122	.0443	.0974	.1525	.1844	.1797	.1443	.0961
	8	.0000	.0002	.0032	.0166	.0487	.0981	.1489	.1797	.1771	.1442
	9	.0000	.0000	.0007	.0051	.0198	.0514	.0980	.1464	.1771	.1762
	10	.0000	.0000	.0001	.0013	.0066	.0220	.0528	.0976	.1449	.1762
	11	.0000	.0000	.0000	.0003	.0018	.0077	.0233	.0532	.0970	.1442
	12	.0000	.0000	.0000	.0000	.0004	.0022	.0083	.0237	.0529	.0961
	13	.0000	.0000	.0000	.0000	.0001	.0005	.0024	.0085	.0233	.0518
	14	.0000	.0000	.0000	.0000	.0000	.0001	.0006	.0024	.0082	.0222
	15	.0000	.0000	.0000	.0000	.0000	.0000	.0001	.0005	.0022	.0074
	16	.0000	.0000	.0000	.0000	.0000	.0000	.0000	.0001	.0005	.0018
	17	.0000	.0000	.0000	.0000	.0000	.0000	.0000	.0000	.0001	.0003
	18	.0000	.0000	.0000	.0000	.0000	.0000	.0000	.0000	.0000	.0000
	19	.0000	.0000	.0000	.0000	.0000	.0000	.0000	.0000	.0000	.0000
20	0	.3585	.1216	.0388	.0115	.0032	.0008	.0002	.0000	.0000	.0000
	1	.3774	.2702	.1368	.0576	.0211	.0068	.0020	.0005	.0001	.0000
	2	.1887	.2852	.2293	.1369	.0669	.0278	.0100	.0031	.0008	.0002
	3	.0596	.1901	.2428	.2054	.1339	.0716	.0323	.0123	.0040	.0011
	4	.0133	.0898	.1821	.2182	.1897	.1304	.0738	.0350	.0139	.0046
	5	.0022	.0319	.1028	.1746	.2023	.1789	.1272	.0746	.0365	.0148
	6	.0003	.0089	.0454	.1091	.1686	.1916	.1712	.1244	.0746	.0370
	7	.0000	.0020	.0160	.0545	.1124	.1643	.1844	.1659	.1221	.0739
	8	.0000	.0004	.0046	.0222	.0609	.1144	.1614	.1797	.1623	.1201
	9	.0000	.0001	.0011	.0074	.0271	.0654	.1158	.1597	.1771	.1602
	10	.0000	.0000	.0002	.0020	.0099	.0308	.0686	.1171	.1593	.1762
	11	.0000	.0000	.0000	.0005	.0030	.0120	.0336	.0710	.1185	.1602
	12	.0000	.0000	.0000	.0001	.0008	.0039	.1036	.0355	.0727	.1201
	13	.0000	.0000	.0000	.0000	.0002	.0010	.0045	.0146	.0366	.0739
	14	.0000	.0000	.0000	.0000	.0000	.0002	.0012	.0049	.0150	.0370
	15	.0000	.0000	.0000	.0000	.0000	.0000	.0003	.0013	.0049	.0148
	16	.0000	.0000	.0000	.0000	.0000	.0000	.0000	.0003	.0013	.0046
	17	.0000	.0000	.0000	.0000	.0000	.0000	.0000	.0000	.0002	.0011
	18	.0000	.0000	.0000	.0000	.0000	.0000	.0000	.0000	.0000	.0002
	19	.0000	.0000	.0000	.0000	.0000	.0000	.0000	.0000	.0000	.0000
	20	.0000	.0000	.0000	.0000	.0000	.0000	.0000	.0000	.0000	.0000

Table 2
Normal Curve Table
$Z = Z$-score

An entry in the table is the proportion under the
curve between $Z = 0$ and a positive value of Z.
Areas for negative values of Z are obtained by
symmetry.

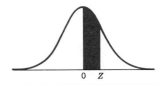

Z	0.00	0.01	0.02	0.03	0.04	0.05	0.06	0.07	0.08	0.09
0.0	0.0000	0.0040	0.0080	0.0120	0.0160	0.0199	0.0239	0.0279	0.0319	0.0359
0.1	0.0398	0.0438	0.0478	0.0517	0.0557	0.0596	0.0636	0.0675	0.0714	0.0753
0.2	0.0793	0.0832	0.0871	0.0910	0.0948	0.0987	0.1026	0.1064	0.1103	0.1141
0.3	0.1179	0.1217	0.1255	0.1293	0.1331	0.1368	0.1406	0.1443	0.1480	0.1517
0.4	0.1554	0.1591	0.1628	0.1664	0.1700	0.1736	0.1772	0.1808	0.1844	0.1879
0.5	0.1915	0.1950	0.1985	0.2019	0.2054	0.2088	0.2123	0.2157	0.2190	0.2224
0.6	0.2257	0.2291	0.2324	0.2357	0.2389	0.2422	0.2454	0.2486	0.2517	0.2549
0.7	0.2580	0.2611	0.2642	0.2673	0.2703	0.2734	0.2764	0.2794	0.2823	0.2852
0.8	0.2881	0.2910	0.2939	0.2967	0.2995	0.3023	0.3051	0.3078	0.3106	0.3133
0.9	0.3159	0.3186	0.3212	0.3238	0.3264	0.3289	0.3315	0.3340	0.3365	0.3389
1.0	0.3413	0.3438	0.3461	0.3485	0.3508	0.3531	0.3554	0.3577	0.3599	0.3621
1.1	0.3642	0.3665	0.3686	0.3708	0.3729	0.3749	0.3770	0.3790	0.3810	0.3830
1.2	0.3849	0.3869	0.3888	0.3907	0.3925	0.3944	0.3962	0.3980	0.3997	0.4015
1.3	0.4032	0.4049	0.4066	0.4082	0.4099	0.4115	0.4131	0.4147	0.4162	0.4177
1.4	0.4192	0.4207	0.4222	0.4236	0.4251	0.4265	0.4279	0.4292	0.4306	0.4319
1.5	0.4332	0.4345	0.4357	0.4370	0.4382	0.4394	0.4406	0.4418	0.4429	0.4441
1.6	0.4452	0.4463	0.4474	0.4484	0.4495	0.4505	0.4515	0.4525	0.4535	0.4545
1.7	0.4554	0.4564	0.4573	0.4582	0.4591	0.4599	0.4608	0.4616	0.4625	0.4633
1.8	0.4641	0.4649	0.4656	0.4664	0.4671	0.4678	0.4686	0.4693	0.4699	0.4706
1.9	0.4713	0.4719	0.4726	0.4732	0.4738	0.4744	0.4750	0.4756	0.4761	0.4767
2.0	0.4772	0.4778	0.4783	0.4788	0.4793	0.4798	0.4803	0.4808	0.4812	0.4817
2.1	0.4821	0.4826	0.4830	0.4834	0.4838	0.4842	0.4846	0.4850	0.4854	0.4857
2.2	0.4861	0.4864	0.4868	0.4871	0.4875	0.4878	0.4881	0.4884	0.4887	0.4890
2.3	0.4893	0.4896	0.4898	0.4901	0.4904	0.4906	0.4909	0.4911	0.4913	0.4916
2.4	0.4918	0.4920	0.4922	0.4925	0.4927	0.4929	0.4931	0.4932	0.4934	0.4936
2.5	0.4938	0.4940	0.4941	0.4943	0.4945	0.4946	0.4948	0.4949	0.4951	0.4952
2.6	0.4953	0.4955	0.4956	0.4957	0.4959	0.4960	0.4961	0.4962	0.4963	0.4964
2.7	0.4965	0.4966	0.4967	0.4968	0.4969	0.4970	0.4971	0.4972	0.4973	0.4974
2.8	0.4974	0.4975	0.4976	0.4977	0.4977	0.4978	0.4979	0.4979	0.4980	0.4981
2.9	0.4981	0.4982	0.4982	0.4983	0.4984	0.4984	0.4985	0.4985	0.4986	0.4986
3.0	0.4987	0.4987	0.4987	0.4988	0.4988	0.4989	0.4989	0.4989	0.4990	0.4990

Table 3
χ^2 Distribution

ν Degree of freedom	$p = 0.99$	0.98	0.95	0.90	0.80	0.70	0.50	0.30	0.20	0.10	0.05	0.02	0.01
1	0.000157	0.000628	0.00393	0.0158	0.0642	0.148	0.455	1.074	1.642	2.706	3.841	5.412	6.635
2	0.0201	0.0404	0.103	0.211	0.446	0.713	1.386	2.408	3.219	4.605	5.991	7.824	9.210
3	0.115	0.185	0.352	0.584	1.005	1.424	2.366	3.665	4.642	6.251	7.815	9.837	11.341
4	0.297	0.429	0.711	1.064	1.649	2.195	3.357	4.878	5.989	7.779	9.488	11.668	13.277
5	0.554	0.752	1.145	1.610	2.343	3.000	4.351	6.064	7.289	9.236	11.070	13.388	15.086
6	0.872	1.134	1.635	2.204	3.070	3.828	5.348	7.231	8.558	10.645	12.592	15.033	16.812
7	1.239	1.564	2.167	2.833	3.822	4.671	6.346	8.383	9.803	12.017	14.067	16.622	18.475
8	1.646	2.032	2.733	3.490	4.594	5.527	7.344	9.524	11.030	13.362	15.507	18.168	20.090
9	2.088	2.532	3.325	4.168	5.380	6.393	8.343	10.656	12.242	14.684	16.919	19.679	21.666
10	2.558	3.059	3.940	4.865	6.179	7.267	9.342	11.781	13.442	15.987	18.307	21.161	23.209
11	3.053	3.609	4.575	5.578	6.989	8.148	10.341	12.899	14.631	17.275	19.675	22.618	24.725
12	3.571	4.178	5.226	6.304	7.807	9.034	11.340	14.011	15.812	18.549	21.026	24.054	26.217
13	4.107	4.765	5.892	7.042	8.634	9.926	12.340	15.119	16.985	19.812	22.362	25.472	27.688
14	4.660	5.368	6.571	7.790	9.467	10.821	13.339	16.222	18.151	21.064	23.685	26.873	29.141
15	5.229	5.985	7.261	8.547	10.307	11.721	14.339	17.322	19.311	22.307	24.996	28.259	30.578
16	5.812	6.614	7.962	9.312	11.152	12.624	15.338	18.418	20.465	23.542	26.296	29.633	32.000
17	6.408	7.255	8.672	10.085	12.002	13.531	16.338	19.511	21.615	24.769	27.587	30.995	33.409
18	7.015	7.906	9.390	10.865	12.857	14.440	17.338	20.601	22.760	25.989	28.869	32.346	34.805
19	7.633	8.567	10.117	11.651	13.716	15.352	18.338	21.689	23.900	27.204	30.144	33.687	36.191
20	8.260	9.237	10.851	12.443	14.578	16.266	19.337	22.775	25.038	28.412	31.410	35.020	37.566
21	8.897	9.915	11.591	13.240	15.445	17.182	20.337	23.858	26.171	29.615	32.671	36.343	38.932
22	9.542	10.600	12.338	14.041	16.314	18.101	21.337	24.939	27.301	30.813	33.924	37.659	40.289
23	10.196	11.293	13.091	14.848	17.187	19.021	22.337	26.018	28.429	32.007	35.172	38.968	41.638
24	10.856	11.992	13.848	15.659	18.062	19.943	23.337	27.096	29.553	33.196	36.415	40.270	42.980
25	11.524	12.697	14.611	16.473	18.940	20.867	24.337	28.172	30.675	34.382	37.652	41.566	44.314
26	12.198	13.409	15.379	17.292	19.820	21.792	25.336	29.246	31.795	35.563	38.885	42.856	45.642
27	12.879	14.125	16.151	18.114	20.703	22.719	26.336	30.319	32.912	36.741	40.113	44.140	46.963
28	13.565	14.847	16.928	18.939	21.588	23.647	27.336	31.391	34.027	37.916	41.337	45.419	48.278
29	14.256	15.574	17.708	19.768	22.475	24.577	28.336	32.461	35.139	39.087	42.557	46.693	49.588
30	14.953	16.306	18.493	20.599	23.364	25.508	29.336	33.530	36.250	40.256	43.773	47.962	50.892

Table 4
Compound Interest
(a)   Annual Compounding

No. of Periods n	$(1 + r)^n$		
	10% per Annum $r = 0.10$	14% per Annum $r = 0.14$	18% per Annum $r = 0.18$
1	1.1	1.14	1.18
2	1.21	1.2996	1.3924
3	1.331	1.48154	1.64303
4	1.4641	1.68896	1.93878
5	1.61051	1.92541	2.28776
6	1.77156	2.19497	2.69955
7	1.94872	2.50227	3.18547
8	2.14359	2.85258	3.75886
9	2.35795	3.25194	4.43546
10	2.59374	3.70722	5.23384
11	2.85312	4.22622	6.17593
12	3.13843	4.8179	7.28759
13	3.45227	5.4924	8.59936
14	3.7975	6.26133	10.1472
15	4.17725	7.13792	11.9738
16	4.59497	8.13723	14.129
17	5.05447	9.27644	16.6723
18	5.55992	10.5751	19.6733
19	6.11591	12.0557	23.2144
20	6.7275	13.7435	27.393
21	7.40025	15.6675	32.3238
22	8.14027	17.861	38.1421
23	8.9543	20.3615	45.0077
24	9.84973	23.2121	53.109
25	10.8347	26.4618	62.6687
26	11.9182	30.1664	73.949
27	13.11	34.3897	87.2598
28	14.421	39.2043	102.967
29	15.8631	44.6929	121.501
30	17.4494	50.9502	143.371
31	19.1943	58.0829	169.177
32	21.1138	66.2145	199.629
33	23.2251	75.4845	235.563
34	25.5477	86.0523	277.964
35	28.1024	98.0996	327.998
36	30.9127	111.833	387.037
37	34.0039	127.49	456.704
38	37.4043	145.339	538.911
39	41.1448	165.686	635.914
40	45.2593	188.884	750.378

Table 4   (continued)
(b)   Monthly Compounding

No. of Periods n	$(1 + r)^n$		
	10% per Annum $r = 0.00833$	14% per Annum $r = 0.01167$	18% per Annum $r = 0.015$
1	1.00833333	1.01166667	1.015
2	1.01673611	1.02346944	1.030225
3	1.02520891	1.03540992	1.04567838
4	1.03375232	1.0474897	1.06136355
5	1.04236693	1.05971042	1.07728401
6	1.05105332	1.07207371	1.09344327
7	1.05981209	1.08458123	1.10984492
8	1.06864386	1.09723468	1.12649259
9	1.07754923	1.11003575	1.14338998
10	1.08652881	1.12298617	1.16054083
11	1.09558321	1.13608767	1.17794894
12	1.10471307	1.14934203	1.19561817
13	1.11391902	1.16275102	1.21355245
14	1.12320168	1.17631645	1.23175574
15	1.13256169	1.19004014	1.25023208
16	1.1419997	1.20392394	1.26898556
17	1.15151637	1.21796972	1.28802034
18	1.16111234	1.23217937	1.30734065
19	1.17078828	1.2465548	1.32695076
20	1.18054485	1.26109794	1.34685502
21	1.19038272	1.27581075	1.36705785
22	1.20030258	1.2906952	1.38756372
23	1.2103051	1.30575331	1.40837717
24	1.22039096	1.3209871	1.42950281
25	1.2305609	1.33639862	1.45094537
26	1.24081557	1.35198994	1.47270956
27	1.2511557	1.36776315	1.4948002
28	1.261582	1.38372039	1.5172222
29	1.27209519	1.39986379	1.53998054
30	1.28269598	1.41619554	1.56308025
31	1.29338511	1.43271782	1.58652645
32	1.30416332	1.44943286	1.61032435
33	1.31503135	1.46634291	1.63447921
34	1.32598995	1.48345025	1.6589964
35	1.33703986	1.50075717	1.68388135
36	1.34818186	1.518266	1.70913957
37	1.35941671	1.5359791	1.73477667
38	1.37074519	1.55389886	1.76079832
39	1.38216806	1.57202768	1.78721029
40	1.39368613	1.590368	1.81401845
41	1.40530018	1.6089223	1.84122872
42	1.41701102	1.62769306	1.86884716
43	1.42881944	1.64668281	1.89687987
44	1.44072627	1.66589411	1.92533306
45	1.45273233	1.68532954	1.95421306
46	1.46483843	1.70499172	1.98352626
47	1.47704542	1.72488329	2.01327915
48	1.48935413	1.74500693	2.04347834
49	1.50176541	1.76536534	2.07413052
50	1.51428013	1.78596127	2.10524248
51	1.52689913	1.80679749	2.13682111

Table 4   (continued)
(b)   Monthly Compounding

No. of Periods	$(1 + r)^n$		
n	10% per Annum $r = 0.00833$	14% per Annum $r = 0.01167$	18% per Annum $r = 0.015$
52	1.53962329	1.82787679	2.16887343
53	1.55245348	1.84920202	2.20140654
54	1.5653906	1.87077604	2.23442764
55	1.57843552	1.89260176	2.26794405
56	1.59158915	1.91468212	2.30196321
57	1.60485239	1.93702008	2.33649266
58	1.61822616	1.95961864	2.37154005
59	1.63171138	1.98248086	2.40711316
60	1.64530893	2.0056098	2.44321978
61	1.65901989	2.02900859	2.47986815
62	1.67284505	2.05268035	2.51706618
63	1.68678543	2.07662829	2.55482217
64	1.70084198	2.10085562	2.5931445
65	1.71501566	2.1253656	2.63204167
66	1.72930746	2.15016154	2.6715223
67	1.74371835	2.17524675	2.71159514
68	1.75824934	2.20062463	2.75226906
69	1.77290142	2.22629859	2.7935531
70	1.7876756	2.25227207	2.8354564
71	1.80257289	2.27854858	2.87798825
72	1.81759434	2.30513164	2.92115807
73	1.83274096	2.33202485	2.96497544
74	1.8480138	2.3592318	3.00945008
75	1.86341391	2.38675618	3.05459183
76	1.87894236	2.41460167	3.10041071
77	1.89460022	2.44277202	3.14691687
78	1.91038855	2.47127103	3.19412063
79	1.92630846	2.50010252	3.24203244
80	1.94236103	2.52927039	3.29066293
81	1.95854737	2.55877854	3.34002287
82	1.9748686	2.58863096	3.39012322
83	1.99132584	2.61883165	3.44097507
84	2.00792022	2.64938469	3.4925897
85	2.02465289	2.68029418	3.54497854
86	2.041525	2.71156427	3.59815322
87	2.05853771	2.74319919	3.65212552
88	2.07569219	2.77520318	3.7069074
89	2.09298963	2.80758055	3.76251102
90	2.11043121	2.84033566	3.81894869
91	2.12801814	2.87347291	3.87623292
92	2.14575162	2.90699676	3.93437642
93	2.16363289	2.94091172	3.99339206
94	2.18166316	2.97522236	4.05329295
95	2.19984369	3.00993329	4.11409234
96	2.21817572	3.04504918	4.17580373
97	2.23666052	3.08057475	4.23844079
98	2.25529936	3.11651479	4.3020174
99	2.27409352	3.15287413	4.36654767
100	2.2930443	3.18965766	4.43204588
101	2.312153	3.22687033	4.49852658

Table 4   **(continued)**

(b)   Monthly Compounding

No. of Periods n	$(1 + r)^n$ 10% per Annum $r = 0.00833$	14% per Annum $r = 0.01167$	18% per Annum $r = 0.015$
102	2.33142095	3.26451715	4.56600448
103	2.35084946	3.30260319	4.63449454
104	2.37043987	3.34113356	4.70401196
105	2.39019354	3.38011345	4.77457215
106	2.41011182	3.41954811	4.84619073
107	2.43019608	3.45944283	4.91888359
108	2.45044772	3.499803	4.99266685
109	2.47086812	3.54063403	5.06755686
110	2.49145868	3.58194143	5.14357021
111	2.51222084	3.62373075	5.22072377
112	2.53315602	3.66600761	5.29903463
113	2.55426565	3.7087777	5.37852015
114	2.5755512	3.75204677	5.45919795
115	2.59701413	3.79582065	5.54108593
116	2.61865591	3.84010523	5.62420222
117	2.64047805	3.88490645	5.70856526
118	2.66248203	3.93023036	5.79419374
119	2.68466938	3.97608305	5.88110665
120	2.70704163	4.02247069	5.96932325
180	4.45391989	8.06750665	14.5843691
240	7.32807437	16.1802704	35.63282
300	12.0569465	32.451309	87.0588133
360	19.8374024	65.0846635	212.703821

Table 4 (continued)
(c) Daily Compounding

No. of Periods n	$(1 + r)^n$ 10% per Annum $r = 0.000274$	14% per Annum $r = 0.0003836$	18% per Annum $r = 0.0004932$
5	1.00137	1.00192	1.00247
10	1.00274	1.00384	1.00494
15	1.00412	1.00577	1.00742
20	1.00549	1.0077	1.00991
25	1.00687	1.00963	1.0124
30	1.00825	1.01157	1.0149
35	1.00963	1.01351	1.01741
40	1.01102	1.01546	1.01992
45	1.0124	1.0174	1.02243
50	1.01379	1.01936	1.02496
55	1.01518	1.02131	1.02749
60	1.01657	1.02327	1.03002
65	1.01796	1.02524	1.03256
70	1.01936	1.0272	1.03511
75	1.02076	1.02918	1.03767
80	1.02216	1.03115	1.04023
85	1.02356	1.03313	1.0428
90	1.02496	1.03511	1.04537
95	1.02636	1.0371	1.04795
100	1.02777	1.03909	1.05054
105	1.02918	1.04108	1.05313
110	1.03059	1.04308	1.05573
115	1.032	1.04508	1.05833
120	1.03342	1.04709	1.06095
125	1.03483	1.0491	1.06356
130	1.03625	1.05111	1.06619
135	1.03767	1.05313	1.06882
140	1.03909	1.05515	1.07146
145	1.04052	1.05717	1.0741
150	1.04194	1.0592	1.07675
155	1.04337	1.06124	1.07941
160	1.0448	1.06327	1.08208
165	1.04623	1.06531	1.08475
170	1.04767	1.06736	1.08742
175	1.0491	1.06941	1.09011
180	1.05054	1.07146	1.0928
185	1.05198	1.07351	1.0955
190	1.05342	1.07557	1.0982
195	1.05487	1.07764	1.10091
200	1.05631	1.07971	1.10363
205	1.05776	1.08178	1.10635
210	1.05921	1.08385	1.10908
215	1.06066	1.08593	1.11182
220	1.06211	1.08802	1.11456
225	1.06357	1.09011	1.11731
230	1.06503	1.0922	1.12007
235	1.06649	1.09429	1.12284
240	1.06795	1.09639	1.12561
245	1.06941	1.0985	1.12839
250	1.07088	1.10061	1.13117

Table 4 (continued)
(c) Daily Compounding

No. of Periods n	$(1 + r)^n$		
	10% per Annum $r = 0.000274$	14% per Annum $r = 0.0003836$	18% per Annum $r = 0.0004932$
255	1.07235	1.10272	1.13396
260	1.07382	1.10483	1.13676
265	1.07529	1.10695	1.13957
270	1.07676	1.10908	1.14238
275	1.07824	1.11121	1.1452
280	1.07971	1.11334	1.14802
285	1.08119	1.11548	1.15086
290	1.08268	1.11762	1.1537
295	1.08416	1.11976	1.15655
300	1.08565	1.12191	1.1594
305	1.08713	1.12406	1.16226
310	1.08862	1.12622	1.16513
315	1.09012	1.12838	1.16801
320	1.09161	1.13055	1.17089
325	1.09311	1.13272	1.17378
330	1.0946	1.13489	1.17668
335	1.0961	1.13707	1.17958
340	1.09761	1.13925	1.18249
345	1.09911	1.14144	1.18541
350	1.10062	1.14363	1.18834
355	1.10213	1.14582	1.19127
360	1.10364	1.14802	1.19421
365	1.10515	1.15022	1.19716
730	1.22135	1.32302	1.43318
1095	1.34978	1.52176	1.71574
1460	1.4917	1.75037	2.05401
1825	1.64855	2.01332	2.45897
2190	1.8219	2.31576	2.94377
2555	2.01347	2.66365	3.52415
2920	2.22518	3.06379	4.21896
3285	2.45915	3.52404	5.05075
3650	2.71773	4.05344	6.04653
4015	3.0035	4.66236	7.23864
4380	3.31931	5.36276	8.66577
4745	3.66833	6.16837	10.3743
5110	4.05405	7.09501	12.4196
5475	4.48033	8.16085	14.8682
5840	4.95143	9.3868	17.7996
6205	5.47206	10.7969	21.3089
6570	6.04744	12.4189	25.51
6935	6.68332	14.2845	30.5395
7300	7.38606	16.4304	36.5605

Table 5
Present Value of $1
(a) Annual Compounding

No. of Periods n	$(1 + r)^{-n}$		
	10% per Annum	14% per Annum	18% per Annum
1	.909091	.877193	.847458
2	.826446	.769468	.718184
3	.751315	.674972	.608631
4	.683014	.592081	.515789
5	.620921	.519369	.437109
6	.564474	.455587	.370432
7	.513158	.399638	.313925
8	.466507	.35056	.266038
9	.424098	.307508	.225456
10	.385543	.269744	.191064
11	.350494	.236618	.161919
12	.318631	.20756	.137219
13	.289664	.18207	.116288
14	.263331	.15971	.0985489
15	.239392	.140097	.083516
16	.217629	.122892	.0707763
17	.197845	.1078	.0599799
18	.179859	.0945614	.0508304
19	.163508	.0829486	.0430766
20	.148644	.072762	.0365056
21	.135131	.0638263	.030937
22	.122846	.055988	.0262178
23	.111678	.0491123	.0222184
24	.101526	.043081	.0188292
25	.092296	.0377903	.0159569
26	.0839055	.0331494	.0135228
27	.0762777	.0290784	.01146
28	.0693434	.0255074	.00971189
29	.0630394	.0223749	.00823041
30	.0573086	.0196271	.00697493
31	.0520987	.0172168	.00591095
32	.0473625	.0151024	.00500928
33	.0430568	.0132478	.00424516
34	.0391425	.0116208	.00359759
35	.0355841	.0101937	.0030488
36	.0323492	.00894187	.00258373
37	.0294084	.00784374	.0021896
38	.0267349	.00688048	.0018556
39	.0243044	.00603551	.00157254
40	.0220949	.0052943	.00133266

Table 5 **(continued)**
(b)   Monthly Compounding

No. of Periods	$(1 + r)^{-n}$		
n	10% per Annum	14% per Annum	18% per Annum
1	.991735537	.988467875	.985221674
2	.983539375	.977068739	.970661748
3	.97541095	.96580106	.956316992
4	.967349702	.954663321	.942184228
5	.959355076	.943654024	.928260323
6	.951426521	.932771688	.91454219
7	.943563492	.922014848	.901026787
8	.935765446	.911382057	.88771112
9	.928031847	.900871885	.874592236
10	.920362162	.890482918	.861667227
11	.912755862	.880213757	.848933228
12	.905212425	.870063022	.836387417
13	.89773133	.860029346	.824027011
14	.890312063	.85011138	.811849271
15	.882954112	.840307789	.799851499
16	.87565697	.830617254	.788031033
17	.868420135	.821038472	.776385253
18	.861243109	.811570153	.764911579
19	.854125397	.802211024	.753607467
20	.847066509	.792959826	.74247041
21	.840065959	.783815315	.731497941
22	.833123265	.774776258	.720687626
23	.826237948	.795841441	.71003707
24	.819409535	.757009662	.699543911
25	.812637555	.748279731	.689205823
26	.805921542	.739650476	.679020515
27	.799261033	.731120734	.668985728
28	.792655569	.722689358	.65909924
29	.786104696	.714355214	.649358856
30	.779607963	.70611718	.63976242
31	.773164922	.697974148	.630307802
32	.766775129	.689925023	.620992908
33	.760438144	.681968721	.611815673
34	.754153531	.674104172	.602774062
35	.747920857	.666330318	.59386607
36	.741739692	.658646114	.585089724
37	.735609612	.651050524	.576443078
38	.729530193	.643543538	.567924214
39	.723501018	.636121115	.559531245
40	.71752167	.628785286	.55126231
41	.711591739	.621534056	.543115576
42	.705710815	.614366447	.535089238
43	.699878494	.607281496	.527181515
44	.694094374	.60027825	.519390655
45	.688358056	.593355766	.51171493
46	.682669146	.586513113	.50415264
47	.677027253	.57974937	.496702109
48	.671431986	.573063628	.489361683
49	.665882961	.566454986	.482129737
50	.660379796	.559922556	.475004666
51	.654922111	.553465459	.467984893

Table 5 **(continued)**
(b) Monthly Compounding

| No. of Periods | $(1 + r)^{-n}$ | | |
n	10% per Annum	14% per Annum	18% per Annum
52	.649509531	.547082826	.46106886
53	.644141684	.540773798	.454255034
54	.638818198	.534537527	.447541905
55	.633538709	.528373174	.440927985
56	.628302851	.522279908	.434411808
57	.623110266	.516256911	.427991928
58	.617960594	.510303371	.421666924
59	.612853481	.504418489	.415435393
60	.607788576	.498601472	.409295954
61	.60276553	.492851537	.403247245
62	.597783996	.487167911	.397287926
63	.592843632	.48154983	.391416676
64	.587944098	.475996537	.385632192
65	.583085056	.470507285	.379933194
66	.578266171	.465081336	.374318418
67	.573487111	.45971796	.368786618
68	.568747548	.454416435	.36333657
69	.564047155	.449176048	.357967063
70	.559385608	.443996093	.35267691
71	.554762586	.438875875	.347464936
72	.550177771	.433814703	.342329985
73	.545630847	.428811897	.337270921
74	.541121501	.423866785	.332286622
75	.536649422	.4189787	.327375982
76	.532214303	.414146985	.322537913
77	.527815837	.40937099	.317771343
78	.523453723	.404650073	.313075215
79	.519127659	.399983597	.308448487
80	.514837347	.395370936	.303890135
81	.510582493	.390811469	.299399148
82	.506362803	.386304582	.294974529
83	.502177986	.38184967	.2906153
84	.498027754	.377446131	.286320492
85	.493911822	.373093375	.282089155
86	.489829906	.368790816	.277920349
87	.485781725	.364537874	.273813152
88	.481767	.360333977	.269766652
89	.477785454	.356178561	.265779953
90	.473836814	.352071065	.26185217
91	.469920807	.348010937	.257982433
92	.466037164	.343997632	.254169885
93	.462185617	.340030608	.25041368
94	.458365901	.336109332	.246712985
95	.454577753	.332233277	.24306698
96	.450820911	.328401922	.239474857
97	.447095119	.324614749	.235935819
98	.443400117	.320871252	.232449083
99	.439735653	.317170924	.229013875
100	.436101474	.313513269	.225629433
101	.43249733	.309897795	.222295008
102	.428922971	.306324015	.21900986

Table 5 (continued)

(b) Monthly Compounding

No. of Periods n	$(1 + r)^{-n}$ 10% per Annum $r = 0.00833$	14% per Annum $r = 0.01167$	18% per Annum $r = 0.015$
103	.425378153	.302791448	.215773261
104	.421862631	.299299619	.212584493
105	.418376163	.295848058	.20944285
106	.414918508	.292436301	.206347636
107	.41148943	.289063889	.203298163
108	.408088691	.285730368	.200293757
109	.404716057	.28243529	.19733375
110	.401371296	.279178211	.194417488
111	.398054177	.275958693	.191544323
112	.394764473	.272776302	.188713619
113	.391501957	.269630612	.185924747
114	.388266403	.266521198	.183177091
115	.38505759	.263447642	.18047004
116	.381875295	.260409531	.177802995
117	.378719301	.257406455	.175175365
118	.375589389	.254438012	.172586566
119	.372485345	.251503801	.170036026
120	.369406953	.248603428	.167523178
180	.224521326	.123954035	.0685665589
240	.136461497	.0618036642	.0280640151
300	.0829397391	.0308153979	.0114864878
360	.0504098259	.0153646028	.00470137299

Table 5 **(continued)**
(c) Daily Compounding

No. of Periods *n*	$(1 + r)^{-n}$		
	10% per Annum	14% per Annum	18% per Annum
5	.998631	.998085	.997538
10	.997264	.996173	.995082
15	.9959	.994265	.992632
20	.994537	.992361	.990188
25	.993175	.99046	.98775
30	.991816	.988563	.985319
35	.990459	.986669	.982893
40	.989103	.984779	.980473
45	.987749	.982893	.978059
50	.986398	.981011	.975651
55	.985048	.979132	.973249
60	.983699	.977256	.970853
65	.982353	.975384	.968462
70	.981008	.973516	.966078
75	.979666	.971651	.9637
80	.978325	.96979	.961327
85	.976986	.967933	.95896
90	.975649	.966079	.956599
95	.974313	.964228	.954244
100	.97298	.962382	.951895
105	.971648	.960538	.949551
110	.970319	.958698	.947213
115	.968991	.956862	.944881
120	.967664	.955029	.942555
125	.96634	.9532	.940234
130	.965017	.951374	.937919
135	.963697	.949552	.93561
140	.962378	.947733	.933307
145	.961061	.945918	.931009
150	.959745	.944106	.928717
155	.958432	.942298	.92643
160	.95712	.940493	.924149
165	.95581	.938692	.921874
170	.954502	.936894	.919605
175	.953195	.935099	.917341
180	.951891	.933308	.915082
185	.950588	.931521	.912829
190	.949287	.929736	.910582
195	.947988	.927956	.90834
200	.94669	.926178	.906103
205	.945394	.924404	.903872
210	.944101	.922634	.901647
215	.942808	.920867	.899427
220	.941518	.919103	.897213
225	.940229	.917342	.895004
230	.938943	.915585	.892801
235	.937658	.913832	.890602
240	.936374	.912081	.88841
245	.935093	.910334	.886223
250	.933813	.908591	.884041
255	.932535	.90685	.881864

Table 5 (continued)

(c) Daily Compounding

No. of Periods	$(1 + r)^{-n}$		
n	10% per Annum	14% per Annum	18% per Annum
260	.931258	.905114	.879693
265	.929984	.90338	.877527
270	.928711	.901649	.875367
275	.92744	.899923	.873211
280	.926171	.898199	.871062
285	.924903	.896478	.868917
290	.923637	.894761	.866778
295	.922373	.893048	.864644
300	.921111	.891337	.862515
305	.91985	.88963	.860392
310	.918591	.887926	.858273
315	.917334	.886225	.85616
320	.916078	.884528	.854052
325	.914824	.882833	.851949
330	.913572	.881142	.849852
335	.912322	.879455	.84776
340	.911073	.87777	.845673
345	.909827	.876089	.843591
350	.908581	.874411	.841514
355	.907338	.872736	.839442
360	.906096	.871064	.837375
365	.904856	.869382	.835313
730	.818764	.755849	.697748
1095	.740863	.657133	.582838
1460	.670374	.571308	.486853
1825	.606592	.496693	.406675
2190	.548878	.431823	.339701
2555	.496656	.375425	.283756
2920	.449402	.326393	.237026
3285	.406644	.283765	.197991
3650	.367954	.246704	.165384
4015	.332945	.214484	.138148
4380	.301267	.186471	.115397
4745	.272604	.162117	.0963922
5110	.246667	.140944	.0805177
5475	.223198	.122536	.0672575
5840	.201962	.106533	.0561811
6205	.182747	.092619	.0469288
6570	.165359	.0805226	.0392003
6935	.149626	.070006	.0327445
7300	.13539	.0608629	.0273519

Table 6
Amount of an Annuity
(a) Annual Compounding

No. of Periods n	10% per Annum A(n, r)	10% per Annum 1/A(n, r)	14% per Annum A(n, r)	14% per Annum 1/A(n, r)	18% per Annum A(n, r)	18% per Annum 1/A(n, r)
1	1.000000	.999999994	1.00000001	.999999993	1	.99999996
2	2.100000	.476190473	2.14000001	.467289717	2.18000001	.458715595
3	3.310000	.302114802	3.43960003	.290731478	3.57240001	.27992386
4	4.641000	.215470802	4.92114404	.203204782	5.21543202	.19173867
5	6.105100	.16379748	6.61010421	.151283545	7.15420979	.13977841
6	7.71561006	.129607379	8.53551881	.117157495	9.44196755	.105910129
7	9.48717108	.105405499	10.7304915	.0931923765	12.1415217	.082361999
8	11.4358882	.0874440168	13.2327603	.0755700232	15.3269956	.0652443586
9	13.579477	.073405385	16.0853467	.0621683833	19.0858549	.0523948237
10	15.9374248	.0627453949	19.3372953	.0517135403	23.5213088	.0425146411
11	18.5311672	.0539631415	23.0445166	.043394271	28.7551443	.034776386
12	21.384284	.0467633146	27.270749	.036693265	34.9310704	.0286278087
13	24.5227124	.0407785234	32.0886539	.0311636631	42.218663	.0236862072
14	27.9749837	.0357462229	37.5810655	.0266091445	50.8180224	.0196780582
15	31.772482	.0314737765	43.3824147	.0228089627	60.9652664	.0164027824
16	35.9497303	.0278166204	50.9803528	.0196153998	72.9390144	.0137100838
17	40.547033	.0246641341	59.1176022	.0169154357	87.0680371	.011485271
18	45.591737	.021930222	68.3940666	.0146211514	103.740284	.00963945696
19	51.1590911	.019546868	78.969236	.0126631591	123.413535	.00810283897
20	57.2750003	.0174596245	91.0249291	.0109860014	146.627971	.00681998115
21	64.0025003	.0156243896	104.768419	.00954486102	174.021006	.0057464327
22	71.4027504	.0140050628	120.435998	.00830316531	206.344787	.00484625763
23	79.5430255	.0125718125	138.297038	.00723081286	244.486849	.00409019955
24	88.4973281	.0112997762	158.658623	.00630284052	289.494482	.00345429727
25	98.3470609	.010168072	181.870831	.00549840783	342.603489	.00291882608
26	109.18767	.00915903842	208.32747	.00480001351	405.272117	.00246747792
27	121.099944	.0082576214	238.499332	.00419288387	479.221098	.00208671948
28	134.209938	.00745101303	272.889238	.00366449042	566.480897	.00176528459
29	148.630932	.0067280746	312.093732	.0032041656	669.447458	.00149376921
30	164.494023	.00607924815	356.786855	.00280279384	790.948001	.00126430562
31	181.943428	.0054962139	407.737015	.00245256124	934.318641	.00107029867
32	201.137771	.00497171662	465.820197	.00214675105	1103.496	.000906210809
33	222.251548	.0044940622	532.035025	.0018795755	1303.12528	.000767385928
34	245.476704	.00407370633	607.519929	.00164603654	1538.68783	.000649904406
35	271.024374	.00368870505	693.57272	.00144180988	1816.65164	.00055046327
36	299.126812	.00334306375	791.672901	.00126314795	2144.64893	.000466276781
37	330.039493	.00302994042	903.507108	.00110679815	2531.68574	.000394993732
38	364.043442	.00274692491	1030.9981	.00096993889	2988.38918	.000334628437
39	401.447787	.00249098397	1176.33784	.000850095922	3527.29923	.000283503025
40	442.592556	.00225941436	1342.02514	.000745142525	4163.21309	.000240199091

Table 6 (continued)
(b) Monthly Compounding

No. of Periods n	10% per Annum		14% per Annum		18% per Annum	
	$A(n,r)$	$1/A(n,r)$	$A(n,r)$	$1/A(n,r)$	$A(n,r)$	$1/A(n,r)$
12	12.5655688	.0795825497	12.80075	.0781204501	13.0412119	.076799899
24	26.4469168	.0378115909	27.5131803	.0363462163	28.633522	.0349241005
36	41.7818235	.0239338525	44.4228	.0225109629	47.2759714	.0211523946
48	58.7224954	.0170292491	63.8577365	.0156598097	69.5652228	.0143749989
60	77.4370772	.0129137105	86.1951261	.0116015841	96.2146569	.0103934269
72	98.1113202	.0101925038	111.868427	.00893907271	128.077205	.00780779064
84	120.950427	.00826785012	141.37583	.00707334485	166.172646	.00601783761
96	146.181086	.00684083026	175.289929	.0057048343	211.720249	.0047232138
108	174.053726	.00574535244	214.268829	.00466703443	266.17779	.0037568745
120	204.844995	.00488173997	259.068916	.00385997678	331.288217	.00301851968
132	238.860513	.0041865438	310.559539	.00321999447	409.135426	.00244417847
144	276.4379	.00361744898	369.739877	.00270460413	502.210965	.00199119508
156	317.950131	.00314514731	437.758327	.0022843654	613.493772	.0016300084
168	363.809235	.00274869328	515.93479	.00193822944	746.545518	.00133950305
180	414.4703	.00241271761	605.786284	.00165074718	905.624605	.00110421028
192	470.436423	.00212568575	709.056383	.00141032508	1095.82245	.000912556589
204	532.262836	.00187877104	827.749049	.00120809562	1323.22646	.000755728541
216	600.563282	.00166510346	964.167517	.00103716417	1595.11482	.000626914118
228	676.015678	.00147925564	1120.959	.00089209329	1920.18949	.000520781937
240	759.368924	.00131688296	1301.16604	.000768541425	2308.85467	.000433115178
252	851.450347	.00117446661	1508.28556	.000663004425	2773.54983	.000360548778
264	953.173898	.00104912651	1746.33673	.000572627249	3329.14781	.000300377171
276	1065.54923	.000938483148	2019.93895	.000495064467	3993.43085	.000250411247
288	1189.69174	.000840553875	2334.40148	.000428375328	4787.65975	.000208870316
300	1326.83359	.000753674018	2695.82648	.000370943755	5737.25423	.000174299405
312	1478.33598	.000676436221	3111.22743	.000321416554	6872.60666	.000145505199
324	1645.70265	.000607643186	3588.6652	.000278655139	8230.05467	.000121505876
336	1830.5948	.000546270536	4137.40449	.000241697422	9853.04419	.000101491476
348	2034.84757	.000491437301	4768.09363	.000209727425	11793.52	.0000847923269
360	2260.48828	.000442382297	5492.97115	.000182050838	14113.5881	.0000708537046

Table 7
Present Value of an Annuity
(a) Annual Compounding

No. of Periods n	10% per Annum		14% per Annum		18% per Annum	
	$P(n, r)$	$1/P(n, r)$	$P(n, r)$	$1/P(n, r)$	$P(n, r)$	$1/P(n, r)$
1	.909091	1.1	.877192	1.14	.847458	1.18
2	1.73554	.576191	1.64666	.60729	1.56564	.638716
3	2.48685	.402115	2.32163	.430732	2.17427	.459924
4	3.16987	.315471	2.91371	.343205	2.69006	.371739
5	3.79079	.263798	3.43308	.291284	3.12717	.319778
6	4.35526	.229607	3.88866	.257158	3.4976	.28591
7	4.86842	.205406	4.2883	.233193	3.81153	.262362
8	5.33493	.187444	4.63886	.21557	4.07757	.245244
9	5.75902	.173641	4.94637	.202169	4.30302	.232395
10	6.14457	.162745	5.21611	.191714	4.49409	.222515
11	6.49506	.153963	5.45273	.183394	4.65601	.214776
12	6.81369	.146763	5.66029	.176669	4.79323	.208628
13	7.10336	.140779	5.84236	.171164	4.90951	.203686
14	7.36669	.135746	6.00207	.166609	5.00806	.199678
15	7.60608	.131474	6.14217	.162809	5.09158	.196403
16	7.82371	.127817	6.26506	.159615	5.16236	.19371
17	8.02155	.124664	6.37286	.156915	5.22233	.191485
18	8.20141	.12193	6.46742	.154621	5.27316	.189639
19	8.36492	.119547	6.55037	.152663	5.31624	.188103
20	8.51356	.11746	6.62313	.150986	5.35275	.18682
21	8.64869	.115624	6.68696	.149545	5.38368	.185746
22	8.77154	.114005	6.74294	.148303	5.4099	.184846
23	8.88322	.112572	6.79206	.147231	5.43212	.18409
24	8.98474	.1113	6.83514	.146303	5.45095	.183454
25	9.07704	.110168	6.87293	.145498	5.46691	.182919
26	9.16095	.109159	6.90608	.1448	5.48043	.182467
27	9.23722	.108258	6.93515	.144193	5.49189	.182087
28	9.30657	.107451	6.96066	.143665	5.5016	.181765
29	9.36961	.106728	6.98304	.143204	5.50983	.181494
30	9.42691	.106079	7.00266	.142803	5.51681	.181264
31	9.47901	.105496	7.01988	.142453	5.52272	.18107
32	9.52638	.104972	7.03498	.142147	5.52773	.180906
33	9.56943	.104499	7.04823	.14188	5.53197	.180767
34	9.60857	.104074	7.05985	.141646	5.53557	.18065
35	9.64416	.10369	7.07004	.141442	5.53862	.18055
36	9.67651	.103343	7.07899	.141263	5.5412	.180466
37	9.70592	.10303	7.08683	.141107	5.54339	.180395
38	9.73265	.102747	7.09371	.14097	5.54525	.180335
39	9.75696	.102491	7.09975	.14085	5.54682	.180284
40	9.77905	.102259	7.10504	.140745	5.54815	.18024

Table 7 **(continued)**
(b) Monthly Compounding

No. of Periods n	10% per Annum		14% per Annum		18% per Annum	
	$P(n, r)$	$1/P(n, r)$	$P(n, r)$	$1/P(n, r)$	$P(n, r)$	$1/P(n, r)$
12	11.3742	.0879182	11.1373	.0897884	10.9074	.0916807
24	21.6703	.0461461	20.8275	.0480135	20.0303	.0499241
36	30.9905	.032268	29.2586	.034178	27.6605	.0361524
48	39.4273	.0253632	36.5941	.0273268	34.0426	.0293752
60	47.0654	.021247	42.9766	.0232685	39.3801	.0253936
72	53.9776	.0185262	48.5297	.0206059	43.8445	.0228079
84	60.2355	.0166015	53.3613	.0187402	47.5784	.0210179
96	65.9003	.0151744	57.5651	.0173716	50.7015	.0197233
108	71.0281	.0140789	61.2227	.0163338	53.3136	.018757
120	75.6712	.0132151	64.405	.0155268	55.4983	.0180186
132	79.8718	.0125201	67.1738	.0148868	57.3256	.017442
144	83.6753	.011951	69.5829	.0143714	58.8539	.0169912
156	87.1184	.0114786	71.6789	.0139511	60.1321	.01663
168	90.235	.0110822	73.5026	.013605	61.2013	.0163395
180	93.0574	.0107461	75.0893	.0133175	62.0955	.0161042
192	95.6102	.0104591	76.4699	.013077	62.8434	.0159126
204	97.922	.0102122	77.6711	.0128748	63.4689	.0157558
216	100.015	.00999854	78.7162	.0127039	63.9921	.0156269
228	101.909	.00981268	79.6255	.0125588	64.4297	.0155208
240	103.625	.0096502	80.4166	.0124352	64.7957	.0154331
252	105.176	.00950788	81.105	.0123297	65.1018	.0153606
264	106.581	.00938253	81.7039	.0122393	65.3578	.0153004
276	107.853	.00927188	82.225	.0121618	65.572	.0152504
288	109.004	.00917395	82.6784	.0120951	65.7511	.0152089
300	110.047	.00908701	83.0728	.0120376	65.9009	.0151743
312	110.99	.00900982	83.4161	.0119881	66.0262	.0151455
324	111.844	.00894103	83.7147	.0119453	66.131	.0151215
336	112.617	.00887965	83.9745	.0119084	66.2186	.0151015
348	113.317	.00882481	84.2006	.0118764	66.2919	.0150848
360	113.95	.00877576	84.3973	.0118487	66.3532	.0150709

Solutions to Odd-Numbered Problems

CHAPTER 1

Exercise 1 (page 10)

1. 0.5 **3.** 1.625 **5.** 1.333... **7.** 0.1666... **9.** 45% **11.** 112% **13.** 6% **15.** 0.25%

17. 0.42 **19.** 0.002 **21.** 0.00001 **23.** 0.734 **25.** $\frac{2}{40} = \frac{1 \cdot 2}{20 \cdot 2} = \frac{1}{20}$ **27.** $\frac{6}{8} = \frac{3 \cdot 2}{4 \cdot 2} = \frac{3}{4}$

29. $0.15 \cdot 1000 = 150$ **31.** $0.18 \cdot 100 = 18$

33. $2x + 5 = 7$
$2x = 7 - 5$
$2x = 2$
$x = 1$

35. $6 - x = 0$
$6 = x$
$x = 6$

37. $3(2 - x) = 9$
$2 - x = 3$
$x = 2 - 3$
$x = -1$

39. $\frac{4x}{3} + \frac{x}{3} = 5$
$4x + x = 3 \cdot 5$
$5x = 15$
$x = 3$

41. $\frac{3x - 5}{x - 3} = 1$
$3x - 5 = x - 3$
$3x - x = -3 + 5$
$2x = 2$
$x = 1$

43. $x^2 - x - 12 = 0$
$(x - 4)(x + 3) = 0$
$x = 4 \quad \text{or} \quad x = -3$

45. $x^2 - 5x + 6 = 0$
$(x - 3)(x - 2) = 0$
$x = 3 \quad \text{or} \quad x = 2$

47. $x = 9$ **49.** $x = \frac{1}{2^3} = \frac{1}{8}$ **51.** $x = -9$ **53.** $x = 2$ **55.** $x = 2$ **57.** $x = 5$

59. $\frac{1}{3} > 0.33 \; (\frac{1}{3} = 0.333\ldots)$ **61.** $3 = \sqrt{9}$

63. $3x + 5 \leq 2$
$3x \leq 2 - 5$
$3x \leq -3$
$x \leq -1$

65. $3x + 5 \geq 2$
$3x \geq -3$
$x \geq -1$

67. $-3x + 5 \leq 2$
$-3x \leq -3$
$3x \geq 3$
$x \geq 1$

69. $6x - 3 \geq 8x + 5$
$6x - 8x \geq 5 + 3$
$-2x \geq 8$
$x \leq -4$

Exercise 2 (page 14)

1. $A = (4, 2); \; B = (6, 2); \; C = (5, 3); \; D = (-2, 1); \; E = (-2, -3); \; F = (3, -2); \; G = (6, -2); \; H = (5, 0)$

3. $\dfrac{f_2 - a_2}{f_1 - a_1} = \dfrac{-2 - 2}{3 - 4} = \dfrac{-4}{-1} = 4$ **5.** $\dfrac{a_2 - c_2}{a_1 - c_1} = \dfrac{2 - 3}{4 - 5} = \dfrac{-1}{-1} = 1$

7. $y = x - 3$

x	0	3	2	−2	4	−4
y	−3	0	−1	−5	1	−7

9. $2x - y = 6$

x	0	3	2	−2	4	−4
y	−6	0	−2	−10	2	−14

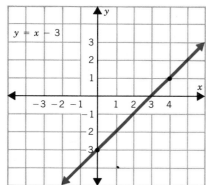

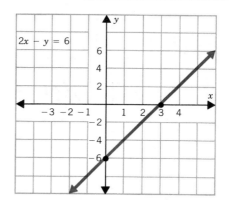

11.

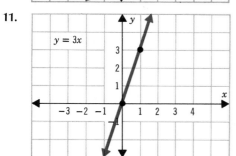

13.

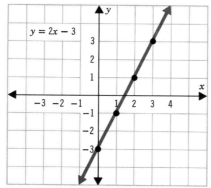

15.

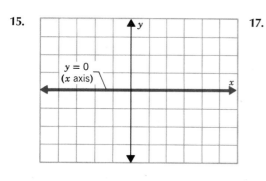

17.

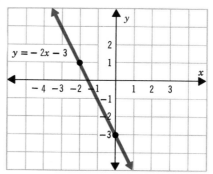

19.

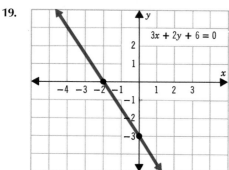

21.

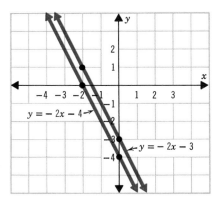

The lines are parallel.

Exercise 3 (page 22)

1. $\dfrac{1-3}{0-2} = \dfrac{-2}{-2} = 1$

3. $\dfrac{-4-0}{-5-(-3)} = \dfrac{-4}{-2} = 2$

5. $\dfrac{4.0-0.3}{1.5-0.1} = \dfrac{3.7}{1.4} = \dfrac{37}{14}$

7. $\begin{aligned} y - 3 &= 2[x - (-2)] \\ y - 3 &= 2(x + 2) \\ 2x - y + 7 &= 0 \end{aligned}$

9. $\begin{aligned} y - (-1) &= -\tfrac{2}{3}(x - 1) \\ y + 1 &= -\tfrac{2}{3}x + \tfrac{2}{3} \\ 2x + 3y + 1 &= 0 \end{aligned}$

11. $m = \dfrac{2-3}{-1-1} = \dfrac{-1}{-2} = \dfrac{1}{2}$
$\begin{aligned} y - 3 &= \tfrac{1}{2}(x - 1) \\ x - 2y + 5 &= 0 \end{aligned}$

13. $\begin{aligned} y &= -3x + 3 \\ 3x + y - 3 &= 0 \end{aligned}$

15. $m = \dfrac{-1-0}{0-2} = \dfrac{-1}{-2} = \dfrac{1}{2}$
$\begin{aligned} y &= \tfrac{1}{2}x - 1 \\ x - 2y - 2 &= 0 \end{aligned}$

17. $x - 1 = 0$

19. Slope $\tfrac{3}{2}$, y-intercept -3

21. Slope $-\tfrac{1}{2}$, y-intercept 2

23. Slope undefined, no y-intercept

25. $x = 2y$ **27.** $x + y = 2$ **29.** $\degree F = \tfrac{9}{5}\degree C + 32$ or $\degree C = \tfrac{5}{9}(F - 32)$; $\tfrac{5}{9}(70 - 32) = \tfrac{190}{9} = 21.111\ldots$

Exercise 4 (page 29)

1. $m_1 = m_2 = -1$

3. $m_1 = m_2 = \tfrac{2}{3}$

5. $\begin{aligned} y &= 5 - x \\ 3x - (5 - x) - 7 &= 0 \\ 3x - 5 + x - 7 &= 0 \\ 4x &= 12 \\ x &= 3 \\ y &= 5 - 3 = 2 \\ (x, y) &= (3, 2) \end{aligned}$

7. $\begin{aligned} y &= 2 - 3x \\ 3x - 2(2 - 3x) + 5 &= 0 \\ 3x - 4 + 6x + 5 &= 0 \\ 9x + 1 &= 0 \\ x &= -\tfrac{1}{9} \\ y &= 2 - 3(-\tfrac{1}{9}) = \tfrac{7}{3} \\ (x, y) &= (-\tfrac{1}{9}, \tfrac{7}{3}) \end{aligned}$

9. $\left.\begin{aligned} 2x - 3y + 4 &= 0 \\ 3x + 2y - 7 &= 0 \end{aligned}\right\}$ $\begin{aligned} 4x - 6y + 8 &= 0 \\ 9x + 6y - 21 &= 0 \\ \hline 13x - 13 &= 0 \\ x &= 1 \end{aligned}$

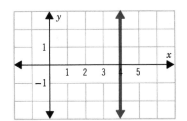

$\begin{aligned} 2(1) - 3y + 4 &= 0 \\ y &= 2 \\ (x, y) &= (1, 2) \end{aligned}$

11. $3x - 4y + 8 = 0$ } $3x - 4y + 8 = 0$
$2x + y - 2 = 0$ } $\underline{8x + 4y - 8 = 0}$
$11x = 0$
$x = 0$

$3(0) - 4y + 8 = 0$
$y = 2$
$(x, y) = (0, 2)$

13. $-2x + 3y - 7 = 0$ } $-6x + 9y - 21 = 0$
$3x + 2y - 9 = 0$ } $\underline{6x + 4y - 18 = 0}$
$13y - 39 = 0$
$y = 3$

$3x + 2(3) - 9 = 0$
$x = 1$
$(x, y) = (1, 3)$

15. $L: \quad 2x - 3y + 6 = 0$ $\qquad M: \quad 4x - 6y + 7 = 0$
$-3y = -2x - 6$ $\qquad\qquad -6y = -4x - 7$
$y = \frac{2}{3}x + 2$ $\qquad\qquad y = \frac{2}{3}x + \frac{7}{6}$

No solution; the lines L and M are parallel; same slope; different y-intercepts.

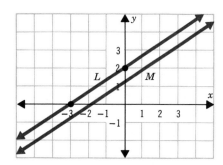

17. $L: \quad -2x + 3y + 6 = 0$ $\qquad M: \quad 4x - 6y - 12 = 0$
$3y = 2x - 6$ $\qquad\qquad -6y = -4x + 12$
$y = \frac{2}{3}x - 2$ $\qquad\qquad y = \frac{2}{3}x - 2$

Infinitely many solutions; the lines L and M are identical; same slope; same y-intercept.

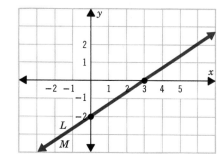

19. $L: \quad 3x - 3y + 10 = 0$ $\qquad M: \quad x + y - 2 = 0$
$-3y = -3x - 10$ $\qquad\qquad y = -x + 2$
$y = x + \frac{10}{3}$

One solution; since the slopes are different, the lines intersect.
$x_0 + \frac{10}{3} = -x_0 + 2$
$2x_0 = -\frac{4}{3}$
$x_0 = -\frac{2}{3}$
$y_0 = \frac{2}{3} + 2 = \frac{8}{3}$

L and M intersect at $\left(-\frac{2}{3}, \frac{8}{3}\right)$.

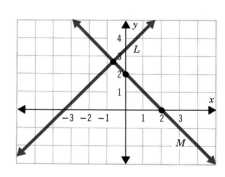

21. $2x - y = 6$
$\quad\quad -y = -2x + 6$
$\quad\quad\quad y = 2x - 6$
A line parallel to this line must have slope 2:
$y - 2 = 2(x - 1)$
$\quad\quad y = 2x$

23. Let x = Number of caramels, y = Number of creams; then $x(0.05) + y(0.10) = 4.0$ and $x + y = 50$:
$5x + 10y = 400$
$\underline{5x + 5y = 250}$

$\quad\quad\quad 5y = 150$
$\quad\quad\quady = 30$
$\quad\quad\quadx = 20$
20 caramels, 30 creams; increase the number of caramels to increase profits.

25. Let x = Bond investment; y = Savings; then $x + y = 50{,}000$ and $0.15x + 0.07y = 6000$:
$0.15x + 0.07(50{,}000 - x) = 6000$
$\quad 0.15x + 3500 - 0.07x = 6000$
$\quad\quad\quad\quad\quad\quad 0.08x = 2500$
$\quad\quad\quad\quad\quad\quad\quad\quad x = \$31{,}250$ in bonds
$\quad\quad\quad\quad\quad\quad\quad\quad y = \$18{,}750$ in savings certificates

27. $x + y = 13$ and $5x + 25y = 165$; solving by substitution:
$5(13 - y) + 25y = 165$
$\quad 65 - 5y + 25y = 165$
$\quad\quad\quad\quad\quad 20y = 100$
$\quad\quad\quad\quad\quady = 5$ quarters
$\quad\quad\quad\quad\quadx = 8$ nickels

29. x = cc of 15% acid; y = cc of 5% acid; then $y = 100 - x$ and $0.15x + 0.05y = (0.08)(100)$:
$0.15x + 0.05(100 - x) = 8$
$\quad 0.15x + 5 - 0.05x = 8$
$\quad\quad\quad\quad\quad\quad 0.1x = 3$
$\quad\quad\quad\quad\quad\quad\quadx = 30$ cc of 15% acid
$\quad\quad\quad\quad\quad\quad\quady = 70$ cc of 5% acid

31. x = Number of adults; y = Number of children; then $y = 5200 - x$ and $2.75x + 1.50y = 11{,}875$:
$2.75x + 1.50(5200 - x) = 11{,}875$
$\quad\quad\quad 1.25x + 7800 = 11{,}875$
$\quad\quad\quad\quad\quad\quad 1.25x = 4075$
$\quad\quad\quad\quad\quad\quad\quad\quad x = 3260$ adults
$\quad\quad\quad\quad\quad\quad\quad\quad y = 1940$ children

Exercise 5 (page 37)

1. (a) $A = 1000(1 + 0.18t) = 1000 + 180t$ (b) $1000 + 180 \cdot \frac{1}{2} = 1090$ (c) 1180   (d) 1360

3. $C = \$10x + \$600,\ R = \$30x$
$\quad 10x + 600 = 30x$
$\quad\quad\quad 600 = 20x$
$\quad\quad\quad\quad30 = x$

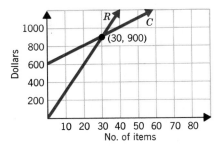

5. $C = \$0.2x + \$50$, $R = \$0.3x$
$0.2x + 50 = 0.3x$
$2x + 500 = 3x$
$500 = x$

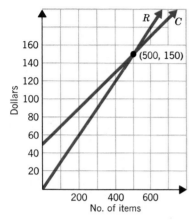

7. $R = \$1x$, $C = 0.75x + 300$
$x = 0.75x + 300$
$0.25x = 300$
$x = 1200$ items

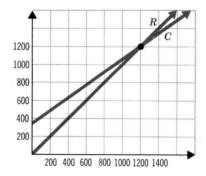

9. (a) \$80,000   (b) \$95,000   (c) \$105,000   (d) \$120,000

11. $S = p + 1$, $D = 3 - p$ **13.** $S = 20p + 500$, $D = 1000 - 30p$
$p + 1 = 3 - p$ $20p + 500 = 1000 - 30p$
$2p = 2$ $50p = 500$
$p = \$1$ $p = \$10$

15. $S = 0.7p + 0.4$, $D = -0.5p + 1.6$
$0.7p + 0.4 = -0.5p + 1.6$
$1.2p = 1.2$
$p = 1$

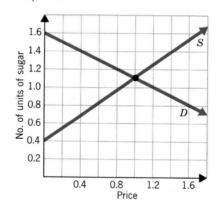

Exercise 6 (page 44)

1. $x \geq 0$

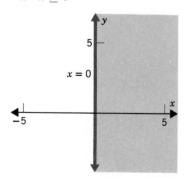

3. $x \geq 0$, $y \geq 0$

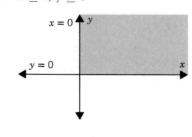

5. $2x - 3y + 6 \leq 0$

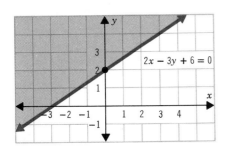

$2x - 3y + 6 = 0$

7. $5x + y + 10 \leq 0$

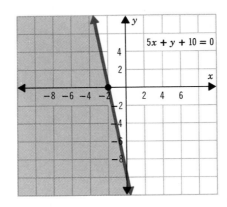

$5x + y + 10 = 0$

9. $x - 5 \geq 0$

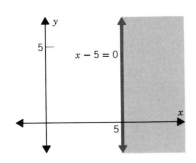

$x - 5 = 0$

11. $x \geq 0, y \geq 0$
$x + y \leq 2$

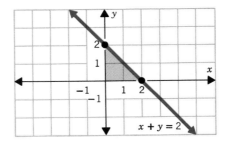

$x + y = 2$

13. $x \geq 0, y \geq 0$
$x + y \geq 2$
$2x + 3y \leq 6$

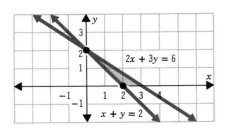

$2x + 3y = 6$

$x + y = 2$

15. $x \geq 0, y \geq 0$
$2 \leq x + y, x + y \leq 8$
$2x + y \leq 10$

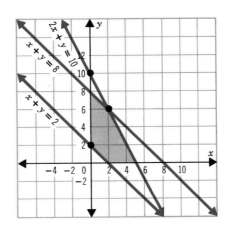

$2x + y = 10$

$x + y = 8$

$x + y = 2$

17. $x \geq 0,\ y \geq 0$
$x + y \geq 2,\ 2x + 3y \leq 12$
$3x + y \leq 12$

19. $x \geq 0,\ y \geq 0$
$1 \leq x + 2y,\ x + 2y \leq 10$

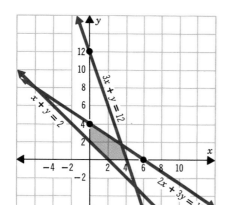

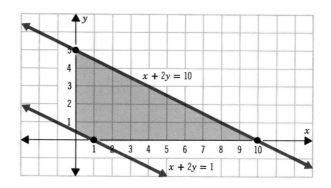

Exercise 7 (page 52)

1. $s = \frac{1}{2}gt^2 = 16t^2$; the ball hits the ground when $s = 16$ feet:
$$16 = 16t^2$$
$$t = 1 \text{ second}$$
When $t = \frac{1}{2},\ s = 16(\frac{1}{2})^2 = 16(\frac{1}{4}) = 4$ feet.

3. $\dfrac{T^2}{1^2} = \dfrac{(483)^3}{(93)^3}$

$T = \left(\dfrac{483}{93}\right)^{3/2} \approx 11.836$ years

5. W_0 is the original weight in pounds; t is time in years:
Weight after t years $= (\frac{1}{2})^{t/2} \cdot W_0$
Weight after 50 years $= (\frac{1}{2})^{50/2} \cdot 2000 = (\frac{1}{2})^{25} \cdot 2000 \approx 0.0000596$ pound
Weight after 200 years $= (\frac{1}{2})^{200/2} \cdot 2000 = (\frac{1}{2})^{100} \cdot 2000 \approx 1.58 \times 10^{-27}$ pound

7. Number of cells after t seconds $= 2^{t/5} \cdot N_0$
When $N_0 = 1000$:   Number of cells after 120 seconds $= 2^{24} \cdot 1000 = 16{,}777{,}216{,}000$
Number of cells after 3600 seconds $= 2^{720} \cdot 1000 \approx 5.52 \times 10^{219}$

Review Exercises (page 54)

1. $3x + 6 = 2x - 1$
$x = -7$

3. $-2(x + 3) = x + 5$
$-2x - 6 = x + 5$
$-3x = 11$
$x = -\frac{11}{3}$

5. $\dfrac{4x - 1}{x + 2} = 5$
$4x - 1 = 5(x + 2)$
$4x - 1 = 5x + 10$
$-x = 11$
$x = -11$

7. $2x - 1 \leq 5$
$2x \leq 6$
$x \leq 3$

9. $3x + 7 \geq -2x + 2$
$5x \geq -5$
$x \geq -1$

11.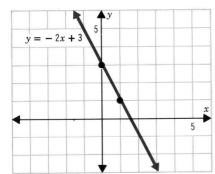

13.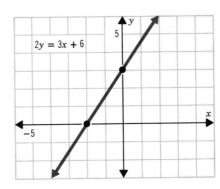

15. Slope $= \dfrac{4 - 2}{-3 - 1} = \dfrac{2}{-4} = \dfrac{-1}{2}$

$$y - 2 = -\tfrac{1}{2}(x - 1)$$
$$2y - 4 = -x + 1$$
$$x + 2y - 5 = 0$$

17. Slope $= \dfrac{3 - 0}{-2 - 0} = \dfrac{-3}{2}$

$$y - 0 = -\tfrac{3}{2}(x - 0)$$
$$2y = -3x$$
$$3x + 2y = 0$$

19. $\qquad y = 2(x + 1)$
$$2x - y + 2 = 0$$

21. $\qquad y - 3 = 1(x - 1)$
$$x - y + 2 = 0$$

23. $-9x - 2y + 18 = 0$
$$2y = -9x + 18$$
$$y = \left(-\tfrac{9}{2}\right)x + 9$$
Slope $= -\tfrac{9}{2}$
y-intercept $= 9$

25. $4x + 2y - 9 = 0$
$$2y = -4x + 9$$
$$y = -2x + \tfrac{9}{2}$$
Slope $= -2$
y-intercept $= \tfrac{9}{2}$

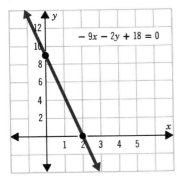

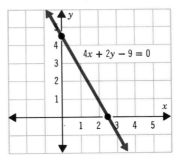

27. $3x - 4y + 12 = 0$
$$-4y = -3x - 12$$
$$y = \tfrac{3}{4}x + 3$$

$6x - 8y + 9 = 0$
$$-8y = -6x - 9$$
$$y = \tfrac{3}{4}x + \tfrac{9}{8}$$

No solution; the lines are parallel.

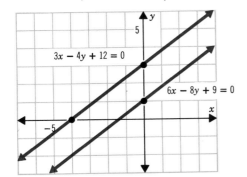

29. $x - y + 2 = 0$ $3x - 4y + 12 = 0$
          $y = x + 2$ $-4y = -3x - 12$
                                                  $y = (\frac{3}{4})x + 3$

The lines intersect.
$3x - 4y + 12 = 0$ $3x - 4y + 12 = 0$
$\underline{\;\;\;x - y + 2 = 0}$ $\underline{\;\;3x - 3y + 6 = 0}$
                                      $-y + 6 = 0$
                                      $y = 6$

$x = 6 - 2 = 4$
One solution; the lines intersect at $(4, 6)$.

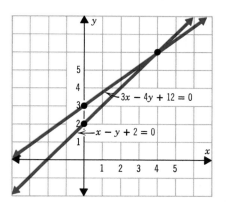

31. $4x + 6y + 12 = 0$ $2x + 3y + 6 = 0$
          $6y = -4x - 12$ $3y = -2x - 6$
          $y = -\frac{2}{3}x - 2$ $y = -\frac{2}{3}x - 2$
Infinitely many solutions; the lines are identical.

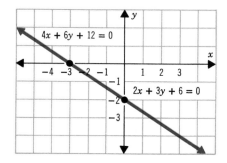

33. $2x - 3y + 6 \geq 0$
          $x \geq 0, y \geq 0$

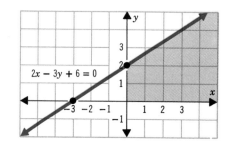

35. $y + 2x \geq 4, x + 2y \geq 4$
          $x \geq 0, y \geq 0$

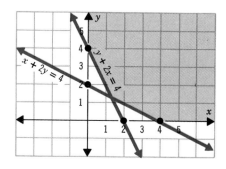

37.   Let x = Amount in bonds, y = Amount in bank; then $y = 90{,}000 - x$ and $0.16x + 0.06y = 10{,}000$:
          $0.16x + (0.06)(90{,}000 - x) = 10{,}000$
          $0.16x - 0.06x + 5400 = 10{,}000$
          $0.10x = 4600$
          $x = \$46{,}000$ in bonds
          $y = \$44{,}000$ in bank

39. (a)
(b)

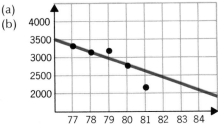

(Using only the last two digits of the date)

(c) We used the points $(80, 2800)$ and $(77, 3400)$. If you chose two different points, your answer may be different.

$$m = \frac{3400 - 2800}{77 - 80} = \frac{600}{-3} = -200$$

$$y - 2800 = -200(x - 78)$$

(d) $y = -200(82 - 78) + 2800 = 2000$

CHAPTER 2

Exercise 1 (page 64)

1. 2×2 **3.** 2×3 **5.** 2×1 **7.** 1×1

9. False; the matrices are not of the same dimension.

11. True; number of rows equals number of columns.

13. True; corresponding entries are equal.

15. True; corresponding entries are equal.

17. Corresponding entries must be equal so $x = 4$ and $z = 3$.

19. $x - 2y = 3$ and $6 = x + y$, so $x = 5$, $y = 1$

21.

$$\begin{array}{c} \\ \text{Steel} \\ \text{Aluminum} \end{array} \begin{array}{ccc} \frac{1}{2}'' & 1'' & 2'' \\ \begin{bmatrix} 25 & 45 & 35 \\ 13 & 20 & 23 \end{bmatrix} \end{array} \quad \text{or} \quad \begin{array}{c} \\ \frac{1}{2}'' \\ 1'' \\ 2'' \end{array} \begin{array}{cc} \text{Steel} & \text{Aluminum} \\ \begin{bmatrix} 25 & 13 \\ 45 & 20 \\ 35 & 23 \end{bmatrix} \end{array}$$

23.

$$\begin{array}{c} \\ \text{Dem} \\ \text{Rep} \\ \text{Ind} \end{array} \begin{array}{cc} {<}\$15{,}000 & {>}\$15{,}000 \\ \begin{bmatrix} 351 & 203 \\ 271 & 215 \\ 73 & 55 \end{bmatrix} \end{array} \quad \text{or} \quad \begin{array}{c} \\ {<}\$15{,}000 \\ {>}\$15{,}000 \end{array} \begin{array}{ccc} \text{Dem} & \text{Rep} & \text{Ind} \\ \begin{bmatrix} 351 & 271 & 73 \\ 203 & 215 & 55 \end{bmatrix} \end{array}$$

Exercise 2 (page 68)

1. $\begin{bmatrix} 2 & -3 & 4 \\ 0 & 2 & 1 \end{bmatrix} + \begin{bmatrix} 1 & -2 & 0 \\ 5 & 1 & 2 \end{bmatrix} = \begin{bmatrix} 3 & -5 & 4 \\ 5 & 3 & 3 \end{bmatrix}$

3. $\begin{bmatrix} 2 & -3 & 4 \\ 0 & 2 & 1 \end{bmatrix} - \begin{bmatrix} -3 & 0 & 5 \\ 2 & 1 & 3 \end{bmatrix} = \begin{bmatrix} 5 & -3 & -1 \\ -2 & 1 & -2 \end{bmatrix}$

5. $\left(\begin{bmatrix} 2 & -3 & 4 \\ 0 & 2 & 1 \end{bmatrix} + \begin{bmatrix} 1 & -2 & 0 \\ 5 & 1 & 2 \end{bmatrix} \right) - \begin{bmatrix} -3 & 0 & 5 \\ 2 & 1 & 3 \end{bmatrix} = \begin{bmatrix} 3 & -5 & 4 \\ 5 & 3 & 3 \end{bmatrix} - \begin{bmatrix} -3 & 0 & 5 \\ 2 & 1 & 3 \end{bmatrix} = \begin{bmatrix} 6 & -5 & -1 \\ 3 & 2 & 0 \end{bmatrix}$

7. $\begin{bmatrix} 2 & -3 & 4 \\ 0 & 2 & 1 \end{bmatrix} + \left(\begin{bmatrix} 1 & -2 & 0 \\ 5 & 1 & 2 \end{bmatrix} + \begin{bmatrix} -3 & 0 & 5 \\ 2 & 1 & 3 \end{bmatrix} \right) = \begin{bmatrix} 2 & -3 & 4 \\ 0 & 2 & 1 \end{bmatrix} + \begin{bmatrix} -2 & -2 & 5 \\ 7 & 2 & 5 \end{bmatrix} = \begin{bmatrix} 0 & -5 & 9 \\ 7 & 4 & 6 \end{bmatrix}$

9. $\left(\begin{bmatrix} 2 & -3 & 4 \\ 0 & 2 & 1 \end{bmatrix} - \begin{bmatrix} 1 & -2 & 0 \\ 5 & 1 & 2 \end{bmatrix} \right) - \begin{bmatrix} -3 & 0 & 5 \\ 2 & 1 & 3 \end{bmatrix} = \begin{bmatrix} 1 & -1 & 4 \\ -5 & 1 & -1 \end{bmatrix} - \begin{bmatrix} -3 & 0 & 5 \\ 2 & 1 & 3 \end{bmatrix} = \begin{bmatrix} 4 & -1 & -1 \\ -7 & 0 & -4 \end{bmatrix}$

11. $[2 + x \quad 3 + y \quad -4 + z] = [6 \quad -8 \quad 2]$

$\qquad 2 + x = 6 \qquad 3 + y = -8 \qquad -4 + z = 2$

$\qquad\qquad x = 4 \qquad\qquad y = -11 \qquad\qquad z = 6$

13. (a)

$\qquad\qquad$ Compact $\quad$ Intermediate $\quad$ Full-size

$$\begin{matrix} A \\ B \end{matrix} \begin{bmatrix} 100 & 50 & 40 \\ 120 & 40 & 35 \end{bmatrix} \text{June}$$

$$\begin{matrix} A \\ B \end{matrix} \begin{bmatrix} 80 & 30 & 10 \\ 70 & 40 & 20 \end{bmatrix} \text{July}$$

$$\begin{matrix} A \\ B \end{matrix} \begin{bmatrix} 300 & 120 & 65 \\ 250 & 100 & 80 \end{bmatrix} \text{June–August}$$

(b) $\begin{bmatrix} 100 & 50 & 40 \\ 120 & 40 & 35 \end{bmatrix} + \begin{bmatrix} 80 & 30 & 10 \\ 70 & 40 & 20 \end{bmatrix} = \begin{bmatrix} 180 & 80 & 50 \\ 190 & 80 & 55 \end{bmatrix}$

(c) $\begin{bmatrix} 300 & 120 & 65 \\ 250 & 100 & 80 \end{bmatrix} - \begin{bmatrix} 180 & 80 & 50 \\ 190 & 80 & 55 \end{bmatrix} = \begin{bmatrix} 120 & 40 & 15 \\ 60 & 20 & 25 \end{bmatrix}$

Exercise 3 (page 78)

1. $(3 \times 3) \quad (3 \times 4) \qquad$ Dimension $BA = 3 \times 4$

$\qquad$ Equal

3. $(3 \times 4) \quad (3 \times 3) \qquad AB$ is not defined.

$\qquad$ Not equal

5. $(3 \times 4) \quad (2 \times 3) \qquad (BA)C$ is not defined.

$\qquad$ Not equal

7. $(3 \times 4) + (3 \times 4) \qquad BA + A$ is defined, since dimensions are equal.

$\qquad\qquad\qquad\qquad\qquad$ Dimension is 3×4.

9. $(3 \times 3) + (3 \times 3) \qquad DC + B$ is defined, since dimensions are equal.

$\qquad\qquad\qquad\qquad\qquad$ Dimension is 3×3.

11. $\begin{bmatrix} 1 & 2 \\ 0 & 4 \end{bmatrix}\begin{bmatrix} 1 & 2 & 3 \\ -1 & 4 & -2 \end{bmatrix} = \begin{bmatrix} -1 & 10 & -1 \\ -4 & 16 & -8 \end{bmatrix}$

13. $\begin{bmatrix} 1 & 2 & 3 \\ -1 & 4 & -2 \end{bmatrix}\begin{bmatrix} 3 & 1 \\ 4 & -1 \\ 0 & 2 \end{bmatrix} = \begin{bmatrix} 11 & 5 \\ 13 & -9 \end{bmatrix}$

15. $\left(\begin{bmatrix} 1 & 0 & 4 \\ 0 & 1 & 2 \\ 0 & -1 & 1 \end{bmatrix} + \begin{bmatrix} 1 & 0 & 0 \\ 0 & 1 & 0 \\ 0 & 0 & 1 \end{bmatrix}\right)\begin{bmatrix} 3 & 1 \\ 4 & -1 \\ 0 & 2 \end{bmatrix} = \begin{bmatrix} 2 & 0 & 4 \\ 0 & 2 & 2 \\ 0 & -1 & 2 \end{bmatrix}\begin{bmatrix} 3 & 1 \\ 4 & -1 \\ 0 & 2 \end{bmatrix} = \begin{bmatrix} 6 & 10 \\ 8 & 2 \\ -4 & 5 \end{bmatrix}$

17. $\left(\begin{bmatrix} 1 & 0 & 4 \\ 0 & 1 & 2 \\ 0 & -1 & 1 \end{bmatrix}\begin{bmatrix} 3 & 1 \\ 4 & -1 \\ 0 & 2 \end{bmatrix}\right)\begin{bmatrix} 1 & 2 & 3 \\ -1 & 4 & -2 \end{bmatrix} = \begin{bmatrix} 3 & 9 \\ 4 & 3 \\ -4 & 3 \end{bmatrix}\begin{bmatrix} 1 & 2 & 3 \\ -1 & 4 & -2 \end{bmatrix} = \begin{bmatrix} -6 & 42 & -9 \\ 1 & 20 & 6 \\ -7 & 4 & -18 \end{bmatrix}$

19. $\begin{bmatrix} 3 & -1 \\ 4 & 2 \end{bmatrix}\begin{bmatrix} 1 & 0 \\ 0 & 1 \end{bmatrix} = \begin{bmatrix} 3 & -1 \\ 4 & 2 \end{bmatrix}$

21. $2\begin{bmatrix} 3 & -1 \\ 4 & 2 \end{bmatrix}\begin{bmatrix} 1 & 2 & 3 \\ -1 & 4 & -2 \end{bmatrix} = \begin{bmatrix} 6 & -2 \\ 8 & 4 \end{bmatrix}\begin{bmatrix} 1 & 2 & 3 \\ -1 & 4 & -2 \end{bmatrix} = \begin{bmatrix} 8 & 4 & 22 \\ 4 & 32 & 16 \end{bmatrix}$

23. $-5\begin{bmatrix} 3 & -1 \\ 4 & 2 \end{bmatrix} + \begin{bmatrix} 1 & 2 \\ 0 & 4 \end{bmatrix} = \begin{bmatrix} -15 & 5 \\ -20 & -10 \end{bmatrix} + \begin{bmatrix} 1 & 2 \\ 0 & 4 \end{bmatrix} = \begin{bmatrix} -14 & 7 \\ -20 & -6 \end{bmatrix}$

25. $\begin{bmatrix} 1 & 2 \\ 2 & 3 \end{bmatrix}\begin{bmatrix} -3 & 2 \\ 2 & -1 \end{bmatrix} = \begin{bmatrix} 1 & 0 \\ 0 & 1 \end{bmatrix} = I_2$

27. $\begin{bmatrix} -1 & -2 \\ 3 & 4 \end{bmatrix}\begin{bmatrix} 2 & 1 \\ -\frac{3}{2} & -\frac{1}{2} \end{bmatrix} = \begin{bmatrix} 1 & 0 \\ 0 & 1 \end{bmatrix} = I_2$

29. $\begin{bmatrix} 1 & 2 & 3 \\ 2 & 3 & 4 \\ 1 & 2 & 1 \end{bmatrix}\begin{bmatrix} -\frac{5}{2} & 2 & -\frac{1}{2} \\ 1 & -1 & 1 \\ \frac{1}{2} & 0 & -\frac{1}{2} \end{bmatrix} = \begin{bmatrix} 1 & 0 & 0 \\ 0 & 1 & 0 \\ 0 & 0 & 1 \end{bmatrix} = I_3$

31. $\begin{bmatrix} 1 & 1 \\ 1 & 2 \end{bmatrix}\begin{bmatrix} a & b \\ c & d \end{bmatrix} = \begin{bmatrix} a+c & b+d \\ a+2c & b+2d \end{bmatrix} = \begin{bmatrix} 1 & 0 \\ 0 & 1 \end{bmatrix}$; solve for a, b, c, d:

$\begin{matrix} a + c = 1 \\ a + 2c = 0 \end{matrix}\Big\} \begin{matrix} a = 2 \\ c = -1 \end{matrix} \qquad \begin{matrix} b + d = 0 \\ b + 2d = 1 \end{matrix}\Big\} \begin{matrix} b = -1 \\ d = 1 \end{matrix}$

$\begin{bmatrix} 1 & 1 \\ 1 & 2 \end{bmatrix}^{-1} = \begin{bmatrix} a & b \\ c & d \end{bmatrix} = \begin{bmatrix} 2 & -1 \\ -1 & 1 \end{bmatrix}$

33. $\begin{bmatrix} 3 & -2 \\ 0 & 2 \end{bmatrix}\begin{bmatrix} a & b \\ c & d \end{bmatrix} = \begin{bmatrix} 3a-2c & 3b-2d \\ 2c & 2d \end{bmatrix} = \begin{bmatrix} 1 & 0 \\ 0 & 1 \end{bmatrix}$

$\begin{matrix} 3a - 2c = 1 \\ 2c = 0 \end{matrix}\Big\} \begin{matrix} a = \frac{1}{3} \\ c = 0 \end{matrix} \qquad \begin{matrix} 3b - 2d = 0 \\ 2d = 1 \end{matrix}\Big\} \begin{matrix} b = \frac{1}{3} \\ d = \frac{1}{2} \end{matrix}$ Hence, $\begin{bmatrix} \frac{1}{3} & \frac{1}{3} \\ 0 & \frac{1}{2} \end{bmatrix}$ is the inverse of $\begin{bmatrix} 3 & -2 \\ 0 & 2 \end{bmatrix}$

35. $\begin{bmatrix} 3 & 2 \\ 6 & 4 \end{bmatrix}\begin{bmatrix} a & b \\ c & d \end{bmatrix} = \begin{bmatrix} 3a+2c & 3b+2d \\ 6a+4c & 6b+4d \end{bmatrix} = \begin{bmatrix} 1 & 0 \\ 0 & 1 \end{bmatrix}$

$\begin{matrix} 3a + 2c = 1 \\ 6a + 4c = 0 \end{matrix} \Longrightarrow \begin{matrix} a = -\frac{2}{3}c + \frac{1}{3} \\ a = -\frac{2}{3}c \end{matrix}$ No solution; hence, no inverse.

37. $AB = \begin{bmatrix} 1 & -1 \\ 2 & 0 \end{bmatrix}\begin{bmatrix} 3 & 2 \\ -1 & 4 \end{bmatrix} = \begin{bmatrix} 4 & -2 \\ 6 & 4 \end{bmatrix}$ $\qquad BA = \begin{bmatrix} 3 & 2 \\ -1 & 4 \end{bmatrix}\begin{bmatrix} 1 & -1 \\ 2 & 0 \end{bmatrix} = \begin{bmatrix} 7 & -3 \\ 7 & 1 \end{bmatrix}$

39. (a) $U + V = \begin{bmatrix} 2 \\ -1 \\ 3 \end{bmatrix} + \begin{bmatrix} \frac{1}{2} \\ 0 \\ 1 \end{bmatrix} = \begin{bmatrix} \frac{5}{2} \\ -1 \\ 4 \end{bmatrix}$ $\qquad$ (b) $U - V = \begin{bmatrix} 2 \\ -1 \\ 3 \end{bmatrix} - \begin{bmatrix} \frac{1}{2} \\ 0 \\ 1 \end{bmatrix} = \begin{bmatrix} \frac{3}{2} \\ -1 \\ 2 \end{bmatrix}$

(c) $\frac{1}{2}(U + V) = \frac{1}{2}\begin{bmatrix} \frac{5}{2} \\ -1 \\ 4 \end{bmatrix} = \begin{bmatrix} \frac{5}{4} \\ -\frac{1}{2} \\ 2 \end{bmatrix}$ $\qquad$ (d) $U + V - W = \begin{bmatrix} \frac{5}{2} \\ -1 \\ 4 \end{bmatrix} - \begin{bmatrix} -3 \\ -7 \\ 0 \end{bmatrix} = \begin{bmatrix} \frac{11}{2} \\ 6 \\ 4 \end{bmatrix}$

(e) $2U - 7V = \begin{bmatrix} 4 \\ -2 \\ 6 \end{bmatrix} - \begin{bmatrix} \frac{7}{2} \\ 0 \\ 7 \end{bmatrix} = \begin{bmatrix} \frac{1}{2} \\ -2 \\ -1 \end{bmatrix}$ $\qquad$ (f) $\frac{1}{4}U - \frac{1}{4}V - \frac{1}{4}W = \frac{1}{4}\left(\begin{bmatrix} \frac{3}{2} \\ -1 \\ 2 \end{bmatrix} - \begin{bmatrix} -3 \\ -7 \\ 0 \end{bmatrix}\right) = \begin{bmatrix} \frac{9}{8} \\ \frac{3}{2} \\ \frac{1}{2} \end{bmatrix}$

41. $\begin{bmatrix} a & b \\ c & d \end{bmatrix}\begin{bmatrix} 0 & 1 \\ 2 & -1 \end{bmatrix} = \begin{bmatrix} 2b & a-b \\ 2d & c-d \end{bmatrix} = \begin{bmatrix} 2 & 1 \\ -1 & 0 \end{bmatrix}$

$\begin{matrix} 2b = 2 \\ 2d = -1 \end{matrix} \qquad \begin{matrix} a - b = 1 \\ c - d = 0 \end{matrix} \qquad a = 2,\ b = 1,\ c = -\frac{1}{2},\ d = -\frac{1}{2}$ $\qquad$ Hence, $A = \begin{bmatrix} 2 & 1 \\ -\frac{1}{2} & -\frac{1}{2} \end{bmatrix}$.

43. $\begin{bmatrix} 1 & 2 & 5 \\ 2 & 4 & 10 \\ -1 & -2 & -5 \end{bmatrix}\begin{bmatrix} 1 & 2 & 5 \\ 2 & 4 & 10 \\ -1 & -2 & -5 \end{bmatrix} = \begin{bmatrix} 0 & 0 & 0 \\ 0 & 0 & 0 \\ 0 & 0 & 0 \end{bmatrix}$

45. $\begin{bmatrix} a & b \\ b & a \end{bmatrix}\begin{bmatrix} a & b \\ b & a \end{bmatrix} + A = \begin{bmatrix} a^2 + b^2 & 2ab \\ 2ab & a^2 + b^2 \end{bmatrix} + \begin{bmatrix} a & b \\ b & a \end{bmatrix} = \begin{bmatrix} a^2 + b^2 + a & 2ab + b \\ 2ab + b & a^2 + b^2 + a \end{bmatrix} = \mathbf{0}$

$2ab + b = 0 \Rightarrow b(2a + 1) = 0 \Rightarrow b = 0$ or $a = -\frac{1}{2}$

If $b = 0$, $a^2 + b^2 + a = 0 \Rightarrow a^2 + a = 0 \Rightarrow a(a + 1) = 0 \Rightarrow a = 0$ or $a = -1$

If $a = -\frac{1}{2}$, $a^2 + b^2 + a = 0 \Rightarrow b^2 = \frac{1}{4} \Rightarrow b = \frac{1}{2}$ or $b = -\frac{1}{2}$

The possibilities are: $a = 0$, $b = 0$; $a = -1$, $b = 0$; $a = -\frac{1}{2}$, $b = \frac{1}{2}$; $a = -\frac{1}{2}$, $b = -\frac{1}{2}$

47. $[x_1 \quad x_2]\begin{bmatrix} \frac{1}{2} & \frac{1}{2} \\ \frac{1}{4} & \frac{3}{4} \end{bmatrix} = [\frac{1}{2}x_1 + \frac{1}{4}x_2 \quad \frac{1}{2}x_1 + \frac{3}{4}x_2] = [x_1 \quad x_2]$

$\left.\begin{array}{l} \frac{1}{2}x_1 + \frac{1}{4}x_2 = x_1 \\ \frac{1}{2}x_1 + \frac{3}{4}x_2 = x_2 \end{array}\right\} \left.\begin{array}{l} x_2 = 2x_1 \\ x_1 + x_2 = 1 \end{array}\right\} x_1 = \frac{1}{3}, x_2 = \frac{2}{3}$

49. (a) PQ represents the matrix of raw material needed to fill order:

$[7 \quad 12 \quad 5]\begin{bmatrix} 2 & 3 & 1 & 12 \\ 7 & 9 & 5 & 20 \\ 8 & 12 & 6 & 15 \end{bmatrix} = [138 \quad 189 \quad 97 \quad 399]$

(b) QC represents the matrix of costs to produce each product:

$\begin{bmatrix} 2 & 3 & 1 & 12 \\ 7 & 9 & 5 & 20 \\ 8 & 12 & 6 & 15 \end{bmatrix}\begin{bmatrix} 10 \\ 12 \\ 15 \\ 20 \end{bmatrix} = \begin{bmatrix} 311 \\ 653 \\ 614 \end{bmatrix}$

(c) PQC represents the total cost to produce the order:

$[138 \quad 189 \quad 97 \quad 399]\begin{bmatrix} 10 \\ 12 \\ 15 \\ 20 \end{bmatrix} = 13{,}083$

51. $k(a_{ij} + b_{ij}) = ka_{ij} + kb_{ij}$

Exercise 4 (page 88)

1. $\begin{array}{l} R_1 = r_2 \\ R_2 = r_1 \end{array}$ Interchange rows **3.** $R_1 = 4r_1$ **5.** $\begin{bmatrix} 3 & 6 & 9 \\ 0 & 1 & 4 \\ 1 & 0 & 2 \end{bmatrix} \rightarrow \begin{bmatrix} 1 & 0 & 2 \\ 0 & 1 & 4 \\ 3 & 6 & 9 \end{bmatrix}$

7. $\begin{bmatrix} 3 & 6 & 9 \\ 0 & 1 & 4 \\ 1 & 0 & 2 \end{bmatrix} \rightarrow \begin{bmatrix} 0 & 6 & 3 \\ 0 & 1 & 4 \\ 1 & 0 & 2 \end{bmatrix}$ **9.** $\begin{bmatrix} 3 & 6 & 9 \\ 0 & 1 & 4 \\ 1 & 0 & 2 \end{bmatrix} \rightarrow \begin{bmatrix} 3 & 6 & 9 \\ 1 & 3 & 7 \\ 1 & 0 & 2 \end{bmatrix}$

11. $\begin{bmatrix} 1 & 1 & | & 6 \\ 2 & -1 & | & 0 \end{bmatrix} \xrightarrow{-2r_1 + r_2} \begin{bmatrix} 1 & 1 & | & 6 \\ 0 & -3 & | & -12 \end{bmatrix} \xrightarrow{-\frac{1}{3}r_2} \begin{bmatrix} 1 & 1 & | & 6 \\ 0 & 1 & | & 4 \end{bmatrix} \xrightarrow{-r_2 + r_1} \begin{bmatrix} 1 & 0 & | & 2 \\ 0 & 1 & | & 4 \end{bmatrix}$; $\begin{array}{l} x = 2 \\ y = 4 \end{array}$

13. $\begin{bmatrix} 2 & 1 & | & 5 \\ 1 & -1 & | & 1 \end{bmatrix} \rightarrow \begin{bmatrix} 1 & -1 & | & 1 \\ 2 & 1 & | & 5 \end{bmatrix} \xrightarrow{-2r_1 + r_2} \begin{bmatrix} 1 & -1 & | & 1 \\ 0 & 3 & | & 3 \end{bmatrix} \rightarrow \begin{bmatrix} 1 & -1 & | & 1 \\ 0 & 1 & | & 1 \end{bmatrix} \rightarrow \begin{bmatrix} 1 & 0 & | & 2 \\ 0 & 1 & | & 1 \end{bmatrix}$; $\begin{array}{l} x = 2 \\ y = 1 \end{array}$

15. $\begin{bmatrix} 2 & 3 & | & 7 \\ 3 & -1 & | & 5 \end{bmatrix} \xrightarrow{\frac{1}{2}r_1} \begin{bmatrix} 1 & 1.5 & | & 3.5 \\ 3 & -1 & | & 5 \end{bmatrix} \xrightarrow{-3r_1 + r_2} \begin{bmatrix} 1 & 1.5 & | & 3.5 \\ 0 & -5.5 & | & -5.5 \end{bmatrix} \rightarrow \begin{bmatrix} 1 & 1.5 & | & 3.5 \\ 0 & 1 & | & 1 \end{bmatrix} \rightarrow \begin{bmatrix} 1 & 0 & | & 2 \\ 0 & 1 & | & 1 \end{bmatrix}$; $\begin{array}{l} x = 2 \\ y = 1 \end{array}$

17. $\begin{bmatrix} 5 & -7 & | & 31 \\ 3 & 2 & | & 0 \end{bmatrix} \xrightarrow{\frac{1}{5}r_1} \begin{bmatrix} 1 & -1.4 & | & 6.2 \\ 3 & 2 & | & 0 \end{bmatrix} \xrightarrow{-3r_1 + r_2} \begin{bmatrix} 1 & -1.4 & | & 6.2 \\ 0 & 6.2 & | & -18.6 \end{bmatrix} \rightarrow$

$\begin{bmatrix} 1 & -1.4 & | & 6.2 \\ 0 & 1 & | & -3 \end{bmatrix} \xrightarrow{1.4r_2 + r_1} \begin{bmatrix} 1 & 0 & | & 2 \\ 0 & 1 & | & -3 \end{bmatrix}$; $\begin{array}{l} x = 2 \\ y = -3 \end{array}$

19. $\begin{bmatrix} 2 & -3 & | & 0 \\ 4 & 9 & | & 5 \end{bmatrix} \xrightarrow{-2r_1 + r_2} \begin{bmatrix} 2 & -3 & | & 0 \\ 0 & 15 & | & 5 \end{bmatrix} \to \begin{bmatrix} 2 & -3 & | & 0 \\ 0 & 1 & | & \frac{1}{3} \end{bmatrix} \to \begin{bmatrix} 2 & 0 & | & 1 \\ 0 & 1 & | & \frac{1}{3} \end{bmatrix} \to \begin{bmatrix} 1 & 0 & | & \frac{1}{2} \\ 0 & 1 & | & \frac{1}{3} \end{bmatrix};$ $\begin{aligned} x &= \frac{1}{2} \\ y &= \frac{1}{3} \end{aligned}$

21. $\begin{bmatrix} 4 & -3 & | & 4 \\ 2 & 6 & | & 7 \end{bmatrix} \xrightarrow{-2r_2 + r_1} \begin{bmatrix} 0 & -15 & | & -10 \\ 2 & 6 & | & 7 \end{bmatrix} \xrightarrow[\frac{1}{2}r_2]{-\frac{1}{15}r_1} \begin{bmatrix} 0 & 1 & | & \frac{2}{3} \\ 1 & 3 & | & \frac{7}{2} \end{bmatrix} \to \begin{bmatrix} 1 & 3 & | & \frac{7}{2} \\ 0 & 1 & | & \frac{2}{3} \end{bmatrix} \xrightarrow{-3r_2 + r_1} \begin{bmatrix} 1 & 0 & | & \frac{3}{2} \\ 0 & 1 & | & \frac{2}{3} \end{bmatrix};$ $\begin{aligned} x &= \frac{3}{2} \\ y &= \frac{2}{3} \end{aligned}$

23. $\begin{bmatrix} \frac{1}{2} & \frac{1}{3} & | & 2 \\ 1 & 1 & | & 5 \end{bmatrix} \to \begin{bmatrix} 1 & 1 & | & 5 \\ \frac{1}{2} & \frac{1}{3} & | & 2 \end{bmatrix} \xrightarrow{-\frac{1}{2}r_1 + r_2} \begin{bmatrix} 1 & 1 & | & 5 \\ 0 & -\frac{1}{6} & | & -\frac{1}{2} \end{bmatrix} \xrightarrow{-6r_2} \begin{bmatrix} 1 & 1 & | & 5 \\ 0 & 1 & | & 3 \end{bmatrix} \xrightarrow{-r_2 + r_1} \begin{bmatrix} 1 & 0 & | & 2 \\ 0 & 1 & | & 3 \end{bmatrix};$ $\begin{aligned} x &= 2 \\ y &= 3 \end{aligned}$

25. $\begin{bmatrix} 1 & 1 & | & 1 \\ 3 & -2 & | & \frac{4}{3} \end{bmatrix} \xrightarrow{-3r_1 + r_2} \begin{bmatrix} 1 & 1 & | & 1 \\ 0 & -5 & | & -\frac{5}{3} \end{bmatrix} \xrightarrow{-\frac{1}{5}r_2} \begin{bmatrix} 1 & 1 & | & 1 \\ 0 & 1 & | & \frac{1}{3} \end{bmatrix} \to \begin{bmatrix} 1 & 0 & | & \frac{2}{3} \\ 0 & 1 & | & \frac{1}{3} \end{bmatrix};$ $\begin{aligned} x &= \frac{2}{3} \\ y &= \frac{1}{3} \end{aligned}$

27. $\begin{bmatrix} 2 & 1 & 1 & | & 6 \\ 1 & -1 & -1 & | & -3 \\ 3 & 1 & 2 & | & 7 \end{bmatrix} \to \begin{bmatrix} 1 & -1 & -1 & | & -3 \\ 2 & 1 & 1 & | & 6 \\ 3 & 1 & 2 & | & 7 \end{bmatrix} \xrightarrow[-3r_1 + r_3]{-2r_1 + r_2} \begin{bmatrix} 1 & -1 & -1 & | & -3 \\ 0 & 3 & 3 & | & 12 \\ 0 & 4 & 5 & | & 16 \end{bmatrix} \to$

$\begin{bmatrix} 1 & -1 & -1 & | & -3 \\ 0 & 1 & 1 & | & 4 \\ 0 & 4 & 5 & | & 16 \end{bmatrix} \xrightarrow{-4r_2 + r_3} \begin{bmatrix} 1 & -1 & -1 & | & -3 \\ 0 & 1 & 1 & | & 4 \\ 0 & 0 & 1 & | & 0 \end{bmatrix} \xrightarrow[-r_3 + r_2]{r_2 + r_1} \begin{bmatrix} 1 & 0 & 0 & | & 1 \\ 0 & 1 & 0 & | & 4 \\ 0 & 0 & 1 & | & 0 \end{bmatrix};$ $\begin{aligned} x &= 1 \\ y &= 4 \\ z &= 0 \end{aligned}$

29. $\begin{bmatrix} 1 & 1 & -1 & | & -2 \\ 3 & 1 & 1 & | & 0 \\ 2 & -1 & 2 & | & 1 \end{bmatrix} \xrightarrow[-2r_1 + r_3]{-3r_1 + r_2} \begin{bmatrix} 1 & 1 & -1 & | & -2 \\ 0 & -2 & 4 & | & 6 \\ 0 & -3 & 4 & | & 5 \end{bmatrix} \xrightarrow{-\frac{1}{2}r_2} \begin{bmatrix} 1 & 1 & -1 & | & -2 \\ 0 & 1 & -2 & | & -3 \\ 0 & -3 & 4 & | & 5 \end{bmatrix} \xrightarrow[3r_2 + r_3]{-r_2 + r_1}$

$\begin{bmatrix} 1 & 0 & 1 & | & 1 \\ 0 & 1 & -2 & | & -3 \\ 0 & 0 & -2 & | & -4 \end{bmatrix} \xrightarrow{-\frac{1}{2}r_3} \begin{bmatrix} 1 & 0 & 1 & | & 1 \\ 0 & 1 & -2 & | & -3 \\ 0 & 0 & 1 & | & 2 \end{bmatrix} \xrightarrow[2r_3 + r_2]{-r_3 + r_1} \begin{bmatrix} 1 & 0 & 0 & | & -1 \\ 0 & 1 & 0 & | & 1 \\ 0 & 0 & 1 & | & 2 \end{bmatrix};$ $\begin{aligned} x &= -1 \\ y &= 1 \\ z &= 2 \end{aligned}$

31. $\begin{bmatrix} 2 & 1 & -1 & | & 2 \\ 1 & 3 & 2 & | & 1 \\ 1 & 1 & 1 & | & 2 \end{bmatrix} \to \begin{bmatrix} 1 & 3 & 2 & | & 1 \\ 2 & 1 & -1 & | & 2 \\ 1 & 1 & 1 & | & 2 \end{bmatrix} \xrightarrow[-r_1 + r_3]{-2r_1 + r_2} \begin{bmatrix} 1 & 3 & 2 & | & 1 \\ 0 & -5 & -5 & | & 0 \\ 0 & -2 & -1 & | & 1 \end{bmatrix} \xrightarrow{-\frac{1}{5}r_2}$

$\begin{bmatrix} 1 & 3 & 2 & | & 1 \\ 0 & 1 & 1 & | & 0 \\ 0 & -2 & -1 & | & 1 \end{bmatrix} \xrightarrow[2r_2 + r_3]{-3r_2 + r_1} \begin{bmatrix} 1 & 0 & -1 & | & 1 \\ 0 & 1 & 1 & | & 0 \\ 0 & 0 & 1 & | & 1 \end{bmatrix} \xrightarrow[-r_3 + r_2]{r_3 + r_1} \begin{bmatrix} 1 & 0 & 0 & | & 2 \\ 0 & 1 & 0 & | & -1 \\ 0 & 0 & 1 & | & 1 \end{bmatrix};$ $\begin{aligned} x &= 2 \\ y &= -1 \\ z &= 1 \end{aligned}$

33. $\begin{bmatrix} 1 & 1 & -1 & | & 0 \\ 2 & 4 & -4 & | & -1 \\ 2 & 1 & 1 & | & 2 \end{bmatrix} \xrightarrow[-2r_1 + r_3]{-2r_1 + r_2} \begin{bmatrix} 1 & 1 & -1 & | & 0 \\ 0 & 2 & -2 & | & -1 \\ 0 & -1 & 3 & | & 2 \end{bmatrix} \xrightarrow{\frac{1}{2}r_2} \begin{bmatrix} 1 & 1 & -1 & | & 0 \\ 0 & 1 & -1 & | & -0.5 \\ 0 & -1 & 3 & | & 2 \end{bmatrix} \xrightarrow[r_2 + r_3]{-r_2 + r_1}$

$\begin{bmatrix} 1 & 0 & 0 & | & 0.5 \\ 0 & 1 & -1 & | & -0.5 \\ 0 & 0 & 2 & | & 1.5 \end{bmatrix} \xrightarrow{0.5r_3} \begin{bmatrix} 1 & 0 & 0 & | & 0.5 \\ 0 & 1 & -1 & | & -0.5 \\ 0 & 0 & 1 & | & 0.75 \end{bmatrix} \xrightarrow{r_3 + r_2} \begin{bmatrix} 1 & 0 & 0 & | & 0.5 \\ 0 & 1 & 0 & | & 0.25 \\ 0 & 0 & 1 & | & 0.75 \end{bmatrix};$ $\begin{aligned} x &= 0.5 \\ y &= 0.25 \\ z &= 0.75 \end{aligned}$

35. $\begin{bmatrix} 3 & 1 & -1 & | & \frac{2}{3} \\ 2 & -1 & 1 & | & 1 \\ 4 & 2 & 0 & | & \frac{8}{3} \end{bmatrix} \xrightarrow{\frac{1}{3}r_1} \begin{bmatrix} 1 & \frac{1}{3} & -\frac{1}{3} & | & \frac{2}{9} \\ 2 & -1 & 1 & | & 1 \\ 4 & 2 & 0 & | & \frac{8}{3} \end{bmatrix} \xrightarrow[-4r_1 + r_3]{-2r_1 + r_2} \begin{bmatrix} 1 & \frac{1}{3} & -\frac{1}{3} & | & \frac{2}{9} \\ 0 & -\frac{5}{3} & \frac{5}{3} & | & \frac{5}{9} \\ 0 & \frac{2}{3} & \frac{4}{3} & | & \frac{16}{9} \end{bmatrix} \xrightarrow{-\frac{3}{5}r_2}$

$\begin{bmatrix} 1 & \frac{1}{3} & -\frac{1}{3} & | & \frac{2}{9} \\ 0 & 1 & -1 & | & -\frac{1}{3} \\ 0 & (\frac{2}{3}) & \frac{4}{3} & | & \frac{16}{9} \end{bmatrix} \xrightarrow[-\frac{2}{3}r_2 + r_3]{-\frac{1}{3}r_2 + r_1} \begin{bmatrix} 1 & 0 & 0 & | & \frac{1}{3} \\ 0 & 1 & -1 & | & -\frac{1}{3} \\ 0 & 0 & 2 & | & 2 \end{bmatrix} \xrightarrow{\frac{1}{2}r_3}$

$\begin{bmatrix} 1 & 0 & 0 & | & \frac{1}{3} \\ 0 & 1 & -1 & | & -\frac{1}{3} \\ 0 & 0 & 1 & | & 1 \end{bmatrix} \xrightarrow{r_3 + r_2} \begin{bmatrix} 1 & 0 & 0 & | & \frac{1}{3} \\ 0 & 1 & 0 & | & \frac{2}{3} \\ 0 & 0 & 1 & | & 1 \end{bmatrix};$ $\begin{aligned} x &= \frac{1}{3} \\ y &= \frac{2}{3} \\ z &= 1 \end{aligned}$

37.
$$\begin{bmatrix} 1 & 1 & 1 & 1 & | & 4 \\ 2 & -1 & 1 & 0 & | & 0 \\ 3 & 2 & 1 & -1 & | & 6 \\ 1 & -2 & -2 & 2 & | & -1 \end{bmatrix} \xrightarrow[\substack{-2r_1+r_2 \\ -3r_1+r_3 \\ -r_1+r_4}]{} \begin{bmatrix} 1 & 1 & 1 & 1 & | & 4 \\ 0 & -3 & -1 & -2 & | & -8 \\ 0 & -1 & -2 & -4 & | & -6 \\ 0 & -3 & -3 & 1 & | & -5 \end{bmatrix} \xrightarrow[-r_3]{} \begin{bmatrix} 1 & 1 & 1 & 1 & | & 4 \\ 0 & -3 & -1 & -2 & | & -8 \\ 0 & 1 & 2 & 4 & | & 6 \\ 0 & -3 & -3 & 1 & | & -5 \end{bmatrix} \xrightarrow[\substack{(r_3) \\ (r_2)}]{}$$

$$\begin{bmatrix} 1 & 1 & 1 & 1 & | & 4 \\ 0 & 1 & 2 & 4 & | & 6 \\ 0 & -3 & -1 & -2 & | & -8 \\ 0 & -3 & -3 & 1 & | & -5 \end{bmatrix} \xrightarrow[\substack{-r_2+r_1 \\ 3r_2+r_3 \\ 3r_2+r_4}]{} \begin{bmatrix} 1 & 0 & -1 & -3 & | & -2 \\ 0 & 1 & 2 & 4 & | & 6 \\ 0 & 0 & 5 & 10 & | & 10 \\ 0 & 0 & 3 & 13 & | & 13 \end{bmatrix} \xrightarrow[\frac{1}{5}r_3]{} \begin{bmatrix} 1 & 0 & -1 & -3 & | & -2 \\ 0 & 1 & 2 & 4 & | & 6 \\ 0 & 0 & 1 & 2 & | & 2 \\ 0 & 0 & 3 & 13 & | & 13 \end{bmatrix} \xrightarrow[\substack{r_3+r_1 \\ -2r_3+r_2 \\ -3r_3+r_4}]{}$$

$$\begin{bmatrix} 1 & 0 & 0 & -1 & | & 0 \\ 0 & 1 & 0 & 0 & | & 2 \\ 0 & 0 & 1 & 2 & | & 2 \\ 0 & 0 & 0 & 7 & | & 7 \end{bmatrix} \xrightarrow[\frac{1}{7}r_4]{} \begin{bmatrix} 1 & 0 & 0 & -1 & | & 0 \\ 0 & 1 & 0 & 0 & | & 2 \\ 0 & 0 & 1 & 2 & | & 2 \\ 0 & 0 & 0 & 1 & | & 1 \end{bmatrix} \xrightarrow[\substack{r_4+r_1 \\ -2r_4+r_3}]{} \begin{bmatrix} 1 & 0 & 0 & 0 & | & 1 \\ 0 & 1 & 0 & 0 & | & 2 \\ 0 & 0 & 1 & 0 & | & 0 \\ 0 & 0 & 0 & 1 & | & 1 \end{bmatrix} ; \begin{matrix} x=1 \\ y=2 \\ z=0 \\ w=1 \end{matrix}$$

39. $\begin{bmatrix} 1 & -1 & | & 5 \\ 2 & -2 & | & 6 \end{bmatrix} \to \begin{bmatrix} 1 & -1 & | & 5 \\ 0 & 0 & | & -4 \end{bmatrix}$; no solution

41. $\begin{bmatrix} 2 & -3 & | & 6 \\ 4 & -6 & | & 12 \end{bmatrix} \to \begin{bmatrix} 2 & -3 & | & 6 \\ 0 & 0 & | & 0 \end{bmatrix}$; infinitely many solutions $(2x - 3y = 6)$

43. $\begin{bmatrix} 5 & -6 & | & 1 \\ -10 & 12 & | & 0 \end{bmatrix} \to \begin{bmatrix} 5 & -6 & | & 1 \\ 0 & 0 & | & 2 \end{bmatrix}$; no solution

45. $\begin{bmatrix} 2 & 3 & | & 5 \\ 4 & 4 & | & 8 \end{bmatrix} \to \begin{bmatrix} 1 & 0 & | & 1 \\ 0 & 1 & | & 1 \end{bmatrix}$; unique solution $(x = 1, y = 1)$

47. $\begin{bmatrix} 2 & -1 & -1 & | & 0 \\ 1 & -1 & -1 & | & 1 \\ 3 & -1 & -1 & | & 2 \end{bmatrix} \to \begin{bmatrix} 1 & -1 & -1 & | & 1 \\ 2 & -1 & -1 & | & 0 \\ 3 & -1 & -1 & | & 2 \end{bmatrix} \xrightarrow[\substack{-2r_1+r_2 \\ -3r_1+r_3}]{} \begin{bmatrix} 1 & -1 & -1 & | & 1 \\ 0 & 1 & 1 & | & -2 \\ 0 & 2 & 2 & | & -1 \end{bmatrix} \xrightarrow[\substack{r_2+r_1 \\ -2r_2+r_3}]{}$

$\begin{bmatrix} 1 & 0 & 0 & | & -1 \\ 0 & 1 & 1 & | & -2 \\ 0 & 0 & 0 & | & 3 \end{bmatrix}$; no solution $(3 \neq 0)$

49. $\begin{bmatrix} 2 & -1 & 1 & | & 6 \\ 3 & -1 & 1 & | & 6 \\ 4 & -2 & 2 & | & 12 \end{bmatrix} \xrightarrow[\frac{1}{2}r_1]{} \begin{bmatrix} 1 & -0.5 & 0.5 & | & 3 \\ 3 & -1 & 1 & | & 6 \\ 4 & -2 & 2 & | & 12 \end{bmatrix} \xrightarrow[\substack{-3r_1+r_2 \\ -4r_1+r_3}]{} \begin{bmatrix} 1 & -0.5 & 0.5 & | & 3 \\ 0 & 0.5 & -0.5 & | & -3 \\ 0 & 0 & 0 & | & 0 \end{bmatrix} \xrightarrow[2r_2]{}$

$\begin{bmatrix} 1 & -0.5 & 0.5 & | & 3 \\ 0 & 1 & -1 & | & -6 \\ 0 & 0 & 0 & | & 0 \end{bmatrix} \xrightarrow[\frac{1}{2}r_2+r_1]{} \begin{bmatrix} 1 & 0 & 0 & | & 0 \\ 0 & 1 & -1 & | & -6 \\ 0 & 0 & 0 & | & 0 \end{bmatrix}$; infinitely many solutions $(x = 0, y = -6 + z)$

51. x = Amount invested at 6% $x + y + z = 5000$
y = Amount invested at 7% $0.06x + 0.07y + 0.08z = 358$
z = Amount invested at 8% $0.06x + 0.07y - 0.08z = 70$

$$\begin{bmatrix} 1 & 1 & 1 & | & 5000 \\ 0.06 & 0.07 & 0.08 & | & 358 \\ 0.06 & 0.07 & -0.08 & | & 70 \end{bmatrix} \to \begin{bmatrix} 1 & 1 & 1 & | & 5000 \\ 0 & 0.01 & 0.02 & | & 58 \\ 0 & 0.01 & -0.14 & | & -230 \end{bmatrix} \to \begin{bmatrix} 1 & 1 & 1 & | & 5000 \\ 0 & 1 & 2 & | & 5800 \\ 0 & 1 & -14 & | & -23,000 \end{bmatrix}$$

$$\to \begin{bmatrix} 1 & 0 & -1 & | & -800 \\ 0 & 1 & 2 & | & 5800 \\ 0 & 0 & -16 & | & -28,800 \end{bmatrix} \to \begin{bmatrix} 1 & 0 & -1 & | & -800 \\ 0 & 1 & 2 & | & 5800 \\ 0 & 0 & 1 & | & 1800 \end{bmatrix} \to \begin{bmatrix} 1 & 0 & 0 & | & 1000 \\ 0 & 1 & 0 & | & 2200 \\ 0 & 0 & 1 & | & 1800 \end{bmatrix}$$

$1000 invested at 6%; $2200 invested at 7%; $1800 invested at 8%

Exercise 5 (page 93)

1. $\begin{bmatrix} 2 & 5 & | & 1 & 0 \\ 1 & 3 & | & 0 & 1 \end{bmatrix} \to \begin{bmatrix} 1 & 3 & | & 0 & 1 \\ 2 & 5 & | & 1 & 0 \end{bmatrix} \to \begin{bmatrix} 1 & 3 & | & 0 & 1 \\ 0 & -1 & | & 1 & -2 \end{bmatrix} \to \begin{bmatrix} 1 & 0 & | & 3 & -5 \\ 0 & 1 & | & -1 & 2 \end{bmatrix}; \quad \begin{bmatrix} 2 & 5 \\ 1 & 3 \end{bmatrix}^{-1} = \begin{bmatrix} 3 & -5 \\ -1 & 2 \end{bmatrix}$

3. $\begin{bmatrix} 1 & -1 & | & 1 & 0 \\ 3 & -4 & | & 0 & 1 \end{bmatrix} \to \begin{bmatrix} 1 & -1 & | & 1 & 0 \\ 0 & -1 & | & -3 & 1 \end{bmatrix} \to \begin{bmatrix} 1 & 0 & | & 4 & -1 \\ 0 & 1 & | & 3 & -1 \end{bmatrix}; \quad \begin{bmatrix} 1 & -1 \\ 3 & -4 \end{bmatrix}^{-1} = \begin{bmatrix} 4 & -1 \\ 3 & -1 \end{bmatrix}$

5. $\begin{bmatrix} 2 & 1 & | & 1 & 0 \\ 4 & 3 & | & 0 & 1 \end{bmatrix} \to \begin{bmatrix} 2 & 1 & | & 1 & 0 \\ 0 & 1 & | & -2 & 1 \end{bmatrix} \to \begin{bmatrix} 2 & 0 & | & 3 & -1 \\ 0 & 1 & | & -2 & 1 \end{bmatrix} \to \begin{bmatrix} 1 & 0 & | & 1.5 & -0.5 \\ 0 & 1 & | & -2 & 1 \end{bmatrix};$

$\begin{bmatrix} 2 & 1 \\ 4 & 3 \end{bmatrix}^{-1} = \begin{bmatrix} 1.5 & -0.5 \\ -2 & 1 \end{bmatrix}$

7. $\begin{bmatrix} 0 & 0 & 1 & | & 1 & 0 & 0 \\ 0 & 1 & 0 & | & 0 & 1 & 0 \\ 1 & 0 & 0 & | & 0 & 0 & 1 \end{bmatrix} \to \begin{bmatrix} 1 & 0 & 0 & | & 0 & 0 & 1 \\ 0 & 1 & 0 & | & 0 & 1 & 0 \\ 0 & 0 & 1 & | & 1 & 0 & 0 \end{bmatrix}; \quad \begin{bmatrix} 0 & 0 & 1 \\ 0 & 1 & 0 \\ 1 & 0 & 0 \end{bmatrix}^{-1} = \begin{bmatrix} 0 & 0 & 1 \\ 0 & 1 & 0 \\ 1 & 0 & 0 \end{bmatrix}$

9. $\begin{bmatrix} 1 & 1 & -1 & | & 1 & 0 & 0 \\ 3 & -1 & 0 & | & 0 & 1 & 0 \\ 2 & -3 & 4 & | & 0 & 0 & 1 \end{bmatrix} \to \begin{bmatrix} 1 & 1 & -1 & | & 1 & 0 & 0 \\ 0 & -4 & 3 & | & -3 & 1 & 0 \\ 0 & -5 & 6 & | & -2 & 0 & 1 \end{bmatrix} \to$

$\begin{bmatrix} 1 & 1 & -1 & | & 1 & 0 & 0 \\ 0 & 1 & -0.75 & | & 0.75 & -0.25 & 0 \\ 0 & -5 & 6 & | & -2 & 0 & 1 \end{bmatrix} \to \begin{bmatrix} 1 & 0 & -0.25 & | & 0.25 & 0.25 & 0 \\ 0 & 1 & -0.75 & | & 0.75 & -0.25 & 0 \\ 0 & 0 & 2.25 & | & 1.75 & -1.25 & 1 \end{bmatrix} \to$

$\begin{bmatrix} 1 & 0 & -0.25 & | & 0.25 & 0.25 & 0 \\ 0 & 1 & -0.75 & | & 0.75 & -0.25 & 0 \\ 0 & 0 & 1 & | & \frac{7}{9} & -\frac{5}{9} & \frac{4}{9} \end{bmatrix} \to \begin{bmatrix} 1 & 0 & 0 & | & \frac{4}{9} & \frac{1}{9} & \frac{1}{9} \\ 0 & 1 & 0 & | & \frac{4}{3} & -\frac{2}{3} & \frac{1}{3} \\ 0 & 0 & 1 & | & \frac{7}{9} & -\frac{5}{9} & \frac{4}{9} \end{bmatrix};$

$\begin{bmatrix} 1 & 1 & -1 \\ 3 & -1 & 0 \\ 2 & -3 & 4 \end{bmatrix}^{-1} = \begin{bmatrix} \frac{4}{9} & \frac{1}{9} & \frac{1}{9} \\ \frac{4}{3} & -\frac{2}{3} & \frac{1}{3} \\ \frac{7}{9} & -\frac{5}{9} & \frac{4}{9} \end{bmatrix}$

11. $\begin{bmatrix} 1 & 1 & -1 & | & 1 & 0 & 0 \\ 2 & 1 & 1 & | & 0 & 1 & 0 \\ 1 & 0 & 1 & | & 0 & 0 & 1 \end{bmatrix} \to \begin{bmatrix} 1 & 1 & -1 & | & 1 & 0 & 0 \\ 0 & -1 & 3 & | & -2 & 1 & 0 \\ 0 & -1 & 2 & | & -1 & 0 & 1 \end{bmatrix} \to \begin{bmatrix} 1 & 0 & 2 & | & -1 & 1 & 0 \\ 0 & 1 & -3 & | & 2 & -1 & 0 \\ 0 & 0 & -1 & | & 1 & -1 & 1 \end{bmatrix} \to$

$\begin{bmatrix} 1 & 0 & 0 & | & 1 & -1 & 2 \\ 0 & 1 & 0 & | & -1 & 2 & -3 \\ 0 & 0 & 1 & | & -1 & 1 & -1 \end{bmatrix}; \quad \begin{bmatrix} 1 & 1 & -1 \\ 2 & 1 & 1 \\ 1 & 0 & 1 \end{bmatrix}^{-1} = \begin{bmatrix} 1 & -1 & 2 \\ -1 & 2 & -3 \\ -1 & 1 & -1 \end{bmatrix}$

13. $\begin{bmatrix} 1 & 1 & 0 & 0 & | & 1 & 0 & 0 & 0 \\ 0 & 1 & -1 & 1 & | & 0 & 1 & 0 & 0 \\ 1 & -1 & 1 & 1 & | & 0 & 0 & 1 & 0 \\ 0 & 1 & 0 & -1 & | & 0 & 0 & 0 & 1 \end{bmatrix} \to \begin{bmatrix} 1 & 1 & 0 & 0 & | & 1 & 0 & 0 & 0 \\ 0 & 1 & -1 & 1 & | & 0 & 1 & 0 & 0 \\ 0 & -2 & 1 & 1 & | & -1 & 0 & 1 & 0 \\ 0 & 1 & 0 & -1 & | & 0 & 0 & 0 & 1 \end{bmatrix} \to$

$\begin{bmatrix} 1 & 0 & 1 & -1 & | & 1 & -1 & 0 & 0 \\ 0 & 1 & -1 & 1 & | & 0 & 1 & 0 & 0 \\ 0 & 0 & -1 & 3 & | & -1 & 2 & 1 & 0 \\ 0 & 0 & 1 & -2 & | & 0 & -1 & 0 & 1 \end{bmatrix} \to \begin{bmatrix} 1 & 0 & 0 & 2 & | & 0 & 1 & 1 & 0 \\ 0 & 1 & 0 & -2 & | & 1 & -1 & -1 & 0 \\ 0 & 0 & 1 & -3 & | & 1 & -2 & -1 & 0 \\ 0 & 0 & 0 & 1 & | & -1 & 1 & 1 & 1 \end{bmatrix} \to$

$\begin{bmatrix} 1 & 0 & 0 & 0 & | & 2 & -1 & -1 & -2 \\ 0 & 1 & 0 & 0 & | & -1 & 1 & 1 & 2 \\ 0 & 0 & 1 & 0 & | & -2 & 1 & 2 & 3 \\ 0 & 0 & 0 & 1 & | & -1 & 1 & 1 & 1 \end{bmatrix}; \quad \begin{bmatrix} 1 & 1 & 0 & 0 \\ 0 & 1 & -1 & 1 \\ 1 & -1 & 1 & 1 \\ 0 & 1 & 0 & -1 \end{bmatrix}^{-1} = \begin{bmatrix} 2 & -1 & -1 & -2 \\ -1 & 1 & 1 & 2 \\ -2 & 1 & 2 & 3 \\ -1 & 1 & 1 & 1 \end{bmatrix}$

15. $\begin{bmatrix} 4 & 6 & | & 1 & 0 \\ 2 & 3 & | & 0 & 1 \end{bmatrix} \rightarrow \begin{bmatrix} 4 & 6 & | & 1 & 0 \\ \boxed{0 & 0} & | & -\frac{1}{2} & 0 \end{bmatrix}$ The 0's in row 2 indicate that I_2 cannot be obtained on the left side of the augmented matrix.

17. $\begin{bmatrix} -8 & 4 & | & 1 & 0 \\ -4 & 2 & | & 0 & 1 \end{bmatrix} \rightarrow \begin{bmatrix} -8 & 4 & | & 1 & 0 \\ \boxed{0 & 0} & | & -\frac{1}{2} & 0 \end{bmatrix}$

19. $\begin{bmatrix} 1 & 1 & 1 & | & 1 & 0 & 0 \\ 3 & -4 & 2 & | & 0 & 1 & 0 \\ \boxed{0 & 0 & 0} & | & 0 & 0 & 1 \end{bmatrix}$

21. $\begin{bmatrix} x \\ y \end{bmatrix} = \begin{bmatrix} 1 & 1 \\ 2 & -1 \end{bmatrix}^{-1} \begin{bmatrix} 6 \\ 0 \end{bmatrix} = \begin{bmatrix} \frac{1}{3} & \frac{1}{3} \\ \frac{2}{3} & -\frac{1}{3} \end{bmatrix} \begin{bmatrix} 6 \\ 0 \end{bmatrix} = \begin{bmatrix} 2 \\ 4 \end{bmatrix}; \quad x = 2, y = 4$

23. $\begin{bmatrix} x \\ y \end{bmatrix} = \begin{bmatrix} 2 & 3 \\ 3 & -1 \end{bmatrix}^{-1} \begin{bmatrix} 7 \\ 5 \end{bmatrix} = \begin{bmatrix} \frac{1}{11} & \frac{3}{11} \\ \frac{3}{11} & -\frac{2}{11} \end{bmatrix} \begin{bmatrix} 7 \\ 5 \end{bmatrix} = \begin{bmatrix} 2 \\ 1 \end{bmatrix}; \quad x = 2, y = 1$

25. $\begin{bmatrix} 2 & -3 \\ 4 & 9 \end{bmatrix}^{-1} \begin{bmatrix} 0 \\ 5 \end{bmatrix} = \begin{bmatrix} \frac{3}{10} & \frac{1}{10} \\ -\frac{2}{15} & \frac{1}{15} \end{bmatrix} \begin{bmatrix} 0 \\ 5 \end{bmatrix} = \begin{bmatrix} \frac{1}{2} \\ \frac{1}{3} \end{bmatrix}; \quad x = \frac{1}{2}, y = \frac{1}{3}$

27. $\begin{bmatrix} \frac{1}{2} & \frac{1}{3} \\ 1 & 1 \end{bmatrix}^{-1} \begin{bmatrix} 2 \\ 5 \end{bmatrix} = \begin{bmatrix} 6 & -2 \\ -6 & 3 \end{bmatrix} \begin{bmatrix} 2 \\ 5 \end{bmatrix} = \begin{bmatrix} 2 \\ 3 \end{bmatrix}; \quad x = 2, y = 3$

29. $\begin{bmatrix} 2 & 1 & 1 \\ 1 & -1 & -1 \\ 3 & 1 & 2 \end{bmatrix}^{-1} \begin{bmatrix} 6 \\ -3 \\ 7 \end{bmatrix} = \begin{bmatrix} \frac{1}{3} & \frac{1}{3} & 0 \\ \frac{5}{3} & -\frac{1}{3} & -1 \\ -\frac{4}{3} & -\frac{1}{3} & 1 \end{bmatrix} \begin{bmatrix} 6 \\ -3 \\ 7 \end{bmatrix} = \begin{bmatrix} 1 \\ 4 \\ 0 \end{bmatrix}; \quad x = 1, y = 4, z = 0$

31. $\begin{bmatrix} 2 & 1 & -1 \\ 1 & 3 & 2 \\ 1 & 1 & 1 \end{bmatrix}^{-1} \begin{bmatrix} 2 \\ 1 \\ 2 \end{bmatrix} = \begin{bmatrix} 0.2 & -0.4 & 1 \\ 0.2 & 0.6 & -1 \\ -0.4 & -0.2 & 1 \end{bmatrix} \begin{bmatrix} 2 \\ 1 \\ 2 \end{bmatrix} = \begin{bmatrix} 2 \\ -1 \\ 1 \end{bmatrix}; \quad x = 2, y = -1, z = 1$

33. $\begin{bmatrix} 3 & 1 & -1 \\ 2 & -1 & 1 \\ 4 & 2 & 0 \end{bmatrix}^{-1} \begin{bmatrix} \frac{2}{3} \\ 1 \\ \frac{8}{3} \end{bmatrix} = \begin{bmatrix} 0.2 & 0.2 & 0 \\ -0.4 & -0.4 & 0.5 \\ -0.8 & 0.2 & 0.5 \end{bmatrix} \begin{bmatrix} \frac{2}{3} \\ 1 \\ \frac{8}{3} \end{bmatrix} = \begin{bmatrix} \frac{1}{3} \\ \frac{2}{3} \\ 1 \end{bmatrix}; \quad x = \frac{1}{3}, y = \frac{2}{3}, z = 1$

35. $A^{-1} = \begin{bmatrix} 5 & -7 \\ -2 & 3 \end{bmatrix}; \quad \begin{bmatrix} 5 & -7 \\ -2 & 3 \end{bmatrix} \begin{bmatrix} 10 \\ 7 \end{bmatrix} = \begin{bmatrix} 1 \\ 1 \end{bmatrix}; \quad x = 1, y = 1$

37. $\begin{bmatrix} 5 & -7 \\ -2 & 3 \end{bmatrix} \begin{bmatrix} 13 \\ 9 \end{bmatrix} = \begin{bmatrix} 2 \\ 1 \end{bmatrix}; x = 2, y = 1$

39. $\begin{bmatrix} a & b \\ c & d \end{bmatrix} \begin{bmatrix} d & -b \\ -c & a \end{bmatrix} = \begin{bmatrix} ad - bc & 0 \\ 0 & -bc + ad \end{bmatrix} = \begin{bmatrix} \Delta & 0 \\ 0 & \Delta \end{bmatrix};$ thus, $\begin{bmatrix} a & b \\ c & d \end{bmatrix} \begin{bmatrix} \frac{d}{\Delta} & \frac{-b}{\Delta} \\ \frac{-c}{\Delta} & \frac{a}{\Delta} \end{bmatrix} = \begin{bmatrix} 1 & 0 \\ 0 & 1 \end{bmatrix}$

Exercise 6 (page 105)

1. Consistent; unique solution   **3.** Inconsistent   **5.** Consistent, solution not unique

7. $A|B = \begin{bmatrix} 1 & 1 & | & 3 \\ 2 & -1 & | & 3 \end{bmatrix} \rightarrow \begin{bmatrix} 1 & 1 & | & 3 \\ 0 & -3 & | & -3 \end{bmatrix} \rightarrow \begin{bmatrix} 1 & 1 & | & 3 \\ 0 & 1 & | & 1 \end{bmatrix} \rightarrow \begin{bmatrix} 1 & 0 & | & 2 \\ 0 & 1 & | & 1 \end{bmatrix}; x = 2, y = 1$

9. $A|B = \begin{bmatrix} 3 & -3 & | & 12 \\ 3 & 2 & | & -3 \end{bmatrix} \rightarrow \begin{bmatrix} 1 & -1 & | & 4 \\ 3 & 2 & | & -3 \end{bmatrix} \rightarrow \begin{bmatrix} 1 & -1 & | & 4 \\ 0 & 5 & | & -15 \end{bmatrix} \rightarrow \begin{bmatrix} 1 & -1 & | & 4 \\ 0 & 1 & | & -3 \end{bmatrix} \rightarrow \begin{bmatrix} 1 & 0 & | & 1 \\ 0 & 1 & | & -3 \end{bmatrix};$

$x = 1, y = -3$

11. $A|B = \begin{bmatrix} 3 & -4 & | & 1 \\ 5 & 2 & | & 19 \end{bmatrix} \rightarrow \begin{bmatrix} 3 & -4 & | & 1 \\ 2 & 6 & | & 18 \end{bmatrix} \rightarrow \begin{bmatrix} 1 & 3 & | & 9 \\ 3 & -4 & | & 1 \end{bmatrix} \rightarrow \begin{bmatrix} 1 & 3 & | & 9 \\ 0 & -13 & | & -26 \end{bmatrix} \rightarrow$

$\begin{bmatrix} 1 & 3 & | & 9 \\ 0 & 1 & | & 2 \end{bmatrix} \rightarrow \begin{bmatrix} 1 & 0 & | & 3 \\ 0 & 1 & | & 2 \end{bmatrix}$; $x_1 = 3$, $x_2 = 2$

13. $A|B = \begin{bmatrix} 2 & 3 & | & 5 \\ 2 & -1 & | & 7 \end{bmatrix} \rightarrow \begin{bmatrix} 1 & \frac{3}{2} & | & \frac{5}{2} \\ 2 & -1 & | & 7 \end{bmatrix} \rightarrow \begin{bmatrix} 1 & \frac{3}{2} & | & \frac{5}{2} \\ 0 & -4 & | & 2 \end{bmatrix} \rightarrow \begin{bmatrix} 1 & \frac{3}{2} & | & \frac{5}{2} \\ 0 & 1 & | & -\frac{1}{2} \end{bmatrix} \rightarrow \begin{bmatrix} 1 & 0 & | & \frac{13}{4} \\ 0 & 1 & | & -\frac{1}{2} \end{bmatrix}$;

$x_1 = \frac{13}{4}$, $x_2 = -\frac{1}{2}$

15. $A|B = \begin{bmatrix} 1 & -1 & 0 & | & 1 \\ 0 & 1 & -1 & | & 6 \\ 1 & 0 & 1 & | & -1 \end{bmatrix} \rightarrow \begin{bmatrix} 1 & -1 & 0 & | & 1 \\ 0 & 1 & -1 & | & 6 \\ 0 & 1 & 1 & | & -2 \end{bmatrix} \rightarrow \begin{bmatrix} 1 & 0 & -1 & | & 7 \\ 0 & 1 & -1 & | & 6 \\ 0 & 0 & 2 & | & -8 \end{bmatrix} \rightarrow \begin{bmatrix} 1 & 0 & -1 & | & 7 \\ 0 & 1 & -1 & | & 6 \\ 0 & 0 & 1 & | & -4 \end{bmatrix} \rightarrow$

$\begin{bmatrix} 1 & 0 & 0 & | & 3 \\ 0 & 1 & 0 & | & 2 \\ 0 & 0 & 1 & | & -4 \end{bmatrix}$; $x_1 = 3$, $x_2 = 2$, $x_3 = -4$

17. $A|B = \begin{bmatrix} 1 & 1 & 0 & 0 & | & 7 \\ 0 & 1 & -1 & 1 & | & 5 \\ 1 & -1 & 1 & 1 & | & 6 \\ 0 & 1 & 0 & -1 & | & 10 \end{bmatrix} \rightarrow \begin{bmatrix} 1 & 1 & 0 & 0 & | & 7 \\ 0 & 1 & -1 & 1 & | & 5 \\ 0 & -2 & 1 & 1 & | & -1 \\ 0 & 1 & 0 & -1 & | & 10 \end{bmatrix} \rightarrow \begin{bmatrix} 1 & 0 & 1 & -1 & | & 2 \\ 0 & 1 & -1 & 1 & | & 5 \\ 0 & 0 & -1 & 3 & | & 9 \\ 0 & 0 & 1 & -2 & | & 5 \end{bmatrix} \rightarrow$

$\begin{bmatrix} 1 & 0 & 0 & 2 & | & 11 \\ 0 & 1 & 0 & -2 & | & -4 \\ 0 & 0 & 1 & -3 & | & -9 \\ 0 & 0 & 0 & 1 & | & 14 \end{bmatrix} \rightarrow \begin{bmatrix} 1 & 0 & 0 & 0 & | & -17 \\ 0 & 1 & 0 & 0 & | & 24 \\ 0 & 0 & 1 & 0 & | & 33 \\ 0 & 0 & 0 & 1 & | & 14 \end{bmatrix}$; $x_1 = -17$, $x_2 = 24$, $x_3 = 33$, $x_4 = 14$

19. $A|B = \begin{bmatrix} 1 & 2 & 3 & -1 & | & 0 \\ 3 & 0 & 0 & -1 & | & 4 \\ 0 & 1 & -1 & -1 & | & 2 \end{bmatrix} \rightarrow \begin{bmatrix} 1 & 2 & 3 & -1 & | & 0 \\ 0 & -6 & -9 & 2 & | & 4 \\ 0 & 1 & -1 & -1 & | & 2 \end{bmatrix} \rightarrow \begin{bmatrix} 1 & 2 & 3 & -1 & | & 0 \\ 0 & 1 & -1 & -1 & | & 2 \\ 0 & -6 & -9 & 2 & | & 4 \end{bmatrix} \rightarrow$

$\begin{bmatrix} 1 & 0 & 5 & 1 & | & -4 \\ 0 & 1 & -1 & -1 & | & 2 \\ 0 & 0 & -15 & -4 & | & 16 \end{bmatrix} \rightarrow \begin{bmatrix} 1 & 0 & 5 & 1 & | & -4 \\ 0 & 1 & -1 & -1 & | & 2 \\ 0 & 0 & 1 & \frac{4}{15} & | & -\frac{16}{15} \end{bmatrix} \rightarrow \begin{bmatrix} 1 & 0 & 0 & -\frac{1}{3} & | & \frac{4}{3} \\ 0 & 1 & 0 & -\frac{11}{15} & | & \frac{14}{15} \\ 0 & 0 & 1 & \frac{4}{15} & | & -\frac{16}{15} \end{bmatrix}$

Rank $A = 3$; Rank $A|B = 3$; number of unknowns $= 4$
There are infinitely many solutions, and we can solve for x_1, x_2, and x_3 in terms of x_4:
$x_1 = \frac{4}{3} + \frac{1}{3}x_4$, $x_2 = \frac{14}{15} + \frac{11}{15}x_4$, $x_3 = -\frac{16}{15} - \frac{4}{15}x_4$

21. $A|B = \begin{bmatrix} 1 & -1 & 1 & | & 5 \\ 2 & -2 & 2 & | & 8 \end{bmatrix} \rightarrow \begin{bmatrix} 1 & -1 & 1 & | & 5 \\ 0 & 0 & 0 & | & -2 \end{bmatrix} \rightarrow \begin{bmatrix} 1 & -1 & 1 & | & 0 \\ 0 & 0 & 0 & | & 1 \end{bmatrix}$

The rank of the coefficient matrix is 1; the rank of the augmented matrix is 2. The system is inconsistent.

23. $A|B = \begin{bmatrix} 3 & -1 & 2 & | & 3 \\ 3 & 3 & 1 & | & 3 \\ 3 & -5 & 3 & | & 12 \end{bmatrix} \rightarrow \begin{bmatrix} 0 & -4 & 1 & | & 0 \\ 1 & 1 & \frac{1}{3} & | & 1 \\ 0 & -8 & 2 & | & 9 \end{bmatrix} \rightarrow \begin{bmatrix} 1 & 1 & \frac{1}{3} & | & 1 \\ 0 & -4 & 1 & | & 0 \\ 0 & -8 & 2 & | & 9 \end{bmatrix} \rightarrow$

$\begin{bmatrix} 1 & 1 & \frac{1}{3} & | & 1 \\ 0 & 1 & -\frac{1}{4} & | & 0 \\ 0 & -8 & 2 & | & 9 \end{bmatrix} \rightarrow \begin{bmatrix} 1 & 0 & \frac{7}{12} & | & 1 \\ 0 & 1 & -\frac{1}{4} & | & 0 \\ 0 & 0 & 0 & | & 9 \end{bmatrix} \rightarrow \begin{bmatrix} 1 & 0 & \frac{7}{12} & | & 0 \\ 0 & 1 & -\frac{1}{4} & | & 0 \\ 0 & 0 & 0 & | & 1 \end{bmatrix}$

The system is inconsistent since the rank of the coefficient matrix is 2 and the rank of the augmented matrix is 3.

Exercise 7.1 (page 111)

1. $A = \frac{1}{2}A + \frac{1}{3}B + \frac{1}{4}C$ $-\frac{1}{2}A + \frac{1}{3}B + \frac{1}{4}C = 0$
   $B = \frac{1}{4}A + \frac{1}{3}B + \frac{1}{4}C$ $\frac{1}{4}A - \frac{2}{3}B + \frac{1}{4}C = 0$
   $C = \frac{1}{4}A + \frac{1}{3}B + \frac{1}{2}C$ $\frac{1}{4}A + \frac{1}{3}B - \frac{1}{2}C = 0$

   The coefficient matrix for the homogeneous system is

$$\begin{bmatrix} -\frac{1}{2} & \frac{1}{3} & \frac{1}{4} \\ \frac{1}{4} & -\frac{2}{3} & \frac{1}{4} \\ \frac{1}{4} & \frac{1}{3} & -\frac{1}{2} \end{bmatrix} \rightarrow \begin{bmatrix} 1 & 0 & -1 \\ 0 & 1 & -\frac{3}{4} \\ 0 & 0 & 0 \end{bmatrix}; \quad A = C = \$10{,}000, \ B = \frac{3}{4}C = \$7500$$

3. $A = 0.2A + 0.3B + 0.1C$ $-0.8A + 0.3B + 0.1C = 0$
   $B = 0.6A + 0.4B + 0.2C$ $0.6A - 0.6B + 0.2C = 0$
   $C = 0.2A + 0.3B + 0.7C$ $0.2A + 0.3B - 0.3C = 0$

   The coefficient matrix is

$$\begin{bmatrix} -0.8 & 0.3 & 0.1 \\ 0.6 & -0.6 & 0.2 \\ 0.2 & 0.3 & -0.3 \end{bmatrix} \rightarrow \begin{bmatrix} 1 & 0 & -\frac{6}{15} \\ 0 & 1 & -\frac{11}{15} \\ 0 & 0 & 0 \end{bmatrix}; \quad A = \frac{6}{15}C, \ B = \frac{11}{15}C, \text{ where } C = \$10{,}000$$

5. $X = (I - A)^{-1} \cdot D_2 = \begin{bmatrix} 1.6048 & 0.3568 & 0.7131 \\ 0.2946 & 1.3363 & 0.3857 \\ 0.3660 & 0.2721 & 1.4013 \end{bmatrix} \begin{bmatrix} 80 \\ 90 \\ 60 \end{bmatrix} = \begin{bmatrix} 203.282 \\ 166.977 \\ 137.847 \end{bmatrix}$

7. Where x_1 = Farmer's income, x_2 = Builder's income, x_3 = Tailor's income, x_4 = Rancher's income, the system of equations is

   $x_1 = 0.3x_1 + 0.3x_2 + 0.3x_3 + 0.2x_4$
   $x_2 = 0.2x_1 + 0.3x_2 + 0.3x_3 + 0.2x_4$
   $x_3 = 0.2x_1 + 0.1x_2 + 0.1x_3 + 0.2x_4$
   $x_4 = 0.3x_1 + 0.3x_2 + 0.3x_3 + 0.4x_4$

   which we may write as

   $-0.7x_1 +\quad 0.3x_2 +\quad 0.3x_3 +\quad 0.2x_4 = 0$
   $0.2x_1 + (-0.7)x_2 +\quad 0.3x_3 +\quad 0.2x_4 = 0$
   $0.2x_1 +\quad 0.1x_2 + (-0.9)x_3 +\quad 0.2x_4 = 0$
   $0.3x_1 +\quad 0.3x_2 +\quad 0.3x_3 + (-0.6)x_4 = 0$

   The coefficient matrix is

$$\begin{bmatrix} -0.7 & 0.3 & 0.3 & 0.2 \\ 0.2 & -0.7 & 0.3 & 0.2 \\ 0.2 & 0.1 & -0.9 & 0.2 \\ 0.3 & 0.3 & 0.3 & -0.6 \end{bmatrix} \rightarrow \begin{bmatrix} 1 & 0 & 0 & -0.8 \\ 0 & 1 & 0 & -0.72 \\ 0 & 0 & 1 & -0.48 \\ 0 & 0 & 0 & 0 \end{bmatrix};$$

   $x_1 = 0.8x_4 = 8000, \ x_2 = 0.72x_4 = 7200, \ x_3 = 0.48x_4 = 4800, \ x_4 = \$10{,}000$

9. $A = \begin{bmatrix} \frac{3}{13} & \frac{4}{7} \\ \frac{2}{13} & \frac{1}{7} \end{bmatrix}; \quad [I - A]^{-1} = \begin{bmatrix} \frac{3}{2} & 1 \\ \frac{7}{26} & \frac{35}{26} \end{bmatrix}; \quad X = \begin{bmatrix} \frac{3}{2} & 1 \\ \frac{7}{26} & \frac{35}{26} \end{bmatrix}\begin{bmatrix} 80 \\ 40 \end{bmatrix} = \begin{bmatrix} 160 \\ 75.38 \end{bmatrix}$

Exercise 7.2 (page 115)

1. (a) (I)   41   23   70   45   41   23   62   41   64   36   19   11   59   39   7   4   94   60
         (II)   13   69   −21   20   98   −35   1   123   18   8   44   −13   1   32   0   1   141   24
   (b) (I)   85   50   71   43   90   54   99   61   43   24   59   32   45   24   69   41   67   43
         (II)   20   140   −27   15   153   −12   15   138   −16   5   62   −5   18   132   −21   13   139   −7

(c) (I) 64 36 49 31 75 47 65 37 72 43 75 47 57 35 77 46 95 57 24 13 39 22

(II) 20 93 −35 13 143 −7 19 141 −23 14 146 −9 9 120 −2 15 159 −11 9 89 −6
5 170 16

3. $A^{-1} = \begin{bmatrix} 1 & 0 & 0 \\ -13 & 1 & -5 \\ 2 & 0 & 1 \end{bmatrix}$; $A^{-1}\begin{bmatrix} 25 \\ 195 \\ -29 \end{bmatrix} = \begin{bmatrix} 25 \\ 15 \\ 21 \end{bmatrix} = \begin{bmatrix} Y \\ O \\ U \end{bmatrix}$; $A^{-1}\begin{bmatrix} 6 \\ 135 \\ 9 \end{bmatrix} = \begin{bmatrix} 6 \\ 12 \\ 21 \end{bmatrix} = \begin{bmatrix} F \\ L \\ U \end{bmatrix}$;

$A^{-1}\begin{bmatrix} 14 \\ 183 \\ -2 \end{bmatrix} = \begin{bmatrix} 14 \\ 11 \\ 26 \end{bmatrix} = \begin{bmatrix} N \\ K \\ Z \end{bmatrix}$; YOU FLUNK

Review Exercises (page 123)

1. $\begin{bmatrix} -1 & 3 & 16 \\ 3 & 15 & 8 \\ 5 & 10 & 29 \end{bmatrix}$ **3.** $\begin{bmatrix} -3 & 9 & 48 \\ 9 & 45 & 24 \\ 15 & 30 & 87 \end{bmatrix}$ **5.** $\begin{bmatrix} -9 & -9 & -6 \\ -3 & 3 & -6 \\ -3 & -6 & 39 \end{bmatrix}$ **7.** $\begin{bmatrix} -20 & 0 & 70 \\ 10 & 80 & 30 \\ 20 & 40 & 210 \end{bmatrix}$

9. $\begin{bmatrix} -\frac{7}{2} & -\frac{3}{2} & \frac{25}{2} \\ 3 & \frac{9}{2} & \frac{11}{2} \\ -\frac{37}{2} & -10 & 19 \end{bmatrix}$ **11.** $\begin{bmatrix} 19 & 36 & 38 \\ 26 & 77 & 73 \\ 73 & 160 & 206 \end{bmatrix}$

13. $\begin{bmatrix} 3 & 3 & 2 \\ 1 & -1 & 2 \\ 1 & 2 & -13 \end{bmatrix}\begin{bmatrix} 0 & 1 & 2 \\ 0 & 5 & 1 \\ 8 & 7 & 9 \end{bmatrix} = \begin{bmatrix} 16 & 32 & 27 \\ 16 & 10 & 19 \\ -104 & -80 & -113 \end{bmatrix}$

15. $\left[\begin{array}{cc|cc} 3 & 0 & 1 & 0 \\ -2 & 1 & 0 & 1 \end{array}\right] \rightarrow \left[\begin{array}{cc|cc} 1 & 0 & \frac{1}{3} & 0 \\ -2 & 1 & 0 & 1 \end{array}\right] \rightarrow \left[\begin{array}{cc|cc} 1 & 0 & \frac{1}{3} & 0 \\ 0 & 1 & \frac{2}{3} & 1 \end{array}\right]$; $\begin{bmatrix} 3 & 0 \\ -2 & 1 \end{bmatrix}^{-1} = \begin{bmatrix} \frac{1}{3} & 0 \\ \frac{2}{3} & 1 \end{bmatrix}$

17. $\begin{bmatrix} 2 & 0 & 1 \\ 3 & 7 & -1 \\ 1 & 0 & 2 \end{bmatrix} \rightarrow \begin{bmatrix} 1 & 0 & 2 \\ 3 & 7 & -1 \\ 2 & 0 & 1 \end{bmatrix} \rightarrow \begin{bmatrix} 1 & 0 & 2 \\ 0 & 7 & -7 \\ 0 & 0 & -3 \end{bmatrix} \rightarrow \begin{bmatrix} 1 & 0 & 2 \\ 0 & 1 & -1 \\ 0 & 0 & 1 \end{bmatrix} \rightarrow \begin{bmatrix} 1 & 0 & 0 \\ 0 & 1 & 0 \\ 0 & 0 & 1 \end{bmatrix}$

19. $\left[\begin{array}{ccc|c} 2 & -1 & 1 & 1 \\ 1 & 1 & -1 & 2 \\ 3 & -1 & 1 & 0 \end{array}\right] \rightarrow \left[\begin{array}{ccc|c} 1 & 1 & -1 & 2 \\ 2 & -1 & 1 & 1 \\ 3 & -1 & 1 & 0 \end{array}\right] \rightarrow \left[\begin{array}{ccc|c} 1 & 1 & -1 & 2 \\ 0 & -3 & 3 & -3 \\ 0 & -4 & 4 & -6 \end{array}\right] \rightarrow \left[\begin{array}{ccc|c} 1 & 1 & -1 & 2 \\ 0 & 1 & -1 & 1 \\ 0 & 1 & -1 & \frac{3}{2} \end{array}\right] \rightarrow$

$\left[\begin{array}{ccc|c} 1 & 1 & -1 & 2 \\ 0 & 1 & -1 & 1 \\ \boxed{0} & 0 & 0 & \frac{1}{2} \end{array}\right]$

There is no solution.

21. $\begin{bmatrix} x & y \\ z & w \end{bmatrix}\begin{bmatrix} 1 & 1 \\ -1 & 1 \end{bmatrix} = \begin{bmatrix} 1 & 1 \\ -1 & 1 \end{bmatrix}\begin{bmatrix} x & y \\ z & w \end{bmatrix}$; $\begin{bmatrix} x-y & x+y \\ z-w & z+w \end{bmatrix} = \begin{bmatrix} x+z & y+w \\ -x+z & -y+w \end{bmatrix}$;

$y = -z, \; x = w$

23. $\begin{bmatrix} 2 & -3 \\ -1 & 2 \end{bmatrix}\begin{bmatrix} 11 \\ 7 \end{bmatrix} = \begin{bmatrix} 1 \\ 3 \end{bmatrix} = \begin{bmatrix} A \\ C \end{bmatrix}$; $\begin{bmatrix} 2 & -3 \\ -1 & 2 \end{bmatrix}\begin{bmatrix} 84 \\ 51 \end{bmatrix} = \begin{bmatrix} 15 \\ 18 \end{bmatrix} = \begin{bmatrix} O \\ R \end{bmatrix}$; $\begin{bmatrix} 2 & -3 \\ -1 & 2 \end{bmatrix}\begin{bmatrix} 51 \\ 28 \end{bmatrix} = \begin{bmatrix} 18 \\ 5 \end{bmatrix} = \begin{bmatrix} R \\ E \end{bmatrix}$;

$\begin{bmatrix} 2 & -3 \\ -1 & 2 \end{bmatrix}\begin{bmatrix} 66 \\ 43 \end{bmatrix} = \begin{bmatrix} 3 \\ 20 \end{bmatrix} = \begin{bmatrix} C \\ T \end{bmatrix}$; $\begin{bmatrix} 2 & -3 \\ -1 & 2 \end{bmatrix}\begin{bmatrix} 44 \\ 29 \end{bmatrix} = \begin{bmatrix} 1 \\ 14 \end{bmatrix} = \begin{bmatrix} A \\ N \end{bmatrix}$; $\begin{bmatrix} 2 & -3 \\ -1 & 2 \end{bmatrix}\begin{bmatrix} 107 \\ 65 \end{bmatrix} = \begin{bmatrix} 19 \\ 23 \end{bmatrix} = \begin{bmatrix} S \\ W \end{bmatrix}$;

$\begin{bmatrix} 2 & -3 \\ -1 & 2 \end{bmatrix}\begin{bmatrix} 64 \\ 41 \end{bmatrix} = \begin{bmatrix} 5 \\ 18 \end{bmatrix} = \begin{bmatrix} E \\ R \end{bmatrix}$; A CORRECT ANSWER

CHAPTER 3

Exercise 2 (page 142)

1. The vertices are $(2, 2)$, $(2, 7)$, $(7, 8)$, $(8, 1)$. Testing these in the objective equation $z = 2x + 3y$, we get:
$z = 2(2) + 3(2) = 4 + 6 = 10$
$z = 2(2) + 3(7) = 4 + 21 = 25$
$z = 2(7) + 3(8) = 14 + 24 = 38$
$z = 2(8) + 3(1) = 16 + 3 = 19$
The maximum is 38 at $(7, 8)$. The minimum is 10 at $(2, 2)$.

3. The vertices are $(2, 2)$, $(2, 7)$, $(7, 8)$, $(8, 1)$.
Testing these in the objective equation
$z = x + 8y$, we get:
$z = 2 + 8(2) = 2 + 16 = 18$
$z = 2 + 8(7) = 2 + 56 = 58$
$z = 7 + 8(8) = 7 + 64 = 71$
$z = 8 + 8(1) = 8 + 8 = 16$
The maximum is 71 at $(7, 8)$.
The minimum is 16 at $(8, 1)$.

5. The vertices are $(2, 2)$, $(2, 7)$, $(7, 8)$, $(8, 1)$.
Testing these in the objective equation
$z = x + 6y$, we get:
$z = 2 + 6(2) = 2 + 12 = 14$
$z = 2 + 6(7) = 2 + 42 = 44$
$z = 7 + 6(8) = 7 + 48 = 55$
$z = 8 + 6(1) = 8 + 6 = 14$
The maximum is 55 at $(7, 8)$.
The minimum is 14 at points on the line
segment joining $(2, 2)$ and $(8, 1)$.

7. The vertices are $(0, 0)$, $(0, 2)$, $(2, 0)$.
Testing these in the objective equation
$z = 5x + 7y$, we get:
$z = 5(0) + 7(0) = 0$
$z = 5(0) + 7(2) = 14$
$z = 5(2) + 7(0) = 10$
The maximum is 14 at $(0, 2)$.

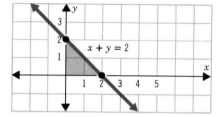

9. $x \geq 0$, $y \geq 0$
① $x + y \geq 2$
② $2x + 3y \leq 6$
The boundary lines for ① and ② intersect when
$\left. \begin{array}{l} x + y = 2 \\ 2x + 3y = 6 \end{array} \right\}$ $\left. \begin{array}{l} y = 2 - x \\ 2x + 3(2 - x) = 6 \end{array} \right\}$ $x = 0, y = 2$

The vertices are $(0, 2)$, $(2, 0)$, $(3, 0)$.
Testing these in the objective equation
$z = 5x + 7y$, we get:
$z = 5(0) + 7(2) = 14$
$z = 5(2) + 7(0) = 10$
$z = 5(3) + 7(0) = 15$
The maximum is 15 at $(3, 0)$.

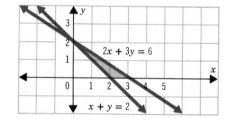

11. $x \geq 0$, $y \geq 0$
① $x + y \leq 8$ ③ $x + y \geq 2$
② $2x + y \leq 10$
The boundary lines for ① and ② cross the axes at $(8, 0)$, $(0, 8)$, $(5, 0)$, and $(0, 10)$. Of these, $(0, 8)$ and $(5, 0)$ are feasible [$(8, 0)$ does not obey ② and $(0, 10)$ does not obey ①]. The boundary lines for ① and ② intersect when
$\begin{array}{l} x + y = 8 \\ \underline{2x + y = 10} \\ \quad -x = -2 \end{array}$ $x = 2, y = 6$

The boundary line for ③ crosses the axes at $(2, 0)$ and $(0, 2)$

The vertices are $(0, 2)$, $(0, 8)$, $(2, 0)$, $(5, 0)$, $(2, 6)$.
Testing these in the objective equation
$z = 5x + 7y$, we get:
$z = 5(0) + 7(2) = 14$
$z = 5(0) + 7(8) = 56$
$z = 5(2) + 7(0) = 10$
$z = 5(5) + 7(0) = 25$
$z = 5(2) + 7(6) = 52$
The maximum is 56 at $(0, 8)$.

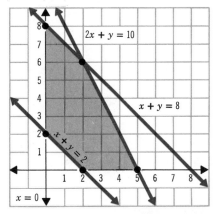

13. $z = 5x + 7y$ has no maximum under these conditions.

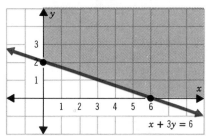

15. The vertices are $(0, 2)$, $(2, 0)$. Testing these in the objective equation
$z = 2x + 3y$, we get:
$z = 2(0) + 3(2) = 6$
$z = 2(2) + 3(0) = 4$
The minimum is 4 at $(2, 0)$.

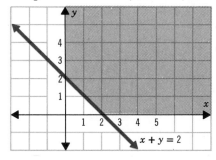

17. Four of the vertices lie on the axes. The other is found by solving
the two equations
$2x + 3y = 12$ ⎫ $2x + 3y = 12$
$3x + \ y = 12$ ⎭ $\underline{9x + 3y = 36}$
$\qquad\qquad\qquad 7x = 24$
$\qquad\qquad\qquad\ x = \frac{24}{7}$
$y = -3(\frac{24}{7}) + 12 = \frac{12}{7}$
The vertices are $(0, 2)$, $(0, 4)$, $(\frac{24}{7}, \frac{12}{7})$, $(4, 0)$, $(2, 0)$.
Testing these in the objective equation $z = 2x + 3y$, we get:
$z = 2(0) + 3(2) = 6$
$z = 2(0) + 3(4) = 12$
$z = 2(\frac{24}{7}) + 3(\frac{12}{7}) = \frac{84}{7} = 12$
$z = 2(4) + 3(0) = 8$
$z = 2(2) + 3(0) = 4$
The minimum is 4 at $(2, 0)$.

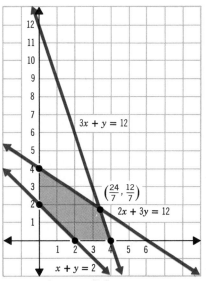

19. The vertices are $(0, \frac{1}{2})$, $(0, 5)$, $(10, 0)$, $(1, 0)$. Testing these in the objective equation $z = 2x + 3y$, we get:

$z = 2(0) + 3(\frac{1}{2}) = \frac{3}{2}$
$z = 2(0) + 3(5) = 15$
$z = 2(10) + 3(0) = 20$
$z = 2(1) + 3(0) = 2$
The minimum is $\frac{3}{2}$ at $(0, \frac{1}{2})$.

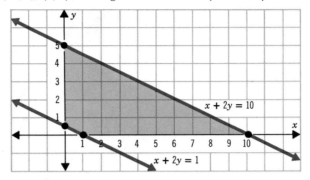

21. $\left. \begin{array}{l} x + 2y = 10 \\ 2x + y = 10 \end{array} \right\}$ $\begin{array}{l} x + 2y = 10 \\ \underline{4x + 2y = 20} \\ 3x = 10 \\ x = \frac{10}{3} \end{array}$

$y = -2(\frac{10}{3}) + 10 = \frac{10}{3}$
The vertices are $(0, 10)$, $(10, 0)$, $(\frac{10}{3}, \frac{10}{3})$.
Testing these in the objective equation $z = x + y$, we get:
$z = 0 + 10 = 10$
$z = 10 + 0 = 10$
$z = \frac{10}{3} + \frac{10}{3} = \frac{20}{3}$
The minimum is $\frac{20}{3}$ at $(\frac{10}{3}, \frac{10}{3})$.
The maximum is 10 at any point on the line segment between $(0, 10)$ and $(10, 0)$.

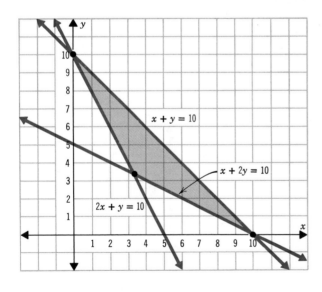

23. (See solution to Problem 21.)
$z = 5x + 2y$
$z = 0 + 2(10) = 20$
$z = 50 + 2(0) = 50$
$z = \frac{50}{3} + \frac{20}{3} = \frac{70}{3}$
The minimum is 20 at $(0, 10)$; the maximum is 50 at $(10, 0)$.

25. (See solution to Problem 21.)

$z = 3x + 4y$

$z = 3(0) + 4(10) = 40$

$z = 3(10) + 4(0) = 30$

$z = 3(\frac{10}{3}) + 4(\frac{10}{3}) = \frac{70}{3}$

The minimum is $\frac{70}{3}$ at $(\frac{10}{3}; \frac{10}{3})$; the maximum is 40 at $(0, 10)$.

27. $P = (\$0.30)x + (\$0.40)y$

$P_1 = 0.3(0) + 0.4(0) = 0$

$P_2 = 0.3(0) + 0.4(150) = \$60.00$

$P_3 = 0.3(160) + 0.4(0) = \$48.00$

$P_4 = 0.3(90) + 0.4(105) = \$69.00$

90 packages of the low-grade mixture and 105 packages of the high-grade mixture.

29. $P = \$4x + \$3y$

$P_1 = 4(0) + 3(0) = 0$

$P_2 = 4(0) + 3(30) = 90$

$P_3 = 4(40) + 3(0) = 160$

$P_4 = 4(20) + 3(20) = 140$

40 standard models and no deluxe models should be manufactured.

31. $x =$ Number of units of first product

$y =$ Number of units of second product

Maximize: $P = 40x + 60y$

Subject to: $x \geq 0, y \geq 0$

① $2x + y \leq 70$

② $x + y \leq 40$

③ $x + 3y \leq 90$

The boundary lines for ① and ② intersect at $(x, y) = (30, 10)$.

The boundary lines for ① and ③ intersect at $(x, y) = (24, 22)$, but this is not a feasible point (① is not satisfied).

The boundary lines for ② and ③ intersect at $(x, y) = (15, 25)$.

The vertices are $(0, 30)$, $(35, 0)$, $(30, 10)$, $(15, 25)$.

Testing each of these in the equation $P = 40x + 60y$, we get:

$P = 40(0) + 60(30) = 1800$

$P = 40(35) + 60(0) = 1400$

$P = 40(30) + 60(10) = 1800$

$P = 40(15) + 60(25) = 2100$

Thus, 15 units of the first product and 25 units of the second product maximizes profit at $2100.

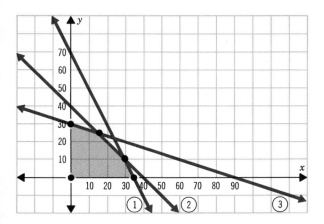

33. $x =$ Ounces of Supplement I
$y =$ Ounces of Supplement II
The problem is to minimize $C = (\$0.03)x + (\$0.04y)$
subject to $x \geq 0$, $y \geq 0$,

① $\quad 5x + 25y \geq 50 \quad$ or $\quad x + 5y \geq 10$
② $\quad 25x + 10y \geq 100 \quad$ or $\quad 5x + 2y \geq 20$
③ $\quad 10x + 10y \geq 60 \quad$ or $\quad x + y \geq 6$
④ $\quad 35x + 20y \geq 180 \quad$ or $\quad 7x + 4y \geq 36$

The vertices are $(0, 10)$, $(10, 0)$, $(5, 1)$, $(4, 2)$, $(\frac{4}{3}, \frac{20}{3})$.
$C_1 = 0.03(0) + 0.04(10) = \$0.40$
$C_2 = 0.03(10) + 0.04(0) = \$0.30$
$C_3 = 0.03(5) + 0.04(1) = \$0.19$
$C_4 = 0.03(4) + 0.04(2) = \$0.20$
$C_5 = 0.03(\frac{4}{3}) + 0.04(\frac{20}{3}) = \$0.307$
He should add 5 ounces of Supplement I and 1 ounce of Supplement II to each 100 ounces of feed.

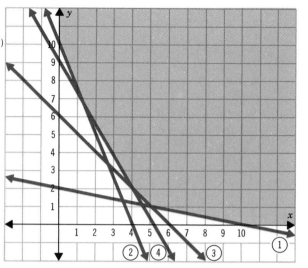

35. Let $P =$ Pounds of pork ground into hamburger and picnic patties
$CS =$ Pounds of chuck steak ground into hamburger and picnic patties
$RS =$ Pounds of round steak ground into hamburger and picnic patties
$x =$ Pounds of hamburger patties made
$y =$ Pounds of picnic patties made
We wish to maximize S, the amount of meat used to make the patties, namely,

$$S = P + CS + RS$$

where $P = 0.3y$, $CS = 0.6x + 0.5y$, $RS = 0.2x$

Thus, the problem is to maximize $S = 0.8x + 0.8y$ subject to
$x \geq 0$, $y \geq 0$,

① $\quad 0.3y \leq 150 \quad$ or $\quad y \leq 500$
② $\quad 0.6x + 0.5y \leq 300 \quad$ or $\quad 6x + 5y \leq 3000$
③ $\quad 0.2x \leq 80 \quad$ or $\quad x \leq 400$

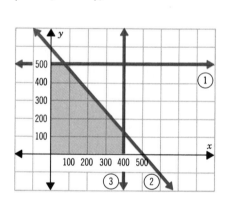

The vertices are $(0, 0)$, $(0, 500)$, $(83\frac{1}{3}, 500)$, $(400, 120)$, $(400, 0)$.
$S_1 = 0.8(0) + 0.8(0) = 0$
$S_2 = 0.8(0) + 0.8(500) = 400$
$S_3 = 0.8(83\frac{1}{3}) + 0.8(500) = 466.67$
$S_4 = 0.8(400) + 0.8(120) = 416$
$S_5 = 0.8(400) + 0.8(0) = 320$
500 pounds of picnic patties and $83\frac{1}{3}$ pounds of hamburger should be made.

37. Let $x =$ Number of rolls of high-grade carpet
$y =$ Number of rolls of low-grade carpet
$p =$ Selling price of high-grade carpet
Revenue $= px + 300y$
Income $I = (p - 420)x + 100y$
The vertices of the set of feasible solutions are $(0, 0)$, $(0, 25)$, $(15, 10)$, and $(20, 0)$; but $(15, 10)$ is the only vertex for which some of each type of carpet is produced. For the vertex $(15, 10)$ to be the one that maximizes I requires that the slope of the objective equation I lie between -1 and -2. Thus, $(p - 420)/(-100)$ must lie between -1 and -2. That is,

$$-2 \leq \frac{p - 420}{-100} \leq -1 \quad \text{or} \quad 100 \leq p - 420 \leq 200$$

The price of the high-grade carpet should be between \$520 and \$620 per roll.

Review Exercises (page 146)

1. (a) $z = 15x + 20y$
The vertices are $(0,0)$, $(0,3)$, $(4,0)$.
$z_1 = 15(0) + 20(0) = 0$
$z_2 = 15(0) + 20(3) = 60$
$z_3 = 15(4) + 20(0) = 60$
Maximum is 60 at any point on the line
$3x + 4y = 12$ between $(0,3)$ and $(4,0)$.
Minimum is 0 at $(0,0)$.

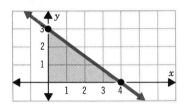

(b) $z = 15x + 20y$
The vertices are $(20,0)$, $(32,4)$, $(40,0)$.
$z_1 = 15(20) + 20(0) = 300$
$z_2 = 15(32) + 20(4) = 560$
$z_3 = 15(40) + 20(0) = 600$
Maximum is 600 at $(40,0)$.
Minimum is 300 at $(20,0)$.

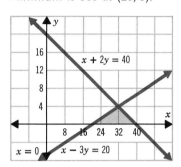

(c) $z = 15x + 20y$.
The vertices are $(0,0)$, $(0,9)$, $(4,5)$, $(6,0)$.
$z_1 = 15(0) + 20(0) = 0$
$z_2 = 15(0) + 20(9) = 180$
$z_3 = 15(4) + 20(5) = 160$
$z_4 = 15(6) + 20(0) = 90$
Maximum is 180 at $(0,9)$.
Minimum is 0 at $(0,0)$.

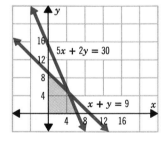

(d) $z = 15x + 20y$
The vertices are $(0,5)$, $(5,0)$, $(20,0)$, $(0,20)$.
$z_1 = 15(0) + 20(5) = 100$
$z_2 = 15(5) + 20(0) = 75$
$z_3 = 15(20) + 20(0) = 300$
$z_4 = 15(0) + 20(20) = 400$
Maximum is 400 at $(0,20)$.
Minimum is 75 at $(5,0)$.

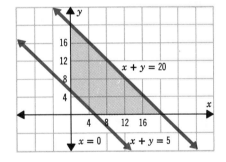

3. $x = $ Pounds of Food A
$y = $ Pounds of Food B
$C = $ Cost of the foods per month
The problem is to minimize $C = \$1.30x + \$0.80y$
subject to $x \geq 0$, $y \geq 0$,
① $5x + 2y \geq 60$
② $3x + 2y \geq 45$
③ $4x + y \geq 30$
The vertices are $(0,30)$, $(\frac{15}{2}, \frac{45}{4})$, $(15,0)$.
$C_1 = 1.3(0) + 0.8(30) = \$24$
$C_2 = 1.3(\frac{15}{2}) + 0.8(\frac{45}{4}) = \$18.75$
$C_3 = 1.3(15) + 0.8(0) = \$19.50$
She should buy 7.5 pounds of A and 11.25 pounds of B.

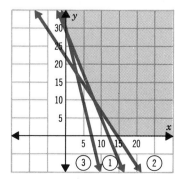

5. $x =$ Number of downhill skis
$y =$ Number of cross-country skis
Maximize $P = 70x + 50y$ subject to $x \geq 0$, $y \geq 0$, $2x + y \leq 40$, $x + y \leq 32$

Vertex	Profit
$(0, 0)$	$P = 0$
$(20, 0)$	$P = \$1400$
$(0, 32)$	$P = \$1600$
$(8, 24)$	$P = \$1760$

Maximum profit of $1760 with 8 downhill skis and 24 cross-country skies.

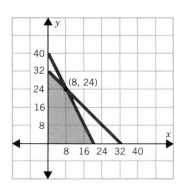

CHAPTER 4

Exercise 1 (page 157)

1. $5x_1 + 2x_2 + x_3 + x_4 = 20$, $x_4 \geq 0$
$6x_1 + x_2 + 4x_3 + x_5 = 24$, $x_5 \geq 0$
$x_1 + x_2 + 4x_3 + x_6 = 16$, $x_6 \geq 0$
$x_1 \geq 0$, $x_2 \geq 0$, $x_3 \geq 0$

$$\begin{array}{ccccccc} x_1 & x_2 & x_3 & x_4 & x_5 & x_6 & P \\ \left[\begin{array}{ccccccc|c} 5 & 2 & 1 & 1 & 0 & 0 & 0 & 20 \\ 6 & 1 & 4 & 0 & 1 & 0 & 0 & 24 \\ 1 & 1 & 4 & 0 & 0 & 1 & 0 & 16 \\ \hline -2 & -1 & -3 & 0 & 0 & 0 & 1 & 0 \end{array}\right] \end{array}$$

3. $2.2x_1 - 1.8x_2 + x_3 = 5$, $x_3 \geq 0$
$0.8x_1 + 1.2x_2 + x_4 = 2.5$, $x_4 \geq 0$
$x_1 + x_2 + x_5 = 0.1$, $x_5 \geq 0$
$x_1 \geq 0$, $x_2 \geq 0$

$$\begin{array}{cccccc} x_1 & x_2 & x_3 & x_4 & x_5 & P \\ \left[\begin{array}{cccccc|c} 2.2 & -1.8 & 1 & 0 & 0 & 0 & 5 \\ 0.8 & 1.2 & 0 & 1 & 0 & 0 & 2.5 \\ 1 & 1 & 0 & 0 & 1 & 0 & 0.1 \\ \hline -3 & -5 & 0 & 0 & 0 & 1 & 0 \end{array}\right] \end{array}$$

5. $x_1 + x_2 + x_3 + x_4 = 50$, $x_4 \geq 0$
$3x_1 + 2x_2 + x_3 + x_5 = 10$, $x_5 \geq 0$
$x_1 \geq 0$, $x_2 \geq 0$, $x_3 \geq 0$

$$\begin{array}{cccccc} x_1 & x_2 & x_3 & x_4 & x_5 & P \\ \left[\begin{array}{ccccc|c} 1 & 1 & 1 & 1 & 0 & 0 & 50 \\ 3 & 2 & 1 & 0 & 1 & 0 & 10 \\ \hline -2 & -3 & -1 & 0 & 0 & 1 & 0 \end{array}\right] \end{array}$$

7. $3x_1 + x_2 + 4x_3 + x_4 = 5$, $x_4 \geq 0$
$x_1 + x_2 + x_5 = 5$, $x_5 \geq 0$
$2x_1 - x_2 + x_3 + x_6 = 6$, $x_6 \geq 0$
$x_1 \geq 0$, $x_2 \geq 0$, $x_3 \geq 0$

$$\begin{array}{ccccccc} x_1 & x_2 & x_3 & x_4 & x_5 & x_6 & P \\ \left[\begin{array}{ccccccc|c} 3 & 1 & 4 & 1 & 0 & 0 & 0 & 5 \\ 1 & 1 & 0 & 0 & 1 & 0 & 0 & 5 \\ 2 & -1 & 1 & 0 & 0 & 1 & 0 & 6 \\ \hline -3 & -4 & -2 & 0 & 0 & 0 & 1 & 0 \end{array}\right] \end{array}$$

Exercise 2 (page 160)

1. x_1 x_2 x_3 x_4

$$\begin{bmatrix} 1 & ② & 1 & 0 & | & 300 \\ 3 & 2 & 0 & 1 & | & 480 \end{bmatrix} \quad \begin{array}{l} x_3 = 300 - x_1 - 2x_2 \\ x_4 = 480 - 3x_1 - 2x_2 \end{array}$$

$$\begin{bmatrix} \frac{1}{2} & 1 & \frac{1}{2} & 0 & | & 150 \\ 3 & 2 & 0 & 1 & | & 480 \end{bmatrix}$$

$$\begin{bmatrix} \frac{1}{2} & 1 & \frac{1}{2} & 0 & | & 150 \\ 2 & 0 & -1 & 1 & | & 180 \end{bmatrix} \quad \begin{array}{l} x_2 = 150 - \frac{1}{2}x_1 - \frac{1}{2}x_3 \\ x_4 = 180 - 2x_1 + x_3 \end{array}$$

3. x_1 x_2 x_3 x_4 x_5 x_6

$$\begin{array}{l} x_4 = 24 - x_1 - 2x_2 - 4x_3 \\ x_5 = 32 - 2x_1 + x_2 - x_3 \\ x_6 = 18 - 3x_1 - 2x_2 - 4x_3 \end{array}$$

$$\begin{bmatrix} 1 & 2 & 4 & 1 & 0 & 0 & | & 24 \\ 2 & -1 & 1 & 0 & 1 & 0 & | & 32 \\ 3 & ② & 4 & 0 & 0 & 1 & | & 18 \end{bmatrix}$$

$$\begin{bmatrix} -2 & 0 & 0 & 1 & 0 & -1 & | & 6 \\ 3.5 & 0 & 3 & 0 & 1 & 0.5 & | & 41 \\ 1.5 & 1 & 2 & 0 & 0 & 0.5 & | & 9 \end{bmatrix} \quad \begin{array}{l} x_4 = 6 + 2x_1 + x_6 \\ x_5 = 41 - 3.5x_1 - 3x_3 - 0.5x_6 \\ x_2 = 9 - 1.5x_1 - 2x_3 - 0.5x_6 \end{array}$$

5. x_1 x_2 x_3 x_4 x_5 x_6 x_7 x_8

$$\begin{array}{l} x_5 = 20 + 3x_1 - x_3 \\ x_6 = 24 - 2x_1 - x_4 \\ x_7 = 28 + 3x_2 - x_3 \\ x_8 = 24 + 3x_2 - x_4 \end{array}$$

$$\begin{bmatrix} -3 & 0 & 1 & 0 & 1 & 0 & 0 & 0 & | & 20 \\ ② & 0 & 0 & 1 & 0 & 1 & 0 & 0 & | & 24 \\ 0 & -3 & 1 & 0 & 0 & 0 & 1 & 0 & | & 28 \\ 0 & -3 & 0 & 1 & 0 & 0 & 0 & 1 & | & 24 \end{bmatrix}$$

$$\begin{bmatrix} -3 & 0 & 1 & 0 & 1 & 0 & 0 & 0 & | & 20 \\ 1 & 0 & 0 & \frac{1}{2} & 0 & \frac{1}{2} & 0 & 0 & | & 12 \\ 0 & -3 & 1 & 0 & 0 & 0 & 1 & 0 & | & 28 \\ 0 & -3 & 0 & 1 & 0 & 0 & 0 & 1 & | & 24 \end{bmatrix}$$

$$\begin{bmatrix} 0 & 0 & 1 & \frac{3}{2} & 1 & \frac{3}{2} & 0 & 0 & | & 56 \\ 1 & 0 & 0 & \frac{1}{2} & 0 & \frac{1}{2} & 0 & 0 & | & 12 \\ 0 & -3 & 1 & 0 & 0 & 0 & 1 & 0 & | & 28 \\ 0 & -3 & 0 & 1 & 0 & 0 & 0 & 1 & | & 24 \end{bmatrix} \quad \begin{array}{l} x_5 = 56 - x_3 - \frac{3}{2}x_4 - \frac{3}{2}x_6 \\ x_1 = 12 - \frac{1}{2}x_4 - \frac{1}{2}x_6 \\ x_7 = 28 + 3x_2 - x_3 \\ x_8 = 24 + 3x_2 - x_4 \end{array}$$

Exercise 3 (page 167)

1. (b) Requires additional pivoting; the pivot element is in row 1, column 1.
3. (a) Final tableau; $P = \frac{256}{7}$; $x_1 = \frac{32}{7}$, $x_2 = 0$
5. (c) No solution; all the entries in the pivot column are negative.

7. x_1 x_2 x_3 x_4

$$\begin{bmatrix} 2 & ③ & 1 & 0 & | & 12 \\ 3 & 1 & 0 & 1 & | & 12 \\ \hline -5 & -7 & 0 & 0 & | & 0 \end{bmatrix} \begin{array}{l} x_3 \\ x_4 \\ \end{array}$$

$$\begin{bmatrix} \frac{2}{3} & 1 & \frac{1}{3} & 0 & | & 4 \\ ⑦\!\!\!/\!\!\!_3 & 0 & -\frac{1}{3} & 1 & | & 8 \\ \hline -\frac{1}{3} & 0 & \frac{7}{3} & 0 & | & 28 \end{bmatrix} \begin{array}{l} x_2 \\ x_4 \\ \end{array}$$

$\downarrow$

9. x_1 x_2 x_3 x_4

$$\begin{bmatrix} 1 & ② & 1 & 0 & | & 2 \\ 2 & 1 & 0 & 1 & | & 2 \\ \hline -5 & -7 & 0 & 0 & | & 0 \end{bmatrix} \begin{array}{l} x_3 \\ x_4 \\ \end{array}$$

$$\begin{bmatrix} \frac{1}{2} & 1 & \frac{1}{2} & 0 & | & 1 \\ ③\!\!\!/\!\!\!_2 & 0 & -\frac{1}{2} & 1 & | & 1 \\ \hline -\frac{3}{2} & 0 & \frac{7}{2} & 0 & | & 7 \end{bmatrix} \begin{array}{l} x_2 \\ x_4 \\ \end{array}$$

$\downarrow$

$$
\begin{array}{cccc}
x_1 & x_2 & x_3 & x_4
\end{array}
$$

$$
\left[\begin{array}{cccc|c}
0 & 1 & \frac{3}{7} & -\frac{2}{7} & \frac{12}{7} \\
1 & 0 & -\frac{1}{7} & \frac{3}{7} & \frac{24}{7} \\
\hline
0 & 0 & \frac{16}{7} & \frac{1}{7} & \frac{204}{7}
\end{array}\right]
\begin{array}{c}
x_2 \\ x_1 \\ \\
\end{array}
$$

$P = \frac{204}{7}, \quad x_1 = \frac{24}{7}, \quad x_2 = \frac{12}{7}$

$$
\begin{array}{cccc}
x_1 & x_2 & x_3 & x_4
\end{array}
$$

$$
\left[\begin{array}{cccc|c}
0 & 1 & \frac{2}{3} & -\frac{1}{3} & \frac{2}{3} \\
1 & 0 & -\frac{1}{3} & \frac{2}{3} & \frac{2}{3} \\
\hline
0 & 0 & 3 & 1 & 8
\end{array}\right]
\begin{array}{c}
x_2 \\ x_1 \\ \\
\end{array}
$$

$P = 8, \quad x_1 = \frac{2}{3}, \quad x_2 = \frac{2}{3}$

11.
$$
\begin{array}{ccccc}
x_1 & x_2 & x_3 & x_4 & x_5
\end{array}
$$

$$
\left[\begin{array}{ccccc|c}
① & 1 & 1 & 0 & 0 & 2 \\
2 & 3 & 0 & 1 & 0 & 12 \\
3 & 1 & 0 & 0 & 1 & 12 \\
\hline
-3 & -1 & 0 & 0 & 0 & 0
\end{array}\right]
\begin{array}{c}
x_3 \\ x_4 \\ x_5 \\ \\
\end{array}
$$

$$
\left[\begin{array}{ccccc|c}
1 & 1 & 1 & 0 & 0 & 2 \\
0 & 1 & -2 & 1 & 0 & 8 \\
0 & -2 & -3 & 0 & 1 & 6 \\
\hline
0 & 2 & 3 & 0 & 0 & 6
\end{array}\right]
\begin{array}{c}
x_1 \\ x_4 \\ x_5 \\ \\
\end{array}
$$

$P = 6, \quad x_1 = 2, \quad x_2 = 0, \quad x_3 = 0$

13.
$$
\begin{array}{ccccc}
x_1 & x_2 & x_3 & x_4 & x_5
\end{array}
$$

$$
\left[\begin{array}{ccccc|c}
-2 & 1 & -2 & 1 & 0 & 4 \\
① & -2 & 1 & 0 & 1 & 2 \\
\hline
-2 & -1 & -1 & 0 & 0 & 0
\end{array}\right]
\begin{array}{c}
x_4 \\ x_5 \\ \\
\end{array}
$$

$$
\left[\begin{array}{ccccc|c}
0 & -3 & 0 & 1 & 2 & 8 \\
1 & -2 & 1 & 0 & 1 & 2 \\
\hline
0 & -5 & 1 & 0 & 2 & 4
\end{array}\right]
\begin{array}{c}
x_4 \\ x_1 \\ \\
\end{array}
$$

No solution, since all the ratios for column 2 are negative.

15.
$$
\begin{array}{ccccc}
x_1 & x_2 & x_3 & x_4 & x_5
\end{array}
$$

$$
\left[\begin{array}{ccccc|c}
1 & 2 & 1 & 1 & 0 & 25 \\
3 & 2 & ③ & 0 & 1 & 30 \\
\hline
-2 & -1 & -3 & 0 & 0 & 0
\end{array}\right]
\begin{array}{c}
x_4 \\ x_5 \\ \\
\end{array}
$$

$$
\left[\begin{array}{ccccc|c}
0 & \frac{4}{3} & 0 & 1 & -\frac{1}{3} & 15 \\
1 & \frac{2}{3} & 1 & 0 & \frac{1}{3} & 10 \\
\hline
1 & 1 & 0 & 0 & 1 & 30
\end{array}\right]
\begin{array}{c}
x_4 \\ x_3 \\ \\
\end{array}
$$

$P = 30, \quad x_1 = 0, \quad x_2 = 0, \quad x_3 = 10$

17.
$$
\begin{array}{ccccccc}
x_1 & x_2 & x_3 & x_4 & x_5 & x_6 & x_7
\end{array}
$$

$$
\left[\begin{array}{ccccccc|c}
2 & 1 & 2 & 3 & 1 & 0 & 0 & 12 \\
0 & ② & 1 & 2 & 0 & 1 & 0 & 20 \\
2 & 1 & 4 & 0 & 0 & 0 & 1 & 16 \\
\hline
-2 & -4 & -1 & -1 & 0 & 0 & 0 & 0
\end{array}\right]
\begin{array}{c}
x_5 \\ x_6 \\ x_7 \\ \\
\end{array}
$$

$$
\left[\begin{array}{ccccccc|c}
② & 0 & \frac{3}{2} & 2 & 1 & -\frac{1}{2} & 0 & 2 \\
0 & 1 & \frac{1}{2} & 1 & 0 & \frac{1}{2} & 0 & 10 \\
2 & 0 & \frac{7}{2} & -1 & 0 & -\frac{1}{2} & 1 & 6 \\
\hline
-2 & 0 & 1 & 3 & 0 & 2 & 0 & 40
\end{array}\right]
\begin{array}{c}
x_5 \\ x_2 \\ x_7 \\ \\
\end{array}
$$

$$
\left[\begin{array}{ccccccc|c}
1 & 0 & \frac{3}{4} & 1 & \frac{1}{2} & -\frac{1}{4} & 0 & 1 \\
0 & 1 & \frac{1}{2} & 1 & 0 & \frac{1}{2} & 0 & 10 \\
0 & 0 & 2 & -3 & -1 & 0 & 1 & 4 \\
\hline
0 & 0 & \frac{5}{2} & 5 & 1 & \frac{3}{2} & 0 & 42
\end{array}\right]
\begin{array}{c}
x_1 \\ x_2 \\ x_7 \\ \\
\end{array}
$$

$P = 42, \quad x_1 = 1, \quad x_2 = 10, \quad x_3 = 0, \quad x_4 = 0$

Exercise 4 (page 174)

1.
$$
\left[\begin{array}{cc|c}
1 & 1 & 2 \\
2 & 3 & 6 \\
\hline
2 & 3 & 0
\end{array}\right];
\left[\begin{array}{cc|c}
1 & 2 & 2 \\
1 & 3 & 3 \\
\hline
2 & 6 & 0
\end{array}\right]
$$

Dual problem:
Maximize $P = 2y_1 + 6y_2$ subject to $y_1 + 2y_2 \le 2$, $y_1 + 3y_2 \le 3$, $y_1 \ge 0$, $y_2 \ge 0$.

3. $\begin{bmatrix} 1 & 1 & 1 & | & 5 \\ 2 & 1 & 0 & | & 4 \\ \hline 3 & 1 & 1 & | & 0 \end{bmatrix}$; $\begin{bmatrix} 1 & 2 & | & 3 \\ 1 & 1 & | & 1 \\ 1 & 0 & | & 1 \\ \hline 5 & 4 & | & 0 \end{bmatrix}$

Dual problem:
Maximize $P = 5y_1 + 4y$ subject to $y_1 + 2y_2 \le 3$, $y_1 + y_2 \le 1$, $y_1 \le 1$, $y_1 \ge 0, y_2 \ge 0$.

5. $\begin{bmatrix} 1 & 1 & | & 2 \\ 2 & 6 & | & 6 \\ \hline 6 & 3 & | & 0 \end{bmatrix}$; $\begin{bmatrix} 1 & 2 & | & 6 \\ 1 & 6 & | & 3 \\ \hline 2 & 6 & | & 0 \end{bmatrix}$

Dual problem:
Maximize $P = 2y_1 + 6y_2$ subject to $y_1 + 2y_2 \le 6$, $y_1 + 6y_2 \le 3$, $y_1 \ge 0, y_2 \ge 0$.

$$\begin{array}{cccc} y_1 & y_2 & u_1 & u_2 \end{array}$$
$$\begin{bmatrix} 1 & 2 & | & 1 & 0 & | & 6 \\ 1 & ⑥ & | & 0 & 1 & | & 3 \\ \hline -2 & -6 & | & 0 & 0 & | & 0 \end{bmatrix} \begin{array}{c} u_1 \\ u_2 \end{array}$$

$$\begin{bmatrix} \frac{2}{3} & 0 & | & 1 & -\frac{1}{3} & | & 5 \\ ⑴⁄₆ & 1 & | & 0 & \frac{1}{6} & | & \frac{1}{2} \\ \hline -1 & 0 & | & 0 & 1 & | & 3 \end{bmatrix} \begin{array}{c} u_1 \\ y_2 \end{array}$$

$$\begin{bmatrix} 0 & -4 & | & 1 & -1 & | & 3 \\ 1 & 6 & | & 0 & 1 & | & 3 \\ \hline 0 & 6 & | & 0 & 2 & | & 6 \end{bmatrix} \begin{array}{c} u_1 \\ y_1 \end{array}$$

$C = 6, \quad x_1 = 0, \quad x_2 = 2$

7. $\begin{bmatrix} 1 & 1 & | & 4 \\ 3 & 4 & | & 12 \\ \hline 6 & 3 & | & 0 \end{bmatrix}$; $\begin{bmatrix} 1 & 3 & | & 6 \\ 1 & 4 & | & 3 \\ \hline 4 & 12 & | & 0 \end{bmatrix}$

Dual problem:
Maximize $P = 4y_1 + 12y_2$ subject to $y_1 + 3y_2 \le 6$, $y_1 + 4y_2 \le 3$, $y_1 \ge 0$, $y_2 \ge 0$.

$$\begin{array}{cccc} y_1 & y_2 & u_1 & u_2 \end{array}$$
$$\begin{bmatrix} 1 & 3 & | & 1 & 0 & | & 6 \\ 1 & ④ & | & 0 & 1 & | & 3 \\ \hline -4 & -12 & | & 0 & 0 & | & 0 \end{bmatrix} \begin{array}{c} u_1 \\ u_2 \end{array}$$

$$\begin{bmatrix} \frac{1}{4} & 0 & | & 1 & -\frac{3}{4} & | & \frac{15}{4} \\ ⑴⁄₄ & 1 & | & 0 & \frac{1}{4} & | & \frac{3}{4} \\ \hline -1 & 0 & | & 0 & 3 & | & 9 \end{bmatrix} \begin{array}{c} u_1 \\ y_2 \end{array}$$

$$\begin{bmatrix} 0 & -1 & | & 1 & -1 & | & 3 \\ 1 & 4 & | & 0 & 1 & | & 3 \\ \hline 0 & 4 & | & 0 & 4 & | & 12 \end{bmatrix} \begin{array}{c} u_1 \\ y_1 \end{array}$$

$C = 12, \quad x_1 = 0, \quad x_2 = 4$

9. $\begin{bmatrix} 1 & -3 & 4 & | & 12 \\ 3 & 1 & 2 & | & 10 \\ 1 & -1 & -1 & | & -8 \\ \hline 1 & 2 & 1 & | & 0 \end{bmatrix}$; $\begin{bmatrix} 1 & 3 & 1 & | & 1 \\ -3 & 1 & -1 & | & 2 \\ 4 & 2 & -1 & | & 1 \\ \hline 12 & 10 & -8 & | & 0 \end{bmatrix}$

Dual problem:
Maximize $P = 12y_1 + 10y_2 - 8y_3$
subject to $y_1 + 3y_2 + y_3 \le 1$, $-3y_1 + y_2 - y_3 \le 2$,
$4y_1 + 2y_2 - y_3 \le 1$, $y_1 \ge 0, y_2 \ge 0, y_3 \ge 0$.

$$\begin{array}{cccccc} y_1 & y_2 & y_3 & u_1 & u_2 & u_3 \end{array}$$
$$\begin{bmatrix} 1 & 3 & 1 & | & 1 & 0 & 0 & | & 1 \\ -3 & 1 & -1 & | & 0 & 1 & 0 & | & 2 \\ ④ & 2 & -1 & | & 0 & 0 & 1 & | & 1 \\ \hline -12 & -10 & 8 & | & 0 & 0 & 0 & | & 0 \end{bmatrix} \begin{array}{c} u_1 \\ u_2 \\ u_3 \end{array}$$

$$
\begin{array}{cccccc}
y_1 & y_2 & y_3 & u_1 & u_2 & u_3
\end{array}
$$

$$
\left[\begin{array}{ccc|ccc|c}
0 & \tfrac{5}{2} & \tfrac{5}{4} & 1 & 0 & -\tfrac{1}{4} & \tfrac{3}{4} \\
0 & \tfrac{5}{2} & -\tfrac{7}{4} & 0 & 1 & \tfrac{3}{4} & \tfrac{11}{4} \\
1 & \tfrac{1}{2} & -\tfrac{1}{4} & 0 & 0 & \tfrac{1}{4} & \tfrac{1}{4} \\
\hline
0 & -4 & 5 & 0 & 0 & 3 & 3
\end{array}\right]
\begin{array}{c}
u_1 \\ u_2 \\ y_1 \\ {}
\end{array}
$$

$$
\left[\begin{array}{ccc|ccc|c}
0 & 1 & \tfrac{1}{2} & \tfrac{2}{5} & 0 & -\tfrac{1}{10} & \tfrac{3}{10} \\
0 & 0 & -3 & -1 & 1 & 1 & 2 \\
1 & 0 & -\tfrac{1}{2} & -\tfrac{1}{5} & 0 & \tfrac{3}{10} & \tfrac{1}{10} \\
\hline
0 & 0 & 7 & \tfrac{8}{5} & 0 & \tfrac{13}{5} & \tfrac{21}{5}
\end{array}\right]
\begin{array}{c}
y_2 \\ u_2 \\ y_1 \\ {}
\end{array}
$$

$C = \tfrac{21}{5}, \quad x_1 = \tfrac{8}{5}, \quad x_2 = 0, \quad x_3 = \tfrac{13}{5}$

Exercise 5 (page 186)

1. Let $x_1 =$ Amount of Food I, $x_2 =$ Amount of Food II, $x_3 =$ Amount of Food III.
Minimize $C = 2x_1 + x_2 + 3x_3$ subject to $2x_1 + 3x_2 + 4x_3 \geq 20$, $4x_1 + 2x_2 + 2x_3 \geq 15$, $x_1 \geq 0, x_2 \geq 0, x_3 \geq 0$.

$$
\begin{array}{ccc}
x_1 & x_2 & x_3
\end{array}
$$

$$
\left[\begin{array}{ccc|c}
2 & 3 & 4 & 20 \\
4 & 2 & 2 & 15 \\
\hline
2 & 1 & 3 & 0
\end{array}\right] ;
\qquad
\left[\begin{array}{cc|c}
2 & 4 & 2 \\
3 & 2 & 1 \\
4 & 2 & 3 \\
\hline
20 & 15 & 0
\end{array}\right]
$$

Dual problem:
Maximize $P = 20y_1 + 15y_2$ subject to $2y_1 + 4y_2 \leq 2$,
$3y_1 + 2y_2 \leq 1$, $4y_1 + 2y_2 \leq 3$, $y_1 \geq 0, y_2 \geq 0$.

$$
\begin{array}{ccccc}
y_1 & y_2 & u_1 & u_2 & u_3
\end{array}
$$

$$
\left[\begin{array}{cc|ccc|c}
2 & 4 & 1 & 0 & 0 & 2 \\
3 & 2 & 0 & 1 & 0 & 1 \\
4 & 2 & 0 & 0 & 1 & 3 \\
\hline
-20 & -15 & 0 & 0 & 0 & 0
\end{array}\right]
\begin{array}{c}
u_1 \\ u_2 \\ u_3 \\ {}
\end{array}
$$

$$
\left[\begin{array}{cc|ccc|c}
0 & \tfrac{8}{3} & 1 & -\tfrac{2}{3} & 0 & \tfrac{4}{3} \\
1 & \tfrac{2}{3} & 0 & \tfrac{1}{3} & 0 & \tfrac{1}{3} \\
0 & -\tfrac{2}{3} & 0 & -\tfrac{4}{3} & 1 & \tfrac{5}{3} \\
\hline
0 & -\tfrac{5}{3} & 0 & \tfrac{20}{3} & 0 & \tfrac{20}{3}
\end{array}\right]
\begin{array}{c}
u_1 \\ y_1 \\ u_3 \\ {}
\end{array}
$$

$$
\left[\begin{array}{cc|ccc|c}
-4 & 0 & 1 & -2 & 0 & 0 \\
\tfrac{3}{2} & 1 & 0 & \tfrac{1}{2} & 0 & \tfrac{1}{2} \\
1 & 0 & 0 & -1 & 1 & 2 \\
\hline
\tfrac{5}{2} & 0 & 0 & \tfrac{15}{2} & 0 & \tfrac{15}{2}
\end{array}\right]
\begin{array}{c}
u_1 \\ y_2 \\ u_3 \\ {}
\end{array}
$$

$C = \$7.50, \quad x_1 = 0, \quad x_2 = 7.5, \quad x_3 = 0$

3. Let $x_1 =$ Amount of ingredient A, $x_2 =$ Amount of ingredient B, $x_3 =$ Amount of ingredient C, $x_4 =$ Amount of ingredient D.

Minimize $C = 3x_1 + 2x_2 + x_3 + 4x_4$ subject to $10x_1 + x_2 + x_3 + 5x_4 \geq 10$,
$2x_1 + 40x_2 + x_3 + 10x_4 \geq 20$, $\tfrac{1}{2}x_1 + 3x_2 + 6x_3 + 3x_4 \geq 6$, $x_1 \geq 0, x_2 \geq 0, x_3 \geq 0, x_4 \geq 0$.

$$
\begin{array}{cccc}
x_1 & x_2 & x_3 & x_4
\end{array}
$$

$$
\left[\begin{array}{cccc|c}
10 & 1 & 1 & 5 & 10 \\
2 & 40 & 1 & 10 & 20 \\
\tfrac{1}{2} & 3 & 6 & 3 & 6 \\
\hline
3 & 2 & 1 & 4 & 0
\end{array}\right] ;
\qquad
\left[\begin{array}{ccc|c}
10 & 2 & \tfrac{1}{2} & 3 \\
1 & 40 & 3 & 2 \\
1 & 1 & 6 & 1 \\
5 & 10 & 3 & 4 \\
\hline
10 & 20 & 6 & 0
\end{array}\right].
$$

Dual problem:
Maximize $P = 10y_1 + 20y_2 + 6y_3$
subject to $10y_1 + 2y_2 + \tfrac{1}{3}y_3 \leq 3$, $y_1 + 40y_2 + 3y_3 \leq 2$,
$y_1 + y_2 + 6y_3 \leq 1$, $5y_1 + 10y_2 + 3y_3 \leq 4$, $y_1 \geq 0$,
$y_2 \geq 0, y_3 \geq 0$.

$$
\begin{array}{ccccccc}
y_1 & y_2 & y_3 & u_1 & u_2 & u_3 & u_4 \\
\end{array}
$$

$$
\left[
\begin{array}{ccc|cccc|c}
10 & 2 & \frac{1}{2} & 1 & 0 & 0 & 0 & 3 \\
1 & \boxed{40} & 3 & 0 & 1 & 0 & 0 & 2 \\
1 & 1 & 6 & 0 & 0 & 1 & 0 & 1 \\
5 & 10 & 3 & 0 & 0 & 0 & 1 & 4 \\
\hline
-10 & -20 & -6 & 0 & 0 & 0 & 0 & 0 \\
\end{array}
\right]
$$

From a computer program, the final tableau is

$$
\begin{array}{ccccccc}
y_1 & y_2 & y_3 & u_1 & u_2 & u_3 & u_4 \\
\end{array}
$$

$$
\left[
\begin{array}{ccc|cccc|c}
1 & 0 & 0 & 0.10109 & -0.00491 & -0.00597 & 0 & 0.28748 \\
0 & 1 & 0 & -0.00128 & 0.02538 & -0.01258 & 0 & 0.03434 \\
0 & 0 & 1 & -0.01663 & -0.00341 & 0.16976 & 0 & 0.11303 \\
0 & 0 & 0 & -0.44274 & -0.21902 & -0.35359 & 1 & 1.88015 \\
\hline
0 & 0 & 0 & 0.88548 & 0.43805 & 0.70719 & 0 & 4.23971 \\
\end{array}
\right]
$$

$C = 4.24, \quad x_1 = 0.89,$
$x_2 = 0.44, \quad x_3 = 0.71, \quad x_4 = 0$

5. Let $x_1 =$ Number of television console cabinets, $x_2 =$ Number of stereo system cabinets, $x_3 =$ Number of radio cabinets.

Maximize $\quad P = 10x_1 + 25x_2 + 3x_3 \quad$ subject to $\quad 3x_1 + 10x_2 + x_3 \le 30{,}000, \quad 5x_1 + 8x_2 + x_3 \le 40{,}000,$
$0.1x_1 + 0.6x_2 + 0.1x_3 \le 120.$

$$
\begin{array}{cccccc}
x_1 & x_2 & x_3 & x_4 & x_5 & x_6 \\
\end{array}
$$

$$
\left[
\begin{array}{cccccc|c}
3 & 10 & 1 & 1 & 0 & 0 & 30{,}000 \\
5 & 8 & 1 & 0 & 1 & 0 & 40{,}000 \\
0.1 & \boxed{0.6} & 0.1 & 0 & 0 & 1 & 120 \\
\hline
-10 & -25 & -3 & 0 & 0 & 0 & 0 \\
\end{array}
\right]
\begin{array}{l}
x_4 \\
x_5 \\
x_6 \\
\\
\end{array}
$$

$$
\left[
\begin{array}{cccccc|c}
\frac{4}{3} & 0 & -\frac{2}{3} & 1 & 0 & -\frac{50}{3} & 28{,}000 \\
\frac{11}{3} & 0 & -\frac{1}{3} & 0 & 1 & -\frac{40}{3} & 38{,}400 \\
\boxed{\frac{1}{6}} & 1 & \frac{1}{6} & 0 & 0 & \frac{5}{3} & 200 \\
\hline
-\frac{35}{6} & 0 & \frac{7}{6} & 0 & 0 & \frac{125}{3} & 5{,}000 \\
\end{array}
\right]
\begin{array}{l}
x_4 \\
x_5 \\
x_2 \\
\\
\end{array}
$$

$$
\left[
\begin{array}{cccccc|c}
0 & -8 & -2 & 1 & 0 & -30 & 26{,}400 \\
0 & -22 & -4 & 0 & 1 & -50 & 34{,}000 \\
1 & 6 & 1 & 0 & 0 & 10 & 1{,}200 \\
\hline
0 & 35 & 7 & 0 & 0 & 100 & 12{,}000 \\
\end{array}
\right]
\begin{array}{l}
x_4 \\
x_5 \\
x_1 \\
\\
\end{array}
$$

$P = \$12{,}000, \quad x_1 = 1200, \quad x_2 = 0, \quad x_3 = 0$

Review Exercises (page 188)

$$
\begin{array}{ccccc}
x_1 & x_2 & x_3 & x_4 & x_5 \\
\end{array}
$$

1.
$$
\left[
\begin{array}{ccccc|c}
2 & \boxed{2} & 1 & 1 & 0 & 8 \\
1 & -4 & 3 & 0 & 1 & 12 \\
\hline
-40 & -60 & -50 & 0 & 0 & 0 \\
\end{array}
\right]
\begin{array}{l}
x_4 \\
x_5 \\
\\
\end{array}
$$

$$
\left[
\begin{array}{ccccc|c}
1 & 1 & \frac{1}{2} & \frac{1}{2} & 0 & 4 \\
5 & 0 & \boxed{5} & 2 & 1 & 28 \\
\hline
20 & 0 & -20 & 30 & 0 & 240 \\
\end{array}
\right]
\begin{array}{l}
x_2 \\
x_5 \\
\\
\end{array}
$$

$$
\left[
\begin{array}{ccccc|c}
\frac{1}{2} & 1 & 0 & \frac{3}{10} & -\frac{1}{10} & \frac{6}{5} \\
1 & 0 & 1 & \frac{2}{5} & \frac{1}{5} & \frac{28}{5} \\
\hline
40 & 0 & 0 & 38 & 4 & 352 \\
\end{array}
\right]
\begin{array}{l}
x_2 \\
x_3 \\
\\
\end{array}
$$

$P = 352, \quad x_1 = 0, \quad x_2 = \frac{6}{5}, \quad x_3 = \frac{28}{5}$

3.
$$\begin{bmatrix} 1 & 1 & 1 & | & 100 \\ 2 & 1 & 0 & | & 50 \\ \hline 5 & 4 & 3 & | & 0 \end{bmatrix} \; ; \; \begin{bmatrix} 1 & 2 & | & 5 \\ 1 & 1 & | & 4 \\ 1 & 0 & | & 3 \\ \hline 100 & 50 & | & 0 \end{bmatrix}$$

Dual problem:
Maximize $P = 100y_1 + 50y_2$
subject to $y_1 + 2y_2 \le 5$, $y_1 + y_2 \le 4$, $y_1 \le 3$, $y_1 \ge 0$, $y_2 \ge 0$.

$$\begin{array}{ccccc} y_1 & y_2 & u_1 & u_2 & u_3 \end{array}$$
$$\begin{bmatrix} 1 & 2 & | & 1 & 0 & 0 & | & 5 \\ 1 & 1 & | & 0 & 1 & 0 & | & 4 \\ \textcircled{1} & 0 & | & 0 & 0 & 1 & | & 3 \\ \hline -100 & -50 & | & 0 & 0 & 0 & | & 0 \end{bmatrix}$$

$$\begin{bmatrix} 0 & 2 & | & 1 & 0 & -1 & | & 2 \\ 0 & \textcircled{1} & | & 0 & 1 & -1 & | & 1 \\ 1 & 0 & | & 0 & 0 & 1 & | & 3 \\ \hline 0 & -50 & | & 0 & 0 & 100 & | & 300 \end{bmatrix}$$

$$\begin{bmatrix} 0 & 0 & | & 1 & -2 & 1 & | & 0 \\ 0 & 1 & | & 0 & 1 & -1 & | & 1 \\ 1 & 0 & | & 0 & 0 & 1 & | & 3 \\ \hline 0 & 0 & | & 0 & 50 & 50 & | & 350 \end{bmatrix}$$

$C = 350$, $x_1 = 0$, $x_2 = 50$, $x_3 = 50$

5. Let $x_1 = $ Acres of corn, $x_2 = $ Acres of wheat, $x_3 = $ Acres of soybeans.

Maximize $P = 30x_1 + 40x_2 + 40x_3$ subject to $x_1 + x_2 + x_3 \le 1000$, $100x_1 + 120x_2 + 70x_3 \le 10{,}000$, $7x_1 + 10x_2 + 8x_3 \le 8000$.

$$\begin{array}{cccccc} x_1 & x_2 & x_3 & x_4 & x_5 & x_6 \end{array}$$
$$\begin{bmatrix} 1 & 1 & 1 & 1 & 0 & 0 & | & 1{,}000 \\ 100 & 120 & \textcircled{70} & 0 & 1 & 0 & | & 10{,}000 \\ 7 & 10 & 8 & 0 & 0 & 1 & | & 8{,}000 \\ \hline -30 & -40 & -40 & 0 & 0 & 0 & | & 0 \end{bmatrix} \begin{array}{l} x_4 \\ x_5 \\ x_6 \end{array}$$

$$\begin{bmatrix} -\frac{3}{7} & -\frac{5}{7} & 0 & 1 & -\frac{1}{70} & 0 & | & \frac{6{,}000}{7} \\ \frac{10}{7} & \frac{12}{7} & 1 & 0 & \frac{1}{70} & 0 & | & \frac{1{,}000}{7} \\ -\frac{31}{7} & -\frac{26}{7} & 0 & 0 & -\frac{8}{70} & 1 & | & \frac{48{,}000}{7} \\ \hline \frac{190}{7} & \frac{200}{7} & 0 & 0 & \frac{4}{7} & 0 & | & \frac{40{,}000}{7} \end{bmatrix} \begin{array}{l} x_4 \\ x_3 \\ x_6 \end{array}$$

$P = \$5714.29$, $x_1 = 0$, $x_2 = 0$, $x_3 = \frac{1000}{7} = 142\frac{6}{7}$

CHAPTER 5

Exercise 1 (page 201)
1. None of these **3.** None of these **5.** $\subset, \subseteq$ **7.** $\subset, \subseteq$ **9.** $\subset, \subseteq$
11. $A \subseteq C$. This is called the *transitive law*.
13. $\{a, b, c, d\}, \{a, b, c\}, \{a, b, d\}, \{a, c, d\}, \{b, c, d\}, \{a, b\}, \{a, c\}, \{a, d\}, \{b, c\}, \{b, d\}, \{c, d\}, \{a\}, \{b\}, \{c\}, \{d\}, \varnothing$
15. $A \cap B = \{3\}$ **17.** $A \cup C = \{1, 2, 3, 5, 7\}$
19. $(A \cup B) \cap C = \{1, 2, 3, 4, 5, 6\} \cap \{3, 5, 7\} = \{3, 5\}$
21. $A \cup (B \cup C) = A \cup \{3, 4, 5, 6, 7\} = \{1, 2, 3, 4, 5, 6, 7\}$

23. (a) $A \cup B = \{0, 1, 2, 3, 5, 7, 8\}$
  (b) $B \cap C = \{5\}$
  (c) $A \cap B = \{5\}$
  (d) $\overline{A \cap B} = \overline{\{5\}} = \{0, 1, 2, 3, 4, 6, 7, 8, 9\}$
  (e) $\bar{A} \cap \bar{B} = \{2, 3, 4, 6, 8, 9\} \cap \{0, 1, 4, 6, 7, 9\} = \{4, 6, 9\}$
  (f) $A \cup (B \cap A) = A = \{0, 1, 5, 7\}$
  (g) $(C \cap A) \cap \bar{A} = \{5\} \cap \{2, 3, 4, 6, 8, 9\} = \varnothing$
  (h) $(A \cap B) \cup (B \cap C) = \{5\} \cup \{5\} = \{5\}$

25. (a) $A \cup B = \{b, c, d, e, f, g\}$
  (b) $A \cap B = \{c\}$
  (c) $\bar{A} \cap \bar{B} = \overline{A \cup B} = \{a, h, i, j, \ldots, z\}$
  (d) $\bar{A} \cup \bar{B} = \overline{A \cap B} = \{a, b, d, e, f, \ldots, z\}$

27. (a) (b) (c) (d)
  (e) (f) (g) (h)

29. $A \cap E = \{x \mid x$ is a customer of IBM and is a member of the Board of Directors of IBM$\}$
31. $A \cup D = \{x \mid x$ is a customer of IBM or is a stockholder of IBM$\}$
33. $M \cap S = \{$All male college students who smoke$\}$
35. $\bar{M} \cap \bar{S} = \{$All female college students who do not smoke$\}$

Exercise 2 (page 206)
 1. $c(\{1, 3, 5, 7\}) = 4$ **3.** $c(\{0, 1, 2, 3, 4, 5, 6, 7, 8, 9\}) = 10$ **5.** $c(A) = 4$
 7. $c(A \cap B) = c(\varnothing) = 0$ **9.** $c[(A \cap B) \cup A] = c(A) = 4$
11. $c[A \cup (B \cap C)] = c(\{1, 3, 6, 8\}) = 4$ **13.** $c[A \cap (B \cap C)] = c(\{8\}) = 1$
15. $c(A \cup B) = 4 + 3 - 2 = 5$ **17.** $7 = 5 + 4 - c(A \cap B); c(A \cap B) = 2$
19. $14 = c(A) + 8 - 4; c(A) = 10$ **21.** $325 + 216 - 89 = 452$
23. (a) $(82 + 152 + 111) + (27 + 33 + 7) + (44 + 47 + 43) = 546$
  (b) $(111 + 15 + 7 + 33) + (33 + 47) + (27 + 44) = 317$
  (c) $(42 + 44) + (15 + 33) = 134$
25. $c(B) = 9 + 8 + 3 + 2 = 22$ **27.** $c(B \cup C) = 22 + (4 + 17) = 43$
29. $c(B \cap \bar{C}) = 9 + 8 = 17$ **31.** $c(\overline{A \cup B \cup C}) = 5$
33. $109 = $ Number of male seniors who are not on the dean's list
   $97 = $ Number of female seniors who are not on the dean's list
  $369 = $ Number of female students who are not seniors and not on the dean's list
   $24 = $ Number of female seniors on the dean's list
   $73 = $ Number of female students on the dean's list who are not seniors
   $89 = $ Number of male students on the dean's list who are not seniors
  $347 = $ Number of male students who are not seniors and not on the dean's list
    $0 = $ Number of male seniors on the dean's list

35. (a) 42
(b) 9
(c) 5
(d) 2
(e) 44
(f) 31

37. Total for English, according to the diagram, is at least 303 whereas the staff member indicated that the total taking English was 281.

39. $143 - 30 - 45 = 68$

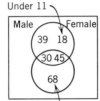

Exercise 3 (page 214)

1. $\dfrac{5!}{2!} = 5 \cdot 4 \cdot 3 = 60$ **3.** $\dfrac{6!}{3!} = 6 \cdot 5 \cdot 4 = 120$ **5.** $\dfrac{10!}{8!} = 10 \cdot 9 = 90$

7. $\dfrac{9!}{8!} = 9$ **9.** $\dfrac{8!}{2!6!} = \dfrac{8 \cdot 7 \cdot 6!}{2 \cdot 6!} = 4 \cdot 7 = 28$ **11.** $P(7, 2) = 7 \cdot 6 = 42$

13. $P(8, 1) = 8$ **15.** $P(5, 0) = 1$ **17.** $4 \cdot 5 = 20$ **19.** $3 \cdot 6 = 18$ **21.** $14 \cdot 13 = 182$

23. $4 \cdot 4 \cdot 4 \cdot 4 = 256$

25. $(5!3!2!) \cdot 3! = 8640$ (First arrange the 5 Math books in order, then the 3 Physics books, then the 2 Computer Science books. Then arrange the 3 groups.)

27. $10 \cdot 9 = 90$ (Suppose each of the 10 teams plays one game at home and one away. There are 10 choices for the home team and 9 teams for the home team to play against.)

Exercise 4 (page 218)

1. $C(6, 4) = \dfrac{6!}{4!2!} = \dfrac{6 \cdot 5}{2} = 15$ **3.** $C(7, 2) = \dfrac{7!}{2!5!} = \dfrac{7 \cdot 6}{2} = 21$

5. $\dbinom{5}{1} = 5$ **7.** $\dbinom{8}{6} = \dfrac{8!}{6!2!} = \dfrac{8 \cdot 7}{2} = 28$

9. $C(8, 3) = \dfrac{8 \cdot 7 \cdot 6}{1 \cdot 2 \cdot 3} = 56$ **11.** $C(17, 4) = \dfrac{17 \cdot 16 \cdot 15 \cdot 14}{1 \cdot 2 \cdot 3 \cdot 4} = 2380$

13. If the 3 officers are of equal rank, the answer is $C(25, 3) = 2300$. If there are 3 distinct offices (e.g., president, vice-president, secretary), the answer is $P(25, 3) = 13{,}800$.

15. $\dbinom{6}{2} = 15$ **17.** $3 \cdot 2 \cdot \dbinom{5}{2} = 3 \cdot 2 \cdot 10 = 60$

19. $\dbinom{3}{1}\dbinom{8}{2}\dbinom{4}{1}\dbinom{20}{7} = 3 \cdot 28 \cdot 4 \cdot (77{,}520) = 26{,}046{,}720$ (Order is not important if we assume that specific positions will be assigned to the 7 linemen after the team is formed.)

21. $\binom{5}{3} = 10$ (The possible sums are 16¢, 31¢, 36¢, 40¢, 56¢, 61¢, 65¢, 76¢, 80¢, and 85¢.)

Exercise 5 (page 223)

1. (a) $2^{10} = 1024$ (b) $\binom{10}{4} = 210$ (c) $\binom{10}{0} + \binom{10}{1} + \binom{10}{2} = 1 + 10 + 45 = 56$

  (d) $1024 - 56 = 968$

3. (a) $C(10, 3) = 120$ (b) $\binom{7}{2}\binom{3}{1} = 21 \cdot 3 = 63$ (c) $\binom{7}{3} = 35$ (d) $\binom{3}{3} = 1$

5. $\dfrac{8!}{4!4!} = 70$ (This is equal to the number of sequences of 8 letters in which A and N each appear 4 times.

  Consider AAAANNNN to be equivalent to AAAA, NAAAANNN to NAAAA, etc.)

7. $\dfrac{9!}{4!3!2!} = 1260$ **9.** $\dfrac{11!}{2!2!2!} = 4,989,600$

11. $\left(\dfrac{10!}{3!3!4!}\right) \div 2 = 2100$

13. (a) $\binom{5}{1}\binom{8}{3} = 280$ (b) $\binom{8}{2}\binom{5}{2} = 280$ (c) $\binom{5}{1}\binom{8}{3} + \binom{5}{2}\binom{8}{2} + \binom{5}{3}\binom{8}{1} = 640$

Exercise 6 (page 226)

1. $(x + y)^5 = x^5 + 5x^4y + 10x^3y^2 + 10x^2y^3 + 5xy^4 + y^5$

3. $(x + 3y)^3 = x^3 + 3x^2(3y) + 3x(3y)^2 + (3y)^3 = x^3 + 9x^2y + 27xy^2 + 27y^3$

5. $(2x - y)^4 = (2x)^4 + 4(2x)^3(-y) + 6(2x)^2(-y)^2 + 4(2x)(-y)^3 + (-y)^4$
$$= 16x^4 - 32x^3y + 24x^2y^2 - 8xy^3 + y^4$$

7. $\binom{5}{2}x^2 = 10x^2$ **9.** $\binom{10}{8} \cdot 3^2 = 405$ **11.** $2^5 = 32$

Review Exercises (page 227)

1. None of these   **3.** None of these   **5.** None of these   **7.** $\in$

9. $\subset, \subseteq$ **11.** None of these   **13.** $\subset, \subseteq$ **15.** None of these

17. (a) $(A \cap B) \cup C = \{3, 6\} \cup \{6, 8, 9\} = \{3, 6, 8, 9\}$

  (b) $(A \cap B) \cap C = \{3, 6\} \cap \{6, 8, 9\} = \{6\}$

  (c) $(A \cup B) \cap B = \{1, 2, 3, 5, 6, 7, 8\} \cap \{2, 3, 6, 7\} = \{2, 3, 6, 7\}$

19. $c(A \cap B) = 24 + 12 - 33 = 3$

21. 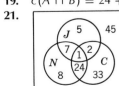   (a) 45   (c) 50

       (b) 33

23. $P(6, 3) = 6 \cdot 5 \cdot 4 = 120$ **25.** $C(5, 3) = \dfrac{5!}{3!2!} = 10$ **27.** $3! = 6$

29. $3 \cdot 4 \cdot 6 = 72$ **31.** Maximum: $P(4, 2) = 12$; $C(4, 2) = 6$ **33.** $\binom{16}{4}\binom{10}{3} = (1820)(120) = 218,400$

35. (a) $\binom{7}{3}\binom{6}{4} = (35)(15) = 525$ (b) $\binom{7}{1}\binom{6}{6} + \binom{7}{2}\binom{6}{5} + \binom{7}{3}\binom{6}{4} + \binom{7}{4}\binom{6}{3} + \binom{7}{5}\binom{6}{2} + \binom{7}{6}\binom{6}{1}$
$$= 7 + 126 + 525 + 700 + 315 + 42 = 1715$$

37. $(3 \cdot 2 \cdot 1)4!5!6! = 3!4!5!6! = 12,441,600$

39. One path from A to B is RRRRRRUUUUUU. All paths from A to B are exactly 12 moves, of which exactly 6 are to the right (R). Thus, in all, there are $\binom{12}{6} = 924$ paths from A to B.

41. $5 \cdot 6 \cdot 8 = 240$ **43.** $\binom{3}{1}\binom{5}{3} = 3 \cdot 10 = 30$

45. Let $AB = X$. We have X, C, D, E to order: $4! = 24$.   **47.** $\dfrac{6!}{3!} = 6 \cdot 5 \cdot 4 = 120$

CHAPTER 6

Exercise 2 (page 243)

1. $\{HHH, HHT, HTH, HTT, THH, THT, TTH, TTT\}$

3. $\{HH1, HH2, HH3, HH4, HH5, HH6, HT1, HT2, HT3, HT4, HT5, HT6, TH1, TH2, TH3, TH4, TH5, TH6, TT1, TT2, TT3, TT4, TT5, TT6\}$

5. $\{RA, RB, RC, GA, GB, GC\}$

7. $\{RR, RG, GR, GG\}$

9. $\{AA1, AA2, AA3, AA4, AB1, AB2, AB3, AB4, AC1, AC2, AC3, AC4, BA1, BA2, BA3, BA4, BB1, BB2, BB3, BB4, BC1, BC2, BC3, BC4, CA1, CA2, CA3, CA4, CB1, CB2, CB3, CB4, CC1, CC2, CC3, CC4\}$

11. $\{RA1, RA2, RA3, RA4, RB1, RB2, RB3, RB4, RC1, RC2, RC3, RC4, GA1, GA2, GA3, GA4, GB1, GB2, GB3, GB4, GC1, GC2, GC3, GC4\}$

13. $2^4 = 16$ **15.** $6^3 = 216$ **17.** $\binom{52}{2} = 1326$ **19.** 1, 2, 3, and 6   **21.** 2

23. $P(HH) = P(HT) = P(TH) = P(TT) = \frac{1}{4}$

25. $P(1H) = P(1T) = P(2H) = P(2T) = P(3H) = P(3T) = P(4H) = P(4T) = P(5H) = P(5T) = P(6H) = P(6T) = \frac{1}{12}$

27. $\{HHHH, HHHT, HHTH, HHTT, HTHH, HTHT, HTTH, HTTT, THHH, THHT, THTH, THTT, TTHH, TTHT, TTTH, TTTT\}$; assign $\frac{1}{16}$ to each simple event

29. $\{HTTT, TTTT\}$

31. $\{HHHT, HHTH, HHTT, HTHH, HTHT, HTTH, THHH, THHT, THTH, TTHH\}$

33. $P(A) = \frac{2}{36} = \frac{1}{18}$ **35.** $P(C) = \frac{4}{36} = \frac{1}{9}$ **37.** $P(E) = \frac{6}{36} = \frac{1}{6}$

39. $P(A) = \frac{1}{2}$ **41.** $P(C) = \frac{5}{6}$ **43.** $P(E) = \frac{1}{2}$

45. (i) $P(E) = \frac{3}{4}$, (ii) $P(E) = \frac{5}{9}$; (i) $P(F) = \frac{1}{2}$; (ii) $P(F) = \frac{4}{9}$; (i) $P(G) = \frac{1}{4}$, (ii) $P(G) = \frac{4}{9}$

47. $\{RRR, RRL, RLR, RLL, LRR, LRL, LLR, LLL\}$. Probability of each simple event is $\frac{1}{8}$. (We assume that the rat does not know left from right.)

   (a) $P(E) = \frac{3}{8}$ (b) $P(F) = \frac{1}{8}$ (c) $P(G) = \frac{1}{2}$ (d) $P(H) = \frac{1}{2}$

49. (a) The number on the red die is three times the number on the green die.

   (b) The number on the red die is 1 larger than the number on the green die.

   (c) The number on the red die is smaller than or equal to the number on the green die.

   (d) The sum of the numbers on the two dice is 8.

   (e) The number on the green die is the square of the number on the red die.

   (f) The numbers on the two dice are the same.

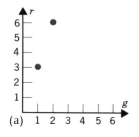

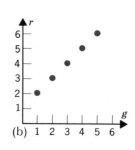

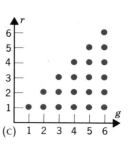

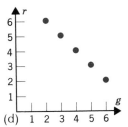
(d)

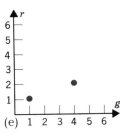
(e)

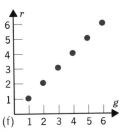
(f)

51. $1 = P(C_1) + P(C_2) + P(C_3) = p + 2p + p = 4p$, so $p = \frac{1}{4}$; then: $P(C_1) = \frac{1}{4}$; $P(C_2) = \frac{2}{4} = \frac{1}{2}$; $P(C_3) = \frac{1}{4}$;
$P(C_1 \cup C_2) = \frac{3}{4}$; $P(C_1 \cup C_3) = \frac{1}{2}$

Exercise 3 (page 252)

1. $P(\bar{A}) = .8$ **3.** $P(A \cup B) = .5$ **5.** $P(A \cup B) = .5 - .15 = .35$
7. The events "Sum is 2" and "Sum is 12" are mutually exclusive. The probability of obtaining a 2 or a 12 is
$\frac{1}{36} + \frac{1}{36} = \frac{1}{18}$.
9. $P(\text{Losing}) = .35$
11. $P(E \cap M) = P(E) + P(M) - P(E \cup M) = .4 + .6 - .8 = .2$
13. (a) $P(A \cup B) = .5 + .3 - .1 = .7$
   (b) $P(A \cap \bar{B}) = .4$
   (c) $P(B \cap \bar{A}) = .2$
   (d) $P(\overline{A \cup B}) = .3$

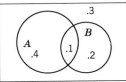

15. Let T = Car needs a tuneup, B = Car needs a brake job.
   (a) $P(T \cup B) = P(T) + P(B) - P(T \cap B)$
      $= .6 + .1 - .02 = .68$
   (b) $P(T \cap \bar{B}) = .58$
   (c) $P(\overline{T \cup B}) = .32$

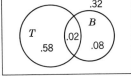

17. (a) $.24 + .33 = .57$ (b) $1 - .05 = .95$ (c) $1 - .17 = .83$ (d) $.21 + .17 = .38$
   (e) $.05 + .24 = .29$ (f) $.05$ (g) $.24 + .33 + .21 = .78$ (h) $1 - .29 = .71$

19. $P(E) = \dfrac{3}{3 + 1} = \frac{3}{4}$ **21.** $P(E) = \dfrac{5}{5 + 7} = \frac{5}{12}$ **23.** $P(E) = \frac{1}{2}$

25. $\dfrac{.7}{1 - .7} = \dfrac{.7}{.3} = \frac{7}{3}$ The odds for E are 7 to 3; the odds against E are 3 to 7.

27. $\dfrac{4}{5} = \dfrac{4}{4 + 1}$ The odds for F are 4 to 1; the odds against F are 1 to 4.

29. $P(7) = \frac{1}{6}$; 1 to 5; $P(11) = \frac{1}{18}$; 1 to 17; $P(7 \text{ or } 11) = \frac{1}{6} + \frac{1}{18} = \frac{2}{9}$, 2 to 7
31. $P(A \text{ or } B) = \frac{1}{3} + \frac{2}{5} = \frac{11}{15}$ The odds are 11 to 4.
33. $P(A \cup B \cup C) = P(A \cup B) + P(C) - P[(A \cup B) \cap C]$
   $= P(A) + P(B) - P(A \cap B) + P(C) - P[(A \cap C) \cup (B \cap C)]$
   $= P(A) + P(B) + P(C) - P(A \cap B) - (P(A \cap C) + P(B \cap C) - P[(A \cap C) \cap (B \cap C)])$
   $= P(A) + P(B) + P(C) - P(A \cap B) - P(A \cap C) - P(B \cap C) + P(A \cap B \cap C)$

Exercise 4 (page 259)

1. $\frac{1}{52}$ **3.** $\frac{13}{52} = \frac{1}{4}$ **5.** $\frac{12}{52} = \frac{3}{13}$ **7.** $\frac{20}{52} = \frac{5}{13}$
9. $\frac{48}{52} = \frac{12}{13}$ **11.** $\frac{3}{23}$ **13.** $\frac{7}{23}$ **15.** $\frac{8}{23}$ **17.** $\frac{11}{23}$
19. $P\{(1, 2), (2, 1), (2, 4), (4, 2), (3, 6), (6, 3)\} = \frac{6}{36} = \frac{1}{6}$

21. Let A = Single, B = College.
$P(A \cup B) = \frac{85}{150} \approx .567$
$P(\overline{A \cup B}) = \frac{65}{150} \approx .433$

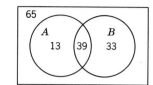

23. $P(\text{At least 2 in same month}) = 1 - P(\text{All different months}) = 1 - \dfrac{(12)(11)(10)}{(12)(12)(12)} = .236$

25. $P(\text{At least 2 have the same number}) = 1 - P(\text{All the numbers are different})$

$$= 1 - \frac{(100)(99)(98)}{(100)(100)(100)} = .0298$$

27. Probability is greater than .99999.

29. Probability that all 5 are defective:

$$\frac{\dbinom{6}{5}}{\dbinom{50}{5}} = \frac{6}{\dfrac{50 \cdot 49 \cdot 48 \cdot 47 \cdot 46}{1 \cdot 2 \cdot 3 \cdot 4 \cdot 5}} = \frac{6 \cdot 5 \cdot 4 \cdot 3 \cdot 2 \cdot 1}{50 \cdot 49 \cdot 48 \cdot 47 \cdot 46} \approx .0000028$$

Probability that at least 2 are defective:

$$\frac{\dbinom{44}{3}\dbinom{6}{2}}{\dbinom{50}{5}} + \frac{\dbinom{44}{2}\dbinom{6}{3}}{\dbinom{50}{5}} + \frac{\dbinom{44}{1}\dbinom{6}{4}}{\dbinom{50}{5}} + \frac{\dbinom{6}{5}}{\dbinom{50}{5}} = \frac{218{,}246}{2{,}118{,}760} \approx .103$$

31. (a) $\dfrac{\dbinom{13}{5}}{\dbinom{52}{5}} = \dfrac{1287}{2{,}598{,}960}$ (b) $\dfrac{\dbinom{13}{4}\dbinom{39}{1}}{\dbinom{52}{5}} \approx 0.0107$ (c) $\dfrac{\dbinom{13}{2}\dbinom{39}{3}}{\dbinom{52}{5}} \approx 0.2743$

33. (a) $\dfrac{4}{\dbinom{52}{5}} \approx .0000015$ (b) $\dfrac{(8)(4)}{\dbinom{52}{5}} = \dfrac{32}{\dbinom{52}{5}} \approx .0000123$ (c) $\dfrac{13 \cdot 48}{\dbinom{52}{5}} \approx .00024$

(d) $\dfrac{13\dbinom{4}{3}12\dbinom{4}{2}}{\dbinom{52}{5}} \approx .0014$ (e) .0076

Exercise 5 (page 265)

1. .40 **3.** .24 **5.** .10 **7.** .08

9. $\dfrac{P(E \cap H)}{P(H)} = \dfrac{.10}{.24} = \dfrac{5}{12}$ **11.** $\dfrac{P(G \cap H)}{P(H)} = \dfrac{.08}{.24} = \dfrac{1}{3}$

13. $P(E|F) = \dfrac{P(E \cap F)}{P(F)} = \dfrac{.1}{.2} = \dfrac{1}{2};\ \ P(F|E) = \dfrac{P(E \cap F)}{P(E)} = \dfrac{.1}{.4} = \dfrac{1}{4}$

15. $P(E|F) = \dfrac{P(E \cap F)}{P(F)}$, so $.2 = \dfrac{.1}{P(F)}$, $P(F) = \dfrac{1}{2}$

17. (a) $\frac{2}{52} = \frac{1}{26}$ **19.** (a) $P(F|I) = \frac{25}{55} = \frac{5}{11}$ **21.** $P(\text{2 girls}|\text{1st girl}) = \frac{1}{2}$
(b) $\frac{1}{2}$ (b) $P(R|F) = \frac{30}{115} = \frac{6}{23}$
(c) $\frac{1}{13}$ (c) $P(M|D) = \frac{50}{110} = \frac{5}{11}$
(d) $P(D|M) = \frac{50}{120} = \frac{5}{12}$
(e) $P(M|R \cup I) = \frac{70}{125} = \frac{14}{25}$
(f) $P(I|M) = \frac{30}{120} = \frac{1}{4}$

23. $P(4 \text{ heads}) = \frac{1}{16};$ $P(4 \text{ heads}|2\text{nd toss head}) = \frac{\frac{1}{16}}{\frac{1}{2}} = \frac{1}{8}$

25. $P(\text{More than } 2|\text{At least } 1) = \frac{.32}{.75} = \frac{32}{75}$

27. Let W = Woman, M = Man, E = Under 160. Assume 1000 people. Then: $P(W|E) = \dfrac{P(W \cap E)}{P(E)} = \dfrac{350}{525} = .67$

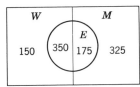

29. Let A = Private, B = Public, E = A average. Assume 100 people for convenience. Then:

$P(A|E) = \dfrac{P(A \cap E)}{P(E)} = \dfrac{12}{24} = .5$

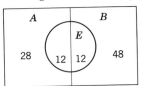

31. $P(F) \cdot P(E|F) = P(E \cap F) = P(E) \cdot P(F|E)$

33. Since $F = (E \cap F) \cup (\overline{E} \cap F)$ and $(E \cap F) \cap (\overline{E} \cap F) = \varnothing$,

$\dfrac{P(E \cap F)}{P(F)} + \dfrac{P(\overline{E} \cap F)}{P(F)} = \dfrac{P(E \cap F) + P(\overline{E} \cap F)}{P(F)} = \dfrac{P(F)}{P(F)} = 1$

Exercise 6 (page 271)

1. $P(E \cap F) = P(E)P(F) = (.3)(.5) = .15$

3. $P(E \cup F) = P(E) + P(F) - P(E \cap F) = P(E) + P(F) - P(E)P(F)$, so $.3 = .2 + P(F) - .2P(F)$

$.1 = .8P(F)$

$P(F) = \frac{1}{8}$

5. $P(E|F) = \dfrac{P(E \cap F)}{P(F)} = \dfrac{P(E) + P(F) - P(E \cup F)}{P(F)} = \dfrac{.3 + .2 - .4}{.2} = \frac{1}{2};$ E and F are not independent

7. $P(E) = \frac{1}{2}$

$P(F) = \frac{1}{2}$

$P(E \cap F) = \frac{1}{6}$

E and F are not independent

9. $P(E) = \frac{4}{8} = \frac{1}{2}$

$P(F) = \frac{3}{4}$

$P(E \cap F) = \frac{3}{8} = \frac{3}{4} \cdot \frac{1}{2}$

E and F are independent

11. (a) $\frac{1}{4}$

(b) $\frac{13}{52} = \frac{1}{4}$

(c) $P(\text{1st club and 2nd heart}) = \frac{1}{4} \cdot \frac{1}{4} = \frac{1}{16}$

13. $E = \{RRR, RRL, LRR\}$

$P(E) = \frac{3}{8}$

$P(F) = \frac{1}{8}$

$P(E \cap F) = P(\varnothing) = 0 \neq P(E)P(F)$

E and F are not independent

15. $P(A) = \frac{1}{4} + \frac{1}{4} = \frac{1}{2}$

$P(B) = \frac{1}{4} + \frac{1}{4} = \frac{1}{2}$

$P(C) = \frac{1}{4} + \frac{1}{4} = \frac{1}{2}$

$P(A \cap B) = P(2) = \frac{1}{4} = P(A)P(B);$ A and B are independent

$P(A \cap C) = P(1) = \frac{1}{4} = P(A)P(C);$ A and C are independent

$P(B \cap C) = P(3) = \frac{1}{4} = P(B)P(C);$ B and C are independent

17. Consider Problem 15.

(a) A and B are not mutually exclusive, but they are independent.

(b) Let $D = \{4\}$. Then: $P(D) = \frac{1}{12};$ $A \cap D = \varnothing$. Hence, they are mutually exclusive, but since $P(A \cap D) = P(\varnothing) = 0 \neq \frac{1}{12} \cdot \frac{1}{2}$, they are not independent.

(c)   Let $E = \{1, 4\}$. Then: $A \cap E = \{1\}$; $P(E) = \frac{1}{4} + \frac{1}{12} = \frac{1}{3}$; $P(A \cap E) = P(1) = \frac{1}{4} \neq \frac{1}{4} \cdot \frac{1}{3}$. Thus, A and E are not independent and are not mutually exclusive.

19. $P(F) = 0$
$E \cap F \subset F$; hence, $P(E \cap F) \leq P(F) = 0$
Thus, $P(E \cap F) = 0$. But $P(E)P(F) = P(E) \cdot 0 = 0$.
Hence, E and F are independent.

21. If $E \cap F = \varnothing$, then $P(E \cap F) = P(\varnothing) = 0$.
But, by independence, $P(E \cap F) = P(E)P(F)$.
Hence, $P(E)P(F) = 0$, which implies that
$P(E) = 0$ or $P(F) = 0$—a contradiction.
Thus, we have $E \cap F \neq \varnothing$.

23. (a)   Let $E = $ At least one ace, $F = $ No ace.
$P(E) = 1 - P(F) = 1 - .4823 = .5177$

(b)   Let $G = $ At least one pair of aces, $H = $ No pair of aces.
$P(G) = 1 - P(H) = 1 - .509 = .491$

Exercise 7 (page 281)

1. $P(C) = P(A \cap C) + P(B \cap C) = (.7)(.9) + (.3)(.2) = .69$ **3.** $P(C|A) = .9$

5. $P(C|D) = \dfrac{P(C \cap D)}{P(D)} = 0$

7. $P(A|E) = \dfrac{P(A \cap E)}{P(E)} = \dfrac{(.3)(.4)}{(.3)(.4) + (.6)(.2) + (.1)(.7)} = \dfrac{.12}{.31} = \frac{12}{31}$

9. $P(C|E) = \dfrac{P(C \cap E)}{P(E)} = \dfrac{(.1)(.7)}{.31} = \frac{7}{31}$

11. $P(B|E) = \dfrac{P(B \cap E)}{P(E)} = \dfrac{.12}{.31} = \frac{12}{31}$

13. $P(E) = P(A_1)P(E|A_1) + P(A_2)P(E|A_2) = (.3)(.01) + (.7)(.02) = .017$
15. $P(E) = P(A_1)P(E|A_1) + P(A_2)P(E|A_2) + P(A_3)P(E|A_3) = (.5)(.01) + (.3)(.03) + (.2)(.02) = .018$

17. $P(A_1|E) = \dfrac{P(E|A_1)P(A_1)}{P(E)} = \dfrac{(.01)(.3)}{.017} = \dfrac{.003}{.017} = \frac{3}{17} \approx .176$

$P(A_2|E) = \dfrac{P(E|A_2)P(A_2)}{P(E)} = \dfrac{(.02)(.7)}{.017} = \dfrac{.014}{.017} = \frac{14}{17} \approx .824$

19. $P(A_1|E) = \dfrac{P(E|A_1)P(A_1)}{P(E)} = \dfrac{(.01)(.5)}{.018} = \dfrac{.005}{.018} = \frac{5}{18} \approx .278$

$P(A_2|E) = \dfrac{P(E|A_2)P(A_2)}{P(E)} = \dfrac{(.03)(.3)}{.018} = \dfrac{.009}{.018} = \frac{9}{18} = .500$

$P(A_3|E) = \dfrac{P(E|A_3)P(A_3)}{P(E)} = \dfrac{(.02)(.2)}{.018} = \dfrac{.004}{.018} = \frac{4}{18} \approx .222$

21. Let $E = $ Item is defective, $A_1 = $ Item is from Machine I, $A_2 = $ Item is from Machine II, $A_3 = $ Item is from Machine III.

$P(A_1|E) = \dfrac{(.02)(.4)}{(.02)(.4) + (.04)(.5) + (.01)(.1)} = \frac{8}{29} \approx .276$

$P(A_2|E) = \dfrac{(.04)(.5)}{(.02)(.4) + (.04)(.5) + (.01)(.1)} = \frac{20}{29} \approx .690$

$P(A_3|E) = \dfrac{(.01)(.1)}{(.02)(.4) + (.04)(.5) + (.01)(.1)} = \frac{1}{29} \approx .034$

23. $P(A_2|E) = 0$; $P(A_3|E) = .065$; $P(A_4|E) = 0$; $P(A_5|E) = .065$

25. $P(U_I|E) = \dfrac{\left(\frac{5}{16}\right)\left(\frac{1}{3}\right)}{\left(\frac{5}{16}\right)\left(\frac{1}{3}\right) + \left(\frac{3}{16}\right)\left(\frac{1}{3}\right) + \left(\frac{7}{16}\right)\left(\frac{1}{3}\right)} = \dfrac{\frac{5}{16}}{\frac{15}{16}} = \frac{1}{3} \approx .333$

$P(U_{II}|E) = .20$
$P(U_{III}|E) = .467$

27. $P(I) = .67;$ $P(II) = .33;$ $P(D|I) = .02;$ $P(D|II) = .01;$

$$P(I|D) = \frac{P(D|I)P(I)}{P(D|I)P(I) + P(D|II)P(II)} = \frac{(.02)(.67)}{(.02)(.67) + (.33)(.01)} = .80$$

29. Let R = Soil is rock, C = Soil is clay, S = Soil is sand, A = Test is positive. Then:
$P(R) = .53;$ $P(C) = .21;$ $P(S) = .26;$ $P(A|R) = .35;$ $P(A|C) = .48;$ $P(A|S) = .75;$

$$P(R|A) = \frac{P(R)P(A|R)}{P(R)P(A|R) + P(C)P(A|C) + P(S)P(A|S)} = \frac{(.53)(.35)}{(.53)(.35) + (.21)(.48) + (.26)(.75)} \approx .39$$

$$P(C|A) = \frac{P(C)P(A|C)}{P(A)} = \frac{.1008}{.4813} \approx .21$$

$$P(S|A) = \frac{P(S)P(A|S)}{P(A)} = \frac{.1950}{.4813} \approx .41$$

31. Let R = Republican.

$$P(R) = P(R|N)P(N) + P(R|S)P(S) + P(R|M)P(M) + P(R|W)P(W)$$
$$= (.4)(.4) + (.56)(.1) + (.48)(.25) + (.52)(.25) = .466$$

$$P(N|R) = \frac{P(R|N)P(R)}{P(R)} = \frac{(.4)(.4)}{.466} \approx .343$$

Exercise 8 (page 290)

1. $b(7, 5; .30) = .0250$

3. $b(15, 8; .70) = b(15, 7; .3) = .0811$

5. $b(15, 10; \frac{1}{2}) = .0916$

7. $b(15, 3; .3) + b(15, 2; .3) + b(15, 1; .3) + b(15, 0; .3)$
$= .1700 + .0916 + .0305 + .0047 = .2968$

9. $b(3, 2; \frac{1}{3}) = \binom{3}{2}(\frac{1}{3})^2(\frac{2}{3}) = 3 \cdot \frac{1}{9} \cdot \frac{2}{3} = \frac{2}{9} = .22\ldots$

11. $b(3, 0; \frac{1}{6}) = (\frac{5}{6})^3 = \frac{125}{216} \approx .5787$

13. $b(5, 3; \frac{2}{3}) = \binom{5}{3}(\frac{2}{3})^3(\frac{1}{3})^2 = 10 \cdot \frac{8}{27} \cdot \frac{1}{9} = \frac{80}{243} \approx .3292$

15. $b(10, 6; .3) = .0368$ **17.** $b(12, 9; .8) = b(12, 3; .2) = .2362$

19. $b(8, 5; .25) + b(8, 6; .25) + b(8, 7; .25) + b(8, 8; .25) = .0231 + .0038 + .0004 + .0000 = .0273$

21. $b(8, 1; \frac{1}{2}) = .03125$

23. $b(8, 5; \frac{1}{2}) + b(8, 6; \frac{1}{2}) + b(8, 7; \frac{1}{2}) + b(8, 8; \frac{1}{2}) = .2188 + .1094 + .0313 + .0039 = .3634$

25. Let A = 2 heads, B = At least 1 head. Then: $P(A) = b(8, 2; \frac{1}{2}) = .1094$ and $P(B) = 1 - P(\bar{B}) = 1 - .0039 = .9961$, so

$$P(A|B) = \frac{P(A \cap B)}{P(B)} = \frac{P(A)}{P(B)}$$

$$P(A|B) = \frac{.1094}{.9961} \approx .1098$$

27. $b(5, 2; \frac{1}{6}) = \binom{5}{2}(\frac{1}{6})^2(\frac{5}{6})^3 = (10)(\frac{1}{36})(\frac{125}{216}) = \frac{625}{3888} \approx .1608$

29. $P(k \text{ items are defective}) = b(8, k; .05)$
   (a) $b(8, 1; .05) = .2793$
   (b) $b(8, 2; .05) = .0515$
   (c) $1 - b(8, 0; .05) = 1 - .6634 = .3366$
   (d) $b(8, 0; .05) + b(8, 1; .05) + b(8, 2; .05) = .6634 + .2793 + .0515 = .9942$

31. $b(6, 3; .5) = .3125$

33. (a)

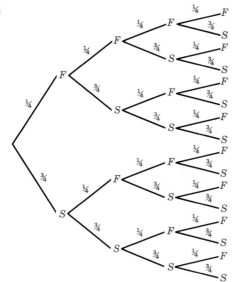

(b) $(\frac{3}{4})(\frac{3}{4})(\frac{1}{4})(\frac{1}{4}) \cdot 6 = \frac{27}{128} = .2109375$

(c) $b(4, 2; \frac{1}{4}) = .2109375$

35. $1 - P(\text{Hitting 0 or 1 time}) = 1 - [(b(10, 0; .2) + b(10, 1; .2)] = 1 - (.1074 + .2684) = .6242$

37. Probability that student gets at least 10 correct answers:
$b(15, 10; .5) + b(15, 11; .5) + b(15, 12; .5) + b(15, 13; .5) + b(15, 14; .5) + b(15, 15; .5) = .0916 + .0417 + .0139 + .0032 + .0005 + .0000 = .1509$
Probability that student gets at least 12 correct answers: .6481

39. (a) $b(6, 5; \frac{1}{2}) + b(6, 6; \frac{1}{2}) = .1094$

(b) $1 - [b(6, 5; .75) + b(6, 6; .75)] = 1 - (.3560 + .1780) = .4660$

41. $P(k \text{ birthdays in January and } 6 - k \text{ in February}) = \dfrac{\binom{6}{k}}{12^6}$ if $1 \leq k \leq 5$. Thus, the solution is

$$\binom{12}{2}\left[\binom{6}{1} + \binom{6}{2} + \binom{6}{3} + \binom{6}{4} + \binom{6}{5}\right]\frac{1}{12^6} = \frac{341}{12^5}$$

43. Investigate the binomial probabilities for $n = 5, 6, 7$; $k = 1, 2, 3$; and $p = \frac{1}{3}$. When $n = 5$, there is a dual maximum for 1 or 2 successes. When $n = 7$, there is a single maximum at 2 successes. We are looking for the smallest n that has a single maximum at 2 successes. Thus, $n = 6$.

Review Exercises (page 292)

1. $S = \{BB, BG, GB, GG\}$

3. (a) $\dfrac{\binom{5}{2}}{\binom{14}{2}} = \frac{10}{91}$ (b) $\dfrac{\binom{5}{1}\binom{9}{1}}{\binom{14}{2}} = \frac{45}{91}$ (c) $\frac{10}{91} + \frac{45}{91} = \frac{55}{91}$

```
      B
   B<
      G
      B
   G<
      G
1st child  2nd child
```

5. $b(4, 3; .5) = .2500$

7. (a) $P(\overline{E}) = 1 - P(E) = 1 - \frac{1}{2} = \frac{1}{2}$

(b) $P(E \cup F) = P(E) + P(F) - P(E \cap F)$
$\frac{5}{8} = \frac{1}{2} + P(F) - \frac{1}{3}$
$P(F) = \frac{1}{8} + \frac{1}{3} = \frac{11}{24}$

(c) $P(\overline{F}) = 1 - P(F) = \frac{13}{24}$

9. There are 3! = 6 ways of putting the letters in the envelopes. There are only 2 ways to have each letter in the wrong envelope. Hence, the probability that at least one person receives the correct letter is $\frac{4}{6} = \frac{2}{3}$.

11. $\dfrac{7}{7 + 6} = \frac{7}{13}$

13. Let M = Failed Math, P = Failed Physics. Then: $P(M) = .38$, $P(P) = .27$, $P(M \cap P) = .09$.

(a) $P(M|P) = \dfrac{P(M \cap P)}{P(P)} = \dfrac{.09}{.27} = \frac{1}{3}$

(b) $P(P|M) = \dfrac{P(M \cap P)}{P(M)} = \dfrac{.09}{.38} = \frac{9}{38}$

(c) $P(M \cup P) = P(M) + P(P) - P(M \cap P) = .38 + .27 - .09 = .56$

15. Let A = Blue-eyed, B = Brown-eyed, L = Left-handed. Then: $P(A) = .25$, $P(B) = .75$, $P(L|A) = .10$, $P(L|B) = .05$.
(a) $P(A \cap L) = P(L|A)P(A) = (.10)(.25) = .0250$
(b) $P(L) = P(A)P(L|A) + P(B)P(L|B) = (.10)(.25) + (.05)(.75) = .0625$

(c) $P(A|L) = \dfrac{P(L|A)P(A)}{P(L)} = \dfrac{.025}{.0625} = .4$

17. Let C = Have cancer, D = Test detects cancer. Then: $P(C) = .018$, $P(\bar{C}) = .982$, $P(D|C) = .85$, $P(D|\bar{C}) = .08$.

$$P(C|D) = \dfrac{P(D|C)P(C)}{P(D|C)P(C) + P(D|\bar{C})P(\bar{C})} = \dfrac{(.85)(.018)}{(.85)(.018) + (.08)(.982)} = .163$$

19. $P(11) = \frac{1}{18}$; $b(5, 3; \frac{1}{18}) + b(5, 4; \frac{1}{18}) + b(5, 5; \frac{1}{18}) = \left[\binom{5}{3} 17^2 + \binom{5}{4} 17 + \binom{5}{5} \right] \dfrac{1}{18^5} \approx 0.00158$

21. $1 - b(5, 0; .05) = 1 - .7738 = .2262$

CHAPTER 7

Exercise 1 (page 304)
1. $(.4)(2) + (.2)(3) + (.1)(-2) + (.3)(0) = 1.2$
3. Expected attendance is $(.08)(35,000) + (.42)(40,000) + (.42)(48,000) + (.08)(60,000) = 44,560$
5. Her expected value is $8(\frac{1}{10}) + (0)(\frac{9}{10}) = .8$. She should pay \$0.80 for a fair game.
7. His expected value is $(\frac{1}{6})(10) + (\frac{5}{6})(0) = \frac{5}{3}$. He should pay \$1.67 for a fair game.
9. Expected value: $(.001)(100) + (.003)(50) + (.996)0 = \$0.25$. If a ticket sells for 60¢, its cost exceeds the expected value by 35¢.
11. (a) $(\frac{1}{8})(3) + (\frac{3}{8})(2) + (\frac{3}{8})(0) + (\frac{1}{8})(-3) = \$0.75$ (b) No   (c) Lose \$2
13. Your expected value is $(\frac{9}{14})(-4) + (\frac{5}{14})(6) = -\frac{6}{14}$. It is not a fair bet.
15. The outcomes are   **17.** \$7
e_1 = Heart not an ace, $p_1 = \frac{12}{52} = \frac{3}{13}$, $m_1 = .25$
e_2 = Ace not ace of hearts, $p_2 = \frac{3}{52}$, $m_2 = .35$
e_3 = Ace of hearts, $p_3 = \frac{1}{52}$, $m_3 = .75$
e_4 = Neither an ace nor a heart, $p_4 = \frac{36}{52} = \frac{9}{13}$, $m_4 = -.15$
Her expected value is

$$\left(\frac{3}{13} \right)(.25) + \left(\frac{3}{52} \right)(.35) + \left(\frac{1}{52} \right)(.75) + \left(\frac{9}{13} \right)(-.15) = -.012$$

No, she should not play the game.
19. The expected profit from the first site is $(\frac{1}{2})(15,000) + (\frac{1}{2})(-3000) = \$6000$. The expected profit from the second site is $(\frac{1}{2})(20,000) + (\frac{1}{2})(-6000) = \$7000$. The second site has a higher expected profit.
21. The sample space is equivalent to a Bernoulli process of 2000 trials where S = Face 5 occurs and F = Any face other than 5 occurs. Then: $p = \frac{1}{6}$ and $E = np = 2000(\frac{1}{6}) \approx 333.3$.

23. $np = (500)(.02) = 10$ **25.** $np = (500)(.002) = 1$

27. $S = \{H, TH, TTH, TTTH, TTTT\}$

$P(H) = \frac{1}{4}$

$P(TH) = \frac{3}{4} \cdot \frac{1}{4} = \frac{3}{16}$

$P(TTH) = \frac{3}{4} \cdot \frac{3}{4} \cdot \frac{1}{4} = \frac{9}{64}$

$P(TTTH) = \frac{3}{4} \cdot \frac{3}{4} \cdot \frac{3}{4} \cdot \frac{1}{4} = \frac{27}{256}$

$P(TTTT) = \frac{3}{4} \cdot \frac{3}{4} \cdot \frac{3}{4} \cdot \frac{3}{4} = \frac{81}{256}$

$E = 1 \cdot \frac{1}{4} + 2 \cdot \frac{3}{16} + 3 \cdot \frac{9}{64} + 4 \cdot \frac{27}{256} + 4 \cdot \frac{81}{256} = \frac{175}{64} \approx 2.73$ tosses

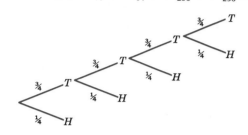

29. $E_1 = m_1 p_1 + m_2 p_2 + \cdots + m_n p_n$. Multiplying each value by k we get:

$E_2 = km_1 p_1 + km_2 p_2 + \cdots + km_n p_n = k[m_1 p_1 + m_2 p_2 + \cdots + m_n p_n] = k \cdot E_1$

Thus, we can see that the expected value of the new experiment, E_2, is k times the original expected value E_1. Add to each outcome used in figuring E_1 the constant k. The new expected value is:

$E_3 = (m_1 + k)p_1 + (m_2 + k)p_2 + \cdots + (m_n + k)p_n = m_1 p_1 + kp_1 + m_2 p_2 + kp_2 + \cdots + m_n p_n + kp_n$

$= m_1 p_1 + m_2 p_2 + \cdots + m_n p_n + kp_1 + kp_2 + \cdots + kp_n = E_1 + k(p_1 + p_2 + \cdots + p_n)$

Since $p_1 + p_2 + \cdots + p_n = 1$, we get $E_3 = E_1 + k$. Thus, we see that the expected value of the new experiment, E_3, is the expected value of the original experiment, E_1, plus k.

Exercise 2 (page 310)

1. The expected number of customers is $(.10)(7) + (.20)(8) + (.40)(9) + (.20)(10) + (.10)(11) = 9$. The optimal number of cars is 9. The expected daily profit is $(.10)(7)(14) + (.20)(8)(14) + (.70)(9)(14) - (9)(8) = 48.40$.

3.

Group size	$p^n - \frac{1}{n}$
2	$(.95)^2 - .5 = .4025$
3	$(.95)^3 - .333 = .524$
4	$(.95)^4 - .25 = .565$
5	$(.95)^5 - .2 = .574$
6	$(.95)^6 - .167 = .568$

5. (a) $E(x) = 75{,}000 - 75{,}000(.05)^x - 500x$.   (b) Two divers should be used.

Review Exercises (page 311)

1. Expected cost for a fair game is $(\frac{1}{3})(89.99) + \frac{1}{3}(49.99) = 29.52$.

3. Let $e_1 = $ Lose all 3 prizes, $p_1 = \dfrac{(995)(994)(993)}{(1000)(999)(998)}$, $m_1 = 0$

$e_2 = $ Win just \$30, $p_2 = \dfrac{(995)(994)(5)}{(1000)(999)(998)}$, $m_2 = 30$

$e_3 = $ Win just \$50, $p_3 = \dfrac{(995)(994)(5)}{(1000)(999)(998)}$, $m_3 = 50$

$e_4 = $ Win just \$100, $p_4 = \dfrac{(995)(994)(5)}{(1000)(999)(998)}$, $m_4 = 100$

$e_5 =$ Win just \$50 and \$30, $p_5 = \dfrac{(995)(5)(4)}{(1000)(999)(998)}$, $m_5 = 80$

$e_6 =$ Win just \$100 and \$30, $p_6 = \dfrac{(995)(5)(4)}{(1000)(999)(998)}$, $m_6 = 130$

$e_7 =$ Win just \$100 and \$50, $p_7 = \dfrac{(995)(5)(4)}{(1000)(999)(998)}$, $m_7 = 150$

$e_8 =$ Win all three, $p_8 = \dfrac{(5)(4)(3)}{(1000)(999)(998)}$, $m_8 = 180$

    (a) Expected value for five tickets is \$0.90.   (b) She paid \$0.35 extra.

5. $S = \{(I, 10), (I, 5), (I, 8), (I, 70), (I, 80), (II, 1), (II, 5)\}$
$P(I, 10) = P(I, 70) = P(I, 80) = \frac{1}{21}$
$P(I, 5) = P(I, 8) = \frac{2}{21}$
$P(II, 1) = P(II, 5) = \frac{2}{6}$
$E = (\frac{1}{21})(10) + (\frac{1}{21})(70) + (\frac{1}{21})(80) + (\frac{2}{21})(5) + (\frac{2}{21})(8) + (\frac{2}{6})(1) + (\frac{2}{6})(5) = \frac{76}{7}$

7. The expected value of the game is $(1)(\frac{18}{37}) + (-1)(\frac{19}{37}) = -\frac{1}{37}$. Game is not fair.

CHAPTER 8

Exercise 1 (page 321)

1. The sum of the entries in row 3 is not equal to 1; there is a negative entry in row 3, column 2.

3. (a) The probability of a change from state 1 to state 2 is $\frac{2}{3}$.

    (b) $\begin{bmatrix} \frac{1}{3} & \frac{2}{3} \end{bmatrix}$ (c) $\begin{bmatrix} \frac{1}{4} & \frac{3}{4} \end{bmatrix}$

    (d) $A^{(0)} = \begin{bmatrix} 0 & 1 \end{bmatrix}$

        $P^{(2)}_{21} = \frac{1}{4} \cdot \frac{1}{3} + \frac{3}{4} \cdot \frac{1}{4} = \frac{13}{38}$

        $P^{(2)}_{22} = \frac{1}{4} \cdot \frac{2}{3} + \frac{3}{4} \cdot \frac{3}{4} = \frac{35}{48}$

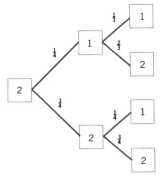

5. $\begin{bmatrix} .25 & .75 \end{bmatrix} \begin{bmatrix} .3 & .7 \\ .4 & .6 \end{bmatrix}^2 = \begin{bmatrix} .375 & .625 \end{bmatrix} \begin{bmatrix} .3 & .7 \\ .4 & .6 \end{bmatrix} = \begin{bmatrix} .3625 & .6375 \end{bmatrix}$

7. $.2 + a + .4 = 1$ $a = .4$
   $b + .6 + .2 = 1$ $b = .2$
         $c = 1$ $c = 1$

9. $A^{(5)} = A^{(0)}P^5 = \begin{bmatrix} .7 & .3 \end{bmatrix} \begin{bmatrix} .7017 & .2983 \\ .0426 & .9574 \end{bmatrix} = \begin{bmatrix} .5040 & .4960 \end{bmatrix}$

11. (a) The probability that a Democratic candidate is elected depends only on whether the previous mayor was a Democrat or a Republican (and similarly for a Republican candidate).

           D R

    (b) $\begin{matrix} D \\ R \end{matrix} \begin{bmatrix} .6 & .4 \\ .3 & .7 \end{bmatrix}$ (c) $\begin{bmatrix} .48 & .52 \\ .39 & .61 \end{bmatrix}$; $\begin{bmatrix} .444 & .556 \\ .417 & .583 \end{bmatrix}$

13. $A^{(2)} = A^{(0)}P^2$, where $P = \begin{matrix} \text{Brand X} \\ \text{Other} \end{matrix} \begin{bmatrix} .75 & .25 \\ .35 & .65 \end{bmatrix}$; $P^2 = \begin{bmatrix} .65 & .35 \\ .49 & .51 \end{bmatrix}$

$[.5 \quad .5]\begin{bmatrix} .65 & .35 \\ .49 & .51 \end{bmatrix} = [.57 \quad .43]$ 57% will drink brand X after 2 months.

15. $\begin{matrix} & T & G & \text{Other} \\ T & & & \\ G & & & \\ \text{Other} & & & \end{matrix}$

$\begin{matrix} T \\ G \\ \text{Other} \end{matrix} \begin{bmatrix} .92 & .08 & 0 \\ .04 & .90 & .06 \\ .10 & .08 & .82 \end{bmatrix} = P$; $[.45 \quad .30 \quad .25] = A^{(0)}$

   (a) $A^{(1)} = A^{(0)}P = [.451 \quad .326 \quad .223]$; $.451 + .326 = .777 = 77.7\%$ (*Check*: $1 - .223 = .777$)

   (b) $A^{(2)} = A^{(1)}P = [.45026 \quad .34732 \quad .20242]$; $.40526 + .34732 = .79758 = 79.758\%$
      (*Check*: $1 - .20242 = .79758$)

17. $uA = [u_1a_{11} + u_2a_{21} \quad u_1a_{12} + u_2a_{22}]$
$(uA)_1 + (uA)_2 = (u_1a_{11} + u_2a_{21}) + (u_1a_{12} + u_2a_{22})$
$= u_1(a_{11} + a_{12}) + u_2(a_{21} + a_{22})$
$= u_1 + u_2 = 1$

Exercise 2 (page 333)

1. $\begin{bmatrix} \frac{1}{2} & \frac{1}{2} \\ 1 & 0 \end{bmatrix}^2 = \begin{bmatrix} \frac{3}{4} & \frac{1}{4} \\ \frac{1}{2} & \frac{1}{2} \end{bmatrix}$; P is regular. If $[t_1 \quad t_2]\begin{bmatrix} \frac{1}{2} & \frac{1}{2} \\ 1 & 0 \end{bmatrix} = [t_1 \quad t_2]$, then $[\frac{1}{2}t_1 + t_2 \quad \frac{1}{2}t_1] = [t_1 \quad t_2]$ or $\frac{1}{2}t_1 = t_2$,
$t_1 + t_2 = 1$, $t_1 = \frac{2}{3}$, $t_2 = \frac{1}{3}$ and $[\frac{2}{3} \quad \frac{1}{3}]$ is the fixed vector.

3. $P^2 = \begin{bmatrix} \frac{1}{4} & \frac{3}{4} \\ \frac{3}{16} & \frac{13}{16} \end{bmatrix}$; P is regular. $[t_1 \quad t_2] = [\frac{1}{5} \quad \frac{4}{5}]$

5. $P^2 = \begin{bmatrix} 1 & 0 & 0 \\ \frac{3}{8} & \frac{1}{2} & \frac{1}{8} \\ \frac{1}{4} & \frac{1}{2} & \frac{1}{4} \end{bmatrix}$ Every power of P will have two 0's in row 1, so the matrix is not regular.

7. If $[t_1 \quad t_2]\begin{bmatrix} 1-p & p \\ p & 1-p \end{bmatrix} = [t_1 \quad t_2]$, then:

$\left.\begin{matrix} (1-p)t_1 + pt_2 = t_1 \\ pt_1 + (1-p)t_2 = t_2 \end{matrix}\right\}$ $t_1 = t_2$, $t_1 + t_2 = 1$, $t_1 = \frac{1}{2}$, $t_2 = \frac{1}{2}$

9. $\begin{matrix} & A & B & C \\ A & & & \\ P = B & & & \\ C & & & \end{matrix}$ $\begin{matrix} A \\ B \\ C \end{matrix}\begin{bmatrix} .7 & .15 & .15 \\ .1 & .8 & .1 \\ .2 & .2 & .6 \end{bmatrix}$ If $[t_1 \quad t_2 \quad t_3]P = [t_1 \quad t_2 \quad t_3]$, then $[t_1 \quad t_2 \quad t_3] = [.3077 \quad .4615 \quad .2308]$. Thus, he stocks Brand A 30.77% of the time, Brand B 46.15% of the time, Brand C 23.08% of the time.

11. The transition matrix is

	Conservative	Labor	Socialist
Conservative	.70	.30	.00
Labor	.40	.50	.10
Socialist	.20	.40	.40

$P^2 = \begin{bmatrix} .61 & .36 & .03 \\ .50 & .41 & .09 \\ .38 & .42 & .20 \end{bmatrix}$

The probability that the grandson of a Laborite will vote Socialist is .09.
The fixed probability vector is $[t_1 \quad t_2 \quad t_3] = [.5532 \quad .3830 \quad .0638]$.

13. Let B, U, R denote Blond, Brunette, and Redhead, respectively.

$$P = \begin{array}{c} \\ B \\ U \\ R \end{array} \begin{array}{ccc} B & U & R \\ \left[\begin{array}{ccc} .6 & .2 & .2 \\ .1 & .7 & .2 \\ .4 & .2 & .4 \end{array}\right] \end{array} \qquad P^2 = \left[\begin{array}{ccc} .46 & .30 & .24 \\ .21 & .55 & .24 \\ .42 & .30 & .28 \end{array}\right] \qquad 30\% \text{ (row 1, column 2 of } P^2\text{)}$$

(a) $[.5 \quad .3 \quad .2] \left[\begin{array}{ccc} .46 & .30 & .24 \\ .21 & .55 & .24 \\ .42 & .30 & .28 \end{array}\right] = [.377 \quad .375 \quad .248]$

(b) $[t_1 \quad t_2 \quad t_3] \left[\begin{array}{ccc} .6 & .2 & .2 \\ .1 & .7 & .2 \\ .4 & .2 & .4 \end{array}\right] = [t_1 \quad t_2 \quad t_3]$

$.6t_1 + .1t_2 + .4t_3 = t_1$
$.2t_1 + .7t_2 + .2t_3 = t_2$
$.2t_1 + .2t_2 + .4t_3 = t_3$
$t_1 + t_2 + t_3 = 1$
$[t_1 \quad t_2 \quad t_3] = [.35 \quad .40 \quad .25]$

Exercise 3 (page 340)
  1. Nonabsorbing (no absorbing states)   **3.** Absorbing
  5. Nonabsorbing (absorbing state 3 is not accessible to states 1 and 2)

7. $\begin{array}{c} \\ 1 \\ 3 \\ 2 \end{array} \begin{array}{ccc} 1 & 3 & 2 \\ \left[\begin{array}{cc|c} 1 & 0 & 0 \\ 0 & 1 & 0 \\ \hline \frac{1}{8} & \frac{2}{8} & \frac{5}{8} \end{array}\right] \end{array}$ $Q = [\frac{5}{8}]; \quad S = [\frac{1}{8} \quad \frac{2}{8}]; \quad T = [1 - \frac{5}{8}]^{-1} = \frac{8}{3}; \quad T \cdot S = [\frac{1}{3} \quad \frac{2}{3}]$

9. (a) $T_{13} = .8$; $T_{23} = .6$ (b) $.3 + 1.8 + 2.1 = 4.2$

11. $\begin{array}{c} \\ 0 \\ 3 \\ 1 \\ 2 \end{array} \begin{array}{cccc} 0 & 3 & 1 & 2 \\ \left[\begin{array}{cc|cc} 1 & 0 & 0 & 0 \\ 0 & 1 & 0 & 0 \\ \hline .6 & 0 & 0 & .4 \\ 0 & .4 & .6 & 0 \end{array}\right] \end{array} = P; \quad Q = \left[\begin{array}{cc} 0 & .4 \\ .6 & 0 \end{array}\right]; \quad S = \left[\begin{array}{cc} .6 & 0 \\ 0 & .4 \end{array}\right]; \quad T = [I_2 - Q]^{-1} = \left[\begin{array}{cc} 1 & -.4 \\ -.6 & 1 \end{array}\right]^{-1} = \left[\begin{array}{cc} \frac{25}{19} & \frac{10}{19} \\ \frac{15}{19} & \frac{25}{19} \end{array}\right];$

$T \cdot S = \begin{array}{cc} 0 & 3 \\ \left[\begin{array}{cc} \frac{15}{19} & \frac{4}{19} \\ \frac{9}{19} & \frac{10}{19} \end{array}\right] \begin{array}{c} 1 \\ 2 \end{array} \end{array}$

With a stake of \$1, the probability is $\frac{4}{19}$. With \$2, the probability is $\frac{10}{19}$.

13. $\begin{array}{c} \\ 0 \\ 1 \\ 2 \\ 4 \end{array} \begin{array}{cccc} 0 & 1 & 2 & 4 \\ \left[\begin{array}{cccc} 1 & 0 & 0 & 0 \\ .6 & 0 & .4 & 0 \\ .6 & 0 & 0 & .4 \\ 0 & 0 & 0 & 1 \end{array}\right] \end{array} \qquad \begin{array}{c} \\ 0 \\ 4 \\ 1 \\ 2 \end{array} \begin{array}{cccc} 0 & 4 & 1 & 2 \\ \left[\begin{array}{cc|cc} 1 & 0 & 0 & 0 \\ 0 & 1 & 0 & 0 \\ \hline .6 & 0 & 0 & .4 \\ .6 & .4 & 0 & 0 \end{array}\right] \end{array}$

$S = \left[\begin{array}{cc} .6 & 0 \\ .6 & .4 \end{array}\right]; \quad Q = \left[\begin{array}{cc} 0 & .4 \\ 0 & 0 \end{array}\right]; \quad T = [I - Q]^{-1} = \left[\begin{array}{cc} 1 & -.4 \\ 0 & 1 \end{array}\right]^{-1} = \left[\begin{array}{cc} 1 & .4 \\ 0 & 1 \end{array}\right]$

(a)   Expected number of wagers is 1.4.

(b) $T \cdot S = \left[\begin{array}{cc} 1 & .4 \\ 0 & 1 \end{array}\right] \left[\begin{array}{cc} .6 & 0 \\ .6 & .4 \end{array}\right] = \left[\begin{array}{cc} .84 & .16 \\ .6 & .4 \end{array}\right]$ The probability that she is wiped out is .84.

(c)   The probability that she wins is .16.

15. $P = \begin{array}{c} \\ 0 \\ 4 \\ 1 \\ 2 \end{array}\begin{array}{cccc} 0 & 4 & 1 & 2 \\ \left[\begin{array}{cccc} 1 & 0 & 0 & 0 \\ 0 & 1 & 0 & 0 \\ .4 & 0 & 0 & .6 \\ .4 & .6 & 0 & 0 \end{array}\right] \end{array};\quad S = \begin{bmatrix} .4 & 0 \\ .4 & .6 \end{bmatrix};\quad Q = \begin{bmatrix} 0 & .6 \\ 0 & 0 \end{bmatrix};\quad T = \begin{bmatrix} 1 & .6 \\ 0 & 1 \end{bmatrix}$

(a) Expected number of wagers is 1.6.

(b) $T \cdot S = \begin{bmatrix} .64 & .36 \\ .4 & .6 \end{bmatrix}$ The probability that she is wiped out is .64.

(c) The probability that she wins is .36.

Exercise 4 (page 345)

1. $\begin{bmatrix} \frac{1}{4} & \frac{1}{2} & \frac{1}{4} \end{bmatrix}\begin{bmatrix} \frac{1}{2} & \frac{1}{2} & 0 \\ \frac{1}{4} & \frac{1}{2} & \frac{1}{4} \\ 0 & \frac{1}{2} & \frac{1}{2} \end{bmatrix} = \begin{bmatrix} \frac{1}{4} & \frac{1}{2} & \frac{1}{4} \end{bmatrix}$

3. (a) $P = \begin{array}{c} D \\ H \\ R \end{array}\begin{array}{c} \begin{array}{ccc} D & H & R \end{array} \\ \left[\begin{array}{ccc} 0 & 1 & 0 \\ 0 & \frac{1}{2} & \frac{1}{2} \\ 0 & 0 & 1 \end{array}\right] \end{array}$

(b) P is not regular, but a fixed probability vector does exist. It is [0   0   1]. This indicates that in the long run the unknown genotype will be R.

(c) $\begin{array}{c} R \\ H \\ D \end{array}\begin{array}{c} \begin{array}{ccc} R & H & D \end{array} \\ \left[\begin{array}{c|cc} 1 & 0 & 0 \\ \hline \frac{1}{2} & \frac{1}{2} & 0 \\ 0 & 1 & 0 \end{array}\right] \end{array}\qquad T = \begin{array}{c} H \\ D \end{array}\begin{array}{c} \begin{array}{cc} H & D \end{array} \\ \left[\begin{array}{cc} 2 & 0 \\ 2 & 1 \end{array}\right] \end{array}$

(d) If the unknown is D to start, three stages are required.
If the unknown is H to start, two stages are required.

Review Exercises (page 346)

1. (a) $\begin{bmatrix} t_1 & t_2 \end{bmatrix}\begin{bmatrix} \frac{1}{4} & \frac{3}{4} \\ \frac{1}{2} & \frac{1}{2} \end{bmatrix} = \begin{bmatrix} \frac{1}{4}t_1 + \frac{1}{2}t_2 & \frac{3}{4}t_1 + \frac{1}{2}t_2 \end{bmatrix} = \begin{bmatrix} t_1 & t_2 \end{bmatrix}$

$\begin{array}{ll} t_1 = \frac{1}{4}t_1 + \frac{1}{2}t_2 & t_1 = \frac{2}{3}t_2 \\ t_2 = \frac{3}{4}t_1 + \frac{1}{2}t_2 & t_1 + t_2 = 1 \\ & t_1 = \frac{2}{5},\ t_2 = \frac{3}{5} \\ & \begin{bmatrix} \frac{2}{5} & \frac{3}{5} \end{bmatrix} \text{ is the fixed vector} \end{array}$

(b) $\begin{bmatrix} t_1 & t_2 \end{bmatrix}\begin{bmatrix} \frac{1}{3} & \frac{2}{3} \\ \frac{2}{3} & \frac{1}{3} \end{bmatrix} = \begin{bmatrix} t_1 & t_2 \end{bmatrix}$

$\begin{array}{ll} \frac{1}{3}t_1 + \frac{2}{3}t_2 = t_1 & t_1 = t_2 \\ \frac{2}{3}t_1 + \frac{1}{3}t_2 = t_2 & \begin{bmatrix} t_1 & t_2 \end{bmatrix} = \begin{bmatrix} \frac{1}{2} & \frac{1}{2} \end{bmatrix} \text{ is the fixed vector} \end{array}$

3. $P = \begin{array}{c} A \\ B \\ C \end{array}\begin{array}{c} \begin{array}{ccc} A & B & C \end{array} \\ \left[\begin{array}{ccc} .5 & .2 & .3 \\ .4 & .4 & .2 \\ .5 & .25 & .25 \end{array}\right] \end{array}\qquad P^2 = \begin{bmatrix} .48 & .255 & .265 \\ .46 & .29 & .25 \\ .475 & .2625 & .2625 \end{bmatrix}\qquad \begin{bmatrix} \frac{1}{3} & \frac{1}{3} & \frac{1}{3} \end{bmatrix} P^2 = \begin{bmatrix} .4717 & .2692 & .2592 \end{bmatrix}$

The fixed vector of P is $\begin{bmatrix} \frac{80}{169} & \frac{45}{169} & \frac{44}{169} \end{bmatrix}$; hence, in the long run, A's share is $\frac{80}{169}$, B's share is $\frac{45}{169}$, and C's share is $\frac{44}{169}$.

$$U_1 \quad U_2 \quad U_3$$

5. The transition matrix is $U_2 \begin{bmatrix} 0 & 1 & 0 \\ \frac{3}{4} & 0 & \frac{1}{4} \\ \frac{3}{4} & \frac{1}{4} & 0 \end{bmatrix}$ The fixed vector is $[\frac{15}{35} \quad \frac{16}{35} \quad \frac{4}{35}]$.

In the long run, she sells $\frac{11}{31}$ of the time at U_1, $\frac{16}{31}$ of the time at U_2, and $\frac{4}{31}$ of the time at U_3.

7. Transition matrix:

$$
\begin{array}{c c}
\begin{array}{ccccccc}
 & 0 & 1 & 2 & 3 & 4 & 5 \\
0 & 1 & 0 & 0 & 0 & 0 & 0 \\
1 & .55 & 0 & .45 & 0 & 0 & 0 \\
2 & 0 & .55 & 0 & .45 & 0 & 0 \\
3 & 0 & 0 & .55 & 0 & .45 & 0 \\
4 & 0 & 0 & 0 & .55 & 0 & .45 \\
5 & 0 & 0 & 0 & 0 & 0 & 1
\end{array}
& \text{or} &
\begin{array}{ccccccc}
 & 0 & 5 & 1 & 2 & 3 & 4 \\
0 & 1 & 0 & 0 & 0 & 0 & 0 \\
5 & 0 & 1 & 0 & 0 & 0 & 0 \\
1 & .55 & 0 & 0 & .45 & 0 & 0 \\
2 & 0 & 0 & .55 & 0 & .45 & 0 \\
3 & 0 & 0 & 0 & .55 & 0 & .45 \\
4 & 0 & .45 & 0 & 0 & .55 & 0
\end{array}
\end{array}
$$

The expected length of the game is $1.298405 + 2.360736 + 1.411736 + .635281 = 5.706158$.

$$T \cdot S = \begin{bmatrix} .87135510 & .12864420 \\ .71412275 & .28587645 \\ .52194450 & .47804895 \\ .28706760 & .71292645 \end{bmatrix}$$ The probability that he is wiped out is .7142275.

CHAPTER 9

Exercise 1 (page 353)

1. Let the entries denote Tami's winnings in cents. Laura chooses columns and Tami chooses rows:

Laura

$$\text{Tami} \quad \begin{array}{c} \text{I} \\ \text{II} \end{array} \begin{array}{cc} \text{I} & \text{II} \\ \begin{bmatrix} -10 & 10 \\ 10 & -10 \end{bmatrix} \end{array}$$

3. The entries denote Tami's winnings in cents.

Laura

$$\text{Tami} \quad \begin{array}{c} 1 \\ 4 \\ 7 \end{array} \begin{array}{ccc} 1 & 4 & 7 \\ \begin{bmatrix} -20 & 50 & -80 \\ 50 & -80 & 110 \\ -80 & 110 & -140 \end{bmatrix} \end{array}$$

5. Strictly determined; value is -1.   **7.** Strictly determined; value is 2.

9. Not strictly determined.   **11.** Strictly determined; value is 2.

13. Not strictly determined.

15. $0 \le a \le 3$ (There is no saddle point in row 1, unless $a \le 3$; in row 2, unless $a \le -9$; in row 3, unless $a \le -5$; in column 1, unless $a \ge 0$; in column 2, unless $a \ge 8$; in column 3, unless $a \ge 5$. Thus, there is no saddle point unless $0 \le a \le 3$. But if $0 \le a \le 3$, then there is a saddle point in row 1, column 1.)

17. $a \le 0 \le b$ or $b \le 0 \le a$ (The matrix $\begin{bmatrix} a & 0 \\ 0 & b \end{bmatrix}$ is strictly determined if and only if there is a saddle point; a is a saddle point if and only if $a = 0$; b is a saddle point if and only if $b = 0$. The 0 in row 1, column 2 is a saddle point if and only if $0 \le a$ and $0 \ge b$. The 0 in row 2, column 1 is a saddle point if and only if $0 \le b$ and $0 \ge a$.)

Exercise 2 (page 357)

1. $P = [.3 \quad .7]$, $Q = \begin{bmatrix} .4 \\ .6 \end{bmatrix}$, $E = [.3 \quad .7]\begin{bmatrix} 6 & 0 \\ -2 & 3 \end{bmatrix}\begin{bmatrix} .4 \\ .6 \end{bmatrix} = .16 + 1.26 = 1.42$

3. $E = [\frac{1}{2} \quad \frac{1}{2}]\begin{bmatrix} 4 & 0 \\ 2 & 3 \end{bmatrix}\begin{bmatrix} \frac{1}{2} \\ \frac{1}{2} \end{bmatrix} = \frac{3}{2} + \frac{3}{4} = \frac{9}{4}$ **5.** $E = [\frac{1}{4} \quad \frac{3}{4}]\begin{bmatrix} 4 & 0 \\ 2 & 3 \end{bmatrix}\begin{bmatrix} \frac{1}{2} \\ \frac{1}{2} \end{bmatrix} = \frac{19}{8}$

7. $E = [\frac{2}{3} \quad \frac{1}{3}]\begin{bmatrix} 4 & 0 \\ -3 & 6 \end{bmatrix}\begin{bmatrix} \frac{1}{3} \\ \frac{2}{3} \end{bmatrix} = \frac{5}{9} + \frac{4}{3} = \frac{17}{9}$

9. $E = [\frac{1}{3} \quad \frac{1}{3} \quad \frac{1}{3}]\begin{bmatrix} 1 & 0 & 0 \\ 0 & 1 & 0 \\ 0 & 0 & 1 \end{bmatrix}\begin{bmatrix} \frac{1}{3} \\ \frac{1}{3} \\ \frac{1}{3} \end{bmatrix} = \frac{1}{3}$

11. The nonstrictly determined games are those without saddle points. If $a_{11} = a_{12}$ or $a_{21} = a_{22}$, then the game is strictly determined. (See Problem 16 in Exercise 1.)
   (a) If $a_{11} > a_{12}$, then $a_{12} < a_{22}$ to prevent a_{12} from being a saddle point. This means that $a_{21} < a_{22}$ to prevent a_{22} from being a saddle point. Also, $a_{11} > a_{21}$ to prevent a_{21} from being a saddle point.
   (b) If $a_{11} < a_{12}$, then $a_{21} > a_{11}$ to prevent a_{11} from being a saddle point. This means that $a_{22} < a_{21}$ to prevent a_{21} from being a saddle point. Also, $a_{12} > a_{22}$ to prevent a_{22} from being a saddle point.

Exercise 3 (page 362)

1. $E_I = p + 4(1 - p) = 4 - 3p$
$E_I = 2p + (1 - p) = p + 1$
The optimal strategy for Player I is $[.75 \quad .25]$.

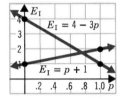
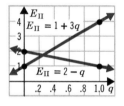

$E_{II} = q + 2(1 - q) = 2 - q$
$E_{II} = 4q + (1 - q) = 1 + 3q$
The optimal strategy for Player II is $[.25 \quad .75]$.
The value of the game is

$E = PAQ = [.75 \quad .25]\begin{bmatrix} 1 & 2 \\ 4 & 1 \end{bmatrix}\begin{bmatrix} .25 \\ .75 \end{bmatrix} = 1.75$

3. $E_I = -3p + (1 - p) = 1 - 4p$
$E_I = 2p - 0(1 - p) = 2p$
The optimum strategy for Player I is $[\frac{1}{6} \quad \frac{5}{6}]$.
$E_{II} = -3q + 2(1 - q) = 2 - 5q$
$E_{II} = q + 0(1 - q) = q$
The optimum strategy for Player II is $[\frac{1}{3} \quad \frac{2}{3}]$.
The value of the game is

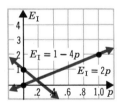
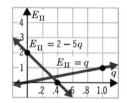

$E = PAQ = [\frac{1}{6} \quad \frac{5}{6}]\begin{bmatrix} -3 & 2 \\ 1 & 0 \end{bmatrix}\begin{bmatrix} \frac{1}{3} \\ \frac{2}{3} \end{bmatrix} = \frac{1}{3}$

5. $E_I = 2p - (1 - p) = 3p - 1$
$E_I = -p + 4(1 - p) = 4 - 5p$
The optimum strategy for Player I is $[\frac{5}{8} \quad \frac{3}{8}]$.
$E_{II} = 2q - (1 - q) = 3q - 1$
$E_{II} = -q + 4(1 - q) = 4 - 5q$
The optimum strategy for Player II is $[\frac{5}{8} \quad \frac{3}{8}]$.
The value of the game is

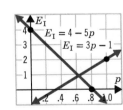

$E = PAQ = [\frac{5}{8} \quad \frac{3}{8}]\begin{bmatrix} 2 & -1 \\ -1 & 4 \end{bmatrix}\begin{bmatrix} \frac{5}{8} \\ \frac{3}{8} \end{bmatrix} = \frac{7}{8}$

7. $\begin{bmatrix} 4 & -1 \\ 0 & 3 \end{bmatrix}$; $p_1 = \dfrac{3-0}{4+3+1} = \tfrac{3}{8}$; $p_2 = \dfrac{4+1}{8} = \tfrac{5}{8}$; $q_1 = \dfrac{3+1}{8} = \tfrac{1}{2}$; $q_2 = \tfrac{4}{8} = \tfrac{1}{2}$; $q_2 = \tfrac{4}{8} = \tfrac{1}{2}$

$V = \begin{bmatrix} \tfrac{3}{8} & \tfrac{5}{8} \end{bmatrix}\begin{bmatrix} 4 & -1 \\ 0 & 3 \end{bmatrix}\begin{bmatrix} \tfrac{1}{2} \\ \tfrac{1}{2} \end{bmatrix} = \begin{bmatrix} \tfrac{3}{2} & \tfrac{3}{2} \end{bmatrix}\begin{bmatrix} \tfrac{1}{2} \\ \tfrac{1}{2} \end{bmatrix} = 1.5$

The game favors the Democrat.

9.

	Opponent	
	Deserted	Busy
Spy Deserted	-100	30
Busy	10	-2

$p_1 = \dfrac{-12}{-142} = \tfrac{6}{71}$; $p_2 = \tfrac{65}{71}$; $q_1 = \dfrac{-32}{-142} = \tfrac{16}{71}$; $q_2 = \tfrac{55}{71}$

The value is $\begin{bmatrix} \tfrac{6}{71} & \tfrac{65}{71} \end{bmatrix}\begin{bmatrix} -100 & 30 \\ 10 & -2 \end{bmatrix}\begin{bmatrix} \tfrac{16}{71} \\ \tfrac{55}{71} \end{bmatrix} = \tfrac{50}{71}$.

11. If $a_{11} + a_{22} - a_{12} - a_{21} = 0$, then the game is strictly determined. Otherwise, from Problem 11 in Exercise 2, we must have either:

(a) $a_{11} - a_{12} > 0$ and $a_{22} - a_{21} > 0$; hence, $a_{11} + a_{22} - a_{12} + a_{21} > 0$, or
(b) $a_{11} - a_{12} < 0$ and $a_{22} - a_{21} < 0$; hence, $a_{11} + a_{22} - a_{12} - a_{21} < 0$.

Exercise 4 (page 373)

1. (a) $\begin{bmatrix} 8 & 3 & 8 \\ 6 & 5 & 4 \\ -2 & 4 & 1 \end{bmatrix}$ Row 2 dominates row 3; the reduced matrix is $\begin{bmatrix} 8 & 3 & 8 \\ 6 & 5 & 4 \end{bmatrix}$.

Column 2 dominates column 1; the reduced matrix is $\begin{bmatrix} 3 & 8 \\ 5 & 4 \end{bmatrix}$.

$p_1 = \dfrac{4-5}{3+4-8-5} = \dfrac{-1}{-6} = \tfrac{1}{6}$ $\qquad$ $q_1 = \dfrac{4-8}{-6} = \dfrac{-4}{-6} = \tfrac{2}{3}$

$p_2 = \dfrac{3-8}{-6} = \dfrac{-5}{-6} = \tfrac{5}{6}$ $\qquad$ $q_2 = \dfrac{3-5}{-6} = \dfrac{-2}{-6} = \tfrac{1}{3}$

$V = \begin{bmatrix} \tfrac{1}{6} & \tfrac{5}{6} \end{bmatrix}\begin{bmatrix} 3 & 8 \\ 5 & 4 \end{bmatrix}\begin{bmatrix} \tfrac{2}{3} \\ \tfrac{1}{3} \end{bmatrix} = \begin{bmatrix} \tfrac{14}{3} & \tfrac{14}{3} \end{bmatrix}\begin{bmatrix} \tfrac{2}{3} \\ \tfrac{1}{3} \end{bmatrix} = \tfrac{14}{3}$

(b) $\begin{bmatrix} 2 & 1 & 0 & 6 \\ 3 & -2 & 1 & 2 \end{bmatrix}$ Column 3 dominates columns 1 and 4; the reduced matrix is $\begin{bmatrix} 1 & 0 \\ -2 & 1 \end{bmatrix}$.

$p_1 = \dfrac{1+2}{1+1+2} = \tfrac{3}{4}$ $\qquad$ $q_1 = \tfrac{1}{4}$

$p_2 = \tfrac{1}{4}$ $\qquad$ $q_2 = \dfrac{1+2}{4} = \tfrac{3}{4}$

$V = \begin{bmatrix} \tfrac{3}{4} & \tfrac{1}{4} \end{bmatrix}\begin{bmatrix} 1 & 0 \\ -2 & 1 \end{bmatrix}\begin{bmatrix} \tfrac{1}{4} \\ \tfrac{3}{4} \end{bmatrix} = \begin{bmatrix} \tfrac{1}{4} & \tfrac{1}{4} \end{bmatrix}\begin{bmatrix} \tfrac{1}{4} \\ \tfrac{3}{4} \end{bmatrix} = \tfrac{1}{4}$

(c) $\begin{bmatrix} 6 & -4 & 2 & -3 \\ -4 & 6 & -5 & 7 \end{bmatrix}$ Column 3 dominates column 1; column 2 dominates column 4; the reduced matrix is $\begin{bmatrix} -4 & 2 \\ 6 & -5 \end{bmatrix}$.

$p_1 = \dfrac{-5-6}{-4-5-2-6} = \tfrac{11}{17}$ $\qquad$ $q_1 = \dfrac{-5-2}{-17} = \tfrac{7}{17}$

$p_2 = \tfrac{6}{17}$ $\qquad$ $q_2 = \tfrac{10}{17}$

$$V = \begin{bmatrix} \frac{11}{7} & \frac{6}{17} \end{bmatrix} \begin{bmatrix} -4 & 2 \\ 6 & -5 \end{bmatrix} \begin{bmatrix} \frac{7}{17} \\ \frac{10}{17} \end{bmatrix} = \begin{bmatrix} -\frac{8}{17} & -\frac{8}{17} \end{bmatrix} \begin{bmatrix} \frac{7}{17} \\ \frac{10}{17} \end{bmatrix} = -\frac{8}{17}$$

(d) $\begin{bmatrix} 4 & -5 & 5 \\ -6 & 3 & 3 \\ 2 & -6 & 3 \end{bmatrix}$ Row 1 dominates row 3; the reduced matrix is $\begin{bmatrix} 4 & -5 & 5 \\ -6 & 3 & 3 \end{bmatrix}$.

Column 2 dominates column 3; the reduced matrix is $\begin{bmatrix} 4 & -5 \\ -6 & 3 \end{bmatrix}$.

$$p_1 = \frac{3+6}{4+3+5+6} = \frac{9}{18} = \frac{1}{2} \qquad q_1 = \frac{3+5}{18} = \frac{8}{18} = \frac{4}{9}$$

$$p_2 = \frac{4+5}{18} = \frac{9}{18} = \frac{1}{2} \qquad q_2 = \frac{4+6}{18} = \frac{10}{18} = \frac{5}{9}$$

$$V = \begin{bmatrix} \frac{1}{2} & \frac{1}{2} \end{bmatrix} \begin{bmatrix} 4 & -5 \\ -6 & 3 \end{bmatrix} \begin{bmatrix} \frac{4}{9} \\ \frac{5}{9} \end{bmatrix} = \begin{bmatrix} -1 & -1 \end{bmatrix} \begin{bmatrix} \frac{4}{9} \\ \frac{5}{9} \end{bmatrix} = -1$$

(e) $\begin{bmatrix} 1 & 3 & 0 \\ 0 & -3 & 1 \\ 0 & 4 & 1 \\ -2 & 1 & 1 \end{bmatrix}$ Row 3 dominates rows 2 and 4; the reduced matrix is $\begin{bmatrix} 1 & 3 & 0 \\ 0 & 4 & 1 \end{bmatrix}$.

Column 1 dominates column 2; the reduced matrix is $\begin{bmatrix} 1 & 0 \\ 0 & 1 \end{bmatrix}$.

$$p_1 = \frac{1-0}{1+1-0-0} = \frac{1}{2} \qquad q_1 = \frac{1-0}{2} = \frac{1}{2}$$

$$p_2 = \frac{1-0}{2} = \frac{1}{2} \qquad q_2 = \frac{1-0}{2} = \frac{1}{2}$$

$$V = \begin{bmatrix} \frac{1}{2} & \frac{1}{2} \end{bmatrix} \begin{bmatrix} 1 & 0 \\ 0 & 1 \end{bmatrix} \begin{bmatrix} \frac{1}{2} \\ \frac{1}{2} \end{bmatrix} = \begin{bmatrix} \frac{1}{2} & \frac{1}{2} \end{bmatrix} \begin{bmatrix} \frac{1}{2} \\ \frac{1}{2} \end{bmatrix} = \frac{1}{2}$$

(f) $\begin{bmatrix} 4 & 3 & -1 \\ 1 & 1 & 4 \\ 1 & 0 & 2 \end{bmatrix}$ Row 2 dominates row 3; the reduced matrix is $\begin{bmatrix} 4 & 3 & -1 \\ 1 & 1 & 4 \end{bmatrix}$.

Column 2 dominates column 1; the reduced matrix is $\begin{bmatrix} 3 & -1 \\ 1 & 4 \end{bmatrix}$.

$$p_1 = \frac{4-1}{3+4-1-(-1)} = \frac{3}{7} \qquad q_1 = \frac{4+1}{7} = \frac{5}{7}$$

$$p_2 = \frac{3+1}{7} = \frac{4}{7} \qquad q_2 = \frac{3-1}{7} = \frac{2}{7}$$

$$V = \begin{bmatrix} \frac{3}{7} & \frac{4}{7} \end{bmatrix} \begin{bmatrix} 3 & -1 \\ 1 & 4 \end{bmatrix} \begin{bmatrix} \frac{5}{7} \\ \frac{2}{7} \end{bmatrix} = \begin{bmatrix} \frac{13}{7} & \frac{13}{7} \end{bmatrix} \begin{bmatrix} \frac{5}{7} \\ \frac{2}{7} \end{bmatrix} = \frac{13}{7}$$

3. Let the thief be in area A with probability q_1. He is then in area B with probability $(1 - q_1)$. The detectives have six choices. The expected values for the probabilities for the detectives to find and arrest a thief for each of the six choices are:

① $E_{\mathrm{I}} = -.24q_1 + .75$

② $E_{\mathrm{I}} = .28q_1 + .36$

③ $E_{\mathrm{I}} = -.72q_1 + .91$

④ $E_I = -.02q_1 + .60$
⑤ $E_I = -.48q_1 + .85$
⑥ $E_I = -.20q_1 + .76$

The intersection of lines 2 and 6 gives the optimum strategy of the thief.

$q_1 = \frac{5}{6}$ $q_2 = 1 - q_1 = \frac{1}{6}$

Eliminating rows 1, 3, 4, and 5, we get:

$p_1 = \frac{5}{12}$ $p_2 = \frac{7}{12}$ $V = .5933\ldots$

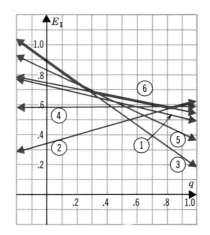

Review Exercises (page 377)

1. (a) Not strictly determined.
(b) Strictly determined; value is 15.
(c) Strictly determined; value is 50.
(d) Strictly determined; value is 9.
(e) Strictly determined; value is 12.

3. Let's first examine the 2×2 matrix $\begin{bmatrix} a & b \\ c & d \end{bmatrix}$.

Let a be the saddle point. We know that $a \leq b$ and $a \geq c$. If $d \leq c$, then $b \geq d$ and row 1 dominates row 2. If $d \geq c$, then column 1 dominates column 2. Similar reasoning would have shown the desired result if we had chosen a saddle point other than a.

Now consider the matrix $\begin{bmatrix} a & b & c \\ d & e & f \end{bmatrix}$.

Let a be the saddle point. We know that $a \leq b$, $a \leq c$, and $a \geq d$. If $d \leq e$, then column 1 dominates column 2. If $d \leq f$, then column 1 dominates column 3. If $d \geq e$ and $d \geq f$, then row 1 dominates row 2. Similar reasoning would have been shown the desired result if we had chosen a saddle point other than a.

5. (a) $\begin{bmatrix} 4 & 6 & 3 \\ 1 & 2 & 5 \end{bmatrix}$ Column 1 dominates column 2; the reduced matrix is $\begin{bmatrix} 4 & 3 \\ 1 & 5 \end{bmatrix}$.

$$p_1 = \frac{5 - 1}{4 + 5 - 3 - 1} = \frac{4}{5} \qquad q_1 = \frac{5 - 3}{5} = \frac{2}{5}$$

$$p_2 = \frac{4 - 3}{5} = \frac{1}{5} \qquad\qquad q_2 = \frac{4 - 1}{5} = \frac{3}{5}$$

$$V = \begin{bmatrix} \frac{4}{5} & \frac{1}{5} \end{bmatrix} \begin{bmatrix} 4 & 3 \\ 1 & 5 \end{bmatrix} \begin{bmatrix} \frac{2}{5} \\ \frac{3}{5} \end{bmatrix} = \begin{bmatrix} \frac{17}{5} & \frac{17}{5} \end{bmatrix} \begin{bmatrix} \frac{2}{5} \\ \frac{3}{5} \end{bmatrix} = \frac{17}{5}$$

(b) $\begin{bmatrix} 1 & 6 \\ 5 & 2 \\ 7 & 4 \end{bmatrix}$ Row 3 dominates row 2; the reduced matrix is $\begin{bmatrix} 1 & 6 \\ 7 & 4 \end{bmatrix}$.

$$p_1 = \frac{4 - 7}{1 + 4 - 7 - 6} = \frac{3}{8} \qquad q_1 = \frac{4 - 6}{-8} = \frac{1}{4}$$

$$p_2 = \frac{5}{8} \qquad\qquad q_2 = \frac{3}{4}$$

$$V = \begin{bmatrix} \frac{3}{8} & \frac{5}{8} \end{bmatrix} \begin{bmatrix} 1 & 6 \\ 7 & 4 \end{bmatrix} \begin{bmatrix} \frac{1}{4} \\ \frac{3}{4} \end{bmatrix} = \frac{19}{4}$$

(c) $\begin{bmatrix} 2 & 1 \\ 4 & 0 \\ 3 & 4 \end{bmatrix}$ Row 3 dominates row 1; the reduced matrix is $\begin{bmatrix} 4 & 0 \\ 3 & 4 \end{bmatrix}$.

$p_1 = \dfrac{4-3}{4+4-3} = \dfrac{1}{5}$ $\qquad q_1 = \dfrac{4-0}{5} = \dfrac{4}{5}$

$p_2 = \dfrac{4}{5}$ $\qquad\qquad q_2 = \dfrac{1}{5}$

$V = \begin{bmatrix} \frac{1}{5} & \frac{4}{5} \end{bmatrix} \begin{bmatrix} 4 & 0 \\ 3 & 4 \end{bmatrix} \begin{bmatrix} \frac{4}{5} \\ \frac{1}{5} \end{bmatrix} = \dfrac{16}{5}$

(d) $\begin{bmatrix} 0 & 3 & 2 \\ 4 & 2 & 3 \end{bmatrix}$

Let Player I play row 1 with probability p. He then plays row 2 with probability $(1-p)$. Player II has 3 choices. The expected earnings for Player I for each of the 3 choices are:

① $E_I = 0p + 4(1-p) = 4 - 4p$
② $E_I = 3p + 2(1-p) = 2 + p$
③ $E_I = 2p + 3(1-p) = 3 - p$

By examining the graphs of these equations, we see that the intersection of lines 1 and 2 gives the optimum strategy for Player I: $p = \frac{2}{5}$, $1 - p = \frac{3}{5}$.

Eliminating column 3, we get $\begin{bmatrix} 0 & 3 \\ 4 & 2 \end{bmatrix}$.

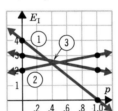

$q_1 = \dfrac{2-3}{2-4-3} = \dfrac{1}{5}$ $\qquad q_2 = \dfrac{4}{5}$

Player I should select row 1 with probability $\frac{2}{5}$ and row 2 with probability $\frac{3}{5}$. Player II should select column 1 with probability $\frac{1}{5}$, column 2 with probability $\frac{4}{5}$, and never select column 3.

$V = \dfrac{12}{5}$

CHAPTER 10

Exercise 1 (page 383)

1. A study of the opinions of people about a certain television program: A poll should be taken either door-to-door or by means of the telephone.

3. A study of the opinions of people toward Medicare: A poll should be taken door-to-door in which people are asked to fill out a questionnaire.

5. A study of the number of savings accounts per family in the United States: The data should be gathered from all different kinds of banks.

7. (a) Asking a group of children if they like candy to determine what percentage of people like candy.
   (b) Asking a group of people over 65 their opinion toward Medicare to determine the opinion of people in general about Medicare.

9. By taking a poll downtown, you would question mostly people who are either shopping or working downtown. For instance, you would question few students.

Exercise 2 (page 389)

1. (a) The lower limit of the 5th class is 250.
   (b) The upper limit of the 4th class is 249.

(c) The midpoint of the 5th class is *275*.
(d) The size of the 5th interval is *50*.
(e) The frequency of the 3rd class is *33*.
(f) The class interval having the largest frequency is the *5th*.
(g) The number of precincts with less than 600 votes is *752*.
(h) Histogram
(i) Frequency polygon

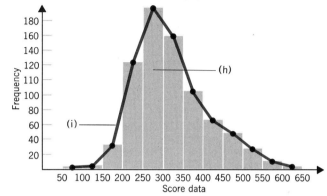

3. (a) Line chart

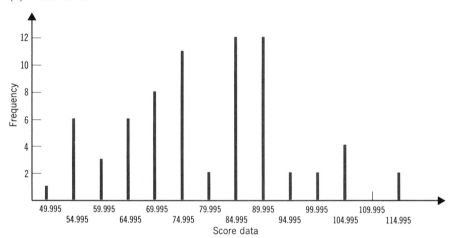

(b) Histogram   (c) Frequency polygon   (d) Cumulative frequency

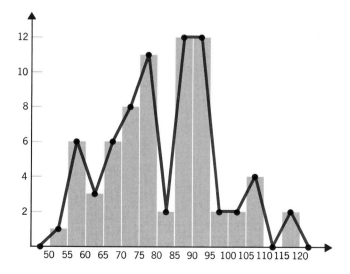

Class Interval	Tally	f	cf
114.995–119.995	||	2	71
109.995–114.995		0	69
104.995–109.995	||||	4	69
99.995–104.995	||	2	65
94.995–99.995	||	2	63
89.995–94.995	⊬⊦⊦ ⊬⊦⊦ ||	12	61
84.995–89.995	⊬⊦⊦ ⊬⊦⊦ ||	12	49
79.995–84.995	||	2	37
74.995–79.995	⊬⊦⊦ ⊬⊦⊦ |	11	35
69.995–74.995	⊬⊦⊦ |||	8	24
64.995–69.995	⊬⊦⊦ |	6	16
59.995–64.995	|||	3	10
54.995–59.995	⊬⊦⊦ |	6	7
49.995–54.995	|	1	1

(e) Cumulative frequency distribution

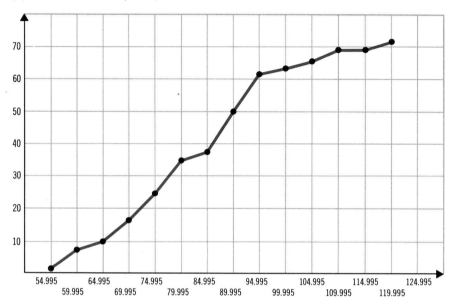

5. (a) Range = 296 − 78 = 218

Score	Tally	f	Score	Tally	f	Score	Tally	f
296	|	1	175	|	1	137	||	2
289	|	1	172	|	1	136	||	2
256	|	1	171	||	2	134	|	1
245	||	2	169	|||	3	132	||	2
240	|	1	166	||	2	131	||||	4
232	|	1	165	||	2	130	|	1
230	|	1	162	|	1	129	|||	3
224	||	2	161	||	2	128	||	2
222	|	1	158	|	1	127	|||	3
218	||	2	157	|	1	126	|	1
212	|	1	156	||	2	123	||	2
211	|	1	155	|	1	122	|	1
207	|	1	154	||	2	119	||	2
204	|	1	153	|||	3	116	|||	3
202	|	1	152	|	1	115	|	1
198	||	2	149	|	1	113	|	1
194	|	1	148	|	1	112	|	1
192	|	1	146	||	2	111	|	1
190	|||	3	145	||	2	110	|	1
188	|	1	144	||	2	108	|	1
185	|||	3	142	|	1	105	|	1
184	|	1	141	|	1	100	|	1
178	|	1	140	|	1	95	|	1
176	||	2	138	|	1	91	|	1
						78	|	1

(b) Line chart

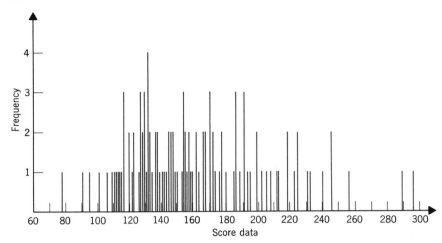

(c) Histogram   (d) Frequency polygon

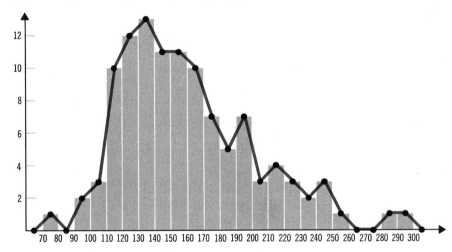

(e) Cumulative (less than) frequency

Class Interval	Tally	f	cf	Class Interval	Tally	f	cf
290.5–300.5	|	1	110	170.5–180.5	┤┤┤ ||	7	80
280.5–290.5	|	1	109	160.5–170.5	┤┤┤ ┤┤┤	10	73
270.5–280.5		0	108	150.5–160.5	┤┤┤ ┤┤┤ |	11	63
260.5–270.5		0	108	140.5–150.5	┤┤┤ ┤┤┤	10	52
250.5–260.5	|	1	108	130.5–140.5	┤┤┤ ┤┤┤ |||	13	42
240.5–250.5	||	2	107	120.5–130.5	┤┤┤ ┤┤┤ ||||	14	29
230.5–240.5	||	2	105	110.5–120.5	┤┤┤ ||||	9	15
220.5–230.5	||||	4	103	100.5–110.5	|||	3	6
210.5–220.5	||||	4	99	90.5–100.5	||	2	3
200.5–210.5	|||	3	95	80.5–90.5		0	1
190.5–200.5	||||	4	92	70.5–80.5	|	1	1
180.5–190.5	┤┤┤ |||	8	88				

(f)

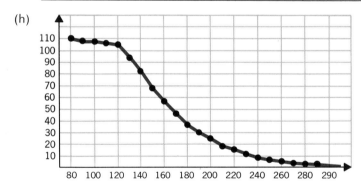

(g)   Cumulative (more than) frequency

Class Interval	Tally	f	cf	Class Interval	Tally	f	cf
70.5–80.5	|	1	110	180.5–190.5	┼┼┼┼ |||	8	30
80.5–90.5		0	109	190.5–200.5	||||	4	22
90.5–100.5	||	2	109	200.5–210.5	|||	3	18
100.5–110.5	|||	3	107	210.5–220.5	||||	4	15
110.5–120.5	┼┼┼┼ ||||	9	104	220.5–230.5	||||	4	11
120.5–130.5	┼┼┼┼ ┼┼┼┼ ||||	14	95	230.5–240.5	||	2	7
130.5–140.5	┼┼┼┼ ┼┼┼┼ |||	13	81	240.5–250.5	||	2	5
140.5–150.5	┼┼┼┼ ┼┼┼┼	10	68	250.5–260.5	|	1	3
150.5–160.5	┼┼┼┼ ┼┼┼┼ |	11	58	260.5–270.5		0	2
160.5–170.5	┼┼┼┼ ┼┼┼┼	10	47	270.5–280.5		0	2
170.5–180.5	┼┼┼┼ ||	7	37	280.5–290.5	|	1	2
				290.5–300.5	|	1	1

(h)

Exercise 3.1 (page 395)

1. Mean $= \bar{X} = \dfrac{21 + 25 + 43 + 36}{4} = \frac{125}{4} = 31.25$; Median $= \dfrac{25 + 36}{2} = 30.5$; no mode

3. Mean = 70.4; Median = 70; Mode = 55.   **5.**   Mean = 76.2; Median = 75; no mode

7. $\bar{X} = \dfrac{(50)(155) + (90)(190) + (120)(210) + (75)(255)}{50 + 90 + 120 + 75} = 206.49$

9. $\bar{X} = \dfrac{14{,}000 + 15{,}000 + 16{,}000 + 16{,}500 + 35{,}000}{5} = 19{,}300$; Median = 16,000

The median describes the situation more realistically, since it is closer to the salary of most of the faculty members in the sample.

11.

	f_i	m_i	$f_i m_i$
Under $100	25	87.50	2,187.50
$100-$125	55	112.50	6,187.50
$125-$150	325	137.50	44,687.50
$150-$175	410	162.50	66,625.00
$175-$200	215	187.50	40,312.50
$200-$225	75	212.50	15,937.50
Over $225	50	237.50	11,875.00
	1,155		187,812.50

Mean = $162.61

Median = $160.52

13. For Table 5, $C_{75} \approx 91.77$, $C_{40} \approx 77.0$. For Table 6, $C_{75} \approx 93.03$, $C_{40} \approx 76.52$.

15. Let 325 be the assumed mean.

	f	x'	fx'
600–649	1	6	6
550–599	9	5	45
500–549	26	4	104
450–499	48	3	144
400–449	67	2	134
350–399	104	1	104
300–349	150	0	0
250–299	190	−1	−190
200–249	120	−2	−240
150–199	33	−3	−99
100–149	4	−4	−16
50–99	1	−5	−5

$n = 753$

$\Sigma \, fx' = -13$

$\overline{X} = 325 + \left(\dfrac{-13}{753}\right)(50) \approx 324.1$

Exercise 3.2 (page 399)

1. $\overline{X} = \dfrac{4 + 5 + 9 + 9 + 10 + 14 + 25}{7} \approx 10.86$

3. $\overline{X} = \dfrac{58 + 62 + 70 + 70}{4} = \dfrac{260}{4} = 65$

x	$x - \overline{X}$	$(x - \overline{X})^2$
4	−6.86	47.0596
5	−5.86	34.3396
9	−1.86	3.4596
9	−1.86	3.4596
10	−.86	.7396
14	3.14	9.8596
25	14.14	199.9396
		298.8572

x	$x - \overline{X}$	$(x - \overline{X})^2$
58	−7	49
62	−3	9
70	5	25
70	5	25
		108

$\sigma = \sqrt{\dfrac{298.8572}{7}} \approx 6.53$

$\sigma = \sqrt{\dfrac{108}{4}} \approx 5.196$

5. $\overline{X} = \dfrac{62 + 75 + 78 + 85 + 100}{5} = 80$

x	$x - \overline{X}$	$(x - \overline{X})^2$
62	-18	324
75	-5	25
78	-2	4
85	5	25
100	20	400
		778

$\sigma = \sqrt{\dfrac{778}{5}} \approx 12.47$

7. $\overline{X} = \dfrac{769 + 815 + 845 + 893 + 922 + 968}{6} \approx 868.67$

x	$x - \overline{X}$	$(x - \overline{X})^2$
769	-99.67	9,934.1089
815	-53.67	2,880.4689
845	-23.67	560.2689
893	24.33	591.9489
922	53.33	2,844.0889
968	99.33	9,866.4489
		26,677.3334

$\sigma = \sqrt{\dfrac{26,677.3334}{6}} \approx 66.68$

9. $\overline{X} = 324.14$

Class Midpoint	f_i	$x - \overline{X}$	$(x - \overline{X})^2$	$(x - \overline{X})^2 \cdot f_i$
625	1	300.86	90,516.7396	90,516.7396
575	9	250.86	62,930.7396	566,376.6564
525	26	200.86	40,344.7396	1,048,963.2296
475	48	150.86	22,758.7396	1,092,419.5008
425	67	100.86	10,172.7396	681,573.5532
375	104	50.86	2,586.7396	269,020.9184
325	150	.86	.7396	110.9400
275	190	-49.14	2,414.7396	458,800.5240
225	120	-99.14	9,828.7396	1,179,448.7520
175	33	-149.14	22,242.7396	734,010.4068
125	4	-199.14	39,656.7396	158,626.9584
75	1	-249.14	62,070.7396	62,070.7396
				6,341,938.9188

$\sigma = \sqrt{\dfrac{6,341,938.9188}{753}} \approx 91.77$

Exercise 4 (page 408)

1. $\overline{X} = 8$; $\sigma = 1$ **3.** $\overline{X} = 18$; $\sigma = 1$

5. $Z = \dfrac{7 - 13.1}{9.3} \approx -.6559$, $\quad Z = \dfrac{9 - 13.1}{9.3} \approx -.4409$, $\quad Z = \dfrac{13 - 13.1}{9.3} \approx -.0108$

$Z = \dfrac{15 - 13.1}{9.3} \approx .2043$, $\quad Z = \dfrac{29 - 13.1}{9.3} \approx 1.7097$, $\quad Z = \dfrac{37 - 13.1}{9.3} \approx 2.5699$

$Z = \dfrac{41 - 13.1}{9.3} = 3.0000$

7. $P(Z \leq -0.5) = \frac{1}{2} - P(-0.5 \leq Z \leq 0) = \frac{1}{2} - P(0 \leq Z \leq 0.5) = \frac{1}{2} - 0.1915 = 0.3085$.

9. $P(Z \geq 1.5) = \frac{1}{2} - P(0 \leq Z \leq 1.5) = \frac{1}{2} - 0.4332 = 0.0688$

11. (a) 0.3133 (b) 0.3642 (c) 0.4938 (d) 0.4987

(e) 0.2734 (f) 0.4896 (g) 0.2881 (h) 0.4988

13. $Z = \dfrac{x - \overline{X}}{\sigma}$; $\overline{X} = 64$, $\sigma = 2$

(a) When $x = 66$, $Z = 1$; when $x = 62$, $Z = -1$;
$P(-1 \leq Z \leq 1) = 2P(0 \leq Z \leq 1) = 0.6826$

This means 68.26% of the women are between 62 and 66 inches tall; $(0.6826)(2000) = 1365.2 \approx 1365$ women

(b) $P(-2 \leq Z \leq 2) = 2(0.4772) = 0.9544$; $(0.9544)(2000) = 1908.8 \approx 1909$ women

(c) $(0.9974)(2000) = 1994.8 \approx 1995$ women

15.   (a) $\dfrac{142 - 130}{5.2} = 2.31$; $P(Z \geq 2.31) = \frac{1}{2} - P(0 \leq Z \leq 2.31) = 0.5 - 0.4896 = 0.0104 = 1.04\%$

(b)   According to the table, Z must be close to 1.04 if the proportional area is 35% (≈ 0.3508).

$(1.04)\sigma = (1.04)(5.2) \approx 5.4$ pounds

Thus, we expect 70% of the students to be within 5.4 pounds of the mean, or between 134.6 and 135.4 pounds.

17.   The Z-score for 1 is $Z = (1 - 2.2)/1.7 = -0.71$; the area under the normal curve between -0.71 and 0 is 0.2611; the area under the normal curve for scores less than -0.71 is $0.5000 - 0.2611 = 0.2389$. The number of shoes he should expect to replace out of 1000 is 239.

19.   Caryl: $Z = (76 - 82)/7 = -0.86$; Mary: $Z = (89 - 93)/2 = -2$, Kathleen: $Z = (21 - 24)/9 = -0.33$; Kathleen has the highest relative standing.

21. $b(15, 0; .3) \approx .0047$
$b(15, 1; .3) \approx .0305$
$b(15, 2; .3) \approx .0916$
$b(15, 3; .3) \approx .1700$
$b(15, 4; .3) \approx .2186$
$b(15, 5; .3) \approx .2061$
$b(15, 6; .3) \approx .1472$
$b(15, 7; .3) \approx .0811$
$b(15, 8; .3) \approx .0348$
$b(15, 9; .3) \approx .0116$
$b(15, 10; .3) \approx .0030$
$b(15, 11; .3) \approx .0006$
$b(15, 12; .3) \approx .0001$
$b(15, 13; .3) \approx .0000$
$b(15, 14; .3) \approx .0000$
$b(15, 15; .3) \approx .0000$

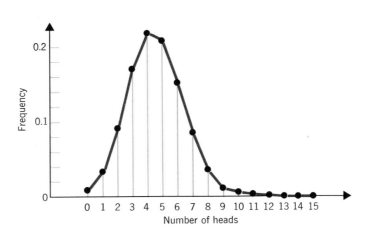

23. $Z(285) = \dfrac{285 - 300}{13} \approx -1.2$

$Z(315) = \dfrac{315 - 300}{13} \approx 1.2$

$P(-1.2 \leq Z \leq 1.2) \approx (2)(0.3849) = 0.7698$

25. $P(Z \geq 0) = 0.5$

27. $Z(325) = \dfrac{325 - 300}{13} \approx 1.9$

$P(Z \geq 1.9) \approx 0.5 - 0.4713 = 0.0287$

Exercise 5 (page 416)

1.

	Disagree	Agree	Totals
Males	540	710	1250
Females	380	870	1250
Totals	920	1580	2500

	Males Disagree	Males Agree	Females Disagree	Females Agree
O	540	710	380	870
E	460	790	460	790

$\chi^2 = \dfrac{(540 - 460)^2}{460} + \dfrac{(710 - 790)^2}{790} + \dfrac{(380 - 460)^2}{460} + \dfrac{(870 - 790)^2}{790} = 13.9 + 8.1 + 13.9 + 8.1 = 44$;

$\nu = 1$ Yes; $\chi^2 = 44 > \chi^2_{.05} = 3.841$

3.

	Red	Yellow	Totals
Boys	60	50	110
Girls	60	30	90
Totals	120	80	200

Probability of red $= \frac{120}{200} = .6$
Probability of yellow $= \frac{80}{200} = .4$

	Boys, Red	Boys, Yellow	Girls, Red	Girls, Yellow
O	60	50	60	30
E	66	44	54	36

$$\chi^2 = \frac{(60-66)^2}{66} + \frac{(50-44)^2}{44} + \frac{(60-54)^2}{54} + \frac{(30-36)^2}{36} = 3.03; \quad \nu = 1$$

At the 5% significance level, $\chi^2 = 3.841 > 3.03$. Color preference is not significant.

5.

	Vac/Cold	Dummy/Cold	Vac/No Cold	Dummy/No Cold	Totals
O	16	20	34	30	100
E	18	18	32	32	100

$$\nu = 1; \quad \chi^2 = \frac{(16-18)^2}{18} + \frac{(20-18)^2}{18} + \frac{(34-32)^2}{32} + \frac{(30-32)^2}{32} = .7$$

No; $\chi^2 = .7$ is much smaller than $\chi^2_{.05} = 3.841$.

7.

	C.B. Male	Normal Male	C.B. Female	Normal Female	Totals
O	40	410	10	540	1000
E	22.5	427.5	27.5	522.5	1000

$$\nu = 1; \quad \chi^2 = \frac{(40-22.5)^2}{22.5} + \frac{(410-427.5)^2}{427.5} + \frac{(10-27.5)^2}{27.5} + \frac{(540-522.5)^2}{522.5} = 26 \quad \text{Yes.}$$

9.

	Bright, Tendril	Bright, Acacia	Dull, Tendril	Dull, Acacia	Totals
O	847	298	300	49	1494
E	840.4	280.1	280.1	93.4	1494

$$\nu = 3; \quad \chi^2 = \frac{(847-840.4)^2}{840.4} + \frac{(298-280.1)^2}{280.1} + \frac{(300-280.1)^2}{280.1} + \frac{(49-93.4)^2}{93.4} \approx 23.72$$

Yes; with $\nu = 3$, the table gives 7.815 at a significance level of 5%; $7.815 < 23.72$.

Review Exercises (page 418)

1. (a)

Score	Tally	Frequency	Score	Tally	Frequency
100	||	2	66	||	2
99	|	1	63	||	2
95	|	1	60		1
92	|	1	55	|	1
90	|	1	52	||	2
89	|	1	48	|	1
87	||	2	44		1
85	||	2	42		1
83	|	1	33		1
82	|	1	30	|	1
80	|||	3	26	|	1
78	||	2	21	|	1
77	|	1	20	|	1
75	|	1	19	|	1
74	|	1	17	|	1
73	||	2	14	||	2
72	||	2	12	|	1
70	|	1	10	|	1
69	|	1	8	|	1

Range $= 100 - 8 = 92$

(b)   Line chart

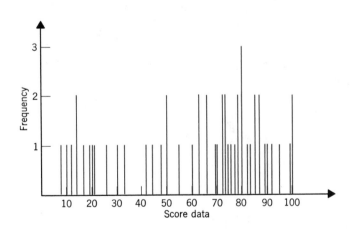

(c)   Histogram

(d)   Frequency
      polygon

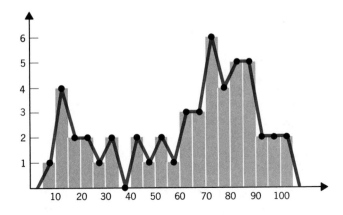

(e) Cumulative (more than) frequency

Class Interval	Tally	f	cf	Class Interval	Tally	f	cf
99.5–104.5	||	2	2	49.5–54.5	||	2	35
94.5–99.5	||	2	4	44.5–49.5	|	1	36
89.5–94.5	||	2	6	39.5–44.5	||	2	38
84.5–89.5	||||	5	11	34.5–39.5		0	38
79.5–84.5	|||||	5	16	29.5–34.5	||	2	40
74.5–79.5	||||	4	20	24.5–29.5	|	1	41
69.5–74.5	||||||	6	26	19.5–24.5	||	2	43
64.5–69.5	|||	3	29	14.5–19.5	||	2	45
59.5–64.5	|||	3	32	9.5–14.5	||||	4	49
54.5–59.5	|	1	33	4.5–9.5	|	1	50

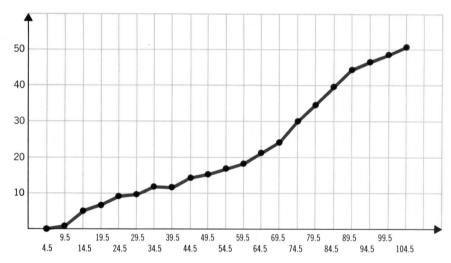

(f) Cumulative (less than) frequency

Class Interval	f	cf	Class Interval	f	cf
99.5–104.5	2	50	49.5–54.5	2	17
94.5–99.5	2	48	44.5–49.5	1	15
89.5–94.5	2	46	39.5–44.5	2	14
84.5–89.5	5	44	34.5–39.5	0	12
79.5–84.5	5	39	29.5–34.5	2	12
74.5–79.5	4	34	24.5–29.5	1	10
69.5–74.5	6	30	19.5–24.5	2	9
64.5–69.5	3	24	14.5–19.5	2	7
59.5–64.5	3	21	9.5–14.5	4	5
54.5–59.5	1	18	4.5–9.5	1	1

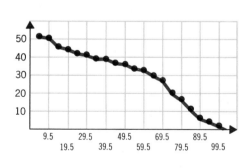

3. The mean is a poor measure in (b) because it gives too much importance to the extreme value 195.

5. $A = \{20, 15, 5, 0\}$; $B = \{12, 11, 10, 9, 8\}$: Both sets have a mean of 10. The standard deviation for the first set is $\sigma_1 = \sqrt{250/5} \approx 7.07$. The standard deviation for the second set is $\sigma_2 = \sqrt{10/5} \approx 1.41$.

7.

$x - \bar{X}$	$(x - \bar{X})^2$
81	5.43	29.48
77	1.43	2.04
76	.43	.18
76	.43	.18
74	−1.57	2.46
73	−2.57	6.60
72	−3.57	12.74
		53.68

Mean = 75.57

$$\sigma = \sqrt{\frac{53.68}{7}} \approx \sqrt{7.67} \approx 2.77$$

9. (a) $(0.6827)(600) = 409.62$
   (b) $[(0.4987) - (0.3413)](600) = 94.44$
   (c) $(0.4972)(600) = 298.32$

11. (a) $(0.4970) - (0.4115) = 0.0855$
   (b) $(0.4599) - (0.3849) = 0.0750$

13.

	P/Rep	C & J/Rep	P/Demo	C & J/Demo	Totals
O	128	101	73	164	466
E	99	130	102	135	466

(a) $\chi^2 = \dfrac{(128 - 99)^2}{99} + \dfrac{(101 - 130)^2}{130} + \dfrac{(73 - 102)^2}{102} + \dfrac{(164 - 135)^2}{135} \approx 29.44$

(b) $\nu = 1$;   there is no evidence for the hypothesis.

CHAPTER 11

Exercise 1 (page 429)

1. $(\$1000)(0.10)(\frac{1}{4}) = \$25$ **3.** $(\$500)(0.12)(\frac{9}{12}) = \$45$

5. $(\$1000)(0.10)(1.5) = \$150$

7. $\$50 = (\$1000)(r)\frac{1}{2}$; $r = 0.10 = 10\%$

9. $\$100 = (\$300)(r)1$; $r = \frac{1}{3} = 33\frac{1}{3}\%$

11. $\$100 = (\$900)(r)\frac{10}{12}$; $r = \frac{1200}{9000} = 13\frac{1}{3}\%$

13. $\$1000\left(1 + \dfrac{0.10}{12}\right)^{36} = \$1348.18$ from Table 4 (10% per annum, compounded monthly, 36 periods)

15. $\$500(1 + 0.18) = \$590$

17. $\$800(1 + r)^n = \$800(1.07971) = \$863.77$

19. $\$100(1 + r)^{-n} = \$100(0.9514) = \$95.14$ from Table 5

21. $\$500(1 + r)^{-n} = \$500(0.835313) = \$417.66$

23. $33\frac{1}{3}\%$ simple interest

25. Between 11 and 12 years (from Table 4)

27. On the simple interest loan, the interest is 24% of $1000, or $240. On the compound interest loan (10%, compounded monthly, 24 months), the interest is

$\$1000(1.22039) - \$1000 = \$220.39$

The 10% compounded loan (b) results in less interest due.

Exercise 2 (page 434)

1. $A = \$100(15.9374) = \$1593.74$ from Table 6 (10% per annum, compounded annually, 10 years)

3. $A = \$400(13.04121) = \$5216.48$ (18% per annum, compounded monthly, 12 months)

5. $A = \$200(41.7818) = \$8356.36$

7. $P = \$100,000\left[\dfrac{1}{A(n,r)}\right] = \$100,000(0.19173867) = \$19,173.87$

9. As in Example 8,

$$0.14p + p\left[\dfrac{1}{A(30, 0.10)}\right] = 30,000$$

$$0.14p + 0.0060792p = 30,000$$

$$p = \dfrac{30,000}{0.1460792} \approx \$205.368$$

Exercise 3 (page 439)

1. $V = (\$500)P\left(36, \dfrac{0.10}{12}\right) = (\$500)(30.9901235) = \$15495.06$ from Table 7

3. $V = (\$100)P\left(9, \dfrac{0.18}{12}\right) = (\$100)(8.36052) = \$836.05$

(using a calculator.)

5. $V = (\$10,000)P(20, 0.10) = (\$10,000)(8.513564) = \$85,135.64$

7. $V = (\$4000)(8.513564) = \$34,054.26$

9. $P = \$10,000\left[\dfrac{1}{P(10, 0.18)}\right] = \$10,000(0.222515) = \$2225.15$

11. 5 years (20 years remaining):
Equity $= \$70,000 - (\$461.56)(111.14495) = \$18,699.94$
10 years (15 years remaining):
Equity $= \$70,000 - (\$461.56)(98.5934) = \$24,493.23$

13. $P = \$15,000\left[\dfrac{1}{P(20, 0.14)}\right] = \$15,000(0.150986) = \$2264.79$

15. $A = \$250P\left(240, \dfrac{0.10}{12}\right) = \$250(103.625) = \$25,906$

17. Use the table on page 437. The principal of either loan is $\$95,000(= \$120,000 - \$25,000)$

	Monthly Payment
8%, 240 months	$(\$95,000)(0.008364) = \$794.58$
9%, 300 months	$(\$95,000)(0.008392) = \$797.24$

The 9% loan requires the larger monthly payment. Since the payments are larger and there are more of them, the total amount of the payments, and therefore the total interest to be paid, is also larger.

	Equity after 10 years
8%, 120 months remaining	$\$120,000 - (\$794.58)(82.42148) = \$54,509.54$
9%, 180 months remaining	$\$120,000 - (\$797.24)(98.5934) = \$41,397.40$

After 10 years, the equity from the 8%, 20 year loan is larger.

Exercise 4 (page 442)
1. The present value of an annuity of $2000 for 5 years at 10% is ($2000)(3.79079) = $7581.58. The corporation should lease the machine.
3. The present value of the annual cost savings of Machine A is ($2000)$P(8, 0.10)$ = ($2000)(5.33493) = $10,669.86. Since the machine costs $10,000, the effective amount saved by its purchase is $669.86. Similarly, the present value of the cost savings of Machine B is ($1800)$P(6, 0.10)$ = $7839.47. Thus, Machine B costs $160.53 more than it will save in labor costs, so Machine A is preferable.
5. The semiannual interest payment is $\frac{1}{2}(0.09)($1000) = $45. The present value of these payments is:

$$($45)P\left(30, \frac{0.08}{2}\right) = ($45)(17.292) = $778.14$$

The present value of the amount payable at maturity is:

$$$1000(1 + 0.04)^{-30} = $308.32$$

Thus, the price of the bond should be $778.14 + $308.32 = $1086.46.

Review Exercises (page 443)
1. $I = Prt = ($400)(\frac{3}{4})(0.12) = $36.00; \quad A = P + I = $400 + $36 = 436
3. $A = P(1 + r)^n = ($100)(1.2511557) = $125 \quad (n = 27)$
5. (a) $I = Prt = ($3000)(0.18)(3) = 1620
   (b) $A = P(1 + r)^n = ($3000)(1.518266) = 4554.80
   $I = A - P = 1554.80
   The compound interest loan costs less.
7. $P = $75(1 + r)^{-n} = ($75)(0.95143) = 71.36

9. From Table 6: $P = $10,000\left[\dfrac{1}{A(n, r)}\right] = ($10,000)(0.037812) = 378.12

11. $P = $60,000\left[\dfrac{1}{P(n, r)}\right] = ($60,000)(0.0090870) = 545.22 monthly payment

   Total interest = (300)($545.22) − $60,000 = $103,566
   Equity after 5 years (n = 240 months remaining):
   $80,000 − ($545.22)$P(n, r)$ = $80,000 − ($545.22)(103.625) = $23,502.

13. $P = $125,000\left[\dfrac{1}{P(n, r)}\right] = ($125,000)(0.008392) = 1049 (using the mortgage table in Section 3)

   $125,000 − ($1049)(98.5934) = $21,575.52

15. $0.15p + p\left[\dfrac{1}{A(n, r)}\right] = $20,000 \qquad (n = 20, r = 10\%)$

   $0.15p + (0.0174596245)p = $20,000$
   $(0.1674596p = $20,000$
   $p = $119,432$

17. $0.20p + p\left[\dfrac{1}{A(n, r)}\right] = $25,000 \qquad (n = 15, r = 10\%)$

   $(0.20 + 0.03147378)p = $25,000$
   $p = $108,004$

CHAPTER 12

Exercise 1 (page 455)
1. Perfect communication, business communication, friendship: A B

3. Dominance, friendship:

5. Dominance, friendship:

7. Perfect communication:

9. Friendship: $\begin{bmatrix} 0 & 0 & 1 & 1 & 0 & 1 \\ 0 & 0 & 1 & 0 & 1 & 1 \\ 0 & 0 & 0 & 0 & 0 & 0 \\ 0 & 0 & 0 & 0 & 0 & 1 \\ 0 & 0 & 0 & 0 & 0 & 0 \\ 0 & 0 & 0 & 0 & 0 & 0 \end{bmatrix}$

11. Friendship: $\begin{bmatrix} 0 & 1 & 1 & 1 \\ 1 & 0 & 1 & 0 \\ 1 & 1 & 0 & 0 \\ 1 & 0 & 1 & 0 \end{bmatrix}$

13. Friendship: $\begin{bmatrix} 0 & 1 & 1 & 0 & 0 & 1 \\ 0 & 0 & 0 & 1 & 1 & 0 \\ 0 & 0 & 0 & 0 & 0 & 1 \\ 0 & 0 & 0 & 0 & 0 & 0 \\ 0 & 0 & 0 & 0 & 0 & 0 \\ 0 & 0 & 0 & 0 & 0 & 0 \end{bmatrix}$

15. Friendship: $\begin{bmatrix} 0 & 1 & 0 & 1 \\ 0 & 0 & 1 & 0 \\ 1 & 0 & 0 & 0 \\ 0 & 0 & 0 & 0 \end{bmatrix}$

Exercise 2 (page 461)

1. Cannot be interpreted as a dominance matrix.

3. Dominance matrix: $M^2 = \begin{bmatrix} 0 & 1 & 0 \\ 0 & 0 & 0 \\ 0 & 0 & 0 \end{bmatrix}$

A dominates B in two ways in one or two stages; A dominates C in one way in one or two stages; B dominates no one in one or two stages; C dominates A in no way and B in one way in one or two stages.

5. Dominance matrix: $M^2 = \begin{bmatrix} 0 & 0 & 0 \\ 1 & 0 & 0 \\ 0 & 0 & 0 \end{bmatrix}$

A dominates no one in one or two stages; B dominates A in two ways in one or two stages and C in one way in one or two stages; C dominates A in one way and B in no way in one or two stages.

7. Dominance matrix: $M^2 = \begin{bmatrix} 0 & 0 & 1 & 1 \\ 0 & 0 & 0 & 1 \\ 1 & 1 & 0 & 0 \\ 0 & 1 & 2 & 0 \end{bmatrix}$

A dominates B in one way, C in two ways, and D in one way in one or two stages; B dominates A in no way and C and D in one way in one or two stages; C dominates A, B, and D in one way in one or two stages; D dominates A in one way and B and C in two ways in one or two stages.

9. $M^2 = \begin{bmatrix} 0 & 0 & 1 \\ 0 & 0 & 0 \\ 0 & 0 & 0 \end{bmatrix}$

A dominates C in one way in two stages; there are no other two-stage dominances. A dominates B in one way and C in two ways in one or two stages; B dominates A in no way and C in one way in one or two stages; C dominates A and B in no way in one or two stages.

11. Team B should be declared the winner since B dominates or has won the most in one or two stages.

13. Let A and B be two countries with A defeating B, A is the strongest in the set $\{A, B\}$. We are going to consider all other countries one at a time by the following process. Let A be the strongest country in a collection C of these countries. Let D be a country not in this collection; then either A defeats D or not. If A defeats D, we are done and A is the strongest in $C \cup \{D\}$. If D defeats A, either D defeats all the countries in C which A defeats, in which case D is the strongest in $C \cup \{D\}$ or there is a country E in C with A defeating E and E defeating D, in which case A is the strongest in $C \cup \{D\}$. We continue this process by adding one country at a time as above and when this process ends we have the strongest. Finding the weakest follows the same process as finding the strongest.

Exercise 3 (page 465)

1. Perfect communication: $M^2 = \begin{bmatrix} 1 & 0 \\ 0 & 1 \end{bmatrix}$

3. Not perfect communication; in fact, this is not the matrix of a graph without loops.

5. Perfect communication: $M^2 = \begin{bmatrix} 1 & 0 & 1 \\ 0 & 2 & 0 \\ 1 & 0 & 1 \end{bmatrix}$

7. Perfect communication: $M^2 = \begin{bmatrix} 5 & 0 & 0 & 2 \\ 0 & 5 & 2 & 0 \\ 0 & 2 & 1 & 0 \\ 2 & 0 & 0 & 1 \end{bmatrix}$

9. $M = \begin{array}{c} \\ A \\ B \\ C \end{array} \begin{array}{c} A \quad B \quad C \\ \begin{bmatrix} 0 & 2 & 2 \\ 2 & 0 & 2 \\ 2 & 2 & 0 \end{bmatrix} \end{array}$; $M^2 = \begin{bmatrix} 8 & 4 & 4 \\ 4 & 8 & 4 \\ 4 & 4 & 8 \end{bmatrix}$

M^2 gives the number of lines connecting two cities passing through exactly one other city.

11. $M = \begin{array}{c} \\ K \\ M \\ D \end{array} \begin{array}{c} K \quad M \quad D \\ \begin{bmatrix} 0 & 1 & 1 \\ 1 & 0 & 1 \\ 1 & 1 & 0 \end{bmatrix} \end{array}$; $M^2 = \begin{bmatrix} 2 & 1 & 1 \\ 1 & 2 & 1 \\ 1 & 1 & 2 \end{bmatrix}$

Katy can communicate with Mike through either one other person or no other person in 2 ways; Mike has 2 ways of getting feedback.

Exercise 4 (page 470)

1. $\begin{array}{c} \\ A \\ B \\ C \\ D \end{array} \begin{array}{c} A \quad B \quad C \quad D \\ \begin{bmatrix} 0 & 1 & 1 & 1 \\ 1 & 0 & 1 & 0 \\ 1 & 1 & 0 & 1 \\ 1 & 0 & 1 & 0 \end{bmatrix} \end{array}$

(a) No

(b) None of them

3. The only difference between the digraph for Problem 2 and that for Problem 3 is in the labeling. In the digraph of Problem 2 replace A by B and B by A.

5. (a)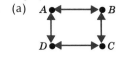

(b) None

Exercise 5 (page 477)

1. *A* is in one clique of 3; *B* is in one clique of 4; *C* is in one clique of 3 and one of 4; *D* is in one clique of 3 and one of 4; *E* is in one clique of 4. The cliques are $\{A, C, D\}$ and $\{B, C, D, E\}$.

3. 1 is in three cliques of 3 people.
2 is in one clique of 3 people.
3 is in three cliques of 3 people.
4 is in one clique of 3 people and one clique of 4 people.
5 is in three cliques of 3 people and one of 4 people.
6 is in one clique of 4 people.
7 is in one clique of 3 people and one clique of 4 people.
The cliques are $\{1, 2, 3\}$, $\{1, 3, 5\}$, $\{1, 5, 7\}$, $\{3, 4, 5\}$, and $\{4, 5, 6, 7\}$.

Review Exercises (page 479)

1. (a) 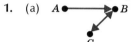 Incidence matrix; friendship

(b)   Perfect communication

(c)  Incidence matrix, dominance or friendship

3. $M = \begin{array}{c} \\ A \\ B \\ C \\ D \\ E \end{array} \begin{array}{cccccc} A & B & C & D & E \\ \begin{bmatrix} 0 & 1 & 1 & 0 & 1 \\ 0 & 0 & 1 & 1 & 1 \\ 0 & 0 & 0 & 1 & 1 \\ 1 & 0 & 0 & 0 & 1 \\ 0 & 0 & 0 & 0 & 0 \end{bmatrix} \end{array}$; $M^2 = \begin{array}{c} \\ A \\ B \\ C \\ D \\ E \end{array} \begin{array}{cccccc} A & B & C & D & E \\ \begin{bmatrix} 0 & 0 & 1 & 2 & 2 \\ 1 & 0 & 0 & 1 & 2 \\ 1 & 0 & 0 & 0 & 1 \\ 0 & 1 & 1 & 0 & 1 \\ 0 & 0 & 0 & 0 & 0 \end{bmatrix} \end{array}$

A and *B* have won the largest number of games. *A* is dominant over 8 teams in two stages; *B* is dominant over 7 teams in two stages. Therefore, *A* should be declared the winner.

5. There are none.

7. (a) $S = \begin{array}{c} \\ A \\ B \\ C \\ D \end{array} \begin{array}{cccc} A & B & C & D \\ \begin{bmatrix} 0 & 1 & 1 & 1 \\ 1 & 0 & 0 & 1 \\ 1 & 0 & 0 & 1 \\ 1 & 1 & 1 & 0 \end{bmatrix} \end{array} = M$; $S^2 = \begin{array}{c} \\ A \\ B \\ C \\ D \end{array} \begin{array}{cccc} A & B & C & D \\ \begin{bmatrix} 3 & 1 & 1 & 2 \\ 1 & 2 & 2 & 1 \\ 1 & 2 & 2 & 1 \\ 2 & 1 & 1 & 3 \end{bmatrix} \end{array}$; $S^3 = \begin{array}{c} \\ A \\ B \\ C \\ D \end{array} \begin{array}{cccc} A & B & C & D \\ \begin{bmatrix} 4 & 5 & 5 & 5 \\ 5 & 2 & 2 & 5 \\ 5 & 2 & 2 & 5 \\ 5 & 5 & 5 & 4 \end{bmatrix} \end{array}$

A is in two cliques of 3 people; *B* is in one clique of 3 people; *C* is in one clique of 3 people; *D* is in two cliques of 3 people. The cliques are $\{A, B, D\}$ and $\{A, C, D\}$.

CHAPTER 13

Exercise 2 (page 484)

1. Proposition **3.** Not a proposition **5.** Proposition **7.** Proposition
9. A fox is not an animal. **11.** I am not buying stocks and bonds.
13. Someone wants to buy my house. **15.** Every person has a car.
17. John is an economics major or a sociology major.
19. John is an economics major and a sociology major.
21. John is not an economics major or he is not a sociology major.
23. John is not an economics major or he is a sociology major.

Exercise 3 (page 496)

1.

p	q	$\sim q$	$p \vee \sim q$
T	T	F	T
T	F	T	T
F	T	F	F
F	F	T	T

3.

p	q	$\sim p$	$\sim q$	$\sim p \wedge \sim q$
T	T	F	F	F
T	F	F	T	F
F	T	T	F	F
F	F	T	T	T

5.

p	q	$\sim p$	$\sim p \wedge q$	$\sim(\sim p \wedge q)$
T	T	F	F	T
T	F	F	F	T
F	T	T	T	F
F	F	T	F	T

7.

p	q	$\sim p$	$\sim q$	$\sim p \vee \sim q$	$\sim(\sim p \vee \sim q)$
T	T	F	F	F	T
T	F	F	T	T	F
F	T	T	F	T	F
F	F	T	T	T	F

9.

p	q	$\sim q$	$p \vee \sim q$	$(p \vee \sim q) \wedge p$
T	T	F	T	T
T	F	T	T	T
F	T	F	F	F
F	F	T	T	F

11.

p	q	$\sim q$	$p \veebar q$	$p \wedge \sim q$	$(p \veebar q) \wedge (p \wedge \sim q)$
T	T	F	F	F	F
T	F	T	T	T	T
F	T	F	T	F	F
F	F	T	F	F	F

13.

p	q	$\sim p$	$\sim q$	$p \wedge q$	$\sim p \wedge \sim q$	$(p \wedge q) \vee (\sim p \wedge \sim q)$
T	T	F	F	T	F	T
T	F	F	T	F	F	F
F	T	T	F	F	F	F
F	F	T	T	F	T	T

15.

p	q	r	$\sim q$	$p \wedge \sim q$	$(p \wedge \sim q) \veebar r$
T	T	T	F	F	T
T	T	F	F	F	F
T	F	T	T	T	F
T	F	F	T	T	T
F	T	T	F	F	T
F	T	F	F	F	F
F	F	T	T	F	T
F	F	F	T	F	F

17.

p	$p \wedge p$	$p \vee p$
T	T	T
F	F	F

Since each column is the same,
$p \equiv p \wedge p \equiv p \vee p$

19.

p	q	r	$p \wedge q$	$q \wedge r$	$(p \wedge q) \wedge r$	$p \wedge (q \wedge r)$
T	T	T	T	T	T	T
T	T	F	T	F	F	F
T	F	T	F	F	F	F
T	F	F	F	F	F	F
F	T	T	F	T	F	F
F	T	F	F	F	F	F
F	F	T	F	F	F	F
F	F	F	F	F	F	F

The last two columns are the same, so
$(p \wedge q) \wedge r \equiv p \wedge (q \wedge r)$

p	q	r	$p \vee q$	$q \vee r$	$(p \vee q) \vee r$	$p \vee (q \vee r)$
T	T	T	T	T	T	T
T	T	F	T	T	T	T
T	F	T	T	T	T	T
T	F	F	T	F	T	T
F	T	T	T	T	T	T
F	T	F	T	T	T	T
F	F	T	F	T	T	T
F	F	F	F	F	F	F

The last two columns are the same, so
$(p \vee q) \vee r \equiv p \vee (q \vee r)$

21.

①	②	③	④	⑤	⑥
p	q	$p \vee q$	$p \wedge q$	$p \wedge (p \vee q)$	$p \vee (p \wedge q)$
T	T	T	T	T	T
T	F	T	F	T	T
F	T	T	F	F	F
F	F	F	F	F	F

Since columns 1 and 5 are the same, $p \equiv p \wedge (p \vee q)$.
Since columns 1 and 6 are the same, $p \equiv p \vee (p \wedge q)$.

23.

①	②	③	④	⑤
p	q	$\sim q$	$\sim q \vee q$	$p \wedge (\sim q \vee q)$
T	T	F	T	T
T	F	T	T	T
F	T	F	T	F
F	F	T	T	F

Since columns 1 and 5 are the same, $p \equiv p \wedge (\sim q \vee q)$.

25.

①	②	③
p	$\sim p$	$\sim(\sim p)$
T	F	T
F	T	F

Since columns 1 and 3 are the same, $p \equiv \sim(\sim p)$

27.

p	q	$\sim p$	$q \wedge (\sim p)$	$p \wedge (q \wedge \sim p)$
T	T	F	F	F
T	F	F	F	F
F	T	T	T	F
F	F	T	F	F

29.

p	q	$\sim p$	$\sim q$	$p \wedge q$	$\sim p \wedge \sim q$	$(p \wedge q) \vee (\sim p \wedge \sim q)$	$[(p \wedge q) \vee (\sim p \wedge \sim q)] \wedge p$
T	T	F	F	T	F	T	T
T	F	F	T	F	F	F	F
F	T	T	F	F	F	F	F
F	F	T	T	F	T	T	F

31. Smith is an exconvict and he is an exconvict. $\equiv$ Smith is an exconvict or he is an exconvict. $\equiv$ Smith is an exconvict.

33. "It is not true that Smith is an exconvict or rehabilitated" means the same as the statement "Smith is not an exconvict and he is not rehabilitated." "It is not true that Smith is an exconvict and he is rehabilitated" means the same as "Smith is not an exconvict or he is not rehabilitated."

35. Katy is not a good volley ball player or she is conceited.

Exercise 4 (page 500)

1. $\sim p \Rightarrow q$; Converse: $q \Rightarrow \sim p$; Contrapositive: $\sim q \Rightarrow p$; Inverse: $p \Rightarrow \sim q$

3. $\sim q \Rightarrow \sim p$; Converse: $\sim p \Rightarrow \sim q$; Contrapositive: $p \Rightarrow q$; Inverse: $q \Rightarrow p$

5. If it is raining, the grass is wet.
Converse: If the grass is wet, it is raining.
Contrapositive: If the grass is not wet, it is not raining.
Inverse: If it is not raining, the grass is not wet.

7. "It is raining or it is cloudy" is equivalent to "If it is not raining, it is cloudy,"
Converse: If it is cloudy, it is not raining.
Contrapositive: If it is not cloudy, it is raining.
Inverse: If it is raining, it is not cloudy.

9. The statement is equivalent to "If it is raining, it is cloudy."
Converse: If it is cloudy, it is raining.
Contrapositive: If it is not cloudy, it is not raining.
Inverse: If it is not raining, it is not cloudy.

11. If it is raining, it is cloudy.
Converse: If it is cloudy, it is raining.
Contrapositive: If it is not cloudy, it is not raining.
Inverse: If it is not raining, it is not cloudy.

13. (a) If Jack studies psychology, then Mary studies sociology.
(b) If Mary studies sociology, then Jack studies psychology.
(c) If Jack does not study psychology, then Mary studies sociology.

Exercise 5 (page 503)

1.

p	q	$\sim p$	$p \wedge q$	$\sim p \vee (p \wedge q)$
T	T	F	T	T
T	F	F	F	F
F	T	T	F	T
F	F	T	F	T

3.

p	q	$\sim p$	$\sim p \wedge q$	$p \vee (\sim p \wedge q)$
T	T	F	F	T
T	F	F	F	T
F	T	T	T	T
F	F	T	F	F

5.

p	q	$\sim p$	$\sim p \Rightarrow q$
T	T	F	T
T	F	F	T
F	T	T	T
F	F	T	F

7.

p	$\sim p$	$\sim p \vee p$
T	F	T
F	T	T

9.

p	q	$p \Rightarrow q$	$p \wedge (p \Rightarrow q)$
T	T	T	T
T	F	F	F
F	T	T	F
F	F	T	F

11.

p	q	r	$q \wedge r$	$p \wedge (q \wedge r)$	$p \wedge q$	$(p \wedge q) \wedge r$	$p \wedge (q \wedge r) \Leftrightarrow (p \wedge q) \wedge r$
T	T	T	T	T	T	T	T
T	T	F	F	F	T	F	T
T	F	T	F	F	F	F	T
T	F	F	F	F	F	F	T
F	T	T	T	F	F	F	T
F	T	F	F	F	F	F	T
F	F	T	F	F	F	F	T
F	F	F	F	F	F	F	T

13.

p	q	$p \vee q$	$p \wedge (p \vee q)$	$p \wedge (p \vee q) \Leftrightarrow p$
T	T	T	T	T
T	F	T	T	T
F	T	T	F	T
F	F	F	F	T

15. $p \Rightarrow q$ **17.** $\sim p \wedge \sim q$ **19.** $q \Rightarrow p$

Exercise 6 (page 510)

1. Let p and q be the statements, p: It is raining, q: John is going to school. Assume that $p \Rightarrow \sim q$ and q are true statements.

Prove: $\sim p$ is true.
Direct: $p \Rightarrow \sim q$ is true.
　Also, its contrapositive $q \Rightarrow \sim p$ is true and q is true.
　Thus, $\sim p$ is true by the law of detachment.
Indirect: Assume $\sim p$ is false.
　Then p is true; $p \Rightarrow \sim q$ is true.
　Thus, $\sim q$ is true by the law of detachment.
　But q is true, and we have a contradiction.
　The assumption is false and $\sim p$ is true.

3. Let p, q, and r be the statements, p: Smith is elected president; q: Kuntz is elected secretary; r: Brown is elected treasurer. Assume that $p \Rightarrow q$, $q \Rightarrow \sim r$, and p are true statements.

Prove: $\sim r$ is true.
Direct: $p \Rightarrow q$ and $q \Rightarrow \sim r$ are true.
　So $p \Rightarrow \sim r$ is true by the law of syllogism, and p is true.
　Thus, $\sim r$ is true by the law of detachment.

Indirect: Assume $\sim r$ is false.

Then r is true; $p \Rightarrow q$ is true; $q \Rightarrow \sim r$ is true.

So, $p \Rightarrow \sim r$ is true by the law of syllogism.

$r \Rightarrow \sim p$, its contrapositive, is true.

Thus, $\sim p$ is true by the law of detachment.

But p is true, and we have a contradiction.

The assumption is false and $\sim r$ is true.

5. Not valid   **7.** Valid

Exercise 7 (page 514)

1.

p	q	r	$\sim p$	$\sim q$	$p \wedge q$	$\sim q \vee r$	$\sim p \wedge (\sim q \vee r)$	$(p \wedge q) \vee [\sim p \wedge (\sim q \vee r)]$
C	C	C	O	O	C	C	O	C
C	C	O	O	O	C	O	O	C
C	O	C	O	C	O	C	O	O
C	O	O	O	C	O	C	O	O
O	C	C	C	O	O	C	C	C
O	C	O	C	O	O	O	O	O
O	O	C	C	C	O	C	C	C
O	O	O	C	C	O	C	C	C

Current flows when any two of the switches p, q, r are closed, or p and q are both open.

3.

p	q	$\sim p$	$\sim q$	$\sim q \vee p$	$q \wedge (\sim q \vee p)$	$[q \wedge (\sim q \vee p)] \vee \sim p$	$p \wedge \{[q \wedge (\sim q \vee p)] \vee \sim p\}$
C	C	O	O	C	C	C	C
C	O	O	C	C	O	O	O
O	C	C	O	O	O	C	O
O	O	C	C	C	O	C	O

p and q must both be closed.

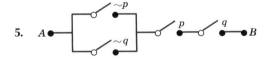

5.

7.

9.

11.

13.

Review Exercises (page 515)
1. (c)   **3.** (a)   **5.** Nobody is rich.   **7.** Danny is tall or Mary is not short.

9.

p	q	$\sim p$	$p \wedge q$	$(p \wedge q) \vee \sim p$
T	T	F	T	T
T	F	F	F	F
F	T	T	F	T
F	F	T	F	T

11.

p	q	$\sim p$	$\sim q$	$p \vee \sim q$	$\sim p \vee (p \vee \sim q)$
T	T	F	F	T	T
T	F	F	T	T	T
F	T	T	F	F	T
F	F	T	T	T	T

13. $q \Rightarrow p$ **15.** $p \Leftrightarrow q$
17. Let p be the statement "I paint the house" and let q be the statement "I go bowling." Assume $\sim p \Rightarrow q$ and $\sim q$ are true.
   Prove: p is true.
   Since $\sim p \Rightarrow q$ is true, its contrapositive $\sim q \Rightarrow p$ is true. We have $\sim q$ is true and hence, by the law of detachment, p is true.

19.

p	q	$\sim p$	$\sim p \vee q$	$p \Rightarrow q$	
T	T	F	T	T	$\sim p \vee q \equiv p \Rightarrow q$
T	F	F	F	F	
F	T	T	T	T	
F	F	T	T	T	

APPENDIX

A Exercises (page 524)
1. (a) $f(3) = 3(3) - 2 = 9 - 2 = 7$ (d) $f(x + 2) = 3(x + 2) - 2 = 3x + 4$
   (b) $f(-2) = 3(-2) - 2 = -8$ (e) $f(x + h) = 3(x + h) - 2 = 3x + 3h - 2$
   (c) $f(0) = 3(0) - 2 = -2$ (f) $f(1/x) = 3(1/x) - 2 = (3/x) - 2$
3. Function   **5.** Function
7. Correspondence does not determine a function, since for $x = 0$, we have $y^2 = 1$, which in turn gives $y = 1$ or $y = -1$. For a given x in the domain we have more than one image y.
9. Function; $f(x) = 1 - x^2$
11. Correspondence does not determine a function, since for $x = 1$, we have two values of y, namely $y = \sqrt{5}$ and $y = -\sqrt{5}$.
13. Function
15. $D =$ all real numbers   **17.** $D = \{x \mid x \geq 1\}$ **19.** $D =$ all real numbers
21. $D = \{x \mid x \neq 2\}$ **23.** $D = \{x \mid x > 0\}$
25. (a) Height when $x = 1$ is $H(1) = 20 - 13(1)^2 = 7$ meters
      $H(1.1) = 20 - 13(1.1)^2 = 4.27$
      $H(1.2) = 20 - 13(1.2)^2 = 1.28$
      $H(1.3) = 20 - 13(1.3)^2 = -1.97$ (the rock is embedded in the surface of the planet)
   (b) The rock hits the ground when $H(x) = 0$; that is, when $x = \sqrt{20/13} \approx 1.24$ seconds.

Answers to Mathematical Questions from CPA, CMA, and Actuary Exams

CHAPTER 1 (page 55)
1. b **2.** d **3.** d **4.** b **5.** b **6.** b **7.** d **8.** c **9.** c **10.** c **11.** b **12.** b

CHAPTER 3 (page 147)
1. b **2.** a **3.** c **4.** c **5.** d **6.** c **7.** c **8.** (a) The problem is not to minimize cost but to maximize profits. Fixed overhead costs should not be included. Machine time constraints should be included. (b) Maximize P = revenue − direct costs − variable overhead = $16.5A + 35B$, subject to $4A + 2B \leq 1800$, $2A + 3B \leq 1200$, $5A + 4B \leq 2400$, $A + B \leq 500$, $B \leq 300$, $A \geq 0$, $B \geq 0$.

CHAPTER 4 (page 189)
1. c **2.** d **3.** c **4.** a **5.** b **6.** a **7.** c **8.** d

CHAPTER 6 (page 295)
1. b **2.** e **3.** b **4.** d **5.** c **6.** d **7.** b **8.** a **9.** d **10.** c **11.** b

CHAPTER 7 (page 312)
1. a **2.** a **3.** b

CHAPTER 10 (page 420)
1. c **2.** e **3.** b **4.** c **5.** b

CHAPTER 11 (page 444)
1. b **2.** c **3.** b **4.** b **5.** d **6.** a **7.** c

Answers to True–False Questions

CHAPTER 1

1. F
2. T
3. T
4. F
5. T

CHAPTER 2

1. T
2. F
3. F
4. T
5. T

CHAPTER 3

1. F
2. T
3. T
4. T
5. F

CHAPTER 4

1. T
2. F
3. T
4. F
5. T

CHAPTER 5

1. T
2. T
3. F
4. F
5. F

CHAPTER 6

1. T
2. F
3. F
4. T
5. F

Answers to Fill-in-the-blanks Questions

CHAPTER 1

1. abscissa, ordinate 2. terminates, repeats 3. undefined, zero 4. negative 5. parallel

CHAPTER 2

1. 3×2 2. one, an infinite number 3. inconsistent 4. rows, columns 5. inconsistent

CHAPTER 3

1. objective 2. feasible solutions 3. convex polyhedral 4. bounded 5. vertex

CHAPTER 4

1. slack variables 2. column 3. $\geq$ 4. dual 5. von Neumann Duality Principle

CHAPTER 5

1. disjoint   **2.** permutation   **3.** combination   **4.** Pascal's   **5.** binomial coefficients

CHAPTER 6

1. for   **2.** equally likely   **3.** disjoint   **4.** Bayes' formula   **5.** independent

Index